Development Centre Seminars

THE WORLD ECONOMY:

A MILLENNIAL PERSPECTIVE

by

Angus Maddison

DEVELOPMENT CENTRE OF THE ORGANISATION
FOR ECONOMIC CO-OPERATION AND DEVELOPMENT

ORGANISATION FOR ECONOMIC CO-OPERATION AND DEVELOPMENT

Pursuant to Article 1 of the Convention signed in Paris on 14th December 1960, and which came into force on 30th September 1961, the Organisation for Economic Co-operation and Development (OECD) shall promote policies designed:

- to achieve the highest sustainable economic growth and employment and a rising standard of living in Member countries, while maintaining financial stability, and thus to contribute to the development of the world economy;
- to contribute to sound economic expansion in Member as well as non-member countries in the process of economic development; and
- to contribute to the expansion of world trade on a multilateral, non-discriminatory basis in accordance with international obligations.

The original Member countries of the OECD are Austria, Belgium, Canada, Denmark, France, Germany, Greece, Iceland, Ireland, Italy, Luxembourg, the Netherlands, Norway, Portugal, Spain, Sweden, Switzerland, Turkey, the United Kingdom and the United States. The following countries became Members subsequently through accession at the dates indicated hereafter: Japan (28th April 1964), Finland (28th January 1969), Australia (7th June 1971), New Zealand (29th May 1973), Mexico (18th May 1994), the Czech Republic (21st December 1995), Hungary (7th May 1996), Poland (22nd November 1996), Korea (12th December 1996) and the Slovak Republic (14th December 2000). The Commission of the European Communities takes part in the work of the OECD (Article 13 of the OECD Convention).

The Development Centre of the Organisation for Economic Co-operation and Development was established by decision of the OECD Council on 23rd October 1962 and comprises twenty-three Member countries of the OECD: Austria, Belgium, Canada, the Czech Republic, Denmark, Finland, France, Germany, Greece, Iceland, Ireland, Italy, Korea, Luxembourg, Mexico, the Netherlands, Norway, Poland, Portugal, Slovak Republic, Spain, Sweden, Switzerland, as well as Argentina and Brazil from March 1994, Chile since November 1998 and India since February 2001. The Commission of the European Communities also takes part in the Centre's Advisory Board.

The purpose of the Centre is to bring together the knowledge and experience available in Member countries of both economic development and the formulation and execution of general economic policies; to adapt such knowledge and experience to the actual needs of countries or regions in the process of development and to put the results at the disposal of the countries by appropriate means.

The Centre has a special and autonomous position within the OECD which enables it to enjoy scientific independence in the execution of its task. Nevertheless, the Centre can draw upon the experience and knowledge available in the OECD in the development field.

 THE OPINIONS EXPRESSED AND ARGUMENTS EMPLOYED IN THIS PUBLICATION ARE THE SOLE RESPONSIBILITY OF THE AUTHOR AND DO NOT NECESSARILY REFLECT THOSE OF THE OECD OR OF THE GOVERNMENTS OF ITS MEMBER COUNTRIES.

*
* *

Publié en français sous le titre :
L'ÉCONOMIE MONDIALE
Une perspective millénaire
Reprinted 2002

Foreword

Shortly after my arrival at the OECD in 1996, I came upon the study by Angus Maddison "Monitoring the World Economy 1820–1992". It is a fascinating and stimulating work providing a complete coverage of the world economy during the period in question. It brought together data of some 56 countries accounting for 93 per cent of the world output and 87 per cent of the world population and world exports. It never left my desk. Probably I was not alone in my appreciation of this quite extraordinary work, as I kept coming on references to it in the work of other authors.

As we were nearing the end of the twentieth century, it seemed to me that this study could undergo some slight revisions to make it more attractive to general readership, and brought up to the close of the century and of the second millennium. I discussed the project with Professor Maddison and, to my delight, he agreed.

From his enormous energy and intellectual capacity emerges a far greater work in depth and scope than anything I had imagined possible. This book covers the development of the entire world economy over the past two thousand years. The author takes a (quite literally) global view of world growth over that period, examining both changes over time and between different regions. The book has a wider ambit than any previous OECD publication or, indeed, than almost any other publication in the market worldwide. First, the scope of the analysis is breath–taking. Second, there must be few (if any) economic history books so wide in their reach, in terms of both geography and history. Third, although his approach is economic, it is not narrowly so and draws on many other subjects — history, geography, demography and more — on the path to its conclusions; this multidisciplinary sweep gives the book great value.

Because of its value and its global reach, I am sure it will find a global readership, as an authoritative reference for academics, students, professionals and general readership.

I predict it will find its place in homes, offices and libraries in every corner of the world, and for many years to come. It will undoubtedly be the foundation for further works of this kind during the millennium we have just entered.

We should all be extremely grateful to Angus Maddison for having taken on this challenge with results which far exceed my original expectations.

John Maynard Keynes wrote that the master economist should "examine the present in light of the past, for the purposes of the future". Never before have we had such a rich resource at our disposal to pursue that objective.

Donald Johnston
OECD Secretary–General

Table of Contents

Text Tables

Appendix Tables

Acknowledgements

I am grateful to Saskia van Bergen, Catherine Girodet, Ly Na Tang Dollon, and Erik Monnikhof for considerable help in processing statistical material and preparing graphs, and to Sheila Lionet for putting the manuscript in a form suitable for publication.

I am particularly indebted to my friend and mentor Moses Abramovitz (1912–2000), for his encouragement, wisdom and generosity in commenting on this manuscript and many others over the past 40 years.

I benefited from discussions that followed the 1998 Kuznets Memorial Lectures which I gave at Yale University, and from comments on presentations on this theme at the Academy of Social Sciences in Australia, the Brazil Forum in Porto Alegre, seminars at the Academia Sinica, Hitotsubashi University, Keio University at Fujisawa, Osaka University and Osaka Gakuin University. I remembered a lot that I learned from a three month stay at the Universita Ca' Foscari in Venice in 1990.

I received useful comments on different drafts from Bart van Ark, Ian Castles, François Crouzet, Charles Feinstein, Colm Foy, David Henderson, Paolo Malanima, Jim Oeppen, Osamu Saito, Graeme Snooks, Victor Urquidi and Sir Tony Wrigley.

I had advice or answers to queries from Michèle Alkilic, Heinz Arndt, Jean–Pascal Bassino, Joel Bergsman, Luis Bertola, Derek Blades, Yves Blayo, Lidia Bratanova, Henk–Jan Brinkman, J.W. Drukker, Nick Eberstadt, Pierre van der Eng, Jean–Yves Garnier, Roland Granier, Maria Alice Gusmâo Veloso, Akira Hayami, André Hofman, Yuri Ivanov, Masaaki Kawagoe, Peter Lindert, Cormac O Grada, Debin Ma, Elizabeth Maddison, Paul McCarthy, Nanno Mulder, Peter Hein van Mulligen, Konosuke Odaka, Dirk Pilat, Richard Ruggles, Serguei Sergueev, Miyohei Shinohara, Siva Sivasubramonian, Marcelo Soto, T.N. Srinivasan, Kaoru Sugihara, Jean–Claude Toutain, Richard Wall, Michael Ward, and Harry X. Wu.

My biggest debts are to my wife, Penelope Maddison, for continuous encouragement, sustained moral and material support.

Preface

Angus Maddison visited Nova University at Lisbon in 1986 and that is where we first met. I already knew of his work, since my late father, himself an economic historian, had mentioned its importance to me many years previously. It was therefore with some nostalgia that, as newly appointed President of the Development Centre, I found myself involved with Angus on a regular basis.

The Development Centre's association with Angus Maddison is a very long one. He was present at the birth of the Development Centre, influenced its evolution and the character of its research. In many ways, the Centre is indissociable from him. This is one reason why the writing of this extraordinary history of the world economy should have been entrusted to him. In addition, Angus is possibly the greatest living *chiffrephile*, as demonstrated by his earlier work for the Centre, most notably: *The World Economy 1820–1992* and *Chinese Economic Performance in the Long Run*, both of which have become works of reference in quantitative economic history the world over.

The Development Centre is preoccupied with the place of governance in the new world order. Our research effort is directed towards helping countries to find ways of reforming governance systems at every level of society. This is also a constant theme in this book. Throughout the thousand years under consideration, governance can be seen as a factor which either advantaged or disadvantaged growth. We therefore remain convinced that this is a vital issue confronting developing societies today. We are also persuaded that OECD countries have themselves a responsibility to implement good governance and to encourage it elsewhere.

Jorge Braga de Macedo
President
OECD Development Centre

April 2001

Introduction and Summary

The Contours of World Development

Over the past millennium, world population rose 22–fold. Per capita income increased 13–fold, world GDP nearly 300–fold. This contrasts sharply with the preceding millennium, when world population grew by only a sixth, and there was no advance in per capita income.

From the year 1000 to 1820 the advance in per capita income was a slow crawl — the world average rose about 50 per cent. Most of the growth went to accommodate a fourfold increase in population.

Since 1820, world development has been much more dynamic. Per capita income rose more than eightfold, population more than fivefold.

Per capita income growth is not the only indicator of welfare. Over the long run, there has been a dramatic increase in life expectation. In the year 1000, the average infant could expect to live about 24 years. A third would die in the first year of life, hunger and epidemic disease would ravage the survivors. There was an almost imperceptible rise up to 1820, mainly in Western Europe. Most of the improvement has occurred since then. Now the average infant can expect to survive 66 years.

The growth process was uneven in space as well as time. The rise in life expectation and income has been most rapid in Western Europe, North America, Australasia and Japan. By 1820, this group had forged ahead to an income level twice that in the rest of the world. By 1998, the gap was 7:1. Between the United States (the present world leader) and Africa (the poorest region) the gap is now 20:1. This gap is still widening. Divergence is dominant but not inexorable. In the past half century, resurgent Asian countries have demonstrated that an important degree of catch–up is feasible. Nevertheless world economic growth has slowed substantially since 1973, and the Asian advance has been offset by stagnation or retrogression elsewhere.

The Purpose of this Study

The purpose of this book is to quantify these long term changes in world income and population in a comprehensive way; identify the forces which explain the success of the rich countries; explore the obstacles which hindered advance in regions which lagged behind; scrutinise the interaction between the rich countries and the rest to assess the degree to which their backwardness may have been due to Western policy.

There is nothing new about long–term surveys of economic performance. Adam Smith had a very broad perspective in his pioneering work in 1776. Others have had an equally ambitious vision. There has been spectacular progress in recent years in historical demography[1]. What is new in this study is systematic quantification of comparative economic performance.

In the past, quantitative research in economic history has been heavily concentrated on the nineteenth and twentieth centuries when growth was fastest. To go back earlier involves use of weaker evidence, greater reliance on clues and conjecture. Nevertheless it is a meaningful, useful and necessary exercise because differences in the pace and pattern of change in major parts of the world economy have deep roots in the past.

Quantification clarifies issues which qualitative analysis leaves fuzzy. It is more readily contestable and likely to be contested. It sharpens scholarly discussion, sparks off rival hypotheses, and contributes to the dynamics of the research process. It can only do this if the quantitative evidence and the nature of proxy procedures is described transparently so that the dissenting reader can augment or reject parts of the evidence or introduce alternative hypotheses. The analysis of Chapters 1, 2 and 3 is underpinned by six appendices which are intended to supply the necessary degree of transparency.

Explaining Economic Performance

Advances in population and income over the past millennium have been sustained by three interactive processes:

a)   Conquest or settlement of relatively empty areas which had fertile land, new biological resources, or a potential to accommodate transfers of population, crops and livestock;

b)   international trade and capital movements;

c)   technological and institutional innovation.

a) Conquest and Settlement

One important instance of this process was Chinese settlement of the relatively empty and swampy lands south of the Yangtse, and introduction of new quick–ripening strains of rice from Vietnam suitable for multicropping. This process occurred between the eighth and thirteenth centuries, during which population growth accelerated, per capita income rose by a third, and the distribution of population and economic activity were transformed. In the eighth century only a quarter of the Chinese population lived south of the Yangtse; in the thirteenth, more than threequarters. The new technology involved higher labour inputs, so productivity rose less than per capita income[2].

An even more dramatic case was the European encounter with the Americas. The existence of this continent was unknown to Europeans before the 1492 voyage of Columbus[3]. The discovery opened up an enormous area, for the most part thinly populated. Mexico and Peru were the most advanced and densely settled, but they were easily conquered and three quarters of their population was wiped out by diseases which the Europeans inadvertently introduced. The new continent offered crops unknown elsewhere — maize, potatoes, sweet potatoes, manioc, chilis, tomatoes, groundnuts, pineapples, cocoa and tobacco. These were introduced in Europe, Africa and Asia, and enhanced their production potential and capacity to sustain population growth. There was a reciprocal transfer to the Americas, which greatly augmented its potential. The new crops were wheat, rice, sugar cane, vines, salad greens, olives, bananas and coffee. The new animals for food were cattle, pigs, chickens, sheep and goats, as well as horses, oxen, asses and donkeys for transport.

The major initial attractions of the Americas were the rich silver resources of Mexico and Peru, and development of plantation agriculture with imports of slave labour from Africa. The neo–European economies of North America and the southern cone of Latin America developed later. The population of the Americas did not recover its 1500 level until the first half of the eighteenth century. The full potential of the Americas began to be realised in the nineteenth century with massive European immigration and the western movement of the production frontier made possible by railways.

The present variation in economic performance within the Americas — between the United States, Latin America and the Caribbean — is partly due to variations in resource endowment, but there are institutional and societal echoes from the past. In North America and Brazil the relatively small indigenous population was marginalised or exterminated, in former Spanish colonies the indigenous population remained as an underclass, and in all the areas where slavery was important their descendants have also remained an underprivileged group. Quite apart from this, there were important differences in the colonial period between Iberian institutions and those of North America. These continued to have an impact on subsequent growth performance[4].

b) International Trade and Capital Movements

International trade was important in the economic ascension of Western Europe, and much less significant in the history of Asia or Africa.

Venice played a key role from 1000 to 1500 in opening up trade within Europe (to Flanders, France, Germany and the Balkans) and in the Mediterranean. It opened trade in Chinese products via the caravan routes to ports in the Black Sea. It traded in Indian and other Asian products via Syria and Alexandria. Trade was important in bringing high value spices and silks to Europe, but it also helped the transfer of technology from Asia, Egypt and Byzantium (silk and cotton textile production, glassblowing, cultivation of rice in Italy, cane sugar production and processing in the Venetian colonies of Crete and Cyprus). To a significant degree the maritime expansion of Venice depended on improved techniques of shipbuilding in its Arsenal, use of the compass and other improvements in navigation. Institutional innovations — the development of banking, accountancy, foreign exchange and credit markets, creation of a solvent system of public finance, creation of a competent diplomatic service were all instrumental in establishing Venice as the lead economy of that epoch. Venice played an important part in fostering the intellectual development of Western Europe. It created manuscript libraries and pioneered in book publishing. Its glass industry was the first to make spectacles on a large scale. It played a leading role in the Renaissance by making Greek works known in the West. The University of Padua was a major centre of European learning, with Galileo as one of its distinguished professors.

Venetian contacts with Asia were eventually blocked by the fall of Byzantium, the rise of the Ottoman Empire, the collapse of the crusader states in the Levant and the Mameluke regime in Egypt. In the second half of the fifteenth century, a much more ambitious interaction between Europe and the rest of the world had started in Portugal.

Portugal played the main role in opening up European trade, navigation and settlement in the Atlantic islands, in developing trade routes around Africa, into the Indian Ocean, to China and Japan. It became the major shipper of spices to Europe for the whole of the sixteenth century, usurping this role from Venice. Its navigators discovered Brazil. Its diplomacy was astute enough to persuade Spain to endorse its territorial claim there, and to let it have a monopoly of trade with the Moluccan spice islands and Indonesia. Although Spain had a bigger empire, its only significant base outside the Americas was the Philippines. Its two most famous navigators were Columbus who was a Genoese with Portuguese training, and Magellan who was Portuguese.

Portugal had major advantages in developing its overseas commerce and empire. There was a clear strategic benefit in being located on the South Atlantic coast of Europe near to the exit of the Mediterranean. Deep–sea fishermen provided an important part of the Portuguese food supply and developed an unrivalled knowledge of Atlantic winds, weather and tides. The value of these skills was greatly enhanced by crown sponsorship of Atlantic exploration, research on navigation, training of pilots, and documentation of maritime experience in the form of route maps with compass bearings (rutters) and cartography. Portuguese shipbuilders in Lisbon and Oporto adapted the design of their ships in the light of increasing knowledge of Atlantic sailing conditions. The biggest changes were in rigging. At first they concentrated on lateen sails, then added a mix of square sails and lateen for deeper penetration into the South Atlantic, with further changes for the much longer route round the Cape. Another element in Portuguese success was the ability to absorb "new Christians" — Jewish merchants and scholars who had played a significant role in Iberia during Muslim rule. They were driven out of Spain, but many took refuge and increased the size of the community in Portugal. They were required to undergo proforma conversion and were subject to a degree of persecution, but they provided important skills in developing Portuguese business interests in Africa, Brazil and Asia, in scientific development, as intermediaries in trade with the Muslim world and in attracting Genoese and Catalan capital to Portuguese business ventures.

Portugal was responsible for transferring cane sugar production and processing technology into the Atlantic islands of Madeira and São Tomé, and later to Brazil. It inaugurated the slave trade to provide a labour force for the industry in the New World. It carried about half of the slaves who were shipped to the Americas from Africa between 1500 and 1870. In the fifteenth century, sugar was a very rare and expensive commodity in Europe; by the end of the eighteenth century it was an item of popular consumption, having grown much more in volume than trade in any other tropical product.

At the time Portugal was pioneering these worldwide linkages, trade relations between different parts of northern Europe were intensified by the phenomenal development of Dutch maritime activity. In 1570, the carrying capacity of Dutch merchant shipping was about the same as the combined fleets of England, France and Germany. Per head of population it was 25 times as big as in these three northern countries.

Development of shipping and shipbuilding, the transformation of Dutch agriculture into horticulture, the creation of a large canal network, use of power derived from windmills and peat made the Netherlands the most dynamic European economy from 1400 to the middle of the seventeenth century. It pushed international specialisation much further than any other country. Shipping and commercial services provided a large part of its income. It imported cereals and live cattle, exported herring and dairy products. In 1700 only 40 per cent of the labour force were in agriculture.

Until 1580 the Netherlands was part of a bigger political entity. It included Flanders and Brabant — the most prosperous industrial area in Europe and a centre for banking, finance and international commerce which was a northern counterpart to Venice. The whole area was under Burgundian control until the late fifteenth century, then fell into the hands of the Habsburgs who were also rulers of Spain. The Dutch revolted against their predatory empire because of its excessive fiscal demands, political and religious repression. They created a modern nation state, which protected property rights of merchants and entrepreneurs, promoted secular education and practised religious tolerance.

Most of the financial and entrepreneurial elite and many of the most skilled artisans of Flanders and Brabant emigrated to the new republic. The Dutch blockaded the river Scheldt and the port of Antwerp for more than 200 years, and destroyed the Iberian monopoly of trade with Africa, Asia and the Americas.

Dutch experience from 1580 to the end of the Napoleonic wars provides a dramatic demonstration of the way in which Western Europe interacted with the world economy in that epoch.

The initial economic success of the Dutch Republic, and its maritime and commercial supremacy, depended to a substantial extent on success in war and beggar–your–neighbour commercial policy in competition with Portugal and Spain. By the eighteenth century it had lost this supremacy, because two new rivals, England and France, had greatly increased their maritime strength, and used the same techniques to push the Dutch out of the markets they sought to dominate. The volume of Dutch foreign trade dropped 20 per cent from 1720 to 1820. During this period, UK exports rose more than sevenfold in volume, and French by two and threequarters. From 1700 to 1820, Dutch per capita income fell by a sixth, British rose by half and French by a quarter.

Britain had faster growth in per capita income from the 1680s to 1820 than any other European country. This was due to improvement of its banking, financial and fiscal institutions and agriculture on lines which the Dutch had pioneered, and to a surge in industrial productivity at the end of the period. It also derived great benefits from its rise to commercial hegemony by adroit use of a beggar–your–neighbour strategy.

Sixty years of armed conflict and the restrictive Navigation Acts pushed competitors out of the markets it sought to monopolise. It took over the leading role in shipping slaves from Africa to the Caribbean and created an overseas empire with a population of about 100 million by 1820.

Other European powers were losers in the British struggle for supremacy. By the end of the Napoleonic wars, the Dutch had lost all their Asian territories except Indonesia. The French were reduced to a token colonial presence in Asia, and lost their major asset in the Caribbean. Shortly after the war, Brazil established its independence from Portugal. Spain lost its huge colonial empire in Latin America, retaining only Cuba, Puerto Rico and the Philippines. Britain took over what the French and Dutch had lost in Asia and Africa, extended its control over India, and established a privileged commercial presence in Latin America.

Other losers included the former rulers of India, whose power and income were usurped in substantial part by the servants of the British East India Company. Under their rule, from 1757 to 1857, Indian per capita income fell, but British gains were substantial.

Between 1820 and 1913, British per capita income grew faster than at any time in the past — three times as fast as in 1700–1820. The basic reason for improved performance was the acceleration of technical progress, accompanied by rapid growth of the physical capital stock and improvement in the education and skills of the labour force, but changes in commercial policy also made a substantial contribution. In 1846 protective duties on agricultural imports were removed and in 1849 the Navigation Acts were terminated. By 1860, all trade and tariff restrictions had been removed unilaterally. In 1860 there were reciprocal treaties for freer trade with France and other European countries. These had most–favoured nation clauses which meant that bilateral liberalisation applied equally to all countries.

Free trade was imposed in India and other British colonies, and the same was true in Britain's informal empire. China, Persia, Thailand and the Ottoman Empire were not colonies, but were obliged to maintain low tariffs by treaties which reduced their sovereignty in commercial matters, and granted extraterritorial rights to foreigners. This regime of free trade imperialism favoured British exports, but was less damaging to the interests of the colonies than in the eighteenth century, when Jamaica could only trade with Britain and its colonies, Guadeloupe only with France.

The British policy of free trade and its willingness to import a large part of its food had positive effects on the world economy. They reinforced and diffused the impact of technical progress. The favourable impact was biggest in North America, the southern cone of Latin America and Australasia which had rich natural resources and received a substantial inflow of capital, but there was also some positive effect in India which was the biggest and poorest part of the Empire.

Innovations in communications played a major part in linking national capital markets and facilitating international capital movements. The United Kingdom already had an important role in international finance, thanks to the soundness of its public credit and monetary system, the size of its

capital market and public debt, and the maintenance of a gold standard. The existence of the empire created a system of property rights which appeared to be as securely protected as those available to investors in British securities. It was a wealthy country operating close to the frontiers of technology, so its rentiers were attracted to foreign investment even when the extra margin of profit was small.

From the 1870s onward, there was a massive outflow of British capital for overseas investment. The United Kingdom directed half its savings abroad. French, German and Dutch investment was also substantial.

The old liberal order was shattered by two world wars and the collapse of capital flows, migration and trade in the beggar–your–neighbour years of the 1930s. Between 1913 and 1950, the world economy grew much more slowly than in 1870–1913, world trade grew much less than world income, and the degree of inequality between regions increased substantially, the setback being biggest in Asia.

By 1950 colonialism was in an advanced state of disintegration. With one or two exceptions, the exit from empire was more or less complete by the 1960s. The British imperial order was finished, as were those of Belgium, France, the Netherlands and Japan. In the West, the United States had emerged as the hegemonial power competing with the Soviet bloc for leverage in the newly independent countries of Asia and Africa.

The world economy grew very much faster from 1950 to 1973 than it had ever done before. It was a golden age of unparalleled prosperity. World per capita GDP rose nearly 3 per cent a year (a rate which implies a doubling every 25 years). World GDP rose by nearly 5 per cent a year and world trade by nearly 8 per cent a year. This dynamism affected all regions. The acceleration was greatest in Europe and Asia. There was also a degree of convergence between regions, though a good part of this was a narrowing of the gap between the United States and the other advanced capitalist countries (Western Europe and Japan).

There were several reasons for unusually favourable performance in the golden age. In the first place, the advanced capitalist countries created a new kind of liberal international order with explicit and rational codes of behaviour, and institutions for co–operation (OEEC, OECD, IMF, World Bank and the GATT) which had not existed before. There was a very serious East–West split from 1948 onwards, but the split reinforced the harmony of interest between capitalist economies, so the beggar–your–neighbour behaviour of pre–war years did not recur. The United States provided a substantial flow of aid for Europe when it was most needed, fostering procedures for articulate co–operation and liberal trading policies. Until the 1970s it also provided the world with a strong anchor for international monetary stability. North–South relations were transformed from the colonial tutelage of pre–war years to a situation where more emphasis was placed on action to stimulate development. The huge expansion of trade in the advanced capitalist economies transmitted a dynamic influence throughout the world economy.

The second new element of strength was the character of domestic policies which were self–consciously devoted to promotion of high levels of demand and employment in the advanced countries. Growth was not only faster than ever before, but the business cycle virtually disappeared. Investment rose to unprecedented levels and expectations became euphoric. Until the 1970s, there was also much milder inflationary pressure than could have been expected in conditions of secular boom.

The third element in this virtuous circle situation was the potential for growth on the supply side. Throughout Europe and Asia there was still substantial scope for "normal" elements of "recovery" from the years of depression and war. Additionally and more importantly, was the continued acceleration of technical progress in the lead country. Furthermore, the United States played a diffusionist role in the golden age in sharp contrast to its role in the interwar years.

Since the golden age, the world picture has changed a great deal. Per capita growth has been less than half as fast. There has been much greater divergence in the performance of different regions. In Western Europe and Japan, per capita growth fell well below that in the golden age, but was appreciably

better than in 1870–1913. In the countries of "resurgent Asia", which have half the world's population, the success was quite extraordinary. Their per capita growth was faster after 1973 than in the golden age, and more than ten times as fast as in the old liberal order.

If the world consisted only of these two groups, the pattern of world development could be interpreted as a clear demonstration of the possibilities for convergence. By success in mobilising and allocating resources efficiently and improving their human and physical capital to assimilate and adapt appropriate technology, the countries of resurgent Asia achieved significant catch–up on the advanced capitalist group.

However, there is another group (168 countries, with about a third of the world's population) where the deterioration in performance since the golden age has been alarming. In Africa there has been no advance in per capita income in the past quarter century. In Eastern Europe and the former USSR, average per capita income in 1998 was about threequarters of that in 1973. In Latin America and in many Asian countries, income gains have been a fraction of what they were in the golden age. The economies of this heterogeneous group of "faltering economies" have been falling behind instead of catching up. Most of them have not been able to adapt successfully to an international economic order which has changed considerably from that in the golden age.

The way in which postwar order now operates is analysed in detail in Chapter 3. The structure of the analysis is based on Table 3–5 which summarises the comparative performance of the major regions.

c) Technological and Institutional Innovation

From the year 1000 to 1820, advances in technology were much slower than they have been since, but they were nevertheless a significant component of the growth process. Without improvements in agriculture, the increase in world population could not have been sustained. Without improvements in maritime technology and commercial institutions the opening up of the world economy could not have been achieved. Technical advance in important areas was dependent on fundamental improvements in scientific method, experimental testing, systematic accumulation and publication of new knowledge. The long centuries of effort provided intellectual and institutional foundations for the much more rapid advances achieved in the nineteenth and twentieth centuries.

This process of cumulative advance is clearly demonstrated in the history of maritime technology and navigation. In the year 1000, European ships and navigation were no better than in the Roman Empire. The advance started when Venice created its public shipyard, the Arsenal, in 1104 to build its oared galleys and improve ship design. The introduction of the compass and the sandglass for measuring time at sea helped to double the productivity of ships. They could navigate in bad weather and make two return journeys a year from Venice to Alexandria instead of one. The Portuguese preparations for the passage to India were a major research project involving years of experimentation in shipping technology, improvement of navigational instruments and charts, applied astronomy, developing knowledge of winds, currents and alternative routes. The Dutch created a new type of factory ship for processing the herring catch at sea. They developed mass production of a cheap general purpose cargo vessel (the fluyt). The British government financed and encouraged research into astronomy, terrestrial magnetism, production of the first reliable maritime chronometer and nautical almanacs. They also demonstrated the efficacy of sauerkraut and citrus juice in preventing scurvy.

By the end of the eighteenth century ships could carry ten times the cargo of a fourteenth century Venetian galley, with a much smaller crew. The safety of long distance sea travel was also greatly improved. In their first voyages to Asia, da Gama and Cabral lost half their crew and more than half of their ships. Magellan lost more than 90 per cent of his crew on the first circumnavigation of the globe. Cook's successful circumnavigation 240 years later approximated modern standards of maritime safety.

Until the fifteenth century, European progress in many fields was dependent on transfers of technology from Asia or the Arab world. In 1405–33, Chinese superiority in shipping technology was evident in seven major expeditions to the "Western Oceans" (see Table 2–11). Chinese ships were much bigger than those of the Portuguese, more seaworthy and more comfortable, with watertight compartments, many more cabins, and a capacity to navigate over large distances to Africa. Thereafter, China turned its back on the world economy, and its maritime technology decayed.

By the end of the seventeenth century, the technological leadership of Europe in shipping and armaments was apparent. There had also been important institutional advances. Banking, credit, foreign exchange markets, financial and fiscal management, accountancy, insurance and corporate governance (by the Dutch and British East India Companies) were more sophisticated than those in Asia, and were essential components of European success in opening up the world economy.

Within Western Europe the diffusion of technology was fairly rapid, and the technological distance between nations was not particularly wide in spite of the frequency of wars. Links were fostered by the growth of humanist scholarship, the creation of universities and the invention of printing.

In the sixteenth and seventeenth centuries, there was a revolutionary change in the quality of western science with close interaction of savants and scientists such as Copernicus, Erasmus, Bacon, Galileo, Hobbes, Descartes, Petty, Leibnitz, Huyghens, Halley and Newton. Many of them were in close contact with colleagues in other countries, or spent years abroad. This type of co–operation was institutionalised by the creation of scientific academies which encouraged discussion and research, and published their proceedings. Much of this work had practical relevance, and many of the leading figures were concerned with matters of public policy.

Diffusion of these advances outside Europe was relatively limited. There were Jesuit scholars in Peking for nearly two centuries, some of them like Ricci, Schall and Verbiest had intimate contact with ruling circles, but there was little curiosity amongst the Chinese elite about intellectual and scientific development in the West. Japanese exposure to western knowledge was more limited than Chinese, but its impact went deeper. The Portuguese and the Jesuits were in Japan for nearly a century, and there was considerable interest in European ships, maps, navigation and guns. After the Portuguese were expelled the only contact Japan had with western learning was with those Dutch East India Company officials who were scientists (Kaempfer, Thunberg and von Siebold). Although these contacts were limited, they helped destroy Japanese respect for "things Chinese" and accentuate their curiosity about "things Western" (see Appendix B).

The East India Company officers who controlled India from 1757 to 1857 had a strong streak of Benthamite radicalism, and a strong urge to modify Indian legal and property institutions. After the Indian Mutiny of 1857 and establishment of direct imperial control, these radical westernising ambitions were dropped. In Indonesia, there were somewhat similar ambitions in the period of British administration during the Napoleonic wars, but Westernisation was abandoned after the Diponogoro revolt in the 1830s.

The only effective overseas transmission of European technology and science by the end of the eighteenth century was to the 13 British colonies in North America. In 1776 they had nine universities for 2.5 million people and an intellectual elite (e.g. Benjamin Franklin and Thomas Jefferson) fully familiar with the activities of their European contemporaries. In the Spanish colonies, Brazil and the Caribbean there were more than 17 million people, but only two universities (in Mexico City and Guadalajara) which concentrated on theology and law.

The reasons for the accelerated growth of technical progress since 1820 are analysed in considerable detail in my earlier study, *Monitoring the World Economy* (1995), particularly in Chapter 2 and pp. 71–3, and are not treated at any length in this volume. However, it is clear that technical progress has slowed down. It was a good deal faster from 1913 to 1973 than it has been since. The slowdown in the past quarter century is one of the reasons for the deceleration of world economic growth. "New economy" pundits find the notion of decelerating technical progress unacceptable and cite anecdotal or microeconomic evidence to argue otherwise. However, the impact of their technological revolution has not been apparent in the macroeconomic statistics until very recently, and I do not share their euphoric expectations[5].

Notes

1. Wrigley and Schofield (1981) and Wrigley and Associates (1997) used techniques of family reconstitution and inverse projection to exploit church records of births, deaths and marriages. As a result, we now have annual estimates of English population and demographic characteristics since 1541. Bagnall and Frier (1994) used remnants of Roman censuses to reconstruct the demography and economy of third century Egypt. Thanks to the work of de Vries (1984) for Europe and Rozman (1973) for Asia one can measure the proportionate importance of urbanisation for long periods in the past. The Chinese bureaucracy kept population registers which go back more than 2 000 years. These bureaucratic records were designed to assess taxable capacity, and include information on cultivated area and crop production, which was used by Perkins (1969) to assess long run movements in Chinese GDP per capita. The work of Perkins encouraged me to write *Chinese Economic Performance in the Long Run* (OECD Development Centre, 1998) which has the same temporal perspective as the present study.

2. See Maddison (1998a), pp. 24–33 for an analysis of the historical development of Chinese agriculture; see Boserup (1965) for a brilliant refutation of the simplistic Malthusian view that population pressure on a fixed stock of natural resources will inevitably produce diminishing returns. She shows how "traditional" Asian agriculture accommodated population pressure by a whole series of changes of technical practice. Intensity of land use progressed from hunter–gatherer activities, to forest fallow, settled farming with improved tools, from dry farming and fallowing to irrigation and multi–cropping. In this process there was probably a significant drop in labour productivity before modern fertilisers and machinery came on the scene.

3. See Morison (1971) on the Norwegian movement from Iceland to Greenland and Leif Ericsson's trip in 1001 via Baffin island, Belle Isle and the Labrador sea to the northern tip of Newfoundland where there was a very brief and long forgotten settlement at l'Anse aux Meadows.

4. Adam Smith *The Wealth of Nations,* 1776, book IV, Chapter VII, Part II contains a prescient assessment of these institutional differences and their implications for subsequent development. Engrossment of land which hindered its development and transfer, the heavy burden taxes to support the pomp of civil and ecclesiastical government, and official control of markets were the shortcomings in the Spanish colonies which he emphasised. See Chapter 2 of this study for my assessment of the Portuguese influence on Brazil, and the difference between the colonial heritage in Mexico and the United States.

5. See the discussion of US economic performance in Chapter 3, and Box 3–1.

Chapter 1

The Contours of World Development

World economic performance was very much better in the second millennium of our era than in the first. Between 1000 and 1998 population rose 22–fold and per capita income 13–fold. In the previous millennium, population rose by a sixth and per capita GDP fell slightly.

The second millennium comprised two distinct epochs. From 1000 to 1820 the upward movement in per capita income was a slow crawl — for the world as a whole the rise was about 50 per cent. Growth was largely "extensive" in character. Most of it went to accommodate a fourfold increase in population. Since 1820, world development has been much more dynamic, and more "intensive". Per capita income rose faster than population; by 1998 it was 8.5 times as high as in 1820; population rose 5.6–fold.

There was a wide disparity in the performance of different regions in both epochs. The most dynamic was Group A: Western Europe, Western Offshoots (the United States, Canada, Australia and New Zealand) and Japan. In 1000–1820, their average per capita income grew nearly four times as fast as the average for the rest of the world. The differential continued between 1820 and 1998 when per capita income of the first group rose 19–fold and 5.4–fold for the second.

There are much wider income gaps today than at any other time in the past. Two thousand years ago the average level for Groups A and B was similar. In the year 1000 the average for Group A was lower as a result of the economic collapse after the fall of the Roman Empire. By 1820, Group A had forged ahead to a level about twice that in the rest of the world. In 1998 the gap was almost 7:1. Between the Western Offshoots and Africa (the richest and poorest regions) it is 19 to one.

Economic performance since 1820 within Group B has not been as closely clustered as in Group A. Per capita income has grown faster in Latin America than Eastern Europe and Asia, and nearly twice as fast as in Africa. Nevertheless, from a Western standpoint, performance in all these regions has been disappointing.

There have been big changes in the weight of different regions. In the year 1000, Asia (except Japan) produced more than two thirds of world GDP, Western Europe less than 9 per cent. In 1820 the proportions were 56 and 24 per cent respectively. In 1998, the Asian share was about 30 per cent compared with 46 per cent for Western Europe and Western Offshoots combined.

Table 1–1. **Level and Rate of Growth of Population: World and Major Regions, 0–1998 A.D.**

	0	1000	1820	1998	0–1000	1000–1820	1820–1998
			(million)		(annual average compound growth rate)		
Western Europe	24.7	25.4	132.9	388	0.00	0.20	0.60
Western Offshoots	1.2	2.0	11.2	323	0.05	0.21	1.91
Japan	3.0	7.5	31.0	126	0.09	0.17	0.79
Total Group A	28.9	34.9	175.1	838	0.02	0.20	0.88
Latin America	5.6	11.4	21.2	508	0.07	0.08	1.80
Eastern Europe & former USSR	8.7	13.6	91.2	412	0.05	0.23	0.85
Asia (excluding Japan)	171.2	175.4	679.4	3 390	0.00	0.17	0.91
Africa	16.5	33.0	74.2	760	0.07	0.10	1.32
Total Group B	202.0	233.4	866.0	5 069	0.01	0.16	1.00
World	230.8	268.3	1 041.1	5 908	0.02	0.17	0.98

Source: Appendix B.

Table 1–2. **Level and Rate of Growth of GDP Per Capita: World and Major Regions, 0–1998 A.D.**

	0	1000	1820	1998	0–1000	1000–1820	1820–1998
		(1990 international dollars)			(annual average compound growth rate)		
Western Europe	450	400	1 232	17 921	−0.01	0.14	1.51
Western Offshoots	400	400	1 201	26 146	0.00	0.13	1.75
Japan	400	425	669	20 413	0.01	0.06	1.93
Average Group A	443	405	1 130	21 470	−0.01	0.13	1.67
Latin America	400	400	665	5 795	0.00	0.06	1.22
Eastern Europe & former USSR	400	400	667	4 354	0.00	0.06	1.06
Asia (excluding Japan)	450	450	575	2 936	0.00	0.03	0.92
Africa	425	416	418	1 368	−0.00	0.00	0.67
Average Group B	444	440	573	3 102	−0.00	0.03	0.95
World	444	435	667	5 709	−0.00	0.05	1.21

Source: Appendix B.

Table 1–3. **Level and Rate of Growth of GDP: World and Major Regions, 0–1998 A.D.**

	0	1000	1820	1998	0–1000	1000–1820	1820–1998
		(billion 1990 international dollars)			(annual average compound growth rate)		
Western Europe	11.1	10.2	163.7	6 961	−0.01	0.34	2.13
Western Offshoots	0.5	0.8	13.5	8 456	0.05	0.35	3.68
Japan	1.2	3.2	20.7	2 582	0.10	0.23	2.75
Total Group A	12.8	14.1	198.0	17 998	0.01	0.32	2.57
Latin America	2.2	4.6	14.1	2 942	0.07	0.14	3.05
Eastern Europe & former USSR	3.5	5.4	60.9	1 793	0.05	0.29	1.92
Asia (excluding Japan)	77.0	78.9	390.5	9 953	0.00	0.20	1.84
Africa	7.0	13.7	31.0	1 939	0.07	0.10	1.99
Total Group B	89.7	102.7	496.5	15 727	0.01	0.19	1.96
World	102.5	116.8	694.4	33 726	0.01	0.22	2.21

Source: Appendix B.

I
The Nature and Welfare Implications of Population Change

The acceleration of population growth over the past millennium could have come from increased fertility or reduced mortality. The evidence (Table 1–4) suggests that a slow and irregular decline in mortality was the predominant cause before 1820. Since 1820 the decline in mortality has been much sharper, and has clearly been the predominant influence. In fact fertility has declined substantially since 1820 (see Table 1–5a). Increases in life expectation are an important manifestation of improvement in human welfare. They are not captured by our measure of GDP, but there has been significant congruence, over time and between regions, in the patterns of improvement in per capita income and life expectation.

Table 1–4. **Life Expectation and Infant Mortality, Both Sexes Combined, 33–1875 A.D.**

Country and period	Years of life expectation at birth	Death rate per 1000 population in lst year of life	Source & authors
Roman Egypt, 33–258	24.0	329	Fragments of Roman Censuses Bagnall and Frier
England, 1301–1425	24.3	218	Very crude estimates derived from fiscal records: Russell
England, 1541–56	33.7	n.a.	Family reconstitution and
England, 1620–26	37.7	171	inverse projection from
England, 1726–51	34.6	195	birth and death records:
England, 1801–26	40.8	144	Wrigley, et al.
France, 1740–49	24.8	296	Family reconstitution:
France, 1820–29	38.8	181	Blayo
Sweden, 1751–55	37.8	203[a]	Parish records & census returns: Gille
Japan, 1776–1875	32.2	277	Temple records: Jannetta
Japan, 1800–50	33.7	295	Temple records: Yasuba
Japan, 1751–1869	37.4	216	Population registers: Saito

a) 1751–1800.

Source: Egypt from Bagnall and Frier (1994), pp. 70 and 100. England 1301–1425 from Russell (1948), pp. 186 and 218. England 1541–1826 (excluding Monmouth) from Wrigley et al. 1997), p.614 for life expectation and p. 219 for infant mortality. France from Blayo (1975), p. 141 for life expectation, pp. 138–9 for infant mortality. Sweden from Gille (1949). Japan from Jannetta and Preston (1991), p. 428 and 433–5, Yasuba (1987), p. 291, deducting a year to adjust to Western reckoning. Saito (1997), p. 143 average for both sexes of his high infant mortality estimate. The first two estimates are derived from temple registers (kakocho), the third from population registers (shumon aratame cho). There is a much greater scarcity of information on infant mortality in Japanese sources than in the European records. Children were not covered in the registers. Temple records provide material on deaths by age but not population. There is a further problem that the Japanese system of counting age was different from that in the West and the degree of ambiguity was large for infants. Japanese children were presumed to be 1 year old at birth and two years old on the following New Year's day. A Japanese child could therefore be anywhere between 2 days and 1 year old when it became 2 years old in the Japanese system (see Saito, 1997). Estimates of infant mortality are therefore hypothetical or inferential. Saito used one of the probability models which Coale and Demeny (1983) constructed to fill gaps in information on deaths by age. Saito (1997), p. 136 shows other estimates with much higher life expectation than the three I show. In my view these are not plausible and either show or infer improbably low infant mortality. Kalland and Pederson (1984) pp. 54 and 61 show life expectation averaging 44 years for 1700–1824 in Kanezaki and an infant mortality rate of less than 100. Smith (1977) pp. 57 and 162 shows a life expectation of 43.2 for 1717–1830 in Nakahara, and a range of alternative infant mortality options which Saito averages at 145. Hanley and Yamamura (1977), p. 222 show a life expectation of 45 for Nishikata 1782–96 and 43 for Fujito 1800–35, without showing infant mortality.

In the year 1000, average life expectation at the world level was probably about 24 years — no better than at the beginning of our era. By 1820, it rose to about 26 years (see Table 1–5a). The rise was biggest — from 24 to 36 years — in Group A, and since then has risen to 78 years. The increase was ten times as fast from 1820 as in the previous eight centuries. In Group B countries, our very crude estimate suggests that there was no improvement between 1000 and 1820. By 1998 it had grown dramatically to an average of 64 years.

Table 1–5a. **Birth Rates and Life Expectation, 1820–1998/9**

	Births per 100 population				*Years of life expectation at birth* (Average for both sexes)			
	1820	*1900*	*1950*	*1998*	*1820*	*1900*	*1950*	*1999*
France	3.19	2.19	2.05	1.26	37	47	65	78
Germany	3.99	3.60	1.65	0.96	41	47	67	77
Italy	3.90	3.30	1.94	0.93	30	43	66	78
Netherlands	3.50	3.16	2.27	1.27	32	52	72	78
Spain	4.00	3.39	2.00	0.92	28	35	62	78
Sweden	3.40	2.69	1.64	1.01	39	56	70	79
United Kingdom	4.02[a]	2.93	1.62	1.30	40[a]	50	69	77
West European Average	3.74	3.08	1.83	1.00	36	46	67	78
United States	5.52	3.23	2.40	1.44	39	47	68	77
Japan	2.62[b]	3.24	2.81	0.95	34	44	61	81
Russia	4.13	4.80	2.65	0.88	28[c]	32	65	67
Brazil	5.43[d]	4.60	4.44	2.10	27[e]	36	45	67
Mexico	n.a.	4.69	4.56	2.70	n.a.	33	50	72
Latin America Average	n.a.	n.a.	4.19	2.51	(27)	(35)	51	69
China	n.a.	4.12[f]	3.70	1.60	n.a.	24[f]	41	71
India	n.a.	4.58[g]	4.50[h]	2.80	21[i]	24g	32[h]	60
Asian Average[j]	n.a.	n.a.	4.28	2.30	(23)	(24)	40	66
African Average	n.a.	n.a.	4.92	3.90	(23)	(24)	38	52
World	n.a.	n.a.	3.74	2.30	26	31	49	66

a) 1821; b) 1811–29; c) 1880; d) 1818; e) 1872; f) 1929–31; g) 1891–1911; h) 1941–51; i) 1833; j) excluding Japan.

Source: Birth rates 1820 and 1900: European countries mostly from Maddison (1991a) p. 241; 1821 for England from Wrigley *et al.* (1997), p. 614; Brazil 1818, from Marcilio (1984), otherwise Brazil and Mexico from Maddison and Associates (1992); United States 1820 and 1900 from *Historical Statistics of the United States*, (1975), vol.1, p. 49; China 1929–31 from Barclay *et al.* (1976); India entries for 1900 and 1950 from Mari Bhat (1989), p. 96; Japan 1816–20 (in Yokoucho) from Hayami (1973), p. 160, 1900 and 1950 from Japan Statistical Association (1987). 1950 generally from OECD (1979) and national sources. 1998 from OECD, *Labour Force Statistics, Population et Sociétés*, INED, Paris July–August 1999, and UN Population Division (1997).
Life expectancy 1820: France from Blayo (1975); Germany from Knodel (1988), p. 59 (average of his alternative estimates); Italy derived from Caselli (1991), p. 73; Spain derived from Livi Bacci and Reher (1993), p. 68; Sweden from Gille (1949), p. 43; the United Kingdom from Wrigley *et al.* (1997), p. 614; Russia (1874–84) from Ohlin (1955), p. 411; the United States from *Historical Statistics of the United States* (1975), vol. 1, p. 56 (refers to Massachusetts in 1850); Japan 1820 — average of three estimates in Table 1–4; Brazil 1872 and 1900 from Merrick and Graham (1979), pp. 41, 42 and 57; China , 1929–31 from Barclay, Coale, Stoto and Trussell (1976, p. 621); India, 1833 for Delhi from Visaria and Visaria (1983), p. 473, 1891–1911 and 1941–51 from Mari Bhat (1989), pp. 92, using an average of the three alternative measures shown. 1900 from Maddison (1995a), p. 27, except for the United Kingdom, from Wrigley *et al.* 1950 for most OECD countries from OECD (1979), Mexico from Maddison and Associates (1992), China from Lee and Wang (forthcoming). India from Mari Bhat (1989). Japan from Japan Statistical Association (1987). Other countries and regions 1950 from UN Population Division (1997). 1999 from *Population et Sociétés*. Regions 1820–1900 derived by weighting country estimates. World averages derived by weighting regional averages by regional population.

Life expectation in 1999 in the Group A countries was fairly closely clustered. In Group B, there was not much difference between Russia, Latin America and Asia, with an average of 67 years. But in Africa, life expectation was significantly lower at 52 years.

Although the pattern of improvement in life expectation and per capita income has been similar, the present interregional dispersions are much bigger for income. In 1999 the gap in life expectation between the lead country, Japan, with 81 years and Africa with 52 years was distressingly wide. But it was much smaller than the 15:1 spread in per capita income level between Japan and Africa.

Table 1–5b. **Average Life Expectation for Groups A and B, 1000–1999**
(years at birth; average for both sexes)

	1000	*1820*	*1900*	*1950*	*1999*
Group A	24	36	46	66	78
Group B	24	24	26	44	64
World	24	26	31	49	66

Source: 1820–1999 from weighted average of regions shown in Table 1–5a. Figure for 1000 is a rough inference from first two entries in Table 1–4 and other fragmentary clues.

Table 1–5c. **Rate of Growth of Life Expectation in Groups A and B, 1000–1999**
(annual average compound growth rate)

	1000–1820	*1820–1900*	*1900–50*	*1950–99*
Group A	0.05	0.31	0.72	0.34
Group B	0.00	0.10	1.06	0.77
World	0.01	0.22	0.92	0.61

West European Experience

Table 1–6 presents the evidence on long run growth of West European population. The pace of change has been very uneven. There were major disasters in the sixth and fourteenth centuries and a substantial setback in several countries in the seventeenth century. Until the nineteenth century population growth was repeatedly interrupted by crises of varying frequency and severity. These were of three main types: hunger crises due to harvest failure, waves of infectious disease, or war. These different types of causality were of course interactive in varying degree.

As European countries operated much nearer to subsistence levels in the past than is now the case, with poor transport and storage facilities, harvest failures could create big spikes in mortality. They also affected birth rates, because dietary deficiencies caused amenorrhea or led young couples to postpone marriage. A major instance of this type of crisis was the potato famine which doubled the normal death rate in Ireland over the six years 1846–51. "Excess" deaths were nearly one million or about 12 per cent of the 1845 population (see Ó Gráda, 1988).

Figure 1-1. **Population of Western Europe: Confrontation of Two Millennia**
(000)

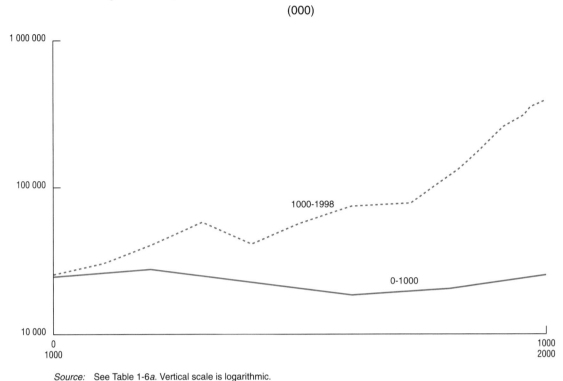

Source: See Table 1-6a. Vertical scale is logarithmic.

Table 1–6a. **West European Population Levels, 0–1998 A.D.**
(000)

0	200	400	600	800	1000	1200
24 700	27 600	22 900	18 600	20 400	25 413	40 885

1300	1400	1500	1600	1700	1820	1998
58 353	41 500	57 268	73 776	81 460	132 888	388 399

Source: McEvedy and Jones (1978) and Appendix B. The share of five Mediterranean countries (France, Greece, Italy, Portugal, Spain) dropped from 77 per cent in the year 0 to 67 per cent in 1000, 60 per cent in 1500, 52 per cent in 1820, and 45 per cent in 1998.

Table 1–6b. **West European Population Growth Rates, 0–1998 A.D.**
(annual average compound growth rates)

0–200	200–600	600–1000	1000–1300	1300–1400
0.06	–0.10	0.08	0.28	–0.34

1400–1500	1500–1600	1600–1700	1700–1820	1820–1998
0.32	0.24	0.08	0.41	0.60

Source: As for 1–6a.

Figure 1-2. **Annual Movement in Swedish Birth and Death Rates, 1736-1987**

(per 1 000 population)

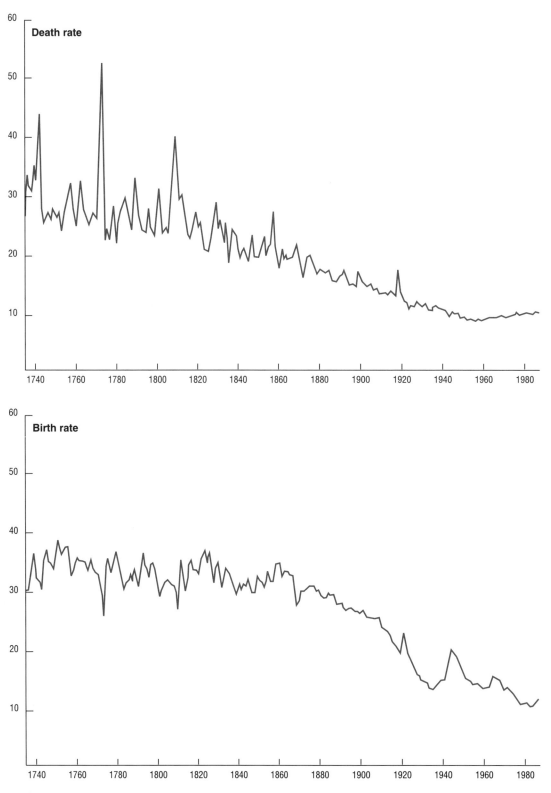

Source: H. Gille "The Demographic History of the Northern Countries in the Eighteenth Century", *Population Studies,* June 1949; *Historical Statistics for Sweden,* vol. i, CBS, Stockholm, 1955; and *OECD Labour Force Statistics,* Paris, various issues.

Recurrent episodes of infectious disease caused major surges in mortality. The worst was bubonic plague which wiped out a third of the European population in the sixth century and again in the fourteenth. The second plague lingered for centuries, finally dying out in England in 1665 and in France in 1720–21. John Graunt, the first scientific demographer, chronicled its impact in London for the years 1592, 1603, 1625, 1630, 1636, and 1665, the worst year, when a total of 97 000 burials were recorded (about 16 per cent of the population). Biraben (1972) estimated a total of 94 000 plague deaths in Provence in 1720–1 (about 32 per cent of the population) due to the arrival of a ship in Marseilles which brought the disease from Syria. The impact of this plague was limited by strict control of movement in and out of the region. The plague disappeared, but many other lethal diseases remained — cholera, diphtheria, dysentery, influenza, measles, smallpox, tuberculosis, typhus and typhoid. Their incidence receded temporarily after epidemics had wiped out the least resistant. In some cases, like the plague, repeated exposure seems to have generated resistance or immunity in the long term. In other cases, the bacterial and viral organisms responsible for infection may have changed. The pattern and duration of acquired immunities varied for reasons not fully understood, but the impact of epidemic disease declined sharply in Western Europe in the late nineteenth and in the twentieth century. However deaths surged again in the global influenza epidemic of 1918–19. The new threat from Aids seems to have been contained in Group A countries.

Until the twentieth century, a major countervailing force in the process of mortality reduction was increased urbanisation. Although city dwellers had higher incomes and better organised food markets than rural areas, their mortality rates were distinctly higher. John Graunt discovered this for London in the seventeenth century where burials were substantially higher than christenings. Mortality rates were a good deal higher in London than in small towns like Romsey, Tiverton and Cranbrook whose experience he also investigated. London's expansion was due to high net immigration, but the big city was a reservoir of infection, with poor sanitation, most lethal in its impact on infants and recent immigrants. Wrigley et al. (1997), p. 218, note that in the early eighteenth century London's infant mortality rate was about twice as high as for the country as a whole. Hayami (1986a) notes the same phenomenon in Japan, citing evidence for the capital city Edo for 1840–68. In the course of the twentieth century this differential has disappeared (see Preston and van der Walle, 1978, for the decline in the differential in nineteenth century France).

Over the long run, in the centuries before 1820, there was a slow increase in agricultural productivity and improvements in food availability. Hunger crises became less frequent or severe. Increased resistance to disease was also helped by rising living standards, substitution of wine, beer and tea for contaminated water, improvements in clothing and bedding. In the nineteenth and twentieth centuries, better sanitation and public health facilities, improvements in medical knowledge and facilities greatly reduced the incidence of premature death by infectious disease (see Fogel, 1986, for a causal analysis of mortality decline). The most striking feature has been the reduction in infant mortality. Around 1820, it was probably between 150–200 per 1 000 population in Western Europe and about 200 in Japan. In the 1990s, it was about seven in Western Europe and four per 1 000 in Japan. The increase in life expectation for the elderly in Western Europe, the Western Offshoots and Japan since 1950 involved a big rise in health expenditure. Earlier decreases in mortality in the nineteenth and twentieth centuries were much cheaper to obtain.

Figure 1–2 provides a fairly representative picture of European mortality and fertility experience since 1736 when such records first became available in Sweden. Vallin (1991) presents similar charts for English, French, Finnish and Norwegian mortality back to 1720. Until the latter half of the nineteenth century, the pattern in all these countries was more irregular than it has been since because crisis mortality has been greatly mitigated. Figure I–2 also shows the demographic transition which started in the mid-nineteenth century throughout most of Western Europe.

Birth rates have fallen more than death rates. In 1998, they were about a third of their 1820 level. As a consequence population growth is much slower and demographic structure has changed dramatically. In England, which is fairly typical of West European experience, nearly 39 per cent of 1821 population were below 15 years of age and less than 5 per cent were 65 or over. In 1998, 19 per cent were below 15 and nearly 16 per cent 65 or over. The proportion aged 15–64 rose from 60 to 65 per cent.

Table 1–7a. Population Growth: Western and Iberian Offshoots in Comparative Perspective, 1500–1998
(annual average compound growth rates)

	1500–1700	1700–1820	1820–1950	1950–73	1973–98
United States	−0.35	1.94	2.12	1.45	0.98
Canada	−0.11	1.18	2.20	2.18	1.19
Australia & New Zealand	0.00	− 0.20	2.45	2.16	1.27
Brazil	0.11	1.07	1.92	2.91	2.00
Other Latin America & Caribbean	−0.21	0.36	1.63	2.65	2.02
Western Europe	0.18	0.41	0.64	0.70	0.32
Japan	0.28	0.12	0.77	1.15	0.61
Rest of World	0.17	0.47	0.58	2.09	1.85

Source: Appendices A and B.

Table 1–7b. Comparative Population Growth in the Americas and Former European Metropoles, 1500–1998

	Population level (million)		Coefficient of multiplication		Population level (million)		Coefficient of multiplication
	1500	1998	1500–1998		1500	1998	1500–1998
Brazil	1	170	170	United States	2.00	271	136
Portugal	1	10	10	United Kingdom	3.94	59	15
Other Latin America	16.5	338	20	Canada	0.25	30	120
Spain	6.8	39	6	France	15.00	59	4

Source: Appendices A and B.

Table 1–7c. Shipment of African Slaves to the Americas, 1500–1870
(000)

	1500–1600	1601–1700	1701–1810	1811–70	1500–1870
Brazil	50	560	1 891	1 145	3 647
Caribbean[a]	–	464	3 234	96	3 793
Spanish America	75	293	579	606	1 552
United States	–	–	348	51	399

a) British, French, Dutch and Danish colonies.
Source: Curtin (1969), p. 268. See also Table 2–5 below.

Table 1–7d. Net Migration to Brazil, Australia and United States and from the United Kingdom, 1500–1998

	1500–1600	1600–1700	1700–1820	1820–69	1870–1913	1913–50	1950–98
Brazil	+40	+60	+400	+400	+2 200	+1 294	n.a.
Australia	–	–	+33	+1 069	+885	+673	+4 184
United States	–	+131	+587	+6 131	+15 820	+6 221	+24 978
United Kingdom	n.a.	−714	−672	−5 548	−6 415	−1 405	+132

Source: Brazil from Marcilio (1984), Merrick and Graham (1979) and IBGE (1960); Australia 1788–1973 from Vamplew (1987), pp. 4–7; thereafter from OECD, *Labour Force Statistics;* United States 1630–1780 from Galenson (1996), p. 178, and Potter (1965) for 1790–1820. I assumed that 1780–90 immigration was the same as Potter's estimate for 1790–1800; United Kingdom 1600–1820 from Henry and Blanchet (1983) who show net migration from England (their figures exclude deaths at sea and in wars abroad; 1820–69 from Mitchell (1975), pp. 137–40, gross emigration 1820–54 was reduced by one sixth, using the same emigrant/immigrant ratio available for 1855–69. United Kingdom and United States for 1870 onwards from Maddison (1991a), p. 240 and from OECD *Labour Force Statistics.*

Figure 1-3. **Comparative Population Levels in the Three Biggest Countries of the Americas and their Former European Metropoles, 1500-1998**

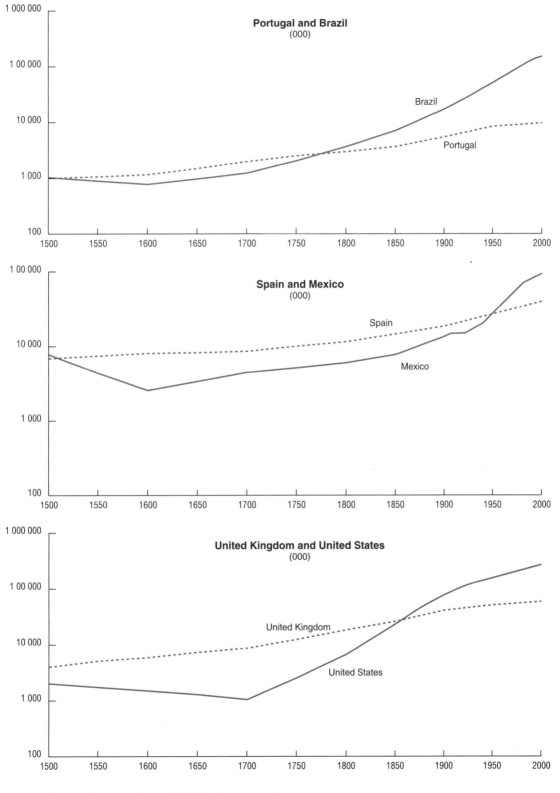

Source: See Appendices A, B, C. Vertical scale is logarithmic.

The Americas and Australasia

The pattern of mortality, migration and population growth in the Americas and Australia was changed drastically by the encounter with Western Europe. The relatively densely populated agrarian civilisations of Mexico and Peru were quickly destroyed by the sixteenth century Spanish conquest mainly because of the inadvertent introduction of European diseases (smallpox, measles, influenza and typhus). Shortly thereafter the traffic in slaves introduced yellow fever and malaria. The consequences were devastating for the indigenous population. At least threequarters of them perished (see Appendix B). In Latin America as a whole, mortality was about twice as big proportionately as Europe's loss from the Black Death.

In parts of the Americas where the population was mainly hunter–gatherers and less densely settled (e.g. Brazil, and the areas that subsequently became Canada and the United States), the impact of disease mortality was somewhat smaller.

Western contact with Australia and other Pacific islands occurred towards the end of the eighteenth century. The impact of disease on mortality was similar to that in the Americas, and there was a more deliberate policy of exterminating the native population than in Spanish America (see Butlin, 1983 and 1993).

Although the initial impact of conquest and colonisation was massively destructive for the indigenous population, the long term economic potential of the Americas was greatly enhanced. Capacity to support a bigger population was augmented by the introduction of new crops and animals (see Crosby, 1972). The new crops were wheat, rice, sugar cane, vines, salad greens, olives, bananas and coffee. The new animals for food were cattle, pigs, chickens, sheep and goats. The introduction of transport and traction animals — horses, oxen, asses and donkeys — along with wheeled vehicles and ploughs (which replaced digging sticks) were another major addition to productive capacity. There was also a reciprocal transfer of New World crops to Europe, Asia and Africa — maize, potatoes, sweet potatoes, manioc, chilis, tomatoes, groundnuts, pineapples, cocoa and tobacco — which enhanced the world's production potential and capacity to sustain population growth.

New economic horizons and acquisition of vast territories led to a large scale transfer of population from Europe and Africa. Between 1500 and 1870 almost nine and a half million African slaves were shipped to work in plantation agriculture (sugar, tobacco, coffee and cotton) in Brazil, the Caribbean and the southern United States.

The migration of Spanish and Portuguese settlers to Latin America in the colonial period (before 1820) was smaller than the movement of slaves. Portuguese emigration was probably about half a million (Marcilio, 1984), and Spanish less than a million (Sanchez–Albornoz, 1984). Galenson (1996) estimates British migration to the Caribbean to have been about a quarter of a million from 1630 to 1780. If we include French and Dutch migration, the net white migration to Latin America probably totalled two million before 1820, compared with imports of 7.5 million slaves. However the life expectation of slaves was a good deal lower. Merrick and Graham (1979, pp. 56–7) estimate 18 years for male slaves in Brazil in 1872, compared with 27 years for the total population. Fertility of slaves was also lower because of the precarious nature of their opportunities for family life. The proportion of females in the white immigrant population was low. Threequarters or more consisted of adult males. Their fertility was quite high because of informal unions with the indigenous and black population. As a result there was a much greater ethnic mix in Latin America than in North America.

Since 1820, Latin American population has grown faster than that of Western Europe. The main reason has been higher birth rates, as the decline in mortality came later and has been smaller. Migration from Europe to Latin America accounted for a substantial part of the differential before 1913, but has been less important since then.

In the area of the United States and Canada, European settlement started in the seventeenth century, and expanded rapidly in the eighteenth, when there was also a large import of slaves. The indigenous population was killed off or pushed out of the areas of European settlement. In 1700,

threequarters of the population had been indigenous, by 1820 they were only 3 per cent (see Table B–15). In the South, there was a heavy concentration on plantation agriculture, with slaves as the main component of the labour force. In the North, white settlers predominated and were mainly occupied on family farms.

White life expectation in North America was similar to that in Western Europe. It was lower for slaves, but the differential was smaller than in Brazil. Merrick and Graham (1979, p. 57) show 35.5 years for slaves in the 1850s and 40.4 for the US population as a whole. Fertility was high. In the United States, the birth rate was 5.5 per 100 population in 1820, in Canada (Quebec) 5.7. This was much higher than the United Kingdom (4.0) or France (3.2).

Since 1820 the US population has grown a good deal faster than that of Western Europe. The death rate has been similar. The birth rate has remained higher but has declined proportionately as much as in Western Europe. Immigration to the United States has continued at a high level. Most of the immigrants came from Europe before the 1960s, so migration explains a good deal of the US/European growth differential.

Japan

From the seventh to the mid–nineteenth century, Japan tried to model its economy, society and institutions on those of China, but its demographic experience was very different:

a)   over the long run, the major check to Japanese population expansion came from famines and hunger crises. Disease and war were much less important than in China (and Europe);

b)   by the second half of the eighteenth century, and perhaps earlier, Japanese life expectation was similar to that in Western Europe, and much higher than in China.

Comparative Incidence of Hunger, Disease and War

Macfarlane (1997) provides a comparative survey of the long run forces affecting mortality in England and Japan; Jannetta (1986) a detailed study of Japanese experience with epidemic disease, and Saito (1996) an assessment of the comparative incidence of famine and disease in Japan over the long term.

The major point which emerges from their work is that Japan was not affected by bubonic plague. The main reason was Japan's isolation. Two hundred kilometres of stormy seas separated it from Korea. The nearest point in China was 750 kilometres away. This sea barrier, and official policy, imposed an effective *cordon sanitaire*. Travel into and out of Japan was very restricted. Foreigners trading with Japan were more or less permanently quarantined in a small area near Nagasaki. There was no import of grain or other products likely to introduce pests. The two Mongol attempts to invade Japan in 1274 and 1281 were unsuccessful. If they had succeeded Japan's demographic history (and much else) would have been very different.

Freedom from the plague was the main reason why Japanese population growth was faster than that of Europe and China in the first millennium and a half of our era.

Smallpox was the most significant cause of Japanese epidemics. Mortality from other diseases — cholera, dysentery, malaria, measles, tuberculosis and typhoid fever was milder than in Europe, and epidemic typhus was absent. This situation was mainly due to hygienic habits, and very limited contact with animals. Japanese had an abundant supply of mountain streams and hot springs, and the Shinto emphasis on physical purity led to daily bathing at home or in bathhouses. Japanese houses were austere but kept spotlessly clean and well ventilated. Shoes were left at the entry, there was

virtually no furniture or hangings except mosquito nets. Most water consumption was in the form of tea made with boiling water. The Japanese diet consisted of rice, fish, soyabeans, a considerable variety of vegetables, bamboo shoots and giant radishes. Buddhist tradition meant that Japanese ate virtually no meat. They had no cows, pigs, sheep, goats or animal dung. Although human wastes were used for manure, the few foreigners who visited Japan were greatly impressed by the immaculate privies, and the sanitary treatment of sewage. In 1853, foreigners were able to force an entry into Japan and greatly increased the range of foreign contacts. This resulted very quickly in a major cholera epidemic in 1858–60, and much greater exposure to influenza, tuberculosis, typhoid, typhus and diphtheria (see Saito, 1996 and Honda, 1997). As a consequence the Japanese death rate rose significantly until the 1890s (see Ishii, 1937, pp. 124–5).

Saito (1996) has collated the historical records of famine and crop failure from the eighth to the twentieth century for Japan. Although it is not possible to measure the intensity of these hunger crises one can get an idea of changes in their frequency. From the eighth to the tenth centuries, there was one every three years, in the eleventh to fifteenth centuries one every five years, in the sixteenth to eighteenth one every four years, in the nineteenth every nine years, and none in the twentieth century.

It is not possible to compare the importance of Japanese hunger crises with those in China or Europe. However, the nature of the Japanese and European diets was very different. Europeans had substantial consumption of meat, milk and other animal products which were absent in Japan. They had sufficient cereal production to make large quantities of ale and beer which the Japanese did not have. Land scarcity was much greater in Japan, and Japanese had to work much more intensively than Europeans. The combination of greater austerity and greater physical strain may well have made Japanese more vulnerable to hunger crises than Europeans, but the susceptibility was probably similar to that of Chinese.

A third major check to population comes from war. Here Japanese experience was very mild compared with China, and probably milder than in Western Europe.

China suffered major losses from the Mongol invasion of North China in 1234. The Mongols razed many cities, inflicted great damage on agriculture, enserfed or enslaved part of the rural population and displaced them by pastoralising cropland to make way for horses. Their later assault on South China in 1279 was much less destructive, but Mongol horsemen brought bubonic plague in 1353. Total population loss from the encounter with the Mongols was around 30 million.

The transition from the Mongol to the Ming dynasty did not involve substantial mortality. The next big disaster was the replacement of the Ming by the Manchus. The Manchu takeover was rapid in North China in 1644, but the struggle with Ming loyalists in the South lasted till 1683. The savagery of war, combined with smallpox and famine, reduced population by more than 20 million. There was also significant migration from mainland China. In the struggle with Koxinga who operated from Taiwan, the Manchus carried out a scorched earth policy on the opposite coasts of Kwangtung, Fukien and Chekiang provinces, burning crops and villages to a depth of about eight to 30 miles. There was significant move of population from this area to Taiwan, and a wave of "overseas" Chinese migrants to Southeast Asia (see Purcell, 1965).

There were other major population losses in the Taiping and other anti–Manchu rebellions in the 1850s and 1860s. As a result of these and associated famine and disease, Chinese population dropped by more than 50 million from 1850 to 1870.

China also suffered significant losses from 1840 to 1945 from aggression by West European countries, Japan and Russia and from its own civil war from 1937 to 1949.

Japan never suffered from foreign invasions, and the two main episodes of civil war in the latter half of the twelfth century when the first (Kamakura) shogunate was established, and from 1467 to 1568, were much smaller in their impact than the wars China experienced.

Table 1–8a. **Comparative Population Growth: Japan, China and Western Europe, 0–1998 A.D.**
(000)

	Japan	China	Western Europe
0	3 000	59 600	24 700
1000	7 500	59 000	25 413
1300	10 500	100 000	58 353
1400	12 700	72 000	41 500
1500	15 400	103 000	57 268
1600	18 500	160 000	73 778
1700	27 500	138 000	81 460
1820	31 000	381 000	132 888
1850	32 000	412 000	164 428
1870	34 437	358 000	187 532
1998	126 469	1 242 700	388 399

Source: China from Appendix B and Maddison (1998a): Western Europe from Table 1–6a: Japan from Farris (1985), Honjo (1935), Taeuber (1958), with some interpolation.

Table 1–8b. **Population Growth Rates: Japan, China and Western Europe, 0–1998 A.D.**
(annual average compound growth rate)

	0–1500	1500–1700	1700–1850	1850–1998
Japan	0.11	0.28	0.10	0.93
China	0.04	0.15	0.73	0.75
Western Europe	0.06	0.18	0.47	0.58

Source: Derived from Table 1–8a.

Table 1–8c. **Urbanisation Ratios: Japan, China and Western Europe, 1000–1890**
(per cent of population in towns of 10 000 inhabitants and more)

	Japan	China	Western Europe
1000	n.a.	3.0	0.0
1500	2.9	3.8	6.1
1820	12.3	3.8	12.3
1890	16.0	4.4	31.0

Source: Appendix Table B–14, de Vries (1984), Perkins (1969) and Ishii (1937).

A Precocious Demographic Transition in Tokugawa Japan

After a century of rapid expansion, Japanese population growth slowed markedly from the early eighteenth to the mid–nineteenth century.

The slowdown reflected a precocious transition to lowered levels of mortality and fertility, and to life expectation higher than the Asian norm. The transition was analogous in some respects to that experienced in West European countries from the mid–nineteenth to the twentieth century.

Japanese demographic records for the eighteenth century have certain deficiencies, but they are much better than those for earlier centuries. In the past 40 years they have been subjected to meticulous scrutiny by a new generation of historical demographers inspired by the pioneering and prolific work of Akira Hayami. As a result the interpretation of this period has changed completely. The eighteenth century slowdown was once attributed to Malthusian immiseration but is now characterised as a period of rising welfare.

There is little doubt that population was stagnant from 1721 to 1846 when the best Tokugawa statistics were available, and there is reasonable evidence that it was expanding much faster in the seventeenth century. There are grounds for believing that birth rates were relatively low and life expectation relatively high, but there is controversy about life expectation. The most credible estimates range from 32 to 37 years. The spread reflects uncertainty which arises from the absence of direct evidence on infant mortality and the need for inferential procedures as explained in the notes to Table 1–4.

The traditional method of family limitation in Japan (as in China) was abortion and infanticide. In the eighteenth century, family size was further reduced by late marriage, and lower levels of marital fertility. The change was induced by new institutional arrangements, rising per capita income and increased per capita labour inputs.

Early in the seventeenth century, the Tokugawa regime compelled its military elite (*daimyo*) to move their vassals (*samurai*) from the countryside to castle towns. The peasantry were no longer closely controlled, and were much freer to capture gains in productivity for themselves. There were large rice levies to provide stipends for the *samurai*, but these were more or less fixed and the tax burden declined over time.

In the seventeenth century, there were large land reclamation and irrigation projects, improved seeds, increased use of fertiliser. The proportion of land devoted to double cropped rice increased significantly, there was a rapid expansion of new commercial crops (cotton, sericulture, oil seeds, sugar and tobacco) and industrial by–employments. These changes brought increased real income, but required more intensive labour, with a particularly heavy additional load for women (Saito, 1996).

In these circumstances, large families came to be regarded as a burden. By reducing dependency, per capita income could be raised or more easily sustained. Family restriction was also socially acceptable. Villages had a collective responsibility to provide the compulsory rice levy, so the welfare of the whole village community was safeguarded by lower dependency rates. The danger that the family line would die out was covered by the widespread practice of adopting adults (e.g. sons–in–law) who would take over the family name and ultimately the family assets. The Japanese inheritance system was more or less equivalent to primogeniture with reversion to a single heir, rather than the system of partible inheritance which prevailed in China.

Japanese death and birth rates increased somewhat in the last quarter of the nineteenth century. Some of the rise may have been more apparent than real because of a change in official attitudes and practice. These changed from Tokugawa tolerance of abortion and infanticide to repression, and these practices were easier to detect because the new Meiji population registration system had much more effective coverage. However, Japanese family size and population growth continued to be fairly modest by subsequent standards elsewhere in Asia.

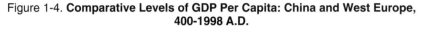

Figure 1-4. **Comparative Levels of GDP Per Capita: China and West Europe, 400-1998 A.D.**

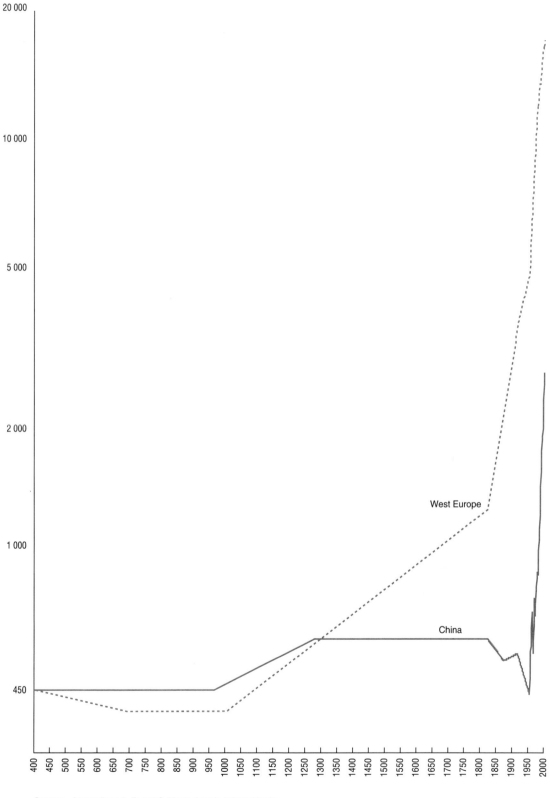

Source: Appendices A, B and C. Vertical scale is logarithmic.

Figure 1-5. **Comparative Levels of GDP Per Capita, China and the United Kingdom, 1700-1998**

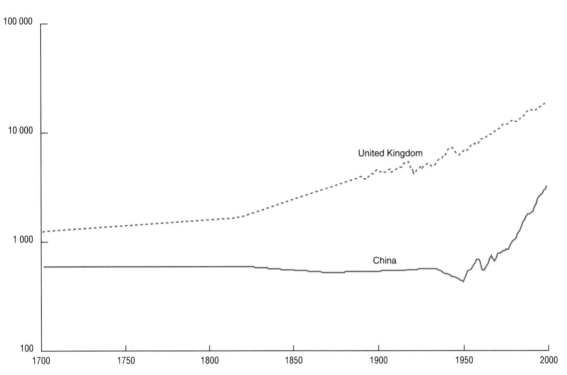

Figure 1.6. **Comparative Levels of GDP Per Capita, China and the United States, 1700-1998**

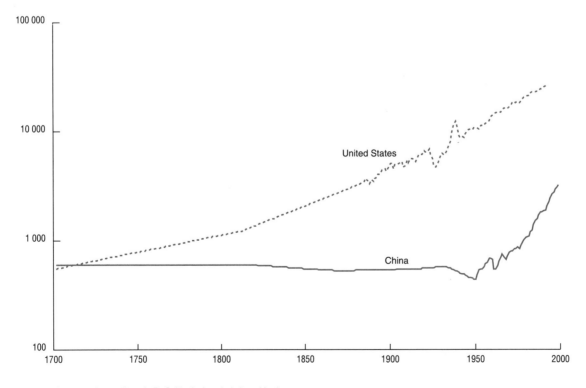

Source: Appendices A, B, C. Vertical scale is logarithmic.

II
GDP Per Capita

Long–term estimates of world GDP are very recent. Research on real income growth by quantitative economic historians has been heavily concentrated on Europe, and generally confined to the past two centuries. Until recently what was known about earlier centuries was in large degree conjectural.

Maddison (1995a) contained detailed estimates for different parts of the world economy for 1820 onwards, with a very crude provisional assessment for 1500 to 1820. Here I have made a much more careful scrutiny of the evidence for centuries before 1820 and incorporated the results of Maddison (1998a) on Chinese economic performance over two millennia. There is still a substantial degree of conjecture, but Appendices A and B present my evidence and assumptions as transparently as possible, so that critical readers can easily modify, adjust or augment my results where they find them open to question.

The level and movement of per capita GDP is the primary general purpose indicator of changes in well–being and production potential, but one should keep in mind that per capita consumption has increased less over the long run because of the increased share of product allocated to investment and government. Labour productivity does not always move parallel to per capita income. The advances achieved in Sung China (960–1279) and in Japan in the seventeenth and eighteenth centuries required substantial increases in per capita labour effort. In the twentieth century we find the opposite phenomenon. Labour input per person fell substantially in Western Europe and Western Offshoots (see Appendix E).

Table 1–8 summarises my findings for the past millennium. It shows clearly the exceptionalism of Western Europe's very lengthy ascension, and origins of the great divergence between the West (Group A) and the rest of the world (Group B).

The major conclusions I draw from the long term quantitative evidence are as follows:

a)   West European income was at a nadir around the year 1000. Its level was significantly lower than it had been in the first century. It was below that in China, India and other parts of East and West Asia;

b)   There was a turning point in the eleventh century when the economic ascension of Western Europe began. It proceeded at a slow pace, but by 1820 real income had tripled. The locus and characteristics of economic leadership changed. The North Italian city states and, in particular, Venice initiated the growth process and reopened Mediterranean trade. Portugal and Spain opened trade routes to the Americas and Asia, but were less dynamic than the Netherlands which became the economic leader around 1600, followed by the United Kingdom in the nineteenth century;

c)   Western Europe overtook China (the leading Asian economy) in per capita performance in the fourteen century (see Figure 1–4). Thereafter China and most of the rest of Asia were more or less stagnant in per capita terms until the second half of the twentieth century. The stagnation was initially due to indigenous institutions and policy, reinforced by colonial exploitation which derived from Western hegemony and was most marked from the eighteenth century onwards;

d)   West European appropriation of the natural resources of North America, introduction of European settlers, technology and organisation added a substantial new dimension to Western economic ascension from the eighteenth century onwards. Towards the end of the nineteenth century, the United States became the world economic leader;

e)   Japan was an exception to the Asian norm. In the course of the seventeenth, eighteenth and the first half of the nineteenth century, it caught up with and overtook China in per capita income. The Meiji takeover in 1868 involved massive institutional change aimed at catching up with the West. This was achieved in income terms in the 1980s, but not yet in productivity;

f) The colonial takeover in Latin America had some analogy to that in North America, but Iberian institutions were less propitious to capitalist development than those in North America. Latin America included a much larger indigenous population which was treated as an underclass without access to land or education. The social order was not greatly changed after independence. Over the long run the rise in per capita income was much smaller than in North America, but faster than in Asia or Africa;

g) African per capita income was lower in 1820 than in the first century. Since then there has been slower advance than in all other regions. The income level in 1998 was little better than that of Western Europe in 1820. Population growth is now faster than in any other region — eight times as fast as in Western Europe;

h) The most dynamic growth performance has been concentrated on the past two centuries. Since 1820 per capita income has risen 19–fold in Group A, and more than 5–fold in the rest of the world — dwarfing any earlier advance and compressing it into a very short time span.

One may ask what is new in these findings. In the first place there is the quantification which clarifies issues that qualitative analysis leaves fuzzy. It helps to separate stylised facts from the stylised fantasies which are sometimes perceived to be reality. It is more readily contestable and likely to be contested. It sharpens scholarly discussion, and contributes to the dynamics of the research process. It is also useful to have a world picture because it helps to identify what is normal and what is exceptional.

My findings differ in some respects from earlier interpretations of the length and pace of Western Europe's economic ascension. There has been a general tendency to date it from 1500 when Europeans encountered America and first made a direct entry into the trading world of Asia. Max Weber attributed Europe's advance to the rise of protestantism, and this thesis attracted attention because it was congruent with the conventional wisdom about the beginning of the European ascension. I no longer believe that there was a sharp break in the pace of advance of per capita income around 1500.

Kuznets (1966, Chapter 1) suggested that "modern economic growth" is a distinctive economic epoch preceded by merchant capitalism in Western Europe "from the end of the fifteenth to the second half of the eighteenth century," and an "antecedent epoch of feudal organisation." In Kuznets (1973, pp. 139–41), he advanced what seemed to be a reasonable view about the rate of per capita GDP growth in Western Europe in the merchant capitalist period. In Maddison (1995a), I accepted Kuznets' hypothesis for his merchant capitalist period, but I now believe that growth was slower then than Kuznets suggested, and that the pace of advance between the eleventh and the fifteenth centuries was not much different. For this reason, it does not seem valid to distinguish between epochs of "feudal organisation" and "merchant capitalism". Instead I would characterise the whole period 1000–1820 as "protocapitalist".

I also differ from Kuznets on the timing of the transition to what he called "modern economic growth" (which I call "capitalist development"). The evidence now available suggests that the transition took place around 1820 rather than in 1760. The revisionist work of Crafts (1983 and 1992) and others has helped to break the old notion of a sudden take–off in the second half of the eighteenth century in England. Recent research on the Netherlands shows income to have been higher there than in the United Kingdom at the end of the eighteenth century. Work in the past twenty years on the quantitative history of other West European countries provides further reason for postdating the transition and modifying the old emphasis on British exceptionalism.

My analysis of US economic performance shows a rapid advance in the eighteenth century in contrast to the findings of Gallman (1972) and Mancall and Weiss (1999). The essential reason for the difference is that I include rough estimates of the indigenous population and its GDP as well as the activity of European settlers (I also did this for Australia, Canada and New Zealand).

My assessment of Japanese development differs from the conventional wisdom. I have quantified its economic performance in the Tokugawa period and compared it with China. Most analysts concentrate on comparisons between Japan and Western Europe in the Meiji period, and ignore the Asian context.

Table 1–9a. **Growth of Per Capita GDP by Major Region, 1000–1998**
(annual average compound growth rate)

	1000–1500	1500–1600	1600–1700	1700–1820	1820–1998
Western Europe	0.13	0.14	0.15	0.15	1.51
Western Offshoots	0.00	0.00	0.17	0.78	1.75
Japan	0.03	0.03	0.09	0.13	1.93
Average Group A	0.11	0.13	0.12	0.18	1.67
Latin America	0.01	0.09	0.19	0.19	1.22
Eastern Europe & former USSR	0.04	0.10	0.10	0.10	1.06
Asia (excluding Japan)	0.05	0.01	–0.01	0.01	0.92
Africa	–0.01	0.00	0.00	0.04	0.67
Average Group B	0.04	0.02	0.00	0.03	0.95

Table 1–9b. **Level of Per Capita GDP, Groups A and B, 1000–1998**
(1990 international dollars)

	1000	1500	1600	1700	1820	1998
Average Group A	405	704	805	907	1 130	21 470
Average Group B	440	535	548	551	573	3 102

Table 1–9c. **Population of Groups A and B, 1000–1998**
(million)

	1000	1500	1600	1700	1820	1998
Total Group A	35	76	95	110	175	838
Total Group B	233	362	461	493	866	5 069

Table 1–9d. **GDP of Groups A and B, 1000–1998**
(billion 1990 international dollars)

	1000	1500	1600	1700	1820	1998
Total Group A	14.1	53.2	76.1	100.0	198.0	17 998
Total Group B	102.7	194.0	252.9	271.8	496.5	15 727

Source for Tables 1–9a to 1–9d: Appendix B.

Gerschenkron (1965) and Rostow (1960 and 1963) both emphasised the idea that "take–offs" were staggered throughout the nineteenth century in West European countries. Kuznets (1979, p. 131) endorsed this view. In fact growth acceleration was more synchronous in Western Europe than they believed.

There are two schools of thought about the relative performance of Europe and Asia. The mainstream view was clearly expressed by Adam Smith in 1776. He was not a practitioner of political arithmetic but on the basis of the "price of labour" and other evidence, his ordinal ranking from the top downwards was as follows for the 1770s:

Netherlands

England

France

British North American colonies

Scotland

Spain

Spanish colonies in America

China

Bengal (depressed by the East India Company's plundering)

This mainstream view is reflected in Landes (1969, p. 13–14) whose overall assessment, like that of Smith, was similar to mine. "Western Europe was already rich before the Industrial Revolution — rich by comparison with other parts of the world of that day. This wealth was the product of centuries of slow accumulation, based in turn on investment, the appropriation of extra–European resources and labour, and substantial technological progress, not only in the production of material goods, but in the organisation and financing of their exchange and distribution ... it seems clear that over the near–millennium from the year 1000 to the eighteenth century, income per head rose appreciably — perhaps tripled."

In Maddison (1983), I contrasted the Landes view with Bairoch's (1981) assessment of relative income per head. He suggested that China was well ahead of Western Europe in 1800, Japan and the rest of Asia only 5 per cent lower than Europe, Latin America well ahead of North America, and Africa about two thirds of the West European level. This highly improbable scenario was never documented in the case of Asia, Latin America or Africa. His figures for these areas were essentially guesstimates. Bairoch consistently took the position that the third world had been impoverished by the rich countries (see Bairoch, 1967), and he was, in fact, fabricating ammunition for this hypothesis (see the critique of Chesnais, 1987).

In spite of its shaky foundations, Bairoch's assessment has been influential. Braudel (1985, vol. 3 pp. 533–4) acknowledged "the great service Paul Bairoch has rendered to historians" and believed "it is virtually beyond question that Europe was less rich than the worlds it was exploiting, even after the fall of Napoleon". Andre Gunder Frank (1998, pp. 171 and 284) cites Bairoch and suggests that "around 1800 Europe and the United States, after long lagging behind, suddenly caught up and then overtook Asia economically and politically". Pomeranz (2000) cites Bairoch more cautiously (p. 16) but his sinophilia drives him to the same conclusion. He suggests (p. 111), there is "little reason to think that West Europeans were more productive than their contemporaries in various other densely populated regions of the Old World prior to 1750 or even 1800."

Maddison (1983) contrasted the assessments of Landes and Bairoch and commented: "These remarkably different quantitative conclusions have very different analytical implications. If Bairoch is right, then much of the backwardness of the third world presumably has to be explained by colonial exploitation, and much less of Europe's advantage can be due to scientific precocity, centuries of slow accumulation, and organisational and financial prosperity."

In view of the laborious efforts I have since made to accumulate quantitative evidence on this topic, I now conclude that Bairoch and his epigoni are quite wrong. To reject them is not to deny the role of colonial exploitation, but this can be better understood by taking a more realistic view of Western strength and Asian weakness around 1800.

The major problem in growth analysis is to explain why such a large divergence developed between the advanced capitalist group and the rest of the world. There are, of course, some examples of past convergence, e.g. Europe's rise from its nadir to overtake China , the Japanese catch–up with China in Tokugawa times, and subsequently with the advanced capitalist group. Western Europe achieved a very substantial degree of catch–up on the United States in the golden age after the second world war; resurgent Asia (China, India, the so–called tigers and others) have narrowed their degree of backwardness substantially over the past quarter century.

In attempting to understand the causes of divergence and the possibilities for catch–up in different parts of the world economy, there is no universal schema which covers the whole millennium. The operative forces have varied between place and period. Chapter 2 attempts to illuminate the changes in the character of economic leadership and backwardness which have occurred over the past millennium.

Chapter 2

The Impact of Western Development on the Rest of the World, 1000–1950

A major feature of world development which emerges from our macro–statistical evidence is the exceptionalism of Western Europe's long–run economic performance. By the year 1000, its income levels had fallen below those in Asia and North Africa. In its lengthy resurrection, it caught up with China (the world leader) in the fourteenth century. By 1820, its levels of income and productivity were more than twice as high as in the rest of the world. By 1913 , the income level in Western Europe and its Western Offshoots was more than six times that in the rest of the world.

In order to understand the forces which made for the Western ascension, and the reasons for its greater dynamism than the rest of the world, it is useful to scrutinise the interaction of the West with the Rest over the long run. It is not feasible to embark on a comprehensive survey of all parts of the world economy. This chapter therefore presents four case histories. A great advantage of this detailed scrutiny is that it demonstrates how misleading it is to treat Western experience as homogeneous or monolithic.

The first deals with the Venetian Republic — the richest and most successful West European economy from the eleventh to the sixteenth century.

Portugal is the second case. It was never as rich as Venice, but developed ship design and navigational techniques which made it possible to open up new routes and commercial contact with Africa and Asia. Portugal pioneered European expansion into the Atlantic, discovered Brazil in 1500 and began three centuries of colonial development in the Americas.

The Netherlands is the third case. It was the European leader in terms of per capita income between 1600 and 1820, with a high degree of international openness and specialisation, and a very large trading empire in Asia.

The United Kingdom is our fourth case. It followed the Dutch model of international specialisation and commercial development, built a much bigger colonial empire, and was a pioneer in industrial and transport technology.

Concentration on Western exceptionalism may be considered Eurocentric, but Western countries were the most successful and their experience is the best basis for understanding the roots of economic growth. Analysis of their interaction with the rest of the world throws light on the origins of economic backwardness, and the extent to which Western advance may have contributed to this.

The process of Western ascension involved violence against other parts of the world. European colonisation of the Americas involved the extermination, marginalisation or conquest of its indigenous populations. European contact with Africa was for three centuries concentrated on the slave trade. There were European wars with Asian countries from the mid–eighteenth to the mid–twentieth century designed to establish or maintain colonies and trading privileges. However, Western economic advance also involved devastating wars and beggar–your–neighbour policies. Venetian advance provoked

conflicts with Genoa, Portugal clashed with the Dutch. The Netherlands was involved in an 80 year struggle for independence from Spain, four wars with Britain and more with France. The United Kingdom was involved in over 60 years of war with other West European countries from 1688 to 1815, and another ten years from 1914 to 1945.

Before starting on the detailed case studies, it is useful to present a brief overview of West European performance from the first to the tenth centuries, and from 1000 to 1500.

I
Europe's Decline from the First to Tenth Centuries

In the first and second centuries, the Roman Empire was at its peak, a political entity that stretched from the Scottish border to Egypt, with a population of 20 million in Europe, another 20 million in Western Asia and 8 million in North Africa[1]. Within this area there was a common legal framework, and the security of the *pax romana*. There were about 40 000 miles of paved road[2]; 5 per cent of the population was urban with an active secular culture[3]. The major cities were supplied with aqueducts, public baths and fountains, amphitheatres, libraries, temples and other public monuments. The Mediterranean was a Roman lake with tribute shipments of grain from Alexandria and Carthage to the Roman ports of Puteoli (near Naples) and Portus Novus (near Rome). Silk and spices from Asia came overland via Antioch, and up the Red Sea to Egypt. By the first century, Roman citizens (Greeks, Syrians and Jews) had discovered how to use the monsoon winds to trade directly with Western India[4].

Roman imperialism was based on plunder, enslavement and ability to exercise control through military force. The strains in running such a large system were already obvious when Diocletian created separate Western and Eastern Empires in 285. Eventually the Western Empire's capacity to levy taxes and tribute eroded. It relied increasingly on barbarians to man its armed forces. When they revolted, the system collapsed.

By the fifth century the West Roman Empire had disintegrated. Gaul, Spain, Carthage and most of Italy were taken over by illiterate barbarian invaders and Britain was abandoned. There was a brief reprise in the sixth century when the East Roman Emperor recovered Italy, Spain and North Africa. The final blow came with the Arab takeover of Egypt, North Africa, Spain, Sicily, Syria and Palestine between 640 and 800. The only remnant of Roman civilisation was the rump of the Byzantine Empire.

The main changes between the first and tenth centuries were *a)* the collapse of a large scale cohesive political unit which was never resurrected, and its replacement by a fragmented, fragile and unstable polity; *b)* disappearance of urban civilisation and predominance of self–sufficient, relatively isolated and ignorant rural communities where a feudal elite extracted an income in kind from a servile peasantry; *c)* the virtual disappearance of trading links between Western Europe, North Africa and Asia[5].

The Belgian historian Pirenne (1939) provided a succinct description of the situation in the ninth century: "If we consider that in the Carolingian epoch, the minting of gold had ceased, the lending of money at interest was prohibited, there was no longer a class of professional merchants, that Oriental products (papyrus, spices and silk) were no longer imported, that the circulation of money was reduced to a minimum, that laymen could neither read or write, that taxes were no longer organised, and that the towns were merely fortresses, we can say without hesitation that we are confronted by a civilisation that had retrogressed to the purely agricultural stage; which no longer needed commerce, credit and regular exchange for the maintenance of the social fabric."[6]

II
Western Europe Recovers and Forges Ahead, 1000–1500

Between the years 1000 and 1500, Western Europe's population grew faster than any other part of the world. Northern countries grew significantly faster than those bordering the Mediterranean. The urban proportion (in terms of towns with more than 10 000 population) rose from zero to 6 per cent, a clear indicator of expansion in manufacturing and commercial activity. Factors making it possible to feed the increased population were an increase in the area of rural settlement, particularly in the Netherlands, Northern Germany and the Baltic coast and the gradual incorporation of technological changes which raised land productivity. The classic analysis of these rural changes is by Lynn White (1962): "...the heavy plough, open fields, the new integration of agriculture and herding, three field rotation, modern horse harness, nailed horseshoes and whipple tree had combined into a total system of agrarian exploitation by the year 1100 to provide a zone of peasant prosperity stretching across Northern Europe from the Atlantic to the Dnieper." White probably exaggerated the precocity of their impact and the degree of prosperity, but these technical improvements were clearly of fundamental importance. The switch from a two–field to a three–field system also increased food security and reduced the incidence of famine. A growing proportion of agricultural output went as inputs into clothing production (wool), wine and beer (cereals and vines) and fodder crops for an increased horse population. There was a degree of regional specialisation in food production with growing international trade in cereals, live cattle, cheese, fish and wine. Increased trade in salt and the reintroduction of spice imports helped improve the palatability and conservation of meat and fish.

Increased use of water and windmills augmented the power available for industrial processes, particularly in new industries such as sugar production and paper making. There was international specialisation in the woollen industry. English wool was exported to Flanders for production of cloth which was traded throughout Europe. The silk industry was introduced in the twelfth century and had grown impressively in Southern Europe by 1500. There were big improvements in the quality of textiles and the varieties of colour and design available. Genoa introduced regular shipments of alum from Chios to Bruges in the thirteenth century. There were improvements in mining and metallurgy which helped transform and expand European weapons production (see Nef, 1987 and Cipolla, 1970). Improvements in shipping and navigation techniques from the eleventh to the fifteenth century underpinned the increase in trade in the Mediterranean, the Baltic, the Atlantic islands and the Northwest coast of Africa.

There were big advances in banking, accountancy, marine insurance, improvements in the quality of intellectual life with the development and spread of universities, the growth of humanist scholarship and, at the end of the fifteenth century, the introduction of printing.

There were important changes in the political order. Scandinavian raiders who had made attacks on England, the low countries, Normandy and deep into Russia had become traders and established effective systems of governance in Scandinavia itself, in England, Normandy and Sicily. The beginnings of a nation state system had emerged, with a reduction in the fragmentation of political power that had characterised the Middle Ages. The hundred years war (1337–1453) was not the last of the conflicts between England and France, but the national identity of the two countries was much more clearly defined after it was over. At the end of the fifteenth century, the *reconquista* had established Spanish identity in its modern form. In the Eastern Mediterranean, the situation was the reverse. The Ottoman Empire had taken Constantinople in 1453, and quickly extended its hegemony to the Balkans, Syria, Palestine, Egypt and North Africa.

Estimates of what happened to GDP in Europe and the rest of the world over this period are obviously subject to a wide margin of error. Chapter 1 and Appendix B explain the basis for my estimates as transparently as possible. I concluded that there was almost a doubling of West European per capita income from 1000 to 1500 compared with an improvement of about a third in China, less elsewhere in Asia, and some regression in Africa. It seems clear that West European levels of income and productivity were higher than in Asia and Africa at the end of the period whereas they had been lower in the year 1000. As far as West Asia and Egypt are concerned, this view seems to be shared by specialists in Muslim history, e.g. Abulafiah (1987) and Abu–Lughod (1989); for China/West European performance the evidence for this conclusion is examined in detail in Maddison (1998a).

Within Europe, the areas which made the most economic progress in this period were i) Flanders, which was the centre for wool production, international banking and commerce in Northern Europe; and ii) Italian city states — Florence, Genoa, Pisa, Milan and Venice. Of these the most successful and the richest was Venice. The dynamic forces of Venetian capitalist development are therefore scrutinised in some detail in the following section.

III
THE VENETIAN REPUBLIC

Venice played a major role in reopening the Mediterranean economy to West European commerce and developing links with Northern Europe. It created an institutional basis for commercial capitalism, made major progress in shipping technology, and helped transfer Asian and Egyptian technology in cane sugar production and processing, silk textiles, glassblowing and jewellery to the West.

Venice was the most successful of the North Italian city states in creating and maintaining a republic dominated by a merchant capitalist elite. Thanks to its geographic position and willingness to defend itself, it was able to guarantee its autonomy and freedom from exactions by feudal landlords and monarchs.

It created political and legal institutions which guaranteed property rights and the enforceability of contracts. It was a pioneer in developing foreign exchange and credit markets, banking and accountancy[7]. It created what was effectively a government bond market, starting with compulsory loans on which interest was paid regularly. Its fiscal system was efficient and favourable to merchant profits and the accumulation of capital. The revenues came from excise levies and property taxes based on cadastral surveys.

It was a tolerant and fairly secular state where foreign merchants (Armenians, Greeks and Jews) could operate as freely as locals. Although it was theoretically part of the catholic world, it enjoyed privileged relations with the Byzantine empire. It buttressed its ecclesiastical independence by acquiring the relics of St. Mark from Alexandria in 828. It was effectively independent of both Pope and Patriarch.

Venetian diplomacy was highly professional, pragmatic, opportunistic and dedicated to the pursuit of its commercial interests. It adjusted amazingly well to political changes. In the ninth and tenth centuries its main commerce was to provision Constantinople with grain and wine from Italy, wood and slaves from Dalmatia and salt from its lagoons, taking silk and spices in return. Towards the end of the eleventh century, Byzantium was under pressure from the Seljuk Turks who seized Anatolia, and Frankish incursions into its Southern Italian territories. Venice secured commercial privileges (exemption from excise taxes) from Byzantium in 1082 in return for help in bolstering its naval defences. In 1204, by contrast, it played a major role in persuading the leaders of the fourth crusade to target Constantinople instead of Islam. As a result Venice acquired bases in Dalmatia and an empire in the Aegean. It took the southern half of the Peloponnese, Corfu and Crete. It occupied nearly half of Constantinople and gained access to trade in the Black Sea and Sea of Azov. In 1261, the Byzantine Emperor recaptured Constantinople and gave trade preferences and a territorial base to Venice's rival, Genoa. However, Venice retained its Greek colonies and Venetian shipping was soon able to re–enter the Black Sea where trade was booming due to the Mongol reopening of the silk route through Central Asia.

West European crusaders successfully attacked the Syrian and Palestinian coast and established small christian states in Antioch, Acre and Jerusalem between 1099 and 1291. They gave commercial privileges to Pisan and Genoan traders who had helped finance their conquest. The Venetians had not helped, but nevertheless managed to establish a trading base in Tyre.

The Turkish Mameluke regime recaptured Syria and Palestine in 1291 and ruled Egypt until 1517. Here too, Venice managed to establish a privileged trading relationship, buying a large part of the Asian spices which the Karimi merchants of Alexandria brought to Egypt from Asia via the Red Sea. In return the Venetians sold metals, armour, woollens and slaves. The slaves came from the Balkans and Russia: males were destined for service in the Mameluke army, females for their harems.

When the Ottoman Turks captured Constantinople in 1453, Venice quickly negotiated the maintenance of its trading rights, but in 1479, the Ottomans closed their access to the Black Sea. In 1517, they took over Egypt and terminated most of the Venetian trade in spices.

Venice had important connections with Northern Europe. Trade with Flanders was carried out mainly at the Champagne fairs where Italian merchants bought woollen goods and sold silk, spices, alum, sugar and lacquer[8]. When the sea route was opened between the Western Mediterranean and the Atlantic, trade with Flanders was carried out directly by ship.

A second route linked Venice with Augsburg, Nuremberg, Prague and Vienna via the Brenner Pass. German merchants brought metals and metal products (including silver). Venetians traded these metals up the Po Valley and in the Mediterranean. In 1318 the Fondaco dei Tedeschi was created in Venice to provide for the trading needs and lodging of German merchants.

In building up its trade, Venice created a political empire. In 1171, the city had about 66 000 inhabitants, and was one of the three biggest in Western Europe until the sixteenth century when its population peaked around 170 000. Venice experienced three demographic catastrophes. In 1347–48, nearly 40 per cent of the population died when a galley brought the plague from the Black Sea port of Caffa. Two other attacks occurred in 1575–77 and 1630; each killing about a third of the population of the city[9].

The Empire overseas (*dominio da mar*) included about half a million people. Between 1388 and 1499, Venice acquired territory on the Italian mainland (*terraferma*) which included Udine, Friuli, Vicenza, Padua, Verona, Bergamo, Rovigo and Cremona. In 1557 the population of these territories was about 1.5 million (see Table 2–1).

The Venetian state played a leading role in commercial activity, being the major shipbuilder, leasing state–owned galleys to private enterprise, arranging the organisation and timing of convoys. It developed types of ship suitable for Venetian commerce and the conditions of trade in the Mediterranean. This state activity reduced costs for private traders by making commerce more secure from enemy attack. It also permitted smaller traders, with limited capital, to participate in international trade.

Table 2–1. **Population of the Venetian Empire in 1557**
(000)

City of Venice	158	Ionia	52
Islands of the Lagoon	50	Crete	194
Istria	52	Terraferma	1 542
Dalmatia	93	Total	2 141

Source: Beloch (1961), pp. 164 and 352. The population of Cyprus (under Venetian control 1489–1573) in the mid–1550s was probably about 160 000, see McEvedy and Jones (1978), p. 119.

Table 2–2. **Size and Carrying Capacity of Venetian Merchant Galleys, 1318–1559**

	Length	*Breadth (metres)*	*Depth*	*Cargo capacity (metric tons)*
1318 for voyages to Cyprus	40.4	5.3	2.4	110
1320 for voyages to Flanders	40.4	5.7	2.4	115
1420 for voyages to Flanders	41.2	6.0	2.7	170
1549–59 merchant galleys	47.8	8.0	3.1	280

Source: Lane (1966), p. 369.

Table 2–3. **Population of 31 Biggest West European Cities, 1500–1800**
(000)

	1500	*1600*	*1700*	*1800*
Italy				
Naples	150	281	216	427
Venice	100	139	138	138
Milan	100	120	124	135
Florence	70	70	72	81
Genoa	60	71	80	91
Rome	55	105	138	163
Bologna	55	63	63	71
Palermo	55	105	100	139
France				
Paris	100	220	510	581
Lyon	50	40	97	100
Rouen	40	60	64	81
Bordeaux	20	40	50	88
Low Countries				
Antwerp	40	47	70	60
Ghent	40	31	51	51
Brussels	35	50	80	74
Bruges	30	27	38	32
Amsterdam	14	65	200	217
Germany and Austria				
Nuremburg	36	40	40	27
Cologne	30	40	42	42
Lubeck	24	23	n.a.	23
Danzig	20	50	50	40
Augsburg	20	48	21	28
Vienna	20	50	114	231
Iberia				
Granada	70	69	n.a.	55
Valencia	40	65	50	80
Lisbon	30	100	165	180
Barcelona	29	43	43	115
Cordoba	27	45	28	40
Seville	25	90	96	96
Madrid	0	49	110	167
Britain				
London	40	200	575	865

Source: de Vries (1984), pp. 270–77.

The biggest enterprise in Venice was the Arsenal, a public shipyard created in 1104. It was operative for centuries, and employed thousands of workers.

There were major changes in ship construction and navigation techniques between the tenth and fourteenth centuries. Roman ships had been constructed hull first, held together by careful watertight cabinetwork of mortice and tenon; the second stage was the insertion of ribs and braces. In the eleventh century there was a switch which made a major reduction in costs. The keel and ribs were made first and a hull of nailed planks was added, using fibre and pitch to make the ships watertight. A later development was the stern–post rudder which replaced trailing oars as a more effective means for steering ships. The power of the rudders was strengthened by use of cranks and pulleys[10]. There were improvements in sails, notably the introduction of a triangular lateen rig set at an angle to the mast instead of a rectangular sail square to the mast. There was a long run increase in the size of ships (see Table 2–2).

Soon after 1270, the compass came into use in the Mediterranean. This, together with improved charts, made it possible to sail all year round. Previously ships trading with Egypt had not ventured out between October and April. With the compass the same ship could make two return trips a year from Venice to Alexandria instead of one.

There were two main kinds of Venetian ship. General purpose cargo ships ("cogs") were built in private shipyards. Their length was about three times their breadth, and they relied entirely on sails. Galleys for passengers, high value cargo and naval duties were built in the Arsenal. These were longer, had a wide beam and a crew of 200 most of whom were oarsmen. Galleys were speedier, more manoeuvrable for entering and leaving harbour, and for occasions when there was no wind. The general Venetian practice was to have 25 benches on each side of the galley, each bench having three oarsmen. The benches were set at an angle and the oars were of different lengths so that the rowers would not interfere with each other. On such a ship there would be 150 oarsmen and about 30 crossbowmen for defence and attack, who would also take turns at rowing. Galleys were owned by the state and rented out for each venture to the highest bidder in public auctions. Galleys also acted as public carriers, as those who leased the ships had to accept goods from other merchants if they had spare capacity.

In 1291, the Genoese defeated a Moroccan fleet controlling the straits of Gibraltar, and opened the way for European commerce from the Mediterranean to the Atlantic[11]. Thereafter Venetian galleys used this route to trade with London and Bruges.

Although international trade, banking, shipbuilding and associated trades in timber, carpentry, rope and sailmaking etc. were the biggest sectors of the Venetian economy, there were also sizeable manufacturing activities producing goods for local use and export. One of the earliest was the glass industry which had already started in the tenth century. Venice was a pioneer in glassblowing technology in Europe and made glasses, goblets, pitchers, dishes, bottles, vases, mirrors, jewellery, candelabra and decorative products of very high quality. From the thirteenth century Venetians produced delicate, carefully blown sand–glasses as a time–keeping device for mariners. From the fourteenth century onwards they started making spectacles — an Italian invention which greatly increased the productivity of artisans and scholars[12]. Angelo Barovier, the most famous glassblower of the fifteenth century, perfected the process for making crystal. By that time, polychrome, engraved, filigree, enamelled and gold–leafed glassware was available in a profuse variety of designs. In 1291 all glassblowing was shifted to the island of Murano by decree of the Maggior Consilio. This enabled Venice to keep tighter control of its trade and technological secrets.

Equally precocious were the skills and products of Venetian goldsmiths, mosaicists, woodcarvers and decorative artists who were in heavy demand in turning the inside of churches, civic monuments and private palaces into works of art. Venetian style was influenced by the work of previous generations of mosaicists and iconographers in Ravenna and the thirteenth century inflow of objects looted from Constantinople.

The trade with Asia in raw silk and silk products eventually led to import substitution in Europe. Silk production had already spread from China to India and Syria, and came to Italy in the twelfth century — initially to Lucca, then to Venice, Florence, Genoa, Milan and Bologna, and later to Lyon in France. Within the Arab world, silk production came to Spain from Syria. Venetian silk production is documented as early as the thirteenth century. The Venetian government regulated production to guarantee quality, keep out competitors and reduce the risk of industrial espionage. The silk, satin and velvet products of Venice were of the highest quality, and designs were a distinctive mix of indigenous creativity and oriental influence. Multicoloured velvet brocades, often executed with gold and silver thread, were produced as items of ceremonial clothing for Venice's governing elite, for furniture, wall hangings, table coverings, decorative items for gondolas etc. These products made a substantial contribution to Venetian exports.

Another important field was book production. In the ninth and tenth centuries, scribes and illuminators were mainly active on sacred books in the scriptoria of monasteries. Later there were civic records, histories, translations of Aristotle and other Greek texts destined for the libraries of San Marco, ducal, civic and private collectors. This gave employment to professional scribes, bookbinders, specialists in ornamented calligraphy and illustration. Less than 15 years after Gutenberg's invention of printing, a German immigrant brought the technique to Venice in 1469. It led to an enormous improvement in the productivity of the industry, with print runs up to 4 500 copies. A very much larger proportion of output was destined for export than had been the case for manuscript books. Venice quickly became the principal Italian typographical centre, and one of the biggest in Europe. By the middle of the sixteenth century, some 20 000 editions had been published. Venetian publishing helped invigorate the cultural and intellectual life of Europe by providing music scores, maps, books on medical matters and translations of the Greek classics. The Aldine Press (set up in 1494) edited and published original Greek texts, and Venice became the major publisher of books for the Greek–speaking world[13].

Sugar was another major product. Venice created plantation agriculture and processing facilities with slave labour in Crete and Cyprus, using techniques borrowed from Syria. Venetian practice was copied later by the Portuguese in Madeira and in Brazil.

The Venetian role in the spice trade was greatly reduced at the beginning of the sixteenth century because of restrictions on trade with Syria and Egypt imposed by the new Ottoman authorities, and competition from direct Portuguese shipments from Asia. Lane (1966, p. 13) suggests that Venetian spice imports fell from around 1 600 tons a year towards the end of the fifteenth century to less than 500 tons by the first decade of the sixteenth century. Lane thought that the absolute size of the pepper component of these shipments had recovered by the 1560s, but Venice's leading role in this trade had obviously evaporated.

Venetian shipping also faced increased competition on Western routes to England and Flanders, and its sugar industry in Crete and Cyprus declined because of competition from Portuguese production in Madeira and later in Brazil.

There were also changes in shipbuilding technology in the Atlantic economies which quickly rendered the oared Venetian galley obsolete. The two main changes were in the rigging of round ships and the development of firearms during the fifteenth century. Lane (1966, pp. 15–16) described these changes as follows: "The transformation of the one–masted cog into a full–rigged, three–masted ship possessed of spritsail, topsail and mizzen lateen occurred about the middle of the century — the sailing ships of 1485 differed less in appearance from the sailing ships of 1785 than they did from those of 1425 — equally important in robbing the merchant galley of the special security which had alone justified its existence was the increase in the use of guns in naval warfare."

As a result there was a sharp decline in the main product of the Arsenal and a rise in the share of cogs in the Venetian merchant fleet. There was increased purchase by Venetian merchants of ships from abroad, as problems of adapting to technological change were compounded by much poorer Venetian access to cheap timber than shipbuilders in the Atlantic economies.

From 1500 onwards, a significant proportion of Venetian capital was reoriented to agrarian reclamation and development and creation of Palladian villas and country estates in the *terraferma*.

Over the sixteenth, seventeenth and eighteenth centuries, Venice did not expand much in population or per capita income, but it remained one of the richest parts of Italy and Europe until overtaken by the Dutch in the seventeenth century.

IV
PORTUGAL

Portugal emerged from Arab rule between 1147 when Lisbon was captured and 1249 when full sovereignty was established in an area corresponding roughly to its present boundaries. Its political regime was very different from that of Venice. Its *reconquista* was due mainly to militant crusading orders of knighthood. The military aristocracy and the church became the major landowners. In Portugal, as in Spain, the interests of church and state were closely linked. The crown was able to nominate bishops and collect ecclesiastical taxes, under a patronage system known as the "padroado real". Although there were some clashes between Portugal and Spain, and for a time (1580–1640) Portugal had a Spanish king, there was a remarkably effective long–term territorial division of interests between the two countries. Under various treaties sanctioned by the Papacy, Portugal was able to develop its commercial and imperial interests in Africa, in the whole of Asia except the Philippines, and in Brazil without significant Spanish interference.

Portugal had three major advantages in developing its overseas commerce and empire. There was a clear strategic benefit in being located on the South Atlantic coast of Europe near to the exit of the Mediterranean. Deep–sea fishermen provided an important part of the Portuguese food supply and developed an unrivalled knowledge of Atlantic winds, weather and tides. The value of these skills was greatly enhanced by crown sponsorship of Atlantic exploration, research on navigation technology, training of pilots, and documentation of maritime experience in the form of route maps with compass bearings (rutters) and cartography. Portuguese shipbuilding in Lisbon and Oporto adapted the design of its ships (caravels) and rigging in the light of increasing knowledge of Atlantic sailing conditions. The biggest changes were in rigging. At first they concentrated on lateen sails, then added a mix of square sails and lateen for deeper penetration into the South Atlantic, with further changes for the much longer route round the Cape. Knowledge of these techniques was protected by forbidding sales of ships to other countries. A third commercial advantage was Portugal's ability to absorb "new Christians" — Jewish merchants and scholars had played a significant role during Muslim rule. They were driven out of Spain, but many took refuge and increased the size of the community in Portugal. They were required to undergo proforma conversion and were subject to a degree of persecution, but they provided important skills in developing Portuguese business interests in Africa, Brazil and Asia, in scientific development, as intermediaries in trade with the Muslim world and in attracting Genoese and Catalan capital to Portuguese business ventures.

A fourth important influence on the pattern of Portuguese business interests was the heritage of slavery. In most parts of Western Europe, slavery had more or less disappeared in the middle ages, though it was a peripheral part of Venetian trade with Byzantium and the Muslim world. Portugal had lived in closer contact with the Muslim world than any other part of Western Europe. Portuguese themselves had had experience of being slaves and about ten per cent of the population in Lisbon were berber or black slaves. They were also used as a labour force in the sugar plantations and sugar mills which Portugal developed in Madeira and São Tomé.

Significant Portuguese activity in slave trading in Africa began around 1445 shortly after Portuguese navigators discovered and settled the Cape Verde islands (opposite Senegal). They were able to buy slaves from African merchants in this region in return for cloth, horses, trinkets and salt. Between 1450 and

Table 2–4. **Sugar Production by Area of Origin, 1456–1894**
(metric tons)

	Cyprus	Madeira	São Tomé	Brazil	British Caribbean	French Caribbean	Other Caribbean	Rest of World
1456	800	80						
1500	375	2 500						
1580		500	2 200[a]	2 300				
1700				20 000	22 000	10 000	5 000	
1760				28 000	71 000	81 000	20 000	
1787				19 000	106 000	125 000	36 000	
1815				75 000	168 000	36 600	66 200	18 500
1894				275 000	260 200	79 400	1 119 000	6 523 600

a) 1550s.

Source: 1486–1787 from Blackburn (1997), pp. 109, 172, 403 and Schwartz (1985), p. 13; 1815–94 from Williams (1970), pp. 366, 377–80. The figure for rest of world includes 10 000 tons of beet sugar in 1815 and 4 725 000 tons in 1894. Sugar beet production started in Europe during the Napoleonic wars.

Table 2–5. **Atlantic Slave Shipments by Portugal and Its Competitors, 1701–1800**
(000)

England	2 532	North America	194
Portugal	1 796	Denmark	74
France	1 180	Other	5
Netherlands	351	Total	6 132

Source: Lovejoy (1982), p. 483.

1600 about 175 000 slaves were shipped to Portugal and its Atlantic islands. Later, as the trade developed, Portugal became more directly involved in capturing slaves further south in Angola. The crown organised the Casa de Escravos in Lisbon in the 1480s. The trade was highly profitable and expanded enormously at the end of the sixteenth and in the seventeenth century when Portugal shipped slaves to Brazil and handled most of the slave shipments to Spanish America (under slave trading permits (*asiento*) sold by the Spanish government). The slave trade received Papal legitimacy in 1455 with the bull *Romanus Pontifex*, which construed it as a form of missionary activity. Between 1500 and 1870, 9.4 million slaves were shipped to the Americas. About 4.5 million of these were supplied by Portugal.

The Portuguese crown took the initiative in exploring and developing the Atlantic islands and their sugar industry, and in creating a maritime bypass of the old caravan route which carried gold from Timbuktu in Mali to the Moroccan coast. This route had supplied two thirds of the gold entering Europe.

The leading role in these two developments was played by Prince Henrique (third son of the Portuguese king, John I, and nephew of the English king, Henry IV). For four decades (1420–1460) he applied his considerable financial resources to these ventures and prepared the ground for the later Portuguese breakthrough into Asian trade by developing navigational expertise[14].

In 1420, the crown took over the administration of the wealthy military orders. Henrique became administrator of the Order of Christ (successor to the Templars in Portugal), and his brother acquired a similar position in the Order of Santiago. Henrique used the assets of his Order to finance ventures in the Atlantic and Africa, and persuaded successive rulers (his brothers) to invest him personally with significant property rights in both areas.

Madeira (about 560 km into the Atlantic from the Moroccan coast) was discovered in 1420. It was uninhabited and extremely fertile. A sugar industry was developed with use of slave labour on similar lines to Venetian practice in Cyprus and Crete. The two sectors of the industry were cane plantations and sugar mills, with the bigger enterprises covering both activities. The industry was developed by leases to Genoese and "new Christian" entrepreneurs. Capital requirements were fairly substantial and the newest techniques were adopted in the mills. Instead of the large circular stone that was rolled over cut cane in the Venetian controlled mills, a new type of press with two cylindrical rollers was able to get more juice from the cane which no longer needed to be cut. The presses were operated with animal or water power rather than manually[15]. Production expanded faster after Henrique's death, when the industry was less tightly controlled. By 1500 Madeiran production was more than six times as big as that of Cyprus where output had plummeted. Portuguese sugar replaced it on the markets of Antwerp and Bristol. In addition to sugar, Madeira was a major source of timber. Wheat and wine production was also significant. The wine was of the malmsey type which the Venetians had brought to Crete from Syria.

The uninhabited Azores were discovered in mid–Atlantic (about 1 300–1 500 km from Portugal) in 1427 and settlement started in 1439. They were not very suitable for sugar production, but were a useful staging post for subsequent Atlantic trade, and augmented Portuguese knowledge of navigation in the Atlantic.

In developing navigation on the African coast, Portugal established settlements in two other significant island outposts. The Cape Verde islands were settled in 1460 and acted as a staging post for the slave trade. In this area, the Portuguese found malaguette (a coarse pepper substitute) and later a better quality pepper in Benin. Further east, São Tomé and Principe (in the Bight of Guinea) were settled after 1480. Sugar production was introduced and by the 1550s had supplemented Madeira as the major centre of Atlantic production.

In 1482, Elmina fort was built on the coast of what is now Ghana. This was centre of the gold trade. Gold became the biggest source of income for the Portuguese crown. At Elmina the main source was Ashanti gold, at trading points on the Guinea coast it was gold diverted to Portuguese traders from the caravan route from Timbuktu to Morocco. Total gold exports of West Africa between 1471 and 1500 amounted to 17 tons. This helped the Portuguese crown to finance its most expensive venture — the opening of a Cape route to Asian trade[16].

Circumnavigation of Africa in order to get direct access to the spices of Asia was not a new idea. The Vivaldi brothers had set out from Genoa in 1291 and disappeared in the attempt. By the end of the fifteenth century, it was clear that such a venture would be very expensive and highly risky, but political developments in the Eastern Mediterranean suggested that the old Venetian route through Egyptian and Syrian middlemen was under threat, and that the potential profits from a new route would be very rewarding.

The Portuguese had an unrivalled knowledge of sailing conditions in the Atlantic and halfway down the African coast. There had been developments in ship design, rigging and seamanship which made it possible to contemplate long–distance trips in stormier seas than the Venetians encountered in the Mediterranean.

The preparations for this venture were carefully planned and spread over a couple of decades. They involved research on techniques of navigation, astronomy and cartography and collection of information on trading conditions in Asia and East Africa. The second component was a series of trial voyages to explore possible routes and wind patterns down the whole length of the African coast. The third component was a voyage to India to explore trading conditions and possibilities for establishing the sort of bases already established on the African coast.

In the Mediterranean, navigators from the thirteenth century had relied on the compass to determine direction, a sandglass to measure time and a traverse board to measure deviations from course. As the main routes had been known since antiquity, they had reasonable charts, a fair idea of the distances they had to travel and rough methods for judging speed.

The Portuguese were now exploring unknown waters, and had to rely much more on celestial navigation. In the Northern hemisphere Portuguese navigators knew that the pole star provided a roughly constant bearing and altitude, maintaining roughly the same height on a particular parallel of latitude. On a north–south passage a navigator could observe the pole star each day at dawn and dusk (when he could see both the star and the horizon). By noting changes in altitude he could get some idea of changes in his position. In sailing east–west, he could keep a steady course by maintaining a constant polar altitude. All this had to be done very crudely using finger spreads or other rough means to estimate changes in altitude. Measurement was greatly refined by the invention of the quadrant, first recorded in 1460 by Gomes, a professional navigator in the employ of Prince Henry. Parry (1974, p. 174) describes the quadrant as follows: "The seaman's quadrant was a very simple device; a quarter of a circle, with a scale marked on the curved edge, and with two pinhole sights along one of the straight edges. A plumb line hung from the apex. The sights were aligned on the star and the reading taken from the point where the plumb line cut the scale. Polar altitude in degrees gave the observer's latitude." This way a navigator could measure his distance from Lisbon, or some other place whose polar altitude he already knew.

In the Southern hemisphere, the pole star was not visible, and there was no other star with the same properties. Instead the altitude of the sun had to be used but one could not study its position with the naked eye. In 1484, John II created a commission of mathematical experts and astronomers to observe and measure solar altitude. The instrument for measuring distance from the equator was the mariner's astrolabe, derived from astrolabes used by medieval astronomers. It was a graduated brass disc, with a bar which was rotated until the point of light shining through the upper sight fell on to the lower one. It was used at midday when the sun was at its zenith. As there were no accurate clocks a series of readings had to be taken around what appeared to be midday, to derive the maximum altitude. As the distance between the equator and the sun changes from day to day and year to year, mariners needed accurate tables of the sun's declination. John II's commission produced a simplified version of the *Almanach* of the Jewish astronomer Zacuto, and successfully tested the possibilities of finding latitude on a trip to the African coast in 1485. Estimates of the sun's declination were incorporated in a navigational manual *Regimento do Astrolabio e do Quadrante* which was available to da Gama when he sailed to India in 1497. Da Gama had direct contact with Zacuto who had come to Lisbon as a refugee from Spain. The *Regimento* also contained a translation of a work by a thirteenth century English mathematician, Holywood (known as Sacrobosco), who was a pioneer of spherical astronomy, pointed out the errors in the Julian calendar and suggested a correction more or less the same as that incorporated in the Gregorian calendar 350 years later. All this Portuguese research and development was done 50 years before Copernicus published his work on celestial orbits in 1543, but the committee would surely have had an immediate understanding of its significance.

There were preparatory voyages to gauge the feasibility of a passage to India by Diogo Câo in 1482–4 and another by Bartolomeu Dias in 1487–8. Câo found the mouth of the Congo river and went past the future sites of Luanda and Benguela in Angola. The voyage of Dias was more rewarding. He had two caravels and a store ship, found a better route to Angola, and at Lüderitz Bay on the coast of Namibia, in the face of adverse winds, discovered it was useful to veer well out west into the Atlantic to catch winds which took him round the Cape. He sailed 1 000 kilometres east of the Cape before turning back. The trip took 18 months. He had sailed nearly 13 000 kilometres from Lisbon. The return passage was somewhat shorter because he found favourable winds from the Cape to the Azores. He had demonstrated that the Atlantic and Indian oceans were connected.

There was also an exploratory trip by land. Pero da Covilhã had been a spy in Spain and Morocco, spoke fluent Arabic and could pass for a Muslim. Armed with letters of credit he went to Cairo via Barcelona, Naples, Rhodes and Alexandria, down the Red Sea coast by caravan, took a ship at Aden for Calicut (in Kerala) which was known to be the major Indian emporium for the spice trade with a hinterland in a rich spice–growing region. He made an extensive reconnaissance of the west coast of India as far north as Goa and the East African coast down to the port of Sofala. He sent a report on his findings in 1490 via a Portuguese emissary in Cairo, and acting on a second set of instructions he visited Hormuz, the centre of the spice trade in the Persian Gulf.

Thus the Portuguese committee was well briefed on trading conditions in India and East Africa and possibilities of navigation in the Atlantic before entrusting Vasco da Gama with a passage to India in 1497–9.

In 1484, John II received a proposition for a westward passage from Christopher Columbus, a Genoese navigator who had spent eight years in Portuguese ships sailing to the Atlantic islands and the Guinea coast. He asked the king "to give him some vessels to go and discover the Ile Cypango by this Western Ocean" (Morison, 1974, p. 31). The committee rejected the proposal because they thought Cypango (Japan) was a fiction of Marco Polo and that Columbus greatly underestimated the distance to Asia. Eventually the Columbus venture was financed by Queen Isabella of Spain. In 1492, he sailed to the Canary Islands, and from there reached the Bahamas in 33 days. He spent more than three months in the Caribbean where he found Cuba and Haiti without realising that the islands were in the middle of a huge unknown continent. Because of stormy weather on his return voyage, he was forced to land in Lisbon in 1493 for refitting, and had to brief John II. The Portuguese did not believe that Columbus had reached Asia, and knew he had not found spices. However, in anticipation of a flurry of Spanish maritime exploration, and to protect Portuguese interests, the Treaty of Tordesillas was negotiated with Spain in 1494. This stipulated that Portugal would not compete in the West Atlantic. On Portuguese insistence, the dividing line was fixed 370 leagues west of the Azores (about 48 degrees west of the Greenwich meridian). Portugal not only got a free hand for its Asian project and African interests, but established a legal claim to Brazil (which was found six years later).

The last step in the preparation for da Gama's voyage was to provide two specially built ships, constructed with advice from Dias. Jones (1978), p. 30, compares them with the caravels used by earlier navigators as follows: "a stouter, roomier craft, standing higher in the water and able successfully to navigate in coastal waters, better able to stand long periods in the ocean, safer in the tempests of the tropics, and with better quarters for the crew. He designed the vessels to have a foremast, and mainmast, square rigged with mainsail and topsail, a square spritsail at the bow and a small lateen–rigged mizzen stepped right aft on the castle. These probably provided a sail area, without bonnets, of about 4 000 sq. feet. Main and fore each had a crow's nest — Length of hull was probably slightly under seventy–five feet, with a beam a third of that." The ships "were about 200 tons register in present day terms", they each had 20 guns firing stone balls weighing a few ounces. In addition, da Gama had a 50 ton caravel and a small supply ship. His crew of about 160 included gunners, musicians and three Arabic interpreters. He carried trade goods of a type used in West Africa (coarse cloth, bells and beads) which were virtually useless in Asia.

Da Gama sailed from Lisbon in July 1497 to Cape Verde. Shortly thereafter (about 150 kilometres off Sierra Leone) instead of heading southeast which was the normal route down the African coast, he veered southwest far into the Atlantic and eventually caught winds which blew him southeast around the Cape. By Christmas he had rounded Africa, and moved up the East coast, visiting Mozambique, Mombasa and Malindi. Economic life there was much more sophisticated than in West Africa. The coastal towns had merchants — Arabs, Indians from Gujarat and Malabar and Persians — who imported silk and cotton textiles, spices and Chinese porcelain and exported cotton, timber and gold. They had professional pilots familiar with monsoon conditions in the Indian ocean. Their ships were sturdy, but the Portuguese noted that they were constructed without nails. Instead the timbers were stitched and bound together with ropes made of coconut fibre (coir) which was widely available in Southern India and Ceylon. The local population were an Afro–Arab mix, speaking Arabic and Swahili, wearing cotton clothing and using coined money. He was able to get a competent Gujarati pilot from the ruler of Malindi (in Kenya), who got him to Calicut (in Kerala) in less than a month.

The Portuguese remained in Calicut for three months, discovered a good deal about prices and conditions in the spice market, but failed to establish amicable relations with the local ruler or to sell their trade goods. The return trip to Malindi took three months. They found it difficult to man the ships as many of the crew had died of scurvy, so they burned the Sao Gabriel (one of the specially built ships). They had already dismantled the supply ship on the outward journey.

The caravel returned to Lisbon in July 1499, and da Gama got back in August (having stopped to bury his brother in the Azores). In the two year voyage, he had lost half the crew and two of the ships, and had very little in the way of cargo. However, he had proved the feasibility of the route, found a new source of gold in East Africa, had established that there were no maritime fleets in the Indian Ocean which could impede Portuguese access to the spice trade. He also let it be known that there were Christians in Kerala[17].

This news was received enthusiastically in Lisbon, and there was a quick follow-up. In March 1500, Pedro Cabral was given command of 12 ships and more than 1 000 men to improve on the route, bring back a significant cargo and establish a base on the Kerala coast. There was fairly extensive private participation in the cost and benefits of the trip.

Cabral went farther west in the Atlantic than da Gama and had the good luck, after a month at sea, to be the first navigator to encounter Brazil. He stayed a few days at a point he called Porto Seguro (about 350 km south of Bahia), and immediately sent a ship back to Lisbon to announce his finding territory which lay well within the area allotted to Portugal in the Treaty of Tordesillas[18].

On the East African coast he stopped off at Sofala and Kilwa which da Gama had missed, got a pilot in Malindi and was in Calicut within six months of leaving Lisbon. He stayed in Calicut for two months and was given a large house as a trading base (known as a factory). However, he had to leave in a hurry. The Portuguese seized a local vessel on its way to Gujarat and another leaving for Jedda on the Red Sea. In retaliation, local muslim traders attacked the Portuguese factory, killed over 50 Portuguese and took the trade goods. In return Cabral captured ten more local vessels and bombarded the unfortified town (see Subramanyam, 1997, pp. 180–1). He sailed 150 kilometres further down the coast to Cochin, where he was able to load additional cargo and create the basis for a permanent factory. He left some of his people behind for this purpose and took three Cochin representatives back to Portugal. Before leaving for Malindi, he stopped in Cannanur (about 70 kilometres north of Calicut) to pick up a cargo of cinnamon.

Cabral arrived back in Lisbon around the beginning of July 1501 with five vessels. The cargo, mostly pepper, appears to have been around 700 tons[19], but the loss of seven ships (six on the way out, one on the way back) and the violence in Calicut were not encouraging.

Da Gama was sent on a second mission to India with a fleet of 20 ships, leaving Lisbon in February 1502. Fifteen of the ships were for the return journey, and another five (under the command of da Gama's uncle) were destined to stay behind to protect Portuguese bases in India and to blockade shipping leaving India for the Red Sea. By June, da Gama had traversed the Cape and stopped at Sofala to buy gold. At Kilwa, he forced the local ruler to agree to pay an annual tribute of pearls and gold, and left there for India. He waited offshore at Cannanur, for ships returning from the Red Sea. He captured one returning from Mecca with pilgrims and a valuable cargo. Part of the cargo was seized and the ship was burned with most of the passengers and crew (see Subrahmanyan, 1997, pp. 205–9). Then he put into Cannanur, and exchanged presents (he offered silver and got precious stones) with the local ruler, but did no business as he found the price of spices too high. He headed in the direction of Cochin, stopped his ships opposite Calicut and demanded that the ruler expel the whole Muslim merchant community (4 000 households) which used the port as a basis for trading with the Red Sea. The Samudri, the local Hindu ruler, refused, so da Gama bombarded the city as Cabral had done. He got to Cochin at the beginning of November, where he was able to buy spices against silver, copper and the textiles he had taken from the ship he sank. A permanent factory was set up in Cochin, and five ships were left to protect Portuguese interests.

Before leaving for home, da Gama's fleet was attacked by more than 30 ships financed by the Muslim traders of Calicut. They were routed after Portuguese bombardment, and part of the Muslim merchant community in Calicut decided to move their operations elsewhere. These naval engagements showed clearly the superiority of armed Portuguese ships over those of Asian countries.

Da Gama returned to Lisbon in October 1503, with 13 of his ships and nearly 1 700 tons of spices, i.e. about the same as annual Venetian imports from the Middle East at the end of the fifteenth century. However, the Portuguese margins on this trade were much bigger than the Venetian. Most of these spices were marketed in Europe via Antwerp, which was the chief port of the Spanish Netherlands.

The voyages of Dias, Cabral and da Gama had laid the foundations of the Portuguese trading empire in East Africa and Asia. Portugal held a monopoly of the traffic round the Cape until the last decade of the sixteenth century.

The Mameluke regime in Egypt sent a fleet in 1509 to try to stop interference with shipping to the Red Sea but they were defeated by the Portuguese at Diu off the coast of Gujarat. However, Portugal did not succeed in establishing a base in the Red Sea, Aden was taken by Turkey in 1538, and the old Asian trade to Egypt was reopened from about the middle of the sixteenth century. Portugal did acquire a fortified position at Hormuz which dominated the entry to the Persian Gulf for about a century. There was no blockade of trade with the newly established regime in Safavid Persia, but traders entering the Gulf and those using other Portuguese bases had to pay for safe–conduct passes (*cartazes*). In addition Portugal levied customs duties on goods travelling through its Asian bases.

Wake (1979), p. 377, provided a rough estimate of annual Portuguese spice imports. In the first half of the sixteenth century they averaged 1 475 metric tons a year, 1 160 in the second half. In 1600, total West European consumption was probably about twice the 1500 level, and per capita consumption had risen by half[20].

Table 2–6. **Number of Ships Sailing to Asia from Seven European Countries, 1500–1800**

	1500–99	*1600–1700*	*1701–1800*
Portugal	705	371	196
Netherlands	65[a]	1 770	2 950
England		811	1 865
France		155	1 300
Other		54	350
Total	770	3 161	6 661

a) 1590s.

Source: Portugal 1500–1800 from Magalhâes Godinho in Bruijn and Gaastra (1993), pp. 7 and 17; otherwise from Bruijn and Gaastra (1993), pp. 178 and 183. "Other" refers to ships of the Danish, Swedish trading companies, and the Ostend Company.

Table 2–7. **Movement of Portuguese Ships to and from Asia, 1500–1800**

	Departures from Lisbon to Indian Ocean	Arrivals in the Orient	Departures from India and Malacca	Arrivals in Lisbon
	(totals for period)			
1500–49	451	403	262	243
1550–99	254	217	212	170
1600–35	207	152	95	74
1636–1700	164	n.a.	n.a.	n.a.
1701–1800	196	n.a.	n.a.	n.a.
	(annual average)			
1500–49	9.0	8.1	5.2	4.9
1550–99	5.1	4.3	4.2	3.4
1600–35	5.8	4.2	2.6	2.1
1636–1700	2.5			
1701–1800	1.9			

Source: Magalhaes in Bruijn and Gaastra (1993), pp. 7 and 17. The difference between departures from Lisbon and returns is due to losses, and in some cases returns to home port, but also to ships which remained in Asia to defend the bases or to participate in intra Asian trade. Once the trade was firmly established, the average duration of the outward trip Lisbon–Cochin was about 5.75 months, and 6.5 months for the return journey. The average size of vessels increased over time with a carrying capacity of 300 tons in the sixteenth century and up to 1 000 tons in the seventeenth.

Table 2–8. **Gold and Silver Shipments from the Americas to Europe, 1500–1800**
(metric tons)

	Gold	Silver
1500–1600	150	7 500
1600–1700	158	26 168
1700–1800	1 400	39 157
Total 1500–1800	2 708	72 825

Source: Morineau (1985), p. 570.

Table 2–9. **Chinese Imports of Silver by Country of Origin, 1550–1700**
(metric tons)

	Japan	Philippines	Portuguese shipments to Macao	Total
1550–1600	1 280	584	380	2 244
1601–40	1 968	719	148	2 835
1641–85	1 586	108	0	1 694
1685–1700	41	137	0	178
Total 1550–1700	4 875	1 548	428	6 951

Source: Von Glahn (1996), pp. 140 and 232.

Table 2–10. **Exports of Silver and Gold from Western Europe, 1601–1780**
(tonnes of "silver equivalent")

	To the Baltic	To Eastern Mediterranean	Dutch (VOC) to Asia	British (EIC) to Asia	Total
1601–50	2 475	2 500	425	250	5 650
1651–1700	2 800	2 500	775	1 050	7 125
1701–50	2 800	2 500	2 200	2 450	9 950
1751–80	1 980	1 500	1 445	1 450	6 375
Total 1601–1780	10 055	9 000	4 845	5 200	29 100

Source: Barrett, in Tracy (1990), p. 251 (he does not show his equivalence conversion ratio for gold).

V
THE TRADING WORLD OF THE INDIAN OCEAN

The population of Asia in 1500 was five times as big as that of Western Europe (284 million compared with 57 million), and the ratio was about the same in 1600. It was a very large market with a network of Asian traders operating between East Africa and India, and from Eastern India to Indonesia. East of the straits of Malacca, trade was dominated by China. Indian ships were not sturdy enough to withstand the typhoons of the China sea, and not adequately armed to deal with pirate activity off the China coast (see Chaudhuri, 1982, p. 410).

The Portuguese displaced Asian traders who had supplied spices to Red Sea and Persian Gulf ports for onward sale to Venetian, Genoese and Catalan traders. But this was only a fraction, perhaps a quarter, of Asian trade in one group of commodities. In addition there was trade within Asian waters in textiles, porcelain, precious metals, carpets, perfume, jewellery, horses, timber, salt, raw silk, gold, silver, medicinal herbs and many other commodities.

Hence, the spice trade was not the only trading opportunity for the Portuguese, or for the other later European traders (Dutch, British, French and others) who followed. Silk and porcelain played an increased role, and in the seventeenth and eighteenth centuries, cotton textiles and tea became very important. There were possibilities of participating in intra–Asian trade as well. In the 1550s to the 1630s this kind of trade between China and Japan was a particularly profitable source of income for Portugal.

Asian merchants were familiar with the seasonal wind patterns and problems of the Indian Ocean, there were experienced pilots, scientific works on astronomy and navigation, and navigational instruments not greatly inferior to those of the Portuguese[21].

From East Africa to Malacca (on the narrow straits between Sumatra and Malaya), Asian trade was conducted by merchant communities which operated without armed vessels or significant interference from governments. Although Southern India, where the Portuguese started their Asian trade, was ruled by the Empire of Vijayanagar, conditions in coastal trade were set by rulers of much smaller political units, who derived income by offering protection and marketing opportunities to traders. The income of the rulers of Vijayanagar and later the Moghul Empire was derived from land taxes, and they had no significant financial interest in foreign trade activities. In China and Japan the situation was different.

Asian merchants operated in mutually interactive community networks with ethnic, religious, family or linguistic ties and an opportunistic concentration on profit. In this respect their trading habits were not very different from those of Venetians or of Jewish traders in the Arab world of the Mediterranean[22]. In Western Asia and the Middle East merchants were generally Arabs and Muslims, but further east they included "Gujarati *vaniyas*, Tamil and Telugu Chettis, Syrian Christians from Southwestern India, Chinese from Fukien and neighbouring provinces"[23]. If they paid for protection and market access, they found that they were free to trade. If the protection became too expensive they usually had some leeway for moving elsewhere.

The Portuguese trading network was different in two respects. It consisted of a string of strongly fortified bases linked by a fleet of armed ships, so market forces were modified by coercion. Unlike the Asian trading communities or in the European trading companies which penetrated Asia at a later date, Portugal was involved in religious evangelism.

The headquarters of the Portuguese trading empire was established in 1510 at the captured Arab port of Goa, an island harbour halfway up the west Indian coast which was a Portuguese colony for nearly 460 years[24]. It was the residence of the Portuguese Viceroy, and from 1542 it was the headquarters of the Jesuit order for all its operations in Asia. Malacca, the port which controlled trade and shipping from India to Indonesia and China, was captured in 1511 and kept until 1641 when it was taken by the Dutch. A base was established at Jaffna in Sri Lanka for trade in cinnamon. Most Portuguese shipments of pepper and ginger originated from the Malabar coast of India, but for higher value spices they obtained a base at Ternate in the Moluccas (between Celebes and New Guinea) for trade in cloves, nutmeg and mace.

VI
THE TRADING WORLD OF CHINA, JAPAN AND THE PHILIPPINES

Trading conditions were very different in Asia east of the Malacca straits. Establishment of trading relations with China and Japan was a much more difficult proposition than with countries in the Indian Ocean. Requests for access to China in 1513 and 1521–22 were rejected. It was not until 1557 that Portugal acquired Macao though it participated earlier in clandestine trade off the Chinese coast. Contact was made with Japan in 1543 and trade started there in earnest in the 1550s from the base in Macao.

China had withdrawn from an active role in Asian trade in the fifteenth century, imposed tight controls on private trade, and an embargo on trade with Japan. In view of the historic importance of this withdrawal, it is worth retracing Chinese experience from the 1100s to 1433 when it was the most dynamic force in Asian trade.

China's exposure to world trade had been greatly enhanced when the Sung dynasty were driven out of North China and relocated their capital at Hangchow, south of the Yangtse. It was a prosperous and densely populated region of rice cultivation. It was not necessary to bring food supplies from distant areas. They relied more heavily on commercial taxes than most Chinese dynasties and fostered the development of ports and foreign trade. Their major port was Ch'üan–chou, about 600 kilometres north of Canton. They developed large scale production of ceramics for the export market, and the kilns of Ching–te–chen (in Kiangsi) prospered greatly.

In order to defend the Yangtse and coastal areas against Mongol attacks the first Chinese professional navy was created in 1232. Within a century it had grown to 20 squadrons with 52 000 men, with its main base near Shanghai. The ships included treadmill operated paddle–wheelers with protective armour plates, for service on the Yangtse. These were armed with powerful catapults to fling heavy stones or other missiles at enemy ships.

After the Sung were defeated, the Mongol (Yuan) dynasty continued with even larger scale shipbuilding activities for foreign trade, for grain transport to Peking (their new capital) in North China, for maritime commerce with Asia and for naval operations. In 1274 and 1281, two massive fleets were assembled in an unsuccessful attempt to invade Japan. The first fleet included 900 ships, the second was much larger and carried an invasion force of quarter of a million soldiers. They reopened overland commerce to Europe and the Middle East on the silk route.

As in the Sung, a large proportion of the trading community in the Yuan dynasty were from all parts of the Muslim world. This is clear from the observations of Marco Polo, the Venetian who came to China in the last quarter of the thirteenth century, and Ibn Battuta from Morocco more than 50 years later. Both left striking testimony to the vigour of the international trade of China at that time.

In the early years of the Ming, the Yung–lo emperor embarked on a series of naval expeditions outside the area of the "Eastern Oceans" which were the traditional Chinese sphere of interest. These expeditions were massive exercises whose basic motivation was political, though they did include an important element of state trading.

Yung–lo was a usurper, who had deposed his nephew in a successful military rebellion. The naval ventures were intended to display China's power and wealth and enhance his own legitimacy. They were also intended to extend Chinese suzerainty over a much wider area. Korea was a permanent member of this system of tributary relationships and Yung–lo persuaded Japan to accept a similar status in 1404 (which lasted with a brief interruption until 1549). In the tribute system, there was an initial exchange of "gifts" (consisting on the Chinese side of specialties such as silk, gold, lacquer and porcelain) and the other side would reciprocate. These exchanges were renewed at intervals of a few years, and in the past had been followed up by private trade relations. However, Yung–lo prohibited private trade.

Table 2–11. **Chinese Naval Diplomacy: Voyages to the "Western Oceans", 1405–33**

Time	Number of ships	Number of naval military & other personnel	Places visited in Western Oceans	Places visited in Eastern Oceans
1405–7	62 large vessels	27 000	Calicut	Champa, Java, Sumatra
1407–9	n.a.	n.a.	Calicut & Cochin	Siam, Sumatra, Java
1409–11	48	30 000	Malacca, Quilon	Sumatra
1413–15	63	29 000	Hormuz, Red Sea, Maldives, Bengal	Champa, Java, Sumatra
1417–19	n.a.	n.a.	Hormuz, Aden, Mogadishu, Malindi	Java, the Ryuku islands, Brunei
1421–2	41	n.a.	Aden, East Africa	Sumatra
1431–33	100	27 500	Ceylon, Calicut, Hormuz, Aden, Jedda, Malindi	Vietnam, Sumatra, Java, Malacca

Source: Needham (1971) and Levathes (1994). The detailed official records of these trips were destroyed later by the bureaucracy who were opposed to renewal of such expeditions. The evidence is based on the writings of participants and later imperial histories.

These tributary relations were conceived as a vehicle for assertion of China's moral and cultural superiority, to act as a civilising force on barbarians at the frontiers, and thereby enhance China's security. For this reason the government expected to play a leading role in developing and supervising the trade relationships. The underlying idea was not to create a colonial empire, but to assert Chinese hegemony. This traditional view of Chinese relations with the outside world was very different from that of the Mongol dynasty whose objective was world conquest, and Yung–lo probably felt the need to re–establish a more attractive image of Chinese civilisation.

Seven expeditions between 1405 and 1433 penetrated very deep into the "Western Oceans". They were commanded by Admiral Cheng–ho, a member of the emperor's household since he was 15 years old who had become a comrade in arms. Cheng–ho was a eunuch. There were thousands of them in the Ming imperial household. Emperors of this dynasty used them as a trusted and loyal counterweight to the power of the bureaucracy. Most of the latter regarded the expeditions as a waste of money, at a time when there were very large commitments in moving the Ming capital from Nanking to Peking and in rebuilding the Grand Canal. They involved very heavy fiscal burdens, and special levies on the coastal provinces. Yung–lo augmented his revenues by printing massive quantities of paper money. The resulting inflation (see Table 2–12) led to a disappearance of paper money transactions in the private economy. From the 1430s, silver became the predominant instrument of exchange and tax payments.

Table 2–12. **Exchange Rates between Ming Paper Currency and Silver, 1376–1426**

	Official	*Market*
1376	1.00	1.00
1397	0.07	
1413	0.05	
1426	0.0025	
1436	n.a.	0.0009

Source: Atwell in Twitchett and Mote (1998), p. 382.

Under the Yung–lo emperor, the Ming navy "consisted of some 3 800 ships in all, 1 350 patrol vessels and 1 350 combat ships attached to guard stations or island bases, a main fleet of 400 large warships stationed near Nanking and 400 grain transport freighters. In addition there were more than 250 long–distance Treasure–ships" (Needham, 1971, p. 484). The treasure ships were the most important vessels in the maritime expeditions to the Western Oceans. They were five times as big as any of the ships of da Gama, 120 metres long and nearly 50 metres broad.

Chinese ships differed substantially from those in the Indian Ocean or Portugal. The treasure ships had nine masts, and smaller ships also had multiple masts. Transverse laths of bamboo attached to the sail fabric permitted precise and stepwise reefing. When sails were furled, they fell immediately into pleats. If tears developed in the sail, the area affected was restricted by the lathing. Big ships had 15 or more watertight compartments, so a partially damaged ship would not sink and could be repaired at sea. They had up to 60 cabins so the crew quarters were more comfortable than on Portuguese ships.

Table 2–11 shows the characteristics of the six naval expeditions of the Yung–lo emperor, and the seventh which was sent after his death. The fleets were very large and the big ships were intended to overawe the rulers of the countries which were visited. The intentions were peaceful but the military force was big enough to deal effectively with attacks on the fleet, which occurred on only three occasions. The first had India and its spices as their destination. The rest explored the East Coast of Africa, the Red Sea and the Persian Gulf.

A major purpose of these voyages was to establish good relations by presentation of gifts and to escort ambassadors or rulers to or from China. There was no attempt to establish bases for trade or for military objectives. There was a search for new plants for medical purposes, and one of the missions was accompanied by 180 medical personnel. There was also an interest in types of African livestock which were unknown in China. The expeditions brought back ostriches, giraffes, zebras, elephant tusks and rhinoceros horns. However, these were exotica, and there was no significant replication of the international interchange of flora and fauna which the European encounter with the Americas inaugurated.

After the death of Cheng–ho, support for this distant diplomacy faded very quickly. The broadening of China's tributary relations with countries of the "Western Oceans" did not enhance China's security and the cost of the naval expeditions had exacerbated a situation of fiscal and monetary crisis. The meritocratic bureaucracy had always opposed a venture which promoted the leverage of the eunuch interest. They consolidated their gains by destroying the official records of the overseas expeditions. There was increasing concern to defend the new northern capital against potential invasions from Mongolia or Manchuria. The new capital's food supply was guaranteed by the Grand Canal which had been reopened in its full length in 1415 (2 300 kilometres — equivalent to the distance from Paris to Istanbul). It functioned better than ever before because of new locks which made it operational on a full–time basis[25]. Grain shipments by sea to the capital had already ceased and sea–going grain ships were replaced by canal barges.

As the oceanic diplomacy had been ended, there was no longer a need for Treasure ships, coastal defences had been reduced and there was strong pressure to reduce the hard core of the navy. By 1474 the fleet of large warships had been cut from 400 to 140. Most of the shipyards were closed, and naval manpower was reduced by retrenchment and desertions.

The tributary arrangements for countries within the Eastern Ocean continued, e.g. ships from Japan were able to come at intervals of several years, but the Yung–lo ban on private trade continued, and sea–going junks with more than two masts were prohibited.

This regime of interdiction and regulation eventually sparked large scale development of illicit private trade and piracy. The coastguards were open to bribery. By the time the Portuguese established their base in Macao in 1557, they were fully aware of the trading situation and had easy contacts with Chinese and Japanese pirates.

In 1567, the Chinese authorities ended the prohibition on private trade but banned trade with Japan. This gave the Portuguese an unbelievably favourable window of opportunity.

Japan

In 1539, the Chinese had confiscated the cargo of Japanese ships participating in the tribute trade. In 1544 they had turned away Japanese attempts to renew the tributary trade. This was enough to induce Japanese hostility, and enmity was further heightened by political changes in Japan. By the middle of the sixteenth century the Ashigawa shogunate which had accepted nominal Chinese suzerainty was on its last legs. It was succeeded by a series of three ruthless military dictators, Nobunaga, Hideyoshi, and Ieyasu, who created a powerful unified system of government. They completely repudiated the idea of Chinese suzerainty.

These political developments occurred at the same time as Japan became a major silver producer. Rich deposits were discovered in the 1530s. The export potential was very large. The Chinese market was hungry for silver, and the gold/silver price ratio was much more favourable to silver in China than in Japan. As the Chinese would not allow Japanese ships to enter their harbours, the main carriers of Japanese silver to China were Chinese pirates and the Portuguese.

Portuguese ships were able to bring Indonesian spices from Malacca to Macao, sell them in China, buy Chinese silks and gold, go from Macao to harbours in the south of Japan (first Hirado and then Nagasaki), sell these products, buy Japanese silver, sell it in Macao, and buy silk again for shipment to Japan or their depot in Goa.

Portuguese trade was also accompanied by Jesuit missions. Francis Xavier was in Japan in 1549–51, and Jesuits were very successful in getting converts in the south of Japan. Eventually, the number of Japanese Christians rose to about 300 000 (many more converts than the Jesuits made in Goa or in China). Japanese were interested in Portuguese ships, maps and navigation, and learned something of these two techniques. They were even more interested in guns. Portuguese technology of that epoch was reproduced in Japanese *namban* (southern barbarian) art which is displayed most clearly in very large multi–panelled lacquer screens. The first Portuguese to arrive in 1543 had firearms which were new to Japan. The potential of this new weaponry was quickly appreciated by the military who managed to copy the guns and manufacture them in Japan. They had an important effect in deciding the outcome of the Japanese civil wars. After 1615, the new shogunate began a successful policy to eliminate firearms and restrict the use of swords to the *samurai*.

In 1596, the Spanish authorities in Manila tried to replicate Portuguese successes in Japan, and sent a mission of Franciscan missionaries to proselytise. The Japanese got the impression that Spain might want to take over as they had the Philippines, and on Hideyoshi's order the Spanish missionaries and 19 of their converts were crucified at Nagasaki. From that point on, Japan became increasingly hostile to Portuguese missionary activities, and made contact with English and Dutch traders who had no religious ambitions. Eventually Christianity became illegal, and the Portuguese were expelled in 1639. Henceforth trade with the Japanese mainland was confined to Chinese and Dutch traders.

Manila

Fernao de Magalhaes had participated in the first Portuguese expedition to the Moluccan spice islands in 1511, and was disappointed with his pay and prospects when he returned to Portugal. In 1517, he defected to Spain, changed his name to Magellan, and persuaded the Spanish crown to finance a voyage by a Western route. The expedition he commanded (1519–22) was the first to circumnavigate the globe. It established a route around the south of Argentina. Magellan was killed in combat in the Philippines, but the voyage continued to the spice islands and eventually got back to Spain. Fifteen men returned, more than 200 failed to survive the voyage.

Spain surrendered its claim to the Moluccas to Portugal for a cash payment, but gained effective control of the Philippines in 1571. It was the only significant part of the Spanish empire outside the Americas. The route between Acapulco (on the west coast of Mexico) and Manila had a monopoly in trading Spanish silver against Chinese silks and porcelain. Spaniards took little direct part in China trade, which was mainly conducted by Chinese ships, using the large overseas Chinese population of Manila as intermediaries. At the end of the sixteenth century there were 2 000 Spanish living in Manila and 10 000 Chinese.

Relations with China were never very friendly. In 1603, a visit by rather pushy Chinese traders representing the provincial authorities of Fukien gave the misleading impression that China intended to invade the Philippines. The Spanish reaction was to attack and kill most of the Chinese community in Manila. The Chinese Wan–li emperor executed the trader who had provoked the Spanish, and the trade with China managed to survive this incident. However, possession of the Philippines was never a particularly profitable venture for Spain, and the flow of silver from Mexico via Manila to China was a good deal smaller than that from Japan (see Table 2–9).

VII
THE PORTUGUESE IN BRAZIL

When the Portuguese arrived in Brazil in 1500, their situation as colonialists was very different from that of Spain in Mexico and Peru. They did not find an advanced civilisation with hoards of precious metals for plunder, or a social discipline and organisation geared to provide steady tribute which they could appropriate. Brazilian Indians were mainly hunter–gatherers, though some were moving towards agriculture using slash–and–burn techniques to cultivate manioc. Their technology and resources meant that they were thin on the ground. They had no towns, no domestic animals. They were stone age men and women, hunting game and fish, naked, illiterate and innumerate.

In the first century of settlement, it became clear that it was difficult to use Indians as slave labour. They were not docile, had high mortality when exposed to Western diseases, could run away and hide rather easily. So Portugal turned to imported African slaves for manual labour. The ultimate fate of Brazilian Indians was rather like that of North American Indians. They were pushed beyond the fringe of colonial society. The main difference was greater miscegenation with the white invaders and with black slaves in Brazil.

A much bigger proportion of Portuguese gains from Brazil came from development of commodity exports and commercial profit than those of Spain from its colonies. In the sixteenth and seventeenth centuries official revenue from Brazil was small — about 3 per cent of Portuguese public revenue in 1588 and 5 per cent in 1619 (see Bethell, 1984, Vol. I, p. 286). In the sixteenth century, economic activity was concentrated on a small population of settlers engaged in a highly profitable export–oriented sugar industry in the Northeast. The techniques for this industry, including negro slavery, had been previously developed in Madeira and São Tomé. Cattle ranching in the dry backlands area (the *sertao*) provided food for those working in sugar production.

Brazilian sugar exports peaked in the 1650s. Earnings fell thereafter because of lower prices and competition from the rapidly growing output in the Caribbean (see Table 2–4).

The setback in sugar caused large parts of the Northeast to lapse into a subsistence economy. In the 1690s, the discovery of gold, and in the 1720s diamonds further south in Minas Gerais, opened new opportunities. During the eighteenth century, there was considerable immigration from Europe, and internal migration from the Northeast to Minas, to engage in gold and diamond development. The eighteenth century prosperity in Minas is obvious even today from the number of elaborate buildings and churches in Ouro Preto which was the centre of mining activity. As Minas Gerais is very barren, the food and transport needs of the mining area stimulated food production in neighbouring provinces to the South and in the Northeast, and mule–breeding in Rio Grande do Sul. The gold industry was at its peak around 1750, with production around 15 tons a year, but as the best deposits were exhausted, output and exports declined. In the first half of the eighteenth century profit remittances from gold averaged 5.23 million milreis (£1.4 million) a year, of which the identifiable royal revenues were around 18 per cent (Alden, 1973, p. 331). Total Brazilian gold shipments over the whole of the eighteenth century were between 800 and 850 tons (see Morineau, 1985).

In the second half of the eighteenth century, Portuguese finances were in desperate straits. Metropolitan revenues from Brazil were squeezed by the decline in gold production. Income from Asia had collapsed and Portugal had to bear the costs of reconstructing Lisbon after the 1755 earthquake. To meet this problem, the Portuguese prime minister, Pombal, expelled the Jesuits from Brazil (1759), confiscated their vast properties, and sold them to wealthy landowners and merchants for the benefit of the crown. Most of the property of other religious orders was taken over a few years later.

Table 2–13. **Commodity Composition of Brazilian Exports, 1821–1951**
(per cent of total)

	Cotton	*Sugar*	*Coffee*	*Rubber*	*Cocoa*
1821–3	25.8	23.1	18.7	0.0	n.a.
1871–3	16.6	12.3	50.2	0.0	n.a.
1901–3	2.6	2.4	55.7	22.5	2.5
1927–9	2.0	0.5	71.1	2.0	3.8
1949–51	10.0	0.3	60.5	0.2	4.8

Source: 1821–73 from Leff (1982), Vol.II, p. 9. 1901–51 from *O Brasil em Numeros*.

When gold production collapsed, Brazil turned back to agricultural exports. At independence in 1822, the three main exports were cotton, sugar and coffee. Coffee production started at the beginning of the nineteenth century after the slave revolt cut output in Haiti. Coffee was grown in the Southeast, whereas sugar and cotton were typical Northeast products.

At the end of the colonial period, half the population were slaves. They were worked to death after a few years of service, and fed on a crude diet of beans and jerked beef. A privileged fraction of the white population enjoyed high incomes but the rest of the population (free blacks, mulattos, Indians and large numbers of the whites) were poor. Landownership was concentrated on slave owners, thus a very unequal distribution of property buttressed a highly unequal distribution of income. There was substantial regional inequality. The poorest area was the Northeast. Minas Gerais had also passed its peak. The most prosperous area was around the new capital, Rio de Janeiro.

Independence came to Brazil very smoothly by Latin American standards. In 1808, the Portuguese Queen and the Regent fled to Rio to escape the French invasion of the motherland. They brought about 10 000 of the mainland establishment with them — the aristocracy, bureaucracy, and some of the military who set up government and court in Rio and Petropolis running Brazil and Portugal as a joint kingdom (both parts by then being about equal in terms of population). After the Napoleonic wars, the two countries split without too much enmity. Brazil became independent with an Emperor who was the son of the Portuguese monarch.

With independence, Brazil ceased remitting official tribute to Portugal, but the large imperial ruling establishment meant a higher internal tax burden. The British, the new protectors of Brazil, took out their growing commercial profits. However, independence meant that the country could create its own banking system, print paper money, indulge in mild inflation and borrow on the international capital market.

There was an intermittent inflow of foreign capital from the 1820s onwards, mostly in the form of direct loans to the government or the proceeds from sales of Brazilian government bonds abroad. There were 17 foreign loans in the Imperial period. There was no default on this debt, and Brazil remained in good standing with its British bankers who supplied all the funds.

There were changes in commercial policy which came with independence. Until 1808, Brazilian ports were open only to British or Portuguese ships[26], and mercantilist restrictions prevented production of manufactured items. These barriers were lifted in 1808, but the United Kingdom retained special extra–territorial rights and tariff preferences until 1827. The preferences were then abolished, but Brazil was obliged to limit tariffs to 15 per cent *ad valorem* until 1844. This was a serious fiscal constraint on a government with all the trappings of a monarchy to support, and without the political clout to impose land or income taxation. It encouraged the trend towards inflationary finance and a depreciating paper currency. In 1844, when Brazil regained its customs autonomy the general tariff level was raised to 30 per cent for manufactured goods, but duties on raw materials and machinery

were lifted. These measures stimulated the creation of the cotton spinning and weaving industry. In the Imperial period, tariff revenue provided two thirds of the government's tax receipts and their effect in protecting local industry was significant. Tariff receipts were a higher proportion of imports than those of any other country except Portugal[27].

In 1833, the United Kingdom abolished slavery in the West Indies and started to interfere actively with the slave trade. Between 1840 and 1851, the inflow of slaves to Brazil was 370 000, but thereafter the British Navy brought it to an end. Slavery continued for almost four more decades, but the economy was modified significantly by the ending of the trade. The immediate effect was to double the price of slaves and make it less profitable to work them to an early death. The sex and age structure of the black population began to change, making for lowered activity rates. In 1888, slavery was abolished without compensation, or any kind of resettlement help for slaves. By that time the slave population was only 7 per cent of the total compared with 13 per cent in the United States in 1860, on the eve of the US civil war.

The Emperor was deposed in 1889 by the military which established an oligarchic republic. Church and state were separated. The franchise was restricted to those with property. The Presidency generally alternated between politicians from São Paulo and Minas Gerais on a prearranged basis. The monarchy had exercised a centralised power, but now the provinces became states with a good deal of autonomy, including control over customs duties which could be levied on both foreign and interstate commerce. At the state level, power was concentrated in the hands of a small political class who favoured their cronies and relatives.

At local level, "coronelismo" (rule of the colonels) prevailed. This semi–bandit gentry built up their landholdings by means not always legal, and exercised seigneurial type power over the less prosperous citizenry.

In the initial years of the Republic, the strains involved in moving from slave to wage labour were obvious. Coffee was no longer profitable in the region around Rio, which switched to cattle raising. The competitive position of São Paulo was strengthened. Its climate and soils were better suited to coffee than the eroded valleys near Rio. It had been building a free labour force of white immigrants since the 1840s, when Senator Vergueiro introduced them to his plantation. The state government subsidised immigration (mainly of Italians) on a large scale from 1880 to 1928. In the 1920s, many of the immigrants to São Paulo were Japanese. This part of the country was further helped by the growth of rail transport and the development of the port of Santos. The average educational level of immigrants was considerably higher than that of native born Brazilians. They had twice the literacy rate and three times the level of secondary and higher education (Merrick and Graham (1979), p. 111). Their wage level made them more expensive than slaves, but their productivity was higher, and their number could be quickly expanded by immigration.

The Northeastern economy stagnated in the Republican period. There and elsewhere, the black and mulatto population generally got little of the benefits of growth in a country where they had no voting rights, access to land, education or any form of governmental help in adjusting to a wage economy.

Portuguese rule in Brazil had several lasting consequences:

a) Brazil is characterised by very wide disparities in income, wealth, education and economic opportunity. These are more extreme than in Asia, Europe or North America. The social structure still has strong echoes of the colonial period, when there was great inequality in access to landed property, and the bulk of the labour force were slaves. The continued neglect of popular education is very marked even by Latin American standards and has hampered the growth of labour productivity. Another aspect of inequality is regional. The per capita income disparity between the poorest state, Piaui, and the federal district is about 7:1. The only other countries with this degree of regional disparity are Mexico and China.

Table 2–14. **Confrontation of Brazilian and US Economic Performance in the Five Major Phases of Brazilian Development, 1500–1998**

Brazilian Growth Record

	Population (000)	GDP (million 1990 int. $	GDP Per Capita (1990 int. $)
1500	1 000	400	400
1820	4 507	2 912	646
1890	14 199	11 267	794
1929	32 894	37 415	1 137
1980	122 936	639 093	5 199
1998	169 807	926 919	5 459

Growth Rates in Each Phase (annual compound rate)

	Population	GDP	GDP Per Capita
1500–1820 Colony	0.47	0.62	0.15
1820–90 Empire	1.65	1.95	0.30
1890–1929 Oligarchic Republic	2.18	3.13	0.92
1929–80 Developmentalist Era	2.62	5.72	3.03
1980–98 Era of "Adjustment"	1.81	2.09	0.27
1500–1998	1.04	1.57	0.53

US Growth Record

	Population (000)	GDP (million 1990 $)	GDP Per Capita (1990 $)
1500	2 000	800	400
1820	9 981	12 548	1 257
1890	63 302	214 714	3 392
1929	122 245	843 335	6 899
1980	227 757	4 239 558	18 575
1998	270 561	7 394 598	27 331

US Growth Rates in Each Phase (annual compound rate)

	Population	GDP	GDP Per Capita
1500–1820	0.50	0.86	0.36
1820–90	2.67	4.14	1.43
1890–1929	1.70	3.57	1.83
1929–80	1.23	3.21	1.96
1980–98	0.96	3.15	2.17
1500–1998	0.99	1.85	0.85

Source: Appendices A, B and C, and Maddison (1995a).

b) Inequalities of income and opportunity in Brazil are closely associated with ethnicity, but the heritage of slavery has produced less social tension than in the United States. Gilberto Freyre (1959) argued that Brazilians are more or less colour blind, and that Brazil is a social continuum from rich to poor with no sharp social antagonisms. Brazil was different from the United States mainly because Portuguese society and mores at the time of colonisation were heavily influenced by close contact with the Muslim world. Florestan Fernandes (1969) took a much more critical view of a Brazilian society that practises *de facto* but generally discreet social discrimination.

c) Brazil has been favoured by softer political transitions than other countries in Latin America. The Treaty of Tordesillas (1494) divided the Americas amicably between Portugal and Spain. Portugal got a slice extending 48 degrees West of the Greenwich meridian, but its present borders encompass nearly three times as much land — a situation peacefully endorsed by the Treaty of Madrid in 1750. Most of the territorial gains were made by frontiersmen. The only substantial invasion was the Dutch occupation of the Northeast (1630–54). Conflicts to preserve boundaries against French or Spanish incursions were insignificant, and the last territorial acquisition, the Acre territory, was by purchase from Bolivia. The biggest foreign war was with Paraguay (1865–70). This is in stark contrast with Mexico, which lost half its territory in wars with the United States, or to European and Asian experience of wars over boundaries.

d) Another striking feature has been the ease of Brazil's domestic political transitions. Independence was gained with no significant struggle, the Portuguese crown prince becoming Emperor of Brazil in 1822. Slavery was abolished without a civil war in 1888. The Empire became a republic without a struggle in 1889. The Vargas dictatorship of 1930–45 began and ended with relatively little violence, and this was also true of military rule from 1964–85.

e) The combination of smooth political transitions, freedom from foreign conflicts and relative ease of social relations between ethnic groups permitted Brazil to assimilate a cosmopolitan mix of the original Portuguese settlers, the descendants of African slaves, later immigrants from Italy, Japan, Germany and the Lebanon. It is a frontier country with a high degree of self–confidence, without a chip–on–the–shoulder feeling of exploitation by powerful neighbours. It is a looser federation than many big countries and has an intellectual life which is multipolar.

VIII
THE NETHERLANDS

From 1400 to 1700, Dutch per capita income growth was the fastest in Europe, and from 1600 to the 1820s its level was the highest. Before 1600 this performance was due to seizure of opportunities for trade in Northern Europe, and success in transforming agriculture by hydraulic engineering. Thereafter prosperity was augmented by its role in world trade.

The Dutch Republic became independent in 1579 by breaking away from a larger "Netherlands" ruled by Spain[28]. The struggle to achieve and maintain independence lasted for nearly 80 years. The Dutch defeated a Spanish empire which included Castile, Aragon, Portugal (from 1580 to 1640), Naples, Sicily, the Duchy of Milan, Franche Comté, Mexico, Peru, the Philippines, West Indies, Tunis, Flanders, Brabant, Luxembourg, Lille, Artois and Hainault.

It is useful to consider the economic and political context from which the Netherlands economy emerged. From the twelfth century onwards, Flanders and Brabant were the most prosperous part of Northern Europe. The leading cities of Flanders (Bruges, Ghent and Ypres) were the major centre of the European woollen textile industry, making very high quality draperies, tapestries and furnishing materials, which were sold all over Europe. The raw materials were to a substantial extent supplied by imports — wool from England and alum (a cleansing agent indispensable in the cloth industry) which Genoese traders brought from Chios. Woad and other dyestuffs, fuller's earth and other items were mainly local products. In the middle of the fourteenth century (see Postan, 1987, p. 180), English wool exports were running at nearly 7 000 tons a year, most going to Flanders via the English port of Calais. By the middle of the fifteenth, English wool exports had dropped by four fifths and the wool imports of Flanders came from Spain, being shipped from Bilbao and other Spanish Atlantic ports. England had become an exporter rather than an importer of woollen textiles, but a substantial part of its cloth exports were undyed and sent to Flanders for finishing. McNeill (1974) pp. 53–4 indicates

the magnitude of the massive Genoese alum shipments to Flanders between the mid–fourteenth to mid–sixteenth century: "Having captured Chios in 1346, they used the island as an entrepôt, collecting the yield of all the mines of Asia Minor there. This assured a constant supply of adequate quantities of alum to fill the holds of vast specialised ships — some twenty such vessels, of a size greater than any wooden ship attained before or afterward, plied regularly between Chios and Bruges, winter and summer, stopping en route only at Cadiz to take on water and other supplies." Postan suggests that the annual production of Flemish woollen cloth in the fourteenth and fifteenth centuries was more than 150 000 pieces of 28 yards (25.8 metres) in length. In addition Flanders produced linens for export, using local supplies of flax.

Flanders was heavily urbanised and much of its food was imported. There were substantial imports of grain (wheat and barley from France and England, rye from the Baltic), fish from the Baltic and Holland, and wine from France. Postan suggests that wine exports from Bordeaux were running at 25 million gallons a year at the beginning of the fourteenth century. A large proportion of this went to England, some to the Baltic, and a substantial amount to Flanders and Brabant.

By the mid–fourteenth century, the cities of Brabant (Antwerp, Leuven and Brussels) gained an economic edge on Flanders, due to the silting up of water routes to Bruges, the greater enterprise of Antwerp and British competition with the Flemish woollen industry. In Flanders, output, marketing and production practices tended to be heavily regulated by guilds. Foreign trade was conducted through periodic fairs or "staple" arrangements which confined international transactions to particular towns and gave privileged access to the consortium of German merchants in the Hanseatic League. Antwerp had a magnificent harbour at the mouth of the Scheldt, and a more commercial, less regulatory approach. It was the major North European centre for international banking, and loans to foreign rulers, e.g. Henry VIII of England. The Antwerp bourse provided a model for the London Exchange.

Both Flanders and Brabant conducted a substantial amount of international business in their high value exports by land, but for heavy imported goods, sea transport was very much cheaper. A large part of these imports came by sea and river in ships and boats from Holland, Zeeland and the Northern Provinces.

The seven Northern Provinces which united to create the Dutch Republic (Holland, Zeeland, Utrecht, Gelderland, Overijssel, Friesland and Groningen successively in 1579–80) were very different from Flanders and Brabant[29]. They occupied a flat amphibious terrain where the relationship between land and water was very close. There were major natural waterways. The Rhine provided transport deep into Germany, to Cologne and Frankfurt–am–Main. Its delta was full of islands and natural harbours. The Ijssel led into the Zuider Zee, the Ems provided an excellent route to the North German coast. In such a setting, the leading industries were fisheries, sea and river transportation and shipbuilding. Agriculture was also deeply marked by the possibilities for hydraulic management and irrigation.

In the fourteenth century, the merchant marine of the Northern Provinces had established a major position in the North Sea and Baltic, carrying rye and timber from East Germany and Poland which was shipped via Danzig; furs, wax, honey, pitch, tar and timber from Russia via Narva and Riga; copper, iron ore, weapons and salt herring from Sweden; salted cod and timber from Bergen in Norway. In return they carried re–exports of English woollen textiles, salt (for preserving fish and meat) and re–exports of wine from France. Apart from these merchanting activities, they acted as carriers, e.g. between Danzig and Riga, when opportunities arose.

Shipping and trade in the Baltic had previously been monopolised by a consortium of German merchants (the Hanseatic League) with headquarters in Lübeck, and commercial bases in London, Bruges, etc. Hanseatic trade from the Baltic had relied to a large extent on the short land route from Lübeck to Hamburg. The Dutch pioneered the sea route through the Danish sound, which though longer, was cheaper. In 1437–41 the Hanseatic League engaged in hostilities to try to drive Dutch ships from the Baltic, but, with support from Danzig, the Dutch kept the right to trade. This trade was

Table 2–15. **Carrying Capacity of Dutch and Other European Merchant Fleets, 1470–1824**
(metric tons)

	1470	1570	1670	1780	1824
Netherlands	60 000	232 000	568 000	450 000	140 000
Germany	60 000	110 000	104 000	155 000	
Britain	n.a.	51 000	260 000	1 000 000	
France	n.a.	80 000	80 000	700 000	
Italy, Portugal, Spain	n.a.	n.a.	250 000	546 000	
Denmark, Norway and Sweden				555 000 [a]	
North America				450 000	

a) 1786–87.

Source: 1470–1670 for Netherlands, Germany and France, and Britain 1570 from Vogel (1915), p. 331. 1670 and 1780 for Britain, 1780 and 1824 for the Netherlands, and 1780 for France from de Vries and van der Woude (1997), pp. 411, 484, 490 and 492. Denmark; Norway and Sweden; and Germany, Italy, Portugal and Spain 1786–87 from Unger (1992), p. 258. Italy, Portugal and Spain 1670 from Petty (1690), p. 251.

Table 2–16. **Dutch Merchant Ships by Area of Operation Around 1670**

	Ships	*Carrying capacity (metric tons)*	*Average capacity per ship (metric tons)*
Norway	200	40 000	200
Archangel	25	9 000	360
Greenland	150	40 000	267
Mediterranean	200	72 000	360
Baltic & Other Europe	735	207 000	282
Herring Fisheries	1 000	60 000	60
Coastal Traffic	1 000	40 000	40
West Africa & West Indies	100	40 000	400
Asia	100	60 000	600
Total	3 510	568 000	162

Source: Vogel (1915), p. 319.

Table 2–17. **Employment in Dutch Shipping by Area of Operation, 1610–1770**

	1610	*1630–40*	*1680*	*1770*
Baltic	4 000	4 000	2 000	n.a.
Norway	4 000	4 200	4 000	n.a.
Archangel	500	1 000	1 200	n.a.
North Sea	500	800	800	n.a.
England	1 000	1 000	500	n.a.
France	4 500	4 500	4 000	n.a.
Iberia & Mediterranean	5 000	6 000	6 000	n.a.
West Africa & Americas	2 000	4 000	2 000	n.a.
Total Merchant Marine	21 500	25 500	22 500	21 000
Asia[a]	2 000	4 000	8 500	11 500
Ocean Fisheries	6 500	7 000	6 500	4 000
Whaling	0	1 500	9 000	6 000
Admiralties[b]	3 000	8 000	11 000[c]	2 000
Total	33 000	46 000	57 500	44 500

a) monopoly of VOC (Dutch East India Company); b) naval defence forces; c),1670.

Source: De Vries and van der Woude (1997), p. 406, see pp. 98–100 for functioning of "admiralties"; figure for 1670 for admiralties is from Israel (1995), p. 263. In time of war, the naval defence forces could be augmented by drawing manpower from the merchant and fishing fleets — see Israel (1995), p. 768.

well documented, because Denmark, whose territory then included Southern Sweden, controlled the entry to the Baltic and levied tolls. In 1500, 300–400 Dutch ships a year entered the Baltic, and by the 1560s, more than 1 300. Grain shipments amounted to about 100 000 tons a year in the latter period.

The Dutch ships involved in this trade operated from the coasts of Zeeland, Holland and Friesland. Dordrecht was the major port for traffic on the Rhine with Germany and with Liège via the Meuse. Middelburg (on the island of Walcheren), opposite the mouth of the Scheldt, imported English woollen cloth, French wine, grains and salt, and in the sixteenth century, spices and sugar from Portugal. The Dutch trading fleet was by far the biggest in Europe. By the 1560s, on the eve of independence, the province of Holland alone had 1 800 seagoing ships (Israel, 1995, p. 117). The carrying capacity of Dutch merchant shipping in 1570 was about the same as the combined fleets of France, Germany and England (see Table 2–15). Per head of population, Dutch shipping capacity was 25 times as big as in these three northern countries.

Herring fisheries were an important part of Dutch shipping activity. The herring were sold fresh or lightly salted near to the ports or were processed and barrelled for international trade. Before 1400, herring shoals best suited for salting were off the Swedish coast, but in the fifteenth century, they migrated into the North Sea, so the bulk of the catch was taken by Dutch ships. A technological breakthrough increased productivity substantially. Dutch shipyards developed a new type of factory ship (a herring "buss"), with nets, rigging and processing facilities which permitted crews of 18 to 30 men to gut, clean, salt and barrel the herring whilst at sea. Vessels of this type could make three trips a year of five to eight weeks during the open season from June to December. By the 1560s there were 400 Dutch vessels of this type operating from the province of Holland, with ownership concentrated on urban investors. At this time, the Dutch were exporting herring to the Baltic rather than importing (see de Vries and van der Woude, 1997, pp. 243–54). In the seventeenth century, Dutch ships embarked on whale fishing off Spitzbergen in the Arctic.

Water control played a major role in Dutch agricultural development. Marshes, bogs, low–lying land subject to frequent flooding were not attractive in their natural state. Agricultural settlers in the Middle Ages occupied mounds and turned them into polders by building dykes to keep off flood waters. In time, skills in hydraulic management improved, and large areas of new land were reclaimed. By the beginning of the sixteenth century, water management and engineering was entrusted to professionals responsible for development and maintenance. Farming communities raised taxes and provided funds for the waterboards. Windmills were used as a source of power for pumps which controlled water flow in canals. As de Vries (1974) p. 27 noted: "Much of fourteenth century Holland was, in effect, a new country. Only in east–Elbian Germany can one find reclamation being carried out in so systematic a manner and over such large tracts."

This conquest of nature had important social implications. Only a small part of the Dutch population was constrained by feudal restrictions. Peasants were freer than anywhere else in Europe. Some were landowners, many more paid money rents or worked for wages. The reliance on water control generated solidaristic attitudes which are still observable in Dutch society.

Dutch agriculture developed a high degree of specialisation. Much of the grain supply came from imports, and domestic production concentrated heavily on meat, milk, butter and cheese. Two features were more developed than elsewhere in Europe: a) stall feeding of cattle through the winter months, and b) large production of vegetables. Over time there was an increased emphasis on industrial crops — hops for the beer industry, flax, hemp and madder for textiles, and later, tobacco and tulip bulbs. There was a gradual transformation of agriculture into horticulture.

In large areas of the Northern Netherlands there were layers of peat several metres deep which were a potential source of cheap energy for many purposes. After 1600, about 275 000 hectares of these peat–bogs were stripped. Engineering skills in land reclamation, drainage, and pumping were easily transferable to peat extraction. In the Groningen area, urban investors set up companies to exploit this resource on a large scale on confiscated monastic lands.

Transport of peat, hay, wheat, cattle, timber, building materials and other heavy freight became a good deal cheaper in the middle of the seventeenth century, because of the creation of a network of canals equipped with tow–paths. Drawn by horses, canal barges carried freight, mail and passengers on regular schedules, at seven kilometres an hour, day and night, at frequent intervals between virtually all areas of the country. "In the 1660s, nearly 300 000 passengers travelled annually on the Amsterdam–Haarlem route, 140 000 glided between Haarlem and Leiden, and some 200 000 between Leiden and the joint destinations of the Hague and Delft" (de Vries and van der Woude, 1997, p. 187). No other country had such a cheap and dense transport network. Road freight carried by carts was slower and much more expensive. As Sir William Temple (1693), p. 152 put it: "one Horse shall draw in a Boat more than fifty can by Cart — And by this easie way of Travelling, an industrious Man loses no time from his Business, for he Writes, or eats, or Sleeps, while he goes."

The biggest industries in the Dutch provinces at the time of independence were shipbuilding, sailcloth, fishing nets, ropes, barrels and associated items, salt refining, breweries, brickworks and timber for buildings, and a substantial woollen and linen textile industry.

The circumstances under which the partition of the Netherlands occurred had an enormous positive impact on the economic potential of the new republic. They were also detrimental to the economic interests of Portugal, Spain and the Spanish Netherlands.

The struggle against the Spanish regime had involved repression and resistance in the Southern Netherlands as well as the North. The inquisition started in 1523 with the burning of two dissident clergy at the stake in Brussels. In the next 50 years more than 2 000 had met the same fate and a large proportion were from the South. The Count of Egmont, the governor of Flanders, a catholic who had been a distinguished general in the Spanish armies, was executed in 1567 because he had protested against Spanish fiscal demands and curtailment of previous political rights of the Southern nobility. Malines (Mechelen) was sacked by Spanish troops and part of its population massacred in 1572. Antwerp suffered deaths and serious property damage from the depredations of riotous Spanish soldiers in 1576. Its losses were even greater during the Spanish siege in 1583–85.

As a result, there was large scale migration from Flanders and Brabant to the new republic. Between 1583 and 1589 the population of Antwerp fell from 84 000 to 42 000. In Bruges and Ghent the exodus of refugees reached the same proportions. In Mechelen, the population fell by two thirds. In the Republic, the population of Middelburg trebled, in Leiden it doubled, 30 000 came to Amsterdam (see Israel, 1995, pp. 307–12). Altogether, the influx was about 150 000, more than 10 per cent of the population of the South, and a bigger proportionate addition to the North. As the North had huge imports of grain and fish which no longer went to the South, there was no problem feeding the new population. The northern confiscation of monastic properties helped in accommodating the influx.

The refugees included a large proportion of the merchant class and bankers of the Southern Netherlands (though some of the latter went to Germany). They brought capital, skills and international contacts. Virtually all of the Jewish population moved to the North. Migration of skilled workers strengthened the textile industry of Leiden. Immigrants also brought skills for other industries including printing, publishing and sugar refining. Before the partition, the only university had been in Leuven (founded 1425). This was one of the largest and most distinguished in Europe, but its freedom was curtailed by the inquisition. The university of Leiden was founded in the North in 1575 followed by Franeker (1585), Harderwijk (1600), Groningen (1614) and Utrecht (1634). Leiden was the biggest with a full range of faculties and offered a humanist education in the tradition of Erasmus. It soon began to attract a large international student body from Germany, Britain and Scandinavia, as well as the refugees from the South.

The political change opened possibilities for a worldwide expansion in Dutch shipping activity to the detriment of Portugal and Spain. In the 1590s, trade with Asia was inaugurated with trial voyages around the Cape into the Indian Ocean to the spice islands, and West via the Magellan Straits to Japan. Barents, 1596–7, made an unsuccessful attempt at a Northeastern passage via Archangel and Novaya

Zemlaya. Hudson discovered New York in 1609 whilst seeking a Northwest passage. Within 30 years the Dutch displaced the Portuguese as the dominant European traders with Asia. They seized Portuguese bases in West Africa, acquiring a substantial share of the trade in gold and slaves. They attacked the Spanish empire in the Americas, occupying Northeast Brazil and its profitable sugar industry from 1630 to 1654 (at that time Portugal was ruled by Spain), then moved their base to the Caribbean (Curaçao and Surinam). There was also significant pirate activity. The greatest coup was Piet Heijn's capture of the whole Spanish silver fleet off Cuba in 1628.

From 1585 to 1795, for reasons of military and naval security and commercial advantage, the Dutch successfully blockaded the mouth of the Scheldt, consolidated the ruin of Antwerp, and imposed a very serious constraint on the economic progress of the Spanish Netherlands. In the course of the seventeenth century, Spanish military potential weakened enormously, but the Dutch had no interest in conquering the Southern Netherlands, which was a useful buffer against French territorial ambitions.

Throughout the seventeenth and for most of the eighteenth century, British economists recognised the superiority of Dutch performance and policy. William Petty's pioneering work on *Political Arithmetick*, written in 1676 and published in 1690 was perhaps the most astute assessment. He demonstrated that a "small country and few people may be equivalent in wealth and strength to a far greater people and territory." He provided a foretaste of the type of reasoning used later by Adam Smith and Douglass North when he compared the performance of France and Holland. The population of France was more than ten times that of the United Provinces, but he estimated the Dutch merchant fleet to be nine times as big as the French, its foreign trade four times as big, its interest rate about half the French level, its foreign assets large, those of France negligible. The Dutch economy was highly specialised, importing a large part of its food, hiring mercenaries to fight its wars, and concentrating its labour force in high productivity sectors. Its flat terrain permitted substantial use of wind power. High density of urban settlement, good ports and internal waterways reduced transport and infastructure costs, cheapened government services and reduced the need for inventories. Dutch institutions favoured economic growth. Religious tolerance encouraged skilled immigration. Property rights were clear and transfers facilitated by maintenance of cadastral registers. An efficient legal system and sound banking favoured economic enterprise. Taxes were high but levied on expenditure rather than income. This encouraged savings, frugality and hard work. Thus the Dutch were a model of economic efficiency with obvious lessons for British policy.

In a similar vein, Gregory King (1696) made a comparative assessment of the resource mobilisation of England, France and the Netherlands in fighting the war of the League of Augsburg. For the nine year conflict, William III, the Dutch stadholder who had become King of England, organised a coalition of the United Kingdom, Netherlands, the German protestant states, Spain and Savoy against France, which had challenged the legitimacy of his succession to the English throne and annoyed its neighbours by trying to expand its frontiers. King estimated French and English per capita fiscal revenues in 1695 to be similar, but in the Netherlands the level was more than two and a half times as large.

The cost of maintaining Dutch independence was high, involving the creation of a chain of fortresses in the South and on the East (where the country was vulnerable from attack via catholic states in Germany — particularly the bishopric of Munster). Its army and naval expenditures were costly. It had to build up an armaments industry. It was involved in a series of wars in which England and France became the main enemies in the seventeenth and eighteenth centuries. Towards the end of the seventeenth century Dutch economic expansion faltered. The Netherlands became the victim rather than the beneficiary of the beggar–your–neighbour policies of the merchant capitalist era. British and French shipping, trade and industry grew much faster than those of the Netherlands. Both countries adopted protectionist policies which damaged Dutch interests. The most important were the British Navigation Acts and similar French provisions. From 1651 onwards Dutch shipping and Dutch ship exports had restricted access to the ports of the United Kingdom and were barred from trade with English and French colonies. When these countries waged war with the Netherlands they did so with the concentrated energy of modern nation states — very different from the way Spain had dissipated its energy.

Table 2–18a. **Dutch Involvement in European Military Conflicts, 1560s–1815**

Wars with Spain to establish and guarantee Independence	Wars of commercial interest with England	Wars over European balance of power, territory & religion
1560s–1609	1652–4	1618–48: 30 Years War
1621–48	1665–7	1686–97: War of League of Augsburg
	1672–4	1701–13: War of Spanish Succession
	1780–3	1756–63: Seven Years War
		1795–1815: Revolutionary & Napoleonic Wars

Source: Israel (1989 and 1995).

Table 2–18b. **Size of European Armies, 1470–1814**
(000)

	France	Spain	Netherlands	United Kingdom	Sweden	Russia
1470s	40	20	0	25	n.a	n.a.
1550s	50	150	0	20	n.a.	n.a.
1590s	80	200	20	30	15	n.a.
1630s	150	300	50	n.a.	45	35
1650s	100	100	29	70	70	n.a.
1670s	120	70	110	15	63	130
1700s	400	50	100	87	100	170
1812–14	600			250		500

Source: 1470s–1700s from Parker (1979), p. 96, except 1650 in the Netherlands which is from Israel (1995), p. 602, and the United Kingdom in 1670s from Brewer (1989), p. 8. 1812–14 from Kennedy (1987), p. 99.

Table 2–19. **Dutch Commodity Trade, 1650s to 1770s**
(million current guilders)

	1650s	1720s	1770s
	Imports		
European Sources	125	84	105 [a]
Other	15	24	38
Total	140	108	143
	Exports and Re–exports[b]		
European Destinations	115	83	92
Other	5	7	8
Total	120	90	100
Of which Re–exports	60	48	69

a) includes colonial products re–exported by Britain (5 million) and France (20 million); b) excludes exports of slaves and ships, earnings from shipping and insurance services, and earnings on foreign loans.

Source: De Vries and van der Woude (1997), p. 498.

The main reason for loss of dynamism in the eighteenth century was the destruction of monopolistic trading privileges in conflicts with France and the United Kingdom, which pushed the Dutch to the sidelines.

Population growth slackened as the economy ceased to attract migrants. There was stagnation in the industrialised western Netherlands and substantial growth in the agricultural province of Overijssel. Agricultural output increased, with a fall in imports and a growth in agricultural exports. There was a decline in production and exports of textiles (particularly the Leiden woollen industry), fisheries and shipbuilding. The volume of foreign trade dropped 20 per cent from 1720 to 1820. During this period UK exports rose more than sevenfold in volume, and French by two and threequarters.

Dutch service industries continued to play an important part in the economy, and there was a large increase in overseas investment. In 1790 total foreign investment probably amounted to 800 million guilders at a time when national income was around 440 million. If the rate of return on foreign investment was around 4 per cent, then foreign income would have been around 30 million guilders, giving a national income about 8 per cent higher than domestic product. The combination of rising rentier incomes, together with pauperism and unemployment in the old industrial areas, increased inequality.

Dutch Economic Activity Outside Europe

a) Africa

Dutch objectives in Africa were to get access to the gold of the Guinea coast, enter the slave trade to the Americas, and acquire a base for ventures in Asia.

They succeeded in capturing Elmina in 1637 and several other Portuguese bases in West Africa for trade in gold and slaves. For a time they captured a foothold in Angola (the main slave base for the Portuguese) but failed to keep it. They also failed to take Mozambique (in East Africa). They established a new base at the Cape in South Africa, introducing European settlers to provide a staging and supply post for their voyages to Asia.

The major economic gain came from participation in the slave trade. Slaves were shipped to Northeastern Brazil and to Surinam for Dutch sugar plantations, and to Curaçao for sale to British and French sugar planters. However, the Dutch role in the trade was a good deal smaller than that of Portugal, England and France (see Table 2–5).

b) Americas

In the Americas, the first major venture was the capture of the sugar producing region of Northeast Brazil (around Recife) from 1630 to 1654. Sugar was transported to the Netherlands where there were 40 refineries by 1650.

The venture in Brazil had substantial military and naval support but the sugar plantations were run by private enterprise. Most were owned by sephardic jews from Amsterdam, many of Portuguese origin. During the period when Portugal was governed by Spain, the Dutch were reasonably well received in Brazil, but after Portugal regained its independence, they were expelled. Many plantation owners then moved to the Caribbean where they introduced the same production techniques and marketing patterns. Their arrival transformed the economy of Barbados which the British had occupied

in 1627 and grew tobacco with white settlers. Within a short time the island had 30 000 slaves and was totally devoted to sugar (see Eltis, 1995, for a proxy assessment of the GDP of Barbados in 1644–1701). Emigrant plantation owners from Brazil had a similar impact in Guadeloupe and Martinique which had been French since 1635 (see Verlinden, 1972, p. 642–4). By the 1660s and 1670s, the British and French had driven out the Dutch, who moved their sugar activities to Surinam.

In the early seventeenth century, sugar production in the Americas had been concentrated on Brazil. But from mid–century, Brazilian production stagnated and a hugely expanded market was dominated by France and Britain. Dutch production in Surinam was on a much smaller scale (see Table 2–4).

Another Dutch venture in the Americas was the inadvertent discovery of a magnificent harbour and huge river by Henry Hudson. He was on a Dutch East India Company mission to try to discover a Northwest passage to Asia in 1609 and hopelessly off course. In 1614 the New Netherlands Company was founded to settle a colony with its capital at New Amsterdam in 1623. In 1664 it was taken over by the British, and in 1674 formally ceded (as New York) in exchange for a free hand for Dutch sugar interests in Surinam (de Vries and van de Woude, 1997, pp. 397 and 467).

c) Asia

The most successful area of Dutch involvement outside Europe was in Asia.

The Dutch were extremely well informed about Asian trading prospects, for many had worked on Portuguese ships. One of them, Jan Huygen van Linschoten, produced two travel journals in 1595 and 1596 with detailed maps, information on markets, winds and potential routes. In 1602, under official pressure, all Dutch merchants in this trade were compelled to join the United East India Company (VOC) which was given monopoly trading rights and authority to establish military outposts and negotiate with foreign rulers. The Company owned and built all its own ships. The comparative volume of Dutch trading activity in Asia can be seen in Table 2–6. In the seventeenth century they sent out nearly five times as many ships as the Portuguese, and in the eighteenth, 15 times as many. The average size of their ships was smaller than the Portuguese who were then using huge carracks of 1 000 tons, against 600 tons for the average Dutch ship. The English East India Company (EIC) was a more important competitor than the Portuguese. They entered the Asian trade at the same time as the Dutch. Their main bases were at two towns they created in India (Madras 1639, and Calcutta in the 1690s) and Bombay which was a wedding gift from Portugal to Charles II in 1661. EIC operations in the seventeenth century were about half the size of those of the VOC, and about two thirds in the eighteenth. The French entered the Asian trade with the *Compagnie des Indes Orientales* which Colbert created in 1664. They established a base at Pondicherry (on the Coromandel coast) in 1673. By the eighteenth century, a new French company, created in 1719, had become a very significant presence. Later participants were Danish and Swedish companies, and from 1715–32, the Ostend company operating from the new port which the Austrian administration had created in the Southern Netherlands.

The total volume of European shipping in Asia in the eighteenth century was about nine times as big as it had been in the sixteenth, but the scope for traditional exports of pepper and spices was limited. This meant that the Dutch, who were more heavily involved in this trade than the English and French and other newcomers, had to be careful to control supply in order to maintain prices. The opportunities for new exports to Europe — a wide variety of cotton textiles, coffee and tea — were much more promising and their share of the trade rose rapidly, for all of the participants in the market (see Table 2–20).

Table 2–20. **Commodity Composition of European Exports from Asia to Europe, 1513–1780**

Portugal (Estado da India — state trading, headquarters Goa)
(per cent by weight)

	1513–19	*1608–10*
Pepper	80.0	69.0
Moluccan Spices	9.0	0.03
Other Spices	9.4	10.9
Textiles	0.2	7.8
Indigo	0.0	7.7
Other	1.4	4.6

Dutch East India Company (VOC corporate monopoly, headquarters Batavia)
(per cent by value)

	1619–21	*1778–801*
Pepper	56.4	11.0
Other Spices	17.6	24.4
Textiles & Raw Silk	16.1	32.7
Coffee & Tea	0.0	22.9
Other	9.9	9.0

English East India Company (EIC corporate monopoly operating
mainly from Bombay, Calcutta and Madras)
(per cent by value)

	1668–70	*1758–60*
Pepper	25.3	4.4
Textiles	56.6	53.5
Raw Silk	0.6	12.3
Tea	0.03	25.3
Other	17.5	4.5

Source: Prakash (1998), pp. 36, 115 and 120.

The initial thrust of the VOC was to bypass the Portuguese, using a new route via the Cape and sailing direct to Indonesia. This brought them directly to the Moluccan islands where the most valuable spices (cloves, nutmeg and mace) could be found. They were also able to get pepper in Indonesia, rather than India. The indigenous rulers in the Indonesian islands were much weaker than those in India, Persia, China and Japan, and more susceptible to Dutch pressure to enforce monopoly rights and low prices. The VOC established its headquarters in 1621 on the Javanese coast at Batavia (present–day Jakarta). They drove the Portuguese out of Ternate in 1603, and destroyed their base at Malacca in 1641. They also expelled the muslim merchants who had previously traded on the Javanese coast.

The population of the spice islands revolted in 1621. They were all killed or deported and replaced by Dutch planters working with slave labour.

In order to help finance its Indonesian operations, the VOC established a base at Masulipatnam on the East (Coromandel) coast of India. Here it obtained the agreement of the King of Golconda, who granted preferential trading conditions. The company's main interest was in cotton textiles, in particular painted chintz, which were in demand in Indonesia. Later the VOC moved further down the coast and shifted their base to Negapatam in 1690 where textiles were cheaper.

In 1617, the VOC obtained permission from the Moghul empire to establish a base in Surat in Gujarat in Northwest India, dislodging Portuguese operations in this area. Here they could exchange pepper and spices for coarse cotton textiles for use as a barter item in the African slave trade.

Later in the seventeenth century, the VOC tried to drive the Portuguese from their bases in Goa and Ceylon. It blockaded but did not capture Goa, but took Jaffna in Ceylon, replaced the Portuguese in the cinnamon trade and as rulers of the island. Portuguese trading on the Malabar coast was harassed, but that area did not have substantial commercial interest for the Dutch.

There was an early move to establish trading links with China and Japan which had been so lucrative for Portugal. Unlike the Portuguese, The Dutch felt no vocation for religious evangelism, and were the only Europeans allowed to trade in Japan between 1639 and 1853. From 1641 they were confined to a very small island (Deshima) in the harbour of Nagasaki. The profitability of this trade faded after a few decades because of a Japanese ban on export of precious metals and Japanese insistence on fixing the prices at which the Dutch could sell their goods. In this trade there was no question of Dutch exploitation. In fact they were used as a conduit by Japanese eager to know about Western technology (see Appendix B).

The VOC did not succeed in dislodging the Portuguese from Macao. In the 1620s they got a base in the Pescadores and from 1624 were allowed to shift to Taiwan. In 1662 they were forced to leave and never acquired another Chinese base. From the 1640s to 1660s the Ming dynasty was in a state of collapse. The great porcelain and pottery town of Ching–te–Chen was devastated and Chinese porcelain exports were interrupted until the 1680s. This encouraged the Dutch to develop their own pottery industry in Delft to produce cheap copies of Chinese blue–and–white ware. At the same time, the Japanese developed their own pottery and porcelain industry to substitute for Chinese imports, and the Dutch also copied Japanese copies of Chinese pottery. European production of porcelain in Sèvres and Meissen started later.

The VOC operated from the 1630s in Bengal because of its rich variety of high quality textiles (cotton and silk). Here they stepped in the shoes of the Portuguese who had been expelled from Hugli by the Moghul authorities in 1632.

At first the VOC concentrated on exporting Bengali raw silk and mixed cotton–silk textiles to Japan, and opium to Indonesia. In exchange they sold Japanese copper, silver and gold in Bengal. The Japanese market declined considerably after 1680, but European demand for Bengali textiles rose very rapidly. Between 1680 and 1740, textiles from Bengal were the largest component of VOC exports to the Netherlands (see Prakash, 1998, pp. 198 and 218). Fine cottons, muslins, silks and mixed piece goods appealed to new European tastes and rising incomes, though it was more difficult to know what the market might be for these fashion items than for raw silk or opium.

Bengali textiles were also of major interest to the British and French companies from the last quarter of the seventeenth century, and their textile exports were even bigger than those of the Dutch. However, both the French (1686) and the British (1700) forbade import of printed and painted cottons in order to protect their domestic textile producers. Both countries continued to import these goods for re–export (though a large part of these were smuggled back into England). The Dutch did not protect their own textile industry, and ended up marketing a large part of French and somewhat less of the British re–exports of Indian textiles within Europe (see Table 2–19). The British greatly increased imports of white bleached cloth from Bengal for processing in England (see Rothermund, 1999).

Towards the second half of the seventeenth century, European demand for coffee grew very fast. The first London café was opened in 1652. The beverage became popular in France in the 1660s and in the Netherlands in the 1670s. The VOC began buying coffee in Mokka in Yemen at the beginning of the eighteenth century, rising from 300 tons in 1711 to 875 tons in 1720. Shrubs were taken for planting in Java and by the late 1720s, Javanese production was about 2 000 tons a year. The VOC

imposed cultivation quotas on petty Javanese rulers who compelled their subjects to raise coffee. From the 1730s there was competition from Surinam where output and exports rose much faster (see Bulbeck and Associates, 1998).

A few years later there was a great surge in European demand for tea, particularly in England and the Netherlands. The Chinese had opened Canton to foreign traders in 1685. British tea imports rose from about 100 kilos in 1669 to 28 000 tons in 1760 (see Chaudhuri, 1978, p. 539). The Dutch bought most of their tea from Chinese junks trading to Batavia, though there was a direct shipment from Canton to Amsterdam in 1729. The English company were able to finance their tea purchases in Canton by selling Bengali opium and raw cotton, but the Dutch were obliged to pay in bullion (see Glamann, 1981, pp. 212–43).

The new European taste for coffee and tea was complementary to the rise of sugar consumption. Growth of these items displaced a significant part of demand for beer and gin, both in England and the Netherlands.

In the second half of the eighteenth century, the VOC ceased to be a profitable organisation. It collapsed in bankruptcy in 1795, after several decades of distributing dividends bigger than its profits.

One of the causes was the disintegration of the Moghul Empire in India and the British takeover of the governance of Bengal in 1757. After that, discrimination against Dutch operations weakened the VOC considerably. Anglo–Dutch hostilities in 1781–84 (when the two countries took opposite sides in the American War of Independence) had serious repercussions in Asia. The outbreak of the Napoleonic wars led to a complete British takeover of Dutch interests in India, Malacca, Ceylon, South Africa and temporarily in Indonesia. It also ended any significant French connection with India.

Contributory factors to the profit decline were the very high overheads for the company in hiring military and naval personnel to run what had become a territorial empire in Java and Ceylon. The officers of the VOC were not well paid and conducted an increasingly large private trade in the company's ships. There was also a good deal of corruption in the administration of Java and Ceylon, which benefited the servants but not the shareholders of the company. Given the changing commodity structure of trade and the locus of operations, Batavia was no longer an ideal headquarters.

After 1815, Indonesia became a colony of the new Dutch kingdom. There was intensive development of tropical crop production for export. During the wartime period of British rule, there had been a policy of westernisation of the administration, property rights and land taxation. The Diponegoro revolt of 1825–30 ended this approach. Thereafter the Dutch stuck consistently to a policy of dual administration, retaining traditional rulers, law and custom as a major instrument of their rule. They also kept their trading monopoly, as most of the profits would have gone to powerful British and American traders under an open–trade regime.

In the 1830s the so–called "Cultivation System" was introduced. The Netherlands exercised its claims on indigenous income by increasing its demand for tribute — forced deliveries of crops or labour services in lieu of land taxation. From 1816 to 1914 movement and residence of the indigenous and Chinese populations were controlled by a system of pass–laws designed to maintain labour discipline and enforce ethnic *apartheid*.

From the 1830s, the Dutch were remarkably successful in raising the income flow from Indonesia. In the 1830–70 period, half of it went directly to the Dutch government as fiscal tribute from the cultivation system. In addition there was monopoly income from transport of export crops by the NHM shipping company owned by the Dutch King, and income from sales of monopoly franchises to dealers in opium. The government dominated production of sugar and coffee, but most of the tobacco crop was in private hands. Favoured individuals were subsidised to create sugar processing factories. There were ample opportunities for corruption in the Dutch administration, amongst the 76 local Regents and heads of the 34 000 villages of Java. In 1844 Indonesia was allocated a fictitious debt of 236 million guilders to cover the costs of liquidating the VOC's debts and those incurred in suppressing the 1825–30 revolt.

Table 2–21a. **The Dutch "Drain" on Indonesia, 1698–1930**

	Indonesian export surplus as per cent of Indonesian net domestic product	Indonesian export surplus as per cent of Dutch net domestic product
1698–1700	0.7	1.1
1778–80	0.9	1.7
1868–72	7.4	5.5
1911–15	7.6	8.7
1926–30	10.3	8.9

Source: Maddison (1989*b*), pp. 646–7. See van der Eng (1998) for a comment on these estimates.

Table 2–21b. **The British "Drain" on India, 1868–1930**

	Indian export surplus as per cent of Indian net domestic product	Indian export surplus as per cent of British net domestic product
1868–72	1.0	1.3
1911–15	1.3	1.2
1926–30	0.9	0.9

Source: Maddison (1989*b*), pp. 647–8 with revision of Indian/British income ratio. The "drain" (i.e. the colonial burden as measured by the trade surplus of the colony) figures prominently in the literature of Indian nationalism, beginning with Naoroji in the 1870s (see Naoroji (1901). I applied the same concept to Indonesia to compare the colonial burden in the two countries as a share of their own national income, and the colonialist's gain as a share of their respective national incomes. See also the discussion in Maddison (1971), pp. 63–6.

Table 2–21c. **Growth of Indonesian Population and Real Income by Ethnic Group, 1700–1929**
(population in 000, per capita income in 1928 guilders)

	Indonesians		Chinese & other foreign Asiatics		Europeans[a]	
	Population	Per capita income	Population	Per capita income	Population	Per capita income
1700	13 015	47	80	156	7.5	1 245
1820	17 829	49	90	193	8.3	2 339
1870	28 594	50	279	187	49.0	2 163
1913	49 066	64	739	240	129.0	3 389
1929	58 297	78	1 334	301	232.0	4 017

a) Includes Eurasians.

Source: Maddison (1989*b*), p. 665, with revised estimates of Indonesian population and income.

Export prices for sugar and coffee rose after the abolition of the African slave trade in the 1830s. This ruined competitors in the Caribbean and raised costs in Brazil.

From 1848, when the Netherlands acquired a more democratic political system, there was growing criticism of exploitative practices and bureaucratic cronyism in Indonesia. These pressures, plus the opening of the Suez Canal and the development of steam shipping, led the Dutch authorities to open the colony to private enterprise and investment. By the 1890s the government share of exports had dropped to zero.

Table 2–21a provides a crude measure of the burden of colonial rule and the colonialist gain for the Netherlands for the period 1700 to 1930. The volume of exports grew very much faster after the demise of the VOC, and became a much greater share of Indonesian GDP. The proportionate gains to the Netherlands also rose greatly. Table 2–21b provides similar estimates for India, where the colonial burden and gain were relatively much smaller.

Table 2–21c provides a crude estimate of population and income levels by ethnic group in Indonesia from 1700 to 1929.

IX
BRITAIN

In considering British economic performance, it is useful to distinguish between Ireland and the rest of the kingdom. Wales was incorporated politically in 1301. The incorporation of Scotland did not take place until 1707, but the ground was prepared by the advent of a Scottish king to the English throne in 1603. Ireland was subject to a brutal conquest in the 1650s. Petty's *Anatomy of Ireland* (1691) suggested that the population fell by a quarter because of war deaths, famine, plague and deportations. The war was followed by a massive confiscation of property and social restructuring. Two thirds of the land fit for agriculture was transferred from Irish to English landlords.

Ireland had a per capita income half of that in the rest of the United Kingdom from 1700 to the 1850s (see Table B–13) and a very different demographic history. As a result of the famine of 1846–51 and massive emigration thereafter, Ireland's population fell by half between 1840 and 1913. It therefore seems legitimate to treat Ireland as a British colony, as I have done in Table 2–22.

Between the Norman conquest of 1066 and 1950 there were several major phases of British economic and political development and overseas involvement.

The Norman–Angevin Regime, 1066–1485

Between the years 1000 and 1500, British population growth was somewhat slower than the West European average, and in all probability this was also true of per capita income. The income level in 1500 (see Tables B–21 and 2–22) was well below that in Italy, Flanders and Brabant which were the European leaders at that time.

From the eleventh to the mid–fifteenth century, British national identity was ambiguous. The monarchy and the ruling elite were Anglo–French warlords whose property rights and income derived initially from territorial conquests in England and France. The resources which the state could mobilise came from tribute received from feudal vassals and their servile peasantry. A fairly submissive church buttressed its political legitimacy and acted as an instrument of social control. William the Conqueror installed his friend Lanfranc as Archbishop of Canterbury, and Norman clergy to fill the other bishoprics. In 1170, when Henry II had problems with Archbishop Becket, he had him murdered. The main investments of the regime were fortified castles (such as those in Carnarvon and Harlech to consolidate the Welsh conquest) or imposing cathedrals and abbeys (such as the the Abbaye des Hommes — the tomb of the conqueror — and the Abbaye des Dames — the tomb of his wife — in Caen).

The acquisition of land and loot in France was pursued by war and matrimony. British possessions were biggest in the second half of the twelfth century after Henry II married Eleonor of Aquitaine, the divorced wife of the French King Louis VII. At that time, half of France was British. There were British victories at Crecy in 1346, Poitiers 1356, and Agincourt in 1415. With Burgundian help the British captured and killed Joan of Arc in 1430. Thereafter the Burgundians changed sides, and at the end of the Hundred Years war in 1453, all that was left was Calais, which the French recuperated in 1558.

There was some economic and political advance in this period. There was an extension of cultivated area by clearing of forests, and increases in land productivity because of changes in agricultural technology of the same kind as those elsewhere in Northern Europe (see White, 1962). There was a big expansion in wool production for export to Flanders, increasingly replaced from the second half of the fourteenth century by export of woollen cloth. However, a good deal of overseas trade was handled by foreign merchants and there was heavy dependence on Antwerp for banking and financial services. The level of urbanisation in 1500 was well below the West European average (see Table B–14). In England and Wales only 3 per cent of the population lived in towns of 10 000 and over compared with 21 per cent in Flanders and Brabant, 16 per cent in the Netherlands and 15 per cent in Italy.

The financial difficulties of the crown provoked a modicum of countervailing power in an emerging parliamentary process. There was some movement away from feudal property rights towards market forces in agriculture which was given a major push by the Black Death when plague reduced the population by a third, increased per capita land availability, and provoked claims for higher labour income.

An important step was taken in the fourteenth century to establish English as the dominant language. Until then French had been used in all legal proceedings, which had a distinctly discriminatory impact on property rights. The situation was changed by the 1362 Statute of Pleading, which stated that "the French tongue is much unknown in the realm, so that the people who do implead, or be impleaded, in the king's court, or in the courts of others, have no knowledge or understanding of that which is said for them or against them" (Baugh and Cable, 1993, p. 145).

Table 2–22a. **Levels of GDP Per Capita in European Colonial Powers and Former Colonies, 1500–1998**
(1990 international dollars)

	1500	*1700*	*1820*	*1913*	*1950*	*1998*
Britain[a]	762	1 405	2 121	5 150	6 907	18 714
France	727	986	1 230	3 485	5 270	19 558
Italy	1 100	1 100	1 117	2 564	3 502	17 759
Netherlands	754	2 110	1 821	4 049	5 996	20 224
Portugal	632	854	963	1 244	2 069	12 929
Spain	698	900	1 063	2 255	2 397	14 227
China	600	600	600	552	439	3 117
India	550	550	533	673	619	1 746
Indonesia	565	580	612	904	840	3 070
Brazil	400	560	646	811	1 672	5 459
Mexico	425	568	759	1 732	2 365	6 655
United States	400	527	1257	5 301	9 561	27 331
Ireland[b]	526	715	880	2 736	3 446	18 183

Table 2–22b. **Growth of Per Capita GDP in European Colonial Powers and Former Colonies, 1500–1998**
(annual average compound growth rates)

	1500–1700	*1700–1820*	*1820–1913*	*1913–50*	*1950–98*
Britain[a]	0.31	0.34	0.96	0.80	2.10
France	0.15	0.18	1.13	1.12	2.77
Italy	0.00	0.01	0.90	0.85	3.44
Netherlands	0.52	–0.12	0.86	1.07	2.56
Portugal	0.15	0.10	0.27	1.38	3.89
Spain	0.13	0.14	0.81	0.17	3.78
China	0.00	0.00	–0.08	–0.62	4.17
India	0.00	–0.03	0.25	–0.23	2.18
Indonesia	0.01	0.04	0.42	–0.20	2.74
Brazil	0.17	0.12	0.24	1.97	2.50
Mexico	0.15	0.24	0.89	0.85	2.18
United States	0.14	0.73	1.56	1.61	2.21
Ireland[b]	0.15	0.17	1.23	0.63	3.53

a) Refers to England, Scotland and Wales for 1500–1913. Northern Ireland is included for 1950 and 1998;
b) refers to all Ireland for 1500–1913, Irish Republic for 1950 and 1998.

Source: Appendices A and B.

Creation of a Modern Nation State and Institutions Favourable to Merchant Capitalism, 1485–1700

From the end of the fifteenth to the end of the seventeenth century, British population rose about fourfold, compared with a doubling in the Netherlands, a rise of less than half in France, and about a quarter in Germany and Italy. There was an increase in life expectation (see Table 1–4), to a level substantially higher than in France. The agricultural share of the labour force dropped considerably (in 1700 it was 56 per cent). Apart from the rise in farm productivity, the reliability of the food supply had been increased (see Wrigley, 1988). This, together with the efficacy of coastal shipping in mitigating local food shortages had more or less eliminated famine–related mortality in England and Wales, at a time when it was still significant in France[30]. The urbanisation ratio rose more than fourfold (Table B–14) and London's population 14–fold (it had become the biggest city in Europe, see Table 2–3).

Per capita income in Britain almost doubled from 1500 to 1700, compared with a rise of a third in France and Germany and stagnation in Italy (see Table B–21). The only country where income grew faster and achieved a higher level by 1700 was the Netherlands. Dutch income performance was better because of higher productivity in agriculture, shipping, banking and commercial services, and a bigger degree of international specialisation. Its shipping fleet was bigger than that of Britain though it had less than a quarter of the population. Only 40 per cent of its labour force was in agriculture.

British economists and diplomats of the seventeenth century (Petty, King, Davenant and Temple) regarded the Netherlands as the economic model to be emulated. To a large extent British economic institutions moved in a Dutch direction — a process which was consolidated in 1688 by the installation of a king who was also the Dutch Stadholder.

There were several stages in the creation of a modern nation state which favoured the interests of merchant capitalism. The old feudal fragmentation of power and resources was replaced by a much more centralised system. Henry VII, a Welshman who emerged as victor in the civil war in 1485, confiscated the estates of many of the feudal aristocracy in favour of the ascendant gentry. He eliminated the right of the nobility to keep armed retainers. Thereafter their country houses were no longer fortified. His son, Henry VIII, broke with the Papacy, created a national church which practised a lukewarm version of protestantism, abolished the monastic orders and seized their property (including about a quarter of English land). His daughter Elizabeth dilapidated the property of the bishops. The great bulk of these ecclesiastical assets fell into the hands of a secular elite of merchants and gentry, through royal sales and largesse.

In the seventeenth century, there were major changes in the British mode of governance (which involved the temporary establishment of a republic and abolition of the House of Lords). It ended with a monarchy dependent for its finance on a House of Commons controlled by a secular elite of landlords and merchants.

In the field of economic policy there was a modernisation of the administration at the end of the seventeenth century. Professional competence was increasingly relevant in public appointments, and improved statistics were becoming a significant guide to policy. Patronage was still important, but political cronyism was replacing nepotism.

The farmers of the hearth tax were obliged to show full accounts from 1679. Tax farming of customs duties was abolished in 1671 and an Inspector General of exports and imports was created in 1696. Tax farming of the excise was abolished in 1683, and the economist Davenant was appointed as the Commissioner. The Board of Trade was created in 1696, with John Locke, the philosopher, as one of the Commissioners. Samuel Pepys carried out a similar modernisation of the naval administration. In 1702, Gregory King, the economist, became Commissioner of Public Accounts. All of these new administrative posts were highly paid to ensure that the occupants were not corruptible. The Bank of England was created in 1694, and a major recoinage took place in 1696. Monetary policy was modernised and a properly managed market for public debt was emerging.

As a result, the British were able to develop a robust system of public finance in the eighteenth century in stark contrast to the weaknesses of the French regime. The government remained solvent with a large part of public debt in the form of perpetual annuities. There were no exemptions for privileged groups, no tax farmers, no sales of public office, no autonomous tax jurisdictions. The political legitimacy of taxes was guaranteed by parliamentary control and the number of public officials per head of population was a fraction of that in France[31].

Intellectual life was very vigorous and increasingly secular in the seventeenth century and there was close interaction with similar developments in Northern Europe. An organisational basis was created in Gresham College by the generous endowment in 1579 of Sir Thomas Gresham, an extremely wealthy banker and royal fiscal agent. The College provided open access to higher education in the form of daily lectures on different topics. It was particularly successful with applied mathematics and practical research into navigational instruments and shipbuilding. In the 1640s and 1650s it became a centre for intensive discussion of new results in experimental science, and was the precursor of the Royal Society which was founded in 1662 on its premises. The leading activists of the Society were Christopher Wren (professor of astronomy at Gresham and Oxford, and the architect who rebuilt London's churches after the great fire); John Wilkins, mathematician and Warden of Wadham College; Robert Boyle, the chemist and anatomist; and William Petty, a former professor of anatomy in Oxford, creator of political economy, director of the cadastral survey of Ireland, and inventor of a double-bottomed ship (like a catamaran), speedier forms of land carriage, schemes for improving the postal service, water pumps and sweetening sea water. In this century of enlightenment, many distinguished intellectuals, e.g. Bacon, Hobbes, Locke and Newton, were involved in practical matters of public policy (Newton was Warden and later Master of the Mint from 1695 to his death). In many cases, their work had an important impact on technology.

The restoration monarchy was interested in promoting research into practical and theoretical work on navigation, created the Royal Observatory and the post of Astronomer Royal. Edmund Halley, mathematician and astronomer, started his fruitful career at the age of 20, laying the foundations of stellar astronomy in the Southern hemisphere in two years of observation in St. Helena, and ended as Astronomer Royal. In 1693, he produced a fundamental paper on the mathematics of life expectation, using mortality data for Breslau supplied by Leibnitz. This laid the scientific foundation for life insurance.

These scientific investigations in England had their counterpart in the Netherlands and to a significant extent in France, but were in sharp contrast with the situation in Spain where religious bigotry and the Inquisition inhibited intellectual curiosity. In Italy too, the counter-reformation harassed Galileo and weakened the creativity of a country which had shown such brilliance in earlier centuries.

In terms of overseas commitments and foreign policy, there were major changes from the 1550s to 1700. The idea of European conquest was abandoned, and the strategic advantages of being an island were intelligently exploited. The British merchant fleet was greatly expanded. Naval forces were developed in the reign of Elizabeth which were adequate to beat off a Spanish attempt at invasion, and by 1700 had considerable offensive power. Gregory King estimated that in 1697 the merchant fleet comprised more than 2 000 vessels with a tonnage of 323 000 tons, and the navy had 189 vessels with a tonnage of 120 000[32]. This was bigger than any other power at that time (except the Netherlands, see Table 2–15).

There was a relatively small British commitment to land forces (see Table 2–18b). From 1688 to 1815 Britain was involved in many wars with continental countries, but most of the burden of land warfare was borne by Britain's allies. This division of effort was ensured by opportunistic diplomacy, subsidies, and the convenient persistence of enmities between major continental countries for dynastic, territorial or religious reasons.

From the sixteenth to the nineteenth century, commercial policy was dominated by mercantilist assumptions. In England and in continental Europe, it was taken for granted that international competition was a beggar–your–neighbour proposition. A major reason for this was that economic

advance before the nineteenth century was based on what seems in retrospect to have been a quite slow pace of advance in technology, with rates of domestic investment which by present standards were low. In England in 1688, Gregory King's estimates suggest that the British investment rate was less than 7 per cent of GDP. The most promising opportunities for raising income were perceived to come from the increased specialisation and division of labour which the Dutch had achieved, or from exploiting new opportunities in the Americas, in the slave trade from Africa, and in imports of spices, textiles and porcelain from Asia. At the levels of income the Dutch and British had achieved there were funds available to finance these overseas ventures and corporate know–how to use them properly. Navigation and shipping technology permitted ventures which could be profitable even when the return voyage might last as much as two years in journeys to East Asia.

Table 2–23. **Structure of British Commodity Trade by Origin and Destination, 1710–1996**

(per cent of total current value)

	Europe	Asia	Africa	North America	British West Indies	Other America	Australia & New Zealand
				Imports			
1710[a]	63.6	6.9	0.4	7.3	21.7	0.1	0.0
1774	46.1	11.4	0.4	12.5	29.3	0.3	0.0
1820	26.8	24.6	0.5	14.6	26.0	7.5	0.0
1913	40.7[b]	15.7	3.0	22.6	0.8[c]	9.6	7.6
1950	27.8[b]	17.2	11.0	15.9	5.1[c]	8.6	14.4
1996	61.7	18.8	2.2	14.1	0.3[c]	1.7	1.2
				Exports and Re–exports			
1710a	87.6	2.1	1.2	5.1	3.4	0.6	0.0
1774	58.5	3.9	6.0	21.5	10.0	0.1	0.0
1820	61.8	7.1	1.1	11.7	9.0	9.3	0.0
1913	37.4[b]	22.7	6.4	13.5	1.0[c]	8.7	10.3
1950	28.8[b]	18.9	13.2	14.4	1.7[c]	7.2	15.8
1996	63.3	16.8	3.0	13.3	0.3[c]	1.5	1.8

a) England and Wales; b) includes North Africa; c) includes all Caribbean.

Source: Mitchell and Deane (1962), pp. 309–11 (for 1710–1820); pp. 317–23 (for 1913). Mitchell and Jones (1971) pp. 136–9 (for 1950). *UN Yearbook of International Trade Statistics* (1996), p. 1065 for 1996. From Mitchell and Deane (1962), pp. 2679–84, it appears that reexports were 58 per cent of domestic exports (i.e. 37 per cent of total exports) in the 1720s and 1770s. This compares with 53 per cent and 220 per cent in the Netherlands for these two periods (see Table 2–19 above). In 1913, British reexports were 20.8 per cent of domestic exports, and in 1950, 3.9 per cent. In 1710, woollen and worsted yarn and manufactures were 78 per cent of domestic exports; in 1774, 49 per cent; in 1820, 12 per cent; and in 1913, 6 per cent. Cotton yarn and manufactures were 2 per cent of domestic exports in 1774; 62 per cent in 1820; 24 per cent in 1913; and 11 per cent in 1938.

Another attraction of such commerce was that it involved new products. In the sixteenth century sugar was virtually unknown as an item of popular consumption. By 1700, consumption was 2.6 kilos per head of population in England and Wales. For tobacco it had risen from zero to about 1 kilo. Tea and coffee had begun to make an appearance[33]. Printed and painted cotton textiles from India had brought major changes in taste and fashion. Porcelain and pottery from China had a similar impact on domestic utensils. The elasticity of demand for these new consumer goods was high, and this category of goods was a very large proportion of personal consumption. Gregory King's estimates suggest that, in 1688, expenditure on food, drink and textiles in England and Wales was 58.5 per cent of gross domestic product (compared with about 16 per cent at the end of the 1990s).

There was an increasing frequency of wars to grab a bigger share of overseas opportunities. There were three Anglo–Dutch wars in the quarter century following 1652. They led to a significant constriction of Dutch trading opportunities in the Americas and Africa. There were also significant net additions to the British merchant fleet from capture of Dutch ships, particularly the Dutch "fluyts" which were designed for cheap mass production and reduced operating costs (through lower manning requirements) but were not armed[34].

Commercial policy reinforced the objective of these trade wars. There was a series of Navigation Acts, starting in 1651 and eventually repealed in 1849. These kept foreign ships from participation in trade with British colonies, and forced the colonies to route their exports through British ports. As a result, a pattern of trade developed which involved large imports of colonial goods for re–export. This pattern was also characteristic of Dutch and French trade (see Table 2–19 and the notes to Table 2–23). Table 2–23 shows clearly the switch in geographic orientation of British trade which had already started in the seventeenth century.

The British Advance to Hegemony, 1700–1820

Between 1700 and 1820, there was a marked acceleration in British population growth to a rate more than twice as fast as in the seventeenth century, when there were losses from civil war and plague. Growth was faster than in any other European country, and the urbanisation ratio rose substantially in all parts of the kingdom; again in sharp contrast to developments elsewhere in Europe (see Table B–14).

Per capita income growth was somewhat faster than in the seventeenth century, and more than twice as fast as the European average. By contrast, Dutch performance was disastrous. Its population growth decelerated sharply and per capita GDP fell. In 1700 British GDP (excluding Ireland) was twice as high as the Dutch. In 1820 it was seven times as big.

There were significant changes in British economic structure, with a substantial decline in the share of the labour force in agriculture, and a big rise in industry and services (see Table 2–24). In the Netherlands there was deindustrialisation, deurbanisation, and a rise in the share of the farm sector.

With the decline in domestic and overseas investment opportunities, Dutch savings were increasingly diverted to foreign investment, much of it in British public debt. Hence British growth was bolstered by Dutch finance (see Maddison, 1991a, pp. 34–5 and 45–6).

Between 1720 and 1820, the volume of British exports rose by 2 per cent a year, and Dutch fell at an annual rate of 0.2 per cent (see Maddison, 1982, p. 247). In 1700, the British share of world shipping capacity was little more than a fifth, the Dutch share more than a quarter. By 1820, the British share was over 40 per cent, and the Dutch little more than 2 per cent (see Tables 2–15 and 2–25a).

This was the period when the United Kingdom rose to world commercial hegemony by adroit use of a beggar–your–neighbour strategy. The Dutch decline was due in substantial part to British and French commercial policy and to the disastrous impact of war in 1795–1815.

From 1700–1820, Britain was involved in a series of major wars with different combinations of European powers (in 1700–13, 1739–48, 1756–63, 1793–1815) as well as the war of American independence (1776–83), which it fought alone against its colonies and their European allies (France, the Netherlands and Spain). British involvement in these conflicts was due in substantial degree to its pursuit of worldwide commercial supremacy. Britain made substantial gains in the peace treaties of 1713 and 1763. The latter eliminated the French from Canada and weakened the Spanish position in the Caribbean and Florida. The war of 1776–83 was a major defeat which involved the loss of the 13 British colonies in North America.

Table 2–24. **Structure of Employment in the Netherlands, the United Kingdom and the United States, 1700–1998**
(per cent of total employment)

		Netherlands	United Kingdom	United States
1700	Agriculture	40	56	n.a.
	Industry	33	22	n.a.
	Services	27	22	n.a.
1820	Agriculture	43[a]	37	70
	Industry	26[a]	33	15
	Services	31[a]	30	15
1890	Agriculture	36[b]	16	38
	Industry	32[b]	43	24
	Services	32[b]	41	38
1998	Agriculture	3	2	3
	Industry	22	26	23
	Services	75	72	74

a) 1807; b) 1889

Source: Maddison (1991a), p. 32 for 1700; Maddison (1995a), p. 253 for the United Kingdom and the United States 1820–90; Netherlands 1807 and 1889 from Smits, Horlings and van Zanden (2000), p. 19; 1998 from OECD, *Labour Force Statistics 1978–1998*. Agriculture includes forestry and fishing; industry includes mining, manufacturing, electricity, gas, water and construction; services is a residual including all other activity, private and governmental (including military).

Table 2–25a. **Carrying Capacity of British and World Shipping, 1470–1913**
(000 tons)

	Sail	Steam	Total carrying capacity in sail equivalent	Sail	Steam	Total carrying capacity in sail equivalent
	United Kingdom			World		
1470	n.a.	0	n.a.	320	0	320
1570	51	0	51	730	0	730
1670	260	0	260	1 450	0	1 450
1780	1 000	0	1 000	3 950	0	3 950
1820	2 436	3	2 448	5 800	20	5 880
1850	3 397	168	4 069	11 400	800	14 600
1900	2 096	7 208	30 928	6 500	22 400	96 100
1913	843	11 273	45 935	4 200	41 700	171 000

Source: UK 1470–1780 from Table 2–15, 1820–1913 from Mitchell and Deane (1962), pp. 217–9. World 1470–1780 from Table 2–15 with upward adjustments for the years 1470, 1570 and 1670 for incomplete coverage of European fleets. The adjustment coefficient for 1470 was 1.85, 1.34 for 1570, and 1.07 for 1670. I also added 100 000 tons as a rough estimate for the ships of Asian countries for 1470–1780. 1800–1913 from Maddison (1989a), p. 145. The equivalence coefficient, 1 steam — 4 sail, from Day (1921), p. 290, allows for the greater speed and regularity of steam ships.

Table 2–25b. **Comparative Rates of Growth of British and World Shipping Capacity and GDP, 1570–1913**
(annual average compound growth rate)

	UK shipping	British GDP	World shipping	World GDP
1570–1820	1.56	0.79	0.84	0.33
1820–1913	3.20	2.13	3.69	1.47

Source: Shipping capacity from Table 2–25a, GDP from Appendix B, Tables B–13 and B–18.

The revolutionary and Napoleonic wars were much less costly in real terms to Britain than to France, the Netherlands, Spain and other continental countries. The Napoleonic campaigns ranged from Moscow to Egypt, Northern Germany to Spain. On the French side more than half a million soldiers were killed, and at least as many in other countries. French troops were financed in substantial degree by levies or billeting soldiers at the cost of occupied territories. And there were swathes of devastation in Germany, Russia and Spain (see Kennedy, 1987, p. 115–39 on the costs of war). The war also involved commercial blockades which retarded industrial development on the continent (as analysed in Crouzet, 1964).

There were huge setbacks to the overseas commercial and colonial interests of the continental powers. The Dutch lost all their Asian territories except Indonesia, and their base in South Africa. The French were reduced to a token colonial presence in Asia, and lost Saint–Domingue, their major asset in the Caribbean. Shortly after the war, Brazil established its independence from Portugal. Spain lost its huge colonial empire in Latin America, retaining only Cuba, Puerto Rico and the Philippines.

Britain took over what the French and Dutch had lost in Asia and Africa, extended its control over India, and established a privileged commercial presence in Latin America.

In 1750, the British Empire included about one and half million people in the Americas (see Table 2–28), about 2.4 million in Ireland, and bases in Calcutta, Madras and Bombay. By 1820, although it had lost its 13 North American colonies, Britain had gained control of Indian territories with a population of about 100 million.

British growth was reinforced from 1700 to 1820 by successful pursuit of its beggar–your–neighbour commercial strategy, but its advance was buttressed by other factors. Unlike its continental counterparts, its domestic development was not disturbed by armed conflict (as it had been in the seventeenth century). The integration of domestic markets was greatly improved by creation of a network of turnpike roads and canals and development of coastal shipping. This permitted a more efficient specialisation and division of labour between different regions. Resource allocation was further strengthened by sound public finance and the growth of the banking sector.

From the 1760s, there was spectacular growth in the cotton textile industry. Demand for cotton clothing and household furnishings had been nurtured by a century and a half of imports from India. The prospects and profitability for domestic expansion were transformed by a wave of technological innovation. Cotton was much easier to manipulate mechanically than wool and mechanisation had a dramatic impact on labour productivity with modest levels of capital investment. Hargreaves' spinning jenny (1764–7) permitted a 16–fold productivity gain in spinning soft weft. Arkwright's spinning frame (1768) could produce a strong warp and used water power. Crompton's 1779 "mule" could produce both weft and warp. Cartwright's 1787 power loom extended the productivity gains to weaving; and, finally, the American Eli Whitney invented the cotton gin in 1793, which substantially reduced the cost of the raw cotton which was imported from America. Between 1774 and 1820, imports of raw cotton increased more than 20–fold. Employment in cotton textiles rose from a negligible level in the 1770s to more than 6 per cent of the labour force in 1820. Cotton yarn and manufactures rose from 2 per cent of British exports in 1774 to 62 per cent in 1820 (even though the price of these exports had fallen sharply). The share of woollen goods in exports fell from 49 per cent in 1774 to 12 per cent in the same period (see notes to Table 2–23).

There was also an expansion in cotton textile production and knowledge of the new techniques in Europe, but French per capita consumption of cotton textiles in 1820 was only about a quarter of that in the United Kingdom.

There were substantial improvements in navigational technology in the eighteenth century thanks to government support for the work of the royal astronomers, and the £20 000 prize offered for the development of a ship's chronometer robust and accurate enough to establish longitude at sea. The first of a series of *Naval Almanacs* (practical guides to navigators) was published in 1767, and the final

instalment of the prize money was paid for John Harrison's chronometer in 1773. Armed with a replica of Harrison's chronometer, and an array of other instruments developed in the eighteenth century, Captain James Cook was able to explore and map the coasts of Australia and New Zealand with great success. He did it without loss of any of his crew to scurvy.

Acceleration of Technical Progress and Real Income Growth, 1820–1913

Between 1820 and 1913, per capita income grew faster than at any time in the past — three times as fast as in 1700–1820. It was a new era for Britain and the rest of Western Europe. The basic reason for improved performance was the acceleration of technical progress, accompanied by rapid growth of the physical capital stock and improvement in the education and skills of the labour force. The efficiency of resource allocation benefited from an improved international division of labour, with Britain's exports rising 3.9 per cent a year (almost twice as fast as the growth in GDP). Economic progress was facilitated by the absence of significant military conflicts. This contrasted sharply with experience from 1688 to 1815, when six major wars — 63 years of conflict — had put serious strains on economic development.

Britain added to its territorial empire from 1820 to 1913. There were major acquisitions from the 1870s in Africa, which included Egypt, Ghana, Kenya, Nigeria, Rhodesia, Sudan, Transvaal, the Orange Free State and Uganda. In Asia, Aden and the sheikdoms around Arabia, Burma, the Malay states, Hong Kong and some Pacific islands were added, and the British raj took control of the whole of India. The population in the African territories was about 52 million in 1913, in Asia about 330 million, in the Caribbean about 1.6 million, and in Australia, Canada, Ireland and New Zealand about 18 million. The total population of the Empire was 412 million — ten times as big as Britain itself. The hard core of the Empire was India, with threequarters of its population. Indian taxation financed a large army under British control, which could be deployed to serve British objectives elsewhere in Asia, the Middle East and eventually in Europe. The security of the Empire was guaranteed by British naval supremacy and a network of military/naval bases in Gibraltar, Malta, Cyprus, Egypt, the Suez Canal, Aden and Hong Kong.

In the course of the nineteenth century, there were major changes in British commercial policy. In 1846 protective duties on agricultural imports were removed and in 1849 the Navigation Acts were terminated. By 1860 all trade and tariff restrictions had been removed unilaterally. Dutch policy was similar to the British. In 1860 there were reciprocal arrangements for freer trade with France under the Cobden–Chevalier Treaty. The French made similar treaties with Belgium, Italy, Spain and Switzerland. These treaties had most–favoured nation clauses which meant that bilateral liberalisation applied equally to all countries. In the continental countries there was a reversal of this liberalisation later in the nineteenth century, but the United Kingdom stuck with free trade until 1931.

Free trade was adopted in India and other British colonies, and the same was true in Britain's informal empire. China, Persia, Thailand and Turkey were not colonies, but were obliged to maintain low tariffs by treaties which reduced their sovereignty in commercial matters, and granted extraterritorial rights to foreigners. In China, Britain took over the administration of its customs service, to ensure that China would service its debts.

Although the British empire was run on a free trade basis from the middle of the nineteenth century, colonialism favoured British exports. In Asian and African countries, British shipping, banking and insurance interests enjoyed a *de facto* monopoly. The colonies were no longer run by monopoly trading companies, but by an imperial bureaucracy which was efficient and free of corruption, but it was rule by white men, living in segregated cantonments, frequenting British clubs, so there was an automatic discrimination in favour of British goods, and some quite overt discrimination in government purchasing policies.

Britain's commercial policy and its willingness to import a large part of its food requirements had important positive effects on the world economy. They reinforced and diffused the impact of technical progress. The impact was biggest in the Western Offshoots which had rich natural resources to be exploited but there was also some positive effect in India which was the biggest and the poorest part of the Empire.

The accelerated technical progress which characterised the world economy from the early nineteenth century onwards is often designated as an "industrial revolution", but the word "industrial" suggests an inappropriately narrow sectoral impact of innovation. The acceleration of technical progress affected a very wide range of economic activity and there were improvements in organisation which also contributed to accelerated growth.

The innovations which were most important in diffusing growth worldwide were the advances in transport and communication. The first ship to use steam power appeared in the United Kingdom in 1812, and by the 1860s virtually all new ships used coal as the source of power. By 1913, less than 2 per cent of British shipping used sail. The power of ships' motors and their fuel efficiency increased steadily over the century. Iron and steel ships became much bigger, quicker and more reliable than wooden vessels. From the 1880s there were regular transatlantic shipping lines, which could get from Liverpool to New York in ten days. The opening of the Suez Canal in 1869 cut the distance from London to Bombay by 41 per cent, to Madras by 35 per cent, Calcutta 32 per cent and Hong Kong 26 per cent. This reduced the fuel costs of steam ships, and put sailing ships at a major disadvantage, because of the lack of wind in the canal.

As a result of cheap and reliable passenger services, there was a huge outflow of European migrants to the United States, Canada, Australia, New Zealand, Argentina and Brazil. The net outflow from the United Kingdom from 1820 to 1913 was about 12 million (half of it from Ireland). From the rest of Europe it was about 14 million. The net outflow from India was over 5 million — about 4.5 million to Burma, Malaya and Sri Lanka, a third of a million to Africa, and another third of a million to the Caribbean (see Davis, 1951, pp. 99–101). The outflow from China to other Asian countries was bigger than that from India (see Purcell, 1965).

Migration from Western Europe to North America, Latin America and Australia speeded the pace at which these areas could exploit their huge natural resources and raised the incomes of those who migrated. Emigrants' remittances helped the countries of emigration. Migration accelerated per capita income growth in Ireland and Italy by reducing excess labour in their impoverished rural areas (see O'Rourke and Williamson, 1999, p. 155). Migration from India and China to the "vent–for–surplus" economies of Southeast Asia (Burma, Malaya, Sri Lanka, Thailand and Vietnam), had a similar impact.

The acceleration in shipping and navigational technology was an extension of a process which had been under way since the thirteenth century[35]. American clipper ships were able to compete with steam in speed up to the 1860s. Long–term advances in land transport had been more modest, and the move from horse–drawn to railway freight was a more dramatic leap. Railway transport started in the North of England in 1826, and by 1913 there were nearly a million kilometres of railway track in service worldwide. Nearly half of these were in the United States and the other Western Offshoots. Another 30 per cent were in Europe, but both India and Argentina had a bigger rail network than the United Kingdom in 1913. This massive and costly railway investment opened up new lands for development, increased the effective size of markets, the scope for internal migration and urbanisation, changed the economics of industrial location, and greatly enhanced the possibilities for international specialisation (see O'Rourke and Williamson, 1999, pp. 41–54 for a detailed analysis of the fall in transport costs and their impact). In this railway development, as in shipbuilding, Britain played a leading part in diffusing and financing the new technology.

Table 2–26a. **Gross Nominal Value of Capital Invested Abroad in 1914**
($ million at current exchange rates)

	Europe	Western Offshoots	Latin America	Asia	Africa	Total
United Kingdom	1 129	8 254	3 682	2 873	2 373	18 311
France	5 250	386	1 158	830	1 023	8 647
Germany	2 979	1 000	905	238	476	5 598
Other	3 377	632	996	1 913	779	7 700
United States	709	900	1 649	246	13	3 514
Total	13 444	11 173	8 390	6 100	4 664	43 770

Source: Maddison (1995a), p. 63. "Other" includes Belgium, Netherlands, Portugal, Russia, Sweden, Switzerland and Japan.

Table 2–26b. **Gross Nominal Value of Capital Invested Abroad in 1938**
($ million at current exchange rates)

	Europe	Western Offshoots	Latin America	Asia	Africa	Total[a]
United Kingdom	1 139	6 562	3 888	3 169	1 848	17 335
France	1 035	582	292	906	1 044	3 859
Germany	274	130	132	140	–	676
Netherlands	1 643	1 016	145	1 998	16	4 818
Other[b]	1 803	1 143	820	101	646	4 579
United States	2 386	4 454	3 496	997	158	11 491
Japan	53	48	1	1 128	–	1 230
Total	8 331	13 935	8 774	8 439	3 712	43 988

a) includes investments not classified by region, of which 729 for the United Kingdom; b) includes 19 European countries.

Source: UK from Bank of England, *United Kingdom Overseas Investments 1938 to 1948,* London, 1950, p. 14; all other countries from C. Lewis, *The United States and Foreign Investment Problems,* Brookings, Washington, 1948, pp. 292 and 294.

Table 2–27. **Gross Nominal Value of Foreign Capital Invested in Nine Major Recipient Countries, 1913**

	Total ($ million at current exchange rates)	Per capita ($)
China	1 600	3.7
India	2 100	6.9
Indonesia	600	12.0
Argentina	3 136	409.8
Brazil	1 932	81.7
Mexico	1 700	113.6
Australia	1 800	373.4
Canada	3 850	490.3
South Africa	1 650	268.2

Source: Stock of foreign capital (portfolio and direct) from Maddison (1989a), p. 45. Population from Appendix A.

The invention of mechanical refrigeration created the possibility of long–distance transport of meat, dairy products and fruit by rail and by sea. In the 1870s refrigerator cars were introduced on US railroads. In 1879 the first shipments of frozen meat reached England from Australia, and in 1882 from New Zealand. In 1882, the first freezing plant was created in Buenos Aires for shipments of meat to England.

Britain created a modern postal service in 1840 which operated a system of standardised charges for letters and parcels throughout the United Kingdom, and exploited the new railway facilities to ensure more rapid deliveries than by stage coach. But introduction of the telegraph in the 1850s had a much more dramatic effect on the communications of business and government. By 1870 the United Kingdom had direct contact with India and North America. This innovation helped greatly to integrate international financial markets because access to information was more or less instantaneous. By 1913 the role of the telegraph had been reinforced by the advent of the telephone, and preliminary developments in radio communication.

Innovations in communications played a major part in linking national capital markets and facilitating international capital movements. The UK already had an important role in international finance, thanks to the soundness of its public credit and monetary system, the size of its capital market and public debt, and the maintenance of a gold standard since 1821 to stabilise its exchange rate. The existence of the empire had created a system of property rights which appeared to be as securely protected as those available to investors in British securities. It was a wealthy country operating close to the frontiers of technology, so its rentiers were attracted by foreign investment opportunities even when the extra margin of profit was small.

From the 1870s onward there was a massive outflow of British capital for overseas investment. The UK directed about half of its savings abroad. French, German and Dutch investment was also substantial. By 1913, British foreign assets were equivalent to one and a half times its GDP, income from them meant that national income was more than 9 per cent greater than its domestic product. Table 2–26a shows the origin and location of this foreign capital as it stood in 1914. Movement of capital made a significant contribution to growth in Australia, Canada, New Zealand, Argentina, Southern Brazil, Uruguay, Russia and South Africa, but its per capita impact was small in Asia (see Table 2–27). Most of it was in the form of bonds and a good deal was in railways.

From 1870 to 1913, world capita GDP rose 1.3 per cent a year compared with 0.5 per cent in 1820–70 and 0.07 per cent in 1700–1820. The acceleration was due to more rapid technological progress, and to the diffusionist forces unleashed by the liberal economic order of which the United Kingdom was the main architect. It was not a process of global equalisation (see Table 3–1b on the widened interregional spread of incomes), but there were significant income gains in all parts of the world. Australia and the United States reached higher levels than the United Kingdom by 1913. Growth was faster than in the United Kingdom in most of Western and Eastern Europe, in Ireland, in all the Western Offshoots, in Latin America and Japan. In India, other Asia (except China) and Africa, the advances were much more modest, but per capita income rose more than a quarter between 1870 to 1913.

Trade grew faster than income on a world basis and in virtually all countries from 1870 to 1913 (see Tables 3–2a and F–4).

In all of these dimensions, the situation was an enormous improvement on the eighteenth century, when shipments of slaves were bigger than the movement of migrants, when capital flows and transfer of technology were of limited significance, and when commercial policy was conducted on a beggar–your–neighbour basis.

Keynes (1919, pp. 9–10) provides an illuminating patrician perspective on the lifestyle and investment opportunities available to people like himself in Britain at the end of the liberal era:

"The inhabitant of London could order by telephone, sipping his morning tea in bed, the various products of the whole earth, in such quantity as he might see fit, and reasonably expect their early delivery on his doorstep; he could at the same moment and by the same means adventure his wealth in the natural resources and new enterprise of any quarter of the world. He could secure forthwith, if he wished it, cheap and comfortable means of transport to any country or climate without passport or other formality, could despatch his servant to the neighbouring office of a bank for such supply of the precious metals as might seem convenient, and then proceed abroad to foreign quarters, without knowledge of their religion, language, or customs, bearing coined wealth upon his person, and would consider himself greatly aggrieved and much surprised at the least interference — He regarded this state of affairs as normal, certain, and permanent."

Wars, Depression and Exit from Empire, 1913–50

This was a complex and dismal period, marked deeply by the shock of two world wars and an intervening depression[36]. The liberal economic order was shattered. World trade was much smaller in relation to world income in 1950 than it had been in 1913. International migration was a fraction of what it had been in the nineteenth century. Most of Western Europe's foreign assets were sold, seized or destroyed. Overseas empires disappeared or were in an advanced state of disintegration.

In spite of these disastrous shocks, and drastic reorientation of economic policy and policy instruments, their impact on world economic growth was smaller than might have been expected because the pace of technological advance was substantially faster in the twentieth century than in the nineteenth.

Development of road vehicles sustained the earlier transport revolution. The number of passenger cars in Western Europe rose from about 300 000 in 1913 to nearly 6 million in 1950, and from 1.1 to 40 million in the United States (see Maddison, 1995a, p. 72). There was a parallel transformation of road freight transport, and tractors had a significant impact in replacing horses in agriculture. Aviation had its main impact before 1950 on the technique of warfare, but its economic role in shrinking the significance of distance was already clear.

Development of electricity to produce heat, light and power also had massive ramifications: "electricity freed the machine and tool from the bondage of place; it made power ubiquitous and placed it within the reach of everyone" (Landes, 1966, p. 509). It made it possible to create new kinds of factories to assemble and mass produce automobiles and a huge range of new household products — sewing machines, refrigerators, washing machines, vacuum cleaners, radios and cameras. It contributed to a vastly popular new brand of popular cinematic entertainment.

There were important advances in chemistry, which made it possible to create synthetic materials, fertilisers, pharmaceuticals which had important implications for economic potential and medicine.

The leading role in developing these twentieth century technologies was played by the United States, which had become the world leader in terms of productivity and per capita income. The driving forces of innovation had changed from the nineteenth century, with a reduced role for the individual inventor, and greater emphasis on applied scientific research of a type which the United States pioneered. It institutionalised innovation in a way the United Kingdom had never done. In 1913, there were about 370 research units in US manufacturing employing 3 500 people. By 1946 there were 2 300 units employing 118 000. In 1946 there were four scientific workers in US manufacturing per 1 000 wage earners, five times the ratio in the United Kingdom. US government–sponsored research played a much more important role in agriculture and mining than in the United Kingdom, and the link between business firms and universities was closer (see Mowery and Rosenberg, 1989).

The United States developed new forms of professional business management, where large enterprises played a strategic role in standardising and enlarging markets. Multi–unit firms coordinated advertising, packaging, transport, sales and marketing. They allocated large amounts of capital, spread risks and increased productivity over a large range of new industries.

It is not easy to provide an aggregative estimate of the pace of technical change or its acceleration, but a rough proxy measure is the pace of advance in total factor productivity (the response of output to combined inputs of labour and capital) in the lead country with the highest productivity level. By 1913, it was the United States, not Britain, which operated closest to the technological frontier. Between 1913 and 1950, US total factor productivity grew by 1.6 per cent a year, more than four times as fast as it or the United Kingdom had achieved from 1870 to 1913. This was the first stage of a technological boom which lasted for 60 years. An acceleration of total factor productivity growth also occurred in the United Kingdom in 1913–50, though to a lesser degree than in the United States (see Maddison 1995a, pp. 40–50, and 252–5). There was also an associated acceleration of growth of labour productivity in most West European countries (see Appendix E, Table E–8).

The importance of this acceleration in growth potential was masked by the interwar behaviour of the United States, and the nature of its economic policy. In the 1930s, it had transmitted a strong deflationary impulse to the world economy by its deep depression which was reinforced by raising its tariffs and withdrawal from foreign investment. In Europe its potential was muted by two world wars which involved diversion of massive resources to mutual destruction.

In the first world war, threequarters of a million British troops were killed in combat, and 7.8 million tons of shipping were lost (mainly in submarine attacks). But these losses were proportionately much smaller than those of France, Germany and Russia. The nominal value of its foreign assets was more or less the same at the end of the war as in 1914, whereas German assets were confiscated as reparations, and two thirds of French were lost through inflation and Russian default. Britain added to its overseas empire by acquiring Germany's former colonies in Tanganyika and Namibia, and took over former Turkish possessions in the Middle East (Iraq, Jordan and Palestine), but a large part of Ireland became an independent republic.

In the 1920s British growth was hampered by highly deflationary policies to drive down wages and maintain an overvalued currency at its prewar parity. Their objective was to restore London's prewar role as an international financial centre and to serve the interests of rentiers who held bonds denominated in sterling. As a consequence, there were high levels of unemployment and loss of competitiveness in export markets. Britain had the worst performance in Western Europe in the 1920s, in terms of GDP growth and exports.

The depression of the 1930s led to devaluation of sterling, a large cut in interest rates, an abandonment of free trade, and creation of a network of imperial preferences. These policies cushioned the impact of the world depression on domestic economy. Housing investment had been depressed by high interest rates in the 1920s, and responded very favourably to their decline. There was no British counterpart to the collapse of the banking system which took place in the United States, Germany and Austria. Exports to the empire were bolstered by devaluation and imperial tariff preferences. As a result the impact of the world depression was milder in the United Kingdom than in all West European countries, except Denmark.

Britain came much closer to defeat in the second world war than in the first because Germany captured the whole of the West European continent in its rapid *blitzkrieg*. The eventual victory was due to very intensive domestic resource mobilisation, sale of foreign assets, financial, material and military support from the United States, Canada, India and Australasia, and Russian resistance to Germany on the Eastern front.

The war changed the economics of empire. The Japanese quickly conquered British colonies in East Asia which could not be adequately defended. The strength of the nationalist movement made it politically necessary to finance military expenditure in India by borrowing rather than local taxation. As a result India was able to liquidate $1.2 billion of prewar debt and acquired sterling balances worth more than $5 billion. The costs of maintaining the empire now greatly outweighed the benefits, and the acceleration of technical progress had reinforced the attractions of domestic investment.

The British withdrawal from India occurred in 1947, from Sri Lanka and Burma in 1948. The withdrawal from the African colonies followed a few years after the United States demanded the withdrawal of British forces from Egypt in 1956. The British imperial order was finished, as were those of Belgium, France, the Netherlands and Japan. In the West, the United States had emerged as the hegemonial power competing with the Soviet bloc for leverage in the newly independent countries of Africa and Asia. The foreign economic and commercial policy of the United States was very different from its prewar stance. It made major efforts to diffuse technology, to promote the outflow of capital and liberalisation of world trade. This new orientation was already manifest in 1948 in Marshall Plan aid for European reconstruction.

X
THE IMPACT OF BRITISH EXPANSION IN THE AMERICAS, AFRICA AND ASIA

As Europe's major offshore island, Britain always had substantial overseas involvements. Until the eleventh century, Britain was a target for conquest and barbarian invasion. Between the twelfth to the fifteenth centuries, under the Norman and Angevin dynasties, it was heavily engaged in attempts to acquire territory in France.

Thereafter Britain was involved in many wars in Europe, mainly with Spain, France and the Netherlands, but the objectives were commercial or diplomatic. By the middle of the sixteenth century, the idea of European conquest had been abandoned. Although trade was developed in the Baltic and Mediterranean overseas ambitions were concentrated on the Americas and Asia. Until the nineteenth century the only significant interest in Africa was the slave trade.

In the sixteenth century, the main activities outside Europe were piracy and reconnoitring voyages to explore the potential for developing a colonial empire. The boldest stroke was royal backing for the 1577–80 voyage of Drake, who took five ships and 116 men, rounded the Straits of Magellan, seized and plundered Spanish treasure ships off the coast of Chile and Peru, made useful contacts in the spice islands of the Moluccas, Java, the Cape of Good Hope and Guinea on his way back.

Piracy and Britain's support of the Dutch Republic provoked war with Spain from 1585 which lasted two decades. By this time, its maritime strength and skill were adequate to defeat the Spanish Armada. This was an invasion force of 130 ships from Cadiz which intended to rendezvous with a fleet of invasion barges in the Spanish Netherlands. The British victory at Gravelines prevented the rendezvous and forced the Spanish fleet to return home around the northwest of Scotland. Spain lost more than half of its fleet, and it was clear that Britain had acquired the naval power to support major ventures in the Americas and Asia.

As overseas ventures were varied in character and became bigger in scope than those of any other European power, our survey is necessarily selective and is presented below under four headings:

a)   development of sugar colonies in the Caribbean and associated participation in the slave trade from Africa from the 1620s onwards;

b)   settlement of 13 colonies in North America between 1607 and 1713 which became the United States in 1776;

c)   creation of an East Indian Trading Company in 1600 and its conquest of an Indian Empire after 1757;

d)   forcible opening of trade with China and establishment of the Treaty Port regime of free trade imperialism.

a) *The Caribbean and the Slave Trade*

The Caribbean islands were the first Spanish possessions in the Americas, but the native Arawaks in Hispaniola (Haiti and Dominican Republic) were quickly wiped out by disease and the Caribs in the Antilles were greatly depleted. Spanish interest switched to Peru and Mexico once large scale silver production started there in the middle of the sixteenth century. The British occupied the uninhabited island of Barbados in 1627 establishing tobacco plantations with a labour force of indentured white settlers. Dutch shippers in the Brazilian sugar trade promoted the idea of developing Caribbean sugar production with slave labour. Dutch entrepreneurs established sugar plantations in Barbados when they were expelled from Brazil. As the island was well watered, and the winds were favourable for a quick passage to Europe, it became Britain's biggest sugar colony until Jamaica was captured from Spain in 1655. With similar help from the Dutch, the French developed sugar production in Martinique and Guadeloupe and later took over a much bigger area in Saint Domingue (Haiti). The Dutch were pushed out of the British and French colonies and created a smaller sugar economy in Surinam. Britain took some French islands (St. Vincent, Grenada, Dominica and Tobago) in 1763, and Trinidad from Spain in 1727.

British entry to the slave trade was pioneered by Hawkins in 1562. Participation reached its peak in the seventeenth and eighteenth centuries when Britain became the main slave shipper, bringing a total of 2.5 million Africans to the Americas (see Table 2–5). The traffic was heaviest to the Caribbean. The British staked out Sierra Leone and the upper Guinea coast in the seventeenth century as their source of supply, the French took slaves mainly from the Senegal–Gambia region and the Dutch from the Gold Coast. The Portuguese operated the Africa–Brazil trade further south in Angola. The Royal Africa Company had a monopoly on British slave trading from 1672 to 1698, but in the eighteenth century "individual entrepreneurs who organised one or several voyages had become the norm in the trade" (see Klein, 1999, p. 80). Apart from European traders, there was financial backing from merchants in New England, Virginia, the West Indies and Brazil. Slavers generally financed their purchases with trade goods (East Indian textiles, alcohol, tobacco, bar iron, weapons, jewellery, or cowrie shells from the Maldives — for use in Africa as currency). "In the overwhelming majority of cases it was the Africans who controlled the slaves until their moment of sale to the captain — African slave traders came down to the coast or the riverbanks in a relatively steady and predictable stream to well–known trading places — European traders tended to spend months on the coast or travelling upriver gathering their slaves a few at a time" (Klein, 1999, pp. 90–1).

Within Africa, slaves were acquired as captives in local wars, as tribute from dependent tribes, or after condemnation as criminals, but there was also large scale slave raiding and kidnapping of individuals within Africa. Klein (1999, p. 129) estimated that of 18 million African slaves exported from 1500 to 1900, "11 million of them were shipped into the Atlantic economy. The other slaves were shipped into the Indian Ocean or across the Sahara to slave markets in the East."

The normal cargo per ship ranged between 400–500 slaves. Klein (1999, p. 139) estimates 12 per cent average mortality on the passage to America over the period 1590–1867 which he compares with 10 per cent in convict ships on the longer voyage to Australia in 1787–1800.

Table 2–28. **Population of British Colonies and Former Colonies in the Americas, 1750 and 1830**
(000)

	1750		1830	

A. 19 Caribbean Slave and Sugar Islands

	Total	Per cent Slaves	Total	Per cent Slaves
1625 St. Kitts	21.8	88.3	23.4	81.6
1627 Barbados	63.4	78.9	102.2	80.3
1632 Antigua	31.1	89.3	37.0	80.0
1655 Jamaica	127.9	90.1	378.1	84.4
1763 Grenada	12.0	87.3	28.4	84.1
1797 Trinidad	0.3	42.4	42.1	54.1
1803 British Guiana	8.0	91.0	100.6	88.1
12 Others	66.0	79.4	132.1	75.6
Total (19)	371.2	85.3	843.7	81.2

B. 13 North American Colonies and USA

	Total	Per cent Black	Total	Per cent Black
1679 New Hampshire	27.5	2.0	269	0.4
1620 Massachusetts	188.0	2.2	610	1.1
1635 Connecticut	111.3	2.7	298	2.7
1644 Rhode Island	33.2	10.1	97	4.1
1664 New York	76.7	14.4	1 919	2.3
1664 New Jersey	71.4	7.5	321	6.5
1681 Pennsylvania	119.7	2.4	1 348	2.8
1704 Delaware	28.7	5.2	77	24.7
1632 Maryland	141.1	30.8	447	34.9
1607 Virginia	231.0	43.9	1 221	42.6
1662 North Carolina	73.0	27.1	738	35.9
1662 South Carolina	64.0	60.4	581	55.6
1713 Georgia	5.2	19.2	517	42.6
Total (13)	1 170.8	20.2	8 443	19.2
Other States			4 458	15.7
Total			12 901	18.1

C. Canada

			143	
1713 Nova Scotia			612	
1759 Lower & Upper Canada			83	
Other			838	
Total Canada				

Source: Panel A: Higman (1996), p. 302. Date of acquisition shown on left. Panel B: *Historical Statistics of the United States* (1975) Part I, pp. 14, 24–37 for 1830, Part 2, pp. 1168 for 1750. Date of acquisition shown on left, countries listed from north to south. The total black population in 1830 was 2.3 million of which 2 million were slaves (15.6 per cent of the total US population). Panel C: Pebrer (1833), p. 386, figures refer to 1829.

The average duration of a slave trading venture from Europe to Africa, the West Indies and back was about 20 months, including several months assembling the cargo in Africa, and two months for the voyage to the West Indies. Evidence for UK and French voyages suggests that the cost of trade goods was twice as big as the costs of shipping, insurance and wages of the crew. Klein (1999, p. 125) suggests that in the late eighteenth century, European trade goods represented less than 5 per cent of West African income. He (pp. 98) suggests that "slave trade profits were not extraordinary by European standards. The average 10 per cent rate obtained was considered a very good profit rate at the time, but not out of the range of other contemporary investments."

The impact of the Atlantic slave trade on African population growth was substantial. Between 1700 and 1800, African population increased from 61 to 70 million (see Table B–9a). In the same period, slavers delivered 6.1 million slaves to the Americas. With 12 per cent mortality on the voyage, this implies a shipment of about 6.9 million. After allowing for births foregone it seems possible that African population would have grown three times as fast in the eighteenth century without the Atlantic slave trade.

If there had been no export of slaves to the Americas, economic development in the Caribbean, in Virginia, Maryland and the Carolinas would have been much more meagre. Smaller profit remittances from the colonies and the absence of income from the slave trade would have slowed British growth and European consumption of sugar would have been much smaller. There would also have been an adverse impact on the New England colonies because their prosperity depended in part on commodity exports and shipping services to the West Indies.

The British abolished the slave trade in 1807, and slavery in 1833, with £20 million compensation to slaveowners and nothing for the slaves. France lost her major sugar colony in Haiti because of the success of the slave revolt which ended with independence in 1804. France abolished the slave trade in 1817 and slavery in 1848.

The British abolition was due in substantial part to the success of humanitarian reformers in convincing public opinion to end a repugnant form of exploitation. The success of independence movements in North America in 1783, and in Latin America in the 1820s, the successful slave revolt in Haiti and the unsuccessful revolt in Jamaica in 1831–2 persuaded the planting lobby that their days were numbered, and that it was in their interest to settle for compensation.

Brazil continued to import slaves until the 1850s when the trade was stopped by British naval intervention. Brazilian slavery was maintained until 1888. Spain restricted slave imports to its colonies until 1789, but thereafter opened them to all slave traders. It made a big push to increase sugar production in the nineteenth century in Cuba and Puerto Rico (the only colonies it retained in the Americas after the others became independent). Slavery was abolished in Puerto Rico in 1873 and in Cuba in 1880. In 1894, Cuban sugar production was 1.1 million tons, in the British Caribbean 260 000, French Caribbean 79 000, Puerto Rico 49 000 and Surinam 8 000 (see Williams, 1970, p. 378).

As a substitute for labour imports from Africa, indentured workers from India were first brought to British Guiana in 1838. From then until 1914, the inflow of Indians to the British Caribbean amounted to 450 000. Javanese were brought to Surinam in large numbers, and Cuba imported 150 000 Chinese on a similar basis from 1849–75. However, the ending of slavery raised costs in the Caribbean sugar industry and weakened its competitive position. In 1787 the Caribbean accounted for 90 per cent of world sugar production. In 1894 its share was only 22 per cent (see Table 2–4). There was a greater diversification of Caribbean production with a greater role for coffee and cotton, but the main impact was stagnant or falling per capita income. Eisner (1961, pp. 119 and 153) shows per capita real income in Jamaica in 1930 about threequarters of that in 1830. Table 2–23 shows the dramatic decline in the importance of British trade with the Caribbean after 1820.

b) The 13 North American Colonies

The situation in North America was very different from that in the Caribbean. In the five colonies which relied most heavily on slave labour (Maryland, Virginia, the Carolinas and Georgia) slaves were about 40 per cent of the population in 1750, compared with 85 per cent in the Caribbean colonies. Whites (indentured servants and others) were a significant part of the labour force. The main crops in plantation agriculture were tobacco, rice and indigo, where work intensity was less than in sugar, and the climate was healthier than in the Caribbean. Life expectation and possibilities for natural growth of the black population were greater than in the Caribbean. Growth of the labour force depended less on the slave trade.

In the Northern colonies, which had 56 per cent of the colonial population in 1750, slaves were less than 5 per cent. A large part of the labour force was employed in agriculture with very much greater land availability per capita than in the United Kingdom. The average family farm in New England, the mid–Atlantic States and Pennsylvania in 1807 had well over 100 acres (Lebergott, 1984, p. 17). Most of the northern colonies had been formed by protestants of various denominations who were keen on education. There were eight universities in the north (Harvard founded in 1636, Yale 1701, University of Pennsylvania 1740, Princeton 1746, Columbia 1754, Brown 1764, Rutgers 1766, Dartmouth 1769), only one (William and Mary, 1693) in the South (and none in the Caribbean). The level of education in the northern colonies was above that in the United Kingdom. Per capita income was about the same level as in the United Kingdom and more evenly distributed.

Although the British Navigation Acts made the colonies route their most important exports to Europe and their imports from Europe through the United Kingdom, they provided favoured access to markets within the empire which were particularly important for exports of shipping services and ships. On the eve of the war of independence, the merchant marine of the colonies was over 450 000 tons, all of which (coastal craft, West Indies schooners, fishing and whaling boats, and ships for trade with England) were built in New England shipyards which had easy access to cheap timber, pitch and tar (see Table 2–15).

In addition, American yards had built an increasing proportion of the British merchant fleet in the course of the eighteenth century. In 1774, 30 per cent of Britain's million–ton merchant fleet was American built (see Davis, 1962, pp. 66–8).

The North American colonies had a significant urban population in Boston, New York and Philadelphia. They had a politically sophisticated elite familiar with the ideas and ideals of the French enlightenment. Their incentive to break the colonial tie was reinforced in 1763, after the Seven Years war, in which the British ended French rule in Canada and French claims to territory west of the 13 colonies. Hitherto, the most likely alternative to British rule had been French rule. Thereafter it was independence.

A striking characteristic of US economic growth after independence was its much greater dynamism than that of its neighbour Mexico, which was a Spanish colony until 1825. It is therefore useful to compare the different institutional, societal and policy influences transmitted by Spain and the United Kingdom.

The main reasons for Mexican backwardness compared with the ex–British colonies in North America were probably as follows:

a)   The Spanish colony was subject to a bigger drain of resources to the metropole. In the first place a considerable part of domestic income went into the pockets of peninsular Spaniards who did not stay in the colony but took their savings back to Spain. Secondly there was official tribute of about 2.7 per cent of GDP (see Maddison, 1995b, pp. 316–7).

b)   The British colonial regime imposed mercantilist restrictions on foreign trade, but they were much lighter than in New Spain. Thomas (1965) has suggested that the net cost of British trade restrictions was about 42 cents per head in the American colonies in 1770 (about 0.6 per cent of GDP).

c)   The British colonies had a better educated population, greater intellectual freedom and social mobility. Education was secular with emphasis on pragmatic skills and yankee ingenuity of which Ben Franklin was the prototype. The 13 British colonies had nine universities in 1776 for 2.5 million people. New Spain, with 5 million, had only two universities in Mexico City and Guadalajara, which concentrated on theology and law. Throughout the colonial period the Inquisition kept a tight censorship and suppressed heterodox thinking.

d)   In New Spain, the best land was engrossed by hacienda owners. In North America the white population had much easier access to land, and in New England family farming enterprise was typical. Restricted access to land in Spanish colonies was recognised as a hindrance to economic growth both by Adam Smith and the Viceroy of New Spain. Rosenzweig (1963) quotes the latter (Revillagigedo) as follows (my translation): "Maldistribution of land is a major obstacle to the progress of agriculture and commerce, particularly with regard to entails with absentee or negligent owners. We have subjects of his majesty here who possess hundreds of square leagues — enough to form a small kingdom — but who produce little of value."

e)   At the top of New Spain there was a privileged upper class, with a sumptuary lifestyle. Differences in status — a hereditary aristocracy, privileged groups of clergy and military with tax exemptions and legal immunities — meant that there was much less entrepreneurial vigour than in the British colonies. The elite in New Spain were rent seekers with a low propensity to productive investment.

f)   In the government of New Spain, power was highly concentrated on the centre, whereas in British North America there were 13 separate colonies, and political power was fragmented, so there was much greater freedom for individuals to pursue their own economic interests.

g)   Another source of advantage for North America was the vigour of its population growth because of the rapid inflow of migrants. Population in North America rose tenfold from 1700 to 1820, and by less than half in Mexico. Economic enterprise was much more dynamic when the market was expanding so rapidly.

c) India

The British connection with India started in 1600 with the creation of a monopoly trading company (the East India Company — EIC). For the first century and a half, it operated around the Indian coast from bases in Calcutta, Madras and Bombay. By the middle of the eighteenth century the main exports were textiles and raw silk from India, and tea from China. Purchases of Indian products were financed mainly by exports of bullion, and from China by export of opium and raw cotton from Bengal (see Table 2–20 and the above discussion of rivalry between the British, Dutch and French trading companies).

Until the eighteenth century the British generally maintained peaceable relations with the Moghul empire whose authority and military power were too great to be challenged. After the death of Aurangzeb in 1707, Moghul control disintegrated. The Moghul emperor became a token suzerain and provincial governors became *de facto* rulers as nawabs of successor states[37].

Given the size of India, with a bigger population than Europe, its racial, linguistic and religious complexity, it is not surprising that it fell apart. At the height of its power, under Akbar, the Moghul Empire practised religious toleration. This is one of the reasons why it was more successful in establishing an extensive domain than the earlier Muslim sultanates of Delhi. Aurangzeb abandoned the policy of religious tolerance, destroyed Hindu temples, reimposed the *jizya* (a capitation tax on non–Muslims) and confiscated some non–Muslim princely states when titles lapsed. After his death, there was a series of wars for the spoils of empire. In Western India, the Mahrattas established an independent

Hindu state with their capital at Poona. The *Nizam–ul–Mulk*, a high Moghul official who foresaw the collapse of the Empire, installed himself as the autonomous ruler of Hyderabad in 1724. In 1739, the Persian emperor Nadir Shah invaded India, massacred the population of Delhi and took away so much booty (including Shah Jehan's peacock throne and the Kohinoor diamond) that he was able to remit Persian taxes for three years. He also annexed Punjab and set up an independent kingdom in Lahore. The Punjab was later captured by the Sikhs. In other areas which nominally remained in the Empire, e.g. Bengal, Mysore and Oudh, the power of the Moghul emperor declined, as did his revenue. Continuous internal warfare greatly weakened the economy and trade of the country.

It was because of these internal political and religious conflicts that the EIC was able to gain control of India. It exploited the differences skilfully by making temporary alliances and picking off local potentates one at a time. Most of its troops were local recruits who were well disciplined and paid regularly. They conquered the Moghul province of Bengal in 1757, took over the provinces of Madras and Bombay in 1803, and seized the Punjab from the Sikhs in 1848. They also succeeded in driving their European commercial rivals — the French and Dutch — from India. The British government did not establish its own direct rule until after the Indian mutiny in 1857 when the East India Company was dissolved.

After its military victory at Plassey in 1757, the EIC operated a dual system in Bengal in which it had control and the nawab was a puppet. The main objectives of the Company were to enrich its officials and finance its exports from the tax revenues of the province instead of shipping bullion to India. The extension of the EIC's territorial conquests changed its role from trading to governance. The Company lost its trading monopoly in 1813 in India and in 1833 for China. Company policy was subjected to parliamentary surveillance in 1773, and the nawab was replaced by a Governor General (Warren Hastings) in direct charge of administration, but with Indian officials. Hastings was dismissed in 1782, and Cornwallis from 1785 created the basis on which colonial India was governed.

All high level posts were reserved for the British, and Indians were excluded. A civil administration was created which was much more effective and cheaper than that of the Moghuls. From 1806 the Company trained its young recruits at Haileybury College near London. From 1833 nominees were selected by competitive examination. After 1853, selection was entirely on merit. In 1829, the system was strengthened by establishing districts throughout British India small enough to be controlled by an individual British official who exercised autocratic power as revenue collector, judge and chief of police.

There was a strong streak of Benthamite radicalism in the EIC administration. James Mill, John Stuart Mill and Macaulay were influential Company officials, and Malthus was the professor of economics at Haileybury College. Bentham himself was consulted on the reform of Indian institutions and the Utilitarians used India to try experiments and ideas (e.g. competitive entry for the civil service) which they would have liked to apply in England. After the Indian Mutiny in 1857, when the British government took over direct control of India, these radical Westernising approaches were dropped, policy became more conservative, and there was no attempt at further extension of direct rule over provinces which were governed by Indian princes with British advisors[38].

The British raj was operated by remarkably few people. There were only 31 000 British in India in 1805 (of which 22 000 in the army, and 2 000 in civil government). In 1931, there were 168 000 (60 000 in the army and police, 4 000 in civil government and 60 000 employed in the private sector). They were never more than 0.05 per cent of the population — a much thinner layer than the Muslim rulers had been.

The changes which the British made in the system of governance had major socioeconomic consequences (see Boxes 2–1 and 2–2 which contrast the Indian social structure at the peak of the Moghul empire and at the end of British rule). The British took over a Moghul tax system which provided a land revenue equal to 15 per cent of national income, but by the end of the colonial period, land tax was only 1 per cent of national income and the total tax burden 6 per cent. The main gains from tax reduction and associated changes in property rights went to upper castes in the village economy, to zamindars who became landlords, and village moneylenders. The wasteful warlord aristocracy of the

Box 2–1. **Social Structure of the Moghul Empire**

Percentage of labour force		*Per cent of national income after tax*
18	*NON–VILLAGE ECONOMY*	52
1	Moghul Emperor and Court Mansabdars Jagirdars Native princes Appointed zamindars Hereditary zamindars	15
17	Merchants and bankers Traditional professions Petty traders & entrepreneurs Soldiers & petty bureaucracy Urban artisans & construction workers Servants Sweepers Scavengers	37
72	*VILLAGE ECONOMY*	45
	Dominant castes Cultivators and rural artisans Landless labourers Servants Sweepers Scavengers	
10	*TRIBAL ECONOMY*	3

Source: Maddison (1971), p. 33.

Box 2–2. **Social Structure at the End of British Rule**

Percentage of labour force		Per cent of national income after tax
18	*NON–VILLAGE ECONOMY*	44
0.05	British officials and military British capitalists, plantation owners, traders, bankers & managers	5
0.95	Native princes Big zamindars and jagirdars	3
	Indian capitalists, merchants and managers	3
	The new Indian professional class	3
17	Petty traders, small entrepreneurs, traditional professions, clerical and manual workers in government, soldiers, railway workers, industrial workers, urban artisans, servants, sweepers & scavengers	37
75	*VILLAGE ECONOMY*	54
9	Village rentiers, rural moneylenders small zamindars, tenants–in–chief	20
20	Working proprietors, protected tenants	18
29	Tenants–at–will, sharecroppers, village artisans and servants	12
17	Landless labourers, scavengers	4
7	*TRIBAL ECONOMY*	2

Source: Maddison (1971), p. 69.

Table 2–29. **Population of British Territories in Asia, Africa, Australia and Europe in 1830**

	Population (000)	Area (Square Miles)
a) Asia		
Bengal Presidency	69 710	220 312
Fort St. George (Madras) Presidency	13 509	141 924
Bombay Presidency	6 252	59 438
Deccan districts	11 000[a]	91 200
Total EIC Territories	100 578	512 874
Areas under EIC "protection"	40 000[a]	614 610
Ceylon	933	
Mauritius	101	
Singapore, Malacca, Penang	107	
b) Africa		
Cape of Good Hope	129	
Sierra Leone	15	
Senegal, Goree and Fernando Po	10	
c) Australia (white population)	70[b]	
d) Europe		
Gibraltar	17	
Malta	120	

a) Pebrer's rough estimates; b) 1839.

Source: India from Pebrer (1833), pp. 454 and 465. EIC armed forces were 223,461 of which 36,606 Europeans. Ceylon and Mauritius from p. 410, Singapore etc. from p. 454. Ceylon was taken from the Dutch in 1795, Malacca in 1825; Mauritius from France 1795. The slave population of Mauritius was 79 000, in Ceylon 20 000. Africa from p. 418; the Cape was taken from the Dutch in 1806; in 1830 the slave population was 36 000. Australia 1839 from Vamplew (1987) p. 44. Gibraltar and Malta from Pebrer (1833), p. 374.

Table 2–30. **Comparative Macroeconomic Performance of India and Britain, 1600–1947**

	1600	1700	1757	1857	1947
Per capita GDP (1990 int. dollars)					
India	550	550	540	520	618
United Kingdom	974	1 250	1 424	2 717	6 361
Population (000)					
India	135 000	165 000	185 000	227 000	414 000
United Kingdom	6 170	8 565	13 180	28 187	49 519
GDP (million 1990 int. dollars)					
India	74 250	90 750	99 900	118 040	255 852
United Kingdom	6 007	10 709	18 768	76 584	314 969

Source: Appendix B and Maddison (1995a).

Moghuls was eliminated, and replaced by a small Westernised elite with a smaller share of national income. Until the 1920s, the new elite was almost entirely British, with British consumption patterns. This greatly reduced the demand for the luxury products of India's traditional handicrafts. The damage to India's main industry was greatly reinforced in the nineteenth century by duty–free imports of British cotton textiles.

In the first century of British rule, the changes in the social structure and replacement of old methods of governance led to continuance of the fall in per capita income which had started at the beginning of the eighteenth century as the Moghul state disintegrated. From 1857 to independence in 1947, there was a slow rise in per capita income, and faster population growth. Table 2–27 gives a rough comparative idea of changes in income and population in India and Britain from 1600 to the end of colonial rule in 1947.

Table 2–21 provides a rough idea of the dimension of the "drain" of resources from India to the United Kingdom as a consequence of having foreign governance. This drain was about 0.9 to 1.3 per cent of Indian national income from 1868 to the 1930s. This meant a transfer of about a fifth of India's net savings which might otherwise have been used to import capital goods. The drain was a major target of criticism by Indian nationalists from the end of the nineteenth century. Even more important from their point of view was the fact that 5 per cent of the national income represented consumption of British personnel in India. Most of this would have gone to an Indian elite if the British had left India 50 years earlier, and a modernising Indian elite might well have pursued policies more conducive to Indian development. However, if the British (or their French rivals) had not ruled India from the mid–eighteenth to late nineteenth century, it seems unlikely that a modernising elite or the legal and institutional framework for its operation would have emerged from the ruins of the Moghul Empire.

As my conclusions on the impact and consequences of British rule are contestable, it seems useful to set out the evidence for my viewpoint in more detail in the following sections on: the socioeconomic structure which the British inherited from Moghul India; the British impact on Indian agriculture; and its impact on industry.

The Socioeconomic Structure of Moghul India

Muslims were the ruling elite in India from the thirteenth century until the British takeover. The Moghuls had the military power to squeeze a large surplus from a passive village society. The ruling class had an extravagant lifestyle whose needs were supplied by urban artisans producing high quality cotton textiles, silks, jewellery, decorative swords and weapons.

The Moghul aristocracy were not landlords but were allotted the tax revenue from a specified area (i.e. they were given a *jagir*). Part of the revenue was for their own sustenance, the rest was paid to the central treasury in cash or in the form of troop support. The aristocracy was not, in principle, hereditary. Moghul practice derived from the traditions of the nomadic societies which had created Islam in Arabia and the Ottoman Empire. Nobles were regularly posted from one *jagir* to another and their estates were liable to royal forfeit on death. This system of warlord predators led to a wasteful use of resources. There was little motive to improve landed property. Moghul officials needed high incomes because they had many dependants to support. They maintained polygamous households with vast retinues of slaves and servants. Military spending was also large because soldiering and wars were the main duty of the Moghul elite. The *jagirdar* had an incentive to squeeze village society close to subsistence, to spend as much as possible on consumption and to die in debt to the state. There were also Hindu nobles (*zamindars*) who retained hereditary control over village revenues, and Hindu princes who continued to rule and collect revenues in autonomous states within the Moghul Empire, e.g. in Rajputana.

113

The reason why the Moghuls could raise so much revenue from taxation, without having a ruling class which directly supervised the production process, was that village society was very docile.

The chief characteristic of Indian society which differentiated it from others was the institution of caste. It segregated the population into mutually exclusive groups whose economic and social functions were clearly defined and hereditary. Old religious texts classify Hindus into four main groups: *brahmins*, a caste of priests at the top of the social scale whose ceremonial purity was not to be polluted by manual labour; next in priority came the *kshatriyas* or warriors, thirdly the *vaishyas* or traders, and finally the *sudras*, or farmers. Below this there were *melechas* or outcastes to perform menial and unclean tasks. Members of different castes did not intermarry or eat together, and kept apart in social life.

The theoretical model of the Rigveda is a very simplified version of the Indian situation. Brahmins and untouchables were distinguishable everywhere, but the hierarchy of intermediate castes was complex and often did not conform to the kshatriya, vaishya, sudra categorisation.

In relations with the state, the village usually acted as a unit. Land taxes were generally paid collectively and the internal allocation of the burden was left to the village headman or accountant. The top group were allies of the state, co–beneficiaries in the system of exploitation. In every village the bottom layer were untouchables squeezed tight against the margin of subsistence. Without the caste sanctions, village society would probably have been more egalitarian, and a more homogeneous peasantry might have been less willing to put up with such heavy fiscal levies.

From an economic point of view, the most interesting feature of caste was that it fixed occupation by heredity. For priests or barbers the prospect of doing the same job as a whole chain of ancestors was perhaps not too depressing, but for those whose hereditary function was to clean latrines, the system offered no joys in this world. One reason they accepted it was the Hindu belief in reincarnation which held out the hope of rebirth in a higher social status to those who acquired merit by loyal performance of their allotted task in this world.

Below the village society, about 10 per cent of the population lived in a large number of tribal communities. Aboriginal tribes led an independent pagan existence as hunters or forest dwellers, completely outside Hindu society and paying no taxes to the Moghuls.

The British Impact on Indian Agriculture

The colonial government modified traditional institutional arrangements in agriculture and created property rights whose character was somewhat closer to those under Western capitalism. Except in the autonomous princely states, the old warlord aristocracy was dispossessed. Their previous income from *jagirs* and that of the Moghul state was appropriated by the British. In the Bengal Presidency (i.e. modern Bengal, Bihar, Orissa and part of Madras) the second layer of Moghul property rights belonging to tax collectors (*zamindars*) was reinforced. They acquired hereditary status, so long as they paid their land taxes, and their tax liabilities were frozen at the 1793 level. In the Madras and Bombay Presidencies the British dispossessed most of the old Moghul and Mahratta nobility and big zamindars, and vested property rights and tax obligations in the traditionally dominant castes in villages. Lower–caste cultivators became their tenants.

Because of the emergence of clearer titles, it was now possible to mortgage land. The status of moneylenders was also improved by the change from Muslim to British law. There had been moneylenders in the Moghul period, but their importance grew substantially under British rule, and over time a considerable amount of land changed hands through foreclosures.

Over time, two forces raised the income of landowners. One of these was the increasing scarcity of land as population expanded. This raised land values and rents. The second was the decline in the incidence of land tax. As a result, there was an increased income and a widening of inequality within villages. The village squirearchy received higher incomes because of the reduced burden of land tax

and the increase in rents; the income of tenants and agricultural labourers declined because their traditional rights were curtailed and their bargaining power was reduced by greater land scarcity. The class of landless agricultural labourers grew in size under British rule.

The colonial government increased the irrigated area about eightfold. Eventually more than a quarter of the land of British India was irrigated, compared with 5 per cent in Moghul India. Irrigation was extended both as a source of revenue and as a measure to mitigate famines. A good deal of the irrigation work was in the Punjab and Sind. The motive here was to provide land for retired Indian army personnel, many of whom came from the Punjab, and to build up population in an area which bordered on the disputed frontier with Afghanistan. These areas, which had formerly been desert, became the biggest irrigated area in the world and major producers of wheat and cotton, both for export and for sale in other parts of India.

Improvements in transport facilities (particularly railways, but also steamships and the Suez canal) helped agriculture by permitting some degree of specialisation on cash crops. This increased yields somewhat, but the bulk of the country stuck to subsistence farming. Plantations were developed for indigo, sugar, jute and tea. These items made a significant contribution to exports, but in the context of Indian agriculture as a whole, they were not very important. In 1946, the two primary export items, tea and jute, were less than 3.5 per cent of gross value of crop output. Thus the enlargement of markets through international trade was less of a stimulus in India than in other Asian countries such as Burma, Ceylon, Indonesia or Thailand.

Under British rule, the Indian population remained subject to recurrent famines and epidemic diseases. In 1876–8 and 1899–1900 famine killed millions of people. In the 1890s there was a widespread outbreak of bubonic plague and in 1919 a great influenza epidemic. In the 1920s and 1930s there were no famines, and the 1944 famine in Bengal was due to war conditions and transport difficulties rather than crop failure. However, the greater stability after 1920 may have been partly due to a lucky break in the weather cycle rather than to a new stability of agriculture.

The British Impact on Indian Industry

Moghul India had a bigger industry than any other country which became a European colony, and was unique in being an industrial exporter in pre–colonial times. A large part of this industry was destroyed as a consequence of British rule.

Between 1757 and 1857 the British wiped out the Moghul court, and eliminated three–quarters of the aristocracy (except those in princely states). They also eliminated more than half of the local chieftainry (zamindars) and in their place established a bureaucracy with European tastes. The new rulers wore European clothes and shoes, drank imported beer, wines and spirits, and used European weapons. Their tastes were mimicked by the male members of the new Indian "middle class" who acted as their clerks and intermediaries. As a result of these political and social changes, about threequarters of the domestic demand for luxury handicrafts was destroyed. This was a shattering blow to manufacturers of fine muslins, jewellery, luxury clothing and footwear, decorative swords and weapons. My own guess would be that the home market for these goods was about 5 per cent of Moghul national income and the export market for textiles probably another 1.5 per cent.

The second blow came from massive imports of cheap textiles from England after the Napoleonic wars. Home spinning, which was a part–time activity of village women, was greatly reduced. Demand for village hand–loom weaving changed with a substantial switch to using factory instead of home–spun yarn.

Modern cotton mills were started in Bombay in 1851, preceding Japan by 20 years and China by 40. Production was concentrated on coarse yarns which were sold domestically and to China and Japan. Exports were half of output. India began to suffer from Japanese competition in the 1890s. Exports to Japan were practically eliminated by 1898. Shortly after, Japanese factories in China began

to reduce India's market there. By the end of the 1930s, Indian exports of yarn to China and Japan had disappeared, piece goods exports had fallen off, and India imported both yarn and piece goods from China and Japan.

If the British had been willing to give tariff protection, India could have copied Lancashire's textile technology more quickly. Instead British imports entered India duty free. By the 1920s when Indian textile imports were coming mainly from Japan, British policy changed. By 1934 the tariff on cotton cloth had been raised to 50 per cent with a margin of preference for British products. As a result there was a considerable substitution of local textiles for imports. In 1896 Indian mills supplied only 8 per cent of Indian cloth consumption, in 1913 20 per cent and in 1945 76 per cent. By the latter date there were no imports of piece goods.

Modern jute manufacturing started in 1854 and the industry expanded rapidly in the vicinity of Calcutta. It was largely in the hands of foreigners (mainly Scots). Between 1879 and 1913 the number of jute spindles rose tenfold — much faster than growth in the cotton textile industry. Most of the jute output was for export.

Coal mining, mainly in Bengal, was another industry which achieved significance. Its output, which by 1914 had reached 15.7 million tons, largely met the demands of the Indian railways.

In 1911 the first Indian steel mill was built by the Tata Company at Jamshedpur in Bihar. The Indian industry started 15 years later than in China, where the first mill was built at Hangyang in 1896. The first Japanese mill was built in 1898. In both China and Japan the first steel mills (and the first textile mills) were government enterprises.

Indian firms in industry, insurance and banking were given a boost from 1905 onwards by the *swadeshi* movement, which was a nationalist boycott of British goods in favour of Indian enterprise. During the First World War, lack of British imports strengthened the hold of Indian firms on the home markets for textiles and steel. After the war, under nationalist pressure, the government started to favour Indian enterprise in its purchase of stores and it agreed to create a tariff commission in 1921 which started raising tariffs for protective reasons.

Many of the most lucrative commercial, financial, business and plantation jobs in the modern sector were occupied by foreigners. Long after the East India Company's legally enforced monopoly privileges were ended, the British continued to exercise effective dominance through their control of the banking sector[39] and the system of "managing agencies". These agencies, originally set up by former employees of the East India Company, were used both to manage industrial enterprise and to handle most of India's international trade. They were closely linked with British banks, insurance and shipping companies. Managing agencies had a quasi–monopoly in access to capital, and they had interlocking directorships which gave them control over supplies and markets. They dominated the foreign markets in Asia. They had better access to government officials than did Indians. The agencies were in many ways able to take decisions favourable to their own interests rather than those of shareholders. They were paid commissions based on gross profits or total sales and were often agents for the raw materials used by the companies they managed. Thus the Indian capitalists who did emerge were highly dependent on British commercial capital and many sectors of industry were dominated by British firms, e.g. shipping, banking, insurance, coal, plantation crops and jute.

Indian industrial efficiency was hampered by the British administration's neglect of technical education, and the reluctance of British firms and managing agencies to provide training or managerial experience to Indians. Even in the Bombay textile industry, where most of the capital was Indian, 28 per cent of the managerial and supervisory staff were British in 1925 (42 per cent in 1895) and the British component was even bigger in more complex industries. This naturally raised Indian production costs[40]. At lower levels in the plant there was widespread use of jobbers for hiring workers and maintaining discipline and workers themselves were a completely unskilled group who had to bribe the jobbers to get and retain their jobs. There were also problems of race, language and caste distinctions

between management, supervisors and workers. The small size and very diversified output of the enterprises hindered efficiency. It is partly for these reasons (and the overvaluation of the currency) that Indian exports had difficulty in competing with Japan.

d) China

Until the nineteenth century China was a much bigger and more powerful state than any in Europe or Asia. Its technical precocity and meritocratic bureaucracy gave it higher levels of income than Europe from the fifth to the fourteenth century (see Figure 1–4). Thereafter Europe slowly forged ahead in terms of per capita income, but Chinese population grew faster. Chinese GDP in 1820 was nearly 30 per cent higher than that of Western Europe and its Western Offshoots combined[41].

In the first three centuries of European trade expansion, China had been much more difficult to penetrate than the Americas, Africa or the rest of Asia. Such trade as there was, was on conditions laid down by China.

Between the 1840s and 1940s, China's economy collapsed. Per capita GDP in 1950 was less than threequarters of the 1820 level. Population growth was interrupted by major military conflict. In 1950, China's GDP was less than a twelfth of that in Western Europe and the Western Offshoots.

The period of China's decline coincided with commercial penetration by foreign powers and the Japanese attempt at conquest. There are clear links between the two processes, but there were also internal forces which contributed to China's retrogression.

China turned its back on the world economy in the early fifteenth century, when its maritime technology was superior to that of Europe (see Table 2–11). Thereafter it was left without naval defences. China's highly educated elite showed no interest in the technological development and military potential of Western Europe. A British mission in 1793 tried to open diplomatic relations and demonstrate the attractions of western science and technology with 600 cases of presents (including chronometers, telescopes, a planetarium, chemical and metal products). The official rebuff stated "there is nothing we lack — we have never set much store on strange or ingenious objects, nor do we want any more of your country's manufactures." China did not start establishing legations abroad until 1877.

The Manchu dynasty was in a state of collapse from the mid–nineteenth century, and the Kuomintang regime which followed was equally incompetent. The dynastic collapse paralleled that of the Moghul regime in India, which led to British takeover there. However, Western colonialism in China was very different from that in India, and it was Japan, not the Western colonial powers, which attempted conquest.

Colonial penetration was inaugurated with the capture of Hong Kong by British gunboats in 1842. The immediate motive was to guarantee free access to Canton to exchange Indian opium for Chinese tea. A second Anglo–French attack in 1858–60 opened access to the interior of China via the Yangtse and the huge network of internal waterways which debouched at Shanghai.

This was the era of free trade imperialism. Western traders were individual firms, not monopoly companies. In sharp contrast to their hostile and mutually exclusive trade regimes in the eighteenth century, the British and French had made their Cobden–Chevalier Treaty to open European commerce on a most–favoured–nation basis. They applied the same principle in the treaties imposed on China. Hence 12 other European countries, Japan, the United States, and three Latin American countries acquired the same trading privileges before the first world war.

The treaties forced China to maintain low tariffs. They legalised the opium trade. They allowed foreigners to travel and trade in China, giving them extra–territorial rights and consular jurisdiction in 92 "treaty ports" which were opened between 1842 and 1917. To monitor the Chinese commitment to

low tariffs, a Maritime Customs Inspectorate was created (with Sir Robert Hart as Inspector General from 1861 to 1908) to collect tariff revenue for the Chinese government. A large part of this was earmarked to pay "indemnities" which the colonialists demanded to defray the costs of their attacks on China.

The centre of this multilateral colonial regime was the international settlement in Shanghai. The British picked the first site in 1843 north of the "native city". The French, Germans, Italians, Japanese and Americans had neighbouring sites along the Whangpoo river opposite Pudong, with extensive grounds for company headquarters, the cricket club, country clubs, tennis clubs, swimming pools, the race course, the golf club, movie theatres, churches, schools, hotels, hospitals, cabarets, brothels, bars, consulates and police stations of the colonial powers. There were similar facilities, on a smaller scale, in Tientsin and Hankow. Most of the Chinese allowed into these segregated settlements were servants[42].

Apart from the British colony of Hong Kong, there were five "leased" territories ceded to Britain, France, Germany, Japan and Russia. These included Britain's 100 year lease on the New Territories adjacent to Hong Kong, granted in 1898.

Foreign residents and trading companies were the main beneficiaries of this brand of free trade imperialism and extra–territorial privilege. The settlements were glittering islands of modernity, but the character of other Chinese cities did not improve, and those which had been damaged by the massive Taiping rebellion of 1850–64 had deteriorated. Chinese agriculture was not significantly affected by the opening of the economy, and the share of exports in Chinese GDP was small (0.7 per cent of GDP in 1870, 1.2 per cent in 1913) — much smaller than in India. China regained its tariff autonomy in 1928 and there was some relaxation of other constraints on its sovereignty in the treaty ports. However, this was offset by intensified pressures from Japan.

The biggest intrusions into Chinese sovereignty and the biggest damage to its economy came from Japan. In the 1590s, Hideyoshi had made an earlier attempt to attack China by invading Korea, and the Meiji regime repeated this strategy with greater success in 1894–5.

There was a gradual build–up of pressure from the 1870s, when Japan sent a punitive force to Taiwan and asserted its suzerainty over the Ryuku islands (Okinawa). In 1876 a Japanese naval force entered Korea and opened the ports of Pusan, Inchon and Wonsan to Japanese consular jursidiction. In 1894, Japan declared war on Korea, and its forces crossed the Yalu river into China. In the Treaty of Shimonoseki, 1895, China was forced to recognise that its suzerainty over Korea had lapsed, Taiwan and the Pescadores were ceded to Japan. Japanese citizens (and hence other foreigners) were now permitted to open factories and manufacture in China. China was forced to pay an indemnity which amounted to a third of Japanese GDP, which China had to finance by foreign borrowing. This sparked off an avalanche of further foreign claims, and a Chinese declaration of war on the foreign powers in 1900. Within two months China was defeated by joint action of the foreign powers and Russia occupied Manchuria. Japan defeated Russia in the war of 1905, and took over Southern Manchuria. Korea became a Japanese protectorate, and in 1910 a Japanese colony.

Japan took Manchuria in 1931 and established a puppet state (Manchukuo) in 1933 which incorporated China's three Manchurian provinces, parts of Inner Mongolia, Hopei and Liaoning. China was obliged to turn the area around Peking and Tientsin into a demilitarised zone, which left North China defenceless. In July 1937, the Japanese attacked again. They presumably expected to take over the whole of North China after a short campaign, and thereafter to dominate a compliant government in the South as part of their new order in Asia. However, the Chinese government reacted strongly, and the war with Japan lasted for eight years. Its impact was compounded by the civil war between the Kuomintang and communist forces. Thus China endured 12 years of war from 1937 to 1949. The destructive impact was similar proportionately to that of the Taiping rebellion of 1850–64.

Notes

1. Beloch (1886, p. 507) estimated a total of 54 million (23 in Europe, 19.5 in West Asia, and 11.5 in Africa). My estimate is derived from Tables B–2, B–8 and B–9b of Appendix B.

2. See Needham, Vol.4 III (*Civil Engineering and Nautics*), 1971, p. 29 for his adjusted figures of paved roads in the 2 million square miles of the Roman Empire. His figure for the 1.5 million square miles of Han dynasty China was 22 000.

3. See Goldsmith (1984), pp. 271–2 for a discussion of the evidence on urbanisation. He suggests a ratio between 9 and 13 per cent, but my 5 per cent ratio refers only to places with 10 000 inhabitants or more.

4. See Warmington (1928) for Roman trade with Asia.

5. Hopkins (1980, p. 105–6) used information on 545 dated sea wrecks from the coasts of Italy, France and Spain to estimate changes in the volume of trade in the Western Mediterranean. He concluded that "in the period of Roman imperial expansion and in the High Empire (200 BC — 200 AD) there was more sea–borne trade in the Mediterranean than ever before and more than there was for the next thousand years." He shows that the level in 400–650 AD was about a fifth of that in the peak period. Ashtor (1976), p. 102 analyses Arab evidence on Mediterranean trade and concludes: "when the Arabs had established their rule over the eastern, southern and western coasts of the Mediterranean, it became the frontier between two civilisations, strange, unknown and hostile to each other. What had been a great lake on whose shores rulers, laws, religion and language were the same or similar became the scene of naval warfare and piracy. Trade disappeared almost entirely in the Mediterranean in the course of the eighth century. Spices, precious silk fabrics and other Oriental articles were hardly to be found in Western Europe."

6. See Pirenne, *Mohammed and Charlemagne* (1939), p. 242. Although Pirenne's description of the ninth century situation is succinct, striking and basically correct, his prior analysis of the timing and causes of Roman decline is difficult to swallow. He argued that the barbarian takeover in Gaul and Italy preserved a good deal of the advantages of Roman civilisation, and that its demolition was due to the Islamic invaders and Charlemagne. Hodges and Whitehouse (1998) summarise modern archaeological evidence and previous critical reactions to Pirenne's thesis. They conclude that Pirenne exaggerated the survival of Roman institutions: "By the end of the sixth century, conditions in the Western Mediterranean bore little resemblance to those in the second century. Before the Arabs arrived the transformation was virtually complete." (p. 53)

7. See Lane and Mueller (1985).

8. These fairs were held six times a year about 40 kilometres southeast of Paris and 110 kilometres from Bruges. Two fairs were held in Troyes, two in Provins, one in Lagny and the other at Bar–sur–Aube. They were the major centres of West European commercial activity from 1200 to 1350. They attracted merchants from all regions of France, northern and central Italy, Flanders, Hainault, Brabant, Spain, England, Germany and Savoy. The lords of the fair were the Counts of Champagne and later the French King. They derived income from taxes, tolls and safe–conduct charges on merchants. In return their agents kept law and order, helped to enforce contracts and kept notarial records. In cases of dispute, most Italian towns were represented by their consuls. The fairs petered out when the sea route from Italy to Flanders was opened (see Verlinden, 1963).

9. See Lane (1973), p. 19.

10. See Lane (1966), pp. 143–252 for an analysis of Venetian shipping techniques and navigation, and Unger (1980), pp. 161–94.

11. Possibilities for trade in the western Mediterranean had already been opened up by the recovery of Sicily (1090), Corsica (1091), Sardinia and Majorca (1232) from Arab control. This benefited the trade of Genoa, Barcelona and Provence.

12. See Landes (1998), pp. 46–7: "By the middle of the fifteenth century, Italy, particularly Florence and Venice, was making thousands of spectacles, fitted with concave as well as convex lenses, for myopes as well as presbyopes."

13. In the field of learning, it should be remembered that the University of Padua was part of the Venetian domain since its foundation in 1405. Its cosmopolitan faculty made major contributions to Renaissance scholarship and to scientific development. Its professors included Galileo, and the Flemish anatomist, Vesalius.

14. Henrique was influential in instigating a Portuguese attack on Morocco in 1415. The strategic port of Ceuta was captured and became a Portuguese stronghold (until 1580 when it was ceded to Spain). Ceuta was one of the terminals of the Sahara gold caravans. It was a useful port for Genoese, Venetian and Catalan merchants moving from the Mediterranean to the Atlantic, and seemed to be a first step in the conquest of Morocco. However, an attempt to take Tangier in 1437 was an ignominious failure. Henrique saved the remnant of his troops by promising to surrender Ceuta and leaving his younger brother as an Arab hostage. He kept Ceuta and left his brother to a nasty death (see Russell, 2000).

15. See Schwartz (1985), pp. 4, 7 and 504.

16. Barrett in Tracy (1990), p. 247, gives figures for West Africa gold exports for 1471 to 1800. From 1471 to 1700 they amounted to 145 tons of which most would have gone to Portugal.

17. The Portuguese were convinced that there were large Christian communities in Africa and Asia, and one of the missions of the explorers was to investigate the myth of the kingdom of Prester John. The Portuguese spy Covilhã went to Ethiopia in 1493 as part of this search. He stayed to work for the negus, the Ethiopian King and was found there in 1520. Elsewhere in Africa the only sizeable community was Copts in Egypt. There were small Christian communities in Southern India.

18. In order to check Cabral's discovery, the Portuguese engaged the Florentine navigator, Amerigo Vespucci to explore the Brazilian coast in 1501. He had carried out an exploratory trip two years earlier along the coast of Venezuela and Guiana for Spain. Needham (1971), Vol.IV:3, p. 513 refers to suggestions that the existence of Brazil was already known to the Portuguese before the Columbus voyage to the Caribbean.

19. Subrahmanyam (1997), p. 182 quotes a figure of "4 000 cantari". This measure has a wide range of possible meanings. Ashtor (1980) pp. 756–7, defines "kintars" (a measure used for Venetian spice exports from Alexandria) as 180 kg. I have assumed that this is the unit used in the source quoted by Subrahmanyam.

20. Needham (who was a biochemist) explains the European demand for spices as follows: "The usual idea is that pepper and spices were simply for table condiments or sauces designed to disguise the taste of tainted meat. But this could never have accounted for the vast imports of the Western Middle Ages –– we are bound to suppose that as in traditional China and the Islamic lands the pepper was actually mixed with the salt for — the meat to be preserved. The addition of spices in the correct amount permitted — inhibition of the autolytic enzymes as well as bacteriostatic action and an anti–oxidant effect on fats" (see Needham, Vol.IV:3, 1971, pp. 520–1). Landes (1998), pp. 132–3 makes the last point in different language: "people of that day could not know this, but the stronger spices worked to kill or weaken the bacteria and viruses that promoted and fed on decay."

21. See Tibbetts (1981) for a translation of the work of the leading Arab navigator Ibn Majid, and Jones (1978) for illustrations of Arab instruments to use stars and the sun for navigation.

22. See Goitein (1967) for the activity of Jewish communities throughout the Arab world of the Mediterranean.

23. See Subrahmanyam (1997), p. 96.

24. Albuquerque was Portuguese Viceroy in Asia in 1509–15. It was he who established the bases in Goa and Malacca. He selected Goa, after an attempt to take Calicut, where the Portuguese made a landing but were cut to pieces. The elimination of the Muslim position in Goa was welcome to the Hindu monarchs of Vijayanagar, with whom the Portuguese established friendly relations (see Panikkar, 1953, pp. 38–9.

25. The Grand Canal was about 10 times the length of the largest European venture — the Canal de Languedoc — built by Colbert and operational from 1681. Its length was 240 kilometres, and was confined to relatively small vessels (see Parry, 1967, p. 215).

26. In 1640 when Portugal regained independence from Spain, it allied itself closely with the United Kingdom. The British were allowed to have merchants in Brazil and Portugal, to engage in the carrying trade, were granted extra–territorial rights, and duties on British goods were bound at a fixed level. In 1703, the Methuen Treaty gave British goods free access to Brazil and the Portuguese market. In return, the United Kingdom propped up the Portuguese Empire with military guarantees.

27. Mulhall (1899), p. 172, shows Brazilian customs receipts equal to 21 per cent of trade turnover (about 37 per cent of imports after allowing for export taxes of about 5 per cent) in 1887 compared with a world average of 5.6 per cent. The ratio of customs receipts to trade turnover was highest in Portugal (41 per cent), next highest in the United States (15 per cent). In Holland it was 0.2 per cent; Belgium 1.1; India 2.2, and the United Kingdom 3.1. Mulhall also shows (p. 258) that in the decade 1871–1880 Brazil received 72 per cent of its revenues from customs duties (higher than any other country). In India it was only 4 per cent (the lowest).

28. From 1384 Flanders and Brabant, and from 1428 the province of Holland, were part of the Duchy of Burgundy whose headquarters were in Brussels. This was the main seat of the Duke and his court, with occasional sorties to Dijon and Bruges. The area of the future Belgium and the Netherlands had 17 provinces (staten) which sent representatives annually to a meeting of the States General where they were told what taxes they had to raise. The provinces were grouped under three governors (stadholders) selected from the nobility. The cities enjoyed considerable "liberties". These rights were exercised by a wealthy commercial elite which regulated industrial standards and arrangements for periodic fairs and staples for exports. There were three bishoprics within the area of the 17 provinces, and two others within the area of northern France under Burgundian control. It was a fragmented, and, by later standards, reasonably benign form of governance. The Duchy recognised French sovereignty, but was in fact autonomous. In 1477 the last Burgundian heir married Maximilian of Habsburg, and after her death in 1482, the territory became effectively a component of the Holy Roman Empire. Maximilian was Emperor from 1493 to 1519 and Charles V from 1519 to 1555. Habsburg rulers curtailed the privileges of the Burgundian nobility and the cities and imposed higher taxes. When the protestant reformation (Lutheran, Anabaptist and Calvinist) affected the provinces, there was a ruthless suppression of heresy. Charles V retired as emperor in 1555, and divided the Empire by giving the Austrian part to his brother, and the rest to his son, Philip II. In fact Philip was effectively in charge of the Netherlands for 50 years from his first visit to Brussels in 1548 until his death in 1598. The Netherlands was the richest region of his colossal empire and his intention was to squeeze it to finance his wider commitments and ambitions — which involved him in war with France, an attempted invasion of England and a massive naval conflict with the Ottoman empire. He used matrimony as well as war to further his ambitions, marrying successively Mary of Portugal (1543); Mary Queen of England (1554); Isabella of France (1559); Anne of Austria (1570). He squandered the silver tribute from Mexico and Peru, and fiscal irresponsibility led to a sequence of defaults on public debt in 1557, 1575, and 1597. The net impact of his activity was to weaken Spain.

Between 1609 and 1621 there was a truce in the war between Spain and the Dutch Republic. Hostilities were renewed in the 1620s when the two countries were on opposite sides in the 30 years struggle between protestant and catholic states in Germany. Spanish forces attacked the Netherlands from Germany, but after the 1630s were never again a serious threat to the Dutch. Spanish sovereignty in Belgium continued until 1714, when it was transferred to Austria, after the war of Spanish succession.

29. The seven provinces of the Netherlands emerged as an independent state with the formation of the Union of Utrecht in 1579, formally rejecting Spanish sovereignty in 1581. The new state was not quite a republic or a monarchy. It incorporated "generality" lands in northern Brabant including Breda, Bergen op Zoom and Maastricht. They were not treated as provinces, partly because the house of Orange enjoyed extensive

seigneurial rights in Breda. William, Prince of Orange, Count of Nassau (1533–84) played a major part in the creation of the new state. He was the wealthiest of the Burgundian–Habsburg nobility, with extensive properties around Breda, in Germany and Provence. He was educated as a catholic in Brussels, served with distinction in the Spanish army against France, enjoyed high standing with the Emperor Charles V for whom he was governor (stadholder) of Holland and Zeeland. When he objected to the repressive policies of Philip II, his properties were seized, and a reward was offered for his assassination. He organised military and naval resistance to the Spanish forces, converted to Calvinism and was recognised as stadholder of the provinces of Holland, Zeeland, Friesland and Utrecht in the new state. He was assassinated in 1584. Thereafter the House of Orange played a leading, but not continuous role as stadholders, and eventually in 1814 became hereditary monarchs of the Kingdom of the Netherlands. Their lands in Orange were seized by Louis XIV who incorporated them into France in 1685. The most prominent members of the house were Count Maurice (who had a leading role as a soldier defending the Republic from 1584 to 1625) and William, Prince of Orange, who was stadholder from 1672 and King of England from 1688 to his death in 1702. The British Ambassador to the Hague, Sir William Temple (1693, p. 133), described the situation in 1670s as follows: "the states general represented the Sovereignty, so did the Prince of Orange the Dignity, of this State, by Public Guards and Attendance of all Military Officers — by the Splendor of his Court, and the Magnificence of his Expence, supported not only by the Pensions and Rights of his several Charges and Commands, but by a mighty Patrimonial Revenue in Lands and Sovereign Principalities, and Lordships, as well in France, Germany, as in several parts of the Seventeen Provinces."

30. See Walter and Schofield (1989), p. 42: "Increased demand for non–cereal foodstuffs and non–agricultural products promoted mixed farming and a diversification of occupations in the countryside, leading to a better balance between cereal growing and animal husbandry, and, more generally to a strengthening of market networks. In addition, the increase in both the acreage and yields of oats and barley created a more advantageous mix to mitigate the impact of harvest failure by preventing the simultaneous failure of all crops." In the same volume (p. 199), Dupaquier makes another important point: "in France there was little movement of grain, and it was difficult to compensate for the effects of a poor regional harvest, whilst in England this could be done, thanks to the strategic role played by coastal shipping."

31. See Brewer (1989), pp. 14–20.

32. See Gregory King's manuscript notebook, p. 208, reproduced in Laslett (1973).

33. See Shammas, in Brewer and Porter (1993) pp. 182 and 184.

34. See Parry (1967) pp. 210–16 on the characteristics of the "fluyt", and Dutch shipbuilding techniques.

35. See North (1968) and Harley (1988) on the pace of decline in shipping costs, and Parry (1967) p. 216–17 on developments in land transport before the railways.

36. For a much more detailed analysis of this period, see Maddison (1976) and (1995a) pp. 65–73.

37. The present analysis of the British impact on India draws heavily on Maddison (1971). See also Habib (1995) and Lal (1988).

38. The "native states" ruled by princes with the guidance of British residents had about a fifth of India's population. There were several hundred of them. The really big ones were Hyderabad, Jammu and Kashmir and Mysore. Portugal retained Goa with 0.15 per cent of India's population, and the French had an even smaller toehold.

39. In 1913, foreign banks held over three–quarters of total deposits, Indian Joint Stock Banks less than one-fourth. In the eighteenth century there had been very powerful Indian banking houses (dominated by the Jagath Seths) which handled revenue remittances and advances for the Moghul Empire, the Nawab of Bengal, the East India Company, other foreign companies, and Indian traders, and which also carried out arbitrage between Indian currency of different areas and vintages. These indigenous banking houses were largely pushed out by the British.

40. See D.H. Buchanan, *The Development of Capitalist Enterprise in India*, Cass, London, 1966, pp. 211 and 321, who gives figures of the cost of European managerial personnel. In the Tata steelworks in 1921–2 the average salary of foreign supervisory staff was 13 527 rupees a year, whereas Indian workers got 240 rupees. These foreigners cost twice as much as in the United States and were usually less efficient. Use of foreign staff often led to inappropriate design, e.g. multi–storey mills in a hot climate or use of mule instead of ring spindles.

41. See Maddison (1998a), pp. 22–3 on the strength and shortcomings of the system of governance in traditional China; and pp. 39–54 on the economic decline and external humiliation of China between 1840 and 1949.

42. See Feuerwerker (1983) pp. 128–207 on the nature of the Treaty ports and settlements in China and on the lifestyle and privileges of the foreign community.

Chapter 3

The World Economy in the Second Half of the Twentieth Century

The world economy performed better in the last half century than at any time in the past. World GDP increased six–fold from 1950 to 1998 with an average growth of 3.9 per cent a year compared with 1.6 from 1820 to 1950, and 0.3 per cent from 1500 to 1820.

Part of the acceleration went to sustain faster population growth, but real per capita income rose by 2.1 per cent a year compared with 0.9 per cent from 1820 to 1950, and 0.05 per cent from 1500 to 1820. Thus per capita growth was 42 times as fast as in the protocapitalist epoch and more than twice as fast as in the first 13 decades of our capitalist epoch.

Interrelations between the different parts of the world economy have greatly intensified. The volume of commodity trade rose faster than GDP. The ratio of exports to world GDP rose from 5.5 per cent in 1950 to 17.2 in 1998 (see Table 3–2). There was a huge increase in international travel, communications and other service transactions. These improved the international division of labour, facilitated the diffusion of ideas and technology, and transmitted high levels of demand from the advanced capitalist group to other areas of the world.

The flow of foreign investment to poorer parts of the world (Africa, Asia excluding Japan, and Latin America) rose at an impressive pace in the past half century (see Table 3–3). As a result, the stock of foreign capital rose from 4 to 22 per cent of their GDP. However, the present ratio is only two thirds of its 1914 level. Most of the huge expansion in international investment in the past half century took place within the advanced capitalist group.

There was a resurgence in international migration. Table 3–4 shows that from 1950 to 1998, West European countries absorbed more than 20 million immigrants, Western Offshoots 34 million. There has been a distinct change in Western Europe. From 1870 to 1949 there was an exodus of people seeking better opportunities elsewhere. Since 1950 the situation has been completely reversed.

Within the capitalist epoch, one can distinguish five distinct phases of development (see Table 3.1a). The "golden age", 1950–73, was by far the best in terms of growth performance. Our age, from 1973 onwards (henceforth characterised as the "neoliberal order") has been second best. The old "liberal order" 1870–1913, was third best, with marginally slower growth than our age. In the fourth best phase (1913–50), growth was obviously below potential because of two world wars and the intervening collapse of world trade, capital markets and migration. The slowest growth was registered in the initial phase of capitalist development (1820–70) when significant growth momentum was largely confined to European countries and Western Offshoots.

Although our age is second best, and international economic relationships have been intensified through continuing liberalisation, the overall momentum of growth has decelerated abruptly, and the divergence in performance in different parts of the world has been sharply disequalising. In the golden age the gap in per capita income between the poorest and the richest regions fell from 15:1 to 13:1. Since then it has risen to 19:1 (see Table 3–1b).

Table 3–1a. Growth of Per Capita GDP, Population and GDP: World and Major Regions, 1000–1998
(annual average compound growth rates)

	1000–1500	1500–1820	1820–70	1870–1913	1913–50	1950–73	1973–98
Per capita GDP							
Western Europe	0.13	0.15	0.95	1.32	0.76	4.08	1.78
Western Offshoots	0.00	0.34	1.42	1.81	1.55	2.44	1.94
Japan	0.03	0.09	0.19	1.48	0.89	8.05	2.34
Asia (excluding Japan)	0.05	0.00	−0.11	0.38	−0.02	2.92	3.54
Latin America	0.01	0.15	0.10	1.81	1.42	2.52	0.99
Eastern Europe & former USSR	0.04	0.10	0.64	1.15	1.50	3.49	−1.10
Africa	−0.01	0.01	0.12	0.64	1.02	2.07	0.01
World	0.05	0.05	0.53	1.30	0.91	2.93	1.33
Population							
Western Europe	0.16	0.26	0.69	0.77	0.42	0.70	0.32
Western Offshoots	0.07	0.43	2.87	2.07	1.25	1.55	1.02
Japan	0.14	0.22	0.21	0.95	1.31	1.15	0.61
Asia (excluding Japan)	0.09	0.29	0.15	0.55	0.92	2.19	1.86
Latin America	0.09	0.06	1.27	1.64	1.97	2.73	2.01
Eastern Europe & former USSR	0.16	0.34	0.87	1.21	0.34	1.31	0.54
Africa	0.07	0.15	0.40	0.75	1.65	2.33	2.73
World	0.10	0.27	0.40	0.80	0.93	1.92	1.66
GDP							
Western Europe	0.30	0.41	1.65	2.10	1.19	4.81	2.11
Western Offshoots	0.07	0.78	4.33	3.92	2.81	4.03	2.98
Japan	0.18	0.31	0.41	2.44	2.21	9.29	2.97
Asia (excluding Japan)	0.13	0.29	0.03	0.94	0.90	5.18	5.46
Latin America	0.09	0.21	1.37	3.48	3.43	5.33	3.02
Eastern Europe & former USSR	0.20	0.44	1.52	2.37	1.84	4.84	−0.56
Africa	0.06	0.16	0.52	1.40	2.69	4.45	2.74
World	0.15	0.32	0.93	2.11	1.85	4.91	3.01

Source: Appendices A and B.

Table 3–1b. Levels of Per Capita GDP and Interregional Spreads, 1000–1998
(1990 international dollars)

	1000	1500	1820	1870	1913	1950	1973	1998
Western Europe	400	774	1 232	1 974	3 473	4 594	11 534	17 921
Western Offshoots	400	400	1 201	2 431	5 257	9 288	16 172	26 146
Japan	425	500	669	737	1 387	1 926	11 439	20 413
Asia (excluding Japan)	450	572	575	543	640	635	1 231	2 936
Latin America	400	416	665	698	1 511	2 554	4 531	5 795
Eastern Europe & former USSR	400	483	667	917	1 501	2 601	5 729	4 354
Africa	416	400	418	444	585	852	1 365	1 368
World	435	565	667	867	1 510	2 114	4 104	5 709
Interregional Spreads	1.1:1	2:1	3:1	5:1	9:1	15:1	13:1	19:1

Table 3–1c. **Shares of World GDP, 1000–1998**
(per cent)

	1000	1500	1820	1870	1913	1950	1973	1998
Western Europe	8.7	17.9	23.6	33.6	33.5	26.3	25.7	20.6
Western Offshoots	0.7	0.5	1.9	10.2	21.7	30.6	25.3	25.1
Japan	2.7	3.1	3.0	2.3	2.6	3.0	7.7	7.7
Asia (excluding Japan)	67.6	62.1	56.2	36.0	21.9	15.5	16.4	29.5
Latin America	3.9	2.9	2.0	2.5	4.5	7.9	8.7	8.7
Eastern Europe & former USSR	4.6	5.9	8.8	11.7	13.1	13.1	12.9	5.3
Africa	11.8	7.4	4.5	3.7	2.7	3.6	3.3	3.1
World	100.0	100.0	100.0	100.0	100.0	100.0	100.0	100.0

Source: Appendices A and B.

Table 3–2a. **Growth in Volume of Merchandise Exports, World and Major Regions, 1870–1998**
(annual average compound growth rates)

	1870–1913	1913–50	1950–73	1973–98
Western Europe	3.24	−0.14	8.38	4.79
Western Offshoots	4.71	2.27	6.26	5.92
Eastern Europe & former USSR	3.37	1.43	9.81	2.52
Latin America	3.29	2.29	4.28	6.03
Asia	2.79	1.64	9.97	5.95
Africa	4.37	1.90	5.34	1.87
World	3.40	0.90	7.88	5.07

Table 3–2b. **Merchandise Exports as Per Cent of GDP in 1990 Prices, World and Major Regions, 1870–1998**

	1870	1913	1950	1973	1998
Western Europe	8.8	14.1	8.7	18.7	35.8
Western Offshoots	3.3	4.7	3.8	6.3	12.7
Eastern Europe & former USSR	1.6	2.5	2.1	6.2	13.2
Latin America	9.7	9.0	6.0	4.7	9.7
Asia	1.7	3.4	4.2	9.6	12.6
Africa	5.8	20.0	15.1	18.4	14.8
World	4.6	7.9	5.5	10.5	17.2

Table 3–2c. **Regional Percentage Shares of World Exports, 1870–1998**

	1870	1913	1950	1973	1998
Western Europe	64.4	60.2	41.1	45.8	42.8
Western Offshoots	7.5	12.9	21.3	15.0	18.4
Eastern Europe & former USSR	4.2	4.1	5.0	7.5	4.1
Latin America	5.4	5.1	8.5	3.9	4.9
Asia	13.9	10.8	14.1	22.0	27.1
Africa	4.6	6.9	10.0	5.8	2.7
World	100.0	100.0	100.0	100.0	100.0

Source: Tables 3–2a and 3–2c are derived from Table F–3. In Table 3–2b, exports in 1990 US dollars from Table F–3 are divided by GDP in 1990 international dollars.

Table 3–3. **Gross Value of Foreign Capital Stock in Developing Countries, 1870–1998**
($ billion at year end and per cent)

	1870	1914	1950	1973	1998
Total in Current Prices	4.1	19.2	11.9	172.0	3 590.2
Total in 1990 Prices	40.1	235.4	63.2	495.2	3 030.7
Stock as per cent of developing country GDP	8.6	32.4	4.4	10.9	21.7

Source: The figures refer to the total for Africa, Asia (except Japan) and Latin America. 1870–1973 stock in current prices from sources cited in Maddison (1989a) p. 30. 1998 stock of foreign direct investment from UNCTAD, *World Investment Report,* Annex B; 1998 debt from World Bank, *Global Development Finance, Country Tables,* 1999; 1998 portfolio equity investment assumed to be $200 billion (derived by cumulating 1988–98 equity flows as shown in World Bank, *op. cit.*). Deflator is the US consumer price index, 1870–1980 from Maddison (1991a), Table E–2, updated from OECD, *Economic Outlook,* December 1999, p. 210. Denominator for third row is GDP in 1990 international dollars from Appendix A. The denominator for 1914 is 1913 GDP — 1914 not being available.

Table 3–4. **Net Migration: Western Europe, Japan and Western Offshoots, 1870–1998**
(000, negative sign means outflow)

	1870–1913	1914–49	1950–73	1974–98
France	890	−236	3 630	1 026
Germany	−2 598	−304[a]	7 070	5 911
Italy	−4 459	−1 771	−2 139	1 617
United Kingdom	−6 415	−1 405[b]	−605	737
Other[c]	−1 414	54	1 425	1 607
Total Western Europe	−13 996	−3 662	9 381	10 898
Japan	n.a.	197	−72	−179
Australia	885	673	2 033	2 151
New Zealand	290	138	247	87
Canada	861	207	2 126	2 680
United States	15 820	6 221	8 257	16 721
Total Western Offshoots	17 856	7 239	12 663	21 639

a) 1922–39; b) excludes 1939–45; c) Includes Belgium, Netherlands, Norway, Sweden and Switzerland.

Source: 1870–1973 generally from Maddison (1991a), p. 240; Australia 1870–73 from Vamplew (1987) pp. 4–7; New Zealand 1870–1973 from Hawke (1985) pp. 11–12; Canada 1870–1950 from Firestone (1958). 1974–98 from OECD, *Labour Force Statistics, 1978–1998.*

Table 3.5 compares the experience of different parts of the world economy in the three most successful phases of capitalist development. Performance in 1973–98 is compared with that of the golden age, and the "liberal order" (1870–1913).

Panel A shows the performance of 49 economies which produce more than threequarters of world GDP, and contain two thirds of world population. The advanced capitalist countries (Western Europe, Western Offshoots and Japan) together produce over half of world GDP. In this group, per capita growth in 1973–98 fell well below that in the golden age, but was appreciably better than in 1870–1913. The second part of Panel A shows the experience of "Resurgent Asia" — 15 countries which produce a quarter of world GDP and have half the world's population. The success of these countries has been extraordinary. Their per capita growth was faster after 1973 than in the golden age, and more than ten times as fast as in the old liberal order. They have achieved significant catch–up on the lead countries, and are replicating (in various degrees of intensity) the big leap forward achieved by Japan in the golden age.

Table 3–5. **Per Capita GDP Performance in the Three Most Successful Phases of the Capitalist Epoch**

	1950–73 (golden age)	1973–98 (neo–liberal order)	1870–1913 (liberal order)	1998 World GDP	1998 World Population
	Annual average compound growth rate of per capita GDP			Per cent share	
Panel A					
Western Europe	4.08	1.78	1.32	20.6	6.6
Western Offshoots	2.44	1.94	1.81	25.1	5.5
Japan	8.05	2.34	1.48	7.7	2.1
Total Advanced Capitalist	3.72	1.98	1.56	53.4	14.2
Resurgent Asia	2.61	4.18	0.38	25.2	50.9
Advanced Capitalist & Resurgent Asia (49)	2.93	1.91	1.36	78.6	65.1
Panel B					
40 Other Asia	4.09	0.59	0.48	4.3	6.5
44 Latin America	2.52	0.99	1.79	8.7	8.6
27 Eastern Europe & former USSR	3.49	−1.10	1.15	5.4	6.9
57 Africa	2.07	0.01	0.64	3.1	12.9
Faltering Economies (168)	2.94	−0.21	1.16	21.4	34.9
World	2.93	1.33	1.30	100.0	100.0

Source: Appendix A. The five phases of the capitalist epoch are the three indicated above, 1820–70, when world per capita growth was 0.53 per cent per annum and 1913–50 when it was 0.91.

If the world consisted only of the two groups of countries in Panel A, the pattern of world development could be interpreted as a clear demonstration of the possibilities for conditional convergence suggested by neo–classic growth theory. This supposes that countries with low incomes have "opportunities of backwardness", and should be able to attain faster growth than more prosperous economies operating much nearer to the technological frontier. This potential can only be realised if such countries are successful in mobilising and allocating resources efficiently, improving their human and physical capital to assimilate and adapt appropriate technology. Resurgent Asia has seized these opportunities. The countries of Panel B have not. Their relative position has deteriorated sharply since 1973.

Panel B shows the experience of "Faltering Economies". Collectively they produce about a fifth of world GDP and have about a third of world population. In all these regions, deterioration in performance since the golden age has been alarming. In the successor states of the former USSR, it has been catastrophic. The aggregate per capita income of Panel B countries actually declined by 0.21 per cent a year in the last quarter century. In the golden age, their aggregate per capita performance was identical with that of the countries in Panel A. In 1870–1913 their aggregate performance was not much below that of Panel A countries.

Before going into a detailed analysis of developments since 1973, one should note four major shocks which interrupted the momentum of growth and impacted unevenly in different parts of the world at different times. The first shock was a threefold challenge to the advanced capitalist group in the early 1970s (greatly accelerated inflation, the collapse of the Bretton Woods international monetary

Table 3–6. **Economic Characteristics of the 20 Biggest Countries, 1998**

	GDP in billion1990 PP dollars	Per capita GDP in 1990 PP dollars	Population million	Per cent of World GDP	Per cent of World Population
United States	7 394.6	27 331	270.6	21.9	4.6
China	3 873.4	3 117	1 242.7	11.5	21.0
Japan	2 581.6	20 410	126.5	7.7	2.1
India	1 702.7	1 746	975.0	5.0	16.5
Germany	1 460.1	17 799	82.0	4.3	1.4
France	1 150.1	19 558	58.8	3.4	1.0
United Kingdom	1 108.6	18 714	59.2	3.3	1.0
Italy	1 022.8	17 759	57.6	3.0	1.0
Brazil	926.9	5 459	169.8	2.7	2.9
Russia	664.5	4 523	146.9	2.0	2.5
Mexico	655.9	6 655	98.6	1.9	1.7
Indonesia	627.5	3 070	204.4	1.9	3.5
Canada	622.9	20 559	30.3	1.8	0.5
South Korea	564.2	12 152	46.4	1.7	0.8
Spain	560.1	14 227	39.4	1.7	0.7
Turkey	423.0	6 552	64.6	1.3	1.1
Australia	382.3	20 390	18.8	1.1	0.3
Thailand	372.5	6 205	60.0	1.1	1.0
Argentina	334.3	9 219	36.3	1.0	0.6
Taiwan	327.0	15 012	21.8	1.0	0.4
Total Top 20	26 755.0	7 023	3 809.7	79.3	64.5
World	33 725.6	5 709	5 907.7	100.0	100.0

Note: 1990 PP dollars are estimated by converting national currencies by purchasing power parities instead of exchange rates. The purchasing power parity estimates were derived mainly from the ICP (International Comparisons Programme) of OECD, Eurostat and the United Nations; see introduction to Appendix A for a detailed explanation.

order, and OPEC action to raise oil prices). The second was the debt crisis which hit Latin America in the early 1980s. A third was the collapse of Japanese asset prices around 1990 which had an extraordinarily deflationary effect on what was formerly the world's most dynamic economy. The fourth was the disintegration of the USSR in 1991. It involved collapse of Soviet control over the East European countries, dismantlement of COMECOM trade arrangements and the Warsaw Pact, and division of the USSR into 15 successor states.

Although these shocks had a profound influence, the liberal international order proved remarkably robust. There was no collapse of world trade or capital markets, and although there were a number of minor wars, the potentially lethal implications for global conflict inherent in the old cold–war standoff were substantially mitigated.

Developments within the fifth phase of capitalist development have been more complex in causality, have differed more between regions, and have been less synchronous than in the golden age. It is therefore necessary to examine the experience of each region separately.

I
ADVANCED CAPITALIST COUNTRIES

Western Europe

From 1973 to 1998, West European GDP grew at 2.1 per cent a year compared with 4.8 in the golden age. The deceleration had three components: a) a slowdown in population growth from 0.7 to 0.3 per cent a year, due to a significant and general fall in birth rates; b) very large rises in unemployment and other dimensions of labour slack; c) deceleration in labour productivity which grew at 2.3 per cent a year compared with 4.8 per cent in the golden age.

It was inevitable that West European productivity growth would decelerate. In 1950–73, once–for–all opportunities for catch–up on the United States were available and were seized, and the rate of technical progress in the lead country (the United States) was then much faster than it has been since 1973. In fact the catch–up process continued after 1973. The average productivity level in Western Europe rose from two thirds of the American level in 1973 to more than four fifths in 1998. However, per capita income in most Western European countries rose more slowly than in the United States because of slack in their labour markets (see Table 3–7).

The most disturbing aspect of West European performance since 1973 has been the staggering rise in unemployment. In 1994–8 the average level was nearly 11 per cent of the labour force (see Table 3–8). This is higher than in the depressed years of the 1930s, and four times the level in the golden age. Unemployment on this scale would have created a major depression if the unemployed had not received substantial income support from social security. The major reason for this rise was a change in macropolicy objectives. Initially, this was dictated by events but its continuance reflected a basic ideological shift.

The "establishment view" of economic policy objectives in the golden age was characterised by Erik Lundberg (1968, p. 37) as follows: "In the postwar period, the achievement of full employment and rapid economic growth have become a primary concern of national governments. Such policy targets did not ... guide government activities during most of the interwar period ... instead there were various policy aims that today would largely be considered as either intermediate, secondary, irrelevant or irrational targets, such as the restoration or preservation of a specific exchange rate, the annual balancing of the government budget, and the stability of the price level at a prevailing or previously reached niveau".

In the course of the 1970s, the objectives of full employment and rapid economic growth were jettisoned, and the major emphasis switched to achieving price stability. Initially, the change had considerable conjunctural validity. After the collapse of the Bretton Woods fixed exchange rate system, policymakers felt disoriented without a monetary anchor. This happened at a time of increased inflationary pressure, and expectations of accelerating inflation were greatly augmented by the first OPEC shock. It was felt that accommodation of inflation beyond a certain point would lead to hyperinflation, and that this would threaten the whole socio–political order. This was the razor's edge theorem. Income policies had been discredited so disinflation seemed the only option.

The change in the attitudes of policymakers was reinforced by changes in academic fashion. The Keynesians were pushed to the periphery, and lost their influence on policy. Politicians sought intellectual sustenance elsewhere. Friedman, Hayek and the neo–Austrians regarded unemployment as a useful corrective. The rational expectations school denied the usefulness of discretionary policy action. They argued that if simple rules were followed long enough, the economy would be self regulating. Responsibility for economic policy action should move from ministers of finance to central bankers. As far as possible, the latter should operate free from political pressure.

Table 3–7. **Western Europe and United States: Degree of Productivity and Per Capita GDP Convergence 1950–98**

	GDP per capita		GDP per hour worked	
	(annual average compound growth)			
	1950–73	1973–98	1959–73	1973–98
France	4.1	1.6	5.0	2.5
Germany	5.0	1.6	5.9	2.4
Italy	5.0	2.1	5.8	2.3
United Kingdom	2.4	1.8	3.1	2.2
12 West Europe	3.9	1.8	4.8	2.3
Ireland	3.0	4.0	4.3	4.1
Spain	5.8	2.0	6.4	2.9
United States	2.5	2.0	2.8	1.5

	Level of GDP per capita			Level of GDP per hour worked		
			US = 100			
	1950	1973	1998	1950	1973	1998
France	55	79	72	46	76	98
Germany	41	72	65	32	62	77
Italy	37	64	65	35	67	81
United Kingdom	72	73	68	63	67	79
12 West Europe	52	73	72	44	68	83
Ireland	36	41	67	29	41	78
Spain	25	52	52	21	46	64

	Employment as per cent of population			Hours worked per head of population		
	1950	1973	1998	1950	1973	1998
France	47.0	41.1	38.6	905	728	580
Germany	42.0	44.9	44.0	974	811	670
Italy	40.1	41.5	42.3	800	669	637
United Kingdom	44.5	44.6	45.8	871	753	682
12 West Europe	43.4	43.3	43.5	904	750	657
Ireland	41.1	34.7	40.6	925	698	672
Spain	41.8	37.4	34.0	921	805	648
United States	40.5	41.0	49.1	756	704	791

Source: Appendices A and E.

By 1983, deflationary policies had been quite successful, and the power of OPEC was greatly reduced. In 1973–83 inflation in Western Europe averaged 11.2 per cent a year, in 1983–93, it was 4.5 per cent. By 1993–8 it had fallen to 2.2 — about half the rate in the golden age (see Table 3–8).

The persistence of deflationary policies in the 1990s in the face of high unemployment and low inflation was due in large measure to a new objective of policy — monetary union.

Monetary union had been advocated within the EEC by the 1970 Werner Report, but this objective was abandoned in the monetary turmoil of the early 1970s and the collapse of the "snake" system (precursor of the EMS) in 1976. The EMS was created in 1979 to establish an area of exchange stability. From 1987 to 1992 it achieved reasonable success. As a result the objective of monetary union was disinterred and put forward in the Delors Report of 1989. This reiterated the importance of policy

Figure 3-1. **Binary Confrontation of United States/Japan, United States/European Per Capita GDP Levels, 1950-98**

(1990 Geary-Khamis dollars)

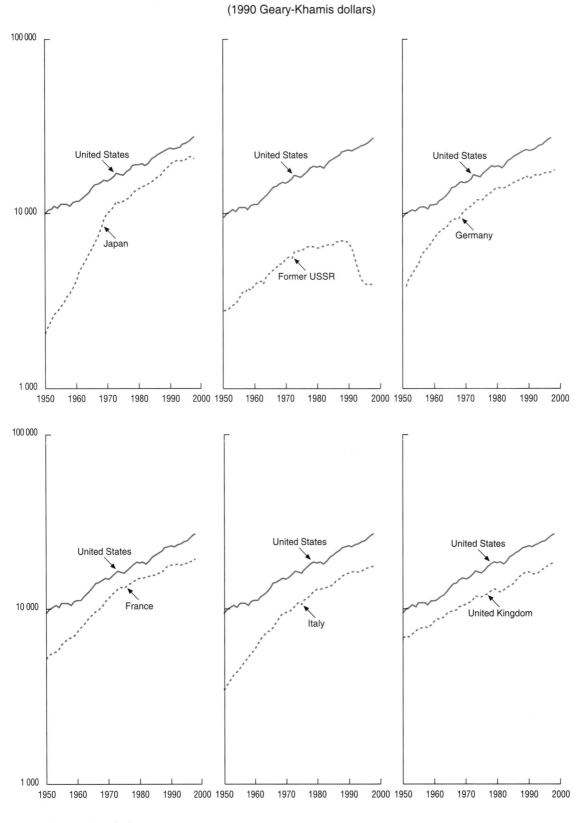

Source: Appendix C.

Table 3–8. **Experience of Unemployment and Inflation in Advanced Capitalist Countries, 1950–98**

	Level of Unemployment (per cent of labour force)				Changes in consumer price index (annual average compound growth rate)			
	1950–73	*1974–83*	*1984–93*	*1994–98*	*1950–73*	*1973–83*	*1983–93*	*1994–98*
Belgium	3.0	8.2	8.8	9.7	2.9	8.1	3.1	1.8
Finland	1.7	4.7	6.9	14.2	5.6	10.5	4.6	1.0
France	2.0	5.7	10.0	12.1	5.0	11.2	3.7	1.5
Germany	2.5	4.1	6.2	9.0	2.7	4.9	2.4	1.7
Italy	5.5	7.2	9.3	11.9	3.9	16.7	6.4	3.5
Netherlands	2.2	7.3	7.3	5.9	4.1	6.5	1.8	2.2
Norway	1.9	2.1	4.1	4.6	4.8	9.7	5.1	2.0
Sweden	1.8	2.3	3.4	9.2	4.7	10.2	6.4	1.5
United Kingdom	2.8	7.0	9.7	8.0	4.6	13.5	5.2	3.0
Ireland	n.a.	8.8	15.6	11.2	4.3	15.7	3.8	2.1
Spain	2.9	9.1	19.4	21.8	4.6	16.4	6.9	3.4
Western Europe Average	**2.6**	**6.0**	**9.2**	**10.7**	**4.3**	**11.2**	**4.5**	**2.2**
Australia	2.1	5.9	8.5	8.6	4.6	11.3	5.6	2.0
Canada	4.7	8.1	9.7	9.4	2.8	9.4	4.0	1.3
United States	4.6	7.4	6.7	5.3	2.7	8.2	3.8	2.4
Average	**3.8**	**7.1**	**8.3**	**7.8**	**3.4**	**9.6**	**4.5**	**1.9**
Japan	**1.6**	**2.1**	**2.3**	**3.4**	**5.2**	**7.6**	**1.7**	**0.6**

Source: Unemployment 1950–83 from Maddison (1995a), p. 84, updated from OECD, *Labour Force Statistics.* Consumer Price index 1950–83 from Maddison (1995a), updated from OECD, *Economic Outlook,* December 1999.

objectives which Lundberg had qualified as secondary or irrational in 1968. It made no mention of employment or growth objectives, nor did it give serious consideration to the institutional, social and economic costs of enforcing convergence and conformity in price, wage, monetary and fiscal behaviour. The major economic gain would be a reduction in transaction costs, improvement in economic stability, and economies of scale in a more integrated and more competitive European market. The proposal was adopted by the EC in 1991, and in the Maastricht Treaty of European Union which was ratified in 1993.

The path to monetary union was not smooth. In 1992 there was a major currency crisis. After a costly defence of their existing exchange rates, there were a number of devaluations. Italy and the United Kingdom left the EMS. In 1993 pressures on the French franc led the EMS authorities to widen the permitted fluctuation band from 2.25 to 15 per cent. Nevertheless, the determination to succeed was very strong, particularly in countries which had historically had the biggest problems of inflation and exchange rate instability and whose long term gains from monetary union seemed most promising. They were willing to prolong the period of high unemployment to fulfil the "convergence" obligations of membership — reducing inflation to what were to them very low levels, maintenance of exchange rate stability and reduction of budget deficits. These policies were successful in achieving a remarkable degree of convergence, and monetary union was inaugurated at the beginning of 1999 with all of the aspirants except Greece being accepted as members (Greece joined in 2001).

Although the intent of government policy in Western Europe was deflationary for a prolonged period, fiscal freedom was substantially constrained by welfare state commitments which are much larger than in the United States and Japan. When unemployment increased, transfer payments were triggered automatically. In many cases, particularly in France and the Netherlands, governments who considered unemployment to be caused by excess labour supply persuaded people to retire early or acquire "handicapped" status. There was also a steady build–up of pension benefits due to the ageing

Table 3-9. **Total Government Expenditure as Per Cent of GDP at Current Prices, Western Europe, the United States and Japan, 1913–1999**

	1913	*1938*	*1950*	*1973*	*1999*
France	8.9	23.2	27.6	38.8	52.4
Germany	17.7	42.4	30.4	42.0	47.6
Netherlands	8.2[a]	21.7	26.8	45.5	43.8
United Kingdom	13.3	28.8	34.2	41.5	39.7
Arithmetic Average	12.0	29.0	29.8	42.0	45.9
United States	8.0	19.8	21.4	31.1	30.1
Japan	14.2	30.3	19.8	22.9	38.1

a) 1910.

Source: 1913–73 from Maddison (1995a, p. 65); 1999 from OECD, *Economic Outlook,* December 1999, Table 28.

of the population. Budget deficits were much higher in 1974–96 than in the golden age. They fell in 1997–98 when the pressure to fulfil the convergence criteria for monetary union was at its height. The deflationary intent of government policy can be more clearly seen in the level of real interest rates. These were very much higher in the period of moderate price rises after 1982 than they were in the golden age and the years of high inflation 1974–81.

Since 1973, West European countries have given greater emphasis to use of market forces to improve efficiency of resource allocation. This was reflected in decisions to remove controls on international capital movements and privatisation of government enterprise. However, agriculture remains highly protected, regulation and tax policy are an impediment to efficient labour market functioning.

United States

American economic policy since 1973 has been much more successful than that of Western Europe and Japan in realising potential for income growth. The level of unemployment fell to less than half of that in Western Europe, whereas in 1950–73 it was usually double the European rate. Labour force participation increased, with employment expanding from 41 per cent of the population in 1973 to 49 per cent in 1998, compared with an average European rise from 42 to 44 per cent (see Table 3–7). Working hours per person rose whereas they fell in Western Europe. High levels of activity were achieved with a rate of inflation which was generally more modest than in Western Europe.

US policymakers have been less inhibited in operating at high levels of demand than their European counterparts. Having the world's major reserve currency, and long used to freedom of international capital movements, they generally treated exchange rate fluctuations with benign neglect. The Reagan administration made major tax cuts, and carried out significant measures of deregulation in the expectation that they would provoke a positive supply response that would outweigh potential inflationary consequences. The US operated with more flexible labour markets. Its capital market was better equipped to supply venture funds to innovators. Its economy was as big as Western Europe but much more closely integrated. Demand buoyancy was sustained by a stock market boom in the 1990s.

The United States was a major gainer from the globalisation of international capital markets. In the postwar period until 1988, US foreign assets always exceeded liabilities, but thereafter its net foreign asset position moved from around zero to minus $1.5 trillion (more than 20 per cent of GDP). Thus the rest of the world helped to sustain the long American boom and financed the large US payments deficit (see Table 3–10).

On the other hand there was a very large rise in US imports which helped to sustain world demand. From 1973 to 1998 import volume rose faster than in Western Europe and Japan. Imports grew at a rate not much less than in 1950–73, whereas in most of Western Europe and Japan there was a substantial deceleration (see Table 3–11). The rise in US imports reflected the strength of demand, and the impact of successive tariff reductions under GATT and WTO auspices, as well as regional arrangements such as the North American Free Trade Area (NAFTA).

In spite of American success in maintaining high levels of demand and activity, economic growth has been slower since 1973 than in 1950–73. The main reason was a sharp deceleration in productivity growth. In 1950–73 labour productivity rose by 2.8 per cent a year. From 1973 to 1998, this fell to 1.5 per cent, which is slower than for any sustained period since 1870. Between 1913 and 1973, US total factor productivity growth (the response of output to the combined inputs of labour and capital) averaged 1.6 to 1.7 per cent a year. From 1973 to 1998 it grew at about a third of this pace.

The productivity slowdown was masked by the improvement in use of potential, but has very serious implications for future growth if it continues, because it cannot continue to be offset by further improvements in the level of demand. The American slowdown probably contributed to slower productivity growth in other advanced capitalist countries which operate at levels of technology nearest to those in the United States. In the long run its impact would trickle down to poorer countries which operate at lower levels of technology.

Many participants in the "new economy" (information technology and associated activities) find the notion of decelerating technical progress unacceptable. It has accelerated dramatically in computer and communications technology and they assume that there have been big spillover effects in the rest of the economy. They justify their position by anecdotal or microeconomic evidence for their favourite sector, and point to the huge increase in share prices on the Nasdaq stock market (which specialises in the "new" economy). However the impact of this technological "revolution" has not been apparent in the macroeconomic statistics until very recently. Nasdaq gives high valuations for many enterprises which have low or no profits, and fell nearly 50 per cent from its peak in the second half of 2000.

New economy pundits argued that the national accounts statistics mismeasured growth. There was some truth in this because the traditional US growth estimates relied on fixed weights for a recent year to measure growth over a period of more than six decades. This did understate US growth compared with the weighting systems in vogue in Western Europe.

In 1993, the traditional approach to GDP measurement was modified by presentation of two new alternative measures: a) one where the weights changed every five years (a procedure then used in most EU countries), and b) a chain index with weights changing every year (a procedure then officially adopted only in the Netherlands). The 5 year segmented index showed the fastest growth (0.28 per cent a year more than the traditional measure and 0.04 per cent faster than the chained index). In Maddison (1995a) I used the 5 year segmented index as far as was then available (back to 1959).

Since then, US national accounts statistics have been further modified in ways which show faster growth and a higher level of GDP. With the new measures, one still finds a marked productivity slowdown from 1973 to 1995, but for 1995–8 there has been an acceleration to rates not far below the golden age. For 1973–95 labour productivity grew at 1.4 per cent, and in 1995–8 at 2.5 per cent. This recent acceleration is largely attributable to the increased weight of the "new" economy. Box 3–1 provides a detailed analysis of these changes in US statistical procedure and their impact. It also demonstrates that they do, in some degree, exaggerate US growth and levels of performance compared with the more conservative approach in measuring the impact of the new economy in European countries and Japan.

Recently, Jorgenson and Stiroh (2000) made an authoritative survey of US growth performance over the past four decades, using the revised GDP estimates. They found that accelerated technological change in computers and communications had its main impact in the production of these goods.

Table 3–10. **Stock of Foreign Assets and Liabilities, the United States, Japan, Germany and the United Kingdom, 1989–98**
($ billion at current exchange rates)

	Assets	*Liabilities*	*Net assets*	*Assets*	*Liabilities*	*Net assets*
	United States			Japan		
1989	2 348	2 397	−49	1 771	1 477	294
1990	2 291	2 459	−168	1 858	1 529	329
1991	2 468	2 731	−263	2 007	1 622	385
1992	2 464	2 919	−455	2 035	1 520	515
1993	3 055	3 237	−182	2 181	1 569	612
1994	3 276	3 450	−174	2 424	1 734	690
1995	3 869	4 292	−423	2 633	1 815	818
1996	4 545	5 092	−547	2 653	1 762	891
1997	5 289	6 355	−1 066	2 737	1 779	958
1998	5 948	7 485	−1 537	2 986	1 833	1 153
	Germany			United Kingdom		
1989	864	595	269	1 514	1 432	82
1990	1 100	751	349	1 728	1 744	−16
1991	1 146	818	328	1 756	1 750	6
1992	1 175	881	294	1 731	1 697	34
1993	1 285	1 080	205	2 001	1 948	53
1994	1 432	1 237	195	2 090	2 096	35
1995	1 656	1 537	119	2 386	2 394	−8
1996	1 691	1 612	79	2 775	2 778	−3
1997	1 759	1 695	64	3 212	3 348	−14
1998				3 521	3 695	−17

Source: IMF, *International Financial Statistics.*

Table 3–11. **Growth in Volume of Merchandise Imports and Ratio of Imports to GDP, Western Europe, Japan and the United States, 1950–98**

	Growth of import volume (annual compound rate)		*Imports as ratio to GDP at 1990 prices*		
	1950–73	*1973–98*	*1950*	*1973*	*1998*
France	9.3	4.6	6.1	15.2	27.7
Germany	12.6	4.7	4.1	17.6	36.1
Italy	11.3	4.0	4.9	16.3	24.9
United Kingdom	4.8	4.0	11.4	17.2	28.2
Japan	16.0	4.0	2.5	9.7	12.4
Arithmetic Average	10.8	4.3	5.8	15.2	25.9
United States	6.6	5.6	3.9	6.9	13.0

Box 3–1. **Impact of Recent Revisions on Measurement of Level and Growth of US GDP, 1929–98**
(million 1990 dollars)

	Maddison1995a updated	BEA (1998)	BEA (1999)	BEA (2000)
1929	844 324	740 311		711 309
1950	1 457 624	1 508 235	(1 455 916)	1 459 127
1959	1 981 830	2 068 828	1 997 061	2 006 235
1973	3 519 224	3 665 799	3 536 622	3 567 274
1990	5 464 795	5 743 800	5 803 200	5 803 200
1991	5 410 089	5 690 540	5 790 784	5 775 948
1992	5 562 302	5 844 986	5 983 457	5 952 089
1993	5 697 296	5 980 898	6 124 987	6 110 061
1994	5 907 953	6 187 856	6 371 321	6 356 710
1995	6 059 772	6 329 197	6 544 370	6 526 361
1996	6 276 136	6 547 387	6 784 105	6 759 427
1997	6 522 904	6 804 797	7 089 655	7 046 304
1998	6 777 297		7 394 598	7 349 878
1999				7 654 836

a) 1950–59 movement from BEA (1998).

Source: Col. 1 1913–90 from Maddison (1995a), updated 1990–7 from OECD *National Accounts 1960–97,* Paris 1999, 1997–8 from OECD, *Economic Outlook,* June 1999. Col. 2 1929–97 from *Survey of Current Business,* August 1998. Col. 3 from Seskin, *Survey of Current Business,* December 1999. Col. 4 from BEA internet web site June 2000. To facilitate comparison, I have converted BEA (1998) estimates from 1992 to 1990 dollars, BEA (1999 and 2000) from 1996 to 1990 dollars. Until the 1990s, the Bureau of Economic Analysis (BEA) published real GDP estimates back to 1929 with a single set of weights for the whole period. In 1993 it published three alternative estimates back to 1959: a) with old style fixed weights; b) a chain procedure where weights changed every year; c) a segmented index with weights changed every five years. In Maddison (1995a) I used the third procedure for reasons of international comparability (it was then standard practice for EU countries). In column 1, I used the 5 year segmented weights for 1959–90; it showed growth 0.28 per cent faster than the fixed weights and 0.04 per cent faster than the chain weights. BEA 1998 (col. 2) did not provide alternatives but switched completely to chain weights back to 1929. BEA (1999) made further changes for 1959–98 (including treatment of computer software as investment). BEA (2000) carried the new estimates back to 1929.

Impact of Recent Revisions on United States GDP Growth Rate
(annual average compound rate)

	Maddison1995a	BEA (1998)	BEA (1999)	BEA (2000)
1929–50	2.63	3.45	n.a.	3.48
1950–73	3.91	3.93	3.93[a]	3.96
1973–98	2.66	2.67[b]	2.96	2.90

a) 1950–59 movement from BEA (1998); b) 1997–98 from BEA (1999).

The impact of the revisions on growth rates is shown in the above table. For 1950–73, the new measures show little difference from those I used in Maddison (1995a). For 1973–98, BEA (1999), which I used in preparing the present study, shows growth about 0.3 percentage points higher than the old measure. However, the revisions for 1929–50 are much bigger. Their acceptance involves a major reinterpretation of American economic history. They imply a GDP level in 1929 16 per cent below the old index and would lower the level for earlier years correspondingly if used as a link. The 1913–50 growth of labour productivity would rise from 2.5 to 3 per cent a year and the 1913 level of labour productivity would be below that in the United Kingdom. The new BEA estimates also change the picture of the war and immediate postwar economy. It seems hazardous to use the new measures for 1929–50 without further investigation of the reasons why their impact is so big. One must also remember that no other country uses the chain index technique or hedonic price indices for such a long period in the past.

Many West European countries have also made recent changes in methods of measuring macroeconomic growth. In particular, most of them have adopted the new SNA recommendations which involve treatment of computer software as investment. However these changes have generally been less far–reaching and have had a smaller impact on growth rates than in the United States. Most other OECD countries have not adopted chain weights and of those which have, only Australia, France and Norway have carried them back very far (France and Netherlands to 1978, Australia to 1960). Most other countries do not use hedonic price deflators (which make a quality adjustment for changing product characteristics). Hedonic price indices are not used in Belgium, Finland, Germany, Greece, Italy, Japan, Spain or the United Kingdom. Wyckoff (1995) contrasted the 13 per cent a year decline in the US price index for computers and office machinery from 1976 to 1993 with the 2 per cent a year fall in Germany for the same period for this category of goods. Most of the difference appears to have been due to the technique of index number construction.

Productivity has continued to lag in the computer–using sectors. They state that "there is no evidence of spillovers from production of information technology to other industries — the empirical record provides little support for the 'new economy' picture of spillovers cascading from information technology producers on to users of this technology."

Oliner and Sichel (2000) reach more or less the same conclusion, as does Robert Gordon (2000), i.e. there has been a belated but positive payoff in macroeconomic productivity from a couple of decades of high investment in the "new economy".

The fact that there have been no very evident spillovers as yet in computer–using industries may well be due to the costs of absorbing new technologies which have involved a large input of highly trained people, rapid obsolescence of equipment and skills, and some serious blunders, such as those connected with the very costly Y2K scare. In the longer run, when the new technology has been fully assimilated, significant spillovers to other sectors of the economy may well occur.

It is too early to judge whether recent productivity improvements portend a return to the pace the US achieved from 1913 to 1973, but there are grounds for hoping that progress may be faster than in 1973–95.

Other Western Offshoots

Australia has been the most buoyant of the other Western Offshoots. It enjoyed favourable results from substantial reduction of trade barriers, increased competition, and its proximity to the fast growing Asian countries. The growth record was much less favourable in Canada and New Zealand.

Japan

During the golden age, the pace of Japanese growth was much faster than in Western Europe. Per capita income increased sixfold from 1950 to 1973, growing at 8 per cent a year compared with 4 per cent in Western Europe. Labour productivity grew by 7.7 per cent a year, compared with 4.8 in Western Europe, total factor productivity at 5.1 per cent a year compared with 2.9 per cent.

Japan did better than Western Europe for several reasons: a) its per capita income and productivity level in 1950 were little more than a third of the European level, so it had greater scope for exploiting opportunities of backwardness; b) the Japanese labour force already had an educational level not very different from the West European norm in 1950, and a huge reserve of technical skills acquired in military service which were fully available for peaceful pursuits; c) Japanese rates of investment were higher than in Western Europe; d) labour input per head of population was higher.

A major reason for Japan's capacity to mount such a large scale investment effort was the very high propensity to save in Japanese households. Horioka (1990) points to a number of complex reasons for this. They include traditional frugality which led to maintenance of modest lifestyles as income rose. Japanese had a high risk aversion and saved as a safeguard against illness and unforeseen risks. The smaller importance of social security than in Europe led to bigger private provision for old age. The significant role of remuneration in the form of twice–yearly lump–sum bonuses and relative scarcity of consumer credit were also contributory factors.

The Japanese catch–up effort was bolstered in unusual degree by government policy. Dedication to this goal was deeply rooted. In the seventeenth and eighteenth centuries, the Tokugawa regime sought successfully to catch up with and overtake Chinese levels of income. From 1868 onwards the objective was to catch up with the West.

In the postwar period, the developmentalist objective was pursued by a comprehensive interactive network of interest groups. There were close solidaristic links between Japan's highly educated bureaucratic elite, politicians of the Liberal Democratic party (in power with one brief interruption since 1955), big business and the banking system. Japan's large corporate groups (*keiretsu*) and banks had close interlocking financial ties. Large corporations often had long–standing symbiotic links with smaller firms. Japanese trade unions were organised on a company basis, workers had long–term job security, and identified their interests with those of their employers. The most successful members of the bureaucratic elite frequently moved into political office or careers of business leadership. MITI (the Ministry of Trade and Industry) provided "administrative guidance" to firms and banks which influenced the allocation of resources to what were considered key industries in terms of growth opportunities or export markets. The consensual character of all these relationships is reflected in the negligible importance of litigation or lawyers.

In the Tokugawa period, foreign trade was tightly controlled in a policy of seclusion (*sakoku*), designed to prevent foreign interference in Japan. In the postwar period trade was more open but the old autarkic emphasis remained. The government played a key role in promoting technological development, and assimilation of foreign technology, using techniques which preserved national independence. Foreign investment in Japan was very limited, and still is. Weak sectors, and some strong ones, were protected by a variety of restrictions on imports.

Although this version of capitalism was highly effective in producing rapid growth and high levels of per capita product it was more costly than it might have been with greater use of market forces, greater representation of consumer interests, and greater openness to foreign trade. By the early 1990s Japan had a capital stock per worker nearly a quarter higher than in Western Europe, but its productivity was substantially lower. Workers and "salarymen" worked very long hours and had little time for holidays. There was much greater unevenness of performance in different sectors than is normal for advanced capitalist countries — with very low productivity in agriculture and distribution, and a world leadership position in autos, steel, machine tools and consumer electronics.

In Japan, as in Western Europe, it was inevitable that the rate of growth would decline after 1973, and likely that the slowdown would be sharper, given the greater success in the golden age. The slowdown was indeed sharp, though per capita GDP and productivity grew faster in Japan than in Western Europe from 1973 to 1990. Thereafter things deteriorated badly. Per capita product rose only 1 per cent a year in 1990–98. Japan was clearly working below potential.

High Japanese investment rates continued in the 1970s and 1980s, and high expectations led to a boom in asset prices. But as the growth potential weakened there were diminishing returns and falling profits. This contributed to a collapse in share prices in 1989–92 from which Japan has not recovered. The Nikkei share price index in 1999 was at half its 1989 level compared with a fourfold rise in the United States, and a two–and–a–half–fold increase in Western Europe.

The stock price collapse was compounded by a fall in the price of residential land by a third from 1990 to 1998. This was proportionately more important than the stock market collapse. Household net worth of all kinds in Japan was 8.5 times as high as disposable income in 1990 and fell to 6.5 in 1998. In the same period the US ratio rose from 4.8 to 5.9, the German from 5.2 to 5.4, the French from 4.2 to 5.2.

The collapse in Japanese profits and asset values created a very deflationary situation. Consumers became extremely cautious in their spending. Many businesses became insolvent or bankrupt and banks found themselves with massive non–performing assets. This restricted their willingness and ability to extend new credits. The rate of price increase fell to 0.6 per cent a year in 1994–98.

Table 3–12. **Indices of Share Prices in National Currencies, Japan, the United States and Western Europe, 1950–99**
(1989 = 100)

	Japan	United States	France	Germany	Italy	United Kingdom
1950	4.4	5.2	2.4	3.6	3.5	3.1
1973	14.1	32.6	19.8	33.5	15.0	15.2
1989	100.0	100.0	100.0	100.0	100.0	100.0
1992	53.1	132.6	104.6	100.8	71.0	112.6
1998	45.9	344.4	209.7	238.7	211.8	217.4
1999	54.0	435.5	260.0	247.4	238.5	

Source: IMF, *International Financial Statistics.* The figures are averages for the years specified.

Table 3–13. **Exchange Rates: Units of National Currency per US Dollar, Japan and Western Europe, 1950–99**
(annual average)

	Japan	France	Germany	Italy	United Kingdom
1950	361	3.5	4.2	625	0.36
1973	272	4.5	2.7	583	0.41
1989	138	6.4	1.9	1 372	0.61
1992	127	5.3	1.6	1 232	0.57
1998	131	5.9	1.8	1 736	0.60
1999	114	6.2	1.8	1 817	0.62

Source: IMF, *International Financial Statistics.*

The government responded to this situation by a massive increase in extravagant public works rather than tax reduction. The Bank of Japan's discount rate fell nine steps from 6 per cent in 1991 to 0.5 per cent in 1995 and remained there for nearly five years. The interbank loan rate was virtually zero for two years from 1998. The government moved very slowly to clear up the mess in the financial system. It aggravated the long term problem by giving financial aid to institutions which should have been allowed to go bankrupt. Government measures prevented a major collapse in the economy, but they failed to revive demand.

The Japanese slowdown was transmitted to the rest of the world in two ways. Import growth was depressed but capital exports increased. Japan's high rate of saving continued but a larger share went to capital exports. Between 1990 and 1998 its net foreign assets rose from 10 to 30 per cent of GDP. Its impact on the world economy was a mirror image of that of the United States (see Table 3–10).

II
RESURGENT ASIA

In the half century since 1950, Asia has been the fastest growing part of the world economy, outperforming all other regions. This was in stark contrast with past experience. In the four and a half centuries from 1500 to 1950, Asia stagnated whilst all other regions progressed. In 1500 Asia accounted for 65 per cent of world GDP, and only 18.5 per cent in 1950. Since 1950, the Asian share has doubled.

In 1950–73, Japan had supergrowth, with per capita income rising over 8 per cent a year compared with the 2.6 per cent for resurgent Asia. In 1973–99 as a whole, per capita growth in resurgent Asia was twice as fast as in Japan. In the 1990s it was four times as fast.

Resurgent Asia consists of the 15 countries shown in Table 3–14. Seven of these (China, Hong Kong, Malaysia, Singapore, South Korea, Taiwan and Thailand) have been the most dynamic element in the world economy. Four now have a per capita income within the West European range. In 1999, the group had an aggregate income of 5.8 trillion international 1990 (PPP adjusted) dollars (not far below the aggregate for the 12 core countries of Western Europe, and more than double Japanese GDP of $2.6 trillion).

There are eight countries in a second group with an aggregate GDP of $3.1 trillion (more than twice as big as Germany). They have lower per capita income than the first group, and for 1950–99 as a whole their per capita growth rate was half as fast, at 2.2 per cent a year. Since 1973, their growth rate has been faster than in any part of the world outside Asia.

Table 3–15 indicates some proximate causes of Asia's growth. Within each category the countries are ranked in descending order of income level. The averages for each category are arithmetic, in contrast to the weighted averages in Table 3–14.

The supergrowth countries in the first group had high investment ratios. The combination of high investment rates and rapid GDP growth means that their physical capital stock was growing more rapidly than in other parts of the world. They also had a relatively high ratio of employment to population. This was partly due to a demographic transition with falling fertility and a rising share of population of working age, but also to the traditionally high labour mobilisation that characterises multicropping rice economies. In all cases which are documented they also had high rates of improvement in the quality of human capital (see Maddison 1995a for estimates of education levels). Equally striking was the rapid growth of exports and the high ratios of exports to GDP. This latter characteristic is in striking contrast to the Japanese model of development. Another contrast with Japan is the willingness of these countries to attract foreign direct investment as a vehicle for assimilation of foreign technology (see Table 3–16).

Countries in the second group have on average much lower income levels than the first, lower investment rates, lower ratios of labour mobilisation and less openness to international trade. To some extent, their slower growth suggests that "opportunities of backwardness" are not inversely related to income level. The ability to mount a successful process of catch–up seems to be greatest at somewhat higher levels of income.

It is difficult to draw sharp conclusions on the role of policy in the seven most successful countries, because their policy mix has been rather heterogeneous.

Three of the supergrowth countries are market oriented, open, highly competitive capitalist countries. *Hong Kong* comes closest to being completely driven by market forces, but its dynamism is also attributable to special circumstances. It was an unusually privileged entrepôt for trade and financial transactions between China and the rest of the world during the US embargo of 1952–73. It still benefits as an intermediary for trade between the Chinese mainland and Taiwan. Its low tax regime is partly attributable to the fact that the government has large revenues from monopoly ownership of

Table 3–14. **Variations in Per Capita GDP Growth Momentum: Resurgent Asia**
in Comparative Perspective, 1913–99
(annual average compound growth rates)

	1913–50	*1950–99*	*1950–73*	*1973–90*	*1990–99*
Japan	0.9	4.9	8.1	3.0	0.9
China	−0.6	4.2	2.9	4.8	6.4
Hong Kong	n.a.	4.6	5.2	5.4	1.7
Malaysia	1.5	3.2	2.2	4.2	4.0
Singapore	1.5	4.9	4.4	5.3	5.7
South Korea	−0.4	6.0	5.8	6.8	4.8
Taiwan	0.6	5.9	6.7	5.3	5.3
Thailand	−0.1	4.3	3.7	5.5	3.6
7 Country Average	**−0.4**	**4.4**	**3.4**	**5.1**	**5.8**
Bangladesh	−0.2	0.9	−0.4	1.5	3.0
Burma	−1.5	2.0	2.0	1.1	3.8
India	−0.2	2.2	1.4	2.6	3.7
Indonesia	−0.2	2.7	2.6	3.1	2.1
Nepal	n.a.	1.4	1.0	1.5	1.9
Pakistan	−0.2	2.3	1.7	3.1	2.3
Philippines	0.0	1.6	2.7	0.7	0.5
Sri Lanka	0.3	2.6	1.9	3.0	3.9
8 Country Average	**−0.3**	**2.2**	**1.7**	**2.5**	**3.0**
15 Resurgent Asia	**−0.3**	**3.4**	**2.5**	**3.9**	**4.6**
Other Asia	1.8	2.3[a]	4.1	0.4	1.1[b]
Latin America	1.4	1.7	2.5	0.7	1.4
Africa	1.0	1.0[a]	2.1	0.1	−0.2[b]
Eastern Europe & former USSR	1.5	1.1[a]	3.5	0.7	−4.8[b]
Western Europe	0.8	2.9[a]	4.1	1.9	1.4[b]
United States	**1.6**	**2.2**	**2.5**	**2.0**	**2.1**

a) 1950–98; b) 1990–98.

Source: Appendix C, updated to 1999 from ADB, *Asian Development Outlook 2000*, Manila, 2000.

undeveloped land. It has access to an enormous pool of cheap labour on its doorstep. It has benefited from very large direct investment from abroad (see Table 3–16), and has made heavy investment in China's neighbouring enterprise zones where its stock of direct investment totalled $155 billion in 1998. In this situation, laisser faire worked wonders in achieving efficient resource allocation. In 1997, sovereignty reverted to China, but the nature of economic institutions and policy were not changed.

The reasons for *Singapore's* ascension resemble those operative in Hong Kong. It is a strategically placed city state with a vocation for entrepôt trade, but its growth got a bigger push from government. Its enlightened authoritarian regime pursued a policy of promoting high savings, improvement of education, encouraging exports and the acquisition of foreign technology. It benefited even more than Hong Kong from foreign direct investment (see Table 3–16). As its own manufacturing production grew more sophisticated, and labour costs rose, it became a major capital exporter, supporting partner enterprises in neighbouring countries. In 1998 its own stock of foreign direct investment abroad was $48 billion.

The third country which is now a market oriented open capitalist economy is *Taiwan*. Its industry is characterised by highly competitive small scale firms with easy freedom of entry, and government willingness to let the failures go bankrupt. In the past two decades, as its manufacturing products became more sophisticated and labour costs rose, domestic investment ratios have fallen and there has been a substantial direct investment abroad, particularly in China. In 1998, its stock of foreign direct investment abroad was $38 billion. The government has maintained very large exchange reserves, as a hedge against its relative political isolation.

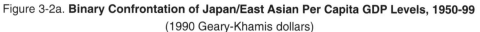

Figure 3-2a. **Binary Confrontation of Japan/East Asian Per Capita GDP Levels, 1950-99**
(1990 Geary-Khamis dollars)

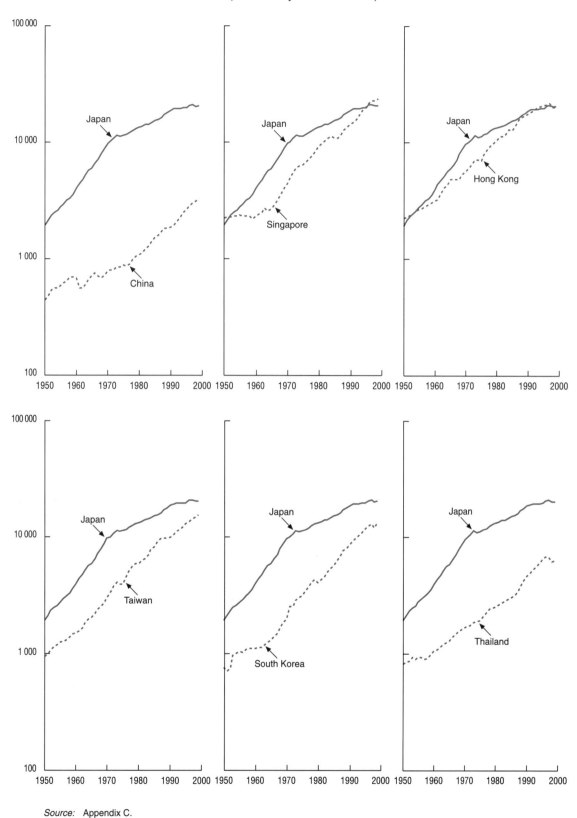

Source: Appendix C.

144

Figure 3-2b. **Binary Confrontation of Japan/East Asian Per Capita GDP Levels, 1950-99**
(1990 Geary-Khamis dollars)

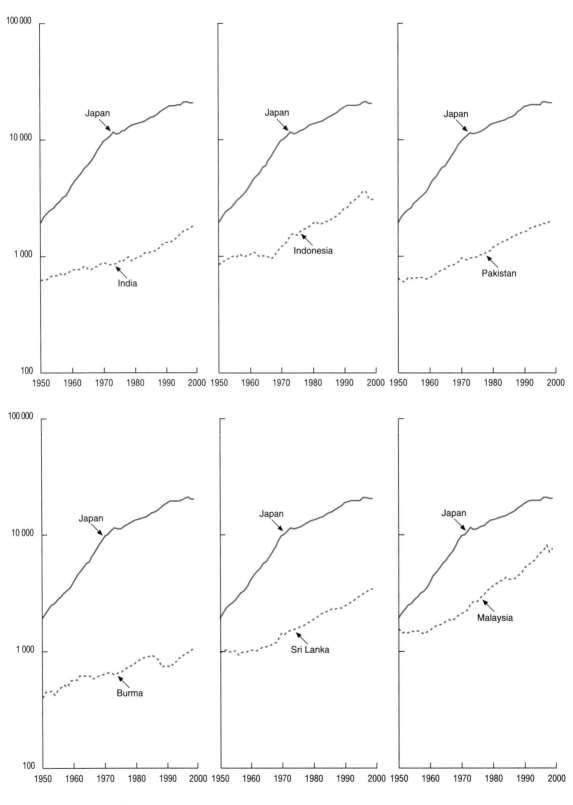

Source: Appendix C.

Table 3–15. **Characteristics of Growth Performance in Resurgent Asia, 1950–99**

	1999 per capita GDP Level	Per capita GDP growth rate	Fixed investment/ GDP Ratio	Annual export volume growth	Export/ GDP ratio	Employment/ population ratio
	1990 int. $	1973–99	1973–97	1973–98	1998	1997
Japan	20 431	2.3	.30	5.3	0.10	0.52
Singapore	23 582	5.4	.38	11.1	1.30	0.49
Hong Kong	20 352	4.1	.27	11.7	1.05	0.48
Taiwan	15 720	5.3	.24	12.1	0.42	0.44
South Korea	13 317	6.1	.31	13.9	0.41	0.46
Malaysia	7 328	4.1	.32	9.5	1.03	0.41
Thailand	6 398	4.8	.31	11.7	0.47	0.55
China	3 259	5.4	.30	11.8	0.19	0.52
Arithmetic Average	**12 851**	**5.0**	**.30**	**11.7**	**0.70**	**0.48**
Sri Lanka	3 451	3.3	.22	5.0	0.30	0.30
Indonesia	3 031	2.7	.24	7.3	0.25[a]	0.43
Philippines	2 291	0.6	.23	9.0	0.31[a]	0.38
Pakistan	1 952	2.8	.17	7.5	0.14	0.26
India	1 818	3.0	.20	5.9	0.08[a]	0.39[b]
Burma	1 050	2.0	.14	6.3	0.01[a]	0.40
Nepal	954	1.7	.17	4.8	0.09	0.39[c]
Bangladesh	835	2.0	.14	9.3	0.12	0.26[d]
Arithmetic Average	**1 923**	**2.3**	**.19**	**6.9**	**0.16**	**0.35**
United States	28 026	2.0	.18	6.0	0.08	0.52
Mexico	6 762	1.3	.19	10.9	0.16[a]	0.40
Brazil	5 421	1.3	.21	6.6	0.07	0.38[e]

a) 1997; b) 1995; c) assumed to be same as India; d) assumed to be same as Pakistan; e) 1994.

Source: Cols. 1 and 2 from Appendix A, updated to 1999 from *Asian Development Outlook 2000*, Manila, 2000. Col. 3 from ADB, *Key Indicators of Developing Asia and Pacific Countries*, Manila, 1999, except China (from *China Statistical Yearbook 1999*, p. 67–8 and Maddison 1998a, p. 164), Taiwan (from *National Income in Taiwan*, Executive Yuan, Taipei) and Japan (from OECD, *National Accounts 1960–97*, vol. 1, Paris 1999). Col. A from IMF, *International Financial Statistics*. Cols. 5 and 6 in most cases from ADB, *Key Statistics*.

China has totally different institutions and policy. Until 1978 virtually the whole economy was under state ownership and control. Economic performance was much better than in the past and the economic structure was transformed. The acceleration was due to a massive increase in inputs of physical and human capital, but there were self–inflicted wounds from the Great Leap Forward and the Cultural Revolution. For most of the Maoist period there was little contact with the outside world. From 1952 to 1973 the United States applied a comprehensive embargo on trade, travel and financial transactions, and from 1960 onwards the USSR did the same. Allocation of resources was extremely inefficient. China grew more slowly than other communist economies and somewhat less than the world average.

Since 1978, Chinese performance has been transformed by liberalisation of the economy. The relaxation of state control in agriculture was a massive success. There was a huge expansion in small–scale industry, particularly in rural areas.

The rigid monopoly of foreign trade and the policy of autarkic self–reliance were abandoned after 1978. Foreign trade decisions were decentralised. The yuan was devalued and China became highly competitive. Special enterprise zones were created as free trade areas. In response to the greater role for market forces, competition emerged, resource allocation improved, and consumer satisfaction increased. There was a massive increase in interaction with the world economy through trade, inflows of direct investment, a very large increase in opportunities for study and travel abroad, and for foreigners to visit China. At the same time, China was prudent in retaining control over the more volatile types of international capital movement. Although it has had to wait 15 years to be admitted to the World Trade Organisation, it is, together with Hong Kong, the world's fourth largest exporter.

Table 3–16. **Stock of Foreign Direct Investment, Total and Per Capita, Major Countries, Regions and World, 1998**

Country	Total ($ million)	Per capita ($)	Country	Total ($ million)	Per capita ($)
Japan	47 856	209			
			United States	875 026	3 234
China	261 117	183	Canada	141 772	4 679
Hong Kong	96 158	14 373	Australia	104 977	5 598
Malaysia	41 005	1 959	New Zealand	34 093	8 946
Singapore	85 855	24 600	Western Offshoots	1 155 868	3 574
South Korea	20 478	441			
Taiwan	20 070	921	Belgium[a]	164 093	15 448
Thailand	19 978	333	France	179 186	3 047
Total/Average	544 661	388	Germany	228 794	2 789
			Ireland	23 871	6 443
Bangladesh	652	5	Italy	105 397	1 830
Burma	1 139	24	Netherlands	164 522	10 798
India	13 231	14	Spain	118 926	3 021
Indonesia	61 116	299	United Kingdom	326 809	5 517
Nepal	81	3	Other Western Europe	264 441	4 311
Pakistan	8 221	61			
Philippines	10 133	130	Argentina	45 466	1 254
Sri Lanka	2 164	114	Brazil	156 758	923
Total/Average	96 737	60	Chile	30 481	2 061
			Mexico	60 783	617
Other Asia	75 492	198	Other Latin America	122 126	649
Total Asia	764 746	217	World	4 088 068	692
Africa	93 994	124			
Eastern Europe	66 397	549			
Former USSR	33 804	116			

a) includes Luxembourg.

Source: UNCTAD, *World Investment Report,* Geneva, 1999.

As a result China has had one of the fastest rates of growth of per capita GDP, and its growth path has been more stable since the 1970s than most of Asia. Its success is in striking contrast to the collapse of activity in the former USSR.

China still has some important problems to solve. It needs to shut down a large proportion of state industrial enterprises which are a hangover from the Maoist period. Most of them make substantial losses. They are kept in operation by government subsidy and default on loans which the state banks are constrained to give them. The relative importance of these enterprises is declining significantly. In 1996 43 million people were employed in the state industrial sector. By 1999 this had fallen to 24 million. Public employment in wholesale and retail trade and restaurants fell from 10.6 million to 6.0 million in the same period.

Another major (and related) problem is the large volume of non–performing loans in the banking sector which is largely controlled by the state. The importance of non–performing loans is smaller than in Japan, but the state does not make efficient allocation of the large funds which it captures from savers and the rapidly burgeoning private sector is starved of funds.

Korea's institutions and policy mix have been somewhat like those of Japan, with close interaction between government and large industrial conglomerates on strategic decisions. There has been a substantial liberalisation of the system in the past decade, with a reduced role for government. A major difference from Japan has been the high export orientation of the economy.

Table 3–17. **Annual Percentage Change in Real GDP Per Capita, Japan and Resurgent Asia, 1997–99**

	Japan	China	Hong Kong	Malaysia	Singapore	South Korea	Taiwan	Thailand
1997	1.2	5.4	2.1	5.4	6.2	3.8	5.8	−1.4
1998	−3.1	4.8	−7.8	−8.7	0.1	−6.7	3.9	−8.9
1999	0.1	4.6	0.8	3.2	4.1	9.6	4.7	3.1

	Bangladesh	Burma	India	Indonesia	Nepal	Pakistan	Philippines	Sri Lanka
1997	3.7	2.8	3.3	2.8	1.4	−0.9	2.9	5.1
1998	3.7	4.5	4.1	−14.1	−0.6	3.1	−2.6	3.6
1999	2.7	2.5	4.1	−1.3	0.7	0.9	1.0	3.0

Source: Appendix C, updated to 1999 from ADB.

Table 3–18. **Exchange Rates: Units of National Currency Per US Dollar in Asian Countries, 1973–99**
(annual average)

	China	Hong Kong	Malaysia	Singapore	South Korea	Taiwan	Thailand
1973	1.99		2.44	2.46	398		20.62
1989	3.77	7.80	2.71	1.95	671	26.41	25.70
1997	8.29	7.74	2.81	1.48	951	28.70	31.36
1998	8.28	7.75	3.92	1.67	1 401	33.46	41.36
1999	8.28	7.76	3.80	1.70	1 189	32.27	37.84

	Bangladesh	Burma	India	Indonesia	Nepal	Pakistan	Philippines	Sri Lanka
1973	7.74	4.93	7.74	415	10.50	9.99	6.76	6.40
1989	32.27	6.70	16.23	1 770	27.19	20.54	21.74	36.05
1997	43.89	6.24	36.31	2 909	58.01	40.87	29.47	59.00
1998	46.91	6.34	41.26	10 014	65.98	44.92	40.89	64.59
1999	49.09	6.29	43.06	7 855	68.25	47.70	39.09	70.40

Source: IMF, *International Financial Statistics,* Hong Kong and Taiwan from national sources and Asian Development Bank.

Korea succeeded in achieving the fastest growth of per capita income in Asia and the world over the past half century. From 1950–73 it grew at 5.8 per cent a year, and from 1973–99 at 6.1 per cent. In the first of these periods it grew more slowly than Japan, in the second more than twice as fast. This was achieved despite very high military expenditure.

In 1998, there was a severe recession with a 6.7 per cent fall in per capita income. This was caused by flight of foreign short term capital in the Asian financial crises of that year. But Korea has a history of successful accommodation to external shocks, and in 1999 per capita income bounced up by 9.6 per cent. As in other Asian countries, the crisis was in large part a consequence of liberalisation of capital transactions in the early 1990s. There were large short term inflows from foreign investors seeking quick gains in a booming economy. The incentive to make such investments was particularly strong for Japanese investors whose own economy was stagnating, whose returns on equity investment were negative and on fixed rate securities virtually zero. In 1997–98, Korea was overexposed to changes in the expectations of foreign short term investors. They were panicked into sudden withdrawal of funds by the contagion effect of the crisis in Thailand.

The 1998 Korean crisis was overcome by substantial borrowing from the IMF, some degree of deflation in policy and the depressing effect of a temporary collapse in profits, stock prices and the exchange rate. There have been some beneficial effects of the crisis. The government is likely to be more cautious in encouraging the more volatile kind of capital inflow. It has moved to encourage bigger flows of foreign direct investment, pushed some of the large conglomerates (*chaebol*) to sell off distressed assets. The banking system has a significant portfolio of non–performing loans but these are proportionately smaller than in Japan.

Table 3–19. **Pre and Post–Crisis Savings as Per Cent of GDP in Five East Asian Countries, 1990–98**

| | 1990–96 | | 1998 | |
	National	*Foreign*	*National*	*Foreign*
Indonesia	29.3	2.6	15.5	−4.9
Korea	35.5	1.8	32.8	−12.8
Malaysia	34.2	6.0	41.8	−13.7
Philippines	19.3	3.9	16.3	−1.9
Thailand	34.8	7.1	32.2	−13.2

Source: Reisen and Soto (2000).

The 1997–98 recession had a serious impact in several Asian countries (see Table 3–17). The adverse effects were greatest in Indonesia where GDP per capita fell by one seventh in 1998. Bankruptcy and the social and political aftermath were much deeper than elsewhere, with negligible signs of recovery. The growth performance of Hong Kong, Malaysia and Thailand was also seriously interrupted. The basic cause was the reversal of massive short term capital inflows which had poured into the region in 1995–97 because of euphoria induced by rapid growth and liberalisation of capital movements (see Table 3–19). All of these countries have made some degree of recovery, but it is too early to assess the degree of damage to their long run growth momentum.

III
PROBLEM ECONOMIES OF EAST ASIA

There are six East Asian economies (Afghanistan, Cambodia, Laos, Mongolia, North Korea and Vietnam) where economic performance since 1950 has been considerably worse than in the rest of Asia, and where income levels are relatively low. Most of these were run for a lengthy period on communist lines, and economic advance was seriously interrupted by war. The worst cases are North Korea and Mongolia which were closely integrated in the Soviet orbit, and where aid and trade were disrupted after the collapse of the USSR in 1991. North Korea is an isolated outpost of Stalinism and has suffered the worst. Mongolia has privatised and marketised its economy and suffers from problems of transition which seem to be smaller than in some of the Asian successor states of the former USSR (see part VI below). Afghanistan has been shattered by foreign invasion and civil war and now has the lowest per capita income in Asia. Cambodia, Laos and Vietnam are making a more successful transition than the successor states of the USSR.

Table 3–20. **Per Capita GDP Performance in Six Problem Economies of East Asia, 1950–98**

| | 1950–73 | 1973–90 | 1990–98 | 1998 per capita GDP Level (1990 int. dollars) |
	(annual average compound growth rates)			
Afghanistan	0.3	−0.8	−1.9	514
Cambodia	2.0	0.9	1.4	1 058
Laos	1.0	1.1	2.1	1 104
Mongolia	3.0	2.6	−2.4	1 094
North Korea	5.8	0.0	−10.4	1 183
Vietnam	1.1	1.3	6.2	1 677

IV
WEST ASIA

West Asia consists of 15 economies. Ten of these are significant oil producers. The importance of oil helps to explain why they have relatively high per capita incomes, and why their growth momentum has differed from that in most of Asia. Per capita income of the oil producers in 1950 was much higher than in prewar years, and higher than in the rest of Asia. Oil production was 16 million metric tons in 1937, 86 million in 1950, and 1 054 million in 1973 — an increase of 11.5 per cent a year from 1950–1973. OPEC action in raising prices and restricting supply meant that aggregate oil production of West Asia was about the same in 1999 as in 1973 (see Table 3–21). Growth was significantly affected by war in Iraq, Iran, Israel, Kuwait, Lebanon, Palestine, Syria and Yemen. The aggregate GDP of this group was about 10 per cent of the Asian total in 1998.

It should be noted that our measure of real GDP per capita is in 1990 prices, and is not adjusted for changes in terms of trade. For most countries this is not important in assessing long term economic performance, but where exports are heavily concentrated on one commodity and prices are highly volatile, these movements are important. The average price of a barrel of crude oil quadrupled from 1972 to 1974. From 1978 to 1980 it rose nearly threefold. Between mid–1997 and mid–1998, it fell by half. At mid–year 2000 it was three times as high as in mid–1998.

Table 3–21. **World Production of Crude Oil and Natural Gas, 1950–99**
(million metric tons)

Country	1950	1973	1999	Country	1950	1973	1999
Bahrain	1.5	3.4	2.2	**Former USSR**	37.9	429.1	370.2
Iran	32.3	293.2	176.2				
Iraq	6.6	99.5	124.7	Romania		14.3	6.6
Kuwait	17.3	150.6	95.6	Other Eastern Europe		8.2	5.6
Oman		14.6	46.1				
Qatar	1.6	27.5	31.2	**Total Eastern Europe**		22.5	12.3
Saudi Arabia	26.6	380.2	426.3				
Syria	–	5.5	29.2	Argentina	3.4	21.9	43.0
United Arab Emirates	–	73.6	101.7	Brazil	–	8.3	57.4
Yemen	–	–	19.4	Colombia	4.7	9.8	41.8
				Ecuador	0.3	10.6	20.7
Total West Asia	85.9	1 054.1	1 052.7	Mexico	10.4	27.2	163.4
				Peru	2.1	3.6	5.3
China	n.a.	53.6	160.6	Venezuela	80.0	178.4	161.7
India	0.3	7.2	38.0	Other Latin America	n.a.	12.3	13.0
Indonesia	6.4	66.1	63.9				
Malaysia	n.a.	4.3	37.6	**Total Latin America**	**n.a.**	**272.1**	**506. 3**
Other East Asia	n.a.	13.6	37.6				
				Algeria	–	51.1	58.5
Total East Asia	**n.a.**	**91.3**	**177.0**	Angola		8.2	37.6
				Congo		2.1	12.9
Norway	–	1.6	149.3	Egypt	2.6	8.5	41.5
United Kingdom	0.2	0.5	139.2	Gabon		7.6	16.8
Other West Europe	n.a.	18.3	31.7	Libya		106.2	65.0
				Nigeria			99.5
Total Western Europe	**n.a.**	**20.4**	**320.2**	Other Africa	–	3.9	17.5
United States	266.7	513.3	359.6	**Total Africa**		**289.0**	**349.3**
Canada		94.1	114.1				
Australia		19.2	24.6	**World**	**523.0**	**2 858.9**	**3 449.5**
New Zealand		0.2	2.1				
Total Western Offshoots		**626.8**	**500.4**				

Source: 1950 from *UN Statistical Yearbook 1955*, New York, pp. 142–5. 1973 and 1999 supplied by International Energy Agency, Paris.

Another feature of the oil producing countries has been extremely rapid population growth as prosperity created a huge demand for foreign workers. Thus the population of Qatar increased 28–fold from 1950 to 1998, UAE 32–fold, Kuwait 13–fold, Saudi Arabia fivefold.

V

LATIN AMERICA

In Latin America, the Bretton Woods collapse and the acceleration of inflation in the early 1970s did not have the same effect on the policy–making establishment that it did in Europe. Most countries had never seriously tried to observe the fixed rate discipline of Bretton Woods. National currencies had been repeatedly devalued, IMF advocacy of fiscal and monetary rectitude had been frequently rebuffed, high rates of inflation had become endemic. The new disturbances were generally viewed as variations on a familiar theme. The acceleration of inflation was not regarded as a razor's edge situation, calling for drastic policy reorientation. The OPEC shock was important for Brazil as a large energy importer, but it brought windfall profits to oil exporting Mexico, Colombia and Venezuela, and was fairly neutral for self sufficient oil producers like Argentina, Chile and Peru.

Hence most countries reacted with insouciance to the worldwide explosion of prices, and governments felt that they could accommodate high rates of inflation. They were able to borrow on a large scale at negative real interest rates to cover external deficits incurred as a result of expansionary policies. As a result their GDP growth rate from 1973 to 1980 did not decelerate.

However, the basic parameters had changed by the early 1980s. By then, the OECD countries were pushing anti–inflationary policy very vigorously. The change to restrictive monetary policy initiated by the United States Federal Reserve pushed up interest rates suddenly and sharply. The dollar appreciated and world export prices began to fall. The average real interest cost of floating rate dollar debt rose to nearly 16 per cent in 1981–83 compared with minus 8.7 per cent in 1977–80. Between 1973 and 1982 external debt had increased sevenfold and the creditworthiness of Latin America as a whole was grievously damaged by Mexico's debt delinquency in 1982. The flow of voluntary private lending stopped abruptly, and created a massive need for retrenchment in economies teetering on the edge of hyperinflation and fiscal crisis. In most countries resource allocation was distorted by subsidies, controls, widespread commitments to government enterprise, and detailed interventionism. Most of them also had serious social tension, and several had unsavoury political regimes.

In the 1930s, most of the Latin American countries resorted to debt default. This path was pursued by some (Bolivia and Peru), but it was not a very attractive option in the 1980s. World trade had not collapsed, international private lending continued on a large scale. The IMF and World Bank had substantial facilities to mitigate the situation, and leverage to pressure Western banks to make involuntary loans and legitimate a substantial degree of delinquency.

In the course of the 1980s, attempts to resolve these problems brought major changes in economic policy. But in most countries, the changes were made reluctantly. After experiments with heterodox policy options in Argentina and Brazil, most countries eventually embraced the neoliberal policy mix pioneered by Chile. They moved towards more market oriented policy, greater openness to international markets, reduced government intervention, trade liberalisation, less distorted exchange rates, better fiscal equilibrium and establishment of more democratic political systems.

In economic terms, the cost of this transition was a decade of falling per capita income. After 1990, economic growth revived substantially but the process was interrupted by contagious episodes of capital flight. The first occurred in 1995 as a reaction to the Mexican debt crisis, the second in 1998 as a reaction to Russian debt default. Growth performance in the 1990s has been disappointing, considering the scope for recovery after the lost decade of the 1980s. For 1980–99 as a whole,

Figure 3-3. **Binary Confrontation of United States/Latin American Per Capita GDP Levels, 1950-98**
(1990 Geary-Khamis dollars)

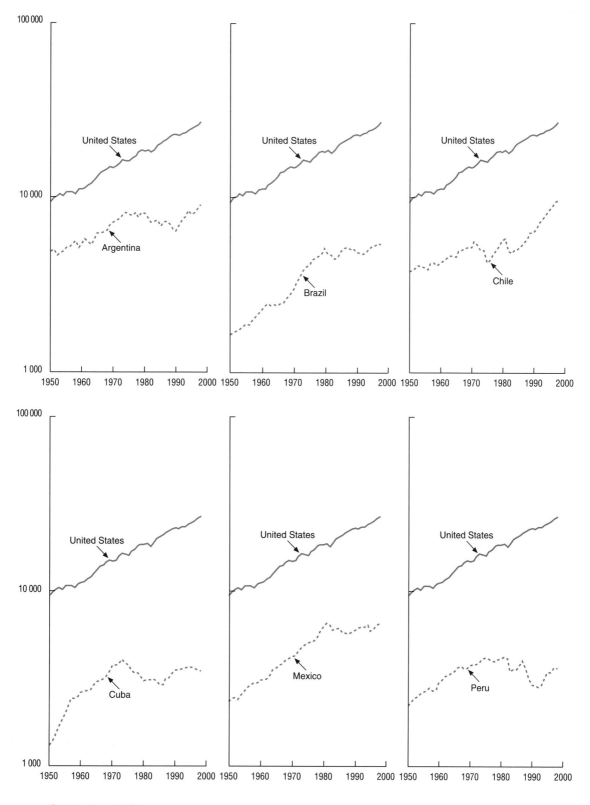

Source: Appendix C.

152

Table 3–22. **Latin American Economic Performance, 1870–1999**

(a) Per capita GDP
(annual average compound growth)

	1950–73	1973–80	1980–90	1990–99	1980–99
Argentina	2.06	0.48	−2.33	3.38	0.33
Brazil	3.73	4.26	−0.54	1.07	0.47
Chile	1.26	1.72	1.10	4.47	2.68
Mexico	3.17	3.80	−0.31	1.16	0.38
40 Other Latin America	2.04	1.19	−0.67	1.28[a]	0.19[b]
Total Latin America	2.52	2.57	−0.68	1.36	0.28

a) 1990–98. b) 1980–98.

(b) Inflation
(annual average compound growth)

	1950–73	1973–94	1994–98	1999
Argentina	26.8	258.4	1.3[a]	−1.7[a]
Brazil	28.4	268.5	19.4[a]	8.0[a]
Chile	48.1[a]	71.8	6.7[a]	2.6[a]
Mexico	5.6	37.6	26.4[a]	13.9[a]
Arithmetic Average	27.2	159.1	13.5	5.7

a) consumer price index; otherwise GDP deflator.

(c) Volume of merchandise exports
(annual average compound growth)

	1870–1913	1913–50	1950–73	1973–98
Argentina	5.2[c]	1.6	3.1	6.7
Brazil	1.9	1.7	4.7	6.7
Chile	3.4[d]	1.4	2.4	9.1
Mexico	5.4[e]	−0.5	4.3	10.9
Total Latin America	3.4	2.3	4.3	6.0

c) 1877–1912; d) 1888–1913; e) 1877/78 to 1910/11.

(d) Ratio of Exports to GDP in 1990 prices
(per cent)

	1870	1913	1950	1973	1998
Argentina	9.4	6.8	2.4	2.0	7.0
Brazil	11.5	9.2	3.9	2.5	5.4
Chile	n.a.	7.5	5.0	4.0	12.6
Mexico	3.1	9.1	3.0	1.9	10.5
Total Latin America	9.2	8.9	6.0	4.7	9.7

per capita income in Latin America has risen by less than 0.3 per cent a year compared with over 2.5 per cent from 1950 to 1980. The earlier growth rate implied a doubling of per capita income every 28 years, the 1980–99 rate implies income doubling over 250 years.

Some idea of the difficulties and costs involved in switching policy regimes can be gained by detailed scrutiny of Chilean experience, where the transformation has been most complete.

The Chilean Paradigm

Chile is the economy with the longest history of substantial inflation. From 1880 to 1913, the annual price rise averaged 5.6 per cent, in 1913–50, 8.3 per cent, in 1950–73 48.1 per cent.

Chile was the heartland of the "structuralist" school which argued that economic rigidities made orthodox monetary remedies inapplicable to its inflationary problems. They argued that inflation could be mitigated by institutional reform, but basically one had to cohabit with it, tolerate or even use it as a positive instrument of policy. Economists of this school also had an instrumental bias towards detailed regulation and subsidies, exchange and trade controls, plus administered internal prices. These views led to early clashes with IMF orthodoxy in the 1950s.

The Allende administration which took over in 1970 was an ideological melange of structuralism, Marxism and a dash of Peronist–style populism. Its policy of nationalising foreign copper interests, increasing social expenditure, land reform and takeover of private business enterprises sapped investor confidence and lowered production at the same time as expansionary fiscal and monetary policies accelerated inflation.

The military who overthrew Allende in 1973 made a complete reversal of policy. They were substantially influenced and aided by Chicago University economists, who saw an opportunity for experiments with monetarism and *laisser faire* in a regime whose "credibility" was high because of its brutal hold on state power.

The new regime privatised the economy, restored land to previous owners, sold 472 of the 507 state enterprises cheaply, and gave gratuities to foreign copper interests deemed to have been inadequately compensated by Allende.

In order to break inflationary momentum shock treatment was applied — curbing public expenditure by a quarter, cutting the tariff level from 94 to 10 per cent, devaluing massively, abolishing exchange controls, suppressing trade union rights, tightening monetary policy, raising indirect taxes and lowering taxes on capital and profits. As a consequence per capita GDP fell by 24 per cent from 1971 to 1975. The rate of inflation was reduced to 375 per cent in 1975 but by 1982 it had fallen to 10 per cent.

After 1975, economic growth resumed, but there was another big recession from 1981 to 1983 when per capita GDP fell by 14 per cent. This setback was due to two major policy errors.

Around 1979, the emphasis in monetarist thinking moved away from controlling domestic monetary supply to fixed exchange rates which were expected to constrain domestic inflation to world rates. However, stable exchange rates and falling prices of copper exports in 1979–81 led to a very big current payments deficit (about 15 per cent of GDP), so the exchange rate was allowed to float sharply downwards.

The fall in the peso had major repercussions for the banks and financieras which had been sold back to private ownership subject to very lax supervision. These institutions made losses which they covered by heavy borrowing abroad. At the new exchange rate they could not service their debts. The government bailed them out and accepted responsibility for all their foreign debts. In this blundering way, there was a significant return to widespread public ownership and control of financial and productive assets (and liabilities).

After this episode the government managed to return to a more respectable growth path, swapped a quarter of the foreign debt for equity, subjected international capital movement to control, and after a short episode of higher tariffs, returned, in chastened mood, to a policy of budget balance, low inflation, floating exchange rates, and a judicious reprivatisation of government assets.

In 1990 the country returned to democratic government. The three successive civilian administrations of Aylwin, Frei, and Lagos have made no basic change to the neoliberal policy mix which they inherited, and in the 1990s it worked reasonably well for them.

VI
THE TRANSITION PROCESS IN THE FORMER USSR AND EASTERN EUROPE

a) Successor States of the Former Soviet Union

15 successor states emerged from the collapse of the former Soviet Union in 1991. In all of them, there had already been a very marked deceleration of economic growth in 1973–90. The reasons for the slowdown (or in some cases, decline) were very different from those in Western Europe. The USSR was relatively isolated from the world economy, and insulated from the inflationary shocks and speculative capital movements which induced caution in Western policy. There was no unemployment, and as the productivity level was less than half of that in Western Europe, the erosion of once–for–all catch–up factors should not have been operative in the USSR. What was most striking after 1973 was that total factor productivity became substantially negative, with labour productivity slowing down dramatically and capital productivity very negative indeed (see Maddison, 1989a, pp. 100–2).

There were three major reasons for the slowdown. One was the decrease in microeconomic efficiency, the second was the increased burden of military expenditure and associated spending. The third was depletion of natural resource advantages, or their destruction by ecological horrors.

The deficiencies in resource allocation were manifest. Average and incremental capital/output ratios were higher than in capitalist countries. Materials were used wastefully as they were supplied below cost. Shortages created a chronic tendency to hoard inventories. The steel consumption/GDP ratio was four times as high as in the United States, the ratio of industrial value added to gross output much lower than in Western countries. In the USSR, the average industrial firm had 814 workers in 1987 compared with an average of 30 in Germany and the United Kingdom. Transfer of technology from the West was hindered by trade restrictions, lack of foreign direct investment and very restricted access to foreign technicians and scholars. Work incentives were poor, malingering on the job was commonplace. The low wages which the system offered had a dulling effect on work incentives.

The quality of consumer goods was poor. Retail outlets and service industries were few. Prices bore little relation to cost. Bread, butter and housing were heavily subsidised. Consumers wasted time queueing, bartering or sometimes bribing their way to the goods and services they wanted. There was an active black market, and special shops for the *nomenklatura*. There was increasing cynicism, frustration, growing alcoholism and a decline in life expectation.

Soviet spending on its military and space effort was around 15 per cent of GDP in the 1970s and 1980s, nearly three times the US ratio and five times as high as in Western Europe. There were significant associated commitments to Afghanistan, Cuba, Mongolia, North Korea, Vietnam and Soviet client states in Africa.

Table 3–23. **Per Capita Growth Performance in Former USSR and Eastern Europe, 1950–98**

	1950–73	1973–90	1990–98	1998 per capita GDP (1990 int. $)	1998 GDP (million 1990 int. $)
	(annual average per capita growth rate)				
Former USSR	**3.36**	**0.74**	**−6.86**	**3 893**	**1 132 434**
Armenia		−0.04	−7.33	3 341	12 679
Azerbaijan		−0.29	−9.35	2 135	16 365
Belarus		1.85	−3.71	5 743	58 799
Estonia		1.27	−0.73	10 118	14 671
Georgia		1.48	−11.94	2 737	14 894
Kazakhstan		−0.23	−5.09	4 809	74 857
Kyrgyzstan		−0.18	−6.82	2 042	9 595
Latvia		1.39	−0.58	6 216	15 222
Lithuania		0.73	−4.55	5 918	21 914
Moldova		0.85	−10.77	2 497	9 112
Russian Federation		0.98	−6.53	4 523	664 495
Tajikistan		−1.84	−14.82	830	5 073
Turkmenistan		−1.67	−8.88	1 723	8 335
Ukraine		1.15	−10.24	2 528	127 151
Uzbekistan		−1.17	−3.32	3 296	79 272
Total Eastern Europe	**3.79**	**0.51**	**0.06**	**5 461**	**660 861**
Albania	3.59	0.57	−0.41	2 401	7 999
Bulgaria	5.19	0.29	−2.36	4 586	37 786
Czechoslovakia	3.08	1.12			
Czech Republic			−0.36	8 643	88 897
Slovak Republic			−0.01	7 754	41 818
Hungary	3.60	0.85	0.05	6 474	66 089
Poland	3.45	−0.35	3.41	6 688	258 220
Romania	4.80	0.08	−2.45	2 890	64 715
Former Yugoslavia	4.49	1.60	−3.45	4 229	95 337
Croatia			−1.93	5 963	27 858
Slovenia			1.09	11 980	23 625
Other former Yugoslavia			−6.37	2 758	43 854

Source: Appendices A and D.

There were increased real costs in exploiting natural resources. In the 1950s a good deal of agricultural expansion was in virgin soil areas, whose fertility was quickly exhausted. Most of the Aral Sea was transformed into a salty desert. Exploitation of mineral and energy resources in Siberia and Central Asia required bigger infrastructure costs than in European Russia. The Chernobyl nuclear accident had a disastrously polluting effect on a large area of the Ukraine.

In 1985–90 Gorbachev established a remarkable degree of political freedom, liberated Eastern Europe and disabled the command economy, but did little to change the economic system. Yeltsin (end 1991 to end 1999) created a market economy and broke up the Soviet Union.

Yeltsin's major initial concerns were to destroy the Soviet economic and political system. The USSR was dissolved at a clandestine meeting of Yeltsin as President of Russia, Kravchuk from the Ukraine and Shuskevich of Belarus early in December 1991. The Baltic states were left free to pursue the capitalist path. The old party bosses of the Asian republics had no prior warning, or ideas for change, but acquiesced, became presidents and entered into a loose federation (the Commonwealth of Independent States). The Soviet Communist Party was dissolved and its assets seized.

Table 3–24. **Changes in Production and Consumption in Belarus, Russia and Ukraine, 1990–98**
(1990 Volume = 100)

	Belarus	*Russian Federation*	*Ukraine*
GDP	80.1	57.7	41.1
Industrial Production	92.7	47.3	31.6
Agricultural Production	65.5	58.1	58.3
Financial Services	196.3	144.7	773.6[a]
Private Consumption	79.0	88.8	51.2
Government Consumption	79.4	70.8	76.9
Fixed Investment	62.9	17.5	15.5
Population	99.8	99.1	96.9

a) 1990–97.

Source: *The Main Macroeconomic Indicators of the Commonwealth of Independent States 1991–1998* (in Russian), Interstate Statistical Committee of the Commonwealth of Independent States, Moscow, 1999.

Table 3–25. **Per Cent of Population in Poverty in Former USSR and Eastern Europe, 1987–88 and 1993–95**

Country	*1987–88*	*1993–95*	*Country*	*1987–88*	*1993–95*
Estonia	1	37	Czech Republic	0	1
Latvia	1	22	Hungary	1	4
Lithuania	1	30	Poland	6	20
Average 3 Baltic States	1	29	Slovakia	0	1
			Slovenia	0	1
			5 Central Europe	1.4	12
Belarus	1	22			
Moldova	4	66	Bulgaria	2	15
Russian Federation	2	50	Romania	6	59
Ukraine	2	63	2 South East Europe	4	37
Average 4 Western CIS	2	52			
Kazakhstan	5	65			
Kyrgyzstan	12	88			
Turkmenistan	12	61			
Uzbekistan	24	63			
Average 4 Central Asian CIS	15	66			

In the Russian republic a government of radical young economic reformers was installed in January 1992, who jettisoned the old command structure, freed most domestic prices, removed obstacles to foreign trade, cut the military budget to a fraction of its earlier level, abolished state trading, legalised all forms of private trading, and began a process of privatisation which eventually sold off most state enterprises at knockdown prices. Between 1990 and 1998, proceeds from Russian privatisation totalled $7.5 billion compared with Brazilian privatisation receipts of $66.7 billion in the same period. The average GDP of these two economies was similar over these years, but Brazilian sales were a very much smaller fraction of its capital stock (see World Bank, 2000, pp. 186-7).

The transition to a market economy was made rather quickly, but the economic outcome was a downward spiral of real income for the mass of the population which lasted almost a decade. In the Russian republic, GDP was 42 per cent lower in 1998 than in 1990. Fixed investment fell precipitously to 17.5 per cent of its 1990 level. There was a big drop in government military spending, so the fall in

Table 3–26. **Annual Average Rate of Change in Consumer Prices: Former USSR and Eastern Europe, 1990–98**

Country	1990–94	1994–98	Country	1990–94	1994–98
Estonia	333.7	15.2	Czech Republic	23.2	8.3
Latvia	320.3	11.5	Hungary	24.0	19.2
Lithuania	435.0	14.9	Poland	42.9	15.5
Average 3 Baltic States	363.0	13.9	Slovakia	26.1	6.2
			Slovenia	95.6	8.3
Belarus	1 402.0	132.1	Average 5 Central Europe	42.4	11.5
Moldova	825.5	17.1			
Russian Federation	927.8	61.5	Albania	96.9	18.6
Ukraine	3 361.8	62.7	Bulgaria	151.0	230.8
Average 4 Western CIS	1 629.3	68.4	Croatia	583.5	4.1
			Macedonia	615.4	2.0
Armenia	3 529.3	14.6	Romania	194.8	69.2
Azerbaijan	1 150.8	20.9	Average South East Europe	328.3	64.9
Georgia	3 817.6	22.4			
Average 3 Caucasus	2 932.6	19.3			
Kazakhstan	1 612.5	25.6			
Kyrgyzstan	721.9	25.0			
Tajikistan	2 228.2	585.0			
Turkmenistan	2 969.3	437.3			
Uzbekistan	811.3	64.3			
Average 5 Central Asia	1 268.6	227.4			

Source: EBRD, *Transition Report 1999*, London, p. 76.

real private consumption per capita was much milder (about 10 per cent) than in per capita GDP. In Belarus it fell by a fifth (see Table 3–24). The situation in the Ukraine was a good deal worse, with a 44 per cent fall in per capita consumption.

The transition to capitalism involved very big changes in income distribution. Under the old system, basic necessities (bread, housing, education, health, crèches and social services) had been highly subsidised by the government or provided free by state enterprises to their workers. These all became relatively more expensive, the real value of wages and pensions was reduced by hyperinflation, and the value of popular savings was destroyed. There were welfare gains from the ending of queueing, the improvement in quality and variety of consumer goods which came from freedom to import, but enjoyment of such gains was felt mainly by people able to succeed in the market economy.

The European Bank for Reconstruction and Development (EBRD) recently estimated changes in the incidence of poverty (see Table 3–25). Between 1987–8 and 1993–5, the poverty ratio in four "Western" CIS countries (whose combined population was 212 million in 1998) had risen from 2 per cent to over half their total population. In four Central Asian states (with a combined population of 49 million), the ratio rose from 15 to 66 per cent, and in the three Baltic States from 1 to 29 per cent. This was much worse than the experience of Central and Southeast Europe, where the only country in a similar situation was Romania. Supplementary evidence of increased impoverishment is evident in reduced life expectation, reduced school attendance, and increased unemployment, though the latter was mitigated by the fact that many workers retained ties with enterprises which provided social benefits, even when their wages had stopped.

There are two major reasons why the transition was more painful in the former USSR than in Eastern Europe. One was the weakness of monetary and fiscal policy which led to hyperinflation. The other was what the EBRD calls the "capture" of the state by a new business oligarchy. Both of these were serious impediments to efficient resource allocation and helped to channel income to a privileged elite.

Macroeconomic Instability

Table 3–26 shows the average rate of inflation in 1990–94, and 1994–98. The first wave of hyperinflation has now been significantly tempered, but the momentum of price increase is still very much higher than the 2 per cent a year in Western capitalist economies (see Table 3–8). In the Baltics and Eastern Europe it is now similar to that in Latin America (13.5 per cent, see Table 3–22).

A bout of hyperinflation was an understandable consequence of the switch from the price structure of a command economy to one governed by market forces, but inflationary momentum was fed by fiscal weakness. This was inevitable in a state which previously derived its income from ownership of assets which had been sold for a song. It was also very difficult to devise and implement a new tax apparatus in an economy where enterprises had rapidly become adept at tax avoidance, tax evasion, concealment of profits at home and in foreign tax havens. In Russia the problem was exacerbated by devolution of spending power to 19 constituent republics and 61 other regional administrations.

Reckless monetary policy was the other major contributor to hyperinflation. In the first reformist phase, the Gaidar government took the advice of international agencies and maintained the rouble as a common currency for the CIS member states until 1993. Thus it had to cover their deficits which amounted to 10 per cent of Russian GDP. Between 1992 and 1994 hyperinflation was fuelled by an enormous increase in the volume of credits at negative real interest rates by the Central Bank to cover the federal budget deficit and to prop up enterprises that should have been forced into bankruptcy. At a later stage, deficits were financed by developing a Treasury Bill market and borrowing abroad. After the re–election of Yeltsin in July 1996, there was a large inflow of foreign investment in Russian equities and Treasury Bills. The stock market rose threefold from mid–1996 to the end of 1997 without much change in the exchange rate. Many foreign investors speculated heavily, hedging the exchange risk by buying forward dollar contracts from Russian banks. The dismissal of prime minister Chernomyrdin in 1998 and the Asian financial crisis caused large withdrawals of foreign funds. The Russian government propped up the exchange rate for a couple of weeks with nearly $5 billion from the IMF, but in mid–August 1998 devalued, defaulted on much of domestic debt and declared a moratorium on debt repayments to foreigners by Russian companies and banks.

The Rise of a New Financial Oligarchy

The other major problem with the Russian transition to capitalism was diagnosed by the EBRD (1999, pp. 110–11) as follows: "under the 'shares for loans' scheme implemented in 1995, many of the key resource–based companies fell into the hands of a small group of financiers, the so–called 'oligarchs'. This has led to very sharp increases in wealth and income inequality — by 1997 the Gini coefficient for income in Russia was around 0.5, a level comparable to those in Colombia or Malaysia. It has also helped to create an investment climate marked by corruption, non–transparent business practices — including barter — and cronyism." "Not only has income inequality increased substantially but spending on social benefits has actually become regressive over the course of the transition. This highlights the capture of the state by narrow interest groups."

There has been legislation to establish Western style property rights, but in practice accountancy is opaque and government interpretation of property rights is arbitrary. Many businesses are subject to criminal pressure. Property owners such as shareholders or investors are uncertain whether their rights will be honoured. Workers are not sure that their wages will be paid. These characteristics make resource allocation very inefficient.

Agriculture Untouched by Reform

A third major failure of transition policy was the treatment of agriculture. In Russia and the Ukraine, 1998 agricultural output was 42 per cent lower than in 1990. This is in startling contrast to China where agricultural output rose 56 per cent in the seven years following the 1978 reforms. Virtually nothing has been done to create dynamism in this backward sector, where effective action is difficult because of the heritage of the past. As Kornai (1992, p. 437) put it: "To this day the Soviet peasantry has not been able to get over the ghastly trauma of collectivisation. Even though the people who experienced it are no longer alive, their children and grandchildren feel there is no security for private property, and the land may be taken from them again. If they were to become prosperous farmers by farming individually, it could mean that they would be branded as *kulaks* again, which could bring persecution, deportation or death."

b) East European Countries

The economic system of the East European countries was similar to that of the former USSR until the end of the 1980s, and so was its macroeconomic performance. In the golden age, 1950–73, East European per capita GDP growth (like that of the USSR) more or less kept pace with that in Western Europe. From 1973 to 1990, it faltered badly as the economic and political system began to crumble, with aggregate per capita growth of about 0.5 per cent per annum compared with 1.9 in Western Europe.

Since 1990, East Europe has experienced major problems in the transition to capitalism, but the process has been much less traumatic than in the former USSR. Average per capita income in 1998 was similar to that in 1990, whereas it was more than 40 per cent lower in the former USSR.

There are in fact big differences in the success of the transition in different East European countries. Poland, by far the biggest economy and the worst performer in 1973–90, has had more rapid income growth since 1990 than any other European country except Ireland. The Czech and Slovak republics and Hungary have more or less recovered their 1990 levels of per capita income. The worst case is the former Yugoslavia which split into five separate states in the course of bloody conflicts. Bulgaria and Romania have also fared badly, in part because their economies were severely affected in various ways by wars in Bosnia and Kosovo, sanctions on Yugoslavia, and bombing of bridges on the Danube.

With the exception of Poland, economic performance has been disappointing. Given the fact that average per capita income in Eastern Europe is about 30 per cent of that in West Europe, there should have been scope for some degree of catch–up.

In fact the problems of transition are very profound. The easiest part was the freeing of prices and the opening of trade with the West. This ended shortages and queueing, improved the quality of goods available and increased consumer welfare in ways not properly captured in the GDP measures. However, much of the old capital stock became junk, the labour force needed to acquire new skills, the legal and administrative system and the tax/social benefit structure had to be transformed, and the distributive and banking system had to be rebuilt from scratch.

It is interesting to compare the situation in Eastern Europe with that in East Germany, which was incorporated into the Bundesrepublik in 1990. In other East European countries, the amount of Western aid has been relatively modest, and their access to Western markets is hampered by the EU's common agricultural policy and restraints on exports of sensitive industrial products. The Länder of East Germany, by contrast, have had completely free access to German and Western markets and have received transfers of various kinds of about a trillion dollars since reunification, but per capita product and labour productivity are still less than half the levels in the rest of Germany. The problem of transforming socialist firms into productive capitalist enterprises was more pronounced than elsewhere because East Germany was incorporated in a monetary union which greatly overvalued the old Ost Mark wages and assets. Most of the industrial capital stock has been scrapped. Employment is down by 30 per cent since 1990, as workers (as well as pensioners and other social categories) became eligible for much higher social security benefits.

The reasons why Eastern European countries have performed better than the states of the former USSR seem to be mainly as follows:

a)   the exposure to the command economy was shorter, about 40 years, as compared with more than 70 in most of the former USSR. This was also true of the Baltic countries, which have been more successful than the other economies of the former USSR;

b)   in several of the East European countries, there had been strong aspirations to break away from the command economy and Soviet hegemony — in Yugoslavia in the 1950s, in Hungary in 1956, in Czechoslovakia in 1968, and in Poland in the 1980s — and there was an active intellectual interest in problems of transition. Yugoslavia, Hungary and Poland were members of the IMF before the collapse of the Soviet system, and had acquired some knowledge of the macroeconomic policy mix and weaponry characteristic of capitalist economies. In the case of Czechoslovakia, Poland, Hungary and Slovenia, there was greater propinquity to and knowledge of Western capitalism than in the former USSR, Bulgaria or Romania;

c)   there was much greater concern to carry out transition policies within a framework of macroeconomic stability in Eastern Europe than in the former USSR. This is particularly true of Poland which started its radical reforms at the beginning of 1990 with an overhang of inflationary pressure engendered by wage indexation and other concessions to the militant trade unionism of the Solidarity movement (see Balcerowicz, 1995, pp. 324–6). Reform policy involved tight monetary and fiscal discipline;

d)   the reform process gave much greater emphasis to creating a transparent legal basis for contracts and property rights, and the privatisation process did not create a new oligarchy of predatory capitalists. Here again, the difference between policy in Poland and in the former Soviet Union is strongly emphasised by Balcerowicz, the main architect of the Polish reforms. As a result there was much less ambiguity about the direction and destination of the reform process.

VII
AFRICA

Africa has nearly 13 per cent of world population, but only 3 per cent of world GDP. It is the world's poorest region, with a 1998 per capita income only 5 per cent of that in the richest region, less than half of that in Asia (excluding Japan). It has the lowest life expectation (52 years compared with 78 in Western Europe). It has the most rapid demographic expansion — about nine times as fast as in Western Europe.

As a result of rapid population growth, age structure is very different from that in Western Europe. In Europe more than two thirds are of working age, in Africa little more than half. 43 per cent of Africans are below 15 years old and 3 per cent 65 or over. In Western Europe 18 per cent are under 15 and 15 per cent 65 or older. Almost half the adult population of Africa are illiterate. They have a high incidence of infectious and parasitic disease (malaria, sleeping sickness, hookworm, river blindness, yellow fever). Over two thirds of HIV infected people live in Africa. As a result the quantity and quality of labour input per head of population is much lower than in other parts of the world.

African economies are more volatile than most others, because their export earnings are concentrated on a few primary commodities, and extremes of weather (droughts and floods) are more severe and have a heavy impact.

Although African levels of performance are low in comparative terms, there has been economic growth in the capitalist epoch. Per capita income rose about 3.5–fold from 1820 to 1980 (see Tables 3–1b and C5–c), which is about the same as in Asia (excluding Japan). Since 1980 African per capita income has declined.

Figure 3-4. **Binary Confrontation of United States/African Per Capita GDP Levels, 1950-98**
(1990 Geary-Khamis dollars)

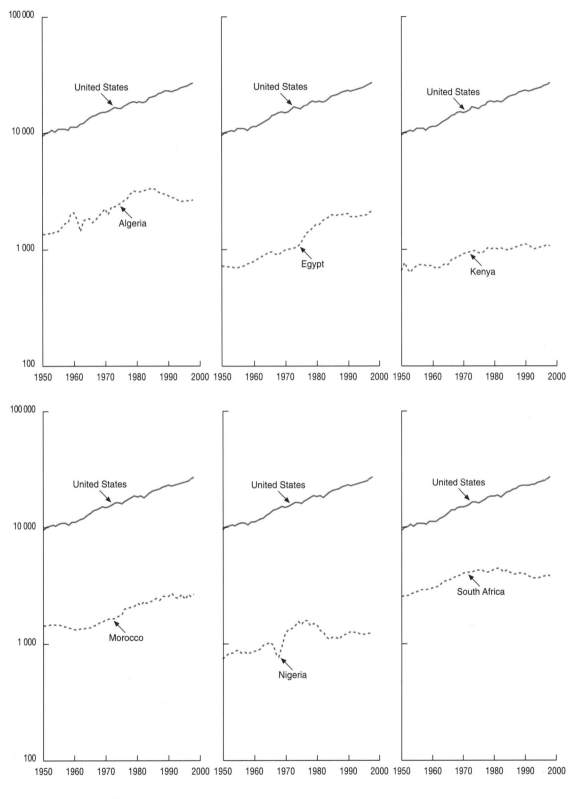

Source: Appendix C.

Table 3–27. **Illiteracy Rates in Africa in 1997**
(percentage of adult population)

Algeria	40	Niger	86
Benin	66	Nigeria	40
Botswana	26	Rwanda	37
Burkina Faso	80	Senegal	65
Burundi	55	South Africa	16
Cameroon	28	Tanzania	28
Central African Rep.	57	Togo	47
Congo	23	Tunisia	33
Côte d'Ivoire	58	Uganda	36
Egypt	48	Zambia	25
Ethiopia	65	Zimbabwe	9
Ghana	33	Arithmetic Average	45
Kenya	21		
Malawi	42	Former USSR	4
Mali	65	Latin America	13
Mauritania	62	China	17
Morocco	54		
Mozambique	59		
Namibia	21		

Source: World Bank, *World Development Report 1999/2000*, Washington, D.C., 2000, pp. 232-3.

Poverty and economic stagnation or decline are predominant characteristics of Africa, but there are important variations in levels of income and growth performance. Table 3–28 distinguishes between the 14 countries where average income is above 2 000 international dollars a head and the 43 countries below this level. In the first group, 1998 per capita income averaged $2 816 and in the rest only $840. Countries in the first group now have an average income like that of Western Europe in 1900, in the rest it is below the Western European level in 1600.

The first relatively prosperous group consists of five countries on the Mediterranean littoral (Algeria, Egypt, Libya, Morocco and Tunisia). Of these Egypt, Morocco and Tunisia had reasonable growth performance in 1973–98, but 1998 per capita income in Algeria was 15 per cent below the 1985 peak, and in Libya about half of the 1973 level.

The second group, at the Southern tip of the continent, consists of Botswana, Namibia, South Africa and Swaziland. Botswana has been one of the world's fastest growing economies (5.4 per cent per capita from 1973 to 1998). Its growth performance was similar to that of Singapore, but was largely based on exploitation of its diamond resources. South Africa's per capita income in 1998 was 14 per cent below its 1981 peak, and Namibia's 9 per cent below 1981.

The third group of five small countries consists of special cases. Gabon and the Congo have relatively high and expanding levels of petroleum production and export. The three others are islands in the Indian Ocean with population growth rates well below the African average. Reunion is a French overseas department with a high degree of subsidy from the metropole. In the Seychelles and Mauritius the majority of the population are of Indian origin, bilingual in English and French. Seychelles has a high tourist income. Mauritius has been successful in developing exports of manufactures.

Threequarters of Africa's population belongs to a fourth group where per capita income peaked in 1980. By 1998 it had fallen by a quarter. This group of countries is the hard core of African poverty.

In explaining the reasons for African poverty, one must distinguish between longer term influences and the reasons for the reversal of economic advance over the past two decades.

Table 3–28. **Variations of Income Level Within Africa, 1998**

	GDP per capita (1990 int. $)	GDP (million 1990 int. $)	Population (000)
Algeria	2 688	81 948	30 481
Egypt	2 128	140 546	66 050
Libya	3 077	15 000	4 875
Morocco	2 693	78 397	29 114
Tunisia	4 190	39 306	9 380
5 Mediterranean Countries	2 539	355 197	139 900
Botswana	4 201	6 803	1 448
Namibia	3 797	6 158	1 622
South Africa	3 858	165 239	42 835
Swaziland	2 794	2 699	966
4 South African Countries	3 860	180 899	46 871
Gabon	4 885	5 901	1 208
Mauritius	9 853	11 508	1 168
Reunion	4 502	3 174	705
Seychelles	5 962	471	79
Congo	2 239	5 951	2 658
5 Special Cases	4 642	27 005	5 818
Total for 14 Countries with per capita GDP above $2000	2 816	563 101	192 589
Total for 43 Other Countries	840	476 307	567 365
Total Africa	1 368	1 039 408	759 954

Source: The estimates of GDP growth for African countries are of poorer quality than for other regions. National accounts were generally introduced by the colonial authorities in the late 1950s, and the quality and staffing of statistical offices since independence has been weak. There are also more serious problems in the estimates of comparative GDP levels than for other regions, see Table A4–g, and the accompanying commentary.

Until late in the nineteenth century, most of the continent was unknown and unexplored, occupied by hunter–gatherers, pastoralists or practitioners of subsistence agriculture. Levels of education and technology were primitive. Land was relatively abundant, was allocated by traditional chiefs, without Western–style property rights. The only territorial units which resembled those of today were Egypt, Ethiopia, Liberia, Morocco and South Africa. Slaves had been the main export.

The European powers became interested in grabbing Africa in the 1880s. France and Britain were the most successful. Twenty–two countries eventually emerged from French colonisation, 21 from British, five from Portuguese, three from Belgian, two from Spanish. Germany lost its colonies after the First World War, Italy after the Second.

The colonialists created boundaries to suit their own convenience, with little regard to local traditions or ethnicity. European law and property rights were introduced with little regard to traditional forms of land allocation. Hence the colonists got the best land and most of the benefits from exploitation of mineral rights and plantation agriculture. African incomes were kept low by forced labour or apartheid practices. Little was done to build a transport infrastructure or to cater for popular education.

European colonisers withdrew from the mid 1950s onwards. The British colonial bond with Egypt and the Sudan was broken in 1956. Ghana became independent in 1957, Nigeria in 1960, Tanzania in 1961, Kenya in 1963. White settler interests retarded the process in Zimbabwe and Namibia. In South Africa, the black population did not get political rights until 1994. French decolonisation

Table 3–29. **Degree and Duration of Per Capita Income Collapse in 13 Biggest African Countries South of the Sahara**

	1998 population (000)	1998 per capita as per cent of peak	Peak year	Distance from peak (years)
Angola	10 865	36.6	1970	28
Cameroon	15 029	60.0	1986	12
Côte d'Ivoire	15 446	64.7	1980	18
Ethiopia	62 232	95.0	1983	15
Kenya	28 337	97.5	1990	8
Madagascar	14 463	55.4	1971	27
Mali	10 109	92.3	1979	19
Mozambique	18 641	63.3	1973	25
Nigeria	110 532	77.1	1977	21
Sudan	33 551	75.5	1977	21
Tanzania	30 609	88.8	1979	19
Zaire	49 001	30.0	1974	24
Zimbabwe	11 004	100.0	1998	0
13 Country Total/Average	409 859	72.0	1980	18

Source: Appendix C.

started with Morocco and Tunisia in 1956. Guinea broke away in 1958, the rest of the sub–Saharan colonies became independent in 1960, and Algeria in 1962. Belgium abandoned Zaire in 1960, Burundi and Rwanda in 1962. Portugal and Spain made their exit in 1975.

In these years, the Cold War was at its height, and Africa became a focus of international rivalry. China, the USSR, Cuba and East European countries supplied economic and military aid to new countries viewed as proxies in a world wide conflict of interest. Western countries, Israel and Taiwan were more generous in supplying aid and less fastidious in its allocation than they might otherwise have been. As a result, Africa accumulated large external debts which had a meagre developmental pay–off.

Independence brought many serious challenges. The political leadership had to try to create elements of national solidarity and stability more or less from scratch. The new national entities were in most cases a creation of colonial rule. There was great ethnic diversity with no tradition or indigenous institutions of nationhood. The linguistic vehicle of administration and education was generally French, English or Portuguese rather than the languages most used by the mass of the population. Thirteen of the new francophone countries had belonged to two large federations whose administrative and transport network had been centred in Dakar and Brazzaville. These networks had to be revamped.

There was a great scarcity of people with education or administrative experience. Suddenly these countries had to create a political elite, staff a national bureaucracy, establish a judiciary, create a police force and armed forces, send out dozens of diplomats. The first big wave of job opportunities strengthened the role of patronage and rent–seeking, and reduced the attractions of entrepreneurship. The existing stock of graduates was too thin to meet the demands and there was heavy dependence on foreign personnel.

The process of state creation involved armed struggle in many cases. In Algeria, Angola, Mozambique, Sudan, Zaire and Zimbabwe, the struggle for independence involved war with the colonial power or the white settler population. A few years later, Nigeria, Uganda and Ethiopia suffered from civil wars and bloody dictators. More recently Burundi, Eritrea, Liberia, Rwanda, Sierra Leone and Somalia have all had the same problem. These wars were a major impediment to development.

Table 3–30. **Total External Debt of Africa, Asia, Latin America, Eastern Europe and former USSR, 1980, 1990 and 1998**
($ million)

	1980	1990	1998		1980	1990	1998
Algeria	19 365	27 877	30 665	Argentina	27 151	62 730	144 050
Angola	n.a.	8 594	12 173	Brazil	71 520	119 877	232 004
Cameroon	2 588	6 679	9 829	Chile	12 081	19 227	36 302
Côte d'Ivoire	7 462	17 251	14 852	Colombia	6 941	17 222	32 263
Egypt	19 131	32 947	31 964	Mexico	57 365	104 431	159 959
Ethiopia	824	8 634	10 351	Peru	9 386	20 967	32 397
Ghana	1 398	3 881	6 884	Venezuela	29 344	33 170	37 003
Kenya	3 387	7 058	7 010	Other Countries	43 471	99 143	112 041
Morocco	9 258	24 458	20 687	**Total Latin America**	**257 259**	**475 867**	**786 019**
Mozambique	n.a.	4 653	8 208				
Nigeria	8 921	33 440	30 315	Bulgaria	n.a.	10 890	9 907
Sudan	5 177	14 762	16 843	Czech Republic	–	6 383	25 301
South Africa	n.a.	n.a.	24 712	Slovakia	–	2 008	9 893
Tanzania	5 322	6 438	7 603	Hungary	9 764	21 277	28 580
Tunisia	3 527	7 691	11 078	Poland	n.a.	49 366	47 708
Zaire	4 770	10 270	12 929	Serbia	18 486	17 837	13 742
Zimbabwe	786	3 247	4 716	Russia[b]	n.a.	59 797	183 601
Other Countries	20 217	52 171	63 999	Other former USSR	–	–	34 888
Total Africa	**112 133**	**270 051**	**324 814**				
				Other Eastern Europe	n.a.	1 489	21 123
				Total Eastern Europe			
China	n.a.	n.a.	154 599	**& former USSR**	**56 263**	**171 004**	**383 842**
India	20 581	83 717	98 232				
Indonesia	20 938	69 872	150 875				
South Korea	29 480	34 986	139 097				
Pakistan	9 931	20 663	32 229				
Turkey	19 131	49 424	102 074				
Other Countries	83 688	284 759	375 775				
Total Asia[a]	**183 749**	**543 421**	**1 052 881**				

a) excludes Brunei, Japan, Hong Kong, Singapore and Taiwan; b) Russia assumed the debts of the former USSR.

Source: World Bank, *Global Development Finance 2000,* Washington, D.C., 2000. The figures are based on data for 137 reporting countries, and World Bank estimates for 12 other countries.

Table 3–31. **Arrears on External Debt in Africa and Other Continents, 1980–98**
($ million)

	1980	1990	1998	1998 Arrears as per cent of 1998 debt
Africa	3 907	32 704	55 335	17.0
Latin America	666	50 119	11 925	1.5
Asia	76	10 067	29 491	2.8
Eastern Europe & former USSR	576	19 509	22 923	6.0

Source: World Bank, *Global Development Finance 2000,* Washington, D.C., 2000. The figures reflect the combined effect of arrears on interest and principal.

Most of the recent attempts to explain Africa's weak economic performance (Bloom and Sachs, 1998; Collier and Gunning, 1999; and Ndulu and O'Connell, 1999) give major emphasis to the problem of "governance".

Ndulu and O'Connell found that in 1988 only five countries "had multi–party systems allowing meaningful political competition at the national level." They categorised 11 as military oligarchies, 16 as plebiscitary one–party states, 13 as competitive one–party, and two as settler oligarchies (Namibia and South Africa, where the situation has now changed). In most of the one–party states, the incumbent ruler sought to keep his position for life. In most states, rulers relied for support on a narrow group who shared the spoils of office. Corruption became widespread, property rights insecure, business decisions risky. Collier and Gunning (p. 93) suggest that nearly two fifths of African private wealth now consists of assets held abroad (compared with 10 per cent in Latin America and 6 per cent in East Asia). Such estimates are necessarily rough, but with Presidents like Mobutu in Zaire or Abacha in Nigeria, it is not difficult to believe that the proportion is high.

A major factor in the slowdown since 1980 has been external debt. As the Cold War faded from the mid 1980s, foreign aid levelled off, and net lending to Africa fell. Although the flow of foreign direct investment has risen it has not offset the fall in other financial flows. Table 3–30 shows clearly that lending to Africa has expanded less since 1990 than the flow to Asia, Latin America, Eastern Europe and the former USSR.

The aggregate external debt of African countries in 1998 was $427 per head of the population. In Asia it was $314, Latin America $1 548, and Eastern Europe and the successor states of the former USSR $932. Asian per capita income is more than twice as high as in Africa, Latin American more than four times as big and in the former communist group three times as big as in Africa. The African burden is clearly the heaviest, and African capacity to finance investment from domestic saving is lower than in other continents.

Although some African countries are scheduled to benefit from debt relief under the 1996 and 1999 HIPC (Heavily Indebted Poor Countries) Initiatives of the World Bank and IMF, and more have benefited from Paris Club debt relief, the scope of these debt restructuring operations has been much smaller in Africa than in Latin America (see Table 3–31). African access to IMF financing has also been much more restricted than that of countries in Asia and the former USSR in their recent debt crises.

Although the setback to African growth in the past two decades has been smaller in quantitative terms than that in the former USSR, the outlook for the future is more depressing. Levels of education and health are much worse, population growth is still explosive, problems of political stability and armed conflict are bigger, and problems of institutional adjustment and integration in a liberal capitalist world order seem just as great. Most of these problems require changes within Africa, but their course could obviously be influenced by outside help in reducing the debt burden.

Appendix A

Growth and Levels of World Population, GDP and GDP Per Capita, Benchmark Years, 1820–1998

This Appendix provides a quantitative picture of the world economy for the period 1820–1998. It presents estimates of population, GDP and GDP per capita for seven benchmark years and their rates of growth in five phases of development 1820–70, 1870–1913, 1913–1950, 1950–73, and 1973–98.

The first section covers Europe and Western Offshoots (the United States, Canada, Australia and New Zealand); the second, Latin America; the third, Asia; and the fourth, Africa. The source notes explain the derivation of the estimates.

Table A–a shows the coverage of our GDP sample. It represents 81 per cent of the world economy for 1820, 93 per cent in 1913, and over 99 per cent for 1950–98. As the objective is comprehensive coverage, proxy measures were needed to fill holes in the data set. The proxy procedures are explained in the text, and generally assume parallelism of per capita growth experience in the missing countries with that in other countries in the same region.

In order to add the individual country GDP estimates to obtain regional or world totals it is necessary to convert them into a common currency. Exchange rate conversion does not provide a satisfactory measure of real values. Purchasing power parity converters (PPPs) are preferable. These have been developed for use by international organisations over the past 50 years, and the best available are those from the International Comparison Programme (ICP) of the United Nations, Eurostat and OECD, though the coverage of these is not yet universal. Table A–b shows the nature of the converters used here. ICP measures were used for 70 countries representing 93.9 per cent of world GDP in the benchmark year 1990. Estimates from the Penn World Tables, version 5.6 (Summers and Heston, 1995) were used for 83 countries, representing 5.5 per cent of the world economy. Proxy measures were used for 45 (most very small) countries for which no ICP or PWT estimates were available. These represented 0.6 per cent of world GDP. 1990 benchmark levels were merged with the GDP time series in constant national prices, thus providing level comparisons for every year in terms of the benchmark *numeraire*. Table A–b also shows the nature of the converters used in Maddison (1995a).

Population figures do not pose the index number and aggregation problems which arise for GDP, and there are fewer holes in the data set. Figures for 1950 onwards were based on official sources, and where these seemed deficient, from the International Programs Center of the US Bureau of the Census. For years before 1950, estimates are based on census material and the work of historical demographers. Pre–1950 estimates are weakest for Africa, considerably better for Asia and Latin America, and best for Europe and Western Offshoots.

The present estimates are an update and revision of those in Maddison (1995a). That study concentrated on a sample of 56 countries, for which full source notes were given. Figures for other countries were given in summary form, with no detailed source notes (see Appendix F of Maddison, 1995a). Here the source notes cover many more countries, for which greater statistical detail is presented.

The revisions and expanded coverage are most significant for Asia; where source notes now cover 37 countries compared with 11 in Maddison (1995a). Estimates are also provided for the 22 new East European countries which emerged from the disintegration of the former USSR, Yugoslavia and Czechoslovakia in the 1990s (see also Appendix D). Estimates for Germany are revised to take account of the integration of new Länder in the East.

For Western Europe, Latin America and Africa, revisions in GDP indices are relatively modest, so for these regions it was not felt necessary to reproduce source notes from Maddison (1995a) *in extenso*, though a full description is given of the derivation of the benchmark levels of GDP in "international" Geary–Khamis dollars for 1990. There are significant revisions in population for Africa and Latin America. Table A–c provides a confrontation of the previous estimates of world and regional population and GDP, with those in the present study.

UPDATING THE ESTIMATES

GDP

The following international sources are useful for those who wish to update the GDP estimates.

For 21 European countries and the 4 Western Offshoots, OECD, *National Accounts of OECD Countries*, Vol. 1, presents the latest available national accounts in current and constant prices in standardised form, and has hitherto given retrospective coverage back to 1960. Because of the significant changes involved in the switchover to the new 1993 SNA system, the latest retrospective view goes back only to 1988 at best. OECD, *Economic Outlook* provides twice yearly provisional estimates of GDP volume change in the current and forthcoming year. These publications also cover Japan, Korea, Mexico and Turkey.

For 11 East European countries and the 15 successor states of the former Soviet Union estimates of GDP are available in constant prices for 1990 onwards (and for material product back to 1980) from the Statistics Division of ECE (Economic Commission for Europe of the United Nations). The Interstate Statistical Committee of CIS (Commonwealth of Independent States) has published detailed national accounts for 12 successor republics of the former USSR, *Osnovie Makroekonomikie Pokazateli Stran Sodruschestva Nezavisimich Gosudarstv 1991–1998*, Moscow, 1999.

For 32 Latin American countries, ECLAC (Economic Commission for Latin America and the Caribbean) publishes estimates of annual volume changes in GDP for the current year and the preceding nine years in its annual end December, *Preliminary Overview of the Economies of Latin America and the Caribbean*.

For 38 East Asian countries, ADB (Asian Development Bank) publishes *Key Indicators of Developing Asian and Pacific Countries* annually. This contains national accounts in some detail in current and constant prices, with an 18 year retrospective coverage.

For 11 West Asian countries and Egypt, ESCWA (Economic and Social Commission for West Asia) publishes *National Accounts Studies of the ESCWA Region* annually. It contains national accounts in current prices and summary annual estimates of GDP volume movement for the previous decade and provisional estimates for the current year.

For 51 African countries, the IMF (International Monetary Fund) twice yearly *World Economic Outlook* shows annual changes in GDP volume for the past decade. It provides similar indicators for the rest of the world. The IMF database is available back to 1970 on internet: http://www.imf.org/external/pubs/ft/weo/2000/01/data/index.htm.

There are two very useful sources of information which have now been discontinued but are still very useful for years before 1990. The OECD Development Centre set up the first international database. It published *National Accounts of Less Developed Countries, 1950–1966* in 1968 and issued 23 annual updates (*Latest Information on National Accounts of Developing Countries*) from 1969 to 1991. The World Bank's *World Tables* were first published in 1976 (with second and third editions in 1980 and 1983) and annually from 1987 to 1995.

Population

The International Programs Center of the US Bureau of the Census provides annual estimates from 1950 onwards, and annual projections to 2050 for all countries. The estimates are revised regularly, and retrospective estimates back to 1950 are included for the new countries which emerged in the 1990s. The estimates are available on internet: http://www.census.gov./ipc. I used their estimates for 1950 onwards for 178 countries (25 European, the United States, 44 Latin American, 51 Asian and 57 African).

Levels of GDP in International Dollars

In this study the benchmark GDP estimates are in 1990 international dollars. I explained the reasons for preferring PPP (purchasing power parity) converters rather than exchange rates, and the advantages of Geary–Khamis multilateral PPPs in Maddison (1995a) pp. 164–79. Such measures are available from the International Comparison Programme (ICP) of the United Nations, Eurostat and OECD.

The ICP exercise was initiated by Irving Kravis, Alan Heston and Robert Summers of the University of Pennsylvania, as a follow up and greatly expanded version of work undertaken in OEEC in the 1950s. Their *magnum opus* was Kravis, Heston and Summers, *World Product and Income: International Comparisons of Real Gross Product* (1982). Their approach was a highly sophisticated comparative pricing exercise in which national accounts expenditure in the participating countries in a given year was decomposed in great detail for representative items of consumption, investment and government services. The results were multilateralised using the Geary–Khamis technique which ensured transitivity, base country invariance and additivity. Their 1982 study covered 34 countries. The Pennsylvania team also created the Penn World Tables which updated and reconciled the material from all the preceding ICP rounds, and added short–cut estimates (using more limited price information) for many countries not covered by ICP. This important supplement to ICP was issued in several successively more ambitious versions from 1978 to 1995.

The ICP was taken over as a co–operative venture by UNSO (United Nations Statistical Office), Eurostat (Statistical Office of the European Union) and OECD in the 1980s. There was a division of labour in which the different agencies made estimates for their respective regions, and the results were adjusted for comparability and consolidated by the UN Statistical Office. UNSO produced such consolidated estimates for 60 countries for 1980 and 57 for 1985. Thereafter the arrangement for consolidating the results on a world–wide basis broke down but the regional exercises continued. For 1990 there were only two regional exercises; OECD estimates on a Geary–Khamis basis for the 22 countries shown in Table A1–g (as well as for Japan and Turkey) and an ECE study for five East European countries and the USSR (shown in Table A1–h).

At the time I wrote Maddison (1995a) there had been several ICP rounds for 87 countries for at least one year. I used the 1990 OECD and ECE estimates for 26 countries, and updated the available results of earlier ICP rounds to 1990 for 14 other countries (seven in Latin America, seven in Asia), and ICP equivalent estimates for East Germany, Bangladesh and Pakistan. Thus I used ICP or ICP equivalent estimates for 43 countries representing 79.7 per cent of world GDP. I used the Penn World Tables of Robert Summers and Alan Heston (version 5.5 issued in 1993) for 106 countries, and their estimate for China. In total the Summers and Heston component represented 19.5 per cent of world GDP in 1990. For the remaining countries, representing 0.8 per cent of world GDP, I used proxy estimates (see Appendix F of Maddison, 1995a).

In the present study, I have continued to use 1990 as the benchmark year for several reasons: it is useful to retain the 1990 benchmark to ensure greater transparency in understanding the nature of the revisions and updating of Maddison (1995a); Maddison (1998a) made a very detailed reconstruction of Chinese GDP on the standardised SNA basis used in Western countries, with an estimate for 1990 in Geary–Khamis dollars; it would be a very complex exercise to switch from a 1990 to a 1993 benchmark on a consistent basis for different parts of the world, and the quality of the result would most likely be inferior to that for 1990.

For 1993 there are regional ICP estimates for 68 countries: OECD results for 24 countries, ESCAP for 14 East Asian countries, ESCWA for eight West Asian countries, and Eurostat for 22 African countries. All of these are available on a Geary–Khamis basis (as well as the EKS basis preferred for political reasons by Eurostat because it gives all countries the same weight). There are considerable problems in putting this material together on a comparable basis. The ESCAP estimates use the Hong Kong rather than the US dollar as a *numeraire*. ESCWA uses a short–cut, reduced information approach. The Eurostat results for Africa are intra–African relatives linked to the US dollar via a standardised exchange rate rather than a purchasing power parity with the United States as the *numeraire* country. To be useable for our purposes they need to be adjusted in the same way as the UN Statistical Office did for earlier Eurostat exercises for Africa (see note to Table A4–g).

OECD has recently published ICP8 estimates for 1996 for a total of 48 countries in two volumes: *Purchasing Power Parities and Real Expenditure*, 1999 covers the 28 OECD member countries and four others (Israel, Slovakia, Slovenia and the Russian Federation); and *A PPP Comparison for the NIS*, 2000. This covers the 15 successor states of the former USSR, Turkey and Mongolia. The ECE has made estimates which include five other East European countries for 1996 (Albania, Bulgaria, Croatia, Macedonia and Romania). The results of these three studies were multilateralised using the EKS procedure. Estimates on a Geary–Khamis basis have not yet been released. No 1996 estimates are available for other parts of the world. Appendix D assesses the results of these studies for Eastern Europe and the former USSR and describes the problems of reconciling them with those used in the present study.

In the present estimates for the 1990 benchmark, I have used the same ICP sources I used in Maddison (1995a), backcast ESCAP and ESCWA results in their 1993 exercise for eight Asian countries to 1990, the OECD 1993 exercise for Turkey and the OECD 1996 results for Mongolia. I dropped the Eurostat estimates for Africa in favour of Penn World Tables (version 5.6).

Table A–a. **Coverage of GDP Sample and the Proportionate Role of Proxy Measures, 1820–1998**

(GDP in billion 1990 international dollars and number of countries)

	1820	*1870*	*1913*	*1950*	*1998*
			Sample GDP		
Europe & Western Offshoots	180.3 (16)	579.5 (21)	1 785.9 (24)	3 729.7 (32)	17 197.1 (50)
Latin America	7.9 (2)	17.2 (5)	101.4 (8)	419.6 (23)	2 919.9 (23)
Asia	371.7 (4)	374.8 (6)	612.3 (12)	981.2 (37)	12 507.9 (37)
Africa	0.0 (0)	0.0 (0)	23.9 (4)	176.9 (42)	961.6 (42)
Total Sample	559.9 (22)	971.5 (32)	2 523.5 (48)	5 307.4 (134)	33 586.5 (152)
			Total GDP (including proxy component)		
Europe & Western Offshoots	238.	611.1	1 845.9	3 732.3 (42)	17 210.0 (60)
Latin America	14.1	27.9	121.7	423.6 (44)	2 941.9 (44)
Asia	411.2	422.2	664.2	985.7 (57)	12 534.6 (56)
Africa	31.0	40.2	72.9	194.6 (56)	1 039.4 (57)
World Total	694.4	1 101.8	2 704.7	5 336.1 (199)	33 725.9 (217)
			Coverage of Sample (Per cent of Regional and World Totals)		
Europe & Western Offshoots	75.8	94.8	96.7	99.9	99.9
Latin America	56.0	61.6	83.3	99.0	99.3
Asia	90.4	88.8	92.2	99.5	99.8
Africa	0.0	0.0	32.8	90.9	92.5
World	80.6	88.2	93.3	99.5	99.6

Source: "Sample" countries are those for which quantitative estimates of the volume movement of GDP are available. Proxy estimates are needed for missing countries in order to derive the regional and world totals (see the detailed explanation of the gap–filling procedure for 1820–1913 for Asian countries in section A–3 of the source notes). Generally proxies were derived by assuming that per capita GDP movement in the country and for period concerned moved parallel with that of other countries within the same region. The proxy GDP can then be derived by multiplying the per capita GDP by population (for which the coverage of the estimates is much more complete). Coverage is much higher for the period since 1950 as national accounts have been produced by official statisticians. For 1913 and earlier, the sample country estimates were mainly by quantitative economic historians. There were major political changes in the 1990s which increased the number of countries from 199 in Maddison (1995a) to 217. The former USSR has split into 15 countries, Yugoslavia into 5, Czechoslovakia into 2, and Eritrea has split from Ethiopia. The 2 Germanies have been reunited, and I have treated the West Bank and Gaza as if they were a consolidated unit. In most cases it is not possible to carry back the estimates for these new countries before 1990. However, the present estimates for new countries (e.g. the 15 successor countries of the former USSR) are (when consolidated) consistent with the historical estimates for the political entity to which they previously belonged.

Table A–b. **Nature of the PPP Converters Used to Estimate Levels of GDP in international dollars in the Benchmark Year 1990**

(billion 1990 Geary–Khamis dollars and number of countries)

	Europe & Western Offshoots	Latin America	Asia	Africa	World
ICP or Equivalent	15 273 (28)	2 131 (18)	8 017 (24)	0 (0)	25 421 (70)
Penn World Tables	59 (3)	71 (14)	524 (16)	846 (50)	1 500 (83)
Proxies	16 (10)	38 (12)	87 (16)	14 (7)	155 (45)
Total	15 349 (41)	2 239 (44)	8 628 (56)	860 (57)	27 076 (198)

Sources: Europe and Western Offshoots: 99.5 per cent of regional GDP from ICP, 28 countries shown in Tables A1–g and A1–h; Penn World Tables for 0.4 per cent of GDP (Bulgaria, Cyprus and Malta); proxy estimates for 0.1 per cent of GDP (Albania, Andorra, Channel Isles, Faeroe Isles, Gibraltar, Greenland, Isle of Man, Liechtenstein, Monaco and San Marino).

Latin America: 95.1 per cent of regional GDP from ICP (18 countries shown in Table A2–g); Penn World Tables for 3.2 per cent of GDP (Bahamas, Barbados, Belize, Dominica, Grenada, Guyana, Haiti, Nicaragua, Puerto Rico, St. Kitts Nevis, St. Lucia, St. Vincent, Suriname, Trinidad and Tobago); proxy estimates for 1.7 per cent of GDP (Antigua and Barbuda, Aruba, Bermuda, Cuba, Falkland Islands, French Guyana, Guadeloupe, Martinique, Neths. Antilles, St. Pierre and Miquelon, Turks and Caicos, and Virgin Islands).

Asia: 65.5 per cent of regional GDP from ICP, 27.4 per cent from ICP equivalent estimates (Bangladesh, China, Pakistan), see 23 countries listed in Tables A3–g, A3–h and A3–i, as well as Mongolia; Penn World Tables for 6.1 per cent of GDP (Bhutan, Burma, Fiji, Iraq, Jordan, Kuwait, Oman, Papua New Guinea, Saudi Arabia, Solomon Islands, Taiwan, Tonga, UAE, Vanuatu, Western Samoa, and Yemen); proxy estimates for 1 per cent of GDP (Afghanistan, American Samoa, Brunei, Cambodia, French Polynesia, Guam, Kiribati, Lebanon, Macao, Maldives, Marshall Islands, Micronesia, New Caledonia, North Korea, Pacific Islands, Wallis and Futuna, see Maddison, 1995a, pp. 214, 219–20).

Africa: Penn World Tables for 98.4 per cent of regional GDP (50 countries); proxy estimates for 1.6 per cent of GDP (Equatorial Guinea, Eritrea, Libya, Mayotte, St. Helena, São Tomé Principe and Western Sahara).

Table A–b cont'd. **Nature of the PPP Converters Used to Estimate Levels of GDP in 1990 international dollars in Maddison (1995a)**

	Europe & Western Offshoots	Latin America	Asia	Africa	World
ICP or Equivalent	14 847 (27)	1 835 (7)	5 111 (9)	0 (0)	21 793 (43)
Penn World Tables	72 (5)	232 (24)	4 211 (28)	813 (50)	5 328 (107)
Proxies	16 (10)	39 (13)	164 (20)	14 (6)	233 (49)
Total	14 941 (42)	2 106 (44)	9 486 (57)	827 (56)	27 359 (199)

Note: In Maddison (1995a), I used the different ICP rounds then available, with adjustment where necessary to 1990, for the 43 of the 56 sample countries. For the non-sample countries, and for the African sample countries (where I had doubts about the quality of the ICP estimates), I used Penn World Tables. In the present study, see Table Al–b above, I used the new estimates for China from Maddison (1998a) and made maximal use of the ICP results available from the 1975, 1980, 1985, and 1990 rounds, and partial use of the PPPs from the 1993 and 1996 rounds. In doing this I adjusted for revisions in nominal GDP in national prices. I did not use the ICP results for African countries (see Table A4–g). In Maddison (1995a) I used the Penn World Tables 5.5 version (1993), whereas the present study uses the PWT 5.6 version (1995) which is the latest available.

Table A–c. **Confrontation of Maddison (1995a) and Present Estimates
of Regional and World Population and GDP, 1820–1990**

Population (million at mid–year)

	Europe & Western Offshoots		Latin America		Asia	
	Maddison (1995a)	*Present*	*Maddison (1995a)*	*Present*	*Maddison (1995a)*	*Present*
1820	228.7	235.3	20.3	21.2	745.8	710.4
1870	360.4	374.5	37.9	40.0	779.0	765.1
1913	595.0	608.2	80.2	80.5	987.0	977.6
1950	748.8	748.5	162.5	165.9	1 377.9	1 381.9
1990	1 087.6	1 086.7	444.8	443.0	3 106.2	3 102.8

	Africa		World	
1820	73.0	74.2	1 067.9	1 041.1
1870	82.8	90.5	1 260.1	1 270.0
1913	109.7	124.7	1 771.9	1 791.0
1950	223.0	228.3	2 512.2	2 524.5
1990	618.9	620.8	5 257.4	5 253.3

GDP (billion 1990 international dollars)

	Europe & Western Offshoots		Latin America		Asia	
1820	239.0	238.1	13.8	14.1	409.2	411.2
1870	607.7	611.5	28.8	27.9	451.7	422.2
1913	1 812.3	1 845.9	115.4	121.7	735.3	664.2
1950	3 718.7	3 732.3	404.0	423.6	1 064.6	985.7
1990	14 940.7	15 348.9	2 105.9	2 239.4	9 485.7	8 627.8

	Africa		World	
1820	32.9	31.0	694.8	694.4
1870	39.8	40.2	1 127.9	1 101.7
1913	63.1	72.9	2 726.1	2 704.8
1950	185.0	194.6	5 372.3	5 336.1
1990	826.7	859.8	27 359.0	27 076.0

Source: Maddison (1995a), and detailed tables and text below. Turkey is included in West Asia in this study; in Maddison (1995a) it was included in Europe. Here the earlier estimates are adjusted to conform with the regionalisation of the present study.

A–1

Population, GDP and GDP Per Capita in Western Europe, Western Offshoots, Eastern Europe and the Successor States of the Former USSR

12 West European Countries

The quantitative historical evidence for these countries is better than for most other parts of the world. It is set out in detail in Maddison (1995a).

GDP and population for Austria, Belgium, Denmark, Finland, France, Norway, Sweden and Switzerland for 1820–1960 and Italy 1820–1970 are from Maddison (1995a), updated (except as noted below for France and Norway) from OECD, *National Accounts 1960–1997*, Vol. 1, Paris 1999 to 1990 and for 1990 onwards from OECD, *National Accounts of OECD Countries, 1988–1998*, vol. 1, 2000. Figures are adjusted to exclude the impact of territorial change and refer to 1998 frontiers, except for Germany and the United Kingdom.

> **Germany:** Figures for 1950 onwards refer to 1991 frontiers, 1820–1913 to Germany within its 1913 boundaries (excluding Alsace–Lorraine). See Table A–d for details.

> **Netherlands:** 1820 1913 GDP movement derived from Smits, Horlings and van Zanden (2000). 1913–60 GDP movement and 1820–1960 population from Maddison (1995a) updated from OECD sources.

> **Switzerland:** It was assumed that the 1820–70 GDP per capita movement paralleled that in Germany.

> **United Kingdom:** 1820–1913 estimates include the whole of Ireland, see Maddison (1995a), p. 232, and Table B–13, those for 1950 onwards include Northern Ireland. 1960 onwards updated from OECD sources.

The latest OECD national accounts publication incorporates new estimates for 15 countries revised to conform with the SNA 1993 standardised system. This involves two significant modifications in statistical practice:

a) treatment of computer software as investment rather than an intermediate product, which along with other changes has raised the 1990 benchmark GDP level as shown in Table A1–g;

b) a recommendation that countries adopt chain–weighted indices to measure the movement in GDP volume. Such indices are now used by France, Greece, Luxembourg, Netherlands, Norway and Sweden. For most countries, the new estimates are available only for very recent years, which is one of the reasons why the new OECD yearbook no longer has the historical depth it has had for the past 30 years. GDP indices based on chain weights for France and Norway for 1978–98 were made available by OECD and used here, together with 1960–78 estimates for these countries from the 1999 OECD national accounts publication. The chain weights seem to make no difference to Norwegian growth, but made French growth slightly faster.

Table A–d. **The Impact of Border Changes in Germany**

	West Germany (1990 frontiers)	East Germany (1990 frontiers)	Germany within 1991 boundaries	Germany within 1936 boundaries	Germany within 1913 frontiers ex. Alsace–Lorraine,
	GDP in million 1990 international dollars				
1820	16 390				26 349
1870	44 094				71 429
1913	145 045			225 008	237 332
1936	192 911	74 652	267 563	299 753	
1950	213 942	51 412	265 354		
1973	814 786	129 969	944 755		
1990	1 182 261	82 177	1 264 438		
1991	1 242 096	85 961	1 328 057		
	(Population (000 at mid–year)				
1820	14 747				24 905
1870	23 055				39 231
1913	37 843			60 227	65 058
1936	42 208	15 614	57 822	67 336	
1950	49 983	18 388	68 371		
1973	61 976	16 890	78 866		
1990	63 254	16 111	79 365		
1991	63 889	15 910	79 799		

Source: West German GDP 1820–60 from Maddison (1995a) updated from OECD sources, with minor adjustment derived from change in 1990 GDP level as noted in Table A1–g. East German GDP index 1950–1991 from Maddison (1995a), p. 132, benchmarked on official estimate for 1991 in 1990 DM (difference between West German and total German 1991 GDP as shown in OECD national accounts). The 1991 official benchmark level for East Germany is lower than I assumed in Maddison (1995a) which lowers the level of East German GDP 1950–91 shown there. 1936 level in East and West Germany, in the territories East of the Oder–Neisse, and for Germany in its 1936 frontiers from Maddison (1995a), p. 131. 1820–1913 levels within 1913 frontiers from Maddison (1995a), p. 231. Population in West Germany 1820–1991 and East Germany 1936–91 derived from Maddison (1995a), p. 104–5, 132 and 231.

Greece, Ireland, Portugal and Spain

Greece: 1900–60 population and 1913–60 GDP from Maddison (1995a) updated from OECD, *National Accounts*. 1820–1913 per capita GDP assumed to move parallel to the aggregate for Eastern Europe. Population movement 1820–1900 derived from Mitchell (1975), p. 21, adjusted to offset changes in Greek territory. This involved a series of adjustments. Greece gained independence from Turkey in the 1820s, and gradually extended its territory to the Ionian Islands (1864), Thessaly (1881), Crete (1898), Epirus, Macedonia, Thrace and the Aegean Islands (1919) and the Dodecanese (1947).

Ireland: 1950–60 from Maddison (1995a), updated from OECD sources.

Portugal: 1820–1970 population and 1950–60 GDP from Maddison (1995a), updated from OECD sources. 1913–50 GDP from D. Batista, C. Martins, M. Pinheiro and J. Reis "New Estimates of Portugal's GDP 1910–1958", Bank of Portugal, October 1997. 1850–1913 derived from Pedro Lains (1989) as described in Maddison (1995a) p. 138. 1820–50 GDP movement assumed to be at same rate as shown by J. Braga de Macedo (1995) for 1834–50.

Spain: 1820–1990 population and 1820–73 GDP movement from Maddison (1995a) updated from OECD sources.

Table A–e. **Population and GDP: 13 Small West European Countries**

	1950	*1973*	*1990*	*1998*
	Population (000 at mid–year)			
Iceland	143	212	255	271
Luxembourg	296	350	382	425
Cyprus	494	634	681	749
Malta	312	322	354	380
9 Other	285	388	483	513
13 Country Total	1 529	1 906	2 155	2 337
	GDP (million 1990 international dollars)			
Iceland	762	2 435	4 596	5 536
Luxembourg	2 481	5 237	8 819	13 324
Cyprus	930	3 207	6 651	8 600
Malta	278	855	2 987	4 424
9 Other	1 429	4 718	8 152	9 615
13 Country Total	5 880	16 452	31 205	41 499
	GDP per capita (1990 international dollars)			
Iceland	5 336	11 472	18 024	20 205
Luxembourg	8 382	14 963	23 086	31 058
Cyprus	1 883	5 058	9 767	11 169
Malta	894	2 655	8 438	11 642
9 Other	5 013	12 159	16 877	18 742
13 Country Average	3 846	8 631	14 480	17 757

13 Small West European Countries

Iceland and Luxembourg 1950–1998 GDP from OECD sources; Cyprus and Malta 1950–90 GDP from Maddison (1995a) updated from IMF. Nine smaller countries (Andorra, Channel Islands, Faeroe Islands, Gibraltar, Greenland, Isle of Man, Liechtenstein, Monaco and San Marino), 1950–98 per capita GDP assumed to be the same as the average for the 12 bigger West European countries. 1950–98 population for the 13 countries from International Programs Center, US Bureau of the Census. 1820–1950, population movement and GDP per capita levels for the 13 country group assumed to move parallel to the average for the 12 bigger West European countries.

Western Offshoots: 4 Countries

United States: Population 1820–1949 from Maddison (1995a), 1820 and 1870 amended to include 325 000 and 180 000 indigenous population (see Maddison, 1995a, p. 97). 1950 onwards from US Bureau of the Census.

1820–1950 GDP movement from Maddison (1995a), amended for 1820–70 to include income of the indigenous population (taken to be $400 per capita in 1820 and 1870).

1950–59 GDP movement from "GDP and Other Major NIPA Series, 1929–97", Survey of Current Business, August 1998. This series is based on a chained index as described in J.S. Landefeld and R.P. Parker, "BEA's Chain Indexes, Time Series and Measures of Long Term Growth", Survey of Current

Business, May 1997, p. 66, Table 5. 1959–98 GDP movement and 1990 benchmark level from the new estimates of BEA in Survey of Current Business, December 1999. The 1959–98 figures implement the recommendation of the new standardised System of National Accounts 1993 (published jointly by Eurostat, IMF, OECD, UN and World Bank) to include computer software as investment rather than intermediate input. The impact of the revisions, which raise the growth rate and the 1990 benchmark GDP level is described in E.P. Seskin, "Improved Estimates of the National Income and Product Accounts for 1959–98: Results of the Comprehensive Revision", *Survey of Current Business*, December 1999.

Australia, New Zealand and Canada: Population 1820–1973 from Maddison (1995a) updated from OECD sources. 1820 and 1870 amended to include indigenous population. Indigenous populations were as follows: Australia 300 000 in 1820, 150 000 in 1870; Canada 75 000 in 1820 and 45 000 in 1870, New Zealand 100 000 in 1820 and 50 000 in 1870 (see Maddison, 1995a, pp. 96–7).

1820–1960 GDP movement from Maddison (1995a) amended for 1820–70 to include income of the indigenous population (taken to be $400 per capita in 1820 and 1870). Canadian and New Zealand GDP movement 1960–98 from OECD sources. New Zealand estimates for 1969–87 refer to fiscal years. Australian GDP movement 1960–98 for calendar years based on the new official chain index (supplied by OECD) which shows slightly faster growth than the old index (annual compound growth of 3.95 per cent a year compared with 3.87 per cent for 1960–90). The Australian and Canadian GDP measures conform to the 1993 system of accounts, which New Zealand has not yet adopted.

Eastern Europe (7/12 Countries)

There have been major changes in the past decade in political and statistical systems which means that the estimates for these countries are of lower quality than for Western Europe.

Population of Albania 1820–1913, Bulgaria 1820, Poland, Romania and Yugoslavia 1820–70 from McEvedy and Jones (1978), otherwise 1820–1949 from Maddison (1995a), p. 110. 1950 onwards from International Programs Center, US Bureau of the Census.

East European GDP to 1990 from Maddison (1995a), Czech Republic, Hungary and Poland updated from OECD sources, other countries from the database of the Statistics Division of ECE (Economic Commission for Europe of the UN). 1820 estimates of GDP were available for only one country (Czechoslovakia); for 1870 for two countries (Czechoslovakia and Hungary); for 1913 for four countries (Bulgaria, Czechoslovakia, Hungary and Yugoslavia). In order to get a rough GDP estimate for the seven countries as a whole for 1820–1913, per capita GDP movement in the missing countries was assumed to move parallel to the average for the countries which were represented. In the 1990s, Czechoslovakia split into the Czech Republic and Slovakia, and Yugoslavia broke up into five republics; 1990–98 GDP volume movement in the five successor republics of Yugoslavia from ECE Statistics Division, 1990 breakdown of GDP by constituent republics derived from the Yugoslav Statistical Yearbook for 1990 (see Table A–f).

Table A–f. **GDP and Population in Successor Republics of Former Yugoslavia, 1990–98**

	1990	*1997*	*1998*
	Population (000 at mid–year)		
Bosnia	4 360	3 223	3 366
Croatia	4 754	4 665	4 672
Macedonia	2 031	1 996	2 009
Slovenia	1 968	1 973	1 972
Serbia–Montenegro	9 705	10 534	10 526
Former Yugoslavia	22 819	22 390	22 545
	GDP (million 1990 international dollars)		
Bosnia	16 530	9 028	9 261
Croatia	33 139	27 182	27 858
Macedonia	7 394	5 706	5 871
Slovenia	21 624	22 730	23 625
Serbia–Montenegro	51 266	28 000	28 722
Former Yugoslavia	129 953	92 646	95 337
	GDP per capita (1990 international dollars)		
Bosnia	3 791	2 801	2 851
Croatia	6 971	5 827	5 963
Macedonia	3 641	2 859	2 922
Slovenia	10 988	11 521	11 980
Serbia–Montenegro	5 282	2 658	2 729
Former Yugoslavia	5 695	4 138	4 229

Source: Population from US Bureau of the Census. 1990 GDP total for Yugoslavia from Table A1–h, broken down by constituent republic by applying the 1988 shares of gross material product shown in *Statisticki Godisnjak Jugoslavije 1990* (Statistical Yearbook of Yugoslavia), Statistical Office, Belgrade, 1990. GDP movement for successor republics 1990–98 from ECE Statistics Division, except for Bosnia, for which figures were not available. Bosnian GDP was assumed to move as in Serbia–Montenegro.

Former USSR

Population 1913–90 from Maddison (1995a), with revised estimates for 1820 and 1870 for the Asian population in the area of the former USSR (see Appendix B). 1950 population in each of the 15 successor republics from *Naselenie SSSR 1987*, Finansi i Statistika, Moscow, 1988, pp. 8–15 adjusted to mid–year; 1973 from *Narodnoe Khoziastvo SSSR*, 1972 and 1973 editions, p. 9, adjusted to mid–year; 1990 from *Mir v Tsifrakh 1992*, Goskomstat CIS, Moscow 1992; movement from 1990 onwards from ECE Statistics Division.

GDP 1870–1990 for the USSR within its 1990 boundaries from Maddison (1995a). Maddison (1998b) provides a detailed analysis of techniques for adjusting the national accounts of the Soviet era from an MPS to an SNA basis. 1820–70 per capita GDP assumed to move in the same proportion as the aggregate for Eastern Europe.

Breakdown of 1991 GDP level by successor republics derived from B.M. Bolotin "The Former Soviet Union as Reflected in National Accounts Statistics", in S. Hirsch, ed., *Memo 3: In Search of Answers in the Post–Soviet Era,* Bureau of National Affairs, Washington DC, 1992, cited in Maddison (1995a), p. 142, backcast to 1990 and adjusted to the USSR GDP total for that year. 1990–98 movement in GDP volume by republic from ECE Statistics Division.

A rough measure of the 1973–90 GDP volume movement in each of the 15 successor states was derived from official Soviet indices of real "national income" (MPS concept) which are available for 1958–90, see *Narodnoe Khoziastvo SSSR*, 1990 ed., p. 13; 1987 ed., p. 123; 1974 ed., p. 574; and 1965 ed., p. 590. Rates of growth of real "national income" 1973–90 were adjusted to a GDP basis, using the ratio which prevailed for the USSR as a whole for this period (.49075). See Maddison (1998*b*), p. 313 for a comparison of these two types of measure for 1913–90.

The official National Accounts of the Russian Federation (*Natsionalnie Schchota Rossii, 1999*) provide a breakdown of Russian GDP and GDP per capita for nine regions, and 90 administrative districts. The five Siberian regions and the Far East region together accounted for 29 per cent of product geographically allocable for 1997, and the Caucasus region 5.8 per cent. Thus, a little more than a third of GDP in the Russian Federation was generated in Asia, or about 232 billion international dollars of the Russian Federation's total GDP of $697 billion in 1997. Eight of the other successor republics of the USSR were in Asia (Armenia, Azerbaijan, Georgia, Kazakhstan, Kyrgyzstan, Tajikistan, Turkmenistan, Uzbekistan). Their total 1997 GDP was 216 billion international dollars. Thus the Asian part of the Russian republic, and the eight other successor republics in Asia together accounted for 448 billion international dollars or about 39 per cent of the total for the former USSR.

The per capita product of the different parts of the Russian Federation is also shown in the 1999 yearbook. In the city of Moscow, per capita income was 2.3 times the national average, in St. Petersburg about the same as the national average. Income levels in Siberia and the Far East were generally well above the national average. The lowest incomes were in the Caucasus region, less than a fifth of the national average in Ingushetia, 28 per cent in Dagestan, not available for Chechnya.

In the present exercise, the 1990 level of GDP in international dollars was derived from the ICP exercise for 1990 as shown in Table A–1h below. The breakdown by successor republic was based on the Bolotin estimates as indicated above. Recently the OECD, ECE, and the governments of most of the successor republics have collaborated on a new PPP exercise for 1996. This exercise was done using the EKS rather than the Geary–Khamis method. The results show significant differences from the ICP 6 estimates which I have used (see Appendix D).

Table A1–a. **Population (000 at mid–year): European Countries, the Former USSR and Western Offshoots**

	1820	1870	1913	1950	1973	1990	1998
Austria	3 369	4 520	6 767	6 935	7 586	7 729	8 078
Belgium	3 434	5 096	7 666	8 640	9 738	9 971	10 197
Denmark	1 155	1 888	2 983	4 269	5 022	5 138	5 303
Finland	1 169	1 754	3 027	4 009	4 666	4 986	5 153
France	31 246	38 440	41 463	41 836	52 118	56 735	58 805
Germany	24 905	39 231	65 058	68 371	78 956	79 364	82 029
Italy	20 176	27 888	37 248	47 105	54 751	56 719	57 592
Netherlands	2 355	3 615	6 164	10 114	13 438	14 947	15 700
Norway	970	1 735	2 447	3 265	3 961	4 241	4 432
Sweden	2 585	4 164	5 621	7 015	8 137	8 566	8 851
Switzerland	1 829	2 664	3 864	4 694	6 441	6 796	7 130
United Kingdom	21 226	31 393	45 649	50 363	56 223	57 561	59 237
12 West Europe	**114 419**	**162 388**	**227 957**	**256 616**	**301 037**	**312 753**	**322 507**
13 Small W.E. Countries	657	933	1 358	1 529	1 907	2 155	2 337
Greece	2 312	3 657	5 425	7 566	8 929	10 161	10 511
Ireland				2 969	3 073	3 506	3 705
Portugal	3 297	4 353	6 004	8 512	8 634	9 899	9 968
Spain	12 203	16 201	20 263	27 868	34 810	38 851	39 371
Total Western Europe	**132 888**	**187 532**	**261 007**	**305 060**	**358 390**	**377 325**	**388 399**
Australia	333	1 770	4 821	8 177	13 505	17 085	18 751
New Zealand	100	341	1 122	1 909	2 971	3 380	3 811
Canada	816	3 781	7 852	13 737	22 560	27 701	30 297
United States	9 981	40 241	97 606	152 271	211 909	249 984	270 561
4 Western Offshoots	**11 230**	**46 133**	**111 401**	**176 094**	**250 945**	**298 150**	**323 420**
Albania	437	603	898	1 227	2 318	3 273	3 331
Bulgaria	2 187	2 586	4 794	7 251	8 621	8 966	8 240
Czechoslovakia	7 190	9 876	13 245	12 389	14 550		
a) Czech Republic						10 310	10 286
b) Slovakia						5 263	5 393
Hungary	4 571	5 717	7 840	9 338	10 426	10 352	10 208
Poland	10 426	17 240	26 710	24 824	33 331	38 109	38 607
Romania	6 389	9 179	12 527	16 311	20 828	22 775	22 396
Former Yugoslavia	5 215	6 981	13 590	15 949	20 416	22 819	22 545
Total East Europe	**36 415**	**52 182**	**79 604**	**87 289**	**110 490**	**121 867**	**121 006**
Former USSR	**54 765**	**88 672**	**156 192**	**180 050**	**249 748**	**289 350**	**290 866**
Armenia				1 355	2 697	3 335	3 795
Azerbaijan				2 900	5 468	7 134	7 666
Belarus				7 755	9 235	10 260	10 239
Estonia				1 115	1 411	1 582	1 450
Georgia				3 261	4 857	5 460	5 442
Kazakhstan				6 711	13 812	16 742	15 567
Kyrgyzstan				1 742	3 182	4 395	4 699
Latvia				1 951	2 442	2 684	2 449
Lithuania				2 570	3 247	3 726	3 703
Moldova				2 344	3 743	4 365	3 649
Russian Federation				102 317	132 651	148 290	146 909
Tajikistan				1 534	3 235	5 303	6 115
Turkmenistan				1 222	2 395	3 668	4 838
Ukraine				36 951	48 280	51 891	50 295
Uzbekistan				6 322	13 093	20 515	24 050

Table A1–b. **GDP Levels (million 1990 international $): European Countries, the Former USSR and Western Offshoots**

	1820	*1870*	*1913*	*1950*	*1973*	*1990*	*1998*
Austria	4 104	8 419	23 451	25 702	85 227	130 476	152 712
Belgium	4 529	13 746	32 347	47 190	118 516	171 442	198 249
Denmark	1 471	3 782	11 670	29 654	70 032	94 863	117 319
Finland	913	1 999	6 389	17 051	51 724	84 103	94 421
France	38 434	72 100	144 489	220 492	683 965	1 026 491	1 150 080
Germany	26 349	71 429	237 332	265 354	944 755	1 264 438	1 460 069
Italy	22 535	41 814	95 487	164 957	582 713	925 654	1 022 776
Netherlands	4 288	9 952	24 955	60 642	175 791	258 094	317 517
Norway	1 071	2 485	6 119	17 838	44 544	78 333	104 860
Sweden	3 098	6 927	17 403	47 269	109 794	151 451	165 385
Switzerland	2 342	5 867	16 483	42 545	117 251	146 900	152 345
United Kingdom	36 232	100 179	224 618	347 850	675 941	944 610	1 108 568
12 West Europe	**145 366**	**338 699**	**840 743**	**1 286 544**	**3 660 253**	**5 276 855**	**6 044 301**
13 Small W.E. Countries	667	1 553	3 843	5 880	16 452	31 205	41 499
Greece	1 539	3 338	8 635	14 489	68 355	101 452	118 433
Ireland				10 231	21 103	41 459	67 368
Portugal	3 175	4 338	7 467	17 615	63 397	107 427	128 877
Spain	12 975	22 295	45 686	66 792	304 220	474 366	560 138
Total Western Europe	**163 722**	**370 223**	**906 374**	**1 401 551**	**4 133 780**	**6 032 764**	**6 960 616**
Australia	172	6 452	27 552	61 274	172 314	291 180	382 335
New Zealand	40	922	5 781	16 136	37 177	46 729	56 322
Canada	729	6 407	34 916	102 164	312 176	524 475	622 880
United States	12 548	98 374	517 383	1 455 916	3 536 622	5 803 200	7 394 598
4 Western Offshoots	**13 489**	**112 155**	**585 632**	**1 635 490**	**4 058 289**	**6 665 584**	**8 456 135**
Albania				1 228	5 219	8 125	7 999
Bulgaria			7 181	11 971	45 557	49 779	37 786
Czechoslovakia	6 106	11 491	27 755	43 368	102 445		
a) Czech Republic						91 706	88 897
b) Slovakia						40 854	41 818
Hungary		7 253	16 447	23 158	58 339	66 990	66 089
Poland				60 742	177 973	194 920	258 220
Romania				19 279	72 411	80 277	64 715
Former Yugoslavia			13 988	25 277	88 813	129 953	95 337
Total East Europe	**23 149**	**45 448**	**121 559**	**185 023**	**550 757**	**662 604**	**660 861**
Former USSR	**37 710**	**83 646**	**232 351**	**510 243**	**1 513 070**	**1 987 995**	**1 132 434**
Armenia					16 691	20 483	12 679
Azerbaijan					24 378	33 397	16 365
Belarus					48 333	73 389	58 799
Estonia					12 214	16 980	14 671
Georgia					28 627	41 325	14 894
Kazakhstan					104 875	122 295	74 857
Kyrgyzstan					11 781	15 787	9 595
Latvia					18 998	26 413	15 222
Lithuania					24 643	32 010	21 914
Moldova					20 134	27 112	9 112
Russian Federation					872 466	1 151 040	664 495
Tajikistan					13 279	15 884	5 073
Turkmenistan					11 483	13 300	8 335
Ukraine					238 156	311 112	127 151
Uzbekistan					67 012	87 468	79 272

Table A1–c. **GDP Per Capita (1990 international $): European Countries, the Former USSR and Western Offshoots**

	1820	1870	1913	1950	1973	1990	1998
Austria	1 218	1 863	3 465	3 706	11 235	16 881	18 905
Belgium	1 319	2 697	4 220	5 462	12 170	17 194	19 442
Denmark	1 274	2 003	3 912	6 946	13 945	18 463	22 123
Finland	781	1 140	2 111	4 253	11 085	16 868	18 324
France	1 230	1 876	3 485	5 270	13 123	18 093	19 558
Germany	1 058	1 821	3 648	3 881	11 966	15 932	17 799
Italy	1 117	1 499	2 564	3 502	10 643	16 320	17 759
Netherlands	1 821	2 753	4 049	5 996	13 082	17 267	20 224
Norway	1 104	1 432	2 501	5 463	11 246	18 470	23 660
Sweden	1 198	1 664	3 096	6 738	13 493	17 680	18 685
Switzerland	1 280	2 202	4 266	9 064	18 204	21 616	21 367
United Kingdom	1 707	3 191	4 921	6 907	12 022	16 411	18 714
12 West Europe	**1 270**	**2 086**	**3 688**	**5 013**	**12 159**	**16 872**	**18 742**
13 Small W.E. Countries	1 015	1 665	2 830	3 846	8 627	14 480	17 757
Greece	666	913	1 592	1 915	7 655	9 984	11 268
Ireland				3 446	6 867	11 825	18 183
Portugal	963	997	1 244	2 069	7 343	10 852	12 929
Spain	1 063	1 376	2 255	2 397	8 739	12 210	14 227
Total Western Europe	**1 232**	**1 974**	**3 473**	**4 594**	**11 534**	**15 988**	**17 921**
Australia	517	3 645	5 715	7 493	12 759	17 043	20 390
New Zealand	400	2 704	5 152	8 453	12 513	13 825	14 779
Canada	893	1 695	4 447	7 437	13 838	18 933	20 559
United States	1 257	2 445	5 301	9 561	16 689	23 214	27 331
4 Western Offshoots	**1 201**	**2 431**	**5 257**	**9 288**	**16 172**	**22 356**	**26 146**
Albania				1 001	2 252	2 482	2 401
Bulgaria				1 651	5 284	5 552	4 586
Czechoslovakia	849	1 164	2 096	3 501	7 041		
a) Czech Republic						8 895	8 643
b) Slovakia						7 762	7 754
Hungary		1 269	2 098	2 480	5 596	6 471	6 474
Poland				2 447	5 340	5 115	6 688
Romania				1 182	3 477	3 525	2 890
Former Yugoslavia			1 029	1 585	4 350	5 695	4 229
Total East Europe	**636**	**871**	**1 527**	**2 120**	**4 985**	**5 437**	**5 461**
Former USSR	**689**	**943**	**1 488**	**2 834**	**6 058**	**6 871**	**3 893**
Armenia					6 189	6 142	3 341
Azerbaijan					4 458	4 681	2 135
Belarus					5 234	7 153	5 743
Estonia					8 656	10 733	10 118
Georgia					5 894	7 569	2 737
Kazakhstan					7 593	7 305	4 809
Kyrgyzstan					3 702	3 592	2 042
Latvia					7 780	9 841	6 216
Lithuania					7 589	8 591	5 918
Moldova					5 379	6 211	2 497
Russian Federation					6 577	7 762	4 523
Tajikistan					4 105	2 995	830
Turkmenistan					4 795	3 626	1 723
Ukraine					4 933	5 995	2 528
Uzbekistan					5 118	4 264	3 296

Table A1–d. **GDP Per Capita Growth Rates: European Countries, the Former USSR and Western Offshoots**

	1820–70	*1870–1913*	*1913–50*	*1950–73*	*1973–98*
Austria	0.85	1.45	0.18	4.94	2.10
Belgium	1.44	1.05	0.70	3.55	1.89
Denmark	0.91	1.57	1.56	3.08	1.86
Finland	0.76	1.44	1.91	4.25	2.03
France	0.85	1.45	1.12	4.05	1.61
Germany	1.09	1.63	0.17	5.02	1.60
Italy	0.59	1.26	0.85	4.95	2.07
Netherlands	0.83	0.90	1.07	3.45	1.76
Norway	0.52	1.30	2.13	3.19	3.02
Sweden	0.66	1.46	2.12	3.07	1.31
Switzerland	1.09	1.55	2.06	3.08	0.64
United Kingdom	1.26	1.01	0.92	2.44	1.79
12 West Europe	**1.00**	**1.33**	**0.83**	**3.93**	**1.75**
13 Small W.E. Countries	0.99	1.24	0.83	3.58	2.93
Greece	0.63	1.30	0.50	6.21	1.56
Ireland				3.04	3.97
Portugal	0.07	0.52	1.39	5.66	2.29
Spain	0.52	1.15	0.17	5.79	1.97
Total Western Europe	**0.95**	**1.32**	**0.76**	**4.08**	**1.78**
Australia	3.99	1.05	0.73	2.34	1.89
New Zealand	3.90	1.51	1.35	1.72	0.67
Canada	1.29	2.27	1.40	2.74	1.60
United States	1.34	1.82	1.61	2.45	1.99
4 Western Offshoots	**1.42**	**1.81**	**1.55**	**2.44**	**1.94**
Albania				3.59	0.26
Bulgaria				5.19	−0.57
Czechoslovakia	0.63	1.38	1.40	3.08	(0.67)
a) Czech Republic					
b) Slovakia					
Hungary		1.18	0.45	3.60	0.59
Poland				3.45	0.91
Romania				4.80	−0.74
Former Yugoslavia			1.17	4.49	−0.11
Total East Europe	**0.63**	**1.31**	**0.89**	**3.79**	**0.37**
Former USSR	**0.63**	**1.06**	**1.76**	**3.36**	**−1.75**
Armenia					−2.44
Azerbaijan					−2.90
Belarus					0.37
Estonia					0.63
Georgia					−3.02
Kazakhstan					−1.81
Kyrgyzstan					−2.35
Latvia					−0.89
Lithuania					−0.99
Moldova					−3.02
Russian Federation					−1.49
Tajikistan					−6.20
Turkmenistan					−4.01
Ukraine					−2.64
Uzbekistan					−1.74

Table A1–e. **GDP Growth Rates: European Countries, the Former USSR and Western Offshoots**

	1820–70	*1870–1913*	*1913–50*	*1950–73*	*1973–98*
Austria	1.45	2.41	0.25	5.35	2.36
Belgium	2.25	2.01	1.03	4.08	2.08
Denmark	1.91	2.66	2.55	3.81	2.09
Finland	1.58	2.74	2.69	4.94	2.44
France	1.27	1.63	1.15	5.05	2.10
Germany	2.01	2.83	0.30	5.68	1.76
Italy	1.24	1.94	1.49	5.64	2.28
Netherlands	1.70	2.16	2.43	4.74	2.39
Norway	1.70	2.12	2.93	4.06	3.48
Sweden	1.62	2.17	2.74	3.73	1.65
Switzerland	1.85	2.43	2.60	4.51	1.05
United Kingdom	2.05	1.90	1.19	2.93	2.00
12 West Europe	**1.71**	**2.14**	**1.16**	**4.65**	**2.03**
13 Small W.E. Countries	1.70	2.13	1.16	4.58	3.77
Greece	1.56	2.23	1.41	6.98	2.22
Ireland				3.20	4.75
Portugal	0.63	1.27	2.35	5.73	2.88
Spain	1.09	1.68	1.03	6.81	2.47
Total Western Europe	**1.65**	**2.10**	**1.19**	**4.81**	**2.11**
Australia	7.52	3.43	2.18	4.60	3.24
New Zealand	6.48	4.36	2.81	3.70	1.68
Canada	4.44	4.02	2.94	4.98	2.80
United States	4.20	3.94	2.84	3.93	2.99
4 Western Offshoots	**4.33**	**3.92**	**2.81**	**4.03**	**2.98**
Albania				6.49	1.72
Bulgaria			1.39	5.98	−0.75
Czechoslovakia	1.27	2.07	1.21	3.81	(0.98)
a) Czech Republic					
b) Slovakia					
Hungary		1.92	0.93	4.10	0.50
Poland				4.78	1.50
Romania				5.92	−0.45
Former Yugoslavia			1.61	5.62	0.28
Total East Europe	**1.36**	**2.31**	**1.14**	**4.86**	**0.73**
Former USSR	**1.61**	**2.40**	**2.15**	**4.84**	**−1.15**
Armenia					−1.09
Azerbaijan					−1.58
Belarus					0.79
Estonia					0.74
Georgia					−2.58
Kazakhstan					−1.34
Kyrgyzstan					−0.82
Latvia					−0.88
Lithuania					−0.47
Moldova					−3.12
Russian Federation					−1.08
Tajikistan					−3.78
Turkmenistan					−1.27
Ukraine					−2.48
Uzbekistan					0.67

Table A1–f. **Population Growth Rates: European Countries, the Former USSR and Western Offshoots**

	1820–70	*1870–1913*	*1913–50*	*1950–73*	*1973–98*
Austria	0.59	0.94	0.07	0.39	0.25
Belgium	0.79	0.95	0.32	0.52	0.18
Denmark	0.99	1.07	0.97	0.71	0.22
Finland	0.81	1.28	0.76	0.66	0.40
France	0.42	0.18	0.02	0.96	0.48
Germany	0.91	1.18	0.13	0.63	0.15
Italy	0.65	0.68	0.64	0.66	0.20
Netherlands	0.86	1.25	1.35	1.24	0.62
Norway	1.17	0.80	0.78	0.84	0.45
Sweden	0.96	0.70	0.60	0.65	0.34
Switzerland	0.75	0.87	0.53	1.39	0.41
United Kingdom	0.79	0.87	0.27	0.48	0.21
12 West Europe	**0.70**	**0.79**	**0.32**	**0.70**	**0.28**
13 Small W.E. Countries	0.70	0.88	0.32	0.97	0.82
Greece	0.92	0.92	0.90	0.72	0.65
Ireland				0.15	0.75
Portugal	0.56	0.75	0.95	0.06	0.58
Spain	0.57	0.52	0.87	0.97	0.49
Total Western Europe	**0.69**	**0.77**	**0.42**	**0.70**	**0.32**
Australia	3.40	2.36	1.44	2.21	1.32
New Zealand	2.48	2.81	1.45	1.94	1.00
Canada	3.11	1.71	1.52	2.18	1.19
United States	2.83	2.08	1.21	1.45	0.98
4 Western Offshoots	**2.87**	**2.07**	**1.25**	**1.55**	**1.02**
Albania	0.65	0.93	0.85	2.80	1.46
Bulgaria	0.34	1.45	1.12	0.76	−0.18
Czechoslovakia	0.64	0.68	−0.18	0.70	(0.30)
a) Czech Republic					
b) Slovakia					
Hungary	0.45	0.74	0.47	0.48	−0.08
Poland	1.01	1.02	−0.20	1.29	0.59
Romania	0.73	0.73	0.72	1.07	0.29
Former Yugoslavia	0.59	1.56	0.43	1.08	0.40
Total East Europe	**0.72**	**0.99**	**0.25**	**1.03**	**0.36**
Former USSR	**0.97**	**1.33**	**0.38**	**1.43**	**0.61**
Armenia				3.04	1.38
Azerbaijan				2.80	1.36
Belarus				0.76	0.41
Estonia				1.03	0.11
Georgia				1.75	0.46
Kazakhstan				3.19	0.48
Kyrgyzstan				2.65	1.57
Latvia				0.98	0.01
Lithuania				1.02	0.53
Moldova				2.06	−0.10
Russian Federation				1.14	0.41
Tajikistan				3.30	2.58
Turkmenistan				2.97	2.85
Ukraine				1.17	0.16
Uzbekistan				3.22	2.46

Table A1–g. Derivation of 1990 Benchmark Levels of GDP in International Dollars, 22 OECD Countries

	GDP in national currency	Geary–Khamis PPP Converter	Exchange rate	GDP in million international dollars	GDP in $ million converted at exchange rate
Austria	1 813 482	13.899	11.370	130 476	159 497
Belgium	6 576 846	38.362	33.418	171 442	196 805
Denmark	825 310	8.700	6.189	94 863	133 351
Finland	523 034	6.219	3.824	84 103	136 777
France	6 620 867	6.450	5.445	1 026 491	1 215 954
West Germany[a]	2 426 000	2.052	1.616	1 182 261	1 501 238
Italy	1 281 207	1384.11	1198.1	925 654	1 069 366
Netherlands	537 867	2.084	1.821	258 094	295 369
Norway	722 705	9.218	6.26	78 333	115 448
Sweden	1 359 879	8.979	5.919	151 451	229 748
Switzerland	317 304	2.160	1.389	146 900	228 441
United Kingdom	554 486	0.587	0.563	944 610	984 877
Luxembourg	345 738	39.203	33.418	8 819	10 346
Iceland	364 402	79.291	58.284	4 596	6 252
Greece	13 143	129.55	158.51	101 452	82 916
Ireland	28 524	0.688	0.605	41 459	47 147
Portugal	9 855	91.737	142.56	107 427	69 129
Spain	501 452	105.71	101.93	474 366	491 957
Australia	393 675	1.352	1.281	291 180	307 319
New Zealand	72 776	1.5574	1.676	46 729	43 422
Canada	668 181	1.274	1.167	524 475	572 563
United States	5 803 200	1.000	1.000	5 803 200	5 803 200

a) East German GDP in international dollars was 82 177 million in 1990.

Source: GDP in national currency from OECD *National Accounts of OECD Countries, 1988–1998*, vol. 1, OECD, Paris, 2000, except for the Netherlands which is from OECD *Quarterly National Accounts* (1999:4), and the United States which is from *Survey of Current Business*, December 1999, p. 132. Official Italian GDP estimates reduced by 3 per cent as explained in Maddison (1995a), p. 133. Geary–Khamis purchasing power converters from the sixth round of the International Comparison Project (ICP) for 1990 — see Maddison (1995a) Table C–6, p. 172; exchange rates from the same source. PPPs and exchange rates are expressed in units of national currency by PPP per US dollar. GDP in million international dollars converted by PPP is derived by dividing column 1 by column 2. GDP in million US dollars converted at exchange rates is derived by dividing column 1 by column 3. When one makes binary comparisons of purchasing power, e.g. of France and the United States, there are three possible approaches. One can a) revalue French expenditure at US prices and get a "Laspeyres" comparison of GDP volume; b) revalue US expenditure at French prices and get a "Paasche" volume comparison; (c) make a compromise "Fisher" geometric average of the Laspeyres and Paasche measures. The results of such binary studies can be used to compare the situation in a number of countries, e.g. France/United States, Germany/United States and United Kingdom/United States comparisons can be linked using the United States as a "star" country. However, the derivative France–Germany, United Kingdom–Germany and France–United Kingdom results are inferential and will not necessarily be the same as one could derive from direct binary comparisons of each pair. Such comparisons are not "transitive", but transitivity and additivity can be achieved by use of a "multilateral" PPP. The Geary–Khamis measure is the multilateral measure I prefer as it gives weights to countries corresponding to the size of their GDP (see Maddison, 1995a, p. 163, for a detailed explanation). For most countries, the new GDP figures in national currencies are higher than those used in Maddison (1995a). They incorporate routine revisions and those resulting from adoption of the 1993 SNA (standardised system of national accounts). This was adopted by Norway in 1995, Denmark and Canada in 1997. Australia, Austria, Belgium, Finland, France, Germany, Greece, Ireland, Italy, Luxembourg, the Netherlands, Portugal, Spain, Sweden and the United Kingdom made the change later, and figures on the new basis were published for these 15 countries for the first time by OECD in the 1988–98 yearbook. The new system involves treatment of expenditure on mineral exploration and computer software as investment rather than intermediate input. In some countries, e.g. France and Italy "entertainment, literary and artistic originals" are also now treated as investment. Iceland, New Zealand and Switzerland still use the old 1968 SNA and have not made these methodological changes. As a result of these revisions the 1990 GDP levels have changed by the following ratios to the level shown in Maddison (1995a):

Austria	1.00676	United Kingdom	1.00928
Belgium	1.02342	Luxembourg	1.15206
Denmark	1.02779	Iceland	1.03700
Finland	1.01591	Greece	0.99539
France	1.01774	Ireland	1.06406
Germany	1.00033	Portugal	1.014765
Italy	1.00668	Spain	1.00051
Netherlands	1.04184	Australia	1.04055
Norway	1.09314	New Zealand	0.99290
Sweden	1.00000	Canada	1.00567
Switzerland	1.01041	United States	1.06192

Table A1–h. **Derivation of 1990 Benchmark Levels of GDP in International Dollars, Five East European Countries and USSR**

	GDP in national currency	Implicit PPP Converter	Exchange rate	GDP in million international dollars	GDP in $ million converted at exchange rate
Czechoslovakia	811 309	6.12	17.95	132 560	45 198
Hungary	1 935 459	28.89	63.206	66 990	30 621
Poland	608 347	3.12	9.5	194 920	64 037
Romania	857 180	10.678	22.43	80 277	38 216
USSR	1 033 222	0.520	1.059	1 987 995	975 658
Yugoslavia	1 113 095	8.565	11.318	129 953	98 347

Source: GDP in national currency from *International Comparison of Gross Domestic Product in Europe 1990*, United Nations Statistical Commission and ECE, Geneva and New York, 1994, p. 61. These comparisons were carried out in cooperation with the national statistical offices, with adjustments to make the coverage of the national accounts conform to the standardised national accounting system used in Western countries. Adjustments were also made to correct for lower quality of goods in the East European countries. The results were multilateralised using the EKS rather than the Geary–Khamis technique, and the PPP adjusted GDPs were expressed in Austrian schillings. The relative volume indices of GDP were converted to an approximate Geary–Khamis basis using Austrian GDP in international dollars in Table 2.4 as a bridge, see *op. cit.*, p. 5. This is how the column 4 results were estimated and the implicit PPP in column 3 was derived by dividing column 1 by column 4. Exchange rates were derived from IMF, *International Financial Statistics*, except for the USSR which is from World Bank, *World Tables 1995*. Since 1990, these six countries have become 25. Czechoslovakia has split into two countries, Yugoslavia into five, and the USSR into 15. In order to get rough provisional estimates for GDP in these 22 new successor states, I assumed that their proportional share in 1990 GDP was the same as it was in national currency. The OECD has released new estimates in international dollars for 20 of these new states (excluding Bosnia and Serbia), using the EKS technique of multilateralisation, see *A PPP Comparison for the NIS, 1994, 1995 and 1996*, OECD, February 2000. See Appendix D for a confrontation of these new estimates with those I use here.

A–2

Population, GDP and GDP Per Capita in 44 Latin American and Caribbean Countries

There are eight core countries for which GDP estimates are available before 1950. 1820–1990 GDP movement for Argentina, Chile, Colombia, Peru and Venezuela from Maddison (1995a), updated from ECLAC, *Economic Survey of Latin America and the Caribbean: Summary 1998–99*, 1999, p. 32. Brazilian GDP 1950–98 as above, 1820–1900 from Maddison (1995a); per capita GDP movement 1900–50 from Maddison and Associates (1992), p. 212. Mexican GDP movement 1870–1910 from Coatsworth (1989), 1910–60 from Maddison (1995a), 1960 onwards from OECD sources. I assumed a smaller drop in Mexican GDP per capita 1820–70 than Coatsworth. GDP 1820–1936 for Uruguay from Luis Bertola and Associates, *PBI de Uruguay 1870–1936*, Montevideo, 1998. 1936–90 GDP supplied by Luis Bertola, 1990 onwards from ECLAC (1999). Benchmark 1990 level of GDP in the eight countries in international dollars from Table A2–g.

Population 1820–1950 from Maddison (1995a) except Uruguay (supplied by Luis Bertola). 1950 onwards from US Bureau of the Census.

There are 15 other countries for which detailed estimates of population and GDP are shown. For 13 of them, 1870–1913 population was derived by interpolating the estimates of N. Sanchez Albornoz, "The Population of Latin America, 1850–1930", in L. Bethell, ed., *The Cambridge History of Latin America*, vol. 4, Cambridge University Press, 1986, p. 122. Jamaica 1870 and 1913 derived from G. Eisner, *Jamaica, 1830–1930: A Study in Economic Growth*, Manchester University Press, 1961, p. 134. 1870–1950 movement in Trinidad and Tobago was assumed to be proportionately the same as in Jamaica. 1820–70 population in the 15 countries assumed to move in the same proportion as the aggregate for the eight core countries. 1950–98 population movement from US Bureau of the Census.

1950–73 GDP movement for 11 of the 15 countries from ECLAC, *Series Historicas del Crecimiento de America Latina*, Santiago, 1978, 1973–90 from World Bank, *World Tables* (1995), and 1990 onwards from ECLAC (1999). Cuba 1950–90 from various ECLAC sources, 1990 onwards from ECLAC, *Preliminary Overview of the Economies of Latin America*, Santiago (1998 and 1999 editions). GDP of Puerto Rico 1950–98 from *PBI Historico*, Junta de Planificación, San José, 1998. Jamaica, Trinidad and Tobago 1950–73 from OECD Development Centre database, 1973–90 from World Bank, *World Tables*, 1990 onwards from ECLAC (1999). 1820–1950 movement in aggregate per capita GDP of the 15 countries assumed to move in the same proportion as the aggregate for the eight core countries.

Aggregate estimates for 21 small Caribbean countries are shown in Tables A–2a to A–2f; country detail for 1950–98 in Table A–g.

Table A2–g shows the derivation of 1990 benchmark GDP levels from ICP studies in 1990 international prices for the eight core countries and ten others. Penn World Tables were used for Bahamas, Barbados, Belize, Dominica, Grenada, Guyana, Haiti, Nicaragua, Puerto Rico, St. Kitts Nevis, St. Lucia, St. Vincent, Suriname, Trinidad and Tobago.

Table A–g. **GDP and Population in 21 Small Caribbean Countries, 1950–98**

	GDP in million 1990 international $				Population (000)			
	1950	**1973**	**1990**	**1998**	**1950**	**1973**	**1990**	**1998**
Bahamas	756	3 159	3 946	4 248	70	182	251	180
Barbados	448	1 595	2 138	2 366	211	243	255	259
Belize	110	341	735	929	66	130	190	230
Dominica	82	182	279	344	51	74	72	66
Grenada	71	180	310	388	76	97	94	96
Guyana	462	1 309	1 159	2 018	428	755	748	708
St. Lucia	61	199	449	508	79	109	140	152
St. Vincent	79	175	392	506	66	90	113	120
Suriname	315	1 046	1 094	1 209	208	384	396	428
Total Group A	2 384	8 186	10 502	12 516	1 255	2 064	2 249	2 339
Antigua & Barbuda	82	328	413	510	46	68	63	64
Bermuda	65	238	310		39	53	58	62
Guadeloupe	359	1 568	1 801		208	329	378	416
Guyana (Fr.)	138	238	516		26	53	116	163
Martinique	293	1 568	1 857		217	332	374	407
Neth. Antilles	393	1 097	980	1 100	159	225	253	274
St. Kitts Nevis	61	215	233	345	44	45	40	42
Total Group B	1 391	5 252	6 110	7 787	739	1 105	1 284	1 428
Other 5 Countries	181	667	1 094	1 446	68	139	183	233
21 Countries	3 956	14 105	17 706	21 749	2 062	3 308	3 726	3 990

Source: 1950–90 GDP movement from Maddison (1995a), p. 218, and the underlying database. For seven of the Group A countries, GDP movement for 1990 onwards from ECLAC, *Economic Survey of Latin America and the Caribbean 1998–1999*, Santiago, 1999, p. 32. 1990–98 per capita GDP movement for Antigua and Barbuda, Bahamas, Netherlands Antilles and St. Kitts Nevis from IMF. For other countries, aggregate GDP per capita movement assumed to be proportionately the same as the Group A average. Population 1950 onwards from the Division of Population Studies, US Bureau of the Census; 1820–50 aggregate population of the 21 countries assumed to move in the same proportion as the aggregate for the 15 countries specified in Table A2–a. The 5 countries in the third group are Aruba, Falkland Islands, St. Pierre and Miquelon, Turks and Caicos Islands and Virgin Islands.

For 11 small Caribbean countries and Cuba, neither ICP nor PWT estimates of PPP were available. It was assumed that the average per capita GDP level for these countries was the same as the average for the 32 countries for which indicators were available, and for Cuba that it was about 15 per cent below the Latin America average.

ICP estimates represented nearly 95.2 per cent of the aggregate GDP for Latin America in 1990, PWT nearly 3.2 per cent, and proxy valuations 1.7 per cent.

It was assumed that the aggregate proportionate GDP per capita movement for the three missing countries for 1870–1913 was the same as the average for the other five core countries. For 1820 it was assumed that the average level of per capita GDP for the missing core countries was the same as the average for Brazil and Mexico.

For the 36 other countries no estimates of GDP movement were available for 1820–1950. Their average per capita GDP movement was assumed to be proportionate to that in the eight sample countries (including the proxy element in the latter). Thus the total proxy component of Latin American aggregate GDP in 1820 was 44.0 per cent, for 1870 38.2 per cent, for 1913 16.7 per cent, and negligible for 1950 onwards.

Table A2–a. **Population (000 at mid–year): 44 Latin American Countries**

	1820	*1870*	*1913*	*1950*	*1973*	*1990*	*1998*
Argentina	534	1 796	7 653	17 150	25 174	32 634	36 265
Brazil	4 507	9 797	23 660	53 443	103 463	151 040	169 807
Chile	885	1 943	3 491	6 091	9 897	13 128	14 788
Colombia	1 206	2 392	5 195	11 592	23 069	32 985	38 581
Mexico	6 587	9 219	14 970	28 485	57 643	84 748	98 553
Peru	1 317	2 606	4 339	7 633	14 350	21 989	26 111
Uruguay	55	373	1 177	2 194	2 834	3 106	3 285
Venezuela	718	1 653	2 874	5 009	11 893	19 325	22 803
Total 8 Countries	**15 809**	**29 779**	**63 359**	**131 597**	**248 323**	**358 955**	**410 193**
Bolivia		1 495	1 881	2 766	4 680	6 620	7 826
Costa Rica		155	372	867	1 886	3 022	3 605
Cuba		1 331	2 469	5 785	9 001	10 545	11 051
Dominican Republic		242	750	2 312	4 781	6 997	7 999
Ecuador		1 013	1 689	3 310	6 629	10 308	12 337
El Salvador		492	1 008	1 940	3 853	5 041	5 752
Guatemala		1 007	1 486	2 969	5 801	9 631	12 008
Haiti		1 150	1 891	3 097	4 748	6 048	6 781
Honduras		404	660	1 431	2 964	4 740	5 862
Jamaica		499	837	1 385	2 036	2 466	2 635
Nicaragua		361	578	1 098	2 241	3 591	4 583
Panama		176	348	893	1 659	2 388	2 736
Paraguay		384	594	1 476	2 692	4 236	5 291
Puerto Rico		645	1 181	2 218	2 863	3 537	3 860
Trinidad & Tobago		210	352	632	985	1 198	1 117
Total 15 other Countries	**5 077**	**9 564**	**16 096**	**32 179**	**56 819**	**80 368**	**93 443**
Total 21 small non sample Countries	**334**	**630**	**1 060**	**2 062**	**3 308**	**3 726**	**3 990**
Total 44 Latin America Countries	**21 220**	**39 973**	**80 515**	**165 837**	**308 450**	**443 049**	**507 623**
Total 43 Latin America Countries (excluding Mexico)	**14 633**	**30 754**	**65 545**	**137 352**	**250 807**	**358 301**	**409 070**

Table A2–b. **GDP Levels (million 1990 international $): 44 Latin American Countries**

	1820	1870	1913	1950	1973	1990	1998
Argentina		2 354	29 060	85 524	200 720	212 518	334 314
Brazil	2 912	6 985	19 188	89 342	401 643	743 765	926 919
Chile			9 261	23 274	50 401	84 038	144 279
Colombia			6 420	24 955	80 728	159 042	205 132
Mexico	5 000	6 214	25 921	67 368	279 302	516 692	655 910
Peru			4 500	17 270	56 713	64 979	95 718
Uruguay		748	3 895	10 224	14 098	20 105	27 313
Venezuela		941	3 172	37 377	126 364	160 648	204 433
Total 8 Countries	**11 275**	**22 273**	**101 417**	**355 334**	**1 209 969**	**1 961 787**	**2 594 018**
Bolivia				5 309	11 030	14 446	19 241
Costa Rica				1 702	8 145	14 370	19 272
Cuba				19 613	29 165	31 087	23 909
Dominican Republic				2 416	9 617	17 503	25 304
Ecuador				6 278	21 337	40 267	51 378
El Salvador				2 888	9 084	10 805	15 627
Guatemala				6 190	18 593	29 050	40 522
Haiti				3 254	4 810	6 323	5 532
Honduras				1 880	4 866	8 898	11 929
Jamaica				1 837	8 411	8 890	9 308
Nicaragua				1 774	6 566	5 297	6 651
Panama				1 710	7 052	10 688	15 609
Paraguay				2 338	5 487	13 923	16 719
Puerto Rico				4 755	20 908	37 277	51 159
Trinidad & Tobago				2 322	8 553	11 110	13 683
Total 15 other Countries	**2 676**	**5 289**	**19 058**	**64 266**	**173 626**	**259 934**	**325 843**
Total 21 small non sample Countries	**169**	**335**	**1 206**	**3 956**	**14 105**	**17 706**	**21 749**
Total 44 Latin America Countries	**14 120**	**27 897**	**121 681**	**423 556**	**1 397 700**	**2 239 427**	**2 941 610**
Total 43 Latin America Countries (excluding Mexico)	**9 120**	**21 683**	**95 760**	**356 188**	**1 118 398**	**1 722 735**	**2 285 700**

Table A2–c. **GDP per Capita (1990 international $): 44 Latin American Countries**

	1820	*1870*	*1913*	*1950*	*1973*	*1990*	*1998*
Argentina		1 311	3 797	4 987	7 973	6 512	9 219
Brazil	646	713	811	1 672	3 882	4 924	5 459
Chile			2 653	3 821	5 093	6 401	9 756
Colombia			1 236	2 153	3 499	4 822	5 317
Mexico	759	674	1 732	2 365	4 845	6 097	6 655
Peru			1 037	2 263	3 952	2 955	3 666
Uruguay		2 005	3 309	4 660	4 975	6 473	8 314
Venezuela		569	1 104	7 462	10 625	8 313	8 965
Total 8 Countries	**713**	**748**	**1 601**	**2 700**	**4 873**	**5 465**	**6 324**
Bolivia				1 919	2 357	2 182	2 459
Costa Rica				1 963	4 319	4 755	5 346
Cuba				3 390	3 240	2 948	2 164
Dominican Republic				1 045	2 012	2 502	3 163
Ecuador				1 897	3 219	3 906	4 165
El Salvador				1 489	2 358	2 143	2 717
Guatemala				2 085	3 205	3 016	3 375
Haiti				1 051	1 013	1 045	816
Honduras				1 314	1 642	1 877	2 035
Jamaica				1 326	4 131	3 605	3 532
Nicaragua				1 616	2 930	1 475	1 451
Panama				1 915	4 251	4 476	5 705
Paraguay				1 584	2 038	3 287	3 160
Puerto Rico				2 144	7 303	10 539	13 254
Trinidad & Tobago				3 674	8 683	9 274	12 250
Total 15 other Countries	**527**	**553**	**1 184**	**1 997**	**3 056**	**3 234**	**3 487**
Total 21 small non sample Countries	**506**	**532**	**1 138**	**1 919**	**4 264**	**4 752**	**5 451**
Total 44 Latin America Countries	**665**	**698**	**1 511**	**2 554**	**4 531**	**5 055**	**5 795**
Total 43 Latin America Countries (excluding Mexico)	**623**	**705**	**1 461**	**2 593**	**4 459**	**4 808**	**5 588**

Table A2–d. **GDP Per Capita Growth Rate: 44 Latin American Countries**

	1820–1870	*1870–1913*	*1913–50*	*1950–73*	*1973–98*
Argentina		2.50	0.74	2.06	0.58
Brazil	0.20	0.30	1.97	3.73	1.37
Chile			0.99	1.26	2.63
Colombia			1.51	2.13	1.69
Mexico	−0.24	2.22	0.85	3.17	1.28
Peru			2.13	2.45	−0.30
Uruguay		1.17	0.93	0.28	2.08
Venezuela			5.30	1.55	−0.68
Total 8 Countries	**0.10**	**1.79**	**1.42**	**2.60**	**1.05**
Bolivia				0.90	0.17
Costa Rica				3.49	0.86
Cuba				−0.20	−1.60
Dominican Republic				2.89	1.83
Ecuador				2.33	1.04
El Salvador				2.02	0.57
Guatemala				1.89	0.21
Haiti				−0.16	−0.86
Honduras				0.97	0.86
Jamaica				5.06	−0.62
Nicaragua				2.62	−2.77
Panama				3.53	1.18
Paraguay				1.10	1.77
Puerto Rico				5.47	2.41
Trinidad & Tobago				3.81	1.39
Total 15 other Countries				**1.87**	**0.53**
Total 21 small non sample Countries				**3.53**	**0.99**
Total 44 Latin America Countries	**0.10**	**1.81**	**1.43**	**2.52**	**0.99**
Total 43 Latin America Countries (excluding Mexico)	**0.25**	**1.71**	**1.56**	**2.38**	**0.91**

Table A2–e. **GDP Growth Rate: 44 Latin American Countries**

	1820–1870	*1870–1913*	*1913–50*	*1950–73*	*1973–98*
Argentina		6.02	2.96	3.78	2.06
Brazil	1.77	2.38	4.24	6.75	3.40
Chile			2.52	3.42	4.30
Colombia			3.74	5.24	3.80
Mexico	0.44	3.38	2.62	6.38	3.47
Peru			3.70	5.31	2.12
Uruguay		3.91	2.64	1.41	2.68
Venezuela			6.89	5.44	1.94
Total 8 Countries	**1.37**	**3.59**	**3.45**	**5.47**	**3.10**
Bolivia				3.23	2.25
Costa Rica				7.04	3.51
Cuba				1.74	−0.79
Dominican Republic				6.19	3.95
Ecuador				5.46	3.58
El Salvador				5.11	2.19
Guatemala				4.90	3.17
Haiti				1.71	0.56
Honduras				4.22	3.65
Jamaica				6.84	0.41
Nicaragua				5.85	0.05
Panama				6.35	3.23
Paraguay				3.78	4.56
Puerto Rico				6.65	3.64
Trinidad & Tobago				5.83	1.90
Total 15 other Countries				**4.42**	**2.55**
Total 21 small non sample Countries				**5.68**	**1.75**
Total 44 Latin America Countries	**1.37**	**3.48**	**3.43**	**5.33**	**3.02**
Total 43 Latin America Countries **(excluding Mexico)**	**1.75**	**3.51**	**3.61**	**5.10**	**2.90**

Table A2–f. **Population Growth Rate: 44 Latin American Countries**

	1820–1870	*1870–1913*	*1913–50*	*1950–73*	*1973–98*
Argentina	2.46	3.43	2.20	1.68	1.47
Brazil	1.57	2.07	2.23	2.91	2.00
Chile	1.59	1.37	1.52	2.13	1.62
Colombia	1.38	1.82	2.19	3.04	2.08
Mexico	0.67	1.13	1.75	3.11	2.17
Peru	1.37	1.19	1.54	2.78	2.42
Uruguay	3.90	2.71	1.70	1.12	0.59
Venezuela	1.68	1.29	1.51	3.83	2.64
Total 8 Countries	**1.27**	**1.77**	**2.00**	**2.80**	**2.03**
Bolivia		0.54	1.05	2.31	2.08
Costa Rica		2.06	2.31	3.44	2.63
Cuba		1.45	2.33	1.94	0.82
Dominican Republic		2.67	3.09	3.21	2.08
Ecuador		1.20	1.84	3.07	2.52
El Salvador		1.68	1.79	3.03	1.62
Guatemala		0.91	1.89	2.96	2.95
Haiti		1.16	1.34	1.88	1.44
Honduras		1.15	2.11	3.22	2.77
Jamaica		1.21	1.37	1.69	1.04
Nicaragua		1.10	1.75	3.15	2.90
Panama		1.60	2.58	2.73	2.02
Paraguay		1.02	2.49	2.65	2.74
Puerto Rico		1.42	1.72	1.12	1.20
Trinidad & Tobago		1.21	1.59	1.95	0.50
Total 15 other Countries	**1.27**	**1.22**	**1.89**	**2.50**	**2.01**
Total 21 small non sample Countries	**1.28**	**1.22**	**1.81**	**2.08**	**0.75**
Total 44 Latin America Countries	**1.27**	**1.64**	**1.97**	**2.73**	**2.01**
Total 43 Latin America Countries (excluding Mexico)	**1.50**	**1.78**	**2.02**	**2.65**	**1.98**

Table A2–g. Derivation of Estimates of 1990 GDP in 1990 International Dollars, 18 Latin American Countries

	GDP in million national currency units in reference year	PPP Converter for reference year (units of national currency per dollar)	GDP in reference year in million Geary–Khamis dollars	1990 GDP in Geary–Khamis dollars of reference year	1990 GDP in million 1990 Geary–Khamis dollars
ICP 3 (Reference Year 1975)					
Jamaica	2 611	0.742	3 519	3 865	8 890
Mexico	1 007 036	7.4	136 086	224 649	516 692
ICP 4 (Reference Year 1980)					
Argentina	3 840	0.02604	147 465	134 607	212 518
Bolivia	128 614	14.51	8 864	9 150	14 446
Brazil	13 164	0.03252	404 797	471 096	743 765
Chile	1 075 269	26.67	40 318	53 299	84 038
Colombia	1 579 130	21.99	71 811	100 736	159 042
Costa Rica	41 406	5.79	7 151	9 102	14 370
Dominican Republic	6 625	0.594	11 153	11 086	17 503
Ecuador	293 337	14.16	20 716	25 505	40 267
El Salvador	8 917	1.31	6 807	6 844	10 805
Guatemala	7 879	0.467	16 871	18 400	29 050
Honduras	4 976	1.12	4 443	5 636	8 898
Panama	3 559	0.564	6 310	6 770	10 688
Paraguay	560 459	83.87	6 682	8 819	13 923
Peru	5 970 000	129.6	46 065	41 157	64 979
Uruguay	92 204	7.58	12 164	12 734	20 105
Venezuela	297 800	3.14	94 841	101 753	160 648

Source: Column 1 shows GDP in the reference year in national currency units, in most cases as specified in the original ICP estimate. For Argentina, Peru and Venezuela, there were upward adjustments to the official estimates of nominal GDP in 1980, after the ICP exercise was conducted. These involved upward adjustments of 36 per cent, 6.5 per cent, and 17.2 per cent respectively to correct for previous underestimates for informal activity. In the case of Mexico my estimate is 12.2 per cent lower than the official 1975 figure shown in OECD, *National Accounts, 1960–97*; the adjustment was made to correct for official exaggeration of output levels in agriculture, manufacturing and some services. The rationale for this change is explained in Maddison (1995a), p. 166. The PPPs in column 2 are from ICP. Column 3 is derived from columns 1 and 2. Column 4 was derived by adjusting column 3 for the volume movement in GDP between the reference year and 1990. Column 5 is column 4 adjusted for the movement in the US GDP deflator from the reference year to 1990.

A–3

Population, GDP and GDP Per Capita in 56 Asian Countries, 1820–1998

The estimates for Asia are an update and substantial revision of those in Maddison (1995a). The biggest revisions to GDP growth are those for China which are described in Maddison (1998a), but there are improvements in those for India, Japan, the Philippines, Taiwan and a number of other countries. Source notes have been added for 26 countries, bringing the detailed coverage from 11 to 37 countries. There are also revisions to the population figures. The 1990 benchmark GDP estimates have been revised: for 24 countries representing 93 per cent of Asian GDP, they are based on ICP or ICP equivalent measures, for 16 countries (6 per cent of Asian GDP) they are derived from Penn World Tables version 5.6, and, for the remaining 1 per cent, GDP levels were measured by proxy estimates (16 countries).

There are three groups of countries. The most reliable estimates of GDP growth are for the first group of 16 East Asian countries for which there has been substantial research on historical national accounts. These countries represented 95 per cent of Asian GDP in 1820, 85 per cent in 1950 and 88.4 per cent in 1998. The proxy estimates used to fill holes in the GDP dataset are shown in Table A–m.

For the second group of 25 East Asian countries, the presently available GDP growth indicators have serious deficiencies and the quality of the 1990 benchmark estimates is poor. Detailed notes are given for Afghanistan, Cambodia, Laos, Mongolia, North Korea and Vietnam which all pose major problems. Conversion of their accounts from Soviet style material product to a GDP basis is one of these, and can only be done in rough fashion. The other countries in this group are Bhutan, Brunei, Macao, the Maldives and 15 Pacific islands. The 25 country group accounted for 3.7 per cent of Asian GDP in 1950 and 1.7 per cent in 1998.

The third group consists of 15 West Asian countries, many of which were provinces of the Ottoman Empire until the end of the first world war. For most of these there has been no quantitative research on their macroeconomic performance before 1950. In ten countries, the postwar economy was strongly affected by the oil industry. Per capita income of the oil producers in 1950 was much higher than in prewar years, and a good deal higher than in the rest of Asia. Oil production in the area was 16 million metric tons in 1937, 86 million in 1950, and 1,053 million in 1973 — an increase of 11.5 per cent a year from 1950 to 1973. OPEC action in raising prices and restricting supply meant that production in 1998 was about the same as in 1973 (see Table 3–21). Growth was also significantly affected by war in Iran, Iraq, Israel, Kuwait, Lebanon, Syria and Yemen. This group represented 11.2 per cent of Asian GDP in 1950, 14.4 per cent in 1973, and 9.9 per cent in 1998.

Our estimates for Asia exclude the eight Asian successor republics of the USSR (Armenia, Azerbaijan, Georgia, Kazakhstan, Kyrgyzstan, Tajikistan, Turkmenistan and Uzbekistan) and the Asian territory of the Russian Federation (see note on former USSR in Section A–1 of this Appendix, and Appendix D.).

16 East Asian Countries

Bangladesh: Maddison (1995a) provides separate GDP and population estimates back to 1820 for Bangladesh and Pakistan. In this study the figures for India 1820–1913 include Bangladesh and Pakistan.

1950–66, volume movement of Bangladesh GDP from A. Maddison, Class *Structure and Economic Growth,* Allen and Unwin, London 1971, p. 171. 1966–78 GDP movement from World Bank, *World Tables,* various issues, 1978 onwards from ADB. Figures for 1967 onwards are for fiscal years. Population 1950 onwards from the Center for International Research, US Bureau of the Census.

For India, Bangladesh, and Pakistan, it is necessary to have benchmark GDP levels which are compatible with the fact that the three countries were united until 1947. The ICP estimates for Bangladesh and Pakistan (see Table A–3g) are not compatible with those for India. I therefore assumed that Pakistan and Bangladesh combined had the same average per capita GDP (in 1990 international dollars) as India in 1950. In 1950 Bangladesh and Pakistan were two "wings" of the former Pakistan. Their relative levels of GDP in 1950 were taken from Planning Commission, Reports of the Advisory Panels for the *Fourth Five–Year Plan,* Government of Pakistan, Islamabad, July 1970, p. 136.

Burma (Myanmar): 1820–70 population movement assumed to be proportionately the same as in India, 1870–1941 population derived from Aye Hlaing (1964), 1950 onwards from US Bureau of the Census. 1901–38 net domestic product by industry of origin at 1901 prices from Aye Hlaing, "Trends of Economic Growth and Income Distribution in Burma 1870–1940", *Journal of the Burma Research Society,* 1964, p. 144 linked to 1938–59 estimates of GDP by industry of origin at 1947/8 prices in E.E. Hagen, *On the Theory of Social Change,* Dorsey, Homewood, Illinois, 1962, linked to OECD Development Centre estimates for 1950–78. GDP from 1978 onwards from ADB. Benchmark 1990 GDP level estimates in 1990 Geary–Khamis dollars derived from R. Summers and A. Heston, *Penn World Tables,* version 5.6.

China: 1820–1995 GDP levels and population from A. Maddison, *Chinese Economic Performance in the Long Run,* OECD Development Centre, 1998, pp. 158–9 and 169, 1950–52 GDP movement from Maddison (1995a). 1995–98 GDP movement derived from *China Statistical Yearbook 1999,* State Statistical Bureau, Beijing, 1999, p. 58. The Chinese authorities show GDP growth averaging 8.7 per cent a year for 1995–98. I reduced this to 6.6 per cent using a correction coefficient derived from Maddison (1998a), p. 160 for 1978–95. See Xu (1999) for a comment on the estimates in Maddison (1998a) by the acting head of national accounts in the Chinese statistical office (SSB). See Table A–3g for 1990 benchmark GDP level.

Hong Kong: 1820–1950 population from Maddison (1998a), p. 170, 1950–89 from US Bureau of the Census, 1990 onwards from ADB. 1950–61 GDP movement from K.R. Chou, *The Hong Kong Economy,* Academic Publications, Hong Kong, 1966, p. 81, and 1961–1998 from *Estimates of Gross Domestic Product 1961 to 1998,* Census and Statistics Dept., Hong Kong, March 1999, p. 14. Benchmark 1990 GDP level derived by updating ICP 5, see Table A3–g.

India: Population 1820–1900 from Maddison (1995a), thereafter from Sivasubramonian, figures refer to October 1st (middle of fiscal year). GDP at 1948/9 prices for fiscal years by industry of origin for undivided India 1900–46, and India 1946–98 from S. Sivasubramonian, "Twentieth Century Economic Performance of India", in A. Maddison, D.S. Prasada Rao and W. Shepherd, eds., *The Asian Economies in the Twentieth Century,* Elgar, Aldershot, London, 2001. 1870–1900 GDP movement derived by linking estimates of net product in nine sectors at constant prices in A. Heston, "National Income", in D. Kumar and M. Desai, *Cambridge Economic History of India,* Vol. 2, Cambridge, 1983, p. 397–8, to the Sivasubramonian estimates of the level of sectoral output in 1900 (see Table A–h). 1820 per capita product assumed to be the same as in 1870. Benchmark 1990 GDP derived from ICP 4, see Table A3–g.

Table A–h. **India: GDP, Population and Per Capita GDP, 1820–1998**[a]

	GDP (1990 million int. $)	Population (million)	Per Capita GDP (1990 int. $)		GDP (1990 million int. $)	Population (million)	Per Capita GDP (1990 int. $)
1820	111 417	209.0	533	1946	212 622	343	620
				1947	213 680	346	618
1870	134 882	253.0	533	1948	215 927	350	617
				1949	221 631	355	624
1900	170 466	284.5	599	1950	222 222	359	619
1901	173 957	286.2	608	1951	227 362	365	623
1902	188 504	288.0	655	1952	234 148	372	629
1903	191 141	289.7	660	1953	248 963	379	657
1904	192 060	291.5	659	1954	259 262	386	672
1905	188 587	293.3	643	1955	265 527	393	676
1906	193 979	295.1	657	1956	280 978	401	701
1907	182 234	296.9	614	1957	277 924	409	680
1908	184 844	298.7	619	1958	299 137	418	716
1909	210 241	300.5	700	1959	305 499	426	717
1910	210 439	302.1	697	1960	326 910	434	753
1911	209 354	303.1	691	1961	336 744	444	758
1912	208 946	303.4	689	1962	344 204	454	758
1913	204 242	303.7	673	1963	361 442	464	779
1914	215 400	304.0	709	1964	389 262	474	821
1915	210 110	304.2	691	1965	373 814	485	771
1916	216 245	304.5	710	1966	377 207	495	762
1917	212 341	304.8	697	1967	408 349	506	807
1918	185 202	305.1	607	1968	418 907	518	809
1919	210 730	305.3	690	1969	446 872	529	845
1920	194 051	305.6	635	1970	469 584	541	868
1921	208 785	307.3	679	1971	474 238	554	856
1922	217 594	310.4	701	1972	472 766	567	834
1923	210 511	313.6	671	1973	494 832	580	853
1924	220 763	316.7	697	1974	500 146	593	843
1925	223 375	319.9	698	1975	544 683	607	897
1926	230 410	323.2	713	1976	551 402	620	889
1927	230 426	326.4	706	1977	593 834	634	937
1928	232 745	329.7	706	1978	625 695	648	966
1929	242 409	333.1	728	1979	594 510	664	895
1930	244 097	336.4	726	1980	637 202	679	938
1931	242 489	341.0	711	1981	675 882	692	977
1932	245 209	345.2	710	1982	697 705	708	985
1933	245 433	345.8	710	1983	753 942	723	1 043
1934	247 712	350.7	706	1984	783 042	739	1 060
1935	245 361	355.6	690	1985	814 344	755	1 079
1936	254 896	360.6	707	1986	848 990	771	1 101
1937	250 768	365.7	686	1987	886 154	788	1 125
1938	251 375	370.9	678	1988	978 822	805	1 216
1939	256 924	376.1	683	1989	1 043 912	822	1 270
1940	265 455	381.4	696	1990	1 098 100	839	1 309
1941	270 531	386.8	699	1991	1 104 114	856	1 290
1942	269 278	391.7	687	1992	1 161 769	872	1 332
1943	279 898	396.3	706	1993	1 233 796	891	1 385
1944	276 954	400.3	692	1994	1 330 036	908	1 465
1945	272 503	405.6	672	1995	1 425 798	927	1 538
1946	258 164	410.4	629	1996	1 532 733	943	1 625
				1997	1 609 371	959	1 678
				1998	1 702 712	975	1 746

a) The figures for 1820–1946 refer to undivided India, 1946–1998 to modern India, 1946 is an overlap year where two figures are given which demonstrate the impact of partition.

Indonesia: 1820–70 real income for three ethnic groups (indigenous, foreign Asiatic, and "European", in A. Maddison, "Dutch Income in and from Indonesia", *Modern Asian Studies,* 23.4 (1989), pp. 663–5. 1870–1900 GDP movement by industry of origin at 1983 prices supplied by Pierre van der Eng. They are a revision of estimates in his article "The Real Domestic Product of Indonesia, 1880–1989", *Explorations in Economic History,* July 1992. 1900–98 from P. van der Eng, "Indonesia's Growth Performance in the Twentieth Century", in A. Maddison, D.S. Prasada Rao and W. Shepherd, eds., *The Asian Economies in the Twentieth Century,* Elgar, Aldershot, 2001. Population 1820–90 from same sources as GDP, 1990 onwards from ADB. Benchmark 1990 GDP level derived from ICP4 (see Table A–3g).

Japan: Population 1820–1960 from Maddison (1995a), updated from OECD sources. 1890–1940 GDP at 1934–36 market prices, by industry of origin, from K. Ohkawa and M. Shinohara, eds., *Patterns of Japanese Development: A Quantitative Appraisal,* Yale, 1979, pp. 278–80. This is a summary of the results of K. Ohkawa, M. Shinohara, and M. Umemura, eds., *Estimates of Long–Term Economic Statistics of Japan since 1868,* (LTES), which appeared in 14 volumes published between 1966 and 1988. Ohkawa and Shinohara (1979) reproduce the GDP by industry of origin estimates in LTES vol. 1 (1974) p. 227 with some tiny modifications. The LTES volumes were originally intended to cover the whole of the Meiji period back to 1868 but GDP aggregates were only published back to 1885, even though some of the volumes contained estimates for earlier years. The main reason for this reticence by Ohkawa and Shinohara was that the estimates in Vol. 9 *on Agriculture and Forestry,* published in 1966 had been criticised by James Nakamura, *Agricultural Production and the Economic Development of Japan, 1873–1922,* Princeton, 1966, for exaggerating the growth of rice production in the early years of the Meiji period. There were also some holes in the data base which reinforced their reluctance to estimate aggregate GDP for years before 1885. In 1979 new estimates of rice production became available for 1874–89 (see Saburo Yamada and Yujiro Hayami, "Agricultural Growth in Japan, 1880–1970", in Y. Hayami, V.W. Ruttan and H.M. Southworth, eds., *Agricultural Growth in Japan, Taiwan, Korea and the Philippines,* Asian Productivity Center, Honolulu, 1979, p. 233). This source was used to revise the LTES GDP estimate for the farm sector, with rough estimates to fill the holes in the data set, GDP for 1874–89 was estimated using the same 1934–36 price weights as in the LTES (see Table A–i). GDP growth 1820–74 from Appendix B.

The LTES (Vol. I, p. 214) GDP estimates for 1940–50 were revised by Toshiyuki Mizoguchi and Noriyuki Nojima, "Nominal and Real GDP in Japan: 1940–55", which was summarised in an English translation in T. Mizoguchi, *Reforms of Statistical System under Socio–Economic Changes,* Maruzen, Tokyo, 1995, p. 225. I used these estimates (at 1955 prices by industry of origin) for the years from 1940 to 1950. 1950–60 from Maddison (1995a), 1960–90 from OECD, *National Accounts 1960–1997,* vol. 1, 1999. 1990 onwards from *National Accounts of OECD Countries 1988–1998,* Vol. 1, 2000. Benchmark GDP level for 1990 derived from ICP6 (see Table A3–g)

Malaysia: Population of modern Malaysia (old federated and unfederated Malay states, Sabah and Sarawak) excluding Brunei and Singapore 1820–1913 from estimates supplied by Don Hoerr, 1913–50 movement kindly supplied by Pierre van der Eng. 1950 onwards from US Bureau of the Census.

GDP movement 1913–90 from provisional estimates by Pierre van der Eng. These are an extension of the estimates by industry of origin for West Malaysia in V.V. Bhanoji Rao, *National Accounts of West Malaysia 1947–1971,* Heinemann, Kuala Lumpur, 1976, adjusted to include Sabah and Sarawak. 1990 onwards from ADB. 1990 GDP benchmark level derived ICP 7, see Table A3–h.

Nepal: 1820–1913 population movement assumed to be proportionately the same as in India. 1913 from League of Nations, *International Statistical Yearbook, 1927,* Geneva, 1928, pp. 2–3; 1950 onwards from US Bureau of the Census. 1950–90 GDP movement from Maddison (1995a) database, 1990 onwards from ADB. 1990 benchmark GDP level derived from ICP 7, see Table A3–h.

Table A–i. Reconstitution of Japanese GDP by Industry of Origin, 1874–90
(million yen at 1934–36 prices)

	FFF (1)	MM (2)	Const. (3)	FI (4)	Subtotal (5)	OS (6)	DRR (7)	GDP (8)
1874	1 300	207	61	28	1 596	1 418	125	3 139
1875	1 444	225	50	30	1 749	1 506	126	3 381
1876	1 388	226	49	31	1 694	1 480	127	3 301
1877	1 437	240	48	33	1 758	1 520	128	3 406
1878	1 416	249	48	35	1 748	1 519	129	3 396
1879	1 514	266	57	38	1 875	1 593	130	3 598
1880	1 580	277	68	40	1 965	1 648	131	3 744
1881	1 497	274	73	42	1 886	1 608	132	3 626
1882	1 537	280	82	45	1 944	1 644	133	3 721
1883	1 529	281	85	48	1 943	1 648	134	3 725
1884	1 426	293	74	51	1 844	1 598	135	3 775
1885	1 637	266	88	54	2 045	1 713	136	3 894
1886	1 748	307	87	58	2 200	1 833	137	4 170
1887	1 808	328	116	60	2 312	1 908	137	4 357
1888	1 749	331	99	65	2 244	1 778	138	4 160
1889	1 578	374	115	67	2 134	2 085	142	4 361
1890	1 848	369	127	73	2 417	2 217	144	4 778

Source: The 1890 benchmark is from Ohkawa, Takamatsu and Yamamoto, National Income (1974) (Vol. 1 of LTES) p. 227. Col. 1 (FFF) refers to gross value added in farming, forestry and fishing. It adjusts the vol. 9, p. 152 estimate of gross farm output 1874–89 in line with the findings of Yamada and Hayami (1979) p. 233. Total farm inputs from vol. 9, p. 186, value added in forestry from p. 234. Value added in fishery from vol. 1, p. 228, linked to estimates for earlier years in Ohkawa (1957), p. 72. Col. 2 (MM) refers to gross value added in manufacturing and mining. 1885–90 from Vol. 1, p. 227; 1874–85 derived from Shinohara's estimates in vol. 10, p. 145 and 243 for gross output and assuming that the 1885 ratio of value added to gross output (30 per cent) was also valid for 1874–84. Col. 3 (Const.) refers to construction; 1885–90 from vol. 1, p. 227, 1874–85 assumed to move in line with investment in construction (vol. 4, p. 230). Col. 4 (FI) refers to transport, communications, electricity, gas and water, which Ohkawa called "facilitating industries". 1885–90 from vol. 1, p. 227, and it was assumed that this sector grew at the same rate in 1874–84. Col. 5 is the subtotal of cols. 1–4. Col. 6 (OS) refers to "other services", i.e. commerce, public administration and military, education, professional services and domestic servants; estimates for 1885–90 are from vol. 1, p. 227. For 1874–84 it was assumed that two thirds of the volume of these services moved parallel to the subtotal in col. 5, and one third in line with population. Col. 7 (DRR) refers to depreciation of residential buildings and "riparian" works. LTES made no imputation for house rent; 1885–90 from vol. 1, p. 227; for 1874–84 it was assumed that DDR rose with population. Col. 8 refers to GDP and is the sum of cols. 5, 6 and 7.

Pakistan: As for Bangladesh.

Philippines: Population 1820–1913 from Maddison (1995a), 1950 onwards from US Bureau of the Census. 1950–90 GDP movement from estimates of the National Statistical Coordination Board, Manila, 1990 onwards from Asian Development Bank (ADB), *Key Indicators of Developing Asian and Pacific Countries,* Manila updated from ADB. In Maddison (1995a), I used the estimates of Hooley (1968) for 1913–50, which showed 1950 per capita GDP well below the 1913 level. He has since made major revisions to his 1968 estimates showing substantially better performance for 1913–50. I have provisionally assumed that the 1950 per capita GDP level was about the same as in 1913. Benchmark GDP level derived from ICP4 (see Table A3–g).

Singapore: 1820–1998 population from same sources as for Malaysia. 1913–50 per capita GDP movement assumed to be proportionately the same as that for Malaysia. 1950–73 GDP movement from Maddison (1995a) database, 1973–90 from World Bank, *World Tables 1995,* 1990 onwards from ADB. 1990 benchmark GDP level derived from ICP 7, see Table A3–h.

South Korea: The estimates refer to the whole of Korea for 1820–1913, South Korea for 1950 onwards. 1820–1906 population movement from T.H. Kwon and Y–H. Shin, "On Population Estimates of the Yi Dynasty, 1392–1910", *Tong–a Munhwa,* 14, 1977, pp. 324–329. 1906–38 from Mizoguchi and Umemura (1988) p. 238. 1940 from Kim and Roemer (1979) p. 23. Population for 1950 onwards from Center for International Research, US Bureau of the Census.

Table A-j. **Japan: GDP, Population and Per Capita GDP, 1820-1998**

	GDP (million int. $)	Population (000)	Per Capita GDP (1990 int. $)		GDP (million int. $)	Population (000)	Per Capita GDP (1990 int. $)
1820	20 739	31 000	669	1934	142 876	68 090	2 098
				1935	146 817	69 238	2 120
1870	25 393	34 437	737	1936	157 493	70 171	2 244
1871		34 648		1937	165 017	71 278	2 315
1872		34 859		1938	176 050	71 879	2 449
1873		35 070		1939	203 780	72 364	2 816
1874	26 644	35 235	756	1940	209 728	72 967	2 874
1875	28 698	35 436	810	1941	214 392	74 005	2 897
1876	28 019	35 713	785	1942	214 853	75 029	2 864
1877	28 910	36 018	803	1943	211 431	76 005	2 782
1878	28 825	36 315	794	1944	206 747	77 178	2 679
1879	30 540	36 557	835	1945	156 805	76 224	2 057
1880	31 779	36 807	863	1946	120 017	77 199	1 555
1881	30 777	37 112	829	1947	125 433	78 119	1 606
1882	31 584	37 414	844	1948	135 352	80 155	1 689
1883	31 618	37 766	837	1949	138 867	81 971	1 694
1884	31 872	38 138	836	1950	160 966	83 563	1 926
1885	33 052	38 427	860	1951	181 025	84 974	2 130
1886	35 395	38 622	916	1952	202 005	86 293	2 341
1887	36 982	38 866	952	1953	216 889	87 463	2 480
1888	35 310	39 251	900	1954	229 151	88 752	2 582
1889	37 016	39 688	933	1955	248 855	89 790	2 772
1890	40 556	40 077	1 012	1956	267 567	90 727	2 949
1891	38 621	40 380	956	1957	287 130	91 513	3 138
1892	41 200	40 684	1 013	1958	303 857	92 349	3 290
1893	41 344	41 001	1 008	1959	331 570	93 237	3 556
1894	46 287	41 350	1 119	1960	375 090	94 053	3 988
1895	46 933	41 775	1 123	1961	420 246	94 890	4 429
1896	44 353	42 196	1 051	1962	457 742	95 797	4 778
1897	45 284	42 643	1 062	1963	496 514	96 765	5 131
1898	53 883	43 145	1 249	1964	554 449	97 793	5 670
1899	49 870	43 626	1 143	1965	586 744	98 883	5 934
1900	52 020	44 103	1 180	1966	649 189	99 790	6 506
1901	53 883	44 662	1 206	1967	721 132	100 850	7 151
1902	51 088	45 255	1 129	1968	813 984	102 050	7 976
1903	54 672	45 841	1 193	1969	915 556	103 231	8 869
1904	55 101	46 378	1 188	1970	1 013 602	104 334	9 715
1905	54 169	46 829	1 157	1971	1 061 230	105 677	10 042
1906	61 263	47 227	1 297	1972	1 150 516	107 179	10 735
1907	63 198	47 691	1 325	1973	1 242 932	108 660	11 439
1908	63 628	48 260	1 318	1974	1 227 706	110 160	11 145
1909	63 556	48 869	1 301	1975	1 265 661	111 520	11 349
1910	64 559	49 518	1 304	1976	1 315 966	112 770	11 669
1911	68 070	50 215	1 356	1977	1 373 741	113 880	12 063
1912	70 507	50 941	1 384	1978	1 446 165	114 920	12 584
1913	71 563	51 672	1 385	1979	1 525 477	115 880	13 164
1914	69 504	52 396	1 327	1980	1 568 457	116 800	13 429
1915	75 952	53 124	1 430	1981	1 618 185	117 650	13 754
1916	87 702	53 815	1 630	1982	1 667 653	118 450	14 079
1917	90 641	54 437	1 665	1983	1 706 380	119 260	14 308
1918	91 572	54 886	1 668	1984	1 773 223	120 020	14 774
1919	100 959	55 253	1 827	1985	1 851 315	120 750	15 332
1920	94 653	55 818	1 696	1986	1 904 918	121 490	15 680
1921	105 043	56 490	1 859	1987	1 984 142	122 090	16 251
1922	104 756	57 209	1 831	1988	2 107 060	122 610	17 185
1923	104 828	57 937	1 809	1989	2 208 858	123 120	17 941
1924	107 766	58 686	1 836	1990	2 321 153	123 540	18 789
1925	112 208	59 522	1 885	1991	2 409 305	123 920	19 442
1926	113 211	60 490	1 872	1992	2 433 924	124 320	19 578
1927	114 859	61 430	1 870	1993	2 441 512	124 670	19 584
1928	124 246	62 361	1 992	1994	2 457 252	124 960	19 664
1929	128 115	63 244	2 026	1995	2 493 399	125 570	19 857
1930	118 800	64 203	1 850	1996	2 591 213	125 864	20 587
1931	119 803	65 205	1 837	1997	2 613 154	126 166	20 712
1932	129 835	66 189	1 962	1998	2 539 986	126 469	20 084
1933	142 589	67 182	2 122				

1911–38 Korean GDP derived from T. Mizoguchi and M. Umemura, *Basic Economic Statistics of Former Japanese Colonies, 1895–1938*, Toyo Keizai Shinposha, Tokyo, 1988, p. 238. They give annual estimates for two aggregate measures: gross domestic expenditure, and net domestic product at factor cost (both at 1934–6 prices). The latter showed a compound growth rate of 3.68 per cent per annum for 1913–38, the former 4.06 per cent. I used the expenditure estimate. Sang–Chul Suh, *Growth and Structural Changes in the Korean Economy, 1910–40*, Harvard University Press, Cambridge, Mass., 1978, p. 171 provides annual estimates of the net value of output for five commodity sectors (agriculture, forestry, fishery, mining, and manufacturing) for 1910–40 at 1936 prices. The aggregate measure shows slower growth for 1913–38 than Mizoguchi and Umemura (growth of 3.07 per cent per annum). I used the Suh commodity estimates together with a rough estimate for the service sector (assuming service output to move parallel to population) as a rough proxy for GDP movement for 1938–40. 1938–40 population movement from Suh, p. 41 adjusted from an end–year to mid–year basis.

In 1945, the Korean economy was split into two occupation zones and the peninsula has since become two very different economies. Suh (p. 136) provided a breakdown of commodity output for his five sectors between North and South Korea for 1934, 1935, 1939 and 1940. The commodity sectors can be aggregated using the current price market shares shown on pp. 160–6. The North Korean share rose from 1934 (37.2 per cent of total commodity output) to 1940 (45.2 per cent). In the same years the Northern share of population rose from 32.4 to 33.6 per cent, so it had higher per capita commodity output than the South in 1934 and the differential had increased very substantially by 1940, owing to the concentration of Japanese investment in Northern manufacturing and mining to complement its activity in Manchukuo. Augmenting Suh's commodity output estimates for North and South Korea by a rough adjustment for service activity, it would seem that in 1940, North Korean per capita GDP was about 49 per cent higher than that in South Korea. Kwang Suk Kim and M. Roemer, *Growth and Structural Transformation,* Harvard University Press, 1979, p. 35 estimate levels of commodity output by sector in South Korea in 1940 and 1953 in 1953 prices which I adjusted to a GDP basis by a rough allowance for service sector output. This link is not very satisfactory as it was made by revaluing Suh's estimate of 1940 South Korean commodity output (in 1940 prices) at 1953 prices, using a variety of price indices, and comparing this with an independently estimated figure of 1953 commodity output in 1953 prices. It would have been more satisfactory if Kim and Roemer had been able to find quantitative indicators of volume changes between the two years. However it is the best link available in the present state of research.

South Korean 1950–53 GDP movement from Maddison (1970) 300–1, 1953–70 from *National Income in Korea 1975*, Bank of Korea, pp. 142–3, 1970–90 from OECD, *National Accounts 1960–97*, vol. 1, Paris, 1999. 1990 onwards from *National Accounts of OECD Countries 1988–1998*, Vol. 1, 2000.

Sri Lanka: 1820–1913 population derived from N.K. Sarkar, *The Demography of Ceylon,* Ceylon Government Press, Colombo, 1957, p. 22, by interpolation of his benchmark estimates for 1814–1921; 1950 onwards from US Bureau of the Census.

GDP movement 1870–1950 derived from the substantial statistical Appendix of D.R. Snodgrass, *Ceylon: An Export Economy in Transition,* Irwin Illinois, 1966. Benchmark 1950 GDP at factor cost by industry of origin at 1950 prices, broken down into 14 sectors (p. 279). Annual volume movement in these sectors 1870–1950, derived as follows: export crops (tea and minor estate crops, rubber, coconut products) from pp. 357–60, food crops from cultivated area of paddy and other crops (p. 333); mining and manufacturing value added assumed to move with employment (p. 322); construction, wholesale and retail trade, banking and insurance assumed to move parallel to aggregate commodity output (in agriculture and industry); transport, communication, and utilities assumed to move parallel to movement of railway freight (p. 351). Other services (including dwellings, public administration and defence) assumed to move parallel with population. These crude estimates for 1870–1950 are provisional, and will be refined in a more careful analysis by Pierre van der Eng and myself. 1950–85 GDP movement

from H.J. Bruton and Associates, *Political Economy of Poverty, Equity and Growth: Sri Lanka and Malaysia*, Oxford University Press, 1992, p. 375, 1985–90 from World Bank, *World Tables* (1995), updated from ADB. GDP level in benchmark year 1990 derived from ICP5 (see Table A3–g).

Taiwan: Population 1820–1990 from Maddison (1998a) updated from ADB. 1913–90 GDP from Toshiyuki Mizoguchi, *Long–Term Economic Statistics of Taiwan: 1905–1990*, Institute of Economic Research, Hitotsubashi University, 1999. There are two aggregate estimates (at 1960 prices), one for gross domestic expenditure, the other for GDP by industry of origin. There is not much difference in the volume movement for 1913–51, but there is a big discrepancy thereafter. I used the volume movement shown by his expenditure measure for 1913–90 and filled the 1950 gap in this series by assuming the same proportionate movement 1950–51 as he shows in his industry of origin estimate. GDP movement from 1990 onwards from ADB. Benchmark 1990 GDP level from Summers and Heston, *Penn World Tables*, version 5.6.

Thailand: Population 1820–1913 from Maddison (1995a), 1950 onwards from US Bureau of the Census. GDP movement 1870–1951 from sources cited in Maddison (1995a), 1951–96 from *National Income of Thailand 1951–1996*, National Economic and Social Development Board, Bangkok, updated from ADB. Benchmark 1990 GDP level from ICP5 (see Table A3–g).

25 East Asian Countries

The quality of the estimates for these countries is distinctly inferior to those for the preceding group of 16 countries.

Afghanistan: 1820–1913 population from McEvedy and Jones (1978), 1950 onwards from US Bureau of the Census. 1950–90 GDP movement from OECD Development Centre database, updated from IMF, World Economic Outlook, May 1999, p. 147. No ICP or PWT estimate of 1990 real product level was available; it was assumed that 1990 per capita GDP was 600 dollars.

Cambodia: 1820–1913 population movement from McEvedy and Jones (1978), 1950 onwards from US Bureau of the Census. 1950–90 GDP movement and level from Maddison (1995a), p. 219 and underlying database, updated from ADB.

Laos: 1820–1913 population movement assumed to be proportionately the same as in Vietnam, 1950 onwards from US Bureau of the Census. The output movement shown in Maddison (1995a) for 1950–90 and for 1990–98 from ADB was based on material product rather than GDP and hence overstated growth. I have adjusted the measure to a GDP basis using the same downward adjustment coefficient as for China. 1990 benchmark GDP level from ICP7, see Table A3–h.

Mongolia: Population 1820–1913 from McEvedy and Jones (1978), 1950 onwards from US Bureau of the Census. 1980–98 GDP movement from ADB. There are no estimates of GDP movement for 1950–80. 1950–80 per capita trend movement was assumed to be the same as in China. 1990 per capita GDP level in international dollars derived from OECD, *A PPP Comparison for the NIS*, Paris, February 2000, p. B–24.

North Korea: For years before 1950, North Korea is included in the estimates for Korea as a whole. Population for 1950 onwards from US Bureau of the Census. No estimates of North Korean GDP or material product have been published for years before 1992, so any estimate is likely to be hazardous. We know that in 1940 North Korean GDP per capita was nearly 50 per cent higher than in the South (see source notes for South Korea), so it seems reasonable to suppose that 1950 North Korean per capita GDP was at least as high as in the South. N. Eberstadt, "Material progress in Korea since Partition", in R.H. Myers, ed., *The Wealth of Nations in the Twentieth Century*, Hoover Institution, 1996 is one of the best informed assessments available. He suggests that North Korea was more productive, and more rapidly developing than the South, for "many years after partition" although the military share was undoubtedly larger in the North. I have assumed that per capita GDP was the same

in the North as in the South from 1950 to 1973, with no progress to 1991. Thereafter, North Korea stopped receiving Soviet aid, and its per capita income has fallen a great deal. GDP volume movement from 1991 was as taken from M.C. Cho and H. Zang, *The Present and Future Prospects of the North Korean Economy,* Discussion Paper D99–3, Institute of Economic Research, Hitotsubashi University, June 1999, p. 5 (taking the Bank of Korea estimates for the 1991–2 and 1996–7 GDP movement, and the estimates which the North Korean authorities reported to the IMF for 1992–6). I assumed no change in per capita GDP from 1997 to 1998.

Vietnam: 1913 population from Banens (2000). His estimate involved a substantial upward revision for the colonial period, using reconstitution techniques based on birth and death rates. 1820–1913 proportionate movement from McEvedy and Jones (1978). Population for 1950 onwards from US Bureau of the Census.

Estimates of 1950–60 material product, using the former Soviet MPS system, were reported by the statistical authorities in Hanoi to the OECD Development Centre. I have used these estimates from the Centre's data files. New GDP estimates for 1960–98 on an SNA basis were kindly provided by Viet Vu of the UN Statistics Division. 1990 benchmark GDP level derived from ICP 7, see Table A–3h.

Jean–Pascal Bassino (Centre for International Economics and Finance, Aix–en–Provence) is conducting a major study of Vietnamese economic history for the Asian Historical Statistics Project of Hitotsubashi University using the French colonial archives. His provisional findings for 1820–1950 imply the following GDP levels, taking 1950 as 100: 1913 84.3; 1870 31.9; 1820 20.7.

19 Small East Asian Countries: 1950–98 population from US Bureau of the Census. 1820–1950 population movement for 15 Pacific islands from McEvedy and Jones (1978), pp. 330–6; Macao 1900–50 from p. 173. 1820–1950 population for Bhutan, Maldives and Brunei assumed to move parallel to India.

GDP movement in Bhutan, Brunei, Macau and Maldives for 1950–90 from Maddison (1995a) database. Update to 1998 from IMF, except for Macau which was assumed to move as in Hong Kong. GDP movement in 15 Pacific islands 1950–90 from Maddison (1995a) database updated from IMF for Fiji, Papua New Guinea, Solomon Islands, Tonga, Vanuatu, Western Samoa, Kiribati, and Micronesia; from ADB for Marshall Islands. GDP movement in French Polynesia, Guam, Pacific Islands, New Caledonia, American Samoa, Wallis and Futuna assumed to move parallel to that in the nine Pacific islands for which estimates were available.

Table A–k. **Population and GDP in 19 Small East Asian Countries, 1950–98**

	Population (000 at mid–year)				*GDP (million 1990 international dollars)*			
	1950	1973	1990	1998	1950	1973	1990	1998
Bhutan	734	1 111	1 585	1 908	369	645	1 407	2 110
Brunei	45	145	254	315	224	1 156	1 663	1 932
Macao	205	259	352	429	127	735	3 078	4 331
Maldives	79	126	218	290	43	107	497	826
Total 4 Countries	1 063	1 641	2 409	2 942	763	2 641	6 645	9 199
Fiji	287	556	738	803	851	2 348	3 440	4 498
Papua New Guinea	1 412	2 477	3 823	4 600	1 356	4 847	5 865	8 625
13 Other Pacific Islands	649	1 210	1 782	2 148	875	2 296	3 496	4 340
15 Pacific Islands Total	2 348	4 243	6 343	7 551	3 082	9 491	12 711	17 463
19 Small Countries	3 411	5 884	8 752	10 493	3 845	11 952	19 356	26 662

1990 benchmark GDP levels in international dollars are from Penn World Tables for Bhutan, Fiji, Papua New Guinea, Solomon Islands, Tonga, Vanuatu and Western Samoa. For ten other countries, proxy estimates were used from Maddison (1995a) pp. 219–220. Macao per capita GDP was taken to be half of that in Hong Kong. In Brunei income levels are dominated by oil production, which was 30.7 tons per capita in 1990, about 6 per cent above that in Kuwait. It was therefore assumed that per capita income was around $6 550 (about 6 per cent higher than in Kuwait).

15 West Asian Countries

1820–1913 population from McEvedy and Jones (1978); 1950 onwards from US Bureau of the Census. The 1820–1913 figures shown for Israel in fact refer to Palestine (including what is now Israel, the West Bank and Gaza).

Volume movement of GDP 1950–90 for Bahrain, Iraq, Jordan, Kuwait, Lebanon, Oman, Qatar, Saudi Arabia, Syria, United Arab Emirates and Yemen from OECD Development Centre database (as in Maddison, 1995a), thereafter from IMF, *World Economic Outlook,* October 1999. For all these countries, except Lebanon and Syria, the benchmark 1990 level of GDP in 1990 international (i.e. Geary–Khamis) dollars was derived from Penn World Tables version 5.6. For Syria the benchmark 1990 GDP level was derived from ICP3 (see Table A3–g). For Lebanon it is conjectural (see Maddison 1995a, p. 214).

Iran: 1950–74 GDP volume movement from OECD Development Centre database, 1974–90 from *World Tables 1995,* 1990 onwards from IMF. Benchmark 1990 GDP level from ICP3 (see Table A3–g).

Turkey: 1950–60 GDP volume movement from Maddison (1995a). 1960–90 from *OECD National Accounts 1960–97,* Vol. 1, 1999, thereafter from *National Accounts of OECD Countries 1988–1998,* vol. 1, 2000. The new figures involve a significant revision of those in Maddison (1995a). The Turkish authorities have revised their estimates, raising the 1990 GDP level substantially and reducing the GDP growth rate from 1968 onwards. 1990 benchmark GDP from ICP7 (see Table A3–g).

Israel: 1950–73 GDP volume movement supplied by the Israeli Central Bureau of Statistics, 1973–90 from World Bank, *World Tables 1995,* 1990 onwards from IMF. Benchmark 1990 GDP derived from ICP 4 (see Table A3–g). For 1922–47 development of Palestine, see entry for the West Bank and Gaza below.

West Bank and Gaza: These areas belonged to the old Palestinian political entity until 1948, when it was split into three parts. Israel got about 75 per cent of the territory, Jordan took over what was then a larger version of the West Bank (including Jerusalem) and Egypt took over the administration of the Gaza strip. In 1967 Israel occupied the West Bank and Gaza, and has been in the process of ceding control of parts of the West Bank to new Palestinian authority since the Oslo Peace accords.

The prepartition characteristics of Palestine are analysed in J. Metzer, *The Divided Economy of Mandatory Palestine,* Cambridge University Press, 1998, who provides annual estimates of population and GDP for the Arab and Jewish sectors for 1922–47 (pp. 29, 217 and 242). These estimates can be extended to 1950, using the 1950 population estimates for the Jewish and non-Jewish population of Israel from D. Patinkin, *The Israel Economy: the First Decade,* Falk Project, Jerusalem, 1960, and estimates of 1947–50 GDP supplied by the Bank of Israel (based mainly on R. Szereszewski, *Essays on the Structure of the Jewish Economy in Palestine and Israel,* Falk Project, Jerusalem, 1968).

From the above sources, it would appear that net domestic product and population moved as in Table A–l:

Table A–I. **Arab and Jewish Population and GDP in Palestine and Israel, 1922–50**

	Net Domestic Product (000 Palestinian pounds at 1936 prices)			Population at mid–year (000)		
	Total	Arab	Jewish	Total	Arab	Jewish
1922	8 360	6 628	1 732	754.6	674.5	80.1
1947	70 877	32 345	38 532	1 942.8	1 333.8	609.0
1950	93 099	3 971	89 128	1 266.8	163.8	1 103.0

N.B.   1922–47 figures refer to the area of mandatory Palestine, 1950 to Israel. The "Arab" population of Israel includes Christians and Druzes.

From Metzer's estimates it appears that Arab per capita income in Palestine rose from 9.83 pounds in 1922 to 24.25 in 1947. In the Jewish economy of Palestine per capita income rose from 24.6 pounds in 1922 to 63.27 in 1947. For 1950, the Bank of Israel GDP estimates cited above are not broken down into the Jewish and non–Jewish groups; but I assumed that non–Jewish real per capita income was the same in 1950 as in 1947. Applying the above 1950 proportionate shares to 1950 Israeli GDP in 1990 international dollars, it would seem that Arab GDP per capita in 1950 was about 950 international dollars.

The Palestine Bureau of Statistics in Ramallah appears to have estimated GDP only in current prices for 1994 onwards. I made a proxy estimate of the trend in real product by linking the 1950 per capita level as derived above, and the 1993 level as estimated by ESCWA (Economic and Social Commission for Western Asia of the United Nations) in the study cited in Table A3–i. These two spot estimates ($950 per capita in 1950 and $4 708 in 1993) are both in 1990 international dollars. I used a logarithmic trend to interpolate between these two years, and to extrapolate from 1993 to 1998, multiplying the per capita estimates by population as estimated by the US Bureau of the Census.

Proxy Procedure to Fill Gaps in the Dataset for 16 Asian Countries

For 1913, there are two gaps in the GDP dataset. I assumed that the 1913–50 movement in per capita GDP in Hong Kong was parallel to that in Japan; in Nepal parallel to India (see Table A–m). For 1870, there were eight holes in the dataset. I assumed that the 1870–1913 per capita GDP movement in Hong Kong and Singapore was proportionately the same as for Japan. In the other six countries (Burma, Korea, Malaysia, Nepal, Philippines and Taiwan), it was assumed to move parallel to the average 1870–1913 per capita movement for Indonesia, Sri Lanka and Thailand see Table A–m). For 1820, there were ten holes in the dataset. Average per capita GDP movement 1820–1870 for these ten countries was assumed to be parallel to that in Japan.

Proxy Procedure to Fill Gaps in the Dataset for 25 East Asian and 16 West Asian Countries

For these countries there were no GDP estimates for any of the years 1820, 1870 and 1913. It was assumed that their average per capita GDP level in 1870 and 1913 was the same as the average for the 16 East Asian countries, and that their 1820 level was the same as in 1870.

Table A–m. **Proxy Entries to Fill Holes in GDP and GDP Per Capita Dataset for 1870 and 1913**

	GDP		GDP per capita	
	1870	*1913*	*1870*	*1913*
Burma	2 156		508	
Hong Kong	106	778	862	1 597
Malaysia	534		667	
Nepal	1 879	3 039	400	539
Philippines	4 005		791	
Singapore	58		691	
South Korea	9 512		663	
Taiwan	1 299		554	
Total Above	19 549	3 817	617	623
25 East Asia	11 050	21 583	552	679
16 West Asia	16 782	26 537	552	679
Total Proxies	47 381	51 937	570	675

Proportionate Importance of the Proxy Estimates

For 1913, the proxy estimates represented 7.8 per cent of the Asian GDP total, for 1870, 11.2 per cent and for 1820, 9.5 per cent. Proxy estimates are contestable, as different analysts may have different ideas about how to fill the gaps. However, the proxy proportion is relatively modest, so the all–Asia results are not too sensitive to variations in procedure. The main task of further research is to fill the gaps by direct estimation, which seems likely to be feasible in a number of cases (see note above on Vietnam).

Table A3–a. **Population in 56 Asian Countries**
(000 at mid–year)

	1820	1870	1913	1950	1973	1990	1998
Bangladesh				45 646	72 471	109 897	125 105
Burma	3 506	4 245	12 326	19 488	29 227	41 068	47 305
China	381 000	358 000	437 140	546 815	881 940	1 135 185	1 242 700
Hong Kong	20	123	487	2 237	4 213	5 704	6 690
India[a]	209 000	253 000	303 700	359 000	580 000	839 000	975 000
Indonesia	17 927	28 922	49 934	79 043	124 271	179 248	204 390
Japan	31 000	34 437	51 672	83 563	108 660	123 540	126 486
Malaysia	287	800	3 084	6 434	11 712	17 507	20 933
Nepal	3 881	4 698	5 639	8 990	12 685	19 333	23 698
Pakistan				39 448	71 121	113 914	135 135
Philippines	2 176	5 063	9 384	21 131	42 094	65 037	77 726
Singapore	30	84	323	1 022	2 193	3 039	3 490
South Korea[b]	13 820	14 347	16 070	20 846	34 073	42 869	46 430
Sri Lanka	1 305	2 786	4 817	7 533	13 246	17 193	18 934
Taiwan	2 000	2 345	3 469	7 882	15 427	20 230	21 780
Thailand	4 665	5 775	8 689	20 042	40 302	55 052	60 037
16 East Asia	**670 617**	**714 625**	**906 734**	**1 269 120**	**2 043 635**	**2 787 816**	**3 135 839**
Afghanistan	3 280	4 207	5 730	8 150	13 421	14 767	24 792
Cambodia	2 090	2 340	3 070	4 163	7 202	8 717	11 340
Laos	470	755	1 387	1 886	3 027	4 191	5 261
Mongolia	619	668	725	779	1 360	2 216	2 579
North Korea				9 471	15 161	20 019	21 234
Vietnam	6 314	10 146	18 638	25 348	45 737	66 315	76 236
19 Small Countries	1 798	1 903	2 237	3 411	5 884	8 752	10 493
25 East Asia	**14 571**	**20 019**	**31 787**	**53 208**	**91 792**	**124 977**	**151 935**
41 East Asia	**685 188**	**734 644**	**938 521**	**1 322 328**	**2 135 427**	**2 912 793**	**3 287 774**
Bahrain			104	115	239	502	616
Iran	6 560	8 415	10 994	16 357	31 491	55 717	64 411
Iraq	1 093	1 580	2 613	5 163	10 402	18 135	21 722
Israel	332	429	700	1 286	3 197	4 512	5 644
Jordan	217	266	348	561	1 674	3 277	4 453
Kuwait				145	894	2 131	1 913
Lebanon	332	476	649	1 364	2 824	3 130	3 506
Oman	317	367	421	489	857	1 773	2 364
Qatar				25	142	482	697
Saudi Arabia	2 123	2 464	2 800	3 860	6 667	15 871	20 786
Syria	1 337	1 582	1 994	3 495	6 931	12 620	16 673
Turkey	10 074	11 793	15 000	21 122	38 503	56 125	64 568
UAE				72	391	1 952	2 303
Yemen	2 953	2 840	3 284	4 461	7 077	12 023	16 388
West Bank + Gaza				1 016	1 098	1 715	2 611
15 West Asia	**25 178**	**30 412**	**39 083**	**59 531**	**112 387**	**189 965**	**228 655**
56 Asia	**710 366**	**765 056**	**977 604**	**1 381 859**	**2 247 814**	**3 102 758**	**3 516 429**
Total excluding Japan	**679 366**	**730 619**	**925 932**	**1 298 296**	**2 139 154**	**2 979 218**	**3 389 943**
Total excluding Japan, China, India	**89 366**	**119 619**	**185 092**	**392 481**	**677 214**	**1 005 033**	**1 172 243**

a) 1820–1913 includes Bangladesh and Pakistan. b) 1820–1913 includes North and South Korea.

Table A3–b. **GDP Levels in 56 Asian Countries**
(million 1990 international $)

	1820	1870	1913	1950	1973	1990	1998
Bangladesh				24 628	35 997	70 320	101 666
Burma			8 445	7 711	18 352	30 834	48 427
China	228 600	189 740	241 344	239 903	740 048	2 109 400	3 873 352
Hong Kong				4 962	29 931	99 770	135 089
India[a]	111 417	134 882	204 241	222 222	494 832	1 098 100	1 702 712
Indonesia	10 970	18 929	45 152	66 358	186 900	450 901	627 499
Japan	20 739	25 393	71 653	160 966	1 242 932	2 321 153	2 581 576
Malaysia			2 773	10 032	29 982	89 823	148 621
Nepal				4 462	7 894	15 609	22 435
Pakistan				25 366	67 828	182 014	261 497
Philippines			10 000	22 616	82 464	143 025	176 246
Singapore			413	2 268	13 108	43 330	79 025
South Korea[b]			14 343	16 045	96 794	373 150	564 211
Sri Lanka		1 782	4 094	7 241	19 759	42 089	63 408
Taiwan			2 591	7 378	63 519	200 477	326 958
Thailand		4 081	7 251	16 375	75 511	255 732	372 509
16 East Asia	**389 305**	**394 356**	**616 117**	**838 533**	**3 205 851**	**7 525 727**	**11 085 231**
Afghanistan				5 255	9 181	8 861	12 744
Cambodia				2 155	5 858	8 235	11 998
Laos				1 156	2 331	3 912	5 806
Mongolia				339	1 170	2 954	2 821
North Korea				7 293	43 072	56 874	25 130
Vietnam	3 453	5 321	14 062	16 681	38 238	68 959	127 851
19 Small Countries				3 845	11 952	19 356	26 662
25 East Asia	**8 043**	**11 050**	**21 583**	**36 724**	**111 802**	**169 151**	**213 012**
41 East Asia	**397 348**	**405 406**	**637 700**	**875 257**	**3 317 653**	**7 694 878**	**11 298 243**
Bahrain				242	1 046	2 054	2 846
Iran				28 128	171 466	199 819	274 695
Iraq				7 041	39 042	44 583	24 564
Israel				3 623	30 839	58 511	85 520
Jordan				933	3 999	12 371	18 313
Kuwait				4 181	23 847	13 111	21 565
Lebanon				3 313	8 915	6 099	12 077
Oman				304	2 809	11 487	17 179
Qatar				763	6 228	3 276	5 091
Saudi Arabia				8 610	73 601	144 438	170 972
Syria				8 418	27 846	70 894	96 112
Turkey				38 408	144 483	305 395	423 018
UAE				1 130	9 739	25 496	31 913
Yemen				4 353	12 431	28 212	37 656
West Bank + Gaza				965	2 455	7 222	14 807
15 West Asia	**13 894**	**16 782**	**26 537**	**110 412**	**558 746**	**932 968**	**1 236 328**
56 Asia	**411 242**	**422 188**	**664 237**	**985 669**	**3 876 399**	**8 627 846**	**12 534 571**
Total excluding Japan	**390 503**	**396 795**	**592 584**	**824 703**	**2 633 467**	**6 306 693**	**9 952 995**
Total excluding Japan, China, India	**50 486**	**72 173**	**146 999**	**362 578**	**1 398 587**	**3 099 193**	**4 376 931**

a) 1820–1913 includes Bangladesh and Pakistan. b) 1820–1913 includes North and South Korea.

Table A3–c. **GDP Per Capita in 56 Asian Countries**
(1990 international $)

	1820	1870	1913	1950	1973	1990	1998
Bangladesh				540	497	640	813
Burma			685	396	628	751	1 024
China	600	530	552	439	839	1 858	3 117
Hong Kong				2 218	7 104	17 491	20 193
India[a]	533	533	673	619	853	1 309	1 746
Indonesia	612	654	904	840	1 504	2 516	3 070
Japan	669	737	1 387	1 926	11 439	18 789	20 410
Malaysia			899	1 559	2 560	5 131	7 100
Nepal				496	622	807	947
Pakistan				643	954	1 598	1 935
Philippines			1 066	1 070	1 959	2 199	2 268
Singapore			1 279	2 219	5 977	14 258	22 643
South Korea[b]			893	770	2 841	8 704	12 152
Sri Lanka		640	850	961	1 492	2 448	3 349
Taiwan			747	936	4 117	9 910	15 012
Thailand		707	835	817	1 874	4 645	6 205
16 East Asia	**581**	**552**	**679**	**661**	**1 569**	**2 700**	**3 535**
Afghanistan				645	684	600	514
Cambodia				518	813	945	1 058
Laos				613	770	933	1 104
Mongolia				435	860	1 333	1 094
North Korea				770	2 841	2 841	1 183
Vietnam	546	524	754	658	836	1 040	1 677
19 Small Countries				1 127	2 031	2 212	2 541
25 East Asia	**552**	**552**	**679**	**690**	**1 218**	**1 353**	**1 402**
41 East Asia	**580**	**552**	**679**	**662**	**1 554**	**2 642**	**3 436**
Bahrain				2 104	4 377	4 092	4 620
Iran				1 720	5 445	3 586	4 265
Iraq				1 364	3 753	2 458	1 131
Israel				2 817	9 646	12 968	15 152
Jordan				1 663	2 389	3 775	4 113
Kuwait				28 834	26 674	6 153	11 273
Lebanon				2 429	3 157	1 949	3 445
Oman				622	3 278	6 479	7 267
Qatar				30 520	43 859	6 797	7 304
Saudi Arabia				2 231	11 040	9 101	8 225
Syria				2 409	4 018	5 618	5 765
Turkey				1 818	3 753	5 441	6 552
UAE				15 694	24 908	13 061	13 857
Yemen				976	1 757	2 347	2 298
West Bank + Gaza				950	2 236	4 211	5 671
15 West Asia	**552**	**552**	**679**	**1 855**	**4 972**	**4 911**	**5 407**
56 Asia	**579**	**552**	**679**	**713**	**1 725**	**2 781**	**3 565**
Total excluding Japan	**575**	**543**	**640**	**635**	**1 231**	**2 117**	**2 936**
Total excluding Japan, China, India	**565**	**603**	**794**	**924**	**2 065**	**3 084**	**3 734**

a) 1820–1913 includes Bangladesh and Pakistan. b) 1820–1913 includes North and South Korea.

Table A3–d. GDP Per Capita Growth Rates in 56 Asian Countries, 1820–1998

	1820–70	*1870–1913*	*1913–50*	*1950–73*	*1973–98*
Bangladesh				−0.36	1.99
Burma			−1.47	2.03	1.97
China	−0.25	0.10	−0.62	2.86	5.39
Hong Kong				5.19	4.27
India[a]	0.00	0.54	−0.22	1.40	2.91
Indonesia	0.13	0.75	−0.20	2.57	2.90
Japan	0.19	1.48	0.89	8.05	2.34
Malaysia			1.50	2.18	4.16
Nepal				0.99	1.69
Pakistan				1.73	2.87
Philippines			0.01	2.66	0.59
Singapore			1.50	4.40	5.47
South Korea[b]			−0.40	5.84	5.99
Sri Lanka			0.33	1.93	3.29
Taiwan			0.61	6.65	5.31
Thailand		0.39	−0.06	3.67	4.91
16 East Asia	**−0.10**	**0.49**	**−0.08**	**3.83**	**3.30**
Afghanistan				0.26	−1.14
Cambodia				1.98	1.06
Laos				1.00	1.45
Mongolia				3.01	0.97
North Korea				5.84	−3.44
Vietnam	−0.08	0.85	−0.37	1.05	2.82
19 Small Countries				2.59	0.90
25 East Asia	**0.00**	**0.48**	**0.04**	**2.50**	**0.56**
41 East Asia	**−0.10**	**0.49**	**−0.07**	**3.78**	**3.23**
Bahrain				3.23	0.22
Iran				5.14	−0.97
Iraq				4.50	−4.69
Israel				5.50	1.82
Jordan				1.59	2.20
Kuwait				−0.34	−3.39
Lebanon				1.15	0.35
Oman				7.50	3.24
Qatar				1.59	−6.92
Saudi Arabia				7.20	−1.17
Syria				2.25	1.45
Turkey				3.20	2.25
UAE				2.03	−2.32
Yemen				2.59	1.08
West Bank + Gaza				3.79	3.79
15 West Asia	**0.00**	**0.48**	**2.75**	**4.38**	**0.34**
56 Asia	**−0.10**	**0.48**	**0.13**	**3.91**	**2.95**
Total excluding Japan	**−0.11**	**0.38**	**−0.02**	**2.92**	**3.54**
Total excluding Japan, China, India	**0.13**	**0.64**	**0.41**	**3.56**	**2.40**

a) 1820–1913 includes Bangladesh and Pakistan. b) 1820–1913 includes North and South Korea.

Table A3–e. GDP Growth Rates in 56 Asian Countries, 1820–1998

	1820–70	*1870–1913*	*1913–50*	*1950–73*	*1973–98*
Bangladesh				1.66	4.24
Burma			−0.25	3.84	3.96
China	−0.37	0.56	−0.02	5.02	6.84
Hong Kong				8.13	6.21
India[a]	0.38	0.97	0.23	3.54	5.07
Indonesia	1.10	2.04	1.05	4.61	4.96
Japan	0.41	2.44	2.21	9.29	2.97
Malaysia			3.54	4.88	6.61
Nepal				2.51	4.27
Pakistan				4.37	5.55
Philippines			2.23	5.79	3.08
Singapore			4.71	7.93	7.45
South Korea[b]			0.30	8.13	7.31
Sri Lanka			1.55	4.46	4.77
Taiwan		1.95	2.87	9.81	6.77
Thailand		1.35	2.23	6.87	6.59
16 East Asia	**0.03**	**1.04**	**0.84**	**6.00**	**5.09**
Afghanistan				2.46	1.32
Cambodia				4.44	2.91
Laos				3.10	3.72
Mongolia				5.53	3.58
North Korea				8.03	−2.13
Vietnam	0.86	2.29	0.46	3.67	4.95
19 Small Countries				5.05	3.26
25 East Asia	**0.64**	**1.57**	**1.45**	**4.96**	**2.61**
41 East Asia	**0.04**	**1.06**	**0.86**	**5.96**	**5.02**
Bahrain				6.57	4.08
Iran				8.18	1.90
Iraq				7.73	−1.84
Israel				9.76	4.16
Jordan				6.53	6.28
Kuwait				7.86	−0.40
Lebanon				4.40	1.22
Oman				10.15	7.51
Qatar				9.56	−0.80
Saudi Arabia				9.78	3.43
Syria				5.34	5.08
Turkey				5.93	4.39
UAE				9.82	4.86
Yemen				4.67	4.53
West Bank + Gaza				4.14	7.45
15 West Asia	**0.38**	**1.07**	**3.93**	**7.30**	**3.23**
56 Asia	**0.05**	**1.06**	**1.07**	**6.13**	**4.81**
Total excluding Japan	**0.03**	**0.94**	**0.90**	**5.18**	**5.46**
Total excluding Japan, China, India	**0.72**	**1.67**	**2.47**	**6.05**	**4.67**

a) 1820–1913 includes Bangladesh and Pakistan. b) 1820–1913 includes North and South Korea.

Table A3–f. **Population Growth Rates in 56 Asian Countries, 1820–1998**

	1820–70	*1870–1913*	*1913–50*	*1950–73*	*1973–98*
Bangladesh				2.03	2.21
Burma	0.38	2.51	1.25	1.78	1.94
China	−0.12	0.47	0.61	2.10	1.38
Hong Kong	3.70	3.25	4.21	2.79	1.87
India[a]	0.38	0.43	0.45	2.11	2.10
Indonesia	0.96	1.28	1.25	1.99	2.01
Japan	0.21	0.95	1.31	1.15	0.61
Malaysia	2.07	3.19	2.01	2.64	2.35
Nepal	0.38	0.43	1.27	1.51	2.53
Pakistan				2.60	2.60
Philippines	1.70	1.45	2.22	3.04	2.48
Singapore	2.08	3.18	3.16	3.38	1.88
South Korea[b]	0.07	0.26	0.71	2.16	1.25
Sri Lanka	1.53	1.28	1.22	2.48	1.44
Taiwan	0.32	0.91	2.24	2.96	1.39
Thailand	0.43	0.95	2.28	3.08	1.61
16 East Asia	**0.13**	**0.56**	**0.91**	**2.09**	**1.73**
Afghanistan	0.50	0.72	0.96	2.19	2.49
Cambodia	0.23	0.63	0.83	2.41	1.83
Laos	0.95	1.42	0.83	2.08	2.24
Mongolia	0.15	0.19	0.19	2.45	2.59
North Korea				2.07	1.36
Vietnam	0.95	1.42	0.83	2.60	2.06
19 Small Countries	0.11	0.38	1.15	2.40	2.34
25 East Asia	**0.64**	**1.08**	**1.40**	**2.40**	**2.04**
41 East Asia	**0.14**	**0.57**	**0.93**	**2.11**	**1.74**
Bahrain			0.27	3.23	3.86
Iran	0.50	0.62	1.08	2.89	2.90
Iraq	0.74	1.18	1.86	3.09	2.99
Israel	0.51	1.15	1.66	4.04	2.30
Jordan	0.41	0.63	1.30	4.87	3.99
Kuwait				8.23	3.09
Lebanon	0.72	0.72	2.03	3.21	0.87
Oman	0.29	0.32	0.41	2.47	4.14
Qatar				7.84	6.57
Saudi Arabia	0.30	0.30	0.87	2.40	4.65
Syria	0.34	0.54	1.53	3.02	3.57
Turkey	0.32	0.56	0.93	2.64	2.09
UAE				7.63	7.35
Yemen	−0.08	0.34	0.83	2.03	3.42
West Bank + Gaza				0.34	3.53
15 West Asia	**0.38**	**0.59**	**1.14**	**2.80**	**2.88**
56 Asia	**0.15**	**0.57**	**0.94**	**2.14**	**1.81**
Total excluding Japan	**0.15**	**0.55**	**0.92**	**2.19**	**1.86**
Total excluding Japan, China, India	**0.58**	**1.02**	**2.05**	**2.40**	**2.22**

a) 1820–1913 includes Bangladesh and Pakistan. b) 1820–1913 includes North and South Korea.

Table A3–g. Derivation of 1990 Benchmark Levels of GDP in 1990 International Dollars for 15 East Asian Countries

	GDP in million national currency units in reference year	PPP Converter for reference year (units of national currency per dollar)	GDP in reference year in million Geary–Khamis dollars	1990 GDP in Geary–Khamis dollars of reference year	1990 GDP in million 1990 Geary–Khamis dollars
ICP 3 (Reference Year 1975)					
Iran	3 377 740	39.7	85 073	86 878	199 819
Syria	20 600	1.48	13 919	23 631	70 894
ICP 4 (Reference Year 1980)					
India	1 360 100	3.37	403 591	695 515	1 098 100
Indonesia	48 914 000	280.0	174 693	285 598	450 901
Israel	107 651	4.14	26 003	37 061	58 511
Philippines	243 750	3.18	76 651	90 591	143 025
South Korea	38 148 400	384.0	99 345	236 350	373 150
ICP 5 (Reference Year 1985)					
Bangladesh	406 930	6.075	66 984	81 779	98 113
Hong Kong	271 655	4.680	58 046	83 160	99 770
Pakistan	472 160	3.761	125 541	166 380	199 611
Sri Lanka	157 763	5.288	29 834	35 082	42 089
Thailand	1 056 496	8.094	130 528	213 158	255 732
ICP 6 (Reference Year 1990)					
China	1 956 038	0.9273			2 109 400
Japan	430 040 000	185.27			2 321 153
ICP 7 (Reference Year 1993)					
Turkey	1 981 867	5 139.3	385 630	333 678	305 395

Source: Column 1 shows GDP in the reference year in national currency units; in most cases the figures are from World Bank, *World Tables* (1995), Japan, Turkey and South Korea from OECD, *National Accounts, 1960–97*, Vol.1 (1999), and Thailand from Asian Development Bank, *Key Indicators* (1999). In most cases these involve minor revisions of the figures used by ICP. Col.2 purchasing power parity (PPP converters) for 1975 from Kravis, Heston and Summers, *World Product and Income* (1982), pp. 176–9; 1980 from UN, *World Comparisons of Purchasing Power and Real Product for 1980* (1987), p. viii; 1985 from UN, *World Comparisons of Real Gross Domestic Product and Purchasing Power, 1985*, (1994), p. 5; 1990 for Japan from OECD, *Purchasing Power Parities and Real Expenditures: GK Results, 1990*, Vol.2 (1993), p. 32 (adjusted to a US PPP = 1.00. Turkey 1993 from *Purchasing Power Parities and Real Expenditures: GK Results, 1993*, vol.2 (1996), p. 35 (adjusted to a US PPP = 1.00). All these PPP converters are multilateral and use the Geary–Khamis method of estimation. The results for China were derived from a 1987 bilateral China/United States comparison, adjusted to a Geary–Khamis basis as described in Maddison, *Chinese Economic Performance in the Long Run* (1998), pp. 153–4, with upward adjustment of the official Chinese GDP estimates in yuan. Column 3 is derived from columns 1 and 2. Column 4 was derived by adjusting column 3 for the volume movement in GDP between the reference year and 1990. Column 5 is column 4 adjusted by the movement in the US GDP deflator from the reference year to 1990.

Table A3–h. **Derivation of 1990 Benchmark Levels of GDP in 1990 International Dollars for Five East Asian Countries**

	GDP in million national currency units in reference year	Implicit Geary–Khamis PPP Converter for reference year (units of national currency per dollar)	GDP in reference year in million Geary–Khamis dollars	1990 GDP in million 1993 Geary–Khamis dollars	1990 GDP in million 1990 Geary–Khamis dollars
		ICP 3 (Reference Year 1993)			
Hong Kong	897 463	6.9486	129 158	109 010	99 770
Laos	950 973	191.0865	4 977	4 274	3 912
Malaysia	165 206	1.32718	124 479	98 142	89 823
Nepal	171 386	8.7553	19 575	17 055	15 609
Singapore	92 905	1.5287	60 774	47 343	43 330
Vietnam	136 571 000	1538.281	88 749	75 345	68 959

Source: Column 1 from ADB, *Key Indicators of Developing Asian and Pacific Countries,* 1999. In most cases these involve minor revisions of the figures cited by ESCAP, except for Singapore, where the figure is 13 per cent lower. ESCAP used an adjusted version of the Geary–Khamis procedure. The estimates for Malaysia and Laos were made by the World Bank and used reduced information techniques (see ESCAP *Comparisons of Real Gross Product and Purchasing Power Parities 1993*). ESCAP took Hong Kong as the numeraire country, and the Hong Kong figures were reported without a PPP adjustment. In column 2 above I derived the implicit 1993 Hong Kong PPP in terms of Hong Kong dollars per US dollar by updating the 1990 result shown in Table A3–g. For other countries ESCAP reported PPP in terms of units of national currency per Hong Kong dollar. In column 2 these PPPs were multiplied by the 1993 Hong Kong/US dollar PPP, to link these regional results to the global ICP exercises in which the United States is the numeraire country. Column 3 is derived from columns 1 and 2. Column 4 was derived by adjusting column 3 for the change in the volume movement of GDP between 1990 and 1993. Column 5 is column 4 adjusted by the movement in the US GDP deflator between 1990 and 1993.

Table A3–i. **Derivation of 1990 Benchmark Levels of GDP in 1990 International Dollars for Three West Asian Countries**

	GDP in million national currency units in reference year	Geary–Khamis PPP Converter for reference year (units of national currency per dollar)	GDP in reference year in million Geary–Khamis dollars	1990 GDP in million 1993 Geary–Khamis dollars	1990 GDP in million 1990 Geary–Khamis dollars
		ICP 3 (Reference Year 1993)			
Bahrain	1 754.2	0.6402	2 740	2 244	2 054
Palestine	8 844.63	0.8698	10 169	7 890	7 222
Qatar	26 183.0	6.5951	3 970	3 579	3 276

Source: First three columns from Geary–Khamis results in *Purchasing Power Parities, Volume and Price Level Comparisons for the Middle East, 1993,* Economic and Social Commission for Western Asia and World Bank, p. 59. This study presented figures for 8 West Asian countries and Egypt for 1993. It used a short–cut, "reduced information" approach, using both the Geary–Khamis and the EKS approach. It should be regarded as a first approximation to a full ICP exercise. The results for some of the countries such as Lebanon and Yemen seemed implausible, so I used the results for only three of the countries. Fourth column derived by adjusting column 3 for the change in the volume of GDP between 1990 and 1993. Column 5 adjusts the column 4 entry for the movement in the US GDP deflator between 1990 and 1993.

A4

Population, GDP and GDP Per Capita in 57 African Countries

Population 1950 onwards from the International Programs Centre, US Bureau of the Census, which provides comprehensive coverage of the African countries on an annual basis back to 1950. Its estimates are updated and revised regularly. Use of this source involved some significant modifications of the figures used in Maddison (1995a), which were a mixture of OECD Development Centre and World Bank sources. 1913 population for the four sample countries from Maddison (1995a). 1820–1913 total African population derived from McEvedy and Jones (1978), p. 206.

Estimates of benchmark 1990 GDP levels in international (Geary–Khamis) dollars were available for 50 African countries from the Penn World Tables of Robert Summers and Alan Heston. In Maddison (1995a), I used the PWT 5.5 estimates. Here I use the 5.6 version. Table A4–g provides a confrontation of the PWT results and those of the three ICP rounds which cover 24 countries. There are seven countries for which no ICP or PWT benchmark was available. For Equatorial Guinea, Mayotte, St. Helena, S. Tome Principe and Western Sahara, 1990 per capita GDP was assumed to be equal to the average for the 50 countries covered by the PWT. For Libya it was assumed to be the same as in Algeria, and for Eritrea the same as Ethiopia.

1990–98 GDP movement for all African countries from IMF, World Economic Outlook, October 1999. GDP movement 1913–90 for Egypt, Ghana, Morocco and South Africa from the sources cited below; 1950–90 GDP movement for other countries (except Botswana, Nigeria and the seven proxy estimates) from the database of the OECD Development Centre.

Egypt: 1913–50 GDP from Hansen and Marzouk (1965), p. 3, 1950–73 from Ikram (1980) p. 398–9; 1973–90 from World Bank, World Tables, 1995

Ghana: GDP 1913–50 from Szereszewski (1965) pp. 74, 92 and 149; 1950–5 from Maddison (1970); 1955–90 from the Government Statistical Service, Republic of Ghana.

Morocco: 1913–50 GDP derived from Amin (1966), 1950–90 GDP from World Bank, World Tables (1983 and 1995 editions).

South Africa: 1913–20 current price GDP divided by cost of living index from Bureau of Census and Statistics, Union Statistics for Fifty Years, Jubilee Issue 1910–1960, Pretoria, 1960; 1920–50 from L.J. Fourie, "Contribution of Factors of Production and Productivity to South African Economic Growth", IARIW, processed, 1971. 1946–70 GDP at 1975 prices from Development Bank of South Africa, 1970–90 from World Bank, World Tables

Botswana: GDP movement in 1950–90 from World Bank, World Tables.

Nigeria: 1950–90 from Bevan, Collier and Gunning (1999).

Estimates for the 15 "non–sample" countries are segregated as they are extremely shaky.

1913–50 per capita GDP for Africa assumed to move parallel to the average for the four countries for which estimates were available. Before 1913 no indicators were available. As a proxy it was assumed that per capita GDP for Africa as a whole moved at the same pace as in "other Asia" (see Table B–21), for 1820–1913.

Table A4–a. **Population of 57 African Countries**
(000 at mid–year)

	1820	1870	1913	1950	1973	1990	1998
Egypt			12 144	21 198	35 480	56 106	66 050
Ghana			2 043	5 297	9 583	15 190	18 497
Morocco			4 500	9 343	16 998	24 685	29 114
South Africa			6 153	13 596	24 549	37 191	42 835
4 Sample Countries			**24 840**	**49 434**	**86 610**	**133 172**	**156 496**
Algeria				8 893	15 198	25 352	30 481
Angola				4 118	6 028	8 430	10 865
Benin				1 673	2 836	4 676	6 101
Botswana				430	643	1 304	1 448
Cameroon				4 888	7 179	11 894	15 029
Cape Verde				146	277	349	400
Central African Rep.				1 260	1 945	2 798	3 376
Chad				2 608	3 995	5 889	7 360
Comoros				148	257	429	546
Congo				768	1 279	2 206	2 658
Côte d'Ivoire				2 860	6 352	11 904	15 446
Djibouti				60	189	370	441
Gabon				416	557	1 078	1 208
Gambia				305	546	964	1 292
Kenya				6 121	12 594	23 674	28 337
Liberia				824	1 528	2 265	2 772
Madagascar				4 620	7 250	11 525	14 463
Mali				3 688	5 909	8 231	10 109
Mauritania				1 006	1 356	1 979	2 511
Mauritius				481	861	1 074	1 168
Mozambique				6 250	10 088	14 056	18 641
Namibia				464	831	1 409	1 622
Niger				2 482	4 559	7 644	9 672
Nigeria				31 797	53 121	86 530	110 532
Reunion				244	469	600	705
Rwanda				2 439	4 110	7 161	7 956
Senegal				2 654	4 727	7 408	9 723
Seychelles				33	58	73	79
Sierra Leone				2 087	2 925	4 283	5 080
Somalia				2 438	3 932	6 675	6 842
Sudan				8 051	15 113	26 628	33 551
Swaziland				277	493	840	966
Tanzania				8 909	15 321	24 886	30 609
Togo				1 172	2 133	3 680	4 906
Tunisia				3 517	5 426	8 207	9 380
Uganda				5 522	10 386	17 227	22 167
Zambia				2 553	4 625	7 957	9 461
Zimbabwe				2 853	6 041	9 958	11 044
38 Other Countries				**129 055**	**221 137**	**361 613**	**448 947**
15 Non–sample Countries				**49 853**	**79 898**	**125 980**	**154 511**
Total 57 Countries	**74 208**	**90 466**	**124 697**	**228 342**	**387 645**	**620 765**	**759 954**
Burkina Faso				4 376	5 947	9 024	11 266
Burundi				2 363	3 529	5 285	5 537
Ethiopia and Eritrea				21 577	34 028	50 960	62 232
Guinea				2 586	3 786	5 936	7 477
Guinea Bissau				573	633	998	1 206
Lesotho				726	1 142	1 744	2 090
Malawi				2 817	4 865	9 139	9 840
Zaire				13 569	23 186	37 978	49 001
6 Other Countries				1 266	2 782	4 916	5 862
15 Non–sample Countries				49 853	79 898	125 980	154 511

Table A4–b. **GDP Levels in 57 African Countries**
(million 1990 international $)

	1820	1870	1913	1950	1973	1990	1998
Egypt			8 891	15 224	36 249	112 873	140 546
Ghana			1 509	5 943	13 484	16 372	23 014
Morocco			3 630	13 598	28 800	64 082	78 397
South Africa			9 857	34 465	102 498	147 509	165 239
4 Sample Countries			**23 887**	**69 230**	**181 031**	**340 836**	**407 196**
Algeria				12 136	35 814	73 934	81 948
Angola				4 331	10 784	7 207	7 029
Benin				1 813	3 011	5 347	7 668
Botswana				150	722	4 178	6 083
Cameroon				3 279	7 201	14 393	15 157
Cape Verde				66	147	430	544
Central African Rep.				972	1 627	1 982	2 203
Chad				1 240	1 726	2 573	3 463
Comoros				83	229	294	285
Congo				990	2 727	5 394	5 951
Côte d'Ivoire				2 977	12 064	16 330	21 201
Djibouti				90	412	530	467
Gabon				1 292	4 086	4 500	5 901
Gambia				165	533	833	1 098
Kenya				3 982	12 107	26 093	30 451
Liberia				869	2 212	2 245	2 580
Madagascar				4 394	8 292	9 210	9 976
Mali				1 685	3 449	6 040	7 917
Mauritania				467	1 309	1 825	2 494
Mauritius				1 198	3 169	7 652	11 508
Mozambique				7 084	18 894	14 105	22 125
Namibia				1 002	2 895	4 619	6 158
Niger				2 018	3 377	4 289	5 149
Nigeria				23 933	76 585	107 459	136 162
Reunion				485	1 771	2 694	3 174
Rwanda				1 334	2 826	6 125	5 605
Senegal				3 341	6 217	10 032	12 659
Seychelles				63	187	366	471
Sierra Leone				1 370	3 180	4 335	2 837
Somalia				2 576	4 625	7 231	6 044
Sudan				6 609	11 783	19 793	29 535
Swaziland				200	1 114	2 154	2 699
Tanzania				3 362	9 007	13 852	16 933
Togo				673	2 245	2 805	3 159
Tunisia				3 920	12 051	27 387	39 306
Uganda				3 793	8 704	10 206	16 082
Zambia				1 687	4 930	6 432	6 374
Zimbabwe				2 000	8 594	13 766	15 990
38 Other Countries				**107 629**	**290 606**	**448 640**	**554 386**
15 Non–sample Countries				**17 710**	**57 548**	**70 352**	**77 826**
Total 57 Countries	**31 010**	**40 172**	**72 948**	**194 569**	**529 185**	**859 828**	**1 039 408**
Burkina Faso				1 686	3 287	5 482	7 613
Burundi				772	1 781	3 520	3 005
Ethiopia and Eritrea				5 394	13 640	18 964	24 833
Guinea				784	1 861	3 304	4 573
Guinea Bissau				166	558	794	736
Lesotho				232	790	1 828	2 451
Malawi				913	2 756	5 146	6 949
Zaire				6 750	16 915	17 394	10 790
6 Other Countries				1 013	15 960	13 920	16 876
15 Non–sample Countries				17 710	57 548	70 352	77 826

Table A4–c. GDP Per Capita in 57 African Countries
(1990 international $)

	1820	1870	1913	1950	1973	1990	1998
Egypt			732	718	1 022	2 012	2 128
Ghana			739	1 122	1 407	1 078	1 244
Morocco			807	1 455	1 694	2 596	2 693
South Africa			1 602	2 535	4 175	3 966	3 858
4 Sample Countries			**962**	**1 400**	**2 090**	**2 559**	**2 602**
Algeria				1 365	2 356	2 916	2 688
Angola				1 052	1 789	855	647
Benin				1 084	1 062	1 143	1 257
Botswana				349	1 123	3 204	4 201
Cameroon				671	1 003	1 210	1 009
Cape Verde				452	531	1 232	1 360
Central African Rep.				771	837	708	653
Chad				475	432	437	471
Comoros				561	891	685	522
Congo				1 289	2 132	2 445	2 239
Côte d'Ivoire				1 041	1 899	1 372	1 373
Djibouti				1 500	2 180	1 432	1 059
Gabon				3 106	7 336	4 174	4 885
Gambia				541	976	864	850
Kenya				651	961	1 102	1 075
Liberia				1 055	1 448	991	931
Madagascar				951	1 144	799	690
Mali				457	584	734	783
Mauritania				464	965	922	993
Mauritius				2 491	3 681	7 125	9 853
Mozambique				1 133	1 873	1 003	1 187
Namibia				2 159	3 484	3 278	3 797
Niger				813	741	561	532
Nigeria				753	1 442	1 242	1 232
Reunion				1 988	3 776	4 490	4 502
Rwanda				547	688	855	704
Senegal				1 259	1 315	1 354	1 302
Seychelles				1 909	3 224	5 014	5 962
Sierra Leone				656	1 087	1 012	558
Somalia				1 057	1 176	1 083	883
Sudan				821	780	743	880
Swaziland				722	2 260	2 564	2 794
Tanzania				377	588	557	553
Togo				574	1 053	762	644
Tunisia				1 115	2 221	3 337	4 190
Uganda				687	838	592	725
Zambia				661	1 066	808	674
Zimbabwe				701	1 423	1 382	1 448
38 Other Countries				**834**	**1 314**	**1 241**	**1 235**
15 Non–sample Countries				**355**	**720**	**558**	**504**
Total 57 Countries	**418**	**444**	**585**	**852**	**1 365**	**1 385**	**1 368**
Burkina Faso				385	553	607	676
Burundi				327	505	666	543
Ethiopia and Eritrea				250	401	372	399
Guinea				303	492	557	612
Guinea Bissau				290	882	796	610
Lesotho				320	692	1 048	1 173
Malawi				324	566	563	706
Zaire				497	730	458	220
6 Other Countries				800	5 737	2 832	2 879
15 Non–sample Countries				355	720	558	504

Table A4–d. **GDP Per Capita Growth Rates in 57 African Countries**

	1820–70	*1870–1913*	*1913–50*	*1950–73*	*1973–98*
Egypt			−0.05	1.54	2.98
Ghana			1.14	0.99	−0.49
Morocco			1.61	0.66	1.87
South Africa			1.25	2.19	−0.32
4 Sample Countries			**1.02**	**1.76**	**0.88**
Algeria				2.40	0.53
Angola				2.34	−3.99
Benin				−0.09	0.68
Botswana				5.21	5.42
Cameroon				1.76	0.02
Cape Verde				0.70	3.84
Central African Rep.				0.35	−0.99
Chad				−0.42	0.34
Comoros				2.03	−2.12
Congo				2.21	0.20
Côte d'Ivoire				2.65	−1.29
Djibouti				1.64	−2.85
Gabon				3.81	−1.61
Gambia				2.60	−0.55
Kenya				1.71	0.45
Liberia				1.39	−1.75
Madagascar				0.81	−2.00
Mali				1.07	1.18
Mauritania				3.23	0.11
Mauritius				1.71	4.02
Mozambique				2.21	−1.81
Namibia				2.10	0.34
Niger				−0.40	−1.31
Nigeria				2.87	−0.63
Reunion				2.83	0.71
Rwanda				1.00	0.10
Senegal				0.19	−0.04
Seychelles				2.30	2.49
Sierra Leone				2.22	−2.63
Somalia				0.47	−1.14
Sudan				−0.22	0.49
Swaziland				5.09	0.85
Tanzania				1.95	−0.24
Togo				2.67	−1.95
Tunisia				3.04	2.57
Uganda				0.87	−0.58
Zambia				2.10	−1.82
Zimbabwe				3.12	0.07
38 Other Countries				**2.00**	**−0.25**
15 Non–sample Countries				**3.12**	**−1.42**
Total 57 Countries	**0.12**	**0.64**	**1.02**	**2.07**	**0.01**
Burkina Faso				1.58	0.81
Burundi				1.91	0.29
Ethiopia and Eritrea				2.07	−0.02
Guinea				2.12	0.88
Guinea Bissau				4.96	−1.46
Lesotho				3.41	2.13
Malawi				2.46	0.89
Zaire				1.68	−4.68
6 Other Countries				8.94	−2.72
15 Non–sample Countries				3.12	−1.42

Table A4-e. **GDP Growth Rates in 57 African Countries**

	1820–70	*1870–1913*	*1913–50*	*1950–73*	*1973–98*
Egypt			1.46	3.84	5.57
Ghana			3.77	3.63	2.16
Morocco			3.63	3.32	4.09
South Africa			3.44	4.85	1.93
4 Sample Countries			**2.92**	**4.27**	**3.30**
Algeria				4.82	3.37
Angola				4.05	−1.70
Benin				2.23	3.81
Botswana				7.07	8.90
Cameroon				3.48	3.02
Cape Verde				3.54	5.37
Central African Rep.				2.26	1.22
Chad				1.45	2.82
Comoros				4.51	0.88
Congo				4.50	3.17
Côte d'Ivoire				6.27	2.28
Djibouti				6.84	0.50
Gabon				5.13	1.48
Gambia				5.23	2.93
Kenya				4.95	3.76
Liberia				4.15	0.62
Madagascar				2.80	0.74
Mali				3.16	3.38
Mauritania				4.58	2.61
Mauritius				4.32	5.29
Mozambique				4.36	0.63
Namibia				4.72	3.07
Niger				2.26	1.70
Nigeria				5.19	2.33
Reunion				5.79	2.36
Rwanda				3.32	2.78
Senegal				2.74	2.89
Seychelles				4.84	3.76
Sierra Leone				3.73	−0.46
Somalia				2.58	1.08
Sudan				2.55	3.74
Swaziland				7.75	3.60
Tanzania				4.38	2.56
Togo				5.38	1.38
Tunisia				5.00	4.84
Uganda				3.68	2.49
Zambia				4.77	1.03
Zimbabwe				6.54	2.51
38 Other Countries				**4.41**	**2.62**
15 Non–sample Countries				**5.26**	**1.21**
Total 57 Countries	**0.52**	**1.40**	**2.69**	**4.45**	**2.74**
Burkina Faso				2.95	3.42
Burundi				3.70	2.11
Ethiopia and Eritrea				4.12	2.43
Guinea				3.83	3.66
Guinea Bissau				5.41	1.11
Lesotho				5.47	4.63
Malawi				4.92	3.77
Zaire				4.08	−1.78
6 Other Countries				12.74	0.22
15 Non–sample Countries				5.26	1.21

Table A4–f. **Population Growth Rates in 57 African Countries**

	1820–70	*1870–1913*	*1913–50*	*1950–73*	*1973–98*
Egypt			1.52	2.26	2.52
Ghana			2.61	2.61	2.67
Morocco			1.99	2.64	2.18
South Africa			2.17	2.60	2.25
4 Sample Countries			**1.88**	**2.47**	**2.39**
Algeria				2.36	2.82
Angola				1.67	2.38
Benin				2.32	3.11
Botswana				1.76	3.30
Cameroon				1.69	3.00
Cape Verde				2.82	1.48
Central African Rep.				1.91	2.23
Chad				1.87	2.47
Comoros				2.43	3.06
Congo				2.24	2.97
Côte d'Ivoire				3.53	3.62
Djibouti				5.12	3.45
Gabon				1.28	3.15
Gambia				2.56	3.51
Kenya				3.19	3.30
Liberia				2.72	2.41
Madagascar				1.98	2.80
Mali				2.07	2.17
Mauritania				1.31	2.50
Mauritius				2.56	1.23
Mozambique				2.10	2.49
Namibia				2.57	2.71
Niger				2.68	3.05
Nigeria				2.26	2.97
Reunion				2.88	1.64
Rwanda				2.29	2.68
Senegal				2.54	2.93
Seychelles				2.48	1.24
Sierra Leone				1.48	2.23
Somalia				2.10	2.24
Sudan				2.78	3.24
Swaziland				2.54	2.73
Tanzania				2.39	2.81
Togo				2.64	3.39
Tunisia				1.90	2.21
Uganda				2.78	3.08
Zambia				2.62	2.90
Zimbabwe				3.32	2.44
38 Other Countries				**2.37**	**2.87**
15 Non–sample Countries				**2.07**	**2.67**
Total 57 Countries	**0.40**	**0.75**	**1.65**	**2.33**	**2.73**
Burkina Faso				1.34	2.59
Burundi				1.76	1.82
Ethiopia and Eritrea				2.00	2.44
Guinea				1.67	2.76
Guinea Bissau				0.43	2.61
Lesotho				1.99	2.45
Malawi				2.40	2.86
Zaire				2.36	3.04
6 Other Countries				3.48	3.03
15 Non–sample Countries				2.07	2.67

Table A4–g. **Alternative Estimates of African 1990 GDP Level by ICP and PWT**
(million international, Geary–Khamis dollars)

	PWT 5.5	*PWT 5.6*	*ICP 4*	*ICP 5*	*ICP 7*
Benin	5 248	5 347	n.a.	6 629	1 227
Botswana	5 479	4 178	5 488	5 662	2 591
Cameroon	17 115	14 393	16 781	41 534	7 123
Congo	5 972	5 394	n.a.	5 358	1 096
Côte d'Ivoire	14 568	16 330	16 655	18 528	5 562
Egypt	105 684	112 873	n.a.	194 267	66 855
Ethiopia	17 891	18 964	16 498	18 622	n.a.
Gabon	3 639	4 500	n.a.	n.a.	2 424
Guinea	3 087	3 304	n.a.	n.a.	2 506
Kenya	26 028	26 093	25 698	31 855	7 358
Madagascar	9 093	9 210	8 001	8 531	3 541
Malawi	4 840	5 146	5 131	6 173	1 582
Mali	5 059	6 040	4 561	5 314	1 485
Mauritius	7 211	7 652	n.a.	7 671	1 796
Morocco	60 193	64 082	56 183	83 696	20 338
Nigeria	96 521	107 459	126 035	139 453	24 349
Rwanda	5 360	6 125	n.a.	5 040	n.a.
Senegal	9 351	10 032	8 627	12 139	3 361
Sierra Leone	4 041	4 325	n.a.	3 021	774
Swaziland	1 580	2 154	n.a.	2 181	611
Tanzania	14 676	13 852	13 388	13 199	2 470
Tunisia	26 421	27 387	28 990	35 312	9 409
Zambia	6 935	6 432	8 358	10 684	2 741
Zimbabwe	14 913	13 766	15 256	20 391	5 559

Source: Col. 1 from Penn World Tables, version 5.5, diskette annex to R.S. Summers and A. Heston, "The Penn World Table (Mark 5): An Expanded Set of International Comparisons, 1950–1988", *Quarterly Journal of Economics,* May 1991. Col. 2 from their diskette of version 5.6a of January 1995. In some cases the PWT estimate referred to a year or two earlier than 1990, and I updated using the volume movement of GDP, and the change in the US GDP deflator between that year and 1990. I used the PWT version 5.5 for 50 countries earlier (see Maddison, 1995a, p. 192 and 221), and here have used version 5.6a. This raised the GDP aggregate for the 50 countries from 812 817 million international (Geary–Khamis) dollars in Maddison (1995a) to 845 908 million here. In addition, there were proxy estimates for six countries amounting to $13 883 million int.dollars in both exercises (see Maddison, 1995a, pp. 214 and 221). The PWT estimates are much more comprehensive than those of the ICP, which covered 15 countries for 1980 (ICP 4), 22 countries in ICP 5 for 1985 and ICP 7 for 1993. There was no ICP 6 round for 1990 for Africa. The ICP results were adjusted to a 1990 basis in the same fashion as those in Tables A3–g and A3–h. The 24 countries shown here include all of those which participated in one or other of the ICP exercises. ICP 4 results are from UN/Eurostat, *World Comparisons of Purchasing Power Parity and Real Product for 1980,* New York, 1987, p. viii; ICP 5 from UN/Eurostat, *World Comparisons of Real GDP and Purchasing Power 1985,* New York, 1994, p. 5; ICP 7 Geary–Khamis results from Eurostat, *Comparisons of Price Levels and Economic Aggregates 1993: The Results of 22 African Countries,* Luxembourg 1996, pp. 43, 145–6. The ICP 7 results in the last column are not comparable with those for earlier years. They are intra–African relatives linked to the US dollar via a standardised exchange rate rather than a purchasing power parity with the United States as the *numeraire* country. As a result they show real product levels which are in the aggregate aout one third of those in the ICP 5 exercise. The ratio of the ICP 7 to ICP 5 results varies from .46 for Botswana to .17 for Cameroon. The ICP 5 result for Cameroon is, in fact, rather odd. However, for the biggest countries, the ratio varies from .17 for Nigeria to .34 for Egypt. A major problem with the ICP exercise is that there is no attempt to reconcile discrepancies between the results of different rounds, whereas this is a fundamental feature of the Summers and Heston approach in the Penn World Tables.

Appendix B

Growth of World Population, GDP and GDP Per Capita before 1820

Maddison (1995a) contained a rough aggregate estimate of world population, GDP and per capita GDP back to 1500 to provide perspective for the detailed analysis of developments after 1820. The main purpose of the brief look backwards was to emphasise the dramatic acceleration of growth in the succeeding capitalist epoch. Maddison (1998a) provided a confrontation of Chinese and Western economic performance over a longer period of two millennia. This demonstrated important differences in the pace and pattern of change in major parts of the world economy, which have roots deep into the past.

The present exercise provides a more detailed and disaggregated scrutiny of the protocapitalist experience from 1500 to 1820, with a rough sketch of the contours of development over the preceding millennium and a half.

The quantitative analysis in this appendix works backward from the 1820 estimates in Appendix A, using the same techniques of analysis — assembling evidence on changes in population, retaining the 1990 international dollar as the temporal and spatial anchor in the estimation of movements in GDP and per capita GDP, filling holes in the evidence with proxy estimates in order to derive world totals. This appendix is divided into two parts. The first deals with population. The second with GDP growth.

POPULATION

The evidence here on the more distant past is weaker than that in Appendix A, and there are more gaps in the database. Nevertheless, the exercise in quantification is not a product of fantasy. The strongest and most comprehensive evidence is that for population, and the population component is of greater proportionate importance in analysis of centuries when per capita income growth was exiguous.

Demographic material is important in providing clues to per capita income development. One striking example is the urbanisation ratio. Thanks to the work of de Vries for Europe and of Rozman for Asia, one can measure the proportion of population living in towns with more than 10 000 inhabitants. In the year 1000, this ratio was zero in Europe (there were only 4 towns with more than 10 000 inhabitants) and in China it was 3 per cent. By 1800 the West European urban ratio was 10.6 per cent, the Chinese 3.8 per cent and the Japanese 12.3 per cent. When countries are able to expand their urban ratios, it indicates that there was a growing surplus beyond subsistence in agriculture, and that the non–agricultural component of economic activity was increasing. These changes were used to infer differences in per capita progress between China and Europe in Maddison (1998a), and such inference is a feature of the present study. The Chinese bureaucracy kept population registers which

go back more than 2 000 years. These bureaucratic records were designed to assess taxable capacity, and include information on cultivated area and crop production, which was used by Perkins (1969) to assess long run movements in Chinese GDP per capita. Bagnall and Frier (1994) have made brilliant use of fragments of ancient censuses to estimate occupational structure, household size, marriage patterns, fertility and life expectation in Roman Egypt of the third century.

Serious work on historical demography started in the seventeenth century with John Graunt (1662). He derived vital statistics, survival tables, and the population of London by processing and analysing christenings and burials recorded in the London bills of mortality from 1603 onwards. Halley (1693) published the first rigorous mathematical analysis of life tables and Gregory King (1696) derived estimates of the population of England and Wales by exploiting information from hearth and poll taxes, a new tax on births, marriages and burials and his own minicensuses for a few towns.

Historical demography gained new vigour in the twentieth century in several important centres: a) the Office of Population Research in Princeton University (established in 1936); b) INED (Institut National des Études Demographiques) founded in the 1950s to exploit family reconstitution techniques developed by Louis Henry; c) the Cambridge Group for the History of Population and Family Structure (established in the 1970s) has carried out a massive research project to reconstitute English population size and structure on an annual basis back to 1541 (Wrigley, et al., 1997); d) research on Japanese population history has blossomed under the leadership of Akira Hayami and Osamu Saito; e) there has been a flood of publications on Latin American demography from the University of California by members of the Berkeley school. For the second half of the twentieth century we have the comprehensive international surveys of the United Nations, and the US Bureau of the Census.

As a result there are now a large number of monographic studies on European, American and Asian countries, and a long series of efforts to construct aggregative estimates of world population. Riccioli (1672) and Gregory King (1696) inaugurated this tradition. Early estimates are usefully surveyed by Willcox (1931) who listed 66 publications between 1650 and 1850. Modern scholarship is represented by Colin Clark (1967), Durand (1974), McEvedy and Jones (1978) and Biraben (1979).

The following detailed estimates for 1500 onwards rely heavily on monographic country studies for the major countries. To fill holes in my dataset I draw on McEvedy and Jones (1978). For the preceding millennium and a half, I used their work extensively.

There are several reasons for preferring McEvedy and Jones rather than Clark, Durand and Biraben. The McEvedy and Jones estimates are the most detailed and best documented. When reconstructing the past, they define countries in terms of 1975 boundaries, which are in most cases identical with the 1990 boundaries I adopted as a general rule (with exceptions for Germany, India, Korea and the United Kingdom). They also show the impact of frontier changes. There are significant differences of judgement amongst the four standard sources on long term population momentum, particularly for Latin America for 1500 and earlier, and for Africa. In both these cases my judgement was closer to that of McEvedy and Jones, than to that of Clark, Durand or Biraben.

Table B–1 summarises my aggregate findings compared with those of McEvedy and Jones, Clark, Durand and Biraben.

Western Europe

Denmark, Finland, Germany, Netherlands, Norway, Sweden and Switzerland 1500–1700 from Maddison (1991) pp. 226–7; Belgium and Italy from de Vries (1984), p. 36. Austria from McEvedy and Jones (1978). France 1500–1700 (refers to present territory) from Bardet and Dupaquier (1997), pp. 446 and 449; 1700–1820 from Henry and Blayo (1975), pp. 97–9. UK estimate is explained in Table B–13 below. Population for the years 0 and 1000 from McEvedy and Jones (1978). Population of 13 small West European countries assumed to move parallel to the total for the 12 countries above.

Portugal 1500–1700 and Spain 1500 from de Vries (1984), p. 36. Spain 1600 and 1700 from *Espana: Anuario Estadistico 1977*, INE, Madrid, p. 49; 0 and 1000 are from McEvedy and Jones. Greece 0–1700 from McEvedy and Jones.

Table B–1. **Alternative Estimates of the Regional Components of World Population, 0–1700 A.D.**
(000)

Year	0	1000	1500	1700
Europe (including area of former USSR)				
Clark	44 500	44 200	73 800	111 800
Durand	42 500	45 500	79 000	n.a.
Biraben	43 000	43 000	84 000	125 000
McEvedy and Jones	32 800	38 800	85 500	126 150
Maddison	33 350	39 013	87 718	126 810
Americas				
Clark	3 000	13 000	41 000	13 000
Durand	12 000	37 500	46 500	n.a.
Biraben	12 000	18 000	42 000	12 000
McEvedy and Jones	4 500	9 000	14 000	13 000
Maddison	6 320	12 860	19 750	13 250
Asia (including Australasia)				
Clark	185 000	173 000	227 000	416 000
Durand	207 000	189 500	304 000	n.a.
Biraben	171 000	152 000	245 000	436 000
McEvedy and Jones	114 200	183 400	277 330	411 250
Maddison	174 650	183 400	284 350	402 350
Africa				
Clark	23 000	50 000	85 000	100 000
Durand	35 000	37 500	54 000	n.a.
Biraben	26 000	38 000	87 000	107 000
McEvedy and Jones	16 500	33 000	46 000	61 000
Maddison	16 500	33 000	46 000	61 000
World				
Clark	225 500	280 200	427 800	640 800
Durand	296 500	310 000	483 500	n.a.
Biraben	252 000	253 000	461 000	680 000
McEvedy and Jones	168 700	264 500	423 600	610 000
Maddison	230 820	268 273	437 818	603 410

Source: Clark (1967), Durand (1974), McEvedy and Jones (1978) and Biraben (1979). The estimates of Durand are high/low ranges. I have taken the mid point of his figures. I included the whole of the former USSR in Europe and the whole of Turkey in Asia, and adjusted the estimates of the other authors to conform to this definition.

Eastern Europe

Population 0 — 1700 of what is now Albania, Bulgaria, Czech Republic, Greece, Hungary, Poland, Romania, Slovakia and the five republics of the former Yugoslavia from McEvedy and Jones (1978).

Table B–2. **Population of Western and Eastern Europe and Western Offshoots, 0–1820 A.D.**
(000)

Year	0	1000	1500	1600	1700	1820
Austria	500	700	2 000	2 500	2 500	3 369
Belgium	300	400	1 400	1 600	2 000	3 434
Denmark	180	360	600	650	700	1 155
Finland	20	40	300	400	400	1 169
France	5 000	6 500	15 000	18 500	21 471	31 246
Germany	3 000	3 500	12 000	16 000	15 000	24 905
Italy	7 000	5 000	10 500	13 100	13 300	20 176
Netherlands	200	300	950	1 500	1 900	2 355
Norway	100	200	300	400	500	970
Sweden	200	400	550	760	1 260	2 585
Switzerland	300	300	650	1 000	1 200	1 829
United Kingdom	800	2 000	3 942	6 170	8 565	21 226
12 Countries	17 600[a]	19 700[b]	48 192	62 580	68 796	114 419
Portugal	500	600	1 000	1 100	2 000	3 297
Spain	4 500	4 000	6 800	8 240	8 770	12 203
Greece	2 000	1 000	1 000	1 500	1 500	2 312
13 Small Countries	100	113	276	358	394	657
Total Western Europe	**24 700**	**25 413**	**57 268**	**73 778**	**81 460**	**132 888**
Albania	200	200	200	200	300	437
Bulgaria	500	800	800	1 250	1 250	2 187
Czechoslovakia	1 000	1 250	3 000	4 500	4 500	7 190
Hungary	300	500	1 250	1 250	1 500	4 571
Poland	450	1 200	4 000	5 000	6 000	10 426
Romania	800	800	2 000	2 000	2 500	6 389
Yugoslavia	1 500	1 750	2 250	2 750	2 750	5 215
Total Eastern Europe	**4 750**	**6 500**	**13 500**	**16 950**	**18 800**	**36 415**
United States	640	1 300	2 000	1 500	1 000	9 981
Canada	80	160	250	250	200	816
Australia & New Zealand	450	500	550	550	550	433
Total Western Offshoots	**1 170**	**1 960**	**2 800**	**2 300**	**1 750**	**11 230**

Table B–3. **European and Asian Population of Russia, 0–1870 A.D.**
(000)

Year	0	1000	1500	1600	1700	1820	1870
European Russia	2 000	4 000	12 000	15 000	20 000	44 161	71 726
Siberia	100	100	200	200	300	1 443	3 272
Caucasus	300	500	1 250	1 500	1 750	2 429	4 587
Turkestan	1 500	2 500	3 500	4 000	4 500	6 732	9 087
Total	**3 900**	**7 100**	**16 950**	**20 700**	**26 550**	**54 765**	**88 672**

Source: McEvedy and Jones (1978).

Former USSR

Table B–3 refers to population in the geographic area that constituted the USSR before it was dissolved in 1991. 0–1870 from McEvedy and Jones (1978), pp. 78–82, 157–63, broken down for European Russia (excluding Finland and the Polish provinces), Siberia, the Caucasus (present republics of Armenia, Azerbaijan and Georgia), and Turkestan (present republics of Kazakhstan, Kyrgyzstan, Tajikistan, Turkmenistan and Uzbekistan).

Western Offshoots

There is a detailed bibliography and survey of the literature on North America in Daniels (1992). Thornton (1987) analyses the process of indigenous depopulation, and cites Ubelaker's (1976) estimates for the Smithsonian Institution. I took a rounded version of the latter as the basis for my estimate of 2 million in 1500 for the United States, and quarter of a million for Canada. Thornton gives no estimates for 1600 and 1700. My assessment for these two years is based on the assumption that the depopulation ratio was smaller than in Mexico (where population density was much greater). Movement of population for 0–1500 assumed to be proportionately the same as the total for Latin America.

For Australia, the conventional official estimate of the aboriginal population at the time of initial contact with Europeans was 250–300 thousand, but Butlin's (1983) detailed modelling of the likely impact of disease, displacement and deliberate extermination in New South Wales and Victoria suggested a considerably higher figure. I assumed a pre–contact population in Australia and New Zealand combined of 550 000 — smaller than Butlin's estimate but bigger than the old official estimates. For 0–1500 I assumed slower growth than in the Americas.

Latin America

The size of the indigenous population at the time of the Spanish conquest is a matter of considerable controversy. Firm evidence is weak, but there are two very distinct schools of thought. It is clear that population declined substantially after the conquest. The native population had been isolated over millennia from foreign microbes, and suffered from major epidemics of smallpox, measles and other deadly diseases against which they had no immunities.

Mexico

In an assessment based on a careful survey of literary evidence of the conquistadores and documents in Spanish archives, Angel Rosenblat (1945) estimated the pre–conquest population of present day Mexico to have been about 4.5 million. He assumed a rather modest rate of depopulation after the conquest — a drop less than 15 per cent in the sixteenth century. The Berkeley school (Cook and Simpson, 1948) had very much higher estimates of the pre–conquest population — their figure for Central Mexico alone (about a quarter of the territory of present day Mexico) was 11 million. This estimate was based on various flimsy suppositions, e.g. multiplying the number of Franciscan monks by baptismal coefficients or inferring population from the size of Aztec armies as estimated by those who fought them. The Borah and Cook (1963) estimate for Central Mexico was even higher — 25 million on the basis of ambiguous pictographs describing the incidence of Aztec fiscal levies. They assumed a 95 per cent depopulation ratio for the indigenous population between 1519 and 1605, and backcast Spanish estimates for 1605 by a multiplier of 25. They give no detailed specification of the different causes of mortality as Butlin (1983) did for Australia. They did not discuss alternative approaches to measurement as Cook (1981) does for Peru, and they never made an adequate response to Rosenblat's (1967) criticism of their work.

There are two reasons for scepticism about the extremely high mortality estimates of the Berkeley school: a) they assume very much higher mortality than European experience in the wake of the Black Death (a one third loss); b) it is implausible that Central Mexican population did not recover its alleged 1519 level until 1970 in spite of the additions the Spanish conquest made to production potential. Before the conquest there were no wheeled vehicles, no ploughs and no metal tools. The basic diet was close to vegetarianism with no cattle, sheep, pigs or hens. The absence of horses, donkeys, oxen and wheeled vehicles meant that land transport possibilities were confined to human porterage. Europe recovered from the Black Death mortality within a century with virtually no change in technology. It seems inconceivable that Mexican recovery took 450 years.

My own judgement is that Berkeley School's estimates for Mexico are far too high. However, I think Rosenblat understates the pre–conquest level and the subsequent rate of depopulation. Zambardino (1980), in a critical review of the Berkeley School, suggests a plausible range of 5–10 million. I took the midpoint of the Zambardino estimate for Mexico (see the discussion in Maddison, 1995b), and assumed a depopulation ratio of two thirds between 1500 and 1600.

Rosenblat (1945) describes the structure of the Mexican population in 1825, at the end of Spanish rule when the total population was 6.8 million. At the top of the scale was a thin layer of 70 000 peninsulares (peninsular Spaniards). The second group consisted of 1.2 million criollos (whites of Spanish extraction). The third group consisted of 1.9 million *mestizos* or *castas*. Most of them originated from unions between whites and Indians, some were Indians who had abandoned their rural lifestyle, wore Spanish–type clothes and lived in urban areas. At the bottom of the social scale were rural Indians (3.7 million) living mostly in nucleated pueblos, engaged in subsistence agriculture, with some hunter–gatherer groups in the North. This group wore traditional dress, maintained their own languages and customs except religion. There was a small group (about 10 000) of negro slaves in the South of the country. This information on social structure is of considerable use in constructing income accounts (see below).

Brazil

I adopted the Rosenblat (1945) estimate for 1500 which was used by McEvedy and Jones. It is close to the Kroeber (1939) estimate based on hypotheses about the nature of land use and technology by a population who were mainly hunter–gatherers (with some slash and burn agriculture in coastal regions). Hemming (1978) estimates a pre–contact population of 2.4 million (a figure he describes as "pure guess–work") derived by blowing up present day figures for 28 regions by assumed depopulation ratios. Denevan (1976) estimates 4.8 million for North and Central Brazil (including Amazonia) but this was based on agricultural potential and inferences from evidence on Peru. Hemming exaggerates the likely depopulation ratio for a country with a thinly settled hunter–gatherer population, and Denevan's reliance on estimates of agricultural potential is not relevant for an Indian population who were predominantly hunter–gatherers.

In the first century of settlement it became clear that it was difficult to use Indians as serf or slave labour. They were not docile, had high mortality when exposed to Western diseases, could run away and hide very easily. So the Portuguese imported large numbers of African slaves for manual labour. The ultimate fate of Brazilian Indians was like that of North American Indians. They were pushed beyond the bounds of colonial society. The main difference was greater miscegenation with the white invaders and black slaves.

Table B–4. **Ethnic Composition of the Brazilian Population, 1500–1870**
(000)

Year	1500	1600	1700	1820	1870
Indigenous	1 000	700	950	500	400
Black and Mixed		70	200	2 500	5 700[a]
European		30	100	1 500	3 700
Total	1 000	800	1 250	4 500	9 800

a) including 1.5 million slaves.

Sources: Rosenblat (1945), Simonsen (1962), Merrick and Graham (1979), Marcilio (1984).

Table B–5. **Alternative Estimates of Latin American Population, 0–1820 A.D.**
(000)

Year	0	1000	1500	1600	1700	1820
			Maddison estimates			
Mexico		4 500	7 500	2 500	4 500	6 587
Brazil		700	1 000	800	1 250	4 507
Peru		3 000	4 000	1 300	1 300	1 317
Other		3 200	5 000	4 000	5 000	8 809
Total	5 600	11 400	17 500	8 600	12 050	21 220
			McEvedy and Jones (1978)			
Mexico	1 500	3 000	5 000	3 500	4 000	6 309[a]
Brazil	400	700	1 000	1 000	1 250	3 827[a]
Peru	750	1 500	2 000	1 500	1 500	1 683[a]
Other	1 550	3 300	5 200	4 500	5 400	10 450[a]
Total	4 200	8 500	13 200	10 500	12 150	22 269[a]
			Rosenblat (1945)			
Mexico			4 500	3 645[b]	n.a.	6 800[c]
Brazil			1 000	886[b]	n.a.	4 000[c]
Peru			2 000	1 591[b]	n.a.	1 400[c]
Other			4 885	4 532[b]	n.a.	10 863[c]
Total			12 385	10 654[b]	n.a.	23 063[c]
			Clark (1967)			
Total	2 900	12 600	40 000	14 000	12 000	
			Biraben (1979)			
Total	10 000	16 000	39 000	10 000	10 000	23 980[a]

a) interpolation of 1800 and 1850 estimates; b) interpolation of 1570 and 1650 estimates; c) 1825.

Sources: My estimates for 1500–1820 (see text above). 0–1500 growth rates from McEvedy and Jones.

Peru

I adopted Cook's (1981, Chapter 7) "minimal" estimate of 4 million. Although he calls it "minimal" he cites lower figures derived by other methods he considers respectable. Cook's approach is like that of the Berkeley school, but he shows alternative estimates derived from a) the "ecological" approach, which assesses population potential (carrying capacity) in terms of resources and the technology available; b) inferences from the extent of archaelogical remains; c) retropolation of assumed depopulation ratios from 1571 when the first reasonably documented Spanish population estimates became available. Cook opts for a pre–conquest figure of 9 million (p. 114) which is near the top of the wide range he shows. I assumed the same depopulation ratio of two thirds between 1500 and 1600, as I did for Mexico.

Other Latin American Countries

I adopted the pre–conquest estimates of McEvedy and Jones (1978) which they derive to a large degree from Rosenblat (1945). I assume a higher depopulation ratio for the sixteenth century than McEvedy and Jones, but less than that for Mexico and Peru (see Table B–5).

Total Latin American Population

Table B–5 compares my estimates, those of McEvedy and Jones and Rosenblat. Mine are higher for 1500 and show bigger depopulation in the sixteenth century, but the differences are modest compared with the Berkeley school. Borah (1976) suggested a population of 100 million upwards for the Americas as a whole in 1500. Colin Clark (1967) and Biraben (1979) were impressed by Borah but obviously felt he exaggerated and adopted compromise estimates (without entering into country detail).

China

Chinese population estimates (see Table B–8) are based on bureaucratic records which go much further back than those in any other country. The type of adjustments which are necessary for intertemporal compatibility are discussed in detail in Bielenstein (1987) and Ho (1959). I have used Ho (1970) p.49 for the population in 2A.D. For 960 onwards see Maddison, 1998a, Appendix D, pp. 167–9. Recently (in volume 8 of the *Cambridge History of China*), Martin Heidra offered a totally different picture of Chinese population with very rapid growth during the Ming dynasty. However, he provides no detail or bibliographic evidence for his revisionism, and shows no decline in the mid seventeenth century wars between the Ming and their Ch'ing successors. His analysis ends in 1650, and his high hypothesis leaves virtually no room for any growth in the Ch'ing period (see Heidra in Twitchett and Mote, 1998, pp. 436–40). It is therefore difficult to give much credence to his views.

Table B–6. **Alternative Estimates of India's Population, 0–1820 A.D.**

(million)

Year	0	1000	1500	1600	1700	1820
Clark (1967)	70	70	79	100	200	190
McEvedy & Jones (1978)	34	77	100	130	160	200
Biraben (1979)	46	40	95	145	175	194
Durand (1974)	75	75	112.5	n.a.	180[a]	n.a.
Maddison	55	75	110	135	165	209

a) 1750.

India

India does not have statistical records of the same sort as Western Europe, China or Japan, and there is consequently a wide range of views. A good deal of discussion has hinged on the year 1600, for which Moreland estimated 100 million, Davis (1951) 125 million, Habib (1982) around 145 million (a range of 140–150). Virtually all of these estimates are based on an assessment of the productive capacity of the cultivated area (see Raychaudhuri and Habib, 1982), so there is an interdependence between what one assumes about demographic and economic performance. I took an average of the Davis and Habib estimate for 1600. For the year 0, I used the estimates of Durand.

Japan

Reasonably firm evidence is available from 1721 onwards from national population surveys at six–yearly intervals. These were taken for the shogun's own domains and those of approximately 250 daimyo in the rest of Japan. The registers excluded samurai households, the imperial nobility, outcastes and beggars (eta and hinin). They understated the female population and (to a degree which varied between different domains) young children as well. Nevertheless they can be adjusted to provide reasonable estimates for 1721 onwards when the aggregate level was about 30 million. Before the six–yearly surveys were instituted, information was available from annual registers of religious affiliation which were instituted after the Portuguese were expelled from Japan and Christianity was made illegal. Hayami (1986a) shows such retrospective daimyo returns for 17 areas for periods varying from 30 to 100 years before the 1730s. Together they covered about 17 per cent of the Japanese population in the 1730s. They show an arithmetic average growth rate of 0.35 per cent a year, and a weighted average of 0.52 per cent. When these rates are backcast they suggest a 1600 population between 16 and 19.7 million, which is close to the Yoshida (1911) estimate of 18.5 million. Yoshida based his estimate on the 1598 cadastral survey which showed 18.5 million koku of grain output. He assumed this would support a population of 18.5 million with a consumption of 1 koku (150 kg.) per head.

Table B–7. **Alternative Estimates of Japanese Population, 0–1820 A.D.**

(000)

Year	0	1000	1500	1600	1700	1820
Maddison	3 000	7 500	15 400	18 500	27 000	31 000
Hayami			10 000	12 000	30 000	31 000

Source: For the first century I took the midpoint of the range cited by Farris (1985) p. 3 for the Yayoi period, and for the year 1000 interpolated between the estimate cited by Farris (p. 175) for the mid 7th and by Taeuber (1958), p. 20, for the mid 13th century. For 1500–1600 I assume the same growth rate as Hayami (0.18 per cent a year).

Yoshida's reasoning was crude but seems more plausible than Hayami's (1986a) range of 10 to 14 million for 1600. Hayami implies a very rapid growth in the seventeenth century with an abrupt change to more or less complete stagnation in the eighteenth century.

Korea

Korea had a system of household population registers (hojok) for purposes of taxation and manpower mobilisation from 1392 to 1910, from which bureaucratic records survive. These registers had very scanty coverage of the child population, there was substantial regional variance, with much better coverage in Seoul, the capital. Kwon (1993) adjusted these records with the help of other

historical documents, and information on family structure from the first modern census of 1925. Kwon and Shin (1977) provide annual estimates for 1392 to 1910. I used their estimates of population movement for 1500, 1600, 1700 and 1910 and linked them to estimates of the 1910 level from Mizoguchi and Umemura (1988) as described in Appendix A. The revised estimates are about twice as high as those used in McEvedy and Jones (1978) which were based on the unadjusted results of the population registers as reported in Lee (1936), pp. 40–1. For 0–1500 I assumed the same proportionate movement as in Japan.

Table B–8. **Population of Asia, 0–1820 A.D.**
(million)

Year	0	1000	1500	1600	1700	1820
China	59.6	59.0	103.0	160.0	138.0	381.0
India	75.0	75.0	110.0	135.0	165.0	209.0
Japan	3.0	7.5	15.4	18.5	27.0	31.0
Korea	1.6	3.9	8.0	10.0	12.2	13.8
Indonesia	2.8	5.2	10.7	11.7	13.1	17.9
Indochina	1.1	2.2	4.5	5.0	5.9	8.9
Other East Asia	5.9	9.8	14.4	16.9	19.8	23.6
Iran	4.0	4.5	4.0	5.0	5.0	6.6
Turkey	6.1	7.3	6.3	7.9	8.4	10.1
Other West Asia	15.1	8.5	7.5	8.5	7.4	8.5
Total Asia	**174.2**	**182.9**	**283.8**	**378.5**	**401.8**	**710.4**

Source: China, India, Japan and Korea as described in text. All 1820 figures are from Appendix A. Indonesia 1700 from Maddison (1989*b*), 0–1700 proportionate movement from McEvedy and Jones. Indochina (area of Cambodia, Laos and Vietnam), 0–1820 proportionate movement from McEvedy and Jones. Other East Asia, Iran, Turkey and Other West Asia 0–1700 from McEvedy and Jones. The geographic coverage of Asia is the same here as in Appendix A. The Asian population in the former USSR is excluded. Turkey, Polynesia and Melanesia are included.

Africa

Except for Egypt there is virtually no documentation on African population. The available estimates are speculative. The first were by Riccioli, an Italian Jesuit, in 1672. He suggested a population of 100 million in his day without explaining the derivation. Gregory King (1696) estimated 70 million, starting with the land area of the continent and a rough assessment of agricultural productivity to estimate what population could be sustained with the available natural resources, levels of technique and organisation.

The leading American demographer Walter Willcox (1931) thought Riccioli's estimate was plausible and assumed no change in seventeenth and eighteenth centuries. Colin Clark (1967) did the same. Carr–Saunders (1964) accepted Riccioli's estimate for the mid–seventeenth century and allowed for some decline thereafter because of the slave trade. Biraben (1979) also allowed for some decline due to the slave trade.

Durand (1974) and McEvedy and Jones (1978) took a very different view. Working backwards from their estimated population level in 1900, they assumed a more dynamic growth process. They took a position on the interaction between population pressure and production which is nearer to that of Boserup (1965 and 1981), than to the Malthusian constraints which the other school had in mind. The hypothesis of McEvedy and Jones seems the more plausible, and I adopted their estimates for 0–1913.

Table B–9a. **Alternative Estimates of African Population, 0–1950 A.D.**
(million)

Year	Willcox (1931)	Carr–Saunders (1964)	Clark (1967)	Biraben (1979)	Durand (1974)	McEvedy & Jones (1978)	Maddison (1999)
0			23	26	35	16.5	16.5
1000			50	39	37.5	33	33
1500			85	87	54	46	46
1600			95	113	55	55	55
1650	100	100	100				
1700			100	107		61	61
1800	100	90	100	102		70	
1820		(92)				(74.2)	74.2
1870		(104.3)				(90.5)	90.5
1900	141	120	122	138	159	110	110.0
1913						(124.7)	124.7
1950		207		219		205	228.3

Sources: Willcox (1931), p.78; Carr–Saunders (1964), p.42; Clark (1967), pp.64, 104 and 108; Biraben (1979), p. 16; Durand (1974), p. 11 (midpoint of his range); McEvedy and Jones (1978), p. 206. Figures in brackets are interpolations.

Table B–9b. **Regional Distribution of African Population 0–1820 A.D**
(000)

Year	0	1000	1500	1600	1700	1820
Egypt	4 000	5 000	4 000	5 000	4 500	4 195
Other North Africa	4 200	5 500	4 300	6 000	4 800	6 790
Other Africa	8 300	22 500	37 700	44 000	51 700	63 223
Total Africa	16 500	33 000	46 000	55 000	61 000	74 208
North African Share %	49.7	31.8	18.0	20.0	13.6	14.8

Source: McEvedy and Jones (1978). Figure for 1820 is an interpolation of their estimates for 1800 and 1850.

McEvedy and Jones (1978) is the only source which provides a detailed analysis of the population of Africa. The most striking aspect of their estimates is the dynamism of the expansion south of the Sahara, and the very large decline in the North African share from about half of the African total in the first century to about one seventh in 1820 (see Table B–9b). For about four millennia Egypt was virtually the only area to practise agriculture, and the rest of the continent was sparsely inhabited by hunter–gatherer populations. In the last millennium B.C., Phoenicians and Greeks settled in North Africa west of Egypt, established cities and brought in sophisticated agricultural techniques. By the first century the whole of the prosperous Mediterranean littoral was under Roman control. Its economy and population declined after the Roman collapse, revived with the seventh century Arab takeover, reaching a new peak around the year 1000 A.D.

The dynamic expansion south of the Sahara was due to the spread of agriculturalists into East and Southern Africa, pushing out hunter— gatherer populations. The introduction of manioc and maize from the Americas in the sixteenth century reinforced the possibilities of agricultural expansion. The introduction of agriculture made it possible to accommodate a substantial increase in population, but per capita income probably did not change much.

The slave trade had a substantial effect on African population growth (see Tables 1–7 and 2–5 and the analysis in Chapter 2). Between 1600 and 1870 more than 9 million slaves were shipped to the Americas. The peak was in the eighteenth century when arrivals in the Americas were over 6 million, and African losses were bigger owing to mortality on the passage. Without this trade, African population growth in the eighteenth century might well have been three times as fast.

Table B–10. World Population, 20 Countries and Regional Totals, 0–1998 A.D.

(000)

Year	0	1000	1500	1600	1700	1820	1870	1913	1950	1973	1998
Austria	500	700	2 000	2 500	2 500	3 369	4 520	6 767	6 935	7 586	8 078
Belgium	300	400	1 400	1 600	2 000	3 434	5 096	7 666	8 640	9 738	10 197
Denmark	180	360	600	650	700	1 155	1 888	2 983	4 269	5 022	5 303
Finland	20	40	300	400	400	1 169	1 754	3 027	4 009	4 666	5 153
France	5 000	6 500	15 000	18 500	21 471	31 246	38 440	41 463	41 836	52 118	58 805
Germany	3 000	3 500	12 000	16 000	15 000	24 905	39 231	65 058	68 371	78 956	82 029
Italy	7 000	5 000	10 500	13 100	13 300	20 176	27 888	37 248	47 105	54 751	57 592
Netherlands	200	300	950	1 500	1 900	2 355	3 615	6 164	10 114	13 438	15 700
Norway	100	200	300	400	500	970	1 735	2 447	3 265	3 961	4 432
Sweden	200	400	550	760	1 260	2 585	4 164	5 621	7 015	8 137	8 851
Switzerland	300	300	650	1 000	1 200	1 829	2 664	3 864	4 694	6 441	7 130
United Kingdom	800	2 000	3 942	6 170	8 565	21 226	31 393	45 649	50 363	56 223	59 237
12 Countries Total	*17 600*	*19 700*	*48 192*	*62 580*	*68 796*	*114 419*	*162 388*	*227 957*	*256 616*	*301 037*	*322 507*
Portugal	500	600	1 000	1 100	2 000	3 297	4 353	6 004	8 512	8 634	9 968
Spain	4 500	4 000	6 800	8 240	8 770	12 203	16 201	20 263	27 868	34 810	39 371
Other	2 100	1 113	1 276	1 858	1 894	2 969	4 590	6 783	12 064	13 909	16 553
Total Western Europe	**24 700**	**25 413**	**57 268**	**73 778**	**81 460**	**132 888**	**187 532**	**261 007**	**305 060**	**358 390**	**388 399**
Eastern Europe	4 750	6 500	13 500	16 950	18 800	36 415	52 182	79 604	87 289	110 490	121 006
Former USSR	3 900	7 100	16 950	20 700	26 550	54 765	88 672	156 192	180 050	249 748	290 866
United States	680	1 300	2 000	1 500	1 000	9 981	40 241	97 606	152 271	211 909	270 561
Other Western Offshoots	490	660	800	800	750	1 249	5 892	13 795	23 823	39 036	52 859
Total Western Offshoots	**1 170**	**1 960**	**2 800**	**2 300**	**1 750**	**11 230**	**46 133**	**111 401**	**176 094**	**250 945**	**323 420**
Mexico	2 200	4 500	7 500	2 500	4 500	6 587	9 219	14 970	28 485	57 643	98 553
Other Latin America	3 400	6 900	10 000	6 100	7 550	14 633	30 754	65 545	137 352	250 807	409 070
Total Latin America	**5 600**	**11 400**	**17 500**	**8 600**	**12 050**	**21 220**	**39 973**	**80 515**	**165 837**	**308 450**	**507 623**
Japan	**3 000**	**7 500**	**15 400**	**18 500**	**27 000**	**31 000**	**34 437**	**51 672**	**83 563**	**108 660**	**126 469**
China	59 600	59 000	103 000	160 000	138 000	381 000	358 000	437 140	546 815	881 940	1 242 700
India	75 000	75 000	110 000	135 000	165 000	209 000	253 000	303 700	359 000	580 000	975 000
Other Asia	36 600	41 400	55 400	65 000	71 800	89 366	119 619	185 092	392 481	677 214	1 172 243
Total Asia (excluding Japan)	**171 200**	**175 400**	**268 400**	**360 000**	**374 800**	**679 366**	**730 619**	**925 932**	**1 298 296**	**2 139 154**	**3 389 943**
Africa	16 500	33 000	46 000	55 000	61 000	74 208	90 466	124 697	228 342	387 645	759 954
World	**230 820**	**268 273**	**437 818**	**555 828**	**603 410**	**1 041 092**	**1 270 014**	**1 791 020**	**2 524 531**	**3 913 482**	**5 907 680**

Table B–11. **Rates of Growth of World Population, 20 Countries and Regional Totals, 0–1998 A.D.**
(annual average compound growth rates)

Year	0–1000	1000–1500	1500–1820	1820–70	1870–1913	1913–50	1950–73	1973–98
Austria	0.03	0.21	0.16	0.59	0.94	0.07	0.39	0.25
Belgium	0.03	0.25	0.28	0.79	0.95	0.32	0.52	0.18
Denmark	0.07	0.10	0.20	0.99	1.07	0.97	0.71	0.22
Finland	0.07	0.40	0.43	0.81	1.28	0.76	0.66	0.40
France	0.03	0.17	0.23	0.42	0.18	0.02	0.96	0.48
Germany	0.02	0.25	0.23	0.91	1.18	0.13	0.63	0.15
Italy	–0.03	0.15	0.20	0.65	0.68	0.64	0.66	0.20
Netherlands	0.04	0.23	0.28	0.86	1.25	1.35	1.24	0.62
Norway	0.07	0.08	0.37	1.17	0.80	0.78	0.84	0.45
Sweden	0.07	0.06	0.48	0.96	0.70	0.60	0.65	0.34
Switzerland	0.00	0.15	0.32	0.75	0.87	0.53	1.39	0.41
United Kingdom	0.09	0.14	0.53	0.79	0.87	0.27	0.48	0.21
12 Countries Total	*0.01*	*0.18*	*0.27*	*0.70*	*0.79*	*0.32*	*0.70*	*0.28*
Portugal	0.02	0.10	0.37	0.56	0.75	0.95	0.06	0.58
Spain	–0.01	0.11	0.18	0.57	0.52	0.87	0.97	0.49
Other	–0.06	0.03	0.26	0.88	0.91	1.57	0.62	0.70
Total Western Europe	**0.00**	**0.16**	**0.26**	**0.69**	**0.77**	**0.42**	**0.70**	**0.32**
Eastern Europe	**0.03**	**0.15**	**0.31**	**0.72**	**0.99**	**0.25**	**1.03**	**0.36**
Former USSR	**0.06**	**0.17**	**0.37**	**0.97**	**1.33**	**0.38**	**1.43**	**0.61**
United States	0.06	0.09	0.50	2.83	2.08	1.21	1.45	0.98
Other Western Offshoots	0.03	0.04	0.14	3.15	2.00	1.49	2.17	1.22
Total Western Offshoots	**0.05**	**0.07**	**0.43**	**2.87**	**2.07**	**1.25**	**1.55**	**1.02**
Mexico	0.07	0.10	–0.04	0.67	1.13	1.75	3.11	2.17
Other Latin America	0.07	0.07	0.12	1.50	1.78	2.02	2.65	1.98
Total Latin America	**0.07**	**0.09**	**0.06**	**1.27**	**1.64**	**1.97**	**2.73**	**2.01**
Japan	**0.09**	**0.14**	**0.22**	**0.21**	**0.95**	**1.31**	**1.15**	**0.61**
China	0.00	0.11	0.41	–0.12	0.47	0.61	2.10	1.38
India	0.00	0.08	0.20	0.38	0.43	0.45	2.11	2.10
Other Asia	0.01	0.06	0.15	0.58	1.02	2.05	2.40	2.22
Total Asia (excluding Japan)	**0.00**	**0.09**	**0.29**	**0.15**	**0.55**	**0.92**	**2.19**	**1.86**
Africa	**0.07**	**0.07**	**0.15**	**0.40**	**0.75**	**1.65**	**2.33**	**2.73**
World	**0.02**	**0.10**	**0.27**	**0.40**	**0.80**	**0.93**	**1.92**	**1.66**

Table B–12. **Shares of World Population, 20 Countries and Regional Totals, 0–1998 A.D.**
(per cent of world total)

Year	0	1000	1500	1600	1700	1820	1870	1913	1950	1973	1998
Austria	0.2	0.3	0.5	0.4	0.4	0.3	0.4	0.4	0.3	0.2	0.1
Belgium	0.1	0.1	0.3	0.3	0.3	0.3	0.4	0.4	0.3	0.2	0.2
Denmark	0.1	0.1	0.1	0.1	0.1	0.1	0.1	0.2	0.2	0.1	0.1
Finland	0.0	0.0	0.1	0.1	0.1	0.1	0.1	0.2	0.2	0.1	0.1
France	2.2	2.4	3.4	3.3	3.6	3.0	3.0	2.3	1.7	1.3	1.0
Germany	1.3	1.3	2.7	2.9	2.5	2.4	3.1	3.6	2.7	2.0	1.4
Italy	3.0	1.9	2.4	2.4	2.2	1.9	2.2	2.1	1.9	1.4	1.0
Netherlands	0.1	0.1	0.2	0.3	0.3	0.2	0.3	0.3	0.4	0.3	0.3
Norway	0.0	0.1	0.1	0.1	0.1	0.1	0.1	0.1	0.1	0.1	0.1
Sweden	0.1	0.1	0.1	0.1	0.2	0.2	0.3	0.3	0.3	0.2	0.1
Switzerland	0.1	0.1	0.1	0.2	0.2	0.2	0.2	0.2	0.2	0.2	0.1
United Kingdom	0.3	0.7	0.9	1.1	1.4	2.0	2.5	2.5	2.0	1.4	1.0
12 Countries Total	*7.6*	*7.3*	*11.0*	*11.3*	*11.4*	*11.0*	*12.8*	*12.7*	*10.2*	*7.7*	*5.5*
Portugal	0.2	0.2	0.2	0.2	0.3	0.3	0.3	0.3	0.3	0.2	0.2
Spain	1.9	1.5	1.6	1.5	1.5	1.2	1.3	1.1	1.1	0.9	0.7
Other	0.9	0.4	0.3	0.3	0.3	0.3	0.4	0.4	0.5	0.4	0.3
Total Western Europe	**10.7**	**9.5**	**13.1**	**13.3**	**13.5**	**12.8**	**14.8**	**14.6**	**12.1**	**9.2**	**6.6**
Eastern Europe	**2.1**	**2.4**	**3.1**	**3.0**	**3.1**	**3.5**	**4.1**	**4.4**	**3.5**	**2.8**	**2.0**
Former USSR	**1.7**	**2.6**	**3.9**	**3.7**	**4.4**	**5.3**	**7.0**	**8.7**	**7.1**	**6.4**	**4.9**
United States	0.3	0.5	0.5	0.3	0.2	1.0	3.2	5.4	6.0	5.4	4.6
Other Western Offshoots	0.2	0.2	0.2	0.1	0.1	0.1	0.5	0.8	0.9	1.0	0.9
Total Western Offshoots	**0.5**	**0.7**	**0.6**	**0.4**	**0.3**	**1.1**	**3.6**	**6.2**	**7.0**	**6.4**	**5.5**
Mexico	1.0	1.7	1.7	0.4	0.7	0.6	0.7	0.8	1.1	1.5	1.7
Other Latin America	1.5	2.6	2.3	1.1	1.3	1.4	2.4	3.7	5.4	6.4	6.9
Total Latin America	**2.4**	**4.2**	**4.0**	**1.5**	**2.0**	**2.0**	**3.1**	**4.5**	**6.6**	**7.9**	**8.6**
Japan	**1.3**	**2.8**	**3.5**	**3.3**	**4.5**	**3.0**	**2.7**	**2.9**	**3.3**	**2.8**	**2.1**
China	25.8	22.0	23.5	28.8	22.9	36.6	28.2	24.4	21.7	22.5	21.0
India	32.5	28.0	25.1	24.3	27.3	20.1	19.9	17.0	14.2	14.8	16.5
Other Asia	15.9	15.4	12.7	11.7	11.9	8.6	9.4	10.3	15.5	17.3	19.8
Total Asia (excluding Japan)	**74.2**	**65.4**	**61.3**	**64.8**	**62.1**	**65.3**	**57.5**	**51.7**	**51.4**	**54.7**	**57.4**
Africa	**7.1**	**12.3**	**10.5**	**9.9**	**10.1**	**7.1**	**7.1**	**7.0**	**9.0**	**9.9**	**12.9**
World	**100.0**	**100.0**	**100.0**	**100.0**	**100.0**	**100.0**	**100.0**	**100.0**	**100.0**	**100.0**	**100.0**

GDP and GDP Per Capita, 1500–1820

Maddison (1995a) pp. 19–20 contained a very crude estimate of the movement of world economic growth from 1500 to 1820, as a supplement to the much more detailed analysis for 1820 onwards. In that study I used three simple hypotheses about the growth of real GDP per capita. For Western Europe it was assumed to rise by 0.2 per cent a year, following the hypothesis of Kuznets (1973), 0.1 per cent a year in the rest of Europe and Latin America, and with zero change in Asia and Africa. Maddison (1998a), pp. 25 and 40 compared the contours of development in China and Europe from the first century of our era to 1995. The evidence for China was examined in considerable detail, but the estimates for Europe contained a large element of conjecture.

This appendix involves a much more detailed scrutiny of the evidence for 1500–1820. It strongly suggests that average per capita West European growth rate was slower (at 0.15 per cent a year) from 1500 to 1820 than the 0.2 per cent which Kuznets hypothesised. Growth was faster in Latin America and in the Western offshoots than was assumed in Maddison (1995a). The hypothesis of a stagnant level of per capita income in Asia is generally confirmed, but Japan is a significant exception.

The last section of this appendix includes rough and tentative estimates of GDP levels by major regions for the first century of our era and for the year 1000. Estimates of world GDP and per capita GDP are set out in Tables B–18 to B–22.

Western Europe

Belgium

Blomme and Van der Wee (1994) provide estimates (for Flanders and Brabant) of GDP by industry of origin for 1510–1812. They give estimates for seven points within the period, which I used to derive approximate estimates for 1500,1600 and 1700.

France

François Perroux, with encouragement and support from Simon Kuznets, set up a group to measure French growth in the 1950s (Marczewski and Toutain were its most productive members). Marczewski (1961) made some preliminary estimates of growth for the eighteenth century which greatly exaggerated industrial performance. These have now been superseded. J.C. Toutain kindly provided me with the revised estimates which I have used here for 1700–1820.

Over the past few decades French economic history has been dominated by members of the *Annales* school who have been rather disdainful of the Kuznetsian approach. From our point of view, there are three main drawbacks to their work: *a)* disinterest in macroquantification; *b)* concentration on regional or supranational characterisations rather than national performance; *c)* Malthusian bias.

Le Roy Ladurie strongly emphasized the long–term stability of the French economy from 1300 to 1700, both in demographic and per capita terms. He first put forward the thesis of stagnant income in a regional study of the peasants of Languedoc (1966) . He argued that there was a tension between the dynamism of population and the rigidity of the agricultural production potential which led to recurrent and prolonged population setbacks. In 1977 he maintained the same conclusions in a survey drawing on a new generation of regional studies.

Braudel's pessimism at one time went further than that of Le Roy Ladurie. In a 1967 article with Spooner, he concluded, after summarising the work of Phelps Brown and other real wage analysts and regional studies of the *Annales* school that: "From the late fifteenth century until well into the beginning of the eighteenth century, the standard of living in Europe progressively declined." Later he changed his mind (Braudel, 1985, Vol.III, p. 314): "Visualizing overall quantities throws into relief clear continuities in European history. The first of these is the regular rise in GNP come hell or high water — if Frank Spooner is correct, France's GNP had been rising since the reign of Louis XII and probably even longer." [Louis XII reigned from 1498 to 1515].

My own view is that Braudel's revised judgement is more acceptable than his earlier position, or that of Le Roy Ladurie. However, the graph which Braudel reproduced from Spooner (1972) did not show real GNP, but the movement in value from 1500 to 1800 of a fixed quantity of wheat, multiplied by population, and by a smoothed index of wheat prices in Paris. The quantitative evidence for assessing aggregate French performance from 1500 to 1700 is therefore still quite weak. Judging from the comparative growth of the urban population ratio (Table B–14), it seems clear that French economic growth was slower than that of England. I have assumed that French per capita growth 1500–1700 was about the same as in Belgium.

Italy

Malanima (1995, p. 600) suggests declining per capita income in Italy for 1570–1700, and stability from 1700 to 1820. These conclusions are based on a variety of indicators of industrial and commercial activity in cities, levels of food consumption and real wages, rather than an articulate estimate of GDP movement. The nature of the approach is explained in his short essay, "Italian Economic Performance: Output and Income 1600–1800" in Maddison and van der Wee (1994). Malanima's assumption of a decline up to 1700 fits with the qualitative indicators and assessment of Cipolla (1976, pp. 236–244), who suggests decline from the late fifteenth to seventeenth century. However, there is some dissent on this in Sella's (1979) assessment of seventeenth century development in Spanish Lombardy (centred in Milan) and Rapp's (1976) judgement on the seventeenth century situation in Venice. Both Sella and Rapp assumed some relative decline compared with more dynamic economies in Northern Europe, but not an absolute decline. I assumed that Italian per capita income was stagnant from 1500 to 1820. Italian population growth was slower than that in the rest of Europe and the urban ratio showed little change from 1500 to 1820.

The Netherlands

Estimates of GDP growth for 1580–1820 are from Maddison (1991a) pp. 205 and 277. They are linked at 1820 to new estimates for 1820–1913 by Smits, Horlings and van Zanden (2000). For 1580–1700, GDP movement was inferred from evidence (on explosive urbanisation, the transformation of the rural economy, and the size of household assets as revealed by probate inventories) provided in de Vries (1974). Van Zanden (1987) presented a wide variety of evidence to document his estimates of agricultural and fishery production, industry, transport and services for 1650–1805. The Dutch estimates show rapid growth to 1700, and a significant fall per capita from 1700 to 1820. De Vries and van der Woude (1997), p. 707 give a graphical representation based on alternative assumptions about the decline of Dutch per capita income from its peak to the nadir at the end of the Napoleonic wars. Their profile is not markedly different from the measure I adopted. I interpolated the 1580–1700 per capita growth rate of 0.43 to derive the estimates for 1600, and assumed that the 1500 level was below that of Belgium.

United Kingdom

1700–1820 GDP growth from Maddison (1991a), p. 220, modified for England and Wales to incorporate the results of Crafts and Harley (1992) rather than Crafts 1983). I assumed that Scottish per capita GDP was three–quarters of the level in England and Wales in 1801 and that its movement 1700–1801 was parallel to the Crafts–Harley estimate for England and Wales. For Ireland 1700–1801 per capita income was assumed to rise half as fast as in England and Wales.

For 1500–1700 there are several indicators which suggest that the United Kingdom was more dynamic than most other European countries. Population rose by 0.39 per cent a year compared with 0.15 per cent in the rest of Western Europe. The urban population ratio (population in cities 10 000 and over as a percentage of total population) rose from 3.1 to 13.3 per cent in England and Wales — about twice as fast as in France or the Netherlands. It seems clear that the ratio of foreign trade to GDP increased from 1500 to 1820. There are no satisfactory aggregate measures of crop output back to 1500 (see Overton, 1996), but the evidence on yields per acre in Clark (1991), on labour productivity in Allen (1991), and occupational structure (Wrigley, 1988) help to explain the growing urban ratio, as per capita crop availability was maintained with a decreasing share of the labour force. The faster growth in animal husbandry than crops (Wrigley, 1988) suggests an improvement in diets. Recent research on the growing variety of consumption items, improvements in housing and increased stocks of furniture and household linen revealed by probate inventories for successive generations also demonstrates a long process of improvement in living standards — see chapters by de Vries, Wills, and Shammas in Brewer and Porter (1993).

For these reasons, it seemed reasonable to assume that the Crafts–Harley rate of growth of per capita income for 1700–1801 was also valid for 1500–1700. For Ireland I assumed per capita growth was half as fast. For the United Kingdom as a whole this implies a per capita growth rate of 0.28 per cent a year for 1500–1700.

Snooks (1993) estimated the growth of total and per capita income in England 1086–1688 by linking the nominal income assessments in the Domesday Book survey of rural England south of the river Tees with Gregory King's estimates for 1688 as adjusted by Lindert and Williamson (1982). He deflated nominal income growth with the price index for household consumables of Phelps Brown and Hopkins (1981), pp. 28–30, supplemented by an index of wheat prices from Thorold Rogers. His estimates imply a growth rate of per capita real income averaging 0.35 per cent a year from 1492 to 1688 (p. 24). At this rate per capita income would have doubled from 1500 to 1700. This is faster growth than I have suggested.

The estimates of per capita GDP in Table B–13 show a very different movement from the frequently quoted real wage index for building workers in Southern England of Phelps Brown and Hopkins (1981). From 1500 to 1800 they suggested that real wages fell by 60 per cent, whereas I show per capita real GDP increasing 2.4 fold.

The tradition in real wage measurement is quite simplistic compared with that in demography or national accounts. Phelps Brown and Hopkins use daily wage rates for craftsmen and labourers hired for building work by Oxford and Cambridge colleges, Eton school and some other employers in Southern England. For the most part they had 15 or more wage quotations a year for craftsmen, and about 3 a year for building labourers. For the period 1500–1800, in which we are most interested, there were 82 years for which they show no wage estimate because of wide variance in the quotes they had or absence of data. They have no data for weekly or annual earnings, or days worked. There is no discussion in Phelps Brown and Hopkins of the representativity of their wage index for building workers. Lindert and Williamson (1982, p. 393), show that 5.3 per cent of families (73 000) derived their livelihood from the building trades in 1688. Even if the Phelps Brown coverage of this group is assumed to be adequate, and even if it is reasonable to assume that building workers were paid mainly in cash and not in kind, this is certainly not true of the bulk of the working population.

People employed in agriculture were 56 per cent of the total in 1700, and most of them were producing and directly consuming cereals, meat, butter and cheese which figure so largely in the price index. Many others such as servants, artisans, the clergy, the armed forces were either not wage earners or received an appreciable part of their remuneration in kind. A large part of the working population were thus sheltered from the impact of price rises.

Table B–13. **Regional Components of British GDP, Population and GDP Per Capita, 1500–1920**

	United Kingdom	*England, Wales & Scotland*	*Ireland*	*Scotland*	*England & Wales*
GDP (million 1990 Geary–Khamis dollars)					
1500	2 815	2 394	421	298	2 096
1600	6 007	5 392	615	566	4 826
1700	10 709	9 332	1 377	1 136	8 196
1801	25 426	21 060	4 366	2 445	18 615
1820	36 232	30 001	6 231		
1870	100 179	90 560	9 619		
1913	224 618	212 727	11 891		
1920	212 938	201 860	11 078		
Population (000)					
1500	3 942	3 142	800	500	2 642
1600	6 170	5 170	1 000	700	4 470
1700	8 565	6 640	1 925	1 036	5 604
1801	16 103	10 902	5 201	1 625	9 277
1820	21 226	14 142	7 084	2 071	12 071
1870	31 393	25 974	5 419	3 337	22 637
1913	45 649	41 303	4 346	4 728	36 575
1920	46 821	42 460	4 361	4 864	37 596
Per Capita GDP (1990 Geary–Khamis dollars)					
1500	714	762	526	596	793
1600	974	1 043	615	809	1 080
1700	1 250	1 405	715	1 096	1 463
1801	1 579	1 931	839	1 505	2 006
1820	1 707	2 121	880		
1870	3 191	3 487	1 775		
1913	4 921	5 150	2 736		
1920	4 568	4 754	2 540		

Source: GDP as explained in the text. Population in England (excluding Monmouth) interpolated from quinquennial estimates in Wrigley *et al.* (1997), pp. 614–5 for 1541–1871. 1500 to 1541 growth at the rate suggested by Wrigley and Schofield (1981), p. 737 for 1471–1541. Monmouth and Wales 1700–1820 population movement from Deane and Cole (1964), p. 103, 1500–1600 assumed to move parallel to England. Ireland 1500 and 1600 derived from O Grada in Bardet and Dupaquier (1997) vol. 1, p. 386, 1700–1821 movement from Dickson, O Grada and Daultrey (1982), p. 156. Scotland 1500–1600 from McEvedy and Jones (1978), pp. 45–7, 1700 from Deane and Cole (1964), p. 6, 1820 from Mitchell (1962), pp. 8–10. 1820–1920 population and GDP movement from Maddison (1995a).

Jan de Vries (1993) is very critical of the real wage approach compared with alternative quantitative methods of measuring well–being. He questions the representativity of construction worker experience in a society with wide income differences. He emphasises the large number of important items left out of the Phelps Brown index and its use of fixed weights for such a long period, but his strongest doubts arise from the conflict between its sombre conclusions with evidence of a different kind which he found in probate inventories "All the studies I have examined for colonial New England and the Chesapeake, England and the Netherlands consistently reveal two features. With very few exceptions, each generation of decedents from the mid–seventeenth to the late eighteenth century left behind more and better possessions."

Aggregate Performance in the West European Core

The aggregate per capita growth rate for the five countries (Belgium, France, Italy, Netherlands and the United Kingdom) where I have given estimates for 1500–1820 is 0.14 per cent per annum, but they are a rather mixed bunch. The growth rate in the United Kingdom was 0.27, the Netherlands 0.28, France 0.16, Belgium 0.13 and zero in Italy. In fact the United Kingdom and the Netherlands are special cases of fast growth. Italian stagnation was also atypical (as is clear from the stability in its urban ratio), and there were special forces retarding Belgian growth. Belgian growth was adversely affected by the break with the Netherlands. Belgium was one of the most prosperous areas of Europe in 1500, as a centre of international trade and banking and substantial textile production. After the Netherlands became independent, the port of Antwerp was blockaded for two centuries, there was substantial migration of capital and skills to Holland. In order to get an approximate picture for Western Europe as a whole, I made proxy estimates for Austria, Denmark, Finland, Norway, Sweden and Switzerland, assuming that per capita real GDP increased at 0.17 per cent a year for 1500–1820. For Germany, a per capita growth rate of 0.14 per cent was assumed, as there was a decline in Germany's role in banking and Hanseatic trade, as well as the impact of the 30 years war. When the proxy estimates are aggregated with the estimates for the 5 countries for which we have better evidence, we find average per capita growth for the 12 West European core countries of 0.15 per cent a year. This is significantly slower than Kuznets' 0.2 per cent hypothesis which I used in Maddison (1995a). I assume here that average per capita growth in "other" Western Europe (Greece and 13 small countries) was the same as the average for the 12 core countries.

Table B–14. **Urbanisation Ratios in Europe and Asia, 1500–1890**
(population in cities 10 000 and over as percentage of total population)

Year	1500	1600	1700	1800	1890
Belgium	21.1	18.8	23.9	18.9	34.5
France	4.2	5.9	9.2	8.8	25.9
Germany	3.2	4.1	4.8	5.5	28.2
Italy	14.9	16.8	14.7	18.3	21.2
Netherlands	15.8	24.3	33.6	28.8	33.4
Scandinavia	0.9	1.4	4.0	4.6	13.2
Switzerland	1.5	2.5	3.3	3.7	16.0
England & Wales	3.1	5.8	13.3	20.3	61.9
Scotland	1.6	3.0	5.3	17.3	50.3
Ireland	0.0	0.0	3.4	7.0	17.6
Western Europe	6.1	7.8	9.9	10.6	31.3
Portugal	3.0	14.1	11.5	8.7	12.7
Spain	6.1	11.4	9.0	11.1	26.8
China	3.8	4.0[a]	n.a.	3.8	4.4
Japan	2.9	4.4	n.a.	12.3	16.0

a) 1650.

Source: European countries from de Vries (1984), pp. 30, 36, 39 and 46 except Italy which is from Malanima (1988b); China and Japan from Rozman (1973) adjusted to refer to the ratio in cities 10 000 and over, see Maddison (1998a) pp. 33–36.

Spain and Portugal

Yun's (1994) rough per capita GDP estimates for Castile (about three–quarters of Spain) suggest a per capita growth rate of about 0.22 per cent for 1580–1630, with a decline thereafter, and a level in 1800 slightly below the 1630 peak. He makes spot estimates of output levels in current prices for 6 benchmark years within the period 1580 to 1800 and deflates with a price index for food products. His firmest evidence relates to agricultural output and food consumption, but his indicators for secondary and tertiary activity are weak. He concludes that his "trajectory seems congruent with what we know about the evolution of the Castilian economy: expansion until the end of the sixteenth century; agrarian recession, decomposition of the urban network and industrial and commercial crisis during the seventeenth, with a subsequent fall of the GDP revealed in our numbers; and growth on the basis of the poorly developed urban structures and the greater dynamism of the outlying areas in the eighteenth century". I assumed a growth rate of Spanish GDP per capita of 0.25 per cent a year for 1500–1600, no advance in the seventeenth century and some mild progress from 1700 to 1820. I adopted a similar profile for Portugal.

Eastern Europe and USSR

For these two areas direct evidence was lacking. As a proxy I assumed slower per capita GDP growth than in Western Europe at 0.1 per cent per annum for 1500–1820 (as I did in Maddison, 1995a).

Western Offshoots

For the United States, Gallman (1972) p. 22 estimated per capita growth in net national product of 0.42 per cent a year between 1710 and 1840 (taking the mid–point of the range he suggests for 1710). Adjusting for the faster growth of per capita income in 1820–40 (see Maddison, 1995a, p. 137), Gallman's estimate implies a per capita growth of about .29 per cent a year for the non–indigenous population, from a level of $909 in 1700 to $1 286 in 1820. Gallman's estimate included only the white and black population. In 1820, the indigenous population was only 3 per cent of the total. In 1700, it was three–quarters of the total (see Table B–15). Assuming the indigenous population had a per capita income of $400 in both 1700 and 1820, the average level for the whole population was $527 in 1700 and $1 257 in 1820. For 1500 and 1600, the population consisted entirely of hunter–gatherer Indians, and an average income of $400 a head was assumed.

Mancall and Weiss (1999) have recently estimated US per capita income for 1700 and 1800, with separate assessments for whites, slaves and Indians. Their "multicultural" estimate (p. 35) shows a per capita growth rate of only 0.28 per cent a year for 1700–1800, compared with my 0.73 per cent a year for 1700–1820. I consider their growth rate to be much too slow, given the huge change in the ethnic composition of the population in the period. They show no figures for population or total GDP, so it is not possible to replicate their "multicultural" measure. They make no reference to the Gallman estimate I used.

For the other Western Offshoots, Canada, Australia and New Zealand, the great bulk of the 1500–1700 population were indigenous hunter–gatherers, and I assumed a per capita GDP of $400 for 1500, 1600, and 1700.

Table B–15. **Ethnic Composition of the US Population, 1700–1820**
(000)

	Indigenous	White	Black	Total
1700	750	223	27	1 000
1820	325	7 884	1 772	9 981

Source: US Bureau of the Census, *Historical Statistics of the United States: Colonial Times to 1970,* 1975, pp. 14 and 18 for 1820, p. 1168 for 1700 white and black populations. Indian population figures from Rosenblat (1945) for 1820; 1700 as explained above.

Table B–16. **Ethnic Composition of Latin American Population in 1820**
(000)

	Indigenous	White	Black	Mixed	Total
Mexico	3 500	1 200	10	1 880	6 590
Brazil	500	1 500	2 200	300	4 500
Caribbean Islands	0	420	1 700	350	2 470
Other Latin America	3 160	1 300	200	3 000	7 660
Total Latin America	7 160	4 420	4 110	5 530	21 220

Source: Table B–4 for Brazil, otherwise from Rosenblat (1945).

Mexico

My per capita income estimate for 1820 is $759 (see Appendix A). At that time the indigenous population was about 53 per cent of the total (see Table B–16). There was a thin layer of "peninsular" Spaniards (about 1 per cent of the population) who ran the army, administration, the church, trading monopolies and part of the professions. They had a baroque life style with sumptuous residences and retinues of servants. About a sixth of the population were *criollos*, i.e. whites of Spanish origin, who had been born in Mexico. They were hacienda owners, merchants, part of the clergy, army and professions. The third social group, over a quarter of the population, were *mestizos* originating from unions between whites and Indians. They were generally workers, farm hands, servants and some were rancheros. I assume a per capita income of $425 for the native population. The aggregate estimate for 1820 implies an average per capita income of $1 140 for the non–native population. 1500–1700 per capita income level of the two segments of the population was assumed to be the same as in 1820, but the average was lower for the two segments combined, because the non–native population was only a quarter of the total in 1700, 4 per cent in 1600, and negligible in 1500.

Other Latin America

In 1500, other parts of Latin America were poorer than Mexico. Except in Peru, most of the inhabitants were hunter gatherers rather than agriculturalists. They also had a lower per capita income than Mexico at the end of the colonial period in 1820. Thus their per capita income grew more slowly than in Mexico from 1500 to 1820. I assumed that the growth differential between Mexico and the rest of Latin America was stable between 1500 and 1820.

China

Maddison (1998a) contains an extensive analysis of the course of population, total output, and per capita product over the past 2000 years. There is a greater mass of survey material on Chinese population for the past two millennia than for any other country, thanks to the bureaucratic system and its efforts to monitor economic activity for tax purposes.

In assessing the growth of agricultural output, Perkins (1969) is a masterpiece of scholarly endeavour, covering the period 1368–1968, on which I relied heavily. Perkins' analysis is basically Boserupian. He feels that China responded successfully to population pressure, and managed to sustain more or less stable per capita consumption over the period he covers. This was achieved by increases in cultivated area, in per capita labour input, and land productivity. It involved heavy inputs of traditional fertilisers, irrigation, development of crop varieties and seeds which permitted multiple cropping, diffusion of best–practice techniques by officially sponsored distribution of agricultural handbooks (available at an early stage due to the precocious development of paper and printing). Crops from the Americas were introduced after the mid–sixteenth century. Maize, peanuts, potatoes and sweet potatoes added significantly to China's output potential because of their heavy yields and the possibility of growing them on inferior land. Tobacco and sugar cane were widely diffused in the Ming period. The pattern of Chinese food consumption was heavily concentrated on proteins and calories supplied by crop production which makes more economic use of land than pastoral activities. Chinese consumption of meat was very much lower than in Europe and concentrated on poultry and pigs which were scavengers rather than grazing animals. Milk and milk products were almost totally absent. Chinese also made very little use of wool. Ordinary clothing came largely from vegetable fibres (hemp, ramie, and then cotton). Quilted clothing supplied the warmth that wool might have provided. The richer part of the population used silk. Silk cocoons were raised on mulberry bushes often grown on hillsides which were not suitable for other crops.

Chinese rural households had many labour–intensive activities outside farming. They raised fish in small ponds, used grass and other biomass for fuel. Important "industrial" activities were centred in rural households. Textile spinning and weaving, making garments and leather goods were largely household activities. The same was true of oil and grain milling; drying and preparation of tea leaves; tobacco products; soybean sauce; candles and tung oil; wine and liqueurs; straw, rattan and bamboo products. Manufacture of bricks and tiles, carts and small boats, and construction of rural housing were also significant village activities. Chinese farmers were engaged in a web of commercial activity carried out in rural market areas to which virtually all villages had access. All these non–farm activities appear to have intensified in the Sung dynasty (960–1280). Thereafter some proportionate increase seems plausible because of the growing importance over the long term of cash crops like cotton, sugar, tobacco and tea. In the nineteenth century well over a quarter of GDP came from traditional handicrafts, transport, trade, construction and housing and most of these were carried out in rural areas. It seems likely that their proportionate importance was just as large in 1500 as it was in 1820.

On the basis of Rozman's (1973) rough estimates, it would seem that there were no dramatic changes in the proportion of the urban population (persons living in towns with a population of 10 000 or more) in China between the Tang dynasty and the beginning of the nineteenth century. This is in striking contrast to the situation in Western Europe, and is a significant piece of corroborative evidence of the comparative performance of China and Europe.

Another type of evidence which is very useful is the detailed documentation and chronology of Chinese technology in Needham's *magnum opus* on Chinese science and civilisation. Although it is weak in analysing the economic impact of invention, it is an invaluable help in assessing comparative development in agriculture, metallurgy, textile production, printing, shipbuilding, navigation etc. and in its assessment of Chinese capacity to develop the fundamentals of science.

The big advance in Chinese land productivity, and the more modest advance in living standards came before the period we are examining here. The big shift from wheat and millet farming in North China, to much more intensive wet rice farming south of the Yangtse came in the Sung dynasty (tenth to thirteenth century). The evidence strongly suggests that per capita GDP stagnated for nearly six centuries thereafter although China was able to accommodate a large rise in population through extensive growth.

India

Maddison (1971) contained an analysis of the social structure and institutions of the Moghul Empire and of British India. For the Moghul period, I relied heavily on the economic survey of Abul Fazl, Akbar's vizier, carried out at the end of the sixteenth century (see translation by Jarrett and Sarkar, 1949). I had no firm conclusions on the growth rate from 1500 to 1820, but there was little evidence to suggest that it was a dynamic economy. There is no reason to think that the British takeover had a positive effect on economic growth before the 1850s.

The Cambridge Economic History of India, Vol.1 (Raychaudhuri and Habib, 1982) does not address the growth question very directly, and deals with India by major area, without trying to generalise for the country as a whole. Habib suggests that farm output per head of population may have been higher in 1595 than in 1870, or 1900, and bases this inference on the availability of more cultivatable land per head at the earlier period and apparently greater relative availability of bullocks and buffaloes as draft animals. On the other hand he also stresses the introduction of new crops in the seventeenth and eighteenth centuries. He is more upbeat about manufacturing: "The expansion of the domestic and foreign markets, and the rising public expenditure on urban developments, public monuments and the army suggest an upward trend in output and possibly labour productivity." (p. 305)

Shireen Moosvi (1987, p. 400) assumes that rural per capita consumption was about the same in 1601 as in 1901, but that urban income was bigger at the earlier date. She therefore assumes an aggregate per capita consumption level 5 per cent higher at the first date. Moreland (1920, p. 274) using the same sort of evidence as Habib and Moosvi, but with less intensive scrutiny, concluded that India was almost certainly not richer at the death of Akbar than in 1910–14, "and probably that she was a little poorer".

My own judgement is that Indian per capita income fell from 1700 to the 1850s due to the collapse of the Moghul Empire and the costs of adjusting to the British regime of governance (see analysis in Chapter 2).

Japan

There are no previous estimates of the long term macroeconomic performance of Japan before the Meiji Restoration of 1868. However, one can get some idea of what happened by comparing Japanese and Chinese experience.

In the seventh century, Japan tried to model its economy, society, religion, literature and institutions on those of China. Admiration for things Chinese continued until the eighteenth century, even though Japan was not integrated into the Chinese international order (with two brief exceptions) as a tributary state. However, Japan never created a meritocratic bureaucracy but let the effective governance of the country fall into the hands of a hereditary and substantially decentralized military elite. The institutional history of Japan from the tenth to the fifteenth century therefore had a closer resemblance to that of feudal Europe than to that of China.

Japan copied the institutions of Tang China in the seventh century, creating a national capital at Nara, on the model of China's Chang–an. It also adopted Chinese style Buddhism, and allowed its religious orders to acquire very substantial properties and economic influence. It adopted Chinese

ideograms, the kanji script, Chinese literary style, Chinese clothing fashions, the Chinese calendar, methods of measuring age and hours. There was already a substantial similarity in the cropping mix and food consumption, with a prevalence of rice agriculture, and much smaller consumption of meat and meat products than in Europe. There was greater land scarcity in Japan and China than in Europe or India, so the agriculture of both countries was very labour–intensive.

Although Japanese emperors continued to be nominal heads of state, governance fell into the hands of a hereditary aristocracy. From 1195 to 1868, the effective head of state was a military overlord known as the *shogun*.

From the seventh to the ninth century, the central government controlled land allocation in imitation of Tang China, but ownership gradually devolved on a rural military elite. The *shoen* was a complex and fragmented feudal system. Many layers of proprietors claimed a share of the surplus from a servile peasantry.

Technological progress and its diffusion were facilitated in China by its bureaucracy to a degree which was not possible in Japan, which had no educated secular elite. Knowledge of printing was available almost as early as in China, but there was little printed matter except for Buddhist tallies and talismans. The Chinese, by comparison, used printed handbooks of best–practice farming to disseminate the methods of multicropping, irrigation and use of quick ripening seeds which the Sung dynasty imported from Vietnam. The degree of urbanisation was smaller in Japan than in China. The division of Japan into particularistic and competing feudal jurisdictions meant that farming and irrigation tended to develop defensively on hillsides. The manorial system also inhibited agricultural specialisation and development of cash crops.

Whilst the Chinese had switched from hemp to cotton clothing in the fourteenth century, the change did not come in Japan until the seventeenth. Until the seventeenth century, Japanese production of silk was small, and consumption depended on imports from China. Shipping and mining technology remained inferior to that in China until the seventeenth century. Rural by–employments were slower to develop than in China.

The old regime collapsed in Japan after a century of civil war (*sengoku*) which started in 1467. The capital city, Kyoto, was destroyed early in these conflicts, with the population reduced from 400 000 to 40 000 by 1500. A new type of regime emerged from the wreckage, with a new type of military elite.

Tokugawa Ieyasu established his shogunal dynasty in 1603, after serving two successive military dictators, Nobunaga (1573–82) and Hideyoshi (1582–98) who had developed some of the techniques of governance which Ieyasu adopted (notably the demilitarisation of rural areas, the *kokudaka* system of fiscal levies based initially on a cadastral survey, the reduction in ecclesiastical properties, and the practice of keeping *daimyo* wives and children as hostages).

The Tokugawa shogun controlled a quarter of the land area directly. The imperial household and aristocracy in Kyoto had only 0.5 per cent of the fiscal revenue, the Shinto and Buddhist temple authorities shared 1.5 per cent. A third was assigned to smaller *daimyo* who were under tight control. The rest was allocated to bigger more autonomous (*tozama*) *daimyo* in rather distant areas who were already feudal lords before the establishment of the Tokugawa regime. These were potential rivals of the shogunate and eventually rebelled in the 1860s. But the shogun in fact held unchallenged hegemonial power after 1615 when he killed Hideyoshi's family and destroyed his castle in Osaka. The Tokugawa shoguns neutered potential *daimyo* opposition by keeping their families hostage, and their incomes precarious (between 1601 and 1705, "some 200 *daimyo* had been destroyed; 172 had been newly created; 200 had received increases in holdings; and 280 had their domains transferred" — Hall, 1991 (pp. 150–1). The shogun's magistrates directly administered the biggest cities (Edo, Kyoto, Osaka and some others), operated as the emperor's delegate, controlled foreign relations and the revenue from gold and silver mines.

The Tokugawa shogunate was not ideal for economic growth or resource allocation but it exercised a more favourable influence than the Kamakura (1192–1338) and Ashikaga (1338–1573) shogunates which preceded it. It initiated a successful process of catch–up and forging ahead. Between 1600 and 1868 Japanese per capita income probably rose by about 40 per cent, moving from a level below China, to a significantly higher position, in spite of the heavy burden of supporting a large and functionally redundant elite.

The Tokugawa established a system of checks and balances between the leading members of the military elite (*daimyo*) who had survived the civil war. It ensured internal peace on a lasting basis. Rural areas were completely demilitarised by Hideyoshi's 1588 sword hunt and the Tokugawa government's gradual suppression of the production and use of Western type firearms which the Portuguese had introduced in 1543.

The *daimyo* and their military vassals (the *samurai*) were compelled to live in a single castle town in each domain, and abandon their previous managerial role in agriculture. As compensation they received stipends in kind (rice), which was supplied by the peasantry in their domain. *Daimyo* had no fixed property rights in land and could not buy or sell it. The shogun could move *daimyo* from one part of the country to another, confiscate, truncate or augment their rice stipends in view of their behaviour (or intentions as determined by shogunal surveillance and espionage). *Daimyo* were also required to spend part of the year in the new capital Edo (present day Tokyo), and to keep their families there permanently as hostages for good behaviour. *Daimyo* were not required to remit revenue on a regular basis to the shogunal authority, though they had to meet the very heavy costs of their compulsory (*sankin kotai*) residence in Edo and respond to ad hoc demands for funds for constructing Edo and rebuilding it after earthquake damage.

This system of goverment was very expensive compared with that of China. The shogunal, *daimyo* and samurai households were about 6.5 per cent of the Japanese population, compared with 2 per cent for the bureaucracy, military and gentry in China. Fiscal levies accounted for 20–25 per cent of Japanese GDP compared with about 5 per cent in China, though the Chinese gentry had rental incomes and the Chinese bureaucracy had a substantial income from non–fiscal exactions. The Tokugawa did, however, achieve some savings by a very substantial reduction in Buddhist income and properties. They also made an ideological shift away from religion towards neo–confucianism. In both respects they were replicating changes which occurred in China in the ninth century.

The economic consequences of these political changes were important for all parts of the economy.

Growth of Farm Output in the Tokugawa Period

The farm population were no longer servile households subjected to arbitrary claims to support feudal notables and military. Rice levies were large but more or less fixed and fell proportionately over time as agriculture expanded. The ending of local warfare meant that it was safer to develop agricultural land in open plains. There was greater scope for land reclamation and increases in area under cultivation. This was particularly true in the previously underdeveloped Kanto plain surrounding the new capital Edo.

Printed handbooks of best practice agriculture started to appear on Chinese lines. *Nogyo Zensho* (Encyclopaedia of Farming, 1697) was the earliest commercial publication, and by the early eighteenth century there were hundreds of such books (see Robertson, 1984). Quick ripening seeds and double cropping were introduced. There was increased use of commercial fertiliser (soybean meal, seaweed etc.), and improvement in tools for threshing. There was a major expansion of commercial crops — cotton, tobacco, oil seeds, sugar (in South Kyushu and the Ryuku islands), and a very substantial increase in silkworm cultivation. Large scale land reclamation was initiated in the 1720s — partly financed by merchants.

Some idea of the progress of agricultural production in Tokugawa Japan can be derived from the *kokudaka* cadastral surveys initiated by Hideyoshi between 1582 and 1590. They assessed the productive capacity of land in terms of *koku* of rice equivalent (i.e. enough to provide subsistence for one person for a year). The *koku* as a volumetric measure equivalent to 5.1 US bushels or to 150 kilograms in terms of weight. This *kokudaka* assessment was the basis on which the shogun allocated income to *daimyo*. The smallest *daimyo* were allocated 10 000 *koku*, the biggest got much larger allocations (over a million *koku* in the Kaga domain at Kanazawa on the Japan Sea coast, 770 000 for the Satsuma domain in Southern Kyushu). In 1598, the total was estimated to be 18.5 million. The official estimate increased over time, as the cultivated area increased, but there were substantial and varying degrees of mismeasurement of the aggregate. Craig (1961, p. 11) gives examples of the difference between nominal and actual productive capacity for the late Tokugawa period; the actual yield for the 9 domains he specifies was one third higher than the official assessment. Nakamura (1968) made an estimate of cereal production for 1600 to 1872 which was adjusted to eliminate these variations in coverage of the official statistics. Table B–17 shows that cereal output per capita increased by 18 per cent from 1600 to 1820, and probably by a quarter over the Tokugawa period as a whole. In 1874, rice and other cereals were 72 per cent of the value of gross farm output, other traditional products 10.7 per cent, and relatively new crops (cotton, sugar, tobacco, oil seeds, silk cocoons and potatoes) 17.2 per cent. Most of the latter were absent in 1600 and most of these escaped taxation, so their production grew faster than cereals. If one assumes that these other items were about 5 per cent of output in 1600, this would imply a growth of total farm output per capita of about a quarter from 1600 to 1820, and over 40 per cent for the Tokugawa period as a whole. For the period before 1600 there is no real quantitative evidence, but it seems likely that there was little growth in agricultural output per head in the sixteenth century which was so severely plagued by civil war.

Table B–17. **Japanese Cereal Production and Per Capita Availability, 1600–1874**

	Cereal Production		*Population*	*Per Capita Availability*
	(000 koku)	*(000 metric tons)*	*(000)*	*(kg)*
1600	19 731	2 960	18 500	160
1700	30 630	4 565	27 000	169
1820	39 017	5 853	31 000	189
1872	46 812	7 022	34 859	201
1874	49 189	7 378	35 235	209

Source: First column for 1600–1872 from Hayami and Miyamoto (1988), p. 44; with 1820 derived by interpolation of their figures for 1800 and 1850. Their estimates were derived from Satoru Nakamura (1968), pp. 169–171. 1874 cereal production from Ohkawa, Shinohara and Umemura (1966), volume 9, *Agriculture and Forestry*, p. 166, with an upward adjustment of rice output by 1 927 *koku* — see Yamada and Hayami (1979), p. 233. In 1874, adjusted cereal output represented 72 per cent of the value of gross agricultural output at 1874–6 prices, other traditional crops 10.8 per cent, and other crops 17.2 per cent (see vol. 9, p. 148). The latter group consisted of industrial crops, potatoes and sericulture, most of which were unimportant in 1600. It seems highly likely therefore that per capita farm output rose more rapidly than cereal output. Col. 2, *koku* (150 kg.) converted into metric tons. Col. 3 is my estimate of population from Table B–7. Col. 4 equals col. 2 divided by col. 3. The standard production measure in Tokugawa Japan was in terms of husked rice, whereas in China the standard unit was unhusked rice. Perkins (1969) assumed a per capita availability of 250 kg. of unhusked rice for China in the period shown here. Using Perkins' (1969, p. 305) coefficient, this meant a per capita availability of 167 kg. of husked rice — higher than Japan in 1600, but lower from 1700 onwards. In 1872, Japan had net imports of rice which raised per capita availability to 219 kg., and in 1874 to 231 kg.

Performance in the Non–Farm Sector

Most analysts of the Tokugawa period (Smith, 1969; Hanley and Yamamura, 1977; Yasuba, 1987) stress the growing importance of industrial and commercial by–employments in rural areas.

Smith (1969) produced the classic analysis of rural non–farm activity, drawing on a 1843 survey of 15 districts of the Choshu domain. Komonoseki county had a population of 6501 families in a region at the extreme south of Honshu, with a big coastline projecting into the inland sea between Kyushu and Shikoku — an area particularly advantageous for trade with other parts of Japan. 82 per cent of the population were farmers, but 55 per cent of net income originated outside agriculture. The arithmetic average of Smith's district ratios suggests that industry produced nearly 28 per cent of family income. I am skeptical of the representativity of the Kaminoseki sample. If it were typical of all rural areas, and urban areas had a proportionately greater commitment to non–agriculture, one could expect over 30 per cent of late Tokugawa GDP to have been derived from industry.

Nishikawa (1987) presents a much more sophisticated and comprehensive account of the Choshu economy in the 1840s. Using the same survey material he constructed a set of aggregate input–output accounts. His analysis covers 107 000 households (520 000 population) including both rural and urban areas, i.e. a sample 16 times bigger than Smith's. His approach is in the national accounting tradition with careful consistency checks, merging of different data sources to estimate the labour force, gross output and value added by economic sector. On a value added basis, manufacturing (including handicrafts) accounts for 18.8 per cent of his aggregate. However, he points out that the survey data were seriously deficient for output. His aggregate therefore excludes *daimyo–samurai* military and civil government services, the activity of monks, nuns, priests and servants, urban services "concentrated in `entertainment' such as inns, restaurants, teahouses, brothels, streetwalking, hair–dressing, massage and so forth". There is no imputation for residential accommodation. The construction sector is also omitted. If we augment Nishikawa's aggregate by a quarter to include the omitted items and bring it to a GDP basis, the structure of value added in Choshu in the 1840s would have been 53 per cent for agriculture, forestry and fisheries, 15 per cent for manufacturing, 32 per cent for the rest (including services and construction). Other very interesting features of the Nishikawa accounts are estimates of Choshu's transactions with other parts of Japan and demonstration of the physiocratic bias in the Tokugawa fiscal regime. 97 per cent of tax revenue consisted of levies on agriculture, 3 per cent was derived from levies on non agriculture. Apart from his structural analysis, Nishikawa also ventures an estimate of the rate of growth of per capita Choshu income between the 1760s and the 1840s of 0.4 per cent a year. However, this is based entirely on land survey estimates for fiscal purposes.

In 1500, less than 3 per cent of Japanese lived in towns of 10 000 population and over. By 1800 more than 12 per cent lived in such cities. Edo which had been a village became a city of a million inhabitants. There were more than two hundred castle towns, half of whose population were *samurai*. Kanazawa and Nagoya were the biggest with a population over 100 000. The old capital, Kyoto, had half a million (being the seat of the Emperor and his court and the centre of a prosperous agricultural area). Osaka became a large commercial metropolis, similar in size to Kyoto. This fourfold increase in the urban proportion contrasted with a stable and much lower ratio in China. Japan had a smaller proportion of small towns than China, because concentration of samurai in one single castle town per domain was accompanied by compulsory destruction of scattered smaller fortified settlements. There was also a decline in the size of Osaka in the eighteenth century as commercial activity increased in smaller towns and rural areas.

The urban centres created a market for the surrounding agricultural areas. They also created a demand for servants, entertainment and theatres. Merchants ceased to be mere quartermasters for the military, and acted as commodity brokers, bankers and money–lenders. They were active in promoting significant expansion of coastal trade and shipping in the inland sea (see Crawcour, 1963). Thus there was clearly a substantial increase in many types of service activity per head of population in Tokugawa Japan. However, the biggest service industry was that of the *samurai* and *daimyo* who supplied an exaggeratedly large amount of military and civil governance. The evidence suggests that they remained a stable proportion of

the population throughout the Tokugawa epoch. Yamamura's (1974) study suggests there was not much change in their household real incomes, and Smith's work on the falling incidence of fiscal levies in agriculture helps to reinforce this latter conclusion.

There was a very substantial increase in levels of education in Tokugawa Japan, and an emphasis on secular neo–confucian values rather than Buddhism. This improved the level of popular culture and knowledge of technology. There was a huge increase in book production and circulation of woodblock prints. Between the eighth century and the beginning of the seventeenth fewer than 100 illustrated books appeared in Japan but by the eighteenth there were large editions of books with polychrome illustrations and 40 per cent literacy of the male population.

In 1639, the Jesuits and the Portuguese traders were expelled from Japan, Christianity was suppressed and contact with Europeans was restricted to the small Dutch trading settlement in the South of Japan, near Nagasaki. This was done because the Portuguese were intrusive and thought to be a political threat. The Togugawa were aware of the Spanish takeover in the Philippines and wanted to avoid this in Japan. The Dutch were only interested in commerce, but in the course of their long stay in Japan, their East India Company appointed three very distinguished doctors in Deshima (Engelbert Kaempfer, 1690–2, an adventurous German savant and scientist; C.P. Thunberg, 1775–6, a distinguished Swedish botanist; and Franz Philipp von Siebold, 1823–9 and 1859–62, a German physician and naturalist). These scholars wrote books which were important sources of Western knowledge about Japan, but they also had a significant impact in transmitting European science and technology to Japan.

The Japanese had depended on Chinese books for knowledge of the West (Chinese translations of works by Matteo Ricci and other Jesuits in Peking), but in 1720 the shogun, Yoshimune, lifted the ban on European books. An important turning point occurred in 1771 when two Japanese doctors observed the dissection of a corpse and compared the body parts (lungs, kidneys and intestines) with those described in a Chinese book and a Dutch anatomy text. The Dutch text corresponded to what they found, and the Chinese text was inaccurate (see Keene, 1969). As a result translations of Dutch learning (*rangaku*) became an important cultural influence. Although they were limited in quantity, they helped destroy Japanese respect for "things Chinese", and accentuate curiosity about "things Western".

Japanese exposure to Western knowledge was more limited than Chinese, but its impact went much deeper. The old tradition was easier to reject in Japan as it was foreign. However, contacts with foreigners and foreign ideas were often frowned upon by the authorities. Von Siebold was expelled from Japan in 1829, and a Japanese friend was executed for giving him copies of Ino Tadataka's magnificent survey maps for the Kuriles and Kamchatka. Nevertheless, the Dutch window into the Western world was important and influential in preparing the ground intellectually for the Meiji Restoration of 1868. Dutch learning (painfully acquired) was the major vehicle of enlightenment for Japan's greatest Westerniser, Yukichi Fukuzawa (1832–1901), whose books sold millions of copies, and who founded Keio University on Western lines.

Although the Tokugawa regime had a positive impact on Japanese growth, it had certain drawbacks.

It involved the maintenance of a large elite whose effective military potential was very feeble in meeting the challenges which came in the nineteenth century, and whose life style involved extremely lavish expenditure. The Meiji regime was able to capture substantial resources for economic development and military modernisation by dismantling these Tokugawa arrangements.

The system of hereditary privilege and big status differentials with virtually no meritocratic element, meant a large waste of potential talent. The frustrations involved are clearly illustrated in Fukuzawa's autobiography. The Tokugawa system was inefficient in its reliance on a clumsy collection of fiscal revenue in kind and overdetailed surveillance of economic activity. It also imposed restrictions on the diffusion of technology. One example of this was the ban on wheeled vehicles on Japanese roads and the virtual absence of bridges. These restrictions were imposed for security reasons, but made journeys

very costly and time consuming. There were also restrictions on the size of boats which inhibited coastal shipping, foreign trade, and naval preparedness. There were restrictions on property rights (buying and selling of land), arbitrary levies by the shogun, cancellation of *daimyo* debts, or defaults by samurai which inhibited private enterprise.

All of these, plus increasing pressures on Japan from Russia, England and the United States, eventually led to the breakdown of the Tokugawa system.

Aggregate Japanese Performance

There has been a good deal of research on the economic history of the Tokugawa period, but hitherto no aggregative quantification of performance except at a regional level. Most of the postwar revisionist historians (Akira Hayami, Yasuba, Nishikawa, Hall, Smith, Hanley and Yamamura) agree (in contrast to earlier Marxists) that there was substantial economic advance.

Levels of income were probably depressed in 1500 as a result of civil war but there may have been a modest increase in Japanese per capita income in the sixteenth century. For 1600–1820, there are indicators of substantial increase in performance in several sectors of the economy. For farming as a whole (including new crops — cotton, sugar, tobacco, oil seeds, silk cocoons and potatoes), gross output per head of population rose by about a quarter (see Table B–17 and accompanying text), and value added by somewhat less. In the early Tokugawa period, agriculture probably represented well over half of GDP.

There is substantial evidence of an expansion in the importance of rural household activity, and the large increase in the size of the urban population led to an increase in commercial activity and urban services. There were substantial improvements in education, and a large increase in book production. It seems likely that all these activities rose faster than agriculture.

An offset to these elements of dynamism was the high cost of the Tokugawa system of governance. The elite of samurai, *daimyo* and the shogunate absorbed nearly a quarter of GDP. Their official function was to provide administrative and military services. But the way this fossilised elite functioned was extremely wasteful and put inreasing strain on the economy. The apparatus of government was a system of checks and balances — an armed truce whose original rationale had been to end the civil wars which lasted from the mid–fifteenth to the mid–sixteenth century.

My overall assessment (see Table B–21) is that from 1500 to 1820 Japanese GDP per capita rose by a third. This was enough to raise its level above that of China and most of the rest of Asia.

Other Asia

Other Asia is a miscellaneous conglomerate of countries with about 12.5 per cent of Asia's population and about 12 per cent of GDP in 1820. For most of them, there is not much hard evidence for assessing their GDP performance from 1500 to 1820.

Indonesia is the largest of these countries. The estimates in Tables 2–21c and 2–22 show that most of the modest rise in per capita income from 1700 to 1820 accrued to European and Chinese trading interests. Boomgaard (1993) pp. 208–210 came to a similar conclusion for 1500–1835. He found that the "Dutch and Chinese introduced new technologies, organisational skills and capital, which strengthened the non–agricultural sectors, and led to the introduction of some cash crops (coffee and sugar). However, they also pushed the Javanese out of the more rewarding economic activities and increased the burden of taxation and corvee levies".

Korea was the second biggest of the "other Asia" countries. Until the 1870s, it was a hermit kingdom with only exiguous contact with the outside world except China. Its social organisation and technology were very close to the Chinese model, and there is reason to suppose that its economic performance was similar to that of China, i.e. stagnant per capita income at a level above the Asian norm. The major disturbances to Korean development because of the Mongol and Japanese invasions happened before 1500.

The Indochinese states were also Chinese tributaries. They were more open to foreign trade than Korea, but there do not seem to be grounds for supposing that per capita income changed much in the period under consideration.

In 1500, the Ottoman Empire had control over a large part of Western Asia and the Balkans. In 1517 it took control of Syria and Egypt and suzerainty of Arabia. The Empire had widespread trading interests in Asia. By the eighteenth century, it had entered a long period of decline, and its trading interests in Asia had been taken over by Europeans. Although estimates of per capita income are not available, there is enough evidence (see Inalcik (1994) and Faroqui *et al.*, 1994) to suggest that it was lower in 1820 than in 1500. In Iran; the second biggest country in West Asia, it also seems very unlikely that per capita income in 1820 was as high as in the heyday of the Safavid dynasty in the sixteenth and seventeenth centuries.

Africa

I assumed that African per capita income did not change from 1500 to 1700.

GDP AND GDP PER CAPITA FROM FIRST CENTURY TO 1000 A.D.

Before 1500, the element of conjecture in the estimates is very large indeed. The derivation of per capita GDP levels for China and Europe are explained in Maddison (1998a), and the conjectures for other areas are explained below. In all cases GDP is derived by multiplying the per capita levels by the independently estimated levels of population.

Maddison (1998a) contained estimates of Chinese economic performance from the first century onwards. The evidence suggested that per capita GDP in the first century (in the Han dynasty) was above subsistence levels — about $450 in our numeraire (1990 international dollars), but did not change significantly until the end of the 10th century.

During the Sung dynasty (960 — 1280) Chinese per capita income increased significantly, by about a third, and population growth accelerated. The main reason for this advance was a major transformation in agriculture. Until the Sung dynasty, large parts of South China had been relatively underdeveloped. Primitive slash and burn agriculture and moving cultivation had been practiced, but the climate and accessibility of water gave great potential for intensive rice cultivation. The Sung rulers developed this potential by introducing quick ripening strains of rice imported from Indochina. They exploited new opportunities to diffuse knowledge of agricultural technology by printing handbooks of best practice in farming. As a result there was a major switch in the centre of gravity, with a substantial rise in the proportion of people in rice growing south of the Yangtse, and a sharp drop in the proportionate importance of the dry farming area (millet and wheat) of North China. Increased density of settlement in the South gave a boost to internal trade, a rise in the proportion of farm output which was marketed, productivity gains from increased specialisation of agricultural production in response to higher living standards. The introduction of paper money facilitated the growth of commerce, and raised the proportion of state income in cash from negligible proportions to more than half.

For most of the rest of Asia, it seemed reasonable here to assume that the level of per capita income was similar to that in China and showed no great change from the first century to the year 1000. The $450 level of per capita income assumed here is sufficiently above subsistence to maintain the governing elite in some degree of luxury and to sustain a relatively elaborate system of governance. Japan was a rather special case. In the first century, it was a subsistence economy in course of transition to agriculture from hunting and gathering, and from wooden to metal tools. By the year 1000, it had made some progress but lagged well behind China.

In Maddison (1998a), pp. 25, 37–38, it was assumed that European per capita income levels in the first century were similar to those in China. Goldsmith (1984) provided a comprehensive assessment of economic performance for the Roman Empire as a whole, and also provided a temporal link, suggesting that Roman levels were about two fifths of Gregory King's estimate of English income for 1688.

The West Asian and North African parts of the Roman Empire were at least as prosperous and urbanised as the European component, which warrants the assumption of similar levels of income there.

Between the first century and the year 1000, there was a collapse in living standards in Western Europe. Urbanisation ratios provide the strongest evidence that the year 1000 was a nadir. The urban ratio of Roman Europe was around 5 per cent in the first century. This compares with zero in the year 1000, when there were only 4 towns with more than 10 000 population (see Maddison, 1998a, p. 35). The urban collapse and other signs of decline warrant the assumption of a relapse more or less to subsistence levels ($400 per capita) in the year 1000.

For the Americas, Australasia, Africa south of the Sahara, Eastern Europe and the area of the former USSR, I have assumed that more or less subsistence levels of income ($400 per capita) prevailed from the first century to the end of the first millennium.

Table B–18. World GDP, 20 Countries and Regional Totals, 0–1998 A.D.
(million 1990 international $)

Year	0	1000	1500	1600	1700	1820	1870	1913	1950	1973	1998
Austria			1 414	2 093	2 483	4 104	8 419	23 451	25 702	85 227	152 712
Belgium			1 225	1 561	2 288	4 529	13 746	32 347	47 190	118 516	198 249
Denmark			443	569	727	1 471	3 782	11 670	29 654	70 032	117 319
Finland			136	215	255	913	1 999	6 389	17 051	51 724	94 421
France			10 912	15 559	21 180	38 434	72 100	144 489	220 492	683 965	1 150 080
Germany			8 112	12 432	13 410	26 349	71 429	237 332	265 354	944 755	1 460 069
Italy			11 550	14 410	14 630	22 535	41 814	95 487	164 957	582 713	1 022 776
Netherlands			716	2 052	4 009	4 288	9 952	24 955	60 642	175 791	317 517
Norway			192	304	450	1 071	2 485	6 119	17 838	44 544	104 860
Sweden			382	626	1 231	3 098	6 927	17 403	47 269	109 794	165 385
Switzerland			482	880	1 253	2 342	5 867	16 483	42 545	117 251	152 345
United Kingdom			2 815	6 007	10 709	36 232	100 179	224 618	347 850	675 941	1 108 568
12 Countries Total			*38 379*	*56 708*	*72 625*	*145 366*	*338 699*	*840 743*	*1 286 544*	*3 660 253*	*6 044 301*
Portugal			632	850	1 708	3 175	4 338	7 467	17 615	63 397	128 877
Spain			4 744	7 416	7 893	12 975	22 295	45 686	66 792	304 220	560 138
Other			590	981	1 169	2 206	4 891	12 478	30 600	105 910	227 300
Total Western Europe	**11 115**	**10 165**	**44 345**	**65 955**	**83 395**	**163 722**	**370 223**	**906 374**	**1 401 551**	**4 133 780**	**6 960 616**
Eastern Europe	**1 900**	**2 600**	**6 237**	**8 743**	**10 647**	**23 149**	**45 448**	**121 559**	**185 023**	**550 757**	**660 861**
Former USSR	**1 560**	**2 840**	**8 475**	**11 447**	**16 222**	**37 710**	**83 646**	**232 351**	**510 243**	**1 513 070**	**1 132 434**
United States			800	600	527	12 548	98 374	517 383	1 455 916	3 536 622	7 394 598
Other Western Offshoots			320	320	300	941	13 781	68 249	179 574	521 667	1 061 537
Total Western Offshoots	**468**	**784**	**1 120**	**920**	**827**	**13 489**	**112 155**	**585 632**	**1 635 490**	**4 058 289**	**8 456 135**
Mexico			3 188	1 134	2 558	5 000	6 214	25 921	67 368	279 302	655 910
Other Latin America			4 100	2 623	3 813	9 120	21 683	95 760	356 188	1 118 398	2 285 700
Total Latin America	**2 240**	**4 560**	**7 288**	**3 757**	**6 371**	**14 120**	**27 897**	**121 681**	**423 556**	**1 397 700**	**2 941 610**
Japan	**1 200**	**3 188**	**7 700**	**9 620**	**15 390**	**20 739**	**25 393**	**71 653**	**160 966**	**1 242 932**	**2 581 576**
China	26 820	26 550	61 800	96 000	82 800	228 600	189 740	241 344	239 903	740 048	3 873 352
India	33 750	33 750	60 500	74 250	90 750	111 417	134 882	204 241	222 222	494 832	1 702 712
Other Asia	16 470	18 630	31 301	36 725	40 567	50 486	72 173	146 999	362 578	1 398 587	4 376 931
Total Asia (excluding Japan)	**77 040**	**78 930**	**153 601**	**206 975**	**214 117**	**390 503**	**396 795**	**592 584**	**824 703**	**2 633 467**	**9 952 995**
Africa	**7 013**	**13 723**	**18 400**	**22 000**	**24 400**	**31 010**	**40 172**	**72 948**	**194 569**	**529 185**	**1 039 408**
World	**102 536**	**116 790**	**247 116**	**329 417**	**371 369**	**694 442**	**1 101 369**	**2 704 782**	**5 336 101**	**16 059 180**	**33 725 635**

Table B–19. **Rates of Growth of World GDP, 20 Countries and Regional Totals, 0–1998 A.D.**
(annual average compound growth rates)

Year	0–1000	1000–1500	1500–1820	1820–70	1870–1913	1913–50	1950–73	1973–98
Austria			0.33	1.45	2.41	0.25	5.35	2.36
Belgium			0.41	2.25	2.01	1.03	4.08	2.08
Denmark			0.38	1.91	2.66	2.55	3.81	2.09
Finland			0.60	1.58	2.74	2.69	4.94	2.44
France			0.39	1.27	1.63	1.15	5.05	2.10
Germany			0.37	2.01	2.83	0.30	5.68	1.76
Italy			0.21	1.24	1.94	1.49	5.64	2.28
Netherlands			0.56	1.70	2.16	2.43	4.74	2.39
Norway			0.54	1.70	2.12	2.93	4.06	3.48
Sweden			0.66	1.62	2.17	2.74	3.73	1.65
Switzerland			0.50	1.85	2.43	2.60	4.51	1.05
United Kingdom			0.80	2.05	1.90	1.19	2.93	2.00
12 Countries Total			*0.42*	*1.71*	*2.14*	*1.16*	*4.65*	*2.03*
Portugal			0.51	0.63	1.27	2.35	5.73	2.88
Spain			0.31	1.09	1.68	1.03	6.81	2.47
Other			0.41	1.61	2.20	2.45	5.55	3.10
Total Western Europe	−0.01	0.30	0.41	1.65	2.10	1.19	4.81	2.11
Eastern Europe	0.03	0.18	0.41	1.36	2.31	1.14	4.86	0.73
Former USSR	0.06	0.22	0.47	1.61	2.40	2.15	4.84	−1.15
United States			0.86	4.20	3.94	2.84	3.93	2.99
Other Western Offshoots			0.34	5.51	3.79	2.65	4.75	2.88
Total Western Offshoots	0.05	0.07	0.78	4.33	3.92	2.81	4.03	2.98
Mexico			0.14	0.44	3.38	2.62	6.38	3.47
Other Latin America			0.25	1.75	3.51	3.61	5.10	2.90
Total Latin America	0.07	0.09	0.21	1.37	3.48	3.43	5.33	3.02
Japan	0.10	0.18	0.31	0.41	2.44	2.21	9.29	2.97
China	0.00	0.17	0.41	−0.37	0.56	−0.02	5.02	6.84
India	0.00	0.12	0.19	0.38	0.97	0.23	3.54	5.07
Other Asia	0.01	0.10	0.15	0.72	1.67	2.47	6.05	4.67
Total Asia (excluding Japan)	0.00	0.13	0.29	0.03	0.94	0.90	5.18	5.46
Africa	0.07	0.06	0.16	0.52	1.40	2.69	4.45	2.74
World	0.01	0.15	0.32	0.93	2.11	1.85	4.91	3.01

Table B–20. **Shares of World GDP, 20 Countries and Regional Totals, 0–1998 A.D.**
(per cent of world total)

Year	0	1000	1500	1600	1700	1820	1870	1913	1950	1973	1998
Austria			0.6	0.6	0.7	0.6	0.8	0.9	0.5	0.5	0.5
Belgium			0.5	0.5	0.6	0.7	1.2	1.2	0.9	0.7	0.6
Denmark			0.2	0.2	0.2	0.2	0.3	0.4	0.6	0.4	0.3
Finland			0.1	0.1	0.1	0.1	0.2	0.2	0.3	0.3	0.3
France			4.4	4.7	5.7	5.5	6.5	5.3	4.1	4.3	3.4
Germany			3.3	3.8	3.6	3.8	6.5	8.8	5.0	5.9	4.3
Italy			4.7	4.4	3.9	3.2	3.8	3.5	3.1	3.6	3.0
Netherlands			0.3	0.6	1.1	0.6	0.9	0.9	1.1	1.1	0.9
Norway			0.1	0.1	0.1	0.2	0.2	0.2	0.3	0.3	0.3
Sweden			0.2	0.2	0.3	0.4	0.6	0.6	0.9	0.7	0.5
Switzerland			0.2	0.3	0.3	0.3	0.5	0.6	0.8	0.7	0.5
United Kingdom			1.1	1.8	2.9	5.2	9.1	8.3	6.5	4.2	3.3
12 Countries Total			*15.5*	*17.2*	*19.5*	*20.9*	*30.7*	*31.1*	*24.1*	*22.8*	*17.9*
Portugal			0.3	0.3	0.5	0.5	0.4	0.3	0.3	0.4	0.4
Spain			1.9	2.1	2.2	1.9	2.0	1.7	1.3	1.9	1.7
Other			0.2	0.3	0.3	0.3	0.4	0.5	0.6	0.7	0.7
Total Western Europe	**10.8**	**8.7**	**17.9**	**19.9**	**22.5**	**23.6**	**33.6**	**33.5**	**26.3**	**25.7**	**20.6**
Eastern Europe	**1.9**	**2.2**	**2.5**	**2.7**	**2.9**	**3.3**	**4.1**	**4.5**	**3.5**	**3.4**	**2.0**
Former USSR	**1.5**	**2.4**	**3.4**	**3.5**	**4.4**	**5.4**	**7.6**	**8.6**	**9.6**	**9.4**	**3.4**
United States			0.3	0.2	0.1	1.8	8.9	19.1	27.3	22.0	21.9
Other Western Offshoots			0.1	0.1	0.1	0.1	1.3	2.5	3.4	3.2	3.1
Total Western Offshoots	**0.5**	**0.7**	**0.5**	**0.3**	**0.2**	**1.9**	**10.2**	**21.7**	**30.6**	**25.3**	**25.1**
Mexico			1.3	0.3	0.7	0.7	0.6	1.0	1.3	1.7	1.9
Other Latin America			1.7	0.8	1.0	1.3	2.0	3.5	6.7	7.0	6.8
Total Latin America	**2.2**	**3.9**	**2.9**	**1.1**	**1.7**	**2.0**	**2.5**	**4.5**	**7.9**	**8.7**	**8.7**
Japan	**1.2**	**2.7**	**3.1**	**2.9**	**4.1**	**3.0**	**2.3**	**2.6**	**3.0**	**7.7**	**7.7**
China	26.2	22.7	25.0	29.2	22.3	32.9	17.2	8.9	4.5	4.6	11.5
India	32.9	28.9	24.5	22.6	24.4	16.0	12.2	7.6	4.2	3.1	5.0
Other Asia	16.1	16.0	12.7	11.2	10.9	7.3	6.6	5.4	6.8	8.7	13.0
Total Asia (excluding Japan)	**75.1**	**67.6**	**62.1**	**62.9**	**57.6**	**56.2**	**36.0**	**21.9**	**15.5**	**16.4**	**29.5**
Africa	**6.8**	**11.8**	**7.4**	**6.7**	**6.6**	**4.5**	**3.6**	**2.7**	**3.6**	**3.3**	**3.1**
World	**100.0**	**100.0**	**100.0**	**100.0**	**100.0**	**100.0**	**100.0**	**100.0**	**100.0**	**100.0**	**100.0**

Table B-21. **World GDP per Capita, 20 Countries and Regional Averages, 0–1998 A.D.**
(1990 international $)

Year	0	1000	1500	1600	1700	1820	1870	1913	1950	1973	1998
Austria			707	837	993	1 218	1 863	3 465	3 706	11 235	18 905
Belgium			875	976	1 144	1 319	2 697	4 220	5 462	12 170	19 442
Denmark			738	875	1 039	1 274	2 003	3 912	6 946	13 945	22 123
Finland			453	538	638	781	1 140	2 111	4 253	11 085	18 324
France			727	841	986	1 230	1 876	3 485	5 270	13 123	19 558
Germany			676	777	894	1 058	1 821	3 648	3 881	11 966	17 799
Italy			1 100	1 100	1 100	1 117	1 499	2 564	3 502	10 643	17 759
Netherlands			754	1 368	2 110	1 821	2 753	4 049	5 996	13 082	20 224
Norway			640	760	900	1 104	1 432	2 501	5 463	11 246	23 660
Sweden			695	824	977	1 198	1 664	3 096	6 738	13 493	18 685
Switzerland			742	880	1 044	1 280	2 202	4 266	9 064	18 204	21 367
United Kingdom			714	974	1 250	1 707	3 191	4 921	6 907	12 022	18 714
12 Countries Total			*796*	*906*	*1 056*	*1 270*	*2 086*	*3 688*	*5 013*	*12 159*	*18 742*
Portugal			632	773	854	963	997	1 244	2 069	7 343	12 929
Spain			698	900	900	1 063	1 376	2 255	2 397	8 739	14 227
Other			462	528	617	743	1 066	1 840	2 536	7 614	13 732
Total Western Europe	450	400	774	894	1 024	1 232	1 974	3 473	4 594	11 534	17 921
Eastern Europe	400	400	462	516	566	636	871	1 527	2 120	4 985	5 461
Former USSR	400	400	500	553	611	689	943	1 488	2 834	6 058	3 893
United States			400	400	527	1 257	2 445	5 301	9 561	16 689	27 331
Other Western Offshoots			400	400	400	753	2 339	4 947	7 538	13 364	20 082
Total Western Offshoots	400	400	400	400	473	1 201	2 431	5 257	9 288	16 172	26 146
Mexico			425	454	568	759	674	1 732	2 365	4 845	6 655
Other Latin America			410	430	505	623	705	1 461	2 593	4 459	5 588
Total Latin America	400	400	416	437	529	665	698	1 511	2 554	4 531	5 795
Japan	400	425	500	520	570	669	737	1 387	1 926	11 439	20 413
China	450	450	600	600	600	600	530	552	439	839	3 117
India	450	450	550	550	550	533	533	673	619	853	1 746
Other Asia	450	450	565	565	565	565	603	794	924	2 065	3 734
Total Asia (excluding Japan)	450	450	572	575	571	575	543	640	635	1 231	2 936
Africa	425	416	400	400	400	418	444	585	852	1 365	1 368
World	444	435	565	593	615	667	867	1 510	2 114	4 104	5 709

Table B–22. **Rates of Growth of World GDP per Capita, 20 Countries and Regional Totals, 0–1998 A.D.**
(annual average compound growth rates)

Year	0–1000	1000–1500	1500–1820	1820–70	1870–1913	1913–50	1950–73	1973–98
Austria			0.17	0.85	1.45	0.18	4.94	2.10
Belgium			0.13	1.44	1.05	0.70	3.55	1.89
Denmark			0.17	0.91	1.57	1.56	3.08	1.86
Finland			0.17	0.76	1.44	1.91	4.25	2.03
France			0.16	0.85	1.45	1.12	4.05	1.61
Germany			0.14	1.09	1.63	0.17	5.02	1.60
Italy			0.00	0.59	1.26	0.85	4.95	2.07
Netherlands			0.28	0.83	0.90	1.07	3.45	1.76
Norway			0.17	0.52	1.30	2.13	3.19	3.02
Sweden			0.17	0.66	1.46	2.12	3.07	1.31
Switzerland			0.17	1.09	1.55	2.06	3.08	0.64
United Kingdom			0.27	1.26	1.01	0.92	2.44	1.79
12 Countries Total			*0.15*	*1.00*	*1.33*	*0.83*	*3.93*	*1.75*
Portugal			0.13	0.07	0.52	1.39	5.66	2.29
Spain			0.13	0.52	1.15	0.17	5.79	1.97
Other			0.15	0.72	1.28	0.87	4.90	2.39
Total Western Europe	**–0.01**	**0.13**	**0.15**	**0.95**	**1.32**	**0.76**	**4.08**	**1.78**
Eastern Europe	**0.00**	**0.03**	**0.10**	**0.63**	**1.31**	**0.89**	**3.79**	**0.37**
Former USSR	**0.00**	**0.04**	**0.10**	**0.63**	**1.06**	**1.76**	**3.36**	**–1.75**
United States			0.36	1.34	1.82	1.61	2.45	1.99
Other Western Offshoots			0.20	2.29	1.76	1.14	2.52	1.64
Total Western Offshoots	**0.00**	**0.00**	**0.34**	**1.42**	**1.81**	**1.55**	**2.44**	**1.94**
Mexico			0.18	–0.24	2.22	0.85	3.17	1.28
Other Latin America			0.13	0.25	1.71	1.56	2.38	0.91
Total Latin America	**0.00**	**0.01**	**0.15**	**0.10**	**1.81**	**1.43**	**2.52**	**0.99**
Japan	**0.01**	**0.03**	**0.09**	**0.19**	**1.48**	**0.89**	**8.05**	**2.34**
China		0.06	0.00	–0.25	0.10	–0.62	2.86	5.39
India		0.04	–0.01	0.00	0.54	–0.22	1.40	2.91
Other Asia		0.05	0.00	0.13	0.64	0.41	3.56	2.40
Total Asia (excluding Japan)	**0.00**	**0.05**	**0.00**	**–0.11**	**0.38**	**–0.02**	**2.92**	**3.54**
Africa	**0.00**	**–0.01**	**0.01**	**0.12**	**0.64**	**1.02**	**2.07**	**0.01**
World	**0.00**	**0.05**	**0.05**	**0.53**	**1.30**	**0.91**	**2.93**	**1.33**

Annual Estimates of Population, GDP and GDP Per Capita for 124 Countries, 7 Regions and the World, 1950–98

This appendix contains annual estimates of population; and levels of GDP and GDP per capita in 1990 international dollars for 1950–98. Annual estimates are given for 124 individual countries, as well as regional, subregional, and world totals. The sources are given in Appendix A.

Annual estimates for population and GDP movement in earlier years can be found in Maddison (1995a) for 46 countries. They have not been included here for lack of space. See Maddison (1995a), Appendix A (pp. 104–107) for annual estimates of population for 12 West European Countries, Western Offshoots and Japan for 1870–1949; pp. 108–109 for five South European Countries, 1900–49; pp. 110–111 for seven East European Countries 1920–49; 1920–49; pp. 112–113 for seven Latin American Countries 1900–49; pp. 114–115 for ten Asian Countries 1900–49. Annual real GDP indices for the same countries and same years are shown (as far as they are available) on pages 148–159 in Appendix B. These GDP indices are generally compatible with the present estimates for 1950 onwards and can be used to backcast the 1950 levels shown here in Tables C–1b, C–2b and C–3b. Revised annual estimates for 1900–50 for India are shown in Table A–h, and for Japan 1870–1950 in Table A–j of the present work.

Table C1–a. Population of European Countries, Annual Estimates, 1950–98
(000 at mid–year)

Year	Austria	Belgium	Denmark	Finland	France	Germany	Italy	Netherlands
1950	6 935	8 640	4 269	4 009	41 836	68 371	47 105	10 114
1951	6 936	8 679	4 304	4 047	42 156	68 863	47 418	10 264
1952	6 928	8 731	4 334	4 091	42 460	69 193	47 666	10 382
1953	6 933	8 778	4 369	4 139	42 752	69 621	47 957	10 494
1954	6 940	8 820	4 406	4 187	43 057	69 937	48 299	10 616
1955	6 947	8 869	4 439	4 235	43 428	70 310	48 633	10 751
1956	6 952	8 924	4 466	4 282	43 843	70 743	48 921	10 888
1957	6 966	8 989	4 488	4 324	44 311	71 134	49 182	11 026
1958	6 987	9 053	4 515	4 360	44 789	71 554	49 476	11 187
1959	7 014	9 104	4 587	4 395	45 240	72 024	49 832	11 348
1960	7 048	9 118	4 581	4 430	45 684	72 674	50 200	11 483
1961	7 087	9 166	4 612	4 461	46 163	73 310	50 536	11 637
1962	7 130	9 218	4 647	4 491	46 998	73 939	50 879	11 801
1963	7 175	9 283	4 684	4 523	47 816	74 544	51 252	11 964
1964	7 224	9 367	4 720	4 549	48 310	74 963	51 675	12 125
1965	7 271	9 488	4 757	4 564	48 758	75 647	52 112	12 293
1966	7 322	9 508	4 797	4 581	49 164	76 214	52 519	12 455
1967	7 377	9 557	4 839	4 606	49 548	76 368	52 901	12 597
1968	7 415	9 590	4 867	4 626	49 915	76 584	53 236	12 726
1969	7 441	9 613	4 893	4 624	50 315	77 143	53 538	12 873
1970	7 467	9 638	4 929	4 606	50 772	77 709	53 822	13 032
1971	7 501	9 673	4 963	4 612	51 251	78 345	54 073	13 194
1972	7 544	9 709	4 992	4 640	51 701	78 715	54 381	13 330
1973	7 586	9 738	5 022	4 666	52 118	78 956	54 751	13 438
1974	7 599	9 768	5 045	4 691	52 460	78 979	55 111	13 543
1975	7 579	9 795	5 060	4 712	52 699	78 679	55 441	13 660
1976	7 566	9 811	5 073	4 726	52 909	78 317	55 718	13 773
1977	7 568	9 822	5 088	4 739	53 145	78 165	55 955	13 856
1978	7 562	9 830	5 104	4 753	53 376	78 082	56 155	13 939
1979	7 549	9 837	5 117	4 765	53 606	78 104	56 318	14 034
1980	7 549	9 847	5 123	4 780	53 880	78 303	56 434	14 148
1981	7 569	9 854	5 122	4 800	54 182	78 418	56 510	14 247
1982	7 576	9 862	5 118	4 827	54 492	78 335	56 579	14 312
1983	7 567	9 867	5 114	4 856	54 772	78 122	56 626	14 368
1984	7 571	9 871	5 112	4 882	55 026	77 846	56 652	14 423
1985	7 578	9 879	5 114	4 902	55 284	77 668	56 674	14 488
1986	7 588	9 888	5 121	4 918	55 547	77 690	56 675	14 567
1987	7 598	9 901	5 127	4 932	55 824	77 718	56 674	14 664
1988	7 615	9 908	5 130	4 946	56 118	78 115	56 629	14 760
1989	7 659	9 941	5 131	4 964	56 423	78 677	56 672	14 846
1990	7 729	9 971	5 138	4 986	56 735	79 364	56 719	14 947
1991	7 813	10 008	5 150	5 014	57 055	79 984	56 751	15 068
1992	7 914	10 051	5 166	5 042	57 374	80 595	56 859	15 182
1993	7 991	10 088	5 185	5 066	57 654	81 180	57 049	15 290
1994	8 030	10 119	5 201	5 089	57 900	81 422	57 204	15 381
1995	8 047	10 137	5 222	5 108	58 138	81 661	57 301	15 460
1996	8 059	10 157	5 256	5 125	58 372	81 896	57 397	15 523
1997	8 072	10 182	5 280	5 140	58 604	82 053	57 512	15 605
1998	8 078	10 197	5 303	5 153	58 805	82 029	57 592	15 700

Table C1–a. **Population of European Countries, Annual Estimates, 1950–98**
(000 at mid–year)

Year	Norway	Sweden	Switzerland	United Kingdom	Total 12 WEC*	Ireland	Greece
1950	3 265	7 015	4 694	50 363	256 616	2 969	7 566
1951	3 296	7 071	4 749	50 574	258 357	2 961	7 659
1952	3 328	7 125	4 815	50 737	259 790	2 953	7 733
1953	3 362	7 171	4 877	50 880	261 333	2 949	7 817
1954	3 395	7 213	4 929	51 066	262 865	2 941	7 893
1955	3 429	7 262	4 980	51 221	264 504	2 921	7 966
1956	3 462	7 315	5 045	51 430	266 271	2 898	8 031
1957	3 494	7 367	5 126	51 657	268 064	2 885	8 096
1958	3 525	7 415	5 199	51 870	269 930	2 853	8 173
1959	3 556	7 454	5 259	52 157	271 970	2 846	8 258
1960	3 585	7 480	5 362	52 373	274 018	2 834	8 327
1961	3 615	7 520	5 512	52 807	276 426	2 819	8 398
1962	3 639	7 562	5 666	53 292	279 262	2 830	8 448
1963	3 667	7 604	5 789	53 625	281 926	2 850	8 480
1964	3 694	7 662	5 887	53 991	284 167	2 864	8 510
1965	3 723	7 734	5 943	54 350	286 640	2 876	8 551
1966	3 753	7 807	5 996	54 643	288 759	2 884	8 614
1967	3 785	7 869	6 063	54 959	290 469	2 900	8 716
1968	3 819	7 912	6 132	55 214	292 036	2 913	8 741
1969	3 851	7 968	6 212	55 461	293 932	2 926	8 773
1970	3 879	8 043	6 267	55 632	295 796	2 950	8 793
1971	3 903	8 098	6 343	55 928	297 884	2 978	8 831
1972	3 933	8 122	6 401	56 097	299 565	3 024	8 889
1973	3 961	8 137	6 441	56 223	301 037	3 073	8 929
1974	3 985	8 160	6 460	56 236	302 037	3 124	8 962
1975	4 007	8 192	6 404	56 226	302 454	3 177	9 046
1976	4 026	8 222	6 333	56 216	302 690	3 228	9 167
1977	4 043	8 251	6 316	56 190	303 138	3 272	9 309
1978	4 060	8 275	6 333	56 178	303 647	3 314	9 430
1979	4 073	8 294	6 351	56 240	304 288	3 368	9 548
1980	4 086	8 311	6 385	56 330	305 176	3 401	9 643
1981	4 100	8 320	6 429	56 352	305 903	3 443	9 729
1982	4 115	8 325	6 467	56 318	306 326	3 480	9 790
1983	4 128	8 329	6 482	56 377	306 608	3 505	9 847
1984	4 140	8 337	6 505	56 506	306 871	3 529	9 896
1985	4 153	8 350	6 534	56 685	307 309	3 541	9 934
1986	4 167	8 370	6 573	56 852	307 956	3 542	9 967
1987	4 187	8 398	6 619	57 009	308 651	3 543	10 001
1988	4 209	8 436	6 671	57 158	309 695	3 531	10 037
1989	4 227	8 493	6 723	57 358	311 114	3 510	10 090
1990	4 241	8 566	6 796	57 561	312 753	3 506	10 161
1991	4 262	8 617	6 873	57 808	314 403	3 526	10 247
1992	4 286	8 668	6 943	58 006	316 086	3 549	10 322
1993	4 312	8 719	6 989	58 191	317 714	3 563	10 379
1994	4 337	8 781	7 037	58 395	318 896	3 583	10 426
1995	4 358	8 827	7 081	58 606	319 946	3 601	10 454
1996	4 381	8 841	7 105	58 801	320 913	3 626	10 476
1997	4 405	8 846	7 113	59 009	321 821	3 661	10 499
1998	4 432	8 851	7 130	59 237	322 507	3 705	10 511

*   WEC = Western European Countries.

Table C1–a. **Population of European Countries, Annual Estimates, 1950–98**
(000 at mid–year)

Year	Portugal	Spain	Total 16 WEC	Total 13 small WEC	Total 29 WEC	Total Eastern Europe	Total former USSR	Total EE and former USSR
1950	8 512	27 868	303 531	1 529	305 060	87 288	180 050	267 338
1951	8 547	28 086	305 610	1 544	307 154	88 374	183 200	271 574
1952	8 563	28 332	307 371	1 559	308 930	89 487	186 400	275 887
1953	8 587	28 571	309 257	1 574	310 831	90 770	189 500	280 270
1954	8 607	28 812	311 118	1 591	312 709	92 045	192 700	284 745
1955	8 657	29 056	313 104	1 600	314 704	93 439	196 150	289 589
1956	8 698	29 355	315 253	1 613	316 866	94 721	199 650	294 371
1957	8 737	29 657	317 439	1 636	319 075	95 801	203 150	298 951
1958	8 789	29 962	319 707	1 661	321 368	96 919	206 700	303 619
1959	8 837	30 271	322 182	1 682	323 864	98 003	210 450	308 453
1960	8 891	30 583	324 653	1 701	326 354	99 056	214 350	313 406
1961	8 944	30 904	327 491	1 717	329 208	100 112	218 150	318 262
1962	9 002	31 158	330 700	1 729	332 429	101 010	221 750	322 760
1963	9 040	31 430	333 726	1 747	335 473	101 914	225 100	327 014
1964	9 053	31 741	336 335	1 759	338 094	102 783	228 150	330 933
1965	8 996	32 085	339 148	1 773	340 921	103 610	230 900	334 510
1966	8 871	32 453	341 581	1 787	343 368	104 412	233 500	337 912
1967	8 798	32 850	343 733	1 803	345 536	105 195	236 000	341 195
1968	8 743	33 240	345 673	1 819	347 492	106 264	238 350	344 614
1969	8 696	33 566	347 893	1 837	349 730	107 101	240 600	347 701
1970	8 663	33 876	350 078	1 853	351 931	107 927	242 757	350 684
1971	8 644	34 190	352 527	1 869	354 396	108 782	245 083	353 865
1972	8 631	34 498	354 607	1 883	356 490	109 628	247 459	357 087
1973	8 634	34 810	356 483	1 907	358 390	110 490	249 747	360 237
1974	8 755	35 147	358 025	1 929	359 954	111 461	252 131	363 592
1975	9 094	35 515	359 286	1 915	361 201	112 468	254 469	366 937
1976	9 356	35 937	360 378	1 914	362 292	113 457	256 760	370 217
1977	9 456	36 367	361 542	1 922	363 464	114 442	259 029	373 471
1978	9 559	36 778	362 728	1 939	364 667	115 300	261 253	376 553
1979	9 662	37 108	363 974	1 957	365 931	116 157	263 425	379 582
1980	9 767	37 510	365 497	1 990	367 487	116 921	265 542	382 463
1981	9 851	37 741	366 667	2 009	368 676	117 661	267 722	385 383
1982	9 912	37 944	367 452	2 020	369 472	118 323	270 042	388 365
1983	9 955	38 123	368 038	2 035	370 073	118 926	272 540	391 466
1984	9 989	38 279	368 564	2 049	370 613	119 503	275 066	394 569
1985	10 011	38 420	369 215	2 067	371 282	120 062	277 537	397 599
1986	10 011	38 537	370 013	2 060	372 073	120 574	280 236	400 810
1987	9 994	38 632	370 821	2 082	372 903	121 051	283 100	404 151
1988	9 968	38 717	371 948	2 105	374 053	121 253	285 463	406 716
1989	9 937	38 792	373 443	2 126	375 569	121 650	287 845	409 495
1990	9 899	38 851	375 170	2 154	377 324	121 866	289 350	411 216
1991	9 871	39 920	377 967	2 183	380 150	122 049	291 060	413 109
1992	9 867	39 008	378 832	2 211	381 043	122 070	292 422	414 492
1993	9 880	39 086	380 622	2 240	382 862	121 632	292 417	414 049
1994	9 902	39 150	381 957	2 264	384 221	121 323	292 407	413 730
1995	9 917	39 210	383 128	2 284	385 412	121 126	292 196	413 322
1996	9 927	39 270	384 212	2 302	386 514	120 980	291 660	412 640
1997	9 946	39 323	385 250	2 320	387 570	120 977	291 027	412 004
1998	9 968	39 371	386 062	2 337	388 399	121 006	290 866	411 872

Table C1–a. **Population of Western Offshoots, Annual Estimates, 1950–98**
(000 at mid–year)

Year	Australia	New Zealand	Canada	United States	Total 4 Western Offshoots
1950	8 177	1 909	13 737	152 271	176 094
1951	8 418	1 948	14 047	154 878	179 291
1952	8 634	1 996	14 491	157 553	182 674
1953	8 821	2 049	14 882	160 184	185 936
1954	8 996	2 095	15 321	163 026	189 438
1955	9 201	2 139	15 730	165 931	193 001
1956	9 421	2 183	16 123	168 903	196 630
1957	9 640	2 233	16 677	171 984	200 534
1958	9 842	2 286	17 120	174 882	204 130
1959	10 056	2 335	17 522	177 830	207 743
1960	10 275	2 377	17 870	180 671	211 193
1961	10 508	2 427	18 238	183 691	214 864
1962	10 700	2 485	18 583	186 538	218 306
1963	10 907	2 537	18 931	189 242	221 617
1964	11 122	2 589	19 290	191 889	224 890
1965	11 341	2 635	19 644	194 303	227 923
1966	11 599	2 683	20 015	196 560	230 857
1967	11 799	2 728	20 378	198 712	233 617
1968	12 009	2 754	20 701	200 706	236 170
1969	12 263	2 780	21 001	202 677	238 721
1970	12 507	2 820	21 297	205 052	241 676
1971	13 067	2 864	22 026	207 661	245 618
1972	13 304	2 913	22 285	209 896	248 398
1973	13 505	2 971	22 560	211 909	250 945
1974	13 723	3 032	22 865	213 854	253 474
1975	13 893	3 087	23 209	215 973	256 162
1976	14 033	3 116	23 518	218 035	258 702
1977	14 192	3 128	23 796	220 239	261 355
1978	14 359	3 129	24 036	222 585	264 109
1979	14 516	3 138	24 277	225 055	266 986
1980	14 695	3 144	24 593	227 726	270 158
1981	14 923	3 157	24 900	229 966	272 946
1982	15 184	3 183	25 202	232 188	275 757
1983	15 393	3 226	25 456	234 307	278 382
1984	15 579	3 258	25 702	236 348	280 887
1985	15 788	3 272	25 942	238 466	283 468
1986	16 018	3 277	26 204	240 651	286 150
1987	16 264	3 304	26 550	242 804	288 922
1988	16 538	3 318	26 798	245 021	291 675
1989	16 833	3 337	27 286	247 342	294 798
1990	17 085	3 380	27 701	249 984	298 150
1991	17 284	3 488	28 031	252 639	301 442
1992	17 489	3 524	28 377	255 374	304 764
1993	17 657	3 567	28 703	258 083	308 010
1994	17 838	3 617	29 036	260 599	311 090
1995	18 072	3 673	29 354	263 044	314 143
1996	18 311	3 729	29 672	265 463	317 175
1997	18 524	3 771	30 008	268 008	320 311
1998	18 751	3 811	30 297	270 561	323 420

Table C1–b. **Levels of GDP in European Countries, Annual Estimates, 1950–98**
(million 1990 international Geary–Khamis dollars)

	Austria	*Belgium*	*Denmark*	*Finland*	*France*	*Germany*	*Italy*	*Netherlands*
1950	25 702	47 190	29 654	17 051	220 492	265 354	164 957	60 642
1951	27 460	49 874	29 852	18 501	234 074	289 679	177 272	61 914
1952	27 484	49 486	30 144	19 121	240 287	314 794	190 541	63 162
1953	28 680	51 071	31 859	19 255	247 223	341 150	204 288	68 652
1954	31 611	53 173	32 478	20 941	259 215	366 584	214 884	73 319
1955	35 105	55 696	32 828	22 008	274 098	406 922	227 389	78 759
1956	37 520	57 313	33 225	22 673	287 969	436 086	237 699	81 654
1957	39 818	58 381	35 746	23 739	305 308	461 071	251 732	83 950
1958	41 272	58 316	36 551	23 867	312 966	481 599	265 192	83 701
1959	42 445	60 160	39 270	25 285	321 924	516 821	281 707	87 793
1960	45 939	63 394	40 367	27 598	344 609	558 482	296 981	95 180
1961	48 378	66 478	42 926	29 701	363 754	581 487	321 992	95 455
1962	49 550	69 904	45 295	30 627	387 937	606 292	347 098	101 993
1963	51 567	72 988	45 579	31 636	408 090	623 382	371 822	105 686
1964	54 662	78 128	49 843	33 235	435 296	661 273	386 333	114 446
1965	56 234	80 870	52 117	35 002	456 456	694 798	395 020	120 435
1966	59 399	83 440	53 539	35 843	479 631	715 393	415 639	123 754
1967	61 205	86 695	55 339	36 600	501 799	717 610	445 232	130 267
1968	63 925	90 293	57 613	37 442	523 967	755 463	482 462	138 627
1969	67 945	96 302	61 283	41 048	560 280	805 410	510 051	147 552
1970	72 785	102 265	62 524	44 114	592 389	843 103	521 506	155 955
1971	76 506	106 103	64 191	45 036	621 055	867 917	531 385	162 539
1972	81 256	111 679	67 578	48 473	648 668	903 739	546 933	167 919
1973	85 227	118 516	70 032	51 724	683 965	944 755	582 713	175 791
1974	88 588	123 494	69 379	53 291	704 012	952 571	610 040	182 763
1975	88 267	121 855	68 921	53 905	699 106	947 383	596 946	182 596
1976	92 307	128 743	73 382	53 676	729 326	993 132	635 737	191 194
1977	96 624	129 549	74 573	53 808	756 545	1 021 710	654 108	196 392
1978	96 273	133 231	75 674	54 934	777 544	1 050 404	678 494	201 024
1979	101 525	136 350	78 356	58 756	802 491	1 092 615	716 984	205 501
1980	103 874	142 458	78 010	61 890	813 763	1 105 099	742 299	207 979
1981	103 771	140 680	77 316	63 043	822 116	1 109 276	745 816	206 925
1982	105 750	142 665	79 650	65 090	842 787	1 099 799	749 233	204 517
1983	108 716	142 648	81 656	66 849	852 644	1 119 394	758 360	208 014
1984	109 077	146 180	85 241	68 866	865 172	1 150 951	777 841	214 854
1985	111 525	147 650	88 897	71 184	877 305	1 176 131	799 697	221 470
1986	114 135	149 854	92 135	72 873	898 129	1 202 151	822 404	227 570
1987	116 053	153 392	92 406	75 861	920 822	1 220 284	847 870	230 788
1988	119 730	160 632	93 482	79 581	961 287	1 260 983	880 671	236 824
1989	124 791	166 396	93 728	84 092	1 000 286	1 302 212	906 053	247 906
1990	130 476	171 442	94 863	84 103	1 026 491	1 264 438	925 654	258 094
1991	134 944	174 880	96 184	78 841	1 036 379	1 328 057	938 522	263 950
1992	136 754	177 695	97 413	76 222	1 051 689	1 357 825	945 660	269 298
1993	137 455	175 072	98 232	75 347	1 041 232	1 343 060	937 303	271 347
1994	140 949	180 312	103 884	78 327	1 061 556	1 374 575	957 993	280 094
1995	143 849	185 047	107 713	81 311	1 079 157	1 398 310	986 004	286 416
1996	146 699	186 661	110 778	84 571	1 091 060	1 408 868	994 537	295 118
1997	148 443	192 652	114 250	89 892	1 112 956	1 429 308	1 009 277	306 297
1998	152 712	198 249	117 319	94 421	1 150 080	1 460 069	1 022 776	317 517

Table C1–b. Levels of GDP in European Countries, Annual Estimates, 1950–1998
(million 1990 international Geary–Khamis dollars)

	Norway	Sweden	Switzerland	United Kingdom	Total 12 WEC	Ireland	Greece
1950	17 838	47 269	42 545	347 850	1 286 544	10 231	14 489
1951	18 665	49 148	45 990	358 234	1 360 663	10 488	15 765
1952	19 332	49 845	46 369	357 585	1 408 150	10 753	15 878
1953	20 225	51 237	48 001	371 646	1 483 287	11 043	18 053
1954	21 229	53 395	50 705	386 789	1 564 323	11 142	18 615
1955	21 639	54 944	54 117	400 850	1 664 355	11 432	20 022
1956	22 771	57 032	57 710	405 825	1 737 477	11 283	21 731
1957	23 432	59 591	60 002	412 315	1 815 085	11 266	23 147
1958	23 218	59 887	58 732	411 450	1 856 751	11 034	24 218
1959	24 411	61 714	62 425	428 107	1 952 062	11 481	25 107
1960	25 813	64 986	66 793	452 768	2 082 910	12 127	26 195
1961	27 377	68 710	72 200	467 694	2 186 152	12 706	28 492
1962	28 159	71 599	75 661	472 454	2 286 569	13 120	29 562
1963	29 254	75 411	79 370	490 625	2 385 410	13 741	32 567
1964	30 662	80 562	83 541	516 584	2 524 565	14 279	35 243
1965	32 305	83 643	86 195	529 996	2 623 071	14 528	38 553
1966	33 556	85 383	88 305	540 163	2 714 045	14 652	40 907
1967	35 690	88 272	91 008	552 277	2 801 994	15 521	43 152
1968	36 498	91 475	94 272	574 775	2 946 812	16 804	46 027
1969	38 140	96 056	99 584	585 207	3 108 858	17 815	50 585
1970	38 902	102 275	105 935	599 016	3 240 769	18 289	54 609
1971	40 683	103 241	110 253	611 705	3 340 614	18 923	58 496
1972	42 785	105 604	113 781	633 352	3 471 767	20 151	65 775
1973	44 544	109 794	117 251	675 941	3 660 253	21 103	68 355
1974	46 858	113 306	118 957	666 755	3 730 014	22 002	65 868
1975	48 811	116 198	110 294	665 984	3 700 266	23 246	69 853
1976	52 135	117 428	108 745	680 933	3 856 738	23 571	74 296
1977	54 002	115 553	111 392	695 699	3 959 955	25 506	76 843
1978	56 453	117 577	111 847	720 501	4 073 956	27 340	81 989
1979	58 894	122 092	114 634	740 370	4 228 568	28 180	85 015
1980	61 811	124 130	119 909	728 224	4 289 446	29 047	86 505
1981	62 406	124 113	121 802	718 733	4 295 997	30 013	86 553
1982	62 514	125 358	120 051	729 861	4 327 275	30 698	86 895
1983	64 729	127 555	120 659	755 779	4 407 003	30 624	87 244
1984	68 530	132 717	124 311	774 665	4 518 405	31 957	89 645
1985	72 105	135 277	128 561	802 000	4 631 802	32 943	92 442
1986	74 687	138 381	130 653	837 280	4 760 252	32 802	93 941
1987	76 203	142 733	131 614	877 143	4 885 169	34 331	93 507
1988	76 117	145 946	135 709	920 841	5 071 803	36 123	97 670
1989	76 818	149 415	141 599	940 908	5 234 204	38 223	101 425
1990	78 333	151 451	146 900	944 610	5 276 855	41 459	101 452
1991	80 774	149 760	145 724	930 493	5 358 508	42 231	104 581
1992	83 413	147 631	145 540	930 975	5 420 115	43 625	105 327
1993	85 694	144 353	144 839	952 554	5 406 488	44 775	103 604
1994	90 400	150 296	145 610	994 384	5 558 380	47 355	105 723
1995	93 879	155 843	146 345	1 022 172	5 686 046	51 855	107 929
1996	98 475	157 523	146 811	1 048 308	5 769 409	55 865	110 474
1997	102 687	160 643	149 273	1 085 122	5 900 800	61 844	114 253
1998	104 860	165 385	152 345	1 108 568	6 044 301	67 368	118 433

Table C1–b. **Levels of GDP in European Countries, Annual Estimates, 1950–98**
(million 1990 International Geary–Khamis dollars)

	Portugal	*Spain*	*Total 16 WEC*	*Total 13 small WEC*	*Total 29 WEC*	*Total Eastern Europe*	*Total former USSR*	*Total EE and former USSR*
1950	17 615	66 792	1 395 671	5 880	1 401 551	185 023	510 243	695 266
1951	18 404	73 874	1 479 194	5 746	1 484 940	195 667	512 566	708 233
1952	18 428	79 676	1 532 885	6 180	1 539 065	198 287	545 792	744 079
1953	19 714	80 589	1 612 686	6 436	1 619 122	209 197	569 260	778 457
1954	20 660	85 204	1 699 944	6 647	1 706 591	218 949	596 910	815 859
1955	21 512	89 635	1 806 956	7 001	1 813 957	233 875	648 027	881 902
1956	22 451	96 077	1 889 019	7 427	1 896 446	239 574	710 065	949 639
1957	23 445	100 188	1 973 131	7 752	1 980 883	257 645	724 470	982 115
1958	23 753	104 666	2 020 422	7 966	2 028 388	272 649	778 840	1 051 489
1959	25 039	102 701	2 116 390	8 279	2 124 669	286 878	770 244	1 057 122
1960	26 711	105 123	2 253 066	8 487	2 261 553	304 633	843 434	1 148 067
1961	28 170	117 549	2 373 069	8 876	2 381 945	322 781	891 763	1 214 544
1962	30 040	128 514	2 487 805	9 269	2 497 074	328 253	915 928	1 244 181
1963	31 823	139 752	2 603 293	9 756	2 613 049	344 112	895 016	1 239 128
1964	33 921	148 387	2 756 395	10 165	2 766 560	364 518	1 010 727	1 375 245
1965	36 446	162 823	2 875 421	10 877	2 886 298	380 016	1 068 117	1 448 133
1966	37 929	179 727	2 987 260	11 398	2 998 658	404 452	1 119 932	1 524 384
1967	40 792	191 468	3 092 927	11 862	3 104 789	420 645	1 169 422	1 590 067
1968	44 421	208 144	3 262 208	12 261	3 274 469	436 444	1 237 966	1 674 410
1969	45 364	231 535	3 454 157	13 144	3 467 301	449 862	1 255 392	1 705 254
1970	49 498	246 976	3 610 141	13 713	3 623 854	465 695	1 351 818	1 817 513
1971	52 781	259 814	3 730 628	14 651	3 745 279	499 790	1 387 832	1 887 622
1972	57 011	281 560	3 896 264	15 548	3 911 812	524 971	1 395 732	1 920 703
1973	63 397	304 220	4 117 328	16 452	4 133 780	550 756	1 513 070	2 063 826
1974	64 122	321 313	4 203 319	16 510	4 219 829	583 528	1 556 984	2 140 512
1975	61 334	323 056	4 177 755	16 005	4 193 760	604 251	1 561 399	2 165 650
1976	65 566	333 729	4 353 900	17 038	4 370 938	619 961	1 634 589	2 254 550
1977	69 239	343 202	4 474 745	18 095	4 492 840	641 681	1 673 159	2 314 840
1978	71 189	348 223	4 602 697	19 058	4 621 755	662 328	1 715 215	2 377 543
1979	75 203	348 367	4 765 333	20 007	4 785 340	672 299	1 707 083	2 379 382
1980	78 655	356 062	4 839 715	20 768	4 860 483	675 819	1 709 174	2 384 993
1981	79 928	355 615	4 848 106	21 257	4 869 363	667 932	1 724 741	2 392 673
1982	81 634	361 106	4 887 608	21 886	4 909 494	674 202	1 767 262	2 441 464
1983	81 492	368 180	4 974 543	22 385	4 996 928	684 326	1 823 723	2 508 049
1984	79 961	374 444	5 094 412	23 512	5 117 924	705 274	1 847 190	2 552 464
1985	82 206	380 795	5 220 188	24 313	5 244 501	706 201	1 863 687	2 569 888
1986	85 610	392 978	5 365 583	25 556	5 391 139	725 733	1 940 363	2 666 096
1987	91 073	415 150	5 519 230	26 754	5 545 984	721 188	1 965 457	2 686 645
1988	97 894	436 576	5 740 066	28 385	5 768 451	727 564	2 007 280	2 734 844
1989	102 922	457 262	5 934 036	30 000	5 964 036	718 039	2 037 253	2 755 292
1990	107 427	474 366	6 001 559	31 205	6 032 764	662 604	1 987 995	2 650 599
1991	110 047	485 126	6 100 493	32 342	6 132 835	590 231	1 863 524	2 453 755
1992	112 134	488 459	6 169 660	33 161	6 202 821	559 157	1 592 085	2 151 242
1993	110 593	482 776	6 148 236	34 633	6 182 869	550 466	1 435 008	1 985 474
1994	113 328	493 643	6 318 429	35 838	6 354 267	572 173	1 235 701	1 807 874
1995	116 640	507 054	6 469 524	36 899	6 506 423	605 352	1 169 446	1 774 798
1996	120 357	518 920	6 575 025	38 136	6 613 161	628 154	1 137 039	1 765 193
1997	124 529	538 824	6 740 250	39 918	6 780 168	646 234	1 156 028	1 802 262
1998	128 877	560 138	6 919 117	41 499	6 960 616	660 861	1 132 434	1 793 295

Table C1–b. **Levels of GDP in Western Offshoots, Annual Estimates, 1950–98**
(million 1990 international Geary–Khamis dollars)

	Australia	New Zealand	Canada	United States	Total 4 Western Offshoots
1950	61 274	16 136	102 164	1 455 916	1 635 490
1951	63 892	14 904	107 960	1 566 784	1 753 540
1952	64 470	15 552	115 816	1 625 245	1 821 083
1953	66 481	16 084	121 228	1 699 970	1 903 763
1954	70 614	18 298	120 390	1 688 804	1 898 106
1955	74 471	18 639	131 633	1 808 126	2 032 869
1956	77 034	19 605	142 282	1 843 455	2 082 376
1957	78 577	20 165	146 402	1 878 063	2 123 207
1958	82 351	20 957	149 021	1 859 088	2 111 417
1959	87 421	22 449	155 062	1 997 061	2 261 993
1960	91 085	22 449	159 880	2 046 727	2 320 141
1961	91 713	23 704	164 598	2 094 396	2 374 411
1962	97 444	24 215	176 130	2 220 732	2 518 521
1963	103 413	25 749	185 041	2 316 765	2 630 968
1964	110 488	27 004	197 098	2 450 915	2 785 505
1965	116 131	28 724	210 203	2 607 294	2 962 352
1966	119 363	30 536	223 832	2 778 086	3 151 817
1967	127 422	29 142	230 647	2 847 549	3 234 760
1968	134 913	29 095	242 703	2 983 081	3 389 792
1969	143 118	32 099	255 497	3 076 517	3 507 231
1970	152 220	31 644	262 098	3 081 900	3 527 862
1971	158 992	33 285	276 694	3 178 106	3 647 077
1972	163 453	34 711	291 314	3 346 554	3 836 032
1973	172 314	37 177	312 176	3 536 622	4 058 289
1974	176 586	39 390	324 928	3 526 724	4 067 628
1975	181 367	38 937	332 269	3 516 825	4 069 398
1976	188 678	39 887	350 467	3 701 163	4 280 195
1977	190 653	37 944	362 245	3 868 829	4 459 671
1978	196 184	38 097	376 894	4 089 548	4 700 723
1979	206 515	38 874	392 561	4 228 647	4 866 597
1980	210 642	39 141	397 814	4 230 558	4 878 155
1981	218 780	41 041	410 164	4 336 141	5 006 126
1982	218 512	41 809	397 671	4 254 870	4 912 862
1983	218 539	42 955	409 246	4 433 129	5 103 869
1984	233 618	45 072	432 711	4 755 958	5 467 359
1985	245 444	45 420	456 107	4 940 383	5 687 354
1986	250 539	46 372	468 055	5 110 480	5 875 446
1987	262 925	46 564	487 138	5 290 129	6 086 756
1988	274 737	46 435	510 815	5 512 845	6 344 832
1989	286 820	46 850	523 177	5 703 521	6 560 368
1990	291 180	46 729	524 475	5 803 200	6 665 584
1991	288 661	45 908	514 459	5 790 784	6 639 812
1992	296 225	46 304	519 148	5 983 457	6 845 134
1993	307 489	48 654	531 096	6 124 987	7 012 226
1994	322 819	51 554	556 209	6 371 321	7 301 903
1995	336 990	53 599	571 447	6 544 370	7 506 406
1996	350 394	55 331	581 118	6 784 105	7 770 948
1997	363 903	56 455	604 180	7 089 655	8 114 193
1998	382 335	56 322	622 880	7 394 598	8 456 135

Table C1–c. **Levels of Per Capita GDP in European Countries, Annual Estimates, 1950–98**
(1990 international Geary–Khamis dollars)

	Austria	*Belgium*	*Denmark*	*Finland*	*France*	*Germany*	*Italy*	*Netherlands*
1950	3 706	5 462	6 946	4 253	5 270	3 881	3 502	5 996
1951	3 959	5 747	6 936	4 572	5 553	4 207	3 738	6 032
1952	3 967	5 668	6 955	4 674	5 659	4 550	3 997	6 084
1953	4 137	5 818	7 292	4 652	5 783	4 900	4 260	6 542
1954	4 555	6 029	7 371	5 001	6 020	5 242	4 449	6 906
1955	5 053	6 280	7 395	5 197	6 312	5 788	4 676	7 326
1956	5 397	6 422	7 440	5 295	6 568	6 164	4 859	7 499
1957	5 716	6 495	7 965	5 490	6 890	6 482	5 118	7 614
1958	5 907	6 442	8 095	5 474	6 988	6 731	5 360	7 482
1959	6 051	6 608	8 561	5 753	7 116	7 176	5 653	7 736
1960	6 518	6 953	8 812	6 230	7 543	7 685	5 916	8 289
1961	6 826	7 253	9 307	6 658	7 880	7 932	6 372	8 203
1962	6 950	7 583	9 747	6 820	8 254	8 200	6 822	8 643
1963	7 187	7 863	9 731	6 994	8 535	8 363	7 255	8 834
1964	7 567	8 341	10 560	7 306	9 010	8 821	7 476	9 439
1965	7 734	8 523	10 956	7 669	9 362	9 185	7 580	9 797
1966	8 112	8 776	11 161	7 824	9 756	9 387	7 914	9 936
1967	8 297	9 071	11 436	7 946	10 128	9 397	8 416	10 341
1968	8 621	9 415	11 837	8 094	10 497	9 865	9 063	10 893
1969	9 131	10 018	12 525	8 877	11 135	10 440	9 527	11 462
1970	9 748	10 611	12 685	9 578	11 668	10 849	9 689	11 967
1971	10 199	10 969	12 934	9 765	12 118	11 078	9 827	12 319
1972	10 771	11 503	13 537	10 447	12 547	11 481	10 057	12 597
1973	11 235	12 170	13 945	11 085	13 123	11 966	10 643	13 082
1974	11 658	12 643	13 752	11 360	13 420	12 061	11 069	13 495
1975	11 646	12 441	13 621	11 440	13 266	12 041	10 767	13 367
1976	12 200	13 122	14 465	11 358	13 785	12 681	11 410	13 882
1977	12 767	13 190	14 657	11 354	14 235	13 071	11 690	14 174
1978	12 731	13 554	14 826	11 558	14 567	13 453	12 083	14 422
1979	13 449	13 861	15 313	12 331	14 970	13 989	12 731	14 643
1980	13 760	14 467	15 227	12 948	15 103	14 113	13 153	14 700
1981	13 710	14 276	15 095	13 134	15 173	14 146	13 198	14 524
1982	13 959	14 466	15 563	13 485	15 466	14 040	13 242	14 290
1983	14 367	14 457	15 967	13 766	15 567	14 329	13 392	14 478
1984	14 407	14 809	16 675	14 106	15 723	14 785	13 730	14 897
1985	14 717	14 946	17 383	14 521	15 869	15 143	14 110	15 286
1986	15 042	15 155	17 992	14 818	16 169	15 474	14 511	15 622
1987	15 274	15 493	18 023	15 381	16 495	15 701	14 960	15 738
1988	15 723	16 212	18 223	16 090	17 130	16 143	15 552	16 045
1989	16 293	16 738	18 267	16 940	17 728	16 551	15 988	16 699
1990	16 881	17 194	18 463	16 868	18 093	15 932	16 320	17 267
1991	17 272	17 474	18 677	15 724	18 165	16 604	16 538	17 517
1992	17 280	17 679	18 857	15 117	18 330	16 848	16 632	17 738
1993	17 201	17 354	18 945	14 873	18 060	16 544	16 430	17 747
1994	17 553	17 819	19 974	15 391	18 334	16 882	16 747	18 210
1995	17 876	18 255	20 627	15 918	18 562	17 123	17 207	18 526
1996	18 203	18 378	21 076	16 502	18 691	17 203	17 327	19 012
1997	18 390	18 921	21 638	17 489	18 991	17 419	17 549	19 628
1998	18 905	19 442	22 123	18 324	19 558	17 799	17 759	20 224

Table C1–c. **Levels of Per Capita GDP in European Countries, Annual Estimates, 1950–98**
(1990 international Geary–Khamis dollars)

	Norway	Sweden	Switzerland	United Kingdom	Total 12 WEC	Ireland	Greece
1950	5 463	6 738	9 064	6 907	5 013	3 446	1 915
1951	5 663	6 951	9 684	7 083	5 267	3 542	2 058
1952	5 809	6 996	9 630	7 048	5 420	3 641	2 053
1953	6 016	7 145	9 842	7 304	5 676	3 745	2 309
1954	6 253	7 403	10 287	7 574	5 951	3 789	2 358
1955	6 311	7 566	10 867	7 826	6 292	3 914	2 513
1956	6 577	7 797	11 439	7 891	6 525	3 893	2 706
1957	6 706	8 089	11 705	7 982	6 771	3 905	2 859
1958	6 587	8 076	11 297	7 932	6 879	3 868	2 963
1959	6 865	8 279	11 870	8 208	7 177	4 034	3 040
1960	7 200	8 688	12 457	8 645	7 601	4 279	3 146
1961	7 573	9 137	13 099	8 857	7 909	4 507	3 393
1962	7 738	9 468	13 354	8 865	8 188	4 636	3 499
1963	7 978	9 917	13 710	9 149	8 461	4 821	3 840
1964	8 300	10 514	14 191	9 568	8 884	4 986	4 141
1965	8 677	10 815	14 504	9 752	9 151	5 051	4 509
1966	8 941	10 937	14 727	9 885	9 399	5 080	4 749
1967	9 429	11 218	15 010	10 049	9 646	5 352	4 951
1968	9 557	11 562	15 374	10 410	10 091	5 769	5 266
1969	9 904	12 055	16 031	10 552	10 577	6 089	5 766
1970	10 029	12 716	16 904	10 767	10 956	6 200	6 211
1971	10 424	12 749	17 382	10 937	11 214	6 354	6 624
1972	10 878	13 002	17 776	11 290	11 589	6 664	7 400
1973	11 246	13 493	18 204	12 022	12 159	6 867	7 655
1974	11 759	13 886	18 414	11 856	12 350	7 043	7 350
1975	12 181	14 184	17 223	11 845	12 234	7 317	7 722
1976	12 950	14 282	17 171	12 113	12 742	7 302	8 105
1977	13 357	14 005	17 636	12 381	13 063	7 795	8 255
1978	13 905	14 209	17 661	12 825	13 417	8 250	8 694
1979	14 460	14 721	18 050	13 164	13 897	8 367	8 904
1980	15 128	14 936	18 780	12 928	14 056	8 541	8 971
1981	15 221	14 917	18 946	12 754	14 044	8 717	8 896
1982	15 192	15 058	18 564	12 960	14 126	8 821	8 876
1983	15 680	15 315	18 614	13 406	14 373	8 737	8 860
1984	16 553	15 919	19 110	13 709	14 724	9 056	9 059
1985	17 362	16 201	19 676	14 148	15 072	9 303	9 306
1986	17 923	16 533	19 877	14 727	15 458	9 261	9 425
1987	18 200	16 996	19 884	15 386	15 827	9 690	9 350
1988	18 084	17 300	20 343	16 110	16 377	10 230	9 731
1989	18 173	17 593	21 062	16 404	16 824	10 890	10 052
1990	18 470	17 680	21 616	16 411	16 872	11 825	9 984
1991	18 952	17 380	21 202	16 096	17 043	11 977	10 206
1992	19 462	17 032	20 962	16 050	17 148	12 292	10 204
1993	19 873	16 556	20 724	16 369	17 017	12 567	9 982
1994	20 844	17 116	20 692	17 029	17 430	13 217	10 140
1995	21 542	17 655	20 667	17 441	17 772	14 400	10 324
1996	22 478	17 817	20 663	17 828	17 978	15 407	10 545
1997	23 311	18 160	20 986	18 389	18 336	16 893	10 882
1998	23 660	18 685	21 367	18 714	18 742	18 183	11 268

Table C1–c. **Levels of Per Capita GDP in European Countries, Annual Estimates, 1950–98**
(million 1990 international Geary–Khamis dollars)

	Portugal	Spain	Total 16 WEC	Total 13 small WEC	Total 29 WEC	Total Eastern Europe	Total former USSR	Total EE and former USSR
1950	2 069	2 397	4 598	3 846	4 594	2 120	2 834	2 601
1951	2 153	2 630	4 840	3 722	4 835	2 214	2 798	2 608
1952	2 152	2 812	4 987	3 964	4 982	2 216	2 928	2 697
1953	2 296	2 821	5 215	4 089	5 209	2 305	3 004	2 778
1954	2 400	2 957	5 464	4 178	5 457	2 379	3 098	2 865
1955	2 485	3 085	5 771	4 376	5 764	2 503	3 304	3 045
1956	2 581	3 273	5 992	4 604	5 985	2 529	3 557	3 226
1957	2 683	3 378	6 216	4 738	6 208	2 689	3 566	3 285
1958	2 703	3 493	6 320	4 796	6 312	2 813	3 768	3 463
1959	2 833	3 393	6 569	4 922	6 560	2 927	3 660	3 427
1960	3 004	3 437	6 940	4 989	6 930	3 075	3 935	3 663
1961	3 150	3 804	7 246	5 169	7 235	3 224	4 088	3 816
1962	3 337	4 125	7 523	5 361	7 512	3 250	4 130	3 855
1963	3 520	4 446	7 801	5 584	7 789	3 376	3 976	3 789
1964	3 747	4 675	8 195	5 779	8 183	3 546	4 430	4 156
1965	4 051	5 075	8 478	6 135	8 466	3 668	4 626	4 329
1966	4 276	5 538	8 745	6 378	8 733	3 874	4 796	4 511
1967	4 637	5 829	8 998	6 579	8 985	3 999	4 955	4 660
1968	5 081	6 262	9 437	6 741	9 423	4 107	5 194	4 859
1969	5 217	6 898	9 929	7 155	9 914	4 200	5 218	4 904
1970	5 714	7 291	10 312	7 400	10 297	4 315	5 569	5 183
1971	6 106	7 599	10 583	7 839	10 568	4 594	5 663	5 334
1972	6 605	8 162	10 988	8 257	10 973	4 789	5 640	5 379
1973	7 343	8 739	11 550	8 627	11 534	4 985	6 058	5 729
1974	7 324	9 142	11 740	8 559	11 723	5 235	6 175	5 887
1975	6 744	9 096	11 628	8 358	11 611	5 373	6 136	5 902
1976	7 008	9 287	12 081	8 902	12 065	5 464	6 366	6 090
1977	7 322	9 437	12 377	9 415	12 361	5 607	6 459	6 198
1978	7 447	9 468	12 689	9 829	12 674	5 744	6 565	6 314
1979	7 783	9 388	13 093	10 223	13 077	5 788	6 480	6 268
1980	8 053	9 492	13 241	10 436	13 226	5 780	6 437	6 236
1981	8 114	9 423	13 222	10 581	13 208	5 677	6 442	6 209
1982	8 236	9 517	13 301	10 835	13 288	5 698	6 544	6 287
1983	8 186	9 658	13 516	11 000	13 503	5 754	6 692	6 407
1984	8 005	9 782	13 822	11 475	13 809	5 902	6 715	6 469
1985	8 212	9 911	14 139	11 762	14 125	5 882	6 715	6 464
1986	8 552	10 197	14 501	12 406	14 489	6 019	6 924	6 652
1987	9 113	10 746	14 884	12 850	14 872	5 958	6 943	6 648
1988	9 821	11 276	15 432	13 485	15 421	6 000	7 032	6 724
1989	10 357	11 788	15 890	14 111	15 880	5 902	7 078	6 729
1990	10 852	12 210	15 997	14 487	15 988	5 437	6 871	6 446
1991	11 149	12 152	16 140	14 815	16 133	4 836	6 403	5 940
1992	11 365	12 522	16 286	14 998	16 279	4 581	5 444	5 190
1993	11 194	12 352	16 153	15 461	16 149	4 526	4 907	4 795
1994	11 445	12 609	16 542	15 830	16 538	4 716	4 226	4 370
1995	11 762	12 932	16 886	16 155	16 882	4 998	4 002	4 294
1996	12 124	13 214	17 113	16 566	17 110	5 192	3 899	4 278
1997	12 521	13 703	17 496	17 206	17 494	5 342	3 972	4 374
1998	12 929	14 227	17 922	17 757	17 921	5 461	3 893	4 354

Table C1–c. **Levels of Per Capita GDP in Western Offshoots, Annual Estimates, 1950–98**
(1990 international Geary–Khamis dollars)

	Australia	*New Zealand*	*Canada*	*United States*	*Total 4 Western Offshoots*
1950	7 493	8 453	7 437	9 561	9 288
1951	7 590	7 651	7 686	10 116	9 780
1952	7 467	7 792	7 992	10 316	9 969
1953	7 537	7 850	8 146	10 613	10 239
1954	7 849	8 734	7 858	10 359	10 020
1955	8 094	8 714	8 368	10 897	10 533
1956	8 177	8 981	8 825	10 914	10 590
1957	8 151	9 030	8 779	10 920	10 588
1958	8 367	9 168	8 704	10 631	10 343
1959	8 693	9 614	8 850	11 230	10 888
1960	8 865	9 444	8 947	11 328	10 986
1961	8 728	9 767	9 025	11 402	11 051
1962	9 107	9 744	9 478	11 905	11 537
1963	9 481	10 149	9 774	12 242	11 872
1964	9 934	10 430	10 218	12 773	12 386
1965	10 240	10 901	10 701	13 419	12 997
1966	10 291	11 381	11 183	14 134	13 653
1967	10 799	10 683	11 318	14 330	13 846
1968	11 234	10 565	11 724	14 863	14 353
1969	11 671	11 546	12 166	15 179	14 692
1970	12 171	11 221	12 307	15 030	14 597
1971	12 167	11 622	12 562	15 304	14 849
1972	12 286	11 916	13 072	15 944	15 443
1973	12 759	12 513	13 838	16 689	16 172
1974	12 868	12 991	14 211	16 491	16 048
1975	13 055	12 613	14 316	16 284	15 886
1976	13 445	12 801	14 902	16 975	16 545
1977	13 434	12 130	15 223	17 567	17 064
1978	13 663	12 175	15 680	18 373	17 798
1979	14 227	12 388	16 170	18 789	18 228
1980	14 334	12 449	16 176	18 577	18 057
1981	14 661	13 000	16 472	18 856	18 341
1982	14 391	13 135	15 779	18 325	17 816
1983	14 197	13 315	16 077	18 920	18 334
1984	14 996	13 834	16 836	20 123	19 465
1985	15 546	13 881	17 582	20 717	20 063
1986	15 641	14 151	17 862	21 236	20 533
1987	16 166	14 093	18 348	21 788	21 067
1988	16 612	13 995	19 062	22 499	21 753
1989	17 039	14 040	19 174	23 059	22 254
1990	17 043	13 825	18 933	23 214	22 356
1991	16 701	13 162	18 353	22 921	22 027
1992	16 938	13 140	18 295	23 430	22 460
1993	17 415	13 640	18 503	23 733	22 766
1994	18 097	14 253	19 156	24 449	23 472
1995	18 647	14 593	19 467	24 879	23 895
1996	19 136	14 838	19 585	25 556	24 501
1997	19 645	14 971	20 134	26 453	25 332
1998	20 390	14 779	20 559	27 331	26 146

Table C2–a. **Population of 8 Latin American Countries, Annual Estimates, 1950–98**
(000 at mid–year)

	Argentina	Brazil	Chile	Colombia	Mexico	Peru	Uruguay	Venezuela	Total
1950	17 150	53 443	6 091	11 592	28 485	7 633	2 194	5 009	131 597
1951	17 517	54 996	6 252	11 965	29 296	7 826	2 223	5 217	135 292
1952	17 877	56 603	6 378	12 351	30 144	8 026	2 253	5 440	139 070
1953	18 231	58 266	6 493	12 750	31 031	8 232	2 284	5 674	142 961
1954	18 581	59 989	6 612	13 162	31 959	8 447	2 317	5 919	146 985
1955	18 928	61 774	6 743	13 588	32 930	8 672	2 353	6 170	151 158
1956	19 272	63 632	6 889	14 029	33 946	8 905	2 389	6 431	155 493
1957	19 611	65 551	7 048	14 486	35 016	9 146	2 425	6 703	159 985
1958	19 947	67 533	7 220	14 958	36 142	9 397	2 460	6 982	164 639
1959	20 281	69 580	7 400	15 447	37 328	9 658	2 495	7 268	169 457
1960	20 616	71 695	7 585	15 953	38 579	9 931	2 531	7 556	174 446
1961	20 951	73 833	7 773	16 476	39 836	10 218	2 564	7 848	179 498
1962	21 284	76 039	7 961	17 010	41 121	10 517	2 598	8 143	184 674
1963	21 616	78 317	8 147	17 546	42 434	10 826	2 632	8 444	189 963
1964	21 949	80 667	8 330	18 090	43 775	11 144	2 664	8 752	195 370
1965	22 283	83 093	8 510	18 646	45 142	11 467	2 693	9 068	200 903
1966	22 612	85 557	8 686	19 202	46 538	11 796	2 721	9 387	206 499
1967	22 934	88 050	8 859	19 764	47 996	12 132	2 749	9 710	212 193
1968	23 261	90 569	9 030	20 322	49 519	12 476	2 777	10 041	217 994
1969	23 600	93 114	9 199	20 869	51 111	12 829	2 802	10 389	223 913
1970	23 962	95 684	9 369	21 430	52 775	13 193	2 824	10 758	229 994
1971	24 352	98 244	9 540	21 993	54 434	13 568	2 826	11 152	236 110
1972	24 757	100 837	9 718	22 543	56 040	13 955	2 830	11 516	242 193
1973	25 174	103 463	9 897	23 069	57 643	14 350	2 834	11 893	248 323
1974	25 598	106 122	10 077	23 593	59 240	14 753	2 838	12 281	254 502
1975	26 021	108 813	10 252	24 114	60 828	15 161	2 842	12 675	260 706
1976	26 457	111 533	10 432	24 620	62 404	15 573	2 857	13 082	266 960
1977	26 895	114 299	10 600	25 094	63 981	15 990	2 874	13 504	273 237
1978	27 338	117 129	10 760	25 543	65 554	16 414	2 889	13 931	279 558
1979	27 785	120 020	10 923	26 031	67 123	16 849	2 905	14 355	285 990
1980	28 237	122 936	11 094	26 583	68 686	17 295	2 920	14 768	292 519
1981	28 701	125 907	11 282	27 159	70 324	17 755	2 936	15 166	299 230
1982	29 151	128 938	11 487	27 764	71 923	18 234	2 954	15 621	306 072
1983	29 584	131 864	11 687	28 388	73 463	18 706	2 973	16 084	312 750
1984	29 993	134 596	11 879	29 026	74 992	19 171	2 990	16 545	319 192
1985	30 407	137 272	12 067	29 675	76 544	19 624	3 008	16 998	325 595
1986	30 853	140 080	12 260	30 339	78 132	20 073	3 027	17 450	332 214
1987	31 303	142 903	12 463	31 011	79 754	20 531	3 045	17 910	338 922
1988	31 749	145 744	12 678	31 681	81 408	21 000	3 064	18 379	345 702
1989	32 194	148 526	12 901	32 341	83 073	21 487	3 084	18 851	352 457
1990	32 634	151 040	13 128	32 985	84 748	21 989	3 106	19 325	358 955
1991	33 083	153 471	13 353	33 629	86 437	22 501	3 128	19 801	365 402
1992	33 531	155 918	13 573	34 296	88 143	23 015	3 149	20 266	371 891
1993	33 963	158 344	13 788	34 979	89 863	23 531	3 172	20 706	378 346
1994	34 412	160 744	14 000	35 679	91 592	24 047	3 194	21 139	384 807
1995	34 877	163 113	14 205	36 397	93 325	24 563	3 216	21 564	391 261
1996	35 335	165 427	14 403	37 124	95 063	25 079	3 239	21 983	397 653
1997	35 798	167 661	14 597	37 852	96 807	25 595	3 262	22 396	403 969
1998	36 265	169 807	14 788	38 581	98 553	26 111	3 285	22 803	410 192

Table C2–a. **Population of 15 Latin American Countries, Annual Estimates, 1950–98**
(000 at mid–year)

	Bolivia	*Costa Rica*	*Cuba*	*Dominican Republic*	*Ecuador*	*El Salvador*	*Guatemala*	*Haiti*
1950	2 766	867	5 785	2 312	3 310	1 940	2 969	3 097
1951	2 824	895	5 892	2 375	3 403	1 989	3 056	3 148
1952	2 883	926	6 008	2 444	3 498	2 042	3 146	3 201
1953	2 945	959	6 129	2 518	3 596	2 097	3 239	3 257
1954	3 009	994	6 254	2 598	3 699	2 156	3 335	3 316
1955	3 074	1 032	6 381	2 685	3 806	2 218	3 434	3 376
1956	3 142	1 072	6 513	2 778	3 918	2 283	3 535	3 441
1957	3 212	1 112	6 641	2 873	4 034	2 351	3 640	3 508
1958	3 284	1 154	6 763	2 968	4 155	2 422	3 749	3 577
1959	3 358	1 200	6 901	3 064	4 281	2 497	3 861	3 648
1960	3 434	1 248	7 027	3 159	4 413	2 574	3 975	3 723
1961	3 513	1 297	7 134	3 225	4 551	2 656	4 090	3 800
1962	3 594	1 345	7 254	3 359	4 696	2 738	4 208	3 880
1963	3 678	1 393	7 415	3 470	4 846	2 825	4 329	3 964
1964	3 764	1 440	7 612	3 588	5 001	2 912	4 454	4 050
1965	3 853	1 488	7 810	3 714	5 162	3 005	4 581	4 137
1966	3 945	1 538	7 985	3 848	5 330	3 114	4 712	4 227
1967	4 041	1 589	8 139	3 981	5 503	3 217	4 847	4 318
1968	4 139	1 638	8 284	4 114	5 682	3 330	4 987	4 412
1969	4 241	1 687	8 421	4 244	5 865	3 450	5 133	4 507
1970	4 346	1 736	8 543	4 373	6 051	3 583	5 287	4 605
1971	4 455	1 786	8 670	4 508	6 240	3 688	5 452	4 653
1972	4 566	1 835	8 831	4 644	6 432	3 767	5 623	4 701
1973	4 680	1 886	9 001	4 781	6 629	3 853	5 801	4 748
1974	4 796	1 938	9 153	4 915	6 829	3 944	5 986	4 795
1975	4 914	1 993	9 290	5 052	7 038	4 042	6 178	4 839
1976	5 025	2 051	9 421	5 192	7 243	4 143	6 375	4 882
1977	5 128	2 112	9 538	5 333	7 455	4 249	6 580	4 925
1978	5 232	2 198	9 634	5 472	7 671	4 361	6 792	4 970
1979	5 335	2 266	9 710	5 613	7 893	4 470	7 009	5 017
1980	5 439	2 307	9 653	5 697	8 123	4 527	7 232	5 056
1981	5 545	2 366	9 712	5 826	8 361	4 475	7 486	5 091
1982	5 653	2 435	9 789	5 957	8 606	4 434	7 710	5 149
1983	5 763	2 506	9 886	6 087	8 831	4 478	7 898	5 248
1984	5 876	2 568	9 982	6 214	9 051	4 543	8 118	5 354
1985	5 992	2 640	10 079	6 343	9 269	4 617	8 351	5 468
1986	6 111	2 716	10 162	6 472	9 484	4 702	8 593	5 588
1987	6 233	2 793	10 240	6 603	9 696	4 791	8 844	5 708
1988	6 359	2 870	10 334	6 734	9 904	4 877	9 103	5 825
1989	6 487	2 947	10 439	6 867	10 110	4 959	9 366	5 939
1990	6 620	3 022	10 545	6 997	10 308	5 041	9 631	6 048
1991	6 756	3 098	10 643	7 127	10 577	5 125	9 901	6 133
1992	6 895	3 172	10 724	7 253	10 852	5 211	10 179	6 215
1993	7 048	3 246	10 789	7 372	11 121	5 301	10 465	6 310
1994	7 202	3 319	10 846	7 489	11 381	5 391	10 759	6 399
1995	7 358	3 391	10 900	7 612	11 629	5 481	11 061	6 488
1996	7 514	3 463	10 952	7 740	11 869	5 571	11 370	6 583
1997	7 670	3 534	11 003	7 869	12 105	5 662	11 686	6 680
1998	7 826	3 605	11 051	7 999	12 337	5 752	12 008	6 781

Table C2–a. **Population of 15 Latin American Countries, Annual Estimates, 1950–98**
(000 at mid–year)

	Honduras	Jamaica	Nicaragua	Panama	Paraguay	Puerto Rico	Trinidad & Tobago	Total
1950	1 431	1 385	1 098	893	1 476	2 218	632	32 178
1951	1 474	1 406	1 131	916	1 515	2 235	649	32 908
1952	1 517	1 426	1 166	940	1 556	2 227	663	33 643
1953	1 562	1 446	1 202	962	1 597	2 204	678	34 393
1954	1 611	1 468	1 239	985	1 640	2 214	698	35 214
1955	1 662	1 489	1 277	1 011	1 683	2 250	721	36 099
1956	1 715	1 510	1 317	1 037	1 727	2 249	743	36 980
1957	1 770	1 535	1 359	1 064	1 771	2 260	765	37 894
1958	1 829	1 566	1 402	1 085	1 816	2 299	789	38 857
1959	1 889	1 599	1 446	1 115	1 862	2 322	817	39 859
1960	1 952	1 632	1 493	1 148	1 910	2 358	841	40 886
1961	2 017	1 648	1 541	1 181	1 959	2 403	861	41 877
1962	2 082	1 665	1 591	1 216	2 010	2 448	887	42 974
1963	2 151	1 698	1 642	1 251	2 062	2 497	904	44 126
1964	2 224	1 739	1 695	1 288	2 115	2 552	924	45 359
1965	2 299	1 777	1 750	1 326	2 170	2 597	939	46 610
1966	2 375	1 820	1 807	1 365	2 228	2 627	953	47 875
1967	2 453	1 861	1 865	1 405	2 288	2 649	960	49 118
1968	2 534	1 893	1 926	1 447	2 349	2 674	963	50 372
1969	2 618	1 920	1 988	1 489	2 412	2 722	963	51 660
1970	2 683	1 944	2 053	1 531	2 477	2 722	955	52 888
1971	2 767	1 967	2 120	1 573	2 545	2 766	962	54 150
1972	2 864	1 998	2 180	1 616	2 614	2 847	975	55 493
1973	2 964	2 036	2 241	1 659	2 692	2 863	985	56 819
1974	3 066	2 071	2 311	1 706	2 773	2 887	995	58 167
1975	3 151	2 105	2 383	1 748	2 850	2 935	1 007	59 525
1976	3 237	2 133	2 458	1 790	2 919	3 026	1 021	60 920
1977	3 326	2 157	2 537	1 840	2 984	3 081	1 039	62 286
1978	3 425	2 179	2 587	1 873	3 051	3 118	1 056	63 619
1979	3 520	2 207	2 663	1 915	3 119	3 168	1 073	64 979
1980	3 625	2 229	2 776	1 956	3 193	3 210	1 091	66 113
1981	3 744	2 258	2 869	1 996	3 276	3 239	1 102	67 346
1982	3 847	2 298	2 945	2 036	3 366	3 279	1 116	68 619
1983	3 946	2 323	3 012	2 077	3 463	3 316	1 133	69 967
1984	4 053	2 348	3 083	2 120	3 564	3 350	1 150	71 375
1985	4 164	2 372	3 152	2 164	3 668	3 382	1 166	72 828
1986	4 277	2 396	3 224	2 208	3 776	3 413	1 180	74 302
1987	4 390	2 415	3 302	2 252	3 887	3 444	1 191	75 788
1988	4 473	2 430	3 387	2 297	4 000	3 475	1 198	77 266
1989	4 604	2 446	3 480	2 342	4 117	3 506	1 200	78 809
1990	4 740	2 466	3 591	2 388	4 236	3 537	1 198	80 368
1991	4 880	2 488	3 708	2 434	4 359	3 571	1 194	81 993
1992	5 021	2 509	3 820	2 480	4 484	3 604	1 186	83 605
1993	5 163	2 529	3 935	2 524	4 612	3 644	1 177	85 236
1994	5 304	2 551	4 057	2 567	4 743	3 687	1 166	86 863
1995	5 445	2 574	4 185	2 609	4 876	3 731	1 155	88 495
1996	5 585	2 595	4 317	2 651	5 012	3 783	1 143	90 148
1997	5 725	2 616	4 450	2 693	5 150	3 828	1 130	91 800
1998	5 862	2 635	4 583	2 736	5 291	3 860	1 117	93 441

Table C2–a. **Total Population of 44 Latin American Countries, Annual Estimates, 1950–98**
(000 at mid–year)

	Total 8 core countries	*Total 15 countries*	*Total 21 small Caribbean countries*	*Total 44 countries*
1950	131 597	32 178	2 062	165 837
1951	135 292	32 908	2 111	170 311
1952	139 070	33 643	2 161	174 875
1953	142 961	34 393	2 211	179 565
1954	146 985	35 214	2 267	184 466
1955	151 158	36 099	2 323	189 580
1956	155 493	36 980	2 378	194 851
1957	159 985	37 894	2 435	200 315
1958	164 639	38 857	2 494	205 990
1959	169 457	39 859	2 555	211 871
1960	174 446	40 886	2 614	217 946
1961	179 498	41 877	2 662	224 038
1962	184 674	42 974	2 711	230 359
1963	189 963	44 126	2 781	236 870
1964	195 370	45 359	2 841	243 570
1965	200 903	46 610	2 900	250 412
1966	206 499	47 875	2 959	257 334
1967	212 193	49 118	3 014	264 325
1968	217 994	50 372	3 071	271 436
1969	223 913	51 660	3 121	278 694
1970	229 994	52 888	3 164	286 046
1971	236 110	54 150	3 214	293 473
1972	242 193	55 493	3 263	300 949
1973	248 323	56 819	3 308	308 451
1974	254 502	58 167	3 340	316 009
1975	260 706	59 525	3 347	323 578
1976	266 960	60 920	3 350	331 230
1977	273 237	62 286	3 364	338 887
1978	279 558	63 619	3 383	346 560
1979	285 990	64 979	3 397	354 366
1980	292 519	66 113	3 410	362 041
1981	299 230	67 346	3 434	370 010
1982	306 072	68 619	3 464	378 155
1983	312 750	69 967	3 494	386 211
1984	319 192	71 375	3 527	394 093
1985	325 595	72 828	3 561	401 985
1986	332 214	74 302	3 593	410 109
1987	338 922	75 788	3 622	418 332
1988	345 702	77 266	3 653	426 621
1989	352 457	78 809	3 684	434 950
1990	358 955	80 368	3 726	443 049
1991	365 402	81 993	3 758	451 153
1992	371 891	83 605	3 790	459 285
1993	378 346	85 236	3 824	467 406
1994	384 807	86 863	3 856	475 526
1995	391 261	88 495	3 889	483 645
1996	397 653	90 148	3 922	491 723
1997	403 969	91 800	3 955	499 724
1998	410 192	93 441	3 990	507 623

Table C2–b. **Levels of GDP in 8 Latin American Countries, Annual Estimates, 1950–98**
(million 1990 international Geary–Khamis dollars)

	Argentina	Brazil	Chile	Colombia	Mexico	Peru	Uruguay	Venezuela	Total
1950	85 524	89 342	23 274	24 955	67 368	17 270	10 224	37 377	355 334
1951	88 866	93 608	24 274	25 726	72 578	18 669	11 015	39 979	374 715
1952	84 333	99 181	25 663	27 350	75 481	19 848	11 167	43 472	386 495
1953	88 866	103 957	27 006	29 026	75 688	20 901	11 736	45 147	402 327
1954	92 528	110 836	27 117	31 042	83 258	22 246	12 488	49 820	429 335
1955	99 125	118 960	27 080	32 242	90 307	23 317	12 593	53 991	457 615
1956	101 856	120 674	27 238	33 539	96 502	24 316	12 807	58 677	475 609
1957	107 087	130 717	30 090	34 766	103 812	25 936	12 932	67 414	512 754
1958	113 655	142 577	30 915	35 639	109 333	25 805	13 292	68 540	539 756
1959	106 303	154 538	30 748	38 207	112 599	26 737	12 125	72 658	553 915
1960	114 614	167 397	32 767	39 831	121 723	30 017	12 554	72 889	591 792
1961	122 809	179 951	34 341	41 847	126 365	32 226	12 912	70 643	621 094
1962	120 833	190 932	35 971	44 120	132 039	34 922	12 624	73 762	645 203
1963	117 927	192 912	38 240	45 571	141 839	36 217	12 686	77 134	662 526
1964	130 074	199 423	39 092	48 389	157 312	38 580	12 940	83 688	709 498
1965	141 960	203 444	39 407	50 136	167 116	40 501	13 088	89 240	744 892
1966	142 919	216 181	43 797	52 806	177 427	43 921	13 536	90 842	781 429
1967	146 755	224 877	45 223	55 028	188 258	45 581	12 975	96 334	815 031
1968	153 002	244 921	46 844	58 398	201 669	45 734	13 181	102 916	866 665
1969	166 080	266 292	48 585	62 116	213 924	47 448	13 984	106 612	925 041
1970	174 972	292 480	49 586	66 308	227 970	50 229	14 638	114 807	990 990
1971	183 458	322 159	54 022	70 250	237 480	52 331	14 498	116 494	1 050 692
1972	189 183	356 880	53 373	75 637	257 636	53 838	13 992	117 982	1 118 521
1973	200 720	401 643	50 401	80 728	279 302	56 713	14 098	126 364	1 209 969
1974	213 739	433 322	50 891	85 370	296 370	61 969	14 541	129 038	1 285 240
1975	211 850	455 918	44 316	87 347	312 998	64 075	15 406	132 728	1 324 638
1976	211 327	498 823	45 881	91 488	326 267	65 334	16 026	142 978	1 398 124
1977	224 084	522 154	50 401	95 283	337 499	65 600	16 205	151 927	1 463 153
1978	214 233	548 342	54 540	103 366	365 340	65 784	17 058	155 528	1 524 191
1979	229 547	587 289	59 060	108 906	398 788	69 609	18 110	156 752	1 628 061
1980	232 802	639 093	63 654	113 375	431 983	72 723	19 205	149 735	1 722 570
1981	219 434	611 007	67 192	115 789	469 972	76 035	19 575	149 253	1 728 257
1982	212 518	614 538	57 634	116 938	466 649	76 147	17 724	146 150	1 708 298
1983	220 016	593 575	57 245	118 806	446 602	66 567	16 688	140 665	1 660 164
1984	224 491	625 438	60 875	123 037	462 678	69 650	16 505	142 664	1 725 338
1985	209 641	675 090	62 366	127 076	475 505	71 247	16 746	144 843	1 782 514
1986	224 985	729 252	65 895	134 844	457 655	77 857	18 231	152 244	1 860 963
1987	230 797	753 685	69 674	142 086	466 148	84 237	19 676	157 698	1 924 001
1988	226 438	751 910	74 814	147 896	471 953	77 285	19 676	166 879	1 936 851
1989	212 373	776 547	82 269	152 686	491 767	68 399	19 930	152 577	1 956 548
1990	212 518	743 765	84 038	159 042	516 692	64 979	20 105	160 648	1 961 787
1991	233 770	751 203	90 173	161 587	538 508	66 603	20 687	177 516	2 040 047
1992	254 575	748 949	100 092	167 889	558 049	66 004	22 218	189 942	2 107 718
1993	269 341	782 652	106 698	175 444	568 934	69 766	22 907	189 182	2 184 924
1994	291 696	831 176	112 139	186 496	594 054	79 254	24 166	182 183	2 301 164
1995	282 653	866 086	122 344	196 567	557 419	86 070	23 683	192 931	2 327 753
1996	295 090	891 202	130 786	200 695	586 144	88 050	24 867	192 160	2 408 994
1997	318 698	925 068	139 941	203 706	625 759	95 622	26 112	204 843	2 539 749
1998	334 314	926 918	144 279	205 132	655 910	95 718	27 313	204 433	2 594 017

Table C2–b. Levels of GDP in 15 Latin American Countries, Annual Estimates, 1950–98
(million 1990 international Geary–Khamis dollars)

	Bolivia	Costa Rica	Cuba	Dominican Republic	Ecuador	El Salvador	Guatemala	Haiti
1950	5 309	1 702	19 613	2 416	6 278	2 888	6 190	3 254
1951	5 683	1 747	19 829	2 701	6 346	2 945	6 277	3 302
1952	5 855	1 958	20 045	2 921	7 129	3 166	6 408	3 489
1953	5 301	2 256	20 281	2 884	7 279	3 392	6 643	3 378
1954	5 412	2 275	20 495	3 049	7 867	3 431	6 767	3 654
1955	5 698	2 538	20 731	3 237	8 074	3 608	6 934	3 507
1956	5 360	2 466	20 966	3 562	8 373	3 891	7 565	3 814
1957	5 183	2 676	21 202	3 787	8 751	4 098	7 992	3 587
1958	5 306	3 007	21 438	3 989	9 007	4 187	8 365	3 871
1959	5 289	3 118	21 672	4 012	9 490	4 375	8 778	3 688
1960	5 516	3 389	21 908	4 209	10 106	4 553	8 992	3 926
1961	5 631	3 530	22 222	4 114	10 360	4 713	9 378	3 767
1962	5 945	3 746	22 556	4 815	10 911	5 276	9 709	4 128
1963	6 327	4 067	22 888	5 129	11 189	5 504	10 635	3 860
1964	6 632	4 265	23 241	5 472	11 977	6 017	11 128	3 772
1965	6 958	4 651	23 595	4 791	13 131	6 340	11 613	3 813
1966	7 461	5 013	23 928	5 434	13 475	6 794	12 255	3 790
1967	7 928	5 320	24 301	5 617	14 188	7 164	12 757	3 713
1968	8 604	5 730	24 653	5 628	14 973	7 396	13 877	3 860
1969	8 989	6 111	25 026	6 244	15 792	7 653	14 532	3 986
1970	9 459	6 515	25 399	6 906	16 899	7 881	15 364	4 174
1971	9 820	6 945	24 046	7 637	17 872	8 245	16 221	4 445
1972	10 321	7 556	23 281	8 581	18 972	8 712	17 412	4 603
1973	11 030	8 145	29 165	9 617	21 337	9 084	18 593	4 810
1974	11 598	8 583	25 870	10 171	22 585	9 675	19 779	5 114
1975	12 364	8 755	24 811	10 659	23 772	10 193	20 164	4 995
1976	13 118	9 231	25 125	11 377	26 075	10 572	21 654	5 422
1977	13 670	10 055	25 458	11 930	27 731	11 189	23 344	5 448
1978	14 128	10 677	25 792	12 207	29 664	11 935	24 511	5 710
1979	14 125	11 207	25 811	12 733	31 274	11 744	25 667	6 127
1980	13 995	11 290	25 850	13 511	32 706	10 748	26 632	6 591
1981	14 124	11 035	26 851	14 069	34 041	9 869	26 804	6 410
1982	13 508	10 266	28 204	14 324	34 421	9 324	25 858	6 191
1983	12 905	10 551	29 754	14 959	33 702	9 386	25 193	6 238
1984	13 034	11 379	31 969	14 999	35 081	9 595	25 321	6 256
1985	12 943	11 475	33 284	14 620	36 570	9 819	25 167	6 269
1986	12 530	12 107	32 538	15 057	37 648	9 926	25 199	6 261
1987	12 858	12 683	30 930	16 189	35 288	10 193	26 094	6 214
1988	13 348	13 114	32 029	16 300	39 060	10 384	27 110	6 263
1989	13 735	13 867	32 048	18 377	39 123	10 491	28 179	6 329
1990	14 446	14 370	31 087	17 503	40 267	10 805	29 050	6 323
1991	15 226	14 686	27 481	17 643	42 280	11 108	30 125	6 329
1992	15 485	15 729	24 238	18 772	43 549	11 918	31 601	5 456
1993	16 135	16 641	21 039	19 148	44 507	12 681	32 865	5 336
1994	16 910	17 357	21 039	19 971	46 465	13 442	34 212	4 893
1995	17 705	17 739	21 417	20 870	47 859	14 275	35 923	5 138
1996	17 670	17 650	22 981	22 289	48 960	14 532	37 001	5 281
1997	18 394	18 268	23 555	23 871	50 869	15 143	38 592	5 361
1998	19 241	19 272	23 909	25 304	51 378	15 627	40 522	5 532

Table C2–b. **Levels of GDP in 15 Latin American Countries, Annual Estimates, 1950–98**
(million 1990 international Geary–Khamis dollars)

	Honduras	Jamaica	Nicaragua	Panama	Paraguay	Puerto Rico	Trinidad & Tobago	Total
1950	1 880	1 837	1 774	1 710	2 338	4 755	2 322	64 266
1951	1 982	1 985	1 894	1 695	2 383	4 929	2 526	66 224
1952	2 058	2 145	2 215	1 787	2 343	5 214	2 612	69 345
1953	2 220	2 446	2 268	1 895	2 410	5 445	2 682	70 780
1954	2 094	2 727	2 480	1 963	2 452	5 669	2 730	73 065
1955	2 149	3 008	2 646	2 077	2 564	5 961	3 111	75 843
1956	2 322	3 307	2 645	2 185	2 672	6 388	3 756	79 272
1957	2 429	3 789	2 868	2 414	2 795	6 708	4 088	82 367
1958	2 506	3 849	2 877	2 432	2 952	6 901	4 423	85 110
1959	2 569	4 064	2 920	2 589	2 944	7 521	4 692	87 721
1960	2 728	4 330	2 960	2 744	2 970	8 066	5 258	91 655
1961	2 798	4 453	3 182	3 040	3 111	8 835	5 488	94 622
1962	2 959	4 533	3 529	3 295	3 330	9 500	5 781	100 013
1963	3 069	4 681	3 912	3 606	3 421	10 488	6 076	104 852
1964	3 229	5 050	4 370	3 761	3 569	11 232	6 283	109 998
1965	3 509	5 456	4 786	4 091	3 773	12 254	6 603	115 364
1966	3 713	5 695	4 944	4 395	3 815	13 119	6 891	120 722
1967	3 922	5 915	5 288	4 762	4 058	13 944	7 035	125 912
1968	4 154	6 218	5 360	5 109	4 202	14 606	7 400	131 770
1969	4 187	6 681	5 716	5 507	4 365	15 899	7 604	138 292
1970	4 296	7 481	5 771	5 839	4 636	17 280	7 873	145 773
1971	4 462	7 481	6 055	6 312	4 839	18 375	7 954	150 709
1972	4 635	7 706	6 248	6 645	5 088	19 732	8 414	157 906
1973	4 866	8 411	6 566	7 052	5 487	20 908	8 553	173 624
1974	4 826	8 095	7 505	7 221	5 945	20 919	9 011	176 897
1975	4 949	8 093	7 493	7 338	6 328	20 388	9 181	179 483
1976	5 467	7 603	7 880	7 458	6 758	21 464	10 059	189 263
1977	6 047	7 443	8 556	7 546	7 478	22 867	10 698	199 460
1978	6 662	7 496	7 884	8 285	8 297	24 379	11 947	209 574
1979	6 976	7 363	5 785	8 651	9 215	25 868	12 500	215 046
1980	7 014	6 957	6 043	9 961	10 549	26 263	13 501	221 611
1981	7 196	7 142	6 367	10 367	11 458	26 544	14 096	226 373
1982	7 078	7 237	6 312	10 939	11 058	25 734	13 271	223 725
1983	7 030	7 405	6 609	11 013	10 724	25 855	12 231	223 555
1984	7 312	7 343	6 474	10 963	11 061	27 747	12 967	231 501
1985	7 640	7 003	6 204	11 480	11 501	28 319	12 436	234 730
1986	7 710	7 119	6 077	11 857	11 486	30 630	12 028	238 173
1987	8 167	7 668	6 035	12 150	11 988	32 136	11 473	240 066
1988	8 571	7 889	5 367	10 256	12 764	34 228	11 027	247 710
1989	8 894	8 428	5 296	10 215	13 509	35 919	10 937	255 347
1990	8 898	8 890	5 297	10 688	13 923	37 277	11 110	259 934
1991	9 138	8 917	5 281	11 650	14 271	38 136	11 499	263 770
1992	9 668	9 140	5 323	12 605	14 514	39 877	11 372	269 247
1993	10 355	9 304	5 302	13 273	15 094	41 729	11 236	274 645
1994	10 158	9 481	5 514	13 685	15 547	43 475	11 708	283 857
1995	10 534	9 642	5 762	13 945	16 247	45 453	12 188	294 697
1996	10 934	9 594	6 050	14 321	16 425	46 706	12 675	303 069
1997	11 481	9 373	6 383	15 009	16 820	48 882	13 208	315 209
1998	11 929	9 308	6 651	15 609	16 719	51 159	13 683	325 843

Table C2–b. **Total GDP in 44 Latin American Countries, Annual Estimates, 1950–98**
(million 1990 international Geary–Khamis dollars)

	Total 8 core countries	*Total 15 countries*	*Total 21 small Caribbean countries*	*Total 44 countries*
1950	355 334	64 266	3 956	423 556
1951	374 715	66 224	4 180	445 119
1952	386 495	69 345	4 418	460 258
1953	402 327	70 780	4 670	477 777
1954	429 335	73 065	4 935	507 335
1955	457 615	75 843	5 215	538 673
1956	475 609	79 272	5 512	560 393
1957	512 754	82 367	5 825	600 946
1958	539 756	85 110	6 156	631 022
1959	553 915	87 721	6 506	648 142
1960	591 792	91 655	6 876	690 323
1961	621 094	94 622	7 266	722 982
1962	645 203	100 013	7 679	752 895
1963	662 526	104 852	8 116	775 494
1964	709 498	109 998	8 577	828 073
1965	744 892	115 364	9 064	869 320
1966	781 429	120 722	9 579	911 730
1967	815 031	125 912	10 124	951 067
1968	866 665	131 770	10 699	1 009 134
1969	925 041	138 292	11 307	1 074 640
1970	990 990	145 773	11 950	1 148 713
1971	1 050 692	150 709	12 629	1 214 030
1972	1 118 521	157 906	13 347	1 289 774
1973	1 209 969	173 624	14 105	1 397 698
1974	1 285 240	176 897	14 295	1 476 432
1975	1 324 638	179 483	14 487	1 518 608
1976	1 398 124	189 263	14 682	1 602 069
1977	1 463 153	199 460	14 880	1 677 493
1978	1 524 191	209 574	15 081	1 748 846
1979	1 628 061	215 046	15 284	1 858 391
1980	1 722 570	221 611	15 489	1 959 670
1981	1 728 257	226 373	15 698	1 970 328
1982	1 708 298	223 725	15 909	1 947 932
1983	1 660 164	223 555	16 124	1 899 843
1984	1 725 338	231 501	16 341	1 973 180
1985	1 782 514	234 730	16 561	2 033 805
1986	1 860 963	238 173	16 784	2 115 920
1987	1 924 001	240 066	17 010	2 181 077
1988	1 936 851	247 710	17 239	2 201 800
1989	1 956 548	255 347	17 471	2 229 366
1990	1 961 787	259 934	17 706	2 239 427
1991	2 040 047	263 770	18 167	2 321 984
1992	2 107 718	269 247	18 640	2 395 605
1993	2 184 924	274 645	19 126	2 478 695
1994	2 301 164	283 857	19 624	2 604 645
1995	2 327 753	294 697	20 135	2 642 585
1996	2 408 994	303 069	20 659	2 732 722
1997	2 539 749	315 209	21 197	2 876 155
1998	2 594 017	325 843	21 749	2 941 609

Table C2–c. **Levels of Per Capita GDP in 8 Latin American Countries, Annual Estimates, 1950–98**
(million 1990 international Geary–Khamis dollars)

	Argentina	Brazil	Chile	Colombia	Mexico	Peru	Uruguay	Venezuela	Average
1950	4 987	1 672	3 821	2 153	2 365	2 263	4 659	7 462	2 700
1951	5 073	1 702	3 883	2 150	2 477	2 385	4 955	7 663	2 770
1952	4 717	1 752	4 024	2 214	2 504	2 473	4 957	7 992	2 779
1953	4 874	1 784	4 159	2 277	2 439	2 539	5 139	7 956	2 814
1954	4 980	1 848	4 101	2 358	2 605	2 634	5 391	8 417	2 921
1955	5 237	1 926	4 016	2 373	2 742	2 689	5 352	8 750	3 027
1956	5 285	1 896	3 954	2 391	2 843	2 731	5 360	9 124	3 059
1957	5 461	1 994	4 269	2 400	2 965	2 836	5 333	10 058	3 205
1958	5 698	2 111	4 282	2 383	3 025	2 746	5 402	9 816	3 278
1959	5 241	2 221	4 155	2 473	3 016	2 768	4 860	9 997	3 269
1960	5 559	2 335	4 320	2 497	3 155	3 023	4 960	9 646	3 392
1961	5 862	2 437	4 418	2 540	3 172	3 154	5 036	9 002	3 460
1962	5 677	2 511	4 518	2 594	3 211	3 321	4 858	9 058	3 494
1963	5 455	2 463	4 694	2 597	3 343	3 345	4 820	9 134	3 488
1964	5 926	2 472	4 693	2 675	3 594	3 462	4 858	9 562	3 632
1965	6 371	2 448	4 631	2 689	3 702	3 532	4 860	9 841	3 708
1966	6 321	2 527	5 042	2 750	3 813	3 723	4 974	9 677	3 784
1967	6 399	2 554	5 105	2 784	3 922	3 757	4 721	9 922	3 841
1968	6 578	2 704	5 188	2 874	4 073	3 666	4 747	10 249	3 976
1969	7 037	2 860	5 281	2 976	4 185	3 698	4 991	10 262	4 131
1970	7 302	3 057	5 293	3 094	4 320	3 807	5 184	10 672	4 309
1971	7 533	3 279	5 663	3 194	4 363	3 857	5 130	10 446	4 450
1972	7 642	3 539	5 492	3 355	4 597	3 858	4 945	10 245	4 618
1973	7 973	3 882	5 093	3 499	4 845	3 952	4 974	10 625	4 873
1974	8 350	4 083	5 050	3 618	5 003	4 200	5 123	10 507	5 050
1975	8 142	4 190	4 323	3 622	5 146	4 226	5 421	10 472	5 081
1976	7 988	4 472	4 398	3 716	5 228	4 195	5 608	10 929	5 237
1977	8 332	4 568	4 755	3 797	5 275	4 103	5 639	11 251	5 355
1978	7 837	4 682	5 069	4 047	5 573	4 008	5 903	11 164	5 452
1979	8 262	4 893	5 407	4 184	5 941	4 131	6 234	10 920	5 693
1980	8 245	5 199	5 738	4 265	6 289	4 205	6 577	10 139	5 889
1981	7 646	4 853	5 956	4 263	6 683	4 283	6 668	9 841	5 776
1982	7 290	4 766	5 017	4 212	6 488	4 176	6 000	9 356	5 581
1983	7 437	4 501	4 898	4 185	6 079	3 559	5 614	8 745	5 308
1984	7 485	4 647	5 125	4 239	6 170	3 633	5 520	8 623	5 405
1985	6 894	4 918	5 168	4 282	6 212	3 631	5 567	8 521	5 475
1986	7 292	5 206	5 375	4 445	5 857	3 879	6 023	8 725	5 602
1987	7 373	5 274	5 590	4 582	5 845	4 103	6 461	8 805	5 677
1988	7 132	5 159	5 901	4 668	5 797	3 680	6 422	9 080	5 603
1989	6 597	5 228	6 377	4 721	5 920	3 183	6 462	8 094	5 551
1990	6 512	4 924	6 402	4 822	6 097	2 955	6 474	8 313	5 465
1991	7 066	4 895	6 753	4 805	6 230	2 960	6 614	8 965	5 583
1992	7 592	4 803	7 374	4 895	6 331	2 868	7 055	9 373	5 668
1993	7 930	4 943	7 738	5 016	6 331	2 965	7 223	9 137	5 775
1994	8 477	5 171	8 010	5 227	6 486	3 296	7 566	8 618	5 980
1995	8 104	5 310	8 612	5 401	5 973	3 504	7 363	8 947	5 949
1996	8 351	5 387	9 080	5 406	6 166	3 511	7 677	8 741	6 058
1997	8 903	5 518	9 587	5 382	6 464	3 736	8 006	9 146	6 287
1998	9 219	5 459	9 757	5 317	6 655	3 666	8 315	8 965	6 324

Table C2–c. **Levels of Per Capita GDP in 15 Latin American Countries, Annual Estimates, 1950–98**
(million 1990 international Geary–Khamis dollars)

	Bolivia	Costa Rica	Cuba	Dominican Republic	Ecuador	El Salvador	Guatemala	Haiti
1950	1 919	1 963	3 390	1 045	1 897	1 489	2 085	1 051
1951	2 013	1 951	3 366	1 137	1 865	1 481	2 054	1 049
1952	2 031	2 114	3 336	1 195	2 038	1 551	2 037	1 090
1953	1 800	2 353	3 309	1 145	2 024	1 617	2 051	1 037
1954	1 799	2 289	3 277	1 174	2 127	1 591	2 029	1 102
1955	1 853	2 460	3 249	1 206	2 121	1 627	2 019	1 039
1956	1 706	2 301	3 219	1 282	2 137	1 704	2 140	1 108
1957	1 614	2 406	3 193	1 318	2 169	1 743	2 195	1 023
1958	1 616	2 605	3 170	1 344	2 168	1 729	2 231	1 082
1959	1 575	2 598	3 140	1 310	2 217	1 752	2 274	1 011
1960	1 606	2 715	3 118	1 332	2 290	1 769	2 262	1 055
1961	1 603	2 723	3 115	1 276	2 276	1 774	2 293	991
1962	1 654	2 785	3 109	1 433	2 324	1 927	2 307	1 064
1963	1 720	2 919	3 087	1 478	2 309	1 948	2 457	974
1964	1 762	2 961	3 053	1 525	2 395	2 066	2 499	931
1965	1 806	3 127	3 021	1 290	2 544	2 110	2 535	922
1966	1 891	3 258	2 997	1 412	2 528	2 182	2 601	897
1967	1 962	3 349	2 986	1 411	2 578	2 227	2 632	860
1968	2 079	3 497	2 976	1 368	2 635	2 221	2 782	875
1969	2 120	3 622	2 972	1 471	2 693	2 218	2 831	884
1970	2 176	3 754	2 973	1 579	2 793	2 199	2 906	906
1971	2 204	3 889	2 774	1 694	2 864	2 236	2 975	955
1972	2 260	4 118	2 636	1 848	2 950	2 313	3 097	979
1973	2 357	4 319	3 240	2 012	3 219	2 358	3 205	1 013
1974	2 418	4 428	2 826	2 069	3 307	2 453	3 304	1 066
1975	2 516	4 392	2 671	2 110	3 378	2 522	3 264	1 032
1976	2 610	4 500	2 667	2 191	3 600	2 551	3 397	1 111
1977	2 666	4 760	2 669	2 237	3 720	2 633	3 547	1 106
1978	2 700	4 859	2 677	2 231	3 867	2 737	3 609	1 149
1979	2 647	4 945	2 658	2 269	3 962	2 627	3 662	1 221
1980	2 573	4 894	2 678	2 372	4 026	2 374	3 683	1 304
1981	2 547	4 664	2 765	2 415	4 071	2 205	3 580	1 259
1982	2 390	4 217	2 881	2 405	4 000	2 103	3 354	1 202
1983	2 239	4 210	3 010	2 458	3 816	2 096	3 190	1 189
1984	2 218	4 432	3 203	2 414	3 876	2 112	3 119	1 168
1985	2 160	4 346	3 302	2 305	3 945	2 127	3 014	1 146
1986	2 050	4 457	3 202	2 326	3 970	2 111	2 933	1 120
1987	2 063	4 541	3 021	2 452	3 640	2 128	2 950	1 089
1988	2 099	4 569	3 099	2 420	3 944	2 129	2 978	1 075
1989	2 117	4 706	3 070	2 676	3 870	2 115	3 009	1 066
1990	2 182	4 754	2 948	2 501	3 906	2 143	3 016	1 045
1991	2 254	4 741	2 582	2 476	3 997	2 168	3 043	1 032
1992	2 246	4 958	2 260	2 588	4 013	2 287	3 105	878
1993	2 289	5 127	1 950	2 597	4 002	2 392	3 141	846
1994	2 348	5 230	1 940	2 667	4 083	2 493	3 180	765
1995	2 406	5 231	1 965	2 742	4 116	2 604	3 248	792
1996	2 352	5 097	2 098	2 880	4 125	2 608	3 254	802
1997	2 398	5 169	2 141	3 034	4 202	2 675	3 302	803
1998	2 458	5 346	2 164	3 163	4 165	2 717	3 375	816

Table C2–c. **Levels of Per Capita GDP in 15 Latin American Countries,**
Annual Estimates, 1950–98
(million 1990 international Geary–Khamis dollars)

	Honduras	Jamaica	Nicaragua	Panama	Paraguay	Puerto Rico	Trinidad & Tobago	Average
1950	1 313	1 327	1 616	1 916	1 584	2 144	3 674	1 997
1951	1 344	1 412	1 674	1 851	1 573	2 205	3 894	2 012
1952	1 356	1 504	1 900	1 901	1 506	2 341	3 941	2 061
1953	1 421	1 691	1 888	1 969	1 509	2 471	3 954	2 058
1954	1 300	1 858	2 002	1 993	1 495	2 561	3 914	2 075
1955	1 293	2 020	2 072	2 055	1 523	2 649	4 316	2 101
1956	1 354	2 190	2 008	2 108	1 547	2 840	5 059	2 144
1957	1 372	2 468	2 111	2 270	1 578	2 968	5 344	2 174
1958	1 370	2 458	2 052	2 241	1 625	3 002	5 609	2 190
1959	1 360	2 541	2 019	2 322	1 581	3 239	5 743	2 201
1960	1 398	2 654	1 983	2 391	1 555	3 421	6 251	2 242
1961	1 387	2 702	2 065	2 574	1 588	3 677	6 371	2 260
1962	1 421	2 722	2 219	2 710	1 657	3 881	6 514	2 327
1963	1 427	2 757	2 382	2 882	1 659	4 201	6 718	2 376
1964	1 452	2 904	2 578	2 920	1 687	4 401	6 801	2 425
1965	1 526	3 070	2 734	3 085	1 739	4 719	7 030	2 475
1966	1 563	3 129	2 736	3 219	1 712	4 993	7 234	2 522
1967	1 599	3 178	2 835	3 388	1 774	5 264	7 327	2 563
1968	1 639	3 284	2 783	3 531	1 789	5 463	7 684	2 616
1969	1 599	3 480	2 875	3 699	1 810	5 840	7 897	2 677
1970	1 601	3 849	2 812	3 814	1 872	6 349	8 244	2 756
1971	1 613	3 803	2 856	4 012	1 902	6 642	8 272	2 783
1972	1 618	3 858	2 867	4 111	1 946	6 930	8 628	2 846
1973	1 642	4 130	2 929	4 250	2 038	7 302	8 685	3 056
1974	1 574	3 908	3 248	4 232	2 144	7 247	9 053	3 041
1975	1 571	3 845	3 144	4 198	2 220	6 946	9 118	3 015
1976	1 689	3 564	3 205	4 167	2 315	7 093	9 847	3 107
1977	1 818	3 451	3 373	4 102	2 506	7 422	10 296	3 202
1978	1 945	3 439	3 047	4 424	2 719	7 819	11 319	3 294
1979	1 982	3 336	2 172	4 518	2 954	8 164	11 649	3 309
1980	1 935	3 121	2 177	5 091	3 304	8 183	12 380	3 352
1981	1 922	3 162	2 219	5 194	3 498	8 195	12 794	3 361
1982	1 840	3 150	2 144	5 372	3 285	7 848	11 888	3 260
1983	1 781	3 188	2 194	5 301	3 097	7 797	10 794	3 195
1984	1 804	3 128	2 100	5 172	3 104	8 283	11 273	3 243
1985	1 835	2 952	1 968	5 306	3 135	8 373	10 664	3 223
1986	1 803	2 972	1 885	5 370	3 042	8 974	10 192	3 205
1987	1 861	3 176	1 828	5 394	3 085	9 330	9 631	3 168
1988	1 916	3 247	1 585	4 465	3 191	9 850	9 202	3 206
1989	1 932	3 445	1 522	4 361	3 282	10 246	9 112	3 240
1990	1 877	3 605	1 475	4 476	3 287	10 539	9 271	3 234
1991	1 873	3 584	1 424	4 786	3 274	10 678	9 630	3 217
1992	1 925	3 643	1 394	5 083	3 237	11 065	9 586	3 220
1993	2 006	3 679	1 347	5 259	3 273	11 453	9 550	3 222
1994	1 915	3 716	1 359	5 332	3 278	11 791	10 038	3 268
1995	1 935	3 746	1 377	5 345	3 332	12 183	10 550	3 330
1996	1 958	3 697	1 401	5 402	3 277	12 347	11 087	3 362
1997	2 006	3 584	1 434	5 572	3 266	12 769	11 685	3 434
1998	2 035	3 533	1 451	5 705	3 160	13 253	12 254	3 487

Table C2–c. **Average Levels of Per Capita GDP in 44 Latin American Countries, Annual Estimates, 1950–98**
(million 1990 international Geary–Khamis dollars)

	Total 8 core countries	*Total 15 countries*	*Total 21 small Caribbean countries*	*Total 44 countries*
1950	2 700	1 997	1 919	2 554
1951	2 770	2 012	1 980	2 614
1952	2 779	2 061	2 044	2 632
1953	2 814	2 058	2 112	2 661
1954	2 921	2 075	2 177	2 750
1955	3 027	2 101	2 245	2 841
1956	3 059	2 144	2 318	2 876
1957	3 205	2 174	2 392	3 000
1958	3 278	2 190	2 468	3 063
1959	3 269	2 201	2 546	3 059
1960	3 392	2 242	2 630	3 167
1961	3 460	2 260	2 730	3 227
1962	3 494	2 327	2 833	3 268
1963	3 488	2 376	2 918	3 274
1964	3 632	2 425	3 019	3 400
1965	3 708	2 475	3 126	3 472
1966	3 784	2 522	3 237	3 543
1967	3 841	2 563	3 359	3 598
1968	3 976	2 616	3 484	3 718
1969	4 131	2 677	3 623	3 856
1970	4 309	2 756	3 777	4 016
1971	4 450	2 783	3 929	4 137
1972	4 618	2 846	4 090	4 286
1973	4 873	3 056	4 264	4 531
1974	5 050	3 041	4 280	4 672
1975	5 081	3 015	4 328	4 693
1976	5 237	3 107	4 383	4 837
1977	5 355	3 202	4 423	4 950
1978	5 452	3 294	4 458	5 046
1979	5 693	3 309	4 499	5 244
1980	5 889	3 352	4 542	5 413
1981	5 776	3 361	4 571	5 325
1982	5 581	3 260	4 593	5 151
1983	5 308	3 195	4 615	4 919
1984	5 405	3 243	4 633	5 007
1985	5 475	3 223	4 651	5 059
1986	5 602	3 205	4 671	5 159
1987	5 677	3 168	4 696	5 214
1988	5 603	3 206	4 719	5 161
1989	5 551	3 240	4 742	5 126
1990	5 465	3 234	4 752	5 055
1991	5 583	3 217	4 834	5 147
1992	5 668	3 220	4 918	5 216
1993	5 775	3 222	5 002	5 303
1994	5 980	3 268	5 089	5 477
1995	5 949	3 330	5 177	5 464
1996	6 058	3 362	5 267	5 557
1997	6 287	3 434	5 360	5 755
1998	6 324	3 487	5 451	5 795

Table C3–a. **Population of 16 East Asian Countries, Annual Estimates 1950–99**
(000 at mid–year)

	China	India	Indonesia	Japan	Philippines	South Korea	Thailand	Taiwan
1950	546 815	359 000	79 043	83 563	21 131	20 846	20 042	7 882
1951	557 480	365 000	80 525	84 974	21 777	20 876	20 653	8 255
1952	568 910	372 000	82 052	86 293	22 443	20 948	21 289	8 541
1953	581 390	379 000	83 611	87 463	23 129	21 060	21 964	8 822
1954	595 310	386 000	85 196	88 752	23 836	21 259	22 685	9 134
1955	608 655	393 000	86 807	89 790	24 565	21 552	23 451	9 480
1956	621 465	401 000	88 456	90 727	25 316	22 031	24 244	9 823
1957	637 408	409 000	90 124	91 513	26 090	22 612	25 042	10 133
1958	653 235	418 000	91 821	92 349	26 888	23 254	25 845	10 460
1959	666 005	426 000	93 565	93 237	27 710	23 981	26 667	10 806
1960	667 070	434 000	95 254	94 053	28 557	24 784	27 513	11 155
1961	660 330	444 000	97 085	94 890	29 443	25 614	28 376	11 510
1962	665 770	454 000	99 028	95 797	30 361	26 420	29 263	11 857
1963	682 335	464 000	101 009	96 765	31 313	27 211	30 174	12 210
1964	698 355	474 000	103 031	97 793	32 299	27 984	31 107	12 570
1965	715 185	485 000	105 093	98 883	33 317	28 705	32 062	12 928
1966	735 400	495 000	107 197	99 790	34 359	29 436	33 036	13 283
1967	754 550	506 000	109 343	100 850	35 416	30 131	34 024	13 617
1968	774 510	518 000	111 532	102 050	36 489	30 838	35 028	13 945
1969	796 025	529 000	113 765	103 231	37 577	31 544	36 050	14 264
1970	818 315	541 000	116 044	104 334	38 680	32 241	37 091	14 565
1971	841 105	554 000	118 368	105 677	39 801	32 883	38 202	14 865
1972	862 030	567 000	121 282	107 179	40 939	33 505	39 276	15 142
1973	881 940	580 000	124 271	108 660	42 094	34 073	40 302	15 427
1974	900 350	593 000	127 338	110 160	43 265	34 692	41 306	15 709
1975	916 395	607 000	130 485	111 520	44 447	35 281	42 272	16 001
1976	930 685	620 000	133 713	112 770	45 692	35 860	43 221	16 329
1977	943 455	634 000	137 026	113 880	46 976	36 436	44 148	16 661
1978	956 165	648 000	140 425	114 920	48 306	37 019	45 057	16 974
1979	969 005	664 000	143 912	115 880	49 680	37 534	46 004	17 308
1980	981 235	679 000	147 490	116 800	51 092	38 124	47 026	17 642
1981	993 861	692 000	150 657	117 650	52 423	38 723	47 924	17 970
1982	1 000 281	708 000	153 894	118 450	53 753	39 326	48 802	18 297
1983	1 023 288	723 000	157 204	119 260	55 079	39 910	49 655	18 596
1984	1 036 825	739 000	160 588	120 020	56 416	40 406	50 481	18 873
1985	1 051 040	755 000	164 047	120 750	57 784	40 806	51 275	19 136
1986	1 066 790	771 000	166 976	121 490	59 185	41 214	52 048	19 357
1987	1 084 035	788 000	169 959	122 090	60 602	41 622	52 813	19 564
1988	1 101 630	805 000	172 999	122 610	62 044	42 031	53 571	19 788
1989	1 118 650	822 000	176 094	123 120	63 529	42 449	54 317	20 006
1990	1 135 185	839 000	179 248	123 540	65 037	42 869	55 052	20 230
1991	1 150 780	856 000	182 223	123 920	66 558	43 246	55 702	20 460
1992	1 164 970	872 000	185 259	124 320	68 100	43 657	56 348	20 660
1993	1 178 440	891 000	188 359	124 670	69 664	44 099	56 988	20 850
1994	1 191 835	908 000	191 524	124 960	71 251	44 556	57 620	21 040
1995	1 204 855	927 000	194 755	125 570	72 860	45 018	58 241	21 220
1996	1 217 550	943 000	198 025	125 864	74 481	45 482	58 851	21 390
1997	1 230 075	959 000	201 350	126 166	76 104	45 991	59 451	21 580
1998	1 242 700	975 000	204 390	126 486	77 726	46 430	60 037	21 780
1999	1 252 704	991 691	207 429	126 737	79 376	46 898	60 609	21 984

Table C3–a. **Population of 16 East Asian Countries, Annual Estimates 1950–99**
(000 at mid–year)

	Bangladesh	Burma	Hong Kong	Malaysia	Nepal	Pakistan	Singapore	Sri Lanka	Total
1950	45 646	19 488	2 237	6 434	8 990	39 448	1 022	7 533	1 269 120
1951	46 152	19 788	2 015	6 582	9 086	40 382	1 068	7 752	1 292 365
1952	46 887	20 093	2 126	6 742	9 183	41 347	1 127	7 982	1 317 963
1953	47 660	20 403	2 242	6 929	9 280	42 342	1 192	8 221	1 344 708
1954	48 603	20 721	2 365	7 118	9 379	43 372	1 248	8 457	1 373 435
1955	49 602	21 049	2 490	7 312	9 479	44 434	1 306	8 679	1 401 651
1956	50 478	21 385	2 615	7 520	9 580	45 536	1 372	8 898	1 430 446
1957	51 365	21 732	2 736	7 739	9 682	46 680	1 446	9 129	1 462 431
1958	52 399	22 088	2 854	7 966	9 789	47 869	1 519	9 362	1 495 698
1959	53 485	22 456	2 967	8 196	9 906	49 104	1 587	9 610	1 525 282
1960	54 622	22 836	3 075	8 428	10 035	50 387	1 646	9 879	1 543 294
1961	55 741	23 229	3 168	8 663	10 176	51 719	1 702	10 152	1 555 798
1962	56 839	23 634	3 305	8 906	10 332	53 101	1 750	10 422	1 580 785
1963	58 226	24 053	3 421	9 148	10 500	54 524	1 795	10 687	1 617 371
1964	59 403	24 486	3 505	9 397	10 677	55 988	1 842	10 942	1 653 379
1965	60 332	24 933	3 598	9 648	10 862	57 495	1 887	11 202	1 691 130
1966	61 548	25 394	3 630	9 900	11 057	59 046	1 934	11 470	1 731 480
1967	62 822	25 870	3 723	10 155	11 262	60 642	1 978	11 737	1 772 120
1968	64 133	26 362	3 803	10 409	11 473	62 282	2 012	12 010	1 814 876
1969	65 483	26 867	3 864	10 662	11 692	63 970	2 043	12 275	1 858 312
1970	67 403	27 386	3 959	10 910	11 919	65 706	2 075	12 532	1 904 160
1971	69 227	27 919	4 045	11 171	12 155	67 491	2 113	12 776	1 951 798
1972	70 759	28 466	4 116	11 441	12 413	69 326	2 152	13 017	1 998 043
1973	72 471	29 227	4 213	11 712	12 685	71 121	2 193	13 246	2 043 635
1974	74 679	29 828	4 320	11 986	12 973	72 912	2 230	13 450	2 088 198
1975	76 253	30 445	4 396	12 267	12 278	74 712	2 263	13 660	2 129 675
1976	77 928	31 080	4 518	12 554	13 599	76 456	2 293	13 887	2 170 585
1977	80 428	31 735	4 584	12 845	13 933	78 153	2 325	14 117	2 210 702
1978	82 936	32 404	4 668	13 139	14 280	80 051	2 354	14 371	2 251 069
1979	85 492	33 081	4 930	13 444	14 641	82 374	2 384	14 649	2 294 318
1980	88 077	33 766	5 063	13 764	15 016	85 219	2 414	14 900	2 336 628
1981	90 666	34 460	5 183	14 097	15 403	88 417	2 470	15 152	2 377 056
1982	93 074	35 162	5 265	14 442	15 796	91 257	2 528	15 410	2 413 737
1983	95 384	35 873	5 345	14 794	16 200	93 720	2 586	15 618	2 465 512
1984	97 612	36 592	5 398	15 158	16 613	96 284	2 644	15 810	2 508 720
1985	99 753	37 319	5 456	15 546	17 037	99 053	2 703	16 021	2 552 726
1986	101 769	38 055	5 525	15 943	17 472	101 953	2 763	16 256	2 597 796
1987	103 764	38 800	5 585	16 334	17 918	104 887	2 824	16 495	2 645 292
1988	105 771	39 551	5 628	16 732	18 376	107 846	2 893	16 735	2 693 205
1989	107 807	40 308	5 661	17 121	18 848	110 848	2 966	16 971	2 740 695
1990	109 897	41 068	5 704	17 507	19 333	113 914	3 039	17 193	2 787 816
1991	111 936	41 834	5 750	17 911	19 831	116 909	3 096	17 391	2 833 547
1992	113 711	42 607	5 800	18 324	20 345	118 852	3 152	17 587	2 875 692
1993	115 453	43 385	5 900	18 753	20 874	120 853	3 209	17 823	2 920 320
1994	117 283	44 169	6 040	19 184	21 414	123 668	3 268	18 066	2 963 878
1995	119 188	44 955	6 160	19 615	21 966	126 404	3 326	18 290	3 009 423
1996	121 140	45 741	6 310	20 052	22 530	129 276	3 383	18 508	3 051 583
1997	123 112	46 525	6 500	20 491	23 107	132 185	3 441	18 721	3 093 799
1998	125 105	47 305	6 690	20 933	23 698	135 135	3 490	18 934	3 135 839
1999	127 118	48 081	6 830	21 376	24 303	138 123	3 532	19 154	3 175 945

Table C3–a. **Population of 25 East Asian Countries, Annual Estimates, 1950–98**
(000 at mid–year)

	Afghanistan	Cambodia	Laos	Mongolia	North Korea	Vietnam	19 small countries	Total
1950	8 150	4 163	1 886	779	9 471	25 348	3 411	53 208
1951	8 284	4 266	1 921	789	9 162	25 794	3 493	53 709
1952	8 425	4 371	1 957	801	8 865	26 247	3 577	54 243
1953	8 573	4 478	1 995	814	8 580	26 724	3 662	54 826
1954	8 728	4 589	2 035	828	8 572	27 210	3 750	55 712
1955	8 891	4 702	2 077	844	8 839	27 738	3 840	56 931
1956	9 062	4 827	2 121	862	9 116	28 327	3 932	58 247
1957	9 241	4 956	2 166	882	9 411	28 999	4 027	59 682
1958	9 429	5 088	2 213	904	9 727	29 775	4 123	61 259
1959	9 625	5 224	2 261	929	10 054	30 683	4 222	62 998
1960	9 829	5 364	2 309	955	10 392	31 656	4 323	64 828
1961	10 043	5 511	2 359	982	10 651	32 701	4 427	66 674
1962	10 267	5 761	2 409	1 010	10 917	33 796	4 533	68 693
1963	10 501	5 919	2 460	1 031	11 210	34 933	4 642	70 696
1964	10 744	6 079	2 512	1 061	11 528	36 099	4 754	72 777
1965	10 998	6 242	2 565	1 090	11 869	37 258	4 868	74 890
1966	11 262	6 408	2 619	1 119	12 232	38 379	4 984	77 003
1967	11 538	6 578	2 674	1 150	12 617	39 464	5 104	79 125
1968	11 825	6 752	2 730	1 181	13 024	40 512	5 226	81 250
1969	12 123	6 931	2 787	1 214	13 455	41 542	5 352	83 404
1970	12 431	6 996	2 845	1 248	13 912	42 577	5 480	85 489
1971	12 749	7 018	2 904	1 283	14 365	43 614	5 612	87 545
1972	13 079	7 112	2 964	1 321	14 781	44 655	5 746	89 658
1973	13 421	7 202	3 027	1 360	15 161	45 737	5 884	91 792
1974	13 772	7 287	3 092	1 403	15 501	46 902	6 023	93 980
1975	14 132	7 179	3 161	1 446	15 801	48 075	6 165	95 959
1976	14 501	6 906	3 176	1 487	16 069	49 273	6 311	97 723
1977	14 880	6 669	3 208	1 528	16 325	50 534	6 460	99 604
1978	15 269	6 460	3 248	1 572	16 580	51 663	6 613	101 405
1979	15 556	6 393	3 268	1 617	16 840	52 668	6 769	103 111
1980	14 985	6 499	3 293	1 662	17 114	53 661	6 929	104 143
1981	14 087	6 681	3 337	1 709	17 384	54 792	7 093	105 083
1982	13 645	6 903	3 411	1 756	17 648	55 972	7 260	106 595
1983	13 709	7 143	3 495	1 805	17 918	57 205	7 432	108 707
1984	13 826	7 286	3 577	1 856	18 196	58 466	6 708	109 915
1985	13 898	7 399	3 657	1 908	18 481	59 730	7 787	112 860
1986	13 937	7 621	3 753	1 961	18 772	61 006	7 971	115 021
1987	14 074	7 883	3 853	2 015	19 068	62 320	8 160	117 373
1988	14 332	8 153	3 960	2 071	19 371	63 630	8 353	119 870
1989	14 646	8 431	4 073	2 159	19 688	64 906	8 550	122 453
1990	14 767	8 717	4 191	2 216	20 019	66 315	8 752	124 977
1991	14 964	9 012	4 314	2 271	20 361	67 684	8 953	127 559
1992	16 624	9 403	4 440	2 320	20 711	69 021	9 159	131 678
1993	18 888	9 858	4 569	2 366	21 064	70 344	9 369	136 458
1994	20 382	10 210	4 702	2 410	21 361	71 617	9 584	140 266
1995	21 571	10 491	4 837	2 454	21 551	72 815	9 804	143 523
1996	22 664	10 773	4 976	2 497	21 512	73 977	10 030	146 429
1997	23 738	11 055	5 117	2 538	21 334	75 124	10 260	149 166
1998	24 792	11 340	5 261	2 579	21 234	76 236	10 493	151 935

Table C3–a. Population of 15 West Asian Countries, Annual Estimates, 1950–98
(000 at mid–year)

	Bahrain	Iran	Iraq	Israel	Jordan	Kuwait	Lebanon	Oman	Qatar
1950	115	16 375	5 163	1 286	561	145	1 364	489	25
1951	118	16 809	5 300	1 490	584	152	1 401	498	27
1952	120	17 272	5 442	1 621	608	160	1 440	508	29
1953	123	17 742	5 589	1 667	633	168	1 479	517	31
1954	127	18 226	5 743	1 712	659	177	1 519	528	33
1955	130	18 729	5 903	1 772	687	187	1 561	539	35
1956	134	19 249	6 073	1 850	716	197	1 604	550	37
1957	139	19 729	6 249	1 944	747	213	1 647	562	39
1958	144	20 326	6 433	2 025	779	235	1 692	573	41
1959	150	20 958	6 625	2 082	813	262	1 739	586	43
1960	157	21 577	6 822	2 141	849	292	1 786	599	45
1961	164	22 214	7 026	2 217	887	325	1 836	614	49
1962	172	22 874	7 240	2 311	934	358	1 887	628	53
1963	179	23 554	7 468	2 407	975	394	1 940	645	58
1964	186	24 264	7 711	2 498	1 017	433	1 996	662	64
1965	191	25 000	7 971	2 578	1 061	476	2 058	679	70
1966	197	25 764	8 240	2 641	1 107	523	2 122	697	77
1967	202	26 538	8 519	2 694	1 255	575	2 187	715	85
1968	208	27 321	8 808	2 747	1 383	632	2 254	735	94
1969	214	28 119	9 106	2 817	1 454	690	2 320	756	103
1970	220	28 933	9 414	2 903	1 503	748	2 383	779	113
1971	225	29 763	9 732	2 997	1 556	793	2 529	803	122
1972	231	30 614	10 062	3 096	1 614	842	2 680	829	132
1973	239	31 491	10 402	3 197	1 674	894	2 824	857	142
1974	248	32 412	10 754	3 286	1 738	948	2 986	884	153
1975	259	33 379	11 118	3 354	1 803	1 007	3 095	913	165
1976	274	34 381	11 494	3 424	1 870	1 072	3 115	956	177
1977	297	35 430	11 883	3 496	1 938	1 140	3 110	1 005	189
1978	323	36 519	12 317	3 570	2 007	1 214	3 102	1 059	202
1979	336	37 772	12 768	3 653	2 077	1 292	3 090	1 116	216
1980	348	39 274	13 233	3 737	2 168	1 370	3 075	1 175	231
1981	363	40 906	13 703	3 801	2 262	1 432	3 068	1 238	242
1982	378	42 555	14 173	3 858	2 357	1 497	3 072	1 301	252
1983	393	44 200	14 652	3 927	2 451	1 566	3 073	1 363	284
1984	408	45 868	15 161	4 005	2 546	1 637	3 072	1 424	315
1985	424	47 533	15 694	4 075	2 646	1 720	3 068	1 482	345
1986	440	49 274	16 247	4 137	2 748	1 799	3 066	1 538	375
1987	455	50 873	16 543	4 203	2 851	1 880	3 068	1 594	402
1988	470	52 435	17 038	4 272	2 956	1 962	3 075	1 652	430
1989	486	53 979	17 568	4 344	3 069	2 045	3 088	1 712	457
1990	502	55 717	18 135	4 512	3 277	2 131	3 130	1 773	482
1991	517	57 492	17 491	4 756	3 562	955	3 179	1 843	505
1992	531	58 905	17 905	4 937	3 762	1 398	3 210	1 915	531
1993	546	59 684	18 480	5 062	3 889	1 467	3 247	1 989	558
1994	561	60 424	19 083	5 185	3 999	1 574	3 291	2 059	587
1995	576	61 528	19 713	5 306	4 099	1 673	3 340	2 131	615
1996	590	62 584	20 367	5 422	4 210	1 754	3 394	2 206	643
1997	603	63 531	21 037	5 535	4 322	1 834	3 450	2 283	670
1998	616	64 411	21 722	5 644	4 435	1 913	3 506	2 364	697
1999	629	65 180	22 427	5 750	4 561	1 991	3 563	2 447	724
2000	642	65 865	23 151	5 852	4 701	2 068	3 620	2 533	750

Table C3–a. **Population of 15 West Asian Countries, Annual Estimates, 1950–98**
(000 at mid–year)

	Saudi Arabia	Syria	Turkey	UAE	Yemen	West Bank and Gaza	Total
1950	3 860	3 495	21 122	72	4 461	1 016	59 549
1951	3 932	3 577	21 669	73	4 546	1 023	61 199
1952	4 006	3 662	22 236	75	4 635	1 031	62 845
1953	4 082	3 750	22 831	77	4 726	1 040	64 455
1954	4 160	3 842	23 464	80	4 820	1 049	66 139
1955	4 243	3 938	24 145	83	4 916	1 054	67 922
1956	4 329	4 041	24 877	86	5 024	1 061	69 828
1957	4 420	4 150	25 671	89	5 134	1 071	71 804
1958	4 514	4 268	26 506	93	5 247	1 078	73 954
1959	4 614	4 395	27 356	98	5 363	1 101	76 185
1960	4 718	4 533	28 217	103	5 483	1 113	78 435
1961	4 828	4 681	29 030	109	5 597	1 110	80 687
1962	4 943	4 835	29 789	116	5 715	1 133	82 988
1963	5 065	4 993	30 509	124	5 834	1 157	85 302
1964	5 129	5 157	31 227	133	5 956	1 182	87 615
1965	5 327	5 326	31 951	144	6 079	1 211	90 122
1966	5 469	5 500	32 678	157	6 186	1 236	92 594
1967	5 618	5 681	33 411	172	6 294	1 143	95 089
1968	5 775	5 867	34 165	191	6 405	1 001	97 586
1969	5 939	6 059	34 952	218	6 516	1 002	100 265
1970	6 109	6 258	35 758	249	6 628	1 022	103 020
1971	6 287	6 479	36 580	288	6 771	1 045	105 970
1972	6 473	6 701	37 493	336	6 916	1 070	109 089
1973	6 667	6 931	38 503	391	7 077	1 098	112 387
1974	6 868	7 169	39 513	453	7 241	1 134	115 787
1975	7 199	7 416	40 530	523	7 409	1 161	119 331
1976	7 608	7 670	41 485	598	7 629	1 183	122 936
1977	8 108	7 933	42 404	684	7 847	1 209	126 673
1978	8 680	8 203	43 317	779	8 068	1 237	130 597
1979	9 307	8 484	44 223	884	8 295	1 263	134 776
1980	9 949	8 774	45 121	1 000	8 527	1 286	139 268
1981	10 565	9 073	46 222	1 100	8 768	1 308	144 051
1982	11 179	9 412	47 329	1 204	9 018	1 336	148 921
1983	11 822	9 762	48 440	1 316	9 278	1 376	153 903
1984	12 502	10 126	49 554	1 438	9 551	1 416	159 023
1985	13 208	10 502	50 669	1 570	9 842	1 457	164 235
1986	13 859	10 892	51 780	1 714	10 149	1 501	169 519
1987	14 465	11 294	52 884	1 779	10 476	1 549	174 316
1988	15 064	11 711	53 976	1 840	10 823	1 603	179 307
1989	15 646	12 141	55 054	1 898	11 192	1 653	184 332
1990	15 871	12 620	56 125	1 952	12 023	1 715	189 965
1991	16 110	13 115	57 198	2 003	12 889	1 797	193 412
1992	16 739	13 589	58 267	2 051	13 379	1 886	199 005
1993	17 386	14 075	59 330	2 097	13 892	1 977	203 679
1994	18 049	14 575	60 387	2 140	14 395	2 085	208 394
1995	18 730	15 087	61 439	2 181	14 862	2 215	213 495
1996	19 409	15 609	62 486	2 222	15 349	2 352	218 597
1997	20 088	16 138	63 530	2 262	15 857	2 484	223 624
1998	20 786	16 673	64 568	2 303	16 388	2 611	228 637
1999	21 505	17 214	65 599	2 344	16 942	2 724	233 600
2000	22 246	17 759	66 620	2 386	17 521	2 825	238 539

Table C3–a. **Population in 56 Asian Countries, Annual Estimates, 1950–98**
(000 at mid–year)

	16 East Asian countries	*25 East Asian countries*	*15 West Asian countries*	*56 Asian countries*
1950	1 269 120	53 208	59 549	1 381 877
1951	1 292 365	53 709	61 199	1 407 273
1952	1 317 963	54 243	62 845	1 435 051
1953	1 344 708	54 826	64 455	1 463 989
1954	1 373 435	55 712	66 139	1 495 286
1955	1 401 651	56 931	67 922	1 526 504
1956	1 430 446	58 247	69 828	1 558 521
1957	1 462 431	59 682	71 804	1 593 917
1958	1 495 698	61 259	73 954	1 630 911
1959	1 525 282	62 998	76 185	1 664 465
1960	1 543 294	64 828	78 435	1 686 557
1961	1 555 798	66 674	80 687	1 703 159
1962	1 580 785	68 693	82 988	1 732 466
1963	1 617 371	70 696	85 302	1 773 369
1964	1 653 379	72 777	87 615	1 813 771
1965	1 691 130	74 890	90 122	1 856 142
1966	1 731 480	77 003	92 594	1 901 077
1967	1 772 120	79 125	95 089	1 946 334
1968	1 814 876	81 250	97 586	1 993 712
1969	1 858 312	83 404	100 265	2 041 981
1970	1 904 160	85 489	103 020	2 092 669
1971	1 951 798	87 545	105 970	2 145 313
1972	1 998 043	89 658	109 089	2 196 790
1973	2 043 635	91 792	112 387	2 247 814
1974	2 088 198	93 980	115 787	2 297 965
1975	2 129 675	95 959	119 331	2 344 965
1976	2 170 585	97 723	122 936	2 391 244
1977	2 210 702	99 604	126 673	2 436 979
1978	2 251 069	101 405	130 597	2 483 071
1979	2 294 318	103 111	134 776	2 532 205
1980	2 336 628	104 143	139 268	2 580 039
1981	2 377 056	105 083	144 051	2 626 190
1982	2 413 737	106 595	148 921	2 669 253
1983	2 465 512	108 707	153 903	2 728 122
1984	2 508 720	109 915	159 023	2 777 658
1985	2 552 726	112 860	164 235	2 829 821
1986	2 597 796	115 021	169 519	2 882 336
1987	2 645 292	117 373	174 316	2 936 981
1988	2 693 205	119 870	179 307	2 992 382
1989	2 740 695	122 453	184 332	3 047 480
1990	2 787 816	124 977	189 965	3 102 758
1991	2 833 547	127 559	193 412	3 154 518
1992	2 875 692	131 678	199 005	3 206 375
1993	2 920 320	136 458	203 679	3 260 457
1994	2 963 878	140 266	208 394	3 312 538
1995	3 009 423	143 523	213 495	3 366 441
1996	3 051 583	146 429	218 597	3 416 609
1997	3 093 799	149 166	223 624	3 466 589
1998	3 135 839	151 935	228 637	3 516 411

Table C3–b. **Levels of GDP in 16 East Asian Countries, Annual Estimates, 1950–99**
(million 1990 international Geary–Khamis dollars)

	China	India	Indonesia	Japan	Philippines	South Korea	Thailand	Taiwan
1950	239 903	222 222	66 358	160 966	22 616	16 045	16 375	7 378
1951	267 228	227 362	71 304	181 025	25 054	14 810	17 532	8 179
1952	305 742	234 148	74 679	202 005	26 609	15 772	18 503	9 093
1953	321 919	248 963	78 394	216 889	28 988	20 345	20 542	10 092
1954	332 326	259 262	83 283	229 151	31 168	21 539	20 381	10 927
1955	350 115	265 527	85 571	248 855	33 331	22 708	22 162	11 853
1956	384 842	280 978	86 700	267 567	35 670	22 815	22 540	12 481
1957	406 222	277 924	92 631	287 130	37 599	24 575	22 792	13 360
1958	452 654	299 137	89 293	303 857	38 900	25 863	23 616	14 510
1959	464 006	305 499	93 129	331 570	41 548	26 865	26 457	15 871
1960	448 727	326 910	97 082	375 090	42 114	27 398	29 665	16 725
1961	368 021	336 744	103 446	420 246	44 480	28 782	31 210	17 931
1962	368 032	344 204	103 332	457 742	46 603	29 654	33 636	19 453
1963	403 732	361 442	99 371	496 514	49 893	32 268	36 360	22 150
1964	452 558	389 262	103 043	554 449	51 613	35 054	38 841	24 971
1965	505 099	373 814	104 070	586 744	54 331	37 166	41 933	26 688
1966	553 676	377 207	104 089	649 189	56 736	41 641	46 654	29 378
1967	536 987	408 349	101 739	721 132	59 756	44 670	50 552	32 688
1968	525 204	418 907	111 662	813 984	62 712	50 371	54 695	35 447
1969	574 669	446 872	125 408	915 556	65 632	58 007	58 980	38 651
1970	640 949	469 584	138 612	1 013 602	68 102	62 988	62 842	43 509
1971	671 780	474 338	146 200	1 061 230	71 799	82 932	65 886	49 591
1972	691 449	472 766	162 748	1 150 516	75 710	85 811	68 666	57 358
1973	740 048	494 832	186 900	1 242 932	82 464	96 794	75 511	63 519
1974	752 734	500 146	196 374	1 227 706	85 398	104 605	78 894	62 384
1975	800 876	544 683	196 374	1 265 661	90 150	111 548	82 799	63 818
1976	793 092	551 402	213 675	1 315 966	98 090	124 664	90 391	75 108
1977	844 157	593 834	230 338	1 373 741	103 585	137 531	99 304	84 267
1978	935 884	625 695	240 853	1 446 165	108 942	150 442	109 112	94 833
1979	1 007 734	594 510	253 961	1 525 477	115 086	161 172	114 828	101 759
1980	1 046 781	637 202	275 805	1 568 457	121 012	156 846	120 116	104 753
1981	1 096 587	675 882	294 768	1 618 185	125 154	166 581	127 211	113 222
1982	1 192 494	697 705	283 922	1 667 653	129 648	179 220	134 020	119 254
1983	1 294 304	753 942	295 296	1 706 380	132 115	199 828	141 504	132 294
1984	1 447 661	783 042	315 677	1 773 223	122 440	217 167	149 644	148 650
1985	1 599 201	814 344	323 451	1 851 315	113 493	231 386	156 598	156 878
1986	1 703 671	848 990	342 452	1 904 918	117 371	258 122	165 264	177 721
1987	1 849 563	886 154	359 323	1 984 142	122 432	287 854	180 996	190 493
1988	2 000 236	978 822	379 917	2 107 060	130 699	320 301	205 047	192 229
1989	2 044 100	1 043 912	414 090	2 208 858	138 809	340 751	230 043	195 311
1990	2 109 400	1 098 100	450 901	2 321 153	143 025	373 150	255 732	200 477
1991	2 232 306	1 104 114	473 680	2 409 304	142 191	407 582	277 618	215 622
1992	2 444 569	1 161 769	524 482	2 433 927	142 668	429 744	300 059	230 203
1993	2 683 336	1 233 796	560 544	2 441 512	145 704	453 344	325 215	244 747
1994	2 950 104	1 330 036	601 301	2 457 252	152 094	490 745	354 283	260 744
1995	3 196 343	1 425 798	648 332	2 493 399	159 199	534 517	385 584	276 463
1996	3 433 255	1 532 733	696 426	2 619 315	168 506	570 598	406 864	292 128
1997	3 657 242	1 609 371	727 953	2 656 686	177 199	599 190	405 097	311 894
1998	3 873 352	1 702 712	627 499	2 581 576	176 246	564 211	372 509	326 958
1999	4 082 513	1 803 172	628 753	2 589 320	181 886	624 582	387 782	345 595

Table C3–b. **Levels of GDP in 16 East Asian Countries, Annual Estimates, 1950–99**
(million 1990 international Geary–Khamis dollars)

	Bangladesh	Burma	Hong Kong	Malaysia	Nepal	Pakistan	Singapore	Sri Lanka	Total
1950	24 628	7 711	4 962	10 032	4 462	25 366	2 268	7 241	838 533
1951	24 974	8 834	4 626	9 478	4 591	24 534	2 406	7 850	899 787
1952	25 706	9 028	5 054	9 930	4 748	24 625	2 569	8 140	976 351
1953	26 072	9 265	5 515	9 977	5 038	26 983	2 758	8 058	1 039 798
1954	26 581	8 690	6 021	10 607	5 145	27 603	2 896	8 295	1 083 875
1955	25 177	9 822	6 564	10 677	5 248	28 238	3 078	8 808	1 137 734
1956	27 821	10 472	7 136	11 320	5 484	29 069	3 200	8 323	1 216 418
1957	27 231	11 089	7 729	11 257	5 484	30 339	3 352	8 862	1 267 576
1958	26 702	10 785	8 345	11 256	5 792	30 762	3 485	9 280	1 354 237
1959	28 126	12 457	8 981	12 026	5 957	31 095	3 470	9 553	1 416 610
1960	29 733	12 871	9 637	12 899	6 091	32 621	3 803	10 081	1 481 447
1961	31 421	13 183	10 276	13 794	6 238	34 602	4 123	10 257	1 474 754
1962	31 258	14 332	12 072	14 578	6 385	37 111	4 411	10 500	1 533 303
1963	34 573	14 737	13 968	15 271	6 537	39 439	4 848	11 168	1 642 271
1964	34 939	14 999	15 165	16 235	6 689	42 417	4 680	11 860	1 796 775
1965	36 647	15 379	17 360	17 405	6 849	44 307	5 033	12 148	1 884 973
1966	37 115	14 737	17 659	18 278	7 331	47 919	5 593	12 772	2 019 974
1967	36 302	15 151	17 959	18 587	7 216	49 718	6 255	13 546	2 120 607
1968	39 678	16 148	18 557	20 217	7 265	53 195	7 123	14 136	2 249 301
1969	40 227	16 815	20 652	21 382	7 590	56 642	8 098	15 292	2 470 473
1970	42 403	17 575	22 548	22 684	7 787	62 522	9 209	17 711	2 702 627
1971	40 552	18 149	24 144	24 359	7 693	62 824	10 362	17 700	2 829 539
1972	35 732	18 284	26 639	26 195	7 934	63 323	11 752	19 087	2 973 970
1973	35 997	18 352	29 931	29 982	7 894	67 828	13 108	19 759	3 205 851
1974	40 817	19 323	30 629	32 222	8 393	70 141	13 994	20 541	3 244 301
1975	40 308	20 125	30 729	32 489	8 518	73 043	14 549	21 504	3 397 174
1976	42 098	21 350	35 718	36 536	8 893	76 898	15 588	22 458	3 521 927
1977	42 525	22 625	39 908	39 513	9 161	79 951	16 797	23 316	3 740 553
1978	45 657	24 086	43 300	42 970	9 563	86 406	18 245	24 943	4 007 096
1979	47 846	25 222	48 289	46 469	9 790	89 580	19 932	26 539	4 188 194
1980	48 239	27 381	53 177	50 333	9 563	98 907	21 865	28 079	4 368 516
1981	49 877	28 930	58 066	53 901	9 563	106 753	23 960	29 707	4 578 347
1982	50 487	30 499	59 662	57 102	10 749	114 852	25 601	31 222	4 784 090
1983	52 961	31 827	63 055	60 588	10 433	122 649	27 695	32 771	5 057 642
1984	55 833	33 397	69 340	65 290	11 441	127 518	30 006	34 103	5 384 432
1985	57 519	34 349	69 639	64 617	12 146	138 632	29 451	35 793	5 688 812
1986	60 011	33 986	77 122	65 434	12 664	147 421	29 975	37 307	5 982 429
1987	62 521	32 624	87 099	68 898	13 164	155 994	32 817	37 752	6 351 826
1988	64 329	28 921	94 083	74 982	14 199	166 031	36 491	38 770	6 832 117
1989	65 948	29 989	96 478	81 996	14 525	174 001	39 857	39 594	7 158 262
1990	70 320	30 834	99 770	89 823	15 609	182 014	43 330	42 089	7 525 727
1991	72 629	30 633	104 858	97 545	16 603	192 138	45 832	44 118	7 866 773
1992	76 245	33 593	111 343	105 151	17 285	206 957	49 399	46 050	8 313 444
1993	79 722	35 622	118 227	113 927	17 950	211 653	55 622	49 235	8 770 156
1994	82 774	38 285	124 613	124 525	19 425	221 260	61 843	52 016	9 321 300
1995	87 355	40 946	129 402	136 182	20 099	232 849	67 066	54 892	9 888 426
1996	91 705	43 584	135 288	147 899	21 170	244 954	72 108	56 955	10 533 488
1997	96 616	45 600	142 372	159 294	22 025	248 142	77 868	60 541	10 997 090
1998	101 666	48 427	135 089	148 621	22 435	261 497	79 025	63 408	11 085 231
1999	106 139	50 606	139 006	156 647	23 175	269 603	83 292	66 071	11 538 142

Table C3–b. **Levels of GDP in 25 East Asian Countries, Annual Estimates, 1950–98**
(million 1990 international Geary–Khamis dollars)

	Afghanistan	Cambodia	Laos	Mongolia	North Korea	Vietnam	19 small countries	Total
1950	5 255	2 155	1 156	339	7 293	16 681	3 845	36 724
1951	5 408	2 228	1 192	353	6 496	17 445	3 987	37 109
1952	5 591	2 368	1 229	370	6 675	18 209	4 225	38 667
1953	5 933	2 392	1 267	387	8 288	19 034	4 316	41 617
1954	6 059	2 670	1 306	406	8 683	19 920	4 471	43 515
1955	6 180	2 614	1 347	426	9 316	20 806	4 636	45 325
1956	6 458	2 963	1 388	448	9 444	21 631	4 820	47 152
1957	6 458	3 163	1 431	473	10 230	22 486	5 012	49 253
1958	6 821	3 322	1 476	499	10 816	23 372	5 200	51 506
1959	7 016	3 646	1 521	528	11 260	24 289	5 403	53 663
1960	7 268	3 863	1 568	559	11 483	25 297	5 640	55 678
1961	7 331	3 827	1 617	592	11 972	26 554	5 938	57 831
1962	7 457	4 139	1 667	627	12 249	29 917	6 130	62 186
1963	7 594	4 451	1 718	660	13 295	30 821	6 496	65 035
1964	7 741	4 331	1 772	699	14 445	32 322	6 794	68 104
1965	7 914	4 538	1 826	740	15 370	32 666	7 172	70 226
1966	7 993	4 744	1 883	782	17 308	32 975	7 561	73 246
1967	8 214	4 988	1 941	828	18 711	28 829	7 854	71 365
1968	8 508	5 214	2 001	876	21 268	28 329	8 347	74 543
1969	8 645	5 292	2 063	927	24 743	30 702	8 750	81 122
1970	8 819	4 785	2 127	982	27 184	31 295	9 581	84 773
1971	8 398	4 546	2 193	1 041	36 229	32 889	10 376	95 672
1972	8 240	4 301	2 261	1 103	37 854	35 815	10 939	100 513
1973	9 181	5 858	2 331	1 170	43 072	38 238	11 952	111 802
1974	9 680	5 007	2 403	1 243	44 038	36 744	12 594	111 709
1975	10 184	4 342	2 477	1 319	44 891	34 130	12 765	110 108
1976	10 694	4 650	2 554	1 396	45 652	39 879	13 181	118 006
1977	9 959	5 016	2 633	1 479	46 379	41 343	13 403	120 212
1978	10 752	5 484	2 714	1 567	47 104	41 622	14 102	123 345
1979	10 715	5 593	2 798	1 661	47 842	41 873	15 175	125 657
1980	10 427	5 705	2 885	1 758	48 621	40 671	14 880	124 947
1981	10 547	5 774	2 974	1 905	49 388	42 103	14 965	127 656
1982	10 726	6 218	3 066	2 064	50 138	45 526	15 226	132 964
1983	11 157	6 660	3 161	2 184	50 905	48 042	15 662	137 771
1984	11 336	7 106	3 258	2 314	51 695	52 355	15 899	143 963
1985	11 299	7 554	3 359	2 446	52 505	55 481	16 565	149 209
1986	12 161	7 998	3 463	2 675	53 331	57 056	17 368	154 052
1987	10 064	7 839	3 570	2 768	54 172	59 127	17 984	155 524
1988	9 228	8 035	3 681	2 909	55 033	62 685	18 633	160 204
1989	9 284	8 233	3 795	3 031	55 934	65 615	19 306	165 198
1990	8 861	8 235	3 912	2 954	56 874	68 959	19 356	169 151
1991	8 932	8 860	4 031	2 681	57 846	72 963	20 212	175 525
1992	9 021	9 482	4 245	2 426	53 391	79 312	21 107	178 984
1993	8 741	9 870	4 674	2 354	53 552	85 718	22 041	186 950
1994	8 479	10 258	4 964	2 408	39 468	93 292	23 016	181 885
1995	10 700	10 940	5 230	2 560	32 758	102 192	24 034	188 414
1996	11 342	11 543	5 355	2 620	27 091	111 736	25 098	194 785
1997	12 023	11 846	5 636	2 726	25 249	120 845	26 208	204 533
1998	12 744	11 998	5 806	2 821	25 130	127 851	26 662	213 012

Table C3–b. **Levels of GDP in 15 West Asian Countries, Annual Estimates, 1950–98**
(million 1990 international Geary–Khamis dollars)

	Bahrain	*Iran*	*Iraq*	*Israel*	*Jordan*	*Kuwait*	*Lebanon*	*Oman*	*Qatar*
1950	242	28 128	7 041	3 623	933	4 181	3 313	304	763
1951	257	28 128	7 661	4 707	990	4 532	2 972	324	827
1952	273	28 128	8 470	4 910	1 049	4 804	3 157	344	876
1953	290	28 156	11 899	4 852	1 112	5 280	3 634	366	963
1954	309	28 156	14 145	5 776	1 178	5 882	4 171	389	1 073
1955	328	28 156	13 568	6 558	1 116	6 020	4 506	413	1 099
1956	349	30 659	14 511	7 142	1 532	6 464	4 399	439	1 180
1957	371	34 939	14 370	7 761	1 571	6 693	4 476	467	1 223
1958	394	39 013	16 039	8 319	1 729	7 024	3 840	496	1 282
1959	419	42 360	16 715	9 370	1 858	7 747	4 164	528	1 415
1960	445	46 467	18 658	9 986	1 977	8 420	4 274	560	1 496
1961	474	50 405	20 806	11 077	2 381	8 495	4 555	567	1 497
1962	504	51 389	21 841	12 171	2 446	9 474	4 731	681	1 555
1963	536	57 043	21 447	13 461	2 582	9 984	4 771	711	1 657
1964	571	61 178	24 024	14 780	3 032	10 962	5 059	712	1 712
1965	607	68 688	26 206	16 171	3 379	11 205	5 569	715	1 837
1966	646	75 579	27 593	16 349	3 474	12 584	5 950	752	2 493
1967	688	84 102	26 953	16 758	3 839	12 885	5 668	1 250	3 014
1968	732	96 759	31 740	19 320	3 696	14 089	6 381	2 274	3 474
1969	779	109 304	32 818	21 755	4 031	14 474	6 520	2 858	3 706
1970	832	120 865	32 691	23 520	3 600	22 944	6 950	2 957	3 756
1971	898	135 829	34 712	26 107	3 682	24 537	7 590	2 983	4 665
1972	969	157 909	33 430	29 342	3 800	25 503	8 514	3 262	5 263
1973	1 046	171 466	39 042	30 839	3 999	23 847	8 915	2 809	6 228
1974	1 136	186 655	41 133	32 941	4 355	20 799	10 465	3 132	5 661
1975	1 015	195 684	47 977	34 038	4 657	18 287	10 724	3 897	5 823
1976	1 180	229 241	57 735	34 480	5 789	19 466	10 989	4 397	6 263
1977	1 322	226 315	59 320	34 480	6 166	18 722	11 260	4 410	5 586
1978	1 424	199 481	70 127	36 144	7 462	20 072	11 539	4 326	6 114
1979	1 419	182 267	86 258	38 416	8 142	22 827	10 873	4 511	6 364
1980	1 525	156 643	84 392	41 053	9 689	18 178	10 879	4 784	6 816
1981	1 568	151 918	69 078	43 173	10 147	14 737	10 366	5 599	5 834
1982	1 669	175 826	68 501	43 948	10 897	13 006	9 680	6 245	4 731
1983	1 785	199 031	62 544	45 496	11 115	14 039	9 584	7 288	4 246
1984	1 860	202 379	62 699	45 905	12 071	14 775	9 786	8 507	4 143
1985	1 854	207 245	61 714	47 489	12 493	14 148	10 028	9 697	3 699
1986	1 897	187 780	61 073	49 760	13 626	15 352	9 581	9 906	3 130
1987	1 935	184 939	62 812	53 344	13 997	14 733	6 705	10 699	3 192
1988	2 003	174 532	49 540	54 417	13 853	15 247	6 099	11 018	3 240
1989	2 053	181 227	45 160	54 895	12 387	16 389	6 106	11 481	3 275
1990	2 054	199 819	44 583	58 511	12 371	13 111	6 099	11 487	3 276
1991	2 148	220 999	16 540	61 848	12 656	7 735	8 429	12 176	3 263
1992	2 316	234 472	21 370	66 051	14 807	13 723	8 808	13 211	3 566
1993	2 508	239 395	21 370	68 298	15 666	18 416	9 425	14 017	3 552
1994	2 568	241 560	21 370	73 012	16 856	19 963	10 179	14 550	3 634
1995	2 622	248 565	19 938	77 977	17 514	20 163	10 840	15 248	3 594
1996	2 704	262 234	19 938	81 639	17 689	20 586	11 274	15 690	3 953
1997	2 788	270 110	21 932	83 846	17 919	21 101	11 725	16 694	4 566
1998	2 846	274 695	24 564	85 520	18 313	21 565	12 077	17 179	5 091

Table C3–b. Levels of GDP in 15 West Asian Countries, Annual Estimates, 1950–98
(million 1990 international Geary–Khamis dollars)

	Saudi Arabia	Syria	Turkey	UAE	Yemen	West Bank and Gaza	Total
1950	8 610	8 418	38 408	1 130	4 353	965	110 412
1951	9 334	8 098	43 329	1 225	4 468	1 009	117 858
1952	9 893	10 202	48 521	1 298	4 584	1 055	127 566
1953	10 875	11 566	53 931	1 427	4 708	1 104	140 163
1954	12 115	13 266	52 393	1 590	4 831	1 157	146 430
1955	12 399	11 970	56 626	1 628	4 959	1 206	150 552
1956	13 312	14 175	58 454	1 749	5 091	1 260	160 716
1957	13 785	15 051	63 103	1 812	5 228	1 321	172 171
1958	14 465	12 972	65 998	1 902	5 367	1 380	180 219
1959	15 955	13 460	69 019	2 097	5 510	1 462	192 079
1960	17 548	13 704	71 064	2 312	5 660	1 534	204 105
1961	19 632	14 832	72 258	2 526	5 810	1 588	216 903
1962	21 974	18 351	76 672	2 809	5 970	1 683	232 248
1963	23 885	18 342	83 890	3 097	6 148	1 783	249 337
1964	25 986	18 755	87 346	3 414	6 307	1 891	265 728
1965	29 137	18 704	89 643	3 762	6 486	2 010	284 120
1966	33 374	17 265	100 137	4 147	6 674	2 130	309 146
1967	36 310	18 696	104 674	4 570	6 868	2 045	328 321
1968	39 547	19 394	111 674	5 037	7 052	1 859	363 029
1969	42 578	23 031	117 624	5 554	7 260	1 931	394 223
1970	46 573	22 155	123 378	6 123	8 731	2 044	427 119
1971	53 289	24 352	130 247	7 147	10 253	2 169	468 459
1972	61 469	30 447	139 919	8 343	11 070	2 306	521 546
1973	73 601	27 846	144 483	9 739	12 431	2 455	558 745
1974	84 700	34 563	152 566	12 894	13 152	2 632	606 784
1975	84 924	41 306	163 510	13 307	14 152	2 797	642 097
1976	92 251	45 834	180 618	15 308	16 363	2 958	722 873
1977	106 191	45 254	186 768	17 978	18 167	3 137	745 076
1978	112 511	49 202	189 577	17 557	19 711	3 332	748 578
1979	120 028	50 986	188 394	21 926	20 805	3 531	766 747
1980	132 160	57 097	183 786	27 717	20 918	3 732	759 370
1981	142 630	62 527	192 709	28 492	22 191	3 940	764 909
1982	144 989	63 857	199 575	26 145	22 563	4 176	795 808
1983	129 404	64 766	209 492	24 833	23 856	4 465	811 944
1984	129 258	62 131	223 552	25 893	24 770	4 769	832 507
1985	120 605	65 928	233 034	25 287	24 578	5 094	842 891
1986	113 260	62 670	249 383	19 919	25 115	5 446	827 898
1987	118 495	63 865	273 031	20 631	26 135	5 834	860 347
1988	122 284	72 342	278 823	20 580	27 249	6 265	857 493
1989	126 701	65 860	279 524	22 766	28 203	6 706	862 733
1990	144 438	70 894	305 395	25 496	28 212	7 222	932 968
1991	156 571	75 927	308 227	25 547	28 297	7 853	948 217
1992	160 955	81 318	326 672	26 237	29 683	8 555	1 011 745
1993	159 989	89 938	352 945	26 001	30 544	9 308	1 061 372
1994	160 789	90 388	333 688	26 573	30 391	10 189	1 055 709
1995	161 593	90 840	357 688	28 194	33 005	11 234	1 099 014
1996	163 855	92 111	382 743	31 041	34 853	12 381	1 152 693
1997	168 279	94 598	411 555	31 786	36 666	13 573	1 207 138
1998	170 972	96 112	423 018	31 913	37 656	14 807	1 236 327

Table C3–b. **Levels of GDP in 56 Asian Countries, Annual Estimates, 1950–98**
(million 1990 international Geary–Khamis dollars)

	16 East Asian countries	*25 East Asian countries*	*15 West Asian countries*	*56 Asian countries*
1950	838 533	36 724	110 412	985 669
1951	899 787	37 109	117 858	1 054 754
1952	976 351	38 667	127 566	1 142 584
1953	1 039 798	41 617	140 163	1 221 578
1954	1 083 875	43 515	146 430	1 273 820
1955	1 137 734	45 325	150 552	1 333 611
1956	1 216 418	47 152	160 716	1 424 286
1957	1 267 576	49 253	172 171	1 489 000
1958	1 354 237	51 506	180 219	1 585 962
1959	1 416 610	53 663	192 079	1 662 352
1960	1 481 447	55 678	204 105	1 741 230
1961	1 474 754	57 831	216 903	1 749 488
1962	1 533 303	62 186	232 248	1 827 737
1963	1 642 271	65 035	249 337	1 956 643
1964	1 796 775	68 104	265 728	2 130 607
1965	1 884 973	70 226	284 120	2 239 319
1966	2 019 974	73 246	309 146	2 402 366
1967	2 120 607	71 365	328 321	2 520 293
1968	2 249 301	74 543	363 029	2 686 873
1969	2 470 473	81 122	394 223	2 945 818
1970	2 702 627	84 773	427 119	3 214 519
1971	2 829 539	95 672	468 459	3 393 670
1972	2 973 970	100 513	521 546	3 596 029
1973	3 205 851	111 802	558 745	3 876 398
1974	3 244 301	111 709	606 784	3 962 794
1975	3 397 174	110 108	642 097	4 149 379
1976	3 521 927	118 006	722 873	4 362 806
1977	3 740 553	120 212	745 076	4 605 841
1978	4 007 096	123 345	748 578	4 879 019
1979	4 188 194	125 657	766 747	5 080 598
1980	4 368 516	124 947	759 370	5 252 833
1981	4 578 347	127 656	764 909	5 470 912
1982	4 784 090	132 964	795 808	5 712 862
1983	5 057 642	137 771	811 944	6 007 357
1984	5 384 432	143 963	832 507	6 360 902
1985	5 688 812	149 209	842 891	6 680 912
1986	5 982 429	154 052	827 898	6 964 379
1987	6 351 826	155 524	860 347	7 367 697
1988	6 832 117	160 204	857 493	7 849 814
1989	7 158 262	165 198	862 733	8 186 193
1990	7 525 727	169 151	932 968	8 627 846
1991	7 866 773	175 525	948 217	8 990 515
1992	8 313 444	178 984	1 011 745	9 504 173
1993	8 770 156	186 950	1 061 372	10 018 478
1994	9 321 300	181 885	1 055 709	10 558 894
1995	9 888 426	188 414	1 099 014	11 175 854
1996	10 533 488	194 785	1 152 693	11 880 966
1997	10 997 090	204 533	1 207 138	12 408 761
1998	11 085 231	213 012	1 236 327	12 534 570

Table C3–c. Levels of Per Capita GDP in 16 East Asian Countries, 1950–99
(1990 international Geary–Khamis dollars)

	China	India	Indonesia	Japan	Philippines	South Korea	Thailand	Taiwan
1950	439	619	840	1 926	1 070	770	817	936
1951	479	623	885	2 130	1 150	709	849	991
1952	537	629	910	2 341	1 186	753	869	1 065
1953	554	657	938	2 480	1 253	966	935	1 144
1954	558	672	978	2 582	1 308	1 013	898	1 196
1955	575	676	986	2 772	1 357	1 054	945	1 250
1956	619	701	980	2 949	1 409	1 036	930	1 271
1957	637	680	1 028	3 138	1 441	1 087	910	1 318
1958	693	716	972	3 290	1 447	1 112	914	1 387
1959	697	717	995	3 556	1 499	1 120	992	1 469
1960	673	753	1 019	3 988	1 475	1 105	1 078	1 499
1961	557	758	1 066	4 429	1 511	1 124	1 100	1 558
1962	553	758	1 043	4 778	1 535	1 122	1 149	1 641
1963	592	779	984	5 131	1 593	1 186	1 205	1 814
1964	648	821	1 000	5 670	1 598	1 253	1 249	1 987
1965	706	771	990	5 934	1 631	1 295	1 308	2 064
1966	753	762	971	6 506	1 651	1 415	1 412	2 212
1967	712	807	930	7 151	1 687	1 483	1 486	2 401
1968	678	809	1 001	7 976	1 719	1 633	1 561	2 542
1969	722	845	1 102	8 869	1 747	1 839	1 636	2 710
1970	783	868	1 194	9 715	1 761	1 954	1 694	2 987
1971	799	856	1 235	10 042	1 804	2 522	1 725	3 336
1972	802	834	1 342	10 735	1 849	2 561	1 748	3 788
1973	839	853	1 504	11 439	1 959	2 841	1 874	4 117
1974	836	843	1 542	11 145	1 974	3 015	1 910	3 971
1975	874	897	1 505	11 349	2 028	3 162	1 959	3 988
1976	852	889	1 598	11 669	2 147	3 476	2 091	4 600
1977	895	937	1 681	12 063	2 205	3 775	2 249	5 058
1978	979	966	1 715	12 584	2 255	4 064	2 422	5 587
1979	1 040	895	1 765	13 164	2 317	4 294	2 496	5 879
1980	1 067	938	1 870	13 429	2 369	4 114	2 554	5 938
1981	1 103	977	1 957	13 754	2 387	4 302	2 654	6 301
1982	1 192	985	1 845	14 079	2 412	4 557	2 746	6 518
1983	1 265	1 043	1 878	14 308	2 399	5 007	2 850	7 114
1984	1 396	1 060	1 966	14 774	2 170	5 375	2 964	7 876
1985	1 522	1 079	1 972	15 332	1 964	5 670	3 054	8 198
1986	1 597	1 101	2 051	15 680	1 983	6 263	3 175	9 181
1987	1 706	1 125	2 114	16 251	2 020	6 916	3 427	9 737
1988	1 816	1 216	2 196	17 185	2 107	7 621	3 828	9 714
1989	1 827	1 270	2 352	17 941	2 185	8 027	4 235	9 763
1990	1 858	1 309	2 516	18 789	2 199	8 704	4 645	9 910
1991	1 940	1 290	2 599	19 442	2 136	9 425	4 984	10 539
1992	2 098	1 332	2 831	19 578	2 095	9 844	5 325	11 142
1993	2 277	1 385	2 976	19 584	2 092	10 280	5 707	11 738
1994	2 475	1 465	3 140	19 664	2 135	11 014	6 149	12 393
1995	2 653	1 538	3 329	19 857	2 185	11 873	6 620	13 028
1996	2 820	1 625	3 517	20 811	2 262	12 546	6 913	13 657
1997	2 973	1 678	3 615	21 057	2 328	13 028	6 814	14 453
1998	3 117	1 746	3 070	20 410	2 268	12 152	6 205	15 012
1999	3 259	1 818	3 031	20 431	2 291	13 317	6 398	15 720

Table C3–c. **Levels of Per Capita GDP in 16 East Asian countries, 1950–99**
(1990 international Geary–Khamis dollars)

	Bangladesh	Burma	Hong Kong	Malaysia	Nepal	Pakistan	Singapore	Sri Lanka	Average	Average ex. Japan
1950	540	396	2 218	1 559	496	643	2 219	961	661	572
1951	541	446	2 296	1 440	505	608	2 253	1 013	696	595
1952	548	449	2 377	1 473	517	596	2 280	1 020	741	629
1953	547	454	2 460	1 440	543	637	2 314	980	773	655
1954	547	419	2 546	1 490	549	636	2 321	981	789	665
1955	508	467	2 636	1 460	554	636	2 357	1 015	812	678
1956	551	490	2 729	1 505	572	638	2 332	935	850	708
1957	530	510	2 825	1 455	566	650	2 318	971	867	715
1958	510	488	2 924	1 413	592	643	2 294	991	905	748
1959	526	555	3 027	1 467	601	633	2 187	994	929	758
1960	544	564	3 134	1 530	607	647	2 310	1 020	960	763
1961	564	568	3 244	1 592	613	669	2 422	1 010	948	722
1962	550	606	3 653	1 637	618	699	2 521	1 007	970	724
1963	594	613	4 083	1 669	623	723	2 701	1 045	1 015	753
1964	588	613	4 327	1 728	626	758	2 541	1 084	1 087	799
1965	607	617	4 825	1 804	631	771	2 667	1 084	1 115	815
1966	603	580	4 865	1 846	663	812	2 892	1 114	1 167	840
1967	578	586	4 824	1 830	641	820	3 162	1 154	1 197	837
1968	619	613	4 880	1 942	633	854	3 540	1 177	1 239	838
1969	614	626	5 345	2 005	649	885	3 964	1 246	1 329	886
1970	629	642	5 695	2 079	653	952	4 438	1 413	1 419	938
1971	586	650	5 969	2 181	633	931	4 904	1 385	1 450	958
1972	505	642	6 472	2 290	639	913	5 461	1 466	1 488	964
1973	497	628	7 104	2 560	622	954	5 977	1 492	1 569	1 014
1974	547	648	7 090	2 688	647	962	6 275	1 527	1 554	1 019
1975	529	661	6 990	2 648	694	978	6 429	1 574	1 595	1 056
1976	540	687	7 906	2 910	654	1 006	6 798	1 617	1 623	1 072
1977	529	713	8 706	3 076	658	1 023	7 225	1 652	1 692	1 129
1978	551	743	9 276	3 270	670	1 079	7 751	1 736	1 780	1 199
1979	560	762	9 795	3 456	669	1 087	8 361	1 812	1 825	1 222
1980	548	811	10 503	3 657	637	1 161	9 058	1 884	1 870	1 261
1981	550	840	11 203	3 824	621	1 207	9 700	1 961	1 926	1 310
1982	542	867	11 332	3 954	680	1 259	10 127	2 026	1 982	1 358
1983	555	887	11 797	4 095	644	1 309	10 710	2 098	2 051	1 428
1984	572	913	12 845	4 307	689	1 324	11 349	2 157	2 146	1 512
1985	577	920	12 764	4 157	713	1 400	10 896	2 234	2 229	1 578
1986	590	893	13 959	4 104	725	1 446	10 849	2 295	2 303	1 647
1987	603	841	15 595	4 218	735	1 487	11 621	2 289	2 401	1 731
1988	608	731	16 717	4 481	773	1 540	12 614	2 317	2 537	1 838
1989	612	744	17 043	4 789	771	1 570	13 438	2 333	2 612	1 891
1990	640	751	17 491	5 131	807	1 598	14 258	2 448	2 700	1 953
1991	649	732	18 236	5 446	837	1 643	14 804	2 537	2 776	2 014
1992	671	788	19 197	5 738	850	1 741	15 672	2 618	2 891	2 137
1993	691	821	20 038	6 075	860	1 751	17 333	2 762	3 003	2 264
1994	706	867	20 631	6 491	907	1 789	18 924	2 879	3 145	2 418
1995	733	911	21 007	6 943	915	1 842	20 164	3 001	3 286	2 564
1996	757	953	21 440	7 376	940	1 895	21 315	3 077	3 452	2 705
1997	785	980	21 903	7 774	953	1 877	22 629	3 234	3 555	2 810
1998	813	1 024	20 193	7 100	947	1 935	22 643	3 349	3 535	2 826
1999	835	1 050	20 352	7 328	954	1 952	23 582	3 451	3 633	2 935

Table C3–c. **Levels of Per Capita GDP in 25 East Asian Countries, Annual Estimates, 1950–98**
(1990 international Geary–Khamis dollars)

	Afghanistan	Cambodia	Laos	Mongolia	North Korea	Vietnam	19 small countries	Total
1950	645	518	613	435	770	658	1 127	690
1951	653	522	621	447	709	676	1 141	691
1952	664	542	628	462	753	694	1 181	713
1953	692	534	635	475	966	712	1 179	759
1954	694	582	642	490	1 013	732	1 192	781
1955	695	556	649	505	1 054	750	1 207	796
1956	713	614	654	520	1 036	764	1 226	810
1957	699	638	661	536	1 087	775	1 245	825
1958	723	653	667	552	1 112	785	1 261	841
1959	729	698	673	568	1 120	792	1 280	852
1960	739	720	679	585	1 105	799	1 305	859
1961	730	694	685	603	1 124	812	1 341	867
1962	726	718	692	621	1 122	885	1 352	905
1963	723	752	698	640	1 186	882	1 399	920
1964	720	712	705	659	1 253	895	1 429	936
1965	720	727	712	679	1 295	877	1 473	938
1966	710	740	719	699	1 415	859	1 517	951
1967	712	758	726	720	1 483	731	1 539	902
1968	719	772	733	742	1 633	699	1 597	917
1969	713	764	740	764	1 839	739	1 635	973
1970	709	684	748	787	1 954	735	1 748	992
1971	659	648	755	811	2 522	754	1 849	1 093
1972	630	605	763	835	2 561	802	1 904	1 121
1973	684	813	770	860	2 841	836	2 031	1 218
1974	703	687	777	886	2 841	783	2 091	1 189
1975	721	605	784	912	2 841	710	2 071	1 147
1976	737	673	804	939	2 841	809	2 089	1 208
1977	669	752	821	968	2 841	818	2 075	1 207
1978	704	849	836	997	2 841	806	2 132	1 216
1979	689	875	856	1 027	2 841	795	2 242	1 219
1980	696	878	876	1 058	2 841	758	2 147	1 200
1981	749	864	891	1 115	2 841	768	2 110	1 215
1982	786	901	899	1 175	2 841	813	2 097	1 247
1983	814	932	904	1 210	2 841	840	2 107	1 267
1984	820	975	911	1 247	2 841	895	2 370	1 310
1985	813	1 021	919	1 282	2 841	929	2 127	1 322
1986	873	1 049	923	1 364	2 841	935	2 179	1 339
1987	715	994	927	1 374	2 841	949	2 204	1 325
1988	644	986	930	1 405	2 841	985	2 231	1 336
1989	634	977	932	1 404	2 841	1 011	2 258	1 349
1990	600	945	933	1 333	2 841	1 040	2 212	1 353
1991	597	983	934	1 181	2 841	1 078	2 258	1 376
1992	543	1 008	956	1 046	2 578	1 149	2 305	1 359
1993	463	1 001	1 023	995	2 542	1 219	2 353	1 370
1994	416	1 005	1 056	999	1 848	1 303	2 402	1 297
1995	496	1 043	1 081	1 043	1 520	1 403	2 451	1 313
1996	500	1 071	1 076	1 049	1 259	1 510	2 502	1 330
1997	506	1 072	1 101	1 074	1 184	1 609	2 554	1 371
1998	514	1 058	1 104	1 094	1 183	1 677	2 541	1 402

Table C3–c. **Levels of Per Capita GDP in 15 West Asian Countries, 1950–98**
(1990 international Geary–Khamis dollars)

	Bahrain	Iran	Iraq	Israel	Jordan	Kuwait	Lebanon	Oman	Qatar
1950	2 102	1 718	1 364	2 818	1 664	28 833	2 429	623	30 510
1951	2 177	1 673	1 445	3 159	1 696	29 816	2 121	650	30 623
1952	2 276	1 629	1 556	3 029	1 726	30 023	2 192	677	30 221
1953	2 360	1 587	2 129	2 910	1 756	31 431	2 457	707	31 076
1954	2 430	1 545	2 463	3 374	1 788	33 234	2 746	736	32 521
1955	2 523	1 503	2 298	3 701	1 625	32 194	2 886	766	31 403
1956	2 603	1 593	2 389	3 860	2 139	32 810	2 743	799	31 891
1957	2 667	1 771	2 300	3 992	2 103	31 425	2 717	831	31 351
1958	2 736	1 919	2 493	4 108	2 219	29 888	2 269	866	31 273
1959	2 792	2 021	2 523	4 501	2 286	29 569	2 395	900	32 905
1960	2 837	2 154	2 735	4 664	2 329	28 836	2 393	935	33 239
1961	2 888	2 269	2 961	4 996	2 685	26 140	2 481	923	30 557
1962	2 928	2 247	3 017	5 267	2 618	26 463	2 507	1 084	29 344
1963	2 996	2 422	2 872	5 592	2 648	25 339	2 459	1 103	28 577
1964	3 068	2 521	3 115	5 917	2 981	25 317	2 534	1 075	26 756
1965	3 180	2 748	3 288	6 273	3 185	23 539	2 706	1 053	26 239
1966	3 278	2 934	3 349	6 190	3 138	24 062	2 804	1 079	32 372
1967	3 405	3 169	3 164	6 221	3 059	22 409	2 592	1 749	35 463
1968	3 517	3 542	3 604	7 033	2 673	22 293	2 831	3 094	36 953
1969	3 639	3 887	3 604	7 723	2 772	20 977	2 810	3 781	35 982
1970	3 780	4 177	3 473	8 102	2 395	30 674	2 917	3 796	33 237
1971	3 989	4 564	3 567	8 711	2 366	30 942	3 001	3 714	38 237
1972	4 194	5 158	3 322	9 478	2 354	30 288	3 177	3 935	39 871
1973	4 375	5 445	3 753	9 646	2 389	26 675	3 157	3 278	43 858
1974	4 580	5 759	3 825	10 025	2 505	21 940	3 505	3 543	37 001
1975	3 919	5 862	4 315	10 149	2 583	18 160	3 465	4 268	35 290
1976	4 308	6 668	5 023	10 070	3 096	18 158	3 528	4 599	35 384
1977	4 450	6 388	4 992	9 863	3 182	16 422	3 621	4 388	29 553
1978	4 409	5 462	5 694	10 124	3 718	16 534	3 720	4 085	30 268
1979	4 223	4 825	6 756	10 516	3 920	17 668	3 519	4 042	29 465
1980	4 383	3 988	6 377	10 986	4 469	13 269	3 538	4 071	29 506
1981	4 318	3 714	5 041	11 358	4 486	10 291	3 379	4 523	24 108
1982	4 414	4 132	4 833	11 392	4 623	8 688	3 151	4 800	18 772
1983	4 542	4 503	4 269	11 585	4 535	8 965	3 119	5 347	14 951
1984	4 560	4 412	4 136	11 462	4 741	9 026	3 186	5 974	13 153
1985	4 374	4 360	3 932	11 654	4 722	8 225	3 269	6 543	10 720
1986	4 312	3 811	3 759	12 028	4 959	8 534	3 125	6 441	8 345
1987	4 253	3 635	3 797	12 692	4 910	7 837	2 186	6 712	7 941
1988	4 263	3 329	2 908	12 738	4 687	7 771	1 983	6 670	7 535
1989	4 225	3 357	2 571	12 637	4 036	8 014	1 977	6 706	7 167
1990	4 092	3 586	2 458	12 968	3 775	6 153	1 949	6 479	6 797
1991	4 156	3 844	946	13 004	3 553	8 100	2 651	6 607	6 461
1992	4 362	3 981	1 194	13 379	3 936	9 816	2 744	6 899	6 716
1993	4 594	4 011	1 156	13 492	4 028	12 553	2 903	7 047	6 366
1994	4 578	3 998	1 120	14 081	4 215	12 683	3 093	7 066	6 190
1995	4 553	4 040	1 011	14 696	4 273	12 052	3 246	7 155	5 844
1996	4 583	4 190	979	15 057	4 202	11 737	3 322	7 113	6 148
1997	4 623	4 252	1 043	15 148	4 146	11 505	3 399	7 313	6 815
1998	4 620	4 265	1 131	15 152	4 129	11 273	3 445	7 267	7 304

Table C3–c. **Levels of Per Capita GDP in 15 West Asian Countries, 1950–98**
(1990 international Geary–Khamis dollars)

	Saudi Arabia	Syria	Turkey	UAE	Yemen	West Bank and Gaza	Average
1950	2 231	2 409	1 818	15 692	976	950	1 854
1951	2 374	2 264	2 000	16 777	983	986	1 926
1952	2 470	2 786	2 182	17 309	989	1 023	2 030
1953	2 664	3 084	2 362	18 532	996	1 062	2 175
1954	2 912	3 453	2 233	19 871	1 002	1 103	2 214
1955	2 922	3 040	2 345	19 616	1 009	1 144	2 217
1956	3 075	3 508	2 350	20 337	1 013	1 188	2 302
1957	3 119	3 627	2 458	20 363	1 018	1 233	2 398
1958	3 205	3 039	2 490	20 446	1 023	1 280	2 437
1959	3 458	3 063	2 523	21 398	1 027	1 328	2 521
1960	3 719	3 023	2 518	22 443	1 032	1 378	2 602
1961	4 066	3 169	2 489	23 177	1 038	1 431	2 688
1962	4 445	3 795	2 574	24 214	1 045	1 485	2 799
1963	4 716	3 674	2 750	24 975	1 054	1 541	2 923
1964	5 066	3 637	2 797	25 672	1 059	1 600	3 033
1965	5 470	3 512	2 806	26 128	1 067	1 660	3 153
1966	6 102	3 139	3 064	26 411	1 079	1 723	3 339
1967	6 463	3 291	3 133	26 571	1 091	1 789	3 453
1968	6 848	3 306	3 269	26 371	1 101	1 857	3 720
1969	7 169	3 801	3 365	25 478	1 114	1 927	3 932
1970	7 624	3 540	3 450	24 589	1 317	2 000	4 146
1971	8 476	3 759	3 561	24 817	1 514	2 076	4 421
1972	9 496	4 544	3 732	24 830	1 601	2 155	4 781
1973	11 040	4 018	3 753	24 909	1 756	2 236	4 972
1974	12 333	4 821	3 861	28 463	1 816	2 321	5 241
1975	11 797	5 570	4 034	25 444	1 910	2 409	5 381
1976	12 126	5 976	4 354	25 599	2 145	2 500	5 880
1977	13 097	5 704	4 404	26 284	2 315	2 595	5 882
1978	12 962	5 998	4 377	22 537	2 443	2 694	5 732
1979	12 897	6 010	4 260	24 803	2 508	2 796	5 689
1980	13 284	6 508	4 073	27 717	2 453	2 902	5 453
1981	13 500	6 892	4 169	25 902	2 531	3 012	5 310
1982	12 970	6 785	4 217	21 715	2 502	3 126	5 344
1983	10 946	6 634	4 325	18 870	2 571	3 245	5 276
1984	10 339	6 136	4 511	18 006	2 594	3 368	5 235
1985	9 131	6 278	4 599	16 106	2 497	3 496	5 132
1986	8 172	5 754	4 816	11 621	2 475	3 628	4 884
1987	8 192	5 655	5 163	11 597	2 495	3 766	4 936
1988	8 118	6 177	5 166	11 185	2 518	3 908	4 782
1989	8 098	5 425	5 077	11 995	2 520	4 057	4 680
1990	9 101	5 618	5 441	13 061	2 347	4 211	4 911
1991	9 719	5 789	5 389	12 754	2 195	4 370	4 903
1992	9 616	5 984	5 606	12 792	2 219	4 536	5 084
1993	9 202	6 390	5 949	12 399	2 199	4 708	5 211
1994	8 908	6 202	5 526	12 417	2 111	4 887	5 066
1995	8 627	6 021	5 822	12 927	2 221	5 027	5 148
1996	8 442	5 901	6 125	13 970	2 271	5 264	5 273
1997	8 377	5 862	6 478	14 052	2 312	5 464	5 398
1998	8 225	5 765	6 552	13 857	2 298	5 671	5 407

Table C3-c. **Average Levels of Per Capita GDP in 56 Asian Countries, Annual Estimates, 1950–98**
(1990 international Geary–Khamis dollars)

	16 East Asian countries	25 East Asian countries	15 West Asian countries	56 Asian countries
1950	661	690	1 854	713
1951	696	691	1 926	750
1952	741	713	2 030	796
1953	773	759	2 175	834
1954	789	781	2 214	852
1955	812	796	2 217	874
1956	850	810	2 302	914
1957	867	825	2 398	934
1958	905	841	2 437	972
1959	929	852	2 521	999
1960	960	859	2 602	1 032
1961	948	867	2 688	1 027
1962	970	905	2 799	1 055
1963	1 015	920	2 923	1 103
1964	1 087	936	3 033	1 175
1965	1 115	938	3 153	1 206
1966	1 167	951	3 339	1 264
1967	1 197	902	3 453	1 295
1968	1 239	917	3 720	1 348
1969	1 329	973	3 932	1 443
1970	1 419	992	4 146	1 536
1971	1 450	1 093	4 421	1 582
1972	1 488	1 121	4 781	1 637
1973	1 569	1 218	4 972	1 725
1974	1 554	1 189	5 241	1 724
1975	1 595	1 147	5 381	1 769
1976	1 623	1 208	5 880	1 824
1977	1 692	1 207	5 882	1 890
1978	1 780	1 216	5 732	1 965
1979	1 825	1 219	5 689	2 006
1980	1 870	1 200	5 453	2 036
1981	1 926	1 215	5 310	2 083
1982	1 982	1 247	5 344	2 140
1983	2 051	1 267	5 276	2 202
1984	2 146	1 310	5 235	2 290
1985	2 229	1 322	5 132	2 361
1986	2 303	1 339	4 884	2 416
1987	2 401	1 325	4 936	2 509
1988	2 537	1 336	4 782	2 623
1989	2 612	1 349	4 680	2 686
1990	2 700	1 353	4 911	2 781
1991	2 776	1 376	4 903	2 850
1992	2 891	1 359	5 084	2 964
1993	3 003	1 370	5 211	3 073
1994	3 145	1 297	5 066	3 188
1995	3 286	1 313	5 148	3 320
1996	3 452	1 330	5 273	3 477
1997	3 555	1 371	5 398	3 580
1998	3 535	1 402	5 407	3 565

Table C4–a. Population in 57 African Countries, Annual Estimates, 1950–98
(000 at mid–year)

	Algeria	Angola	Benin	Botswana	Cameroon	Cape Verde	Central African Republic	Chad
1950	8 893	4 118	1 673	430	4 888	146	1 260	2 608
1951	9 073	4 173	1 705	436	4 947	151	1 275	2 644
1952	9 280	4 232	1 738	442	5 009	155	1 292	2 682
1953	9 532	4 294	1 773	448	5 074	160	1 309	2 722
1954	9 611	4 358	1 809	455	5 141	164	1 328	2 763
1955	9 842	4 423	1 846	461	5 211	169	1 348	2 805
1956	10 057	4 491	1 885	468	5 284	174	1 370	2 849
1957	10 271	4 561	1 925	475	5 360	180	1 392	2 895
1958	10 485	4 636	1 967	482	5 439	185	1 416	2 942
1959	10 696	4 715	2 010	489	5 522	191	1 441	2 991
1960	10 909	4 797	2 055	497	5 609	197	1 467	3 042
1961	11 122	4 752	2 102	505	5 699	203	1 495	3 095
1962	11 001	4 826	2 152	513	5 794	210	1 523	3 150
1963	11 273	4 920	2 203	521	5 892	217	1 553	3 208
1964	11 613	5 026	2 256	530	5 996	224	1 585	3 271
1965	11 963	5 135	2 311	538	6 104	232	1 628	3 342
1966	12 339	5 201	2 368	546	6 217	239	1 683	3 416
1967	12 760	5 247	2 427	554	6 336	247	1 729	3 492
1968	13 146	5 350	2 489	562	6 460	254	1 756	3 570
1969	13 528	5 472	2 553	572	6 590	262	1 785	3 650
1970	13 932	5 606	2 620	584	6 727	269	1 827	3 733
1971	14 335	5 753	2 689	600	6 870	273	1 869	3 818
1972	14 761	5 896	2 761	620	7 021	275	1 910	3 905
1973	15 198	6 028	2 836	643	7 179	277	1 945	3 995
1974	15 653	5 988	2 914	672	7 346	279	1 983	4 087
1975	16 140	5 892	2 996	705	7 522	280	2 031	4 181
1976	16 635	5 955	3 080	742	7 723	283	2 071	4 278
1977	17 153	6 184	3 168	783	7 966	286	2 111	4 378
1978	17 703	6 311	3 260	824	8 214	289	2 153	4 480
1979	18 266	6 493	3 355	864	8 461	292	2 197	4 518
1980	18 862	6 794	3 444	903	8 761	296	2 244	4 507
1981	19 484	6 951	3 540	937	9 044	300	2 291	4 606
1982	20 132	7 114	3 642	972	9 280	305	2 338	4 826
1983	20 803	7 260	3 750	1 009	9 563	309	2 385	5 014
1984	21 488	7 400	3 864	1 047	9 870	314	2 451	5 054
1985	22 182	7 572	3 984	1 087	10 199	320	2 516	5 089
1986	22 844	7 750	4 109	1 129	10 544	325	2 556	5 223
1987	23 485	7 913	4 241	1 171	10 890	331	2 600	5 396
1988	24 102	8 090	4 379	1 215	11 236	337	2 653	5 559
1989	24 725	8 249	4 524	1 259	11 562	343	2 727	5 720
1990	25 352	8 430	4 676	1 304	11 894	349	2 798	5 889
1991	25 983	8 671	4 834	1 323	12 261	356	2 870	6 046
1992	26 618	8 960	4 998	1 342	12 636	362	2 946	6 218
1993	27 257	9 232	5 167	1 360	13 017	369	3 032	6 402
1994	27 898	9 494	5 342	1 379	13 405	375	3 117	6 590
1995	28 539	9 877	5 523	1 397	13 800	381	3 183	6 784
1996	29 183	10 250	5 710	1 415	14 202	388	3 243	6 977
1997	29 830	10 549	5 902	1 432	14 611	394	3 308	7 166
1998	30 481	10 865	6 101	1 448	15 029	400	3 376	7 360

Table C4–a. **Population in 57 African Countries, Annual Estimates, 1950–98**
(000 at mid–year)

	Comoros	Congo	Côte d'Ivoire	Djibouti	Egypt	Gabon	Gambia	Ghana
1950	148	768	2 860	60	21 198	416	305	5 297
1951	151	781	2 918	62	21 704	418	313	5 437
1952	154	794	2 977	63	22 223	421	321	5 581
1953	157	809	3 037	65	22 755	423	329	5 731
1954	160	824	3 099	66	23 299	426	337	5 887
1955	164	840	3 164	68	23 856	429	346	6 049
1956	167	856	3 231	70	24 426	432	354	6 217
1957	171	874	3 300	72	25 010	435	363	6 391
1958	175	892	3 374	74	25 608	438	372	6 573
1959	179	911	3 463	76	26 220	442	381	6 761
1960	183	931	3 576	78	26 847	446	391	6 958
1961	187	952	3 700	84	27 523	450	401	7 154
1962	192	974	3 832	90	28 173	456	411	7 355
1963	196	996	3 985	96	28 821	461	421	7 564
1964	201	1 020	4 148	103	29 533	468	432	7 782
1965	206	1 044	4 327	111	30 265	474	443	8 010
1966	212	1 070	4 527	119	30 986	482	454	8 245
1967	217	1 097	4 745	128	31 681	489	465	8 490
1968	223	1 124	4 984	137	32 338	497	477	8 744
1969	230	1 153	5 235	147	32 966	504	489	9 009
1970	236	1 183	5 504	158	33 574	514	502	8 789
1971	243	1 214	5 786	169	34 184	525	515	9 040
1972	250	1 246	6 072	179	34 807	536	529	9 306
1973	257	1 279	6 352	189	35 480	557	546	9 583
1974	265	1 314	6 622	198	36 216	591	563	9 823
1975	273	1 358	6 889	208	36 952	640	581	10 023
1976	281	1 406	7 151	217	37 737	676	599	10 229
1977	305	1 456	7 419	229	38 754	709	618	10 427
1978	314	1 509	7 692	248	39 940	760	637	10 604
1979	324	1 563	7 973	263	41 123	786	656	10 753
1980	334	1 620	8 261	279	42 441	808	676	10 880
1981	341	1 680	8 558	294	43 941	854	696	11 027
1982	349	1 742	8 866	306	45 361	904	717	11 236
1983	357	1 807	9 185	316	46 703	947	739	11 982
1984	366	1 883	9 517	289	48 088	984	767	12 653
1985	375	1 936	9 864	297	49 514	1 015	796	13 050
1986	385	1 989	10 221	305	50 974	1 037	827	13 597
1987	395	2 043	10 585	312	52 252	1 050	859	13 985
1988	406	2 097	10 956	329	53 487	1 059	893	14 379
1989	417	2 151	11 362	353	54 704	1 068	928	14 778
1990	429	2 206	11 904	370	56 106	1 078	964	15 190
1991	441	2 261	12 430	381	57 512	1 090	1 001	15 614
1992	454	2 315	12 796	391	58 723	1 106	1 040	16 039
1993	468	2 371	13 223	402	59 929	1 123	1 080	16 461
1994	482	2 427	13 731	413	61 150	1 139	1 121	16 878
1995	497	2 484	14 204	421	62 374	1 156	1 163	17 291
1996	513	2 542	14 653	428	63 599	1 173	1 205	17 698
1997	529	2 600	15 075	434	64 824	1 190	1 248	18 101
1998	546	2 658	15 446	441	66 050	1 208	1 292	18 497

Table C4–a. **Population in 57 African Countries, Annual Estimates, 1950–98**
(000 at mid–year)

	Kenya	Liberia	Madagascar	Mali	Mauritania	Mauritius	Morocco	Mozambique
1950	6 121	824	4 620	3 688	1 006	481	9 343	6 250
1951	6 289	843	4 690	3 761	1 014	499	9 634	6 346
1952	6 464	863	4 763	3 835	1 023	517	9 939	6 446
1953	6 646	884	4 839	3 911	1 032	536	10 206	6 552
1954	6 836	906	4 919	3 988	1 042	554	10 487	6 664
1955	7 034	928	5 003	4 067	1 053	572	10 782	6 782
1956	7 240	952	5 090	4 148	1 065	592	11 089	6 906
1957	7 455	976	5 182	4 230	1 077	610	11 406	7 038
1958	7 679	1 001	5 277	4 314	1 090	628	11 735	7 177
1959	7 913	1 028	5 378	4 399	1 103	645	12 074	7 321
1960	8 157	1 055	5 482	4 486	1 117	663	12 423	7 472
1961	8 412	1 083	5 590	4 576	1 132	681	12 736	7 628
1962	8 679	1 113	5 703	4 668	1 147	701	13 057	7 789
1963	8 957	1 144	5 821	4 763	1 162	715	13 385	7 957
1964	9 248	1 175	5 944	4 862	1 178	736	13 722	8 127
1965	9 549	1 209	6 070	4 963	1 195	756	14 066	8 301
1966	9 864	1 243	6 200	5 068	1 212	774	14 415	8 486
1967	10 192	1 279	6 335	5 177	1 231	789	14 770	8 681
1968	10 532	1 317	6 473	5 289	1 249	804	15 137	8 884
1969	10 888	1 356	6 616	5 405	1 269	816	15 517	9 093
1970	11 272	1 397	6 766	5 525	1 289	830	15 909	9 304
1971	11 685	1 439	6 920	5 649	1 311	841	16 313	9 539
1972	12 126	1 483	7 082	5 777	1 333	851	16 661	9 810
1973	12 594	1 528	7 250	5 909	1 356	861	16 998	10 088
1974	13 090	1 575	7 424	6 046	1 380	873	17 335	10 370
1975	13 615	1 625	7 604	6 188	1 404	885	17 687	10 433
1976	14 171	1 675	7 805	6 334	1 430	898	18 043	10 770
1977	14 762	1 728	8 007	6 422	1 457	913	18 397	11 128
1978	15 386	1 783	8 217	6 517	1 485	929	18 758	11 466
1979	16 045	1 840	8 443	6 620	1 516	947	19 126	11 828
1980	16 685	1 900	8 678	6 731	1 550	964	19 487	12 103
1981	17 341	1 961	8 922	6 849	1 585	979	19 846	12 450
1982	18 015	2 025	9 174	6 975	1 622	992	20 199	12 794
1983	18 707	2 092	9 436	7 110	1 661	1 002	20 740	13 137
1984	19 419	2 161	9 706	7 255	1 702	1 012	21 296	13 487
1985	20 149	2 233	9 987	7 408	1 745	1 022	21 857	13 839
1986	20 890	2 308	10 277	7 569	1 791	1 032	22 422	14 122
1987	21 620	2 386	10 577	7 738	1 838	1 043	22 987	14 066
1988	22 330	2 467	10 885	7 884	1 888	1 052	23 555	13 882
1989	23 016	2 551	11 201	8 051	1 932	1 063	24 122	13 906
1990	23 674	2 265	11 525	8 231	1 979	1 074	24 685	14 056
1991	24 493	2 005	11 858	8 417	2 035	1 085	25 242	14 293
1992	25 410	2 145	12 201	8 574	2 113	1 096	25 797	14 522
1993	26 071	2 271	12 555	8 732	2 198	1 107	26 352	15 047
1994	26 496	2 304	12 917	8 930	2 272	1 118	26 907	16 159
1995	26 864	2 282	13 289	9 182	2 334	1 128	27 461	17 150
1996	27 316	2 397	13 671	9 485	2 389	1 140	28 013	17 694
1997	27 839	2 602	14 062	9 789	2 449	1 154	28 565	18 165
1998	28 337	2 772	14 463	10 109	2 511	1 168	29 114	18 641

Table C4–a. **Population in 57 African Countries, Annual Estimates, 1950–98**
(000 at mid–year)

	Namibia	Niger	Nigeria	Reunion	Rwanda	Senegal	Seychelles	Sierra Leone
1950	464	2 482	31 797	244	2 439	2 654	33	2 087
1951	475	2 538	32 449	251	2 486	2 703	33	2 115
1952	486	2 597	33 119	258	2 535	2 756	33	2 143
1953	497	2 659	33 809	266	2 587	2 810	34	2 172
1954	509	2 723	34 518	274	2 641	2 867	35	2 202
1955	522	2 790	35 248	286	2 698	2 927	36	2 233
1956	535	2 859	36 000	296	2 759	2 989	38	2 264
1957	548	2 931	36 774	309	2 822	3 055	38	2 296
1958	562	3 007	37 569	318	2 889	3 123	39	2 328
1959	576	3 085	38 388	327	2 959	3 195	40	2 362
1960	591	3 168	39 230	338	3 032	3 270	42	2 396
1961	606	3 253	40 096	348	3 046	3 348	43	2 432
1962	621	3 343	40 989	359	3 051	3 430	44	2 468
1963	637	3 437	41 908	371	3 129	3 516	45	2 505
1964	654	3 533	42 854	384	3 184	3 636	47	2 543
1965	671	3 633	43 829	393	3 265	3 744	48	2 582
1966	689	3 735	44 838	403	3 358	3 857	49	2 622
1967	707	3 842	45 887	414	3 451	3 966	50	2 662
1968	725	3 951	46 977	425	3 548	4 074	51	2 704
1969	745	4 064	48 110	436	3 657	4 193	53	2 746
1970	765	4 182	49 309	445	3 769	4 318	54	2 789
1971	786	4 303	50 540	453	3 880	4 450	56	2 834
1972	808	4 429	51 796	462	3 992	4 589	57	2 879
1973	831	4 559	53 121	469	4 110	4 727	58	2 925
1974	854	4 695	54 600	475	4 226	4 872	59	2 974
1975	879	4 836	56 224	481	4 357	4 989	61	3 027
1976	905	4 984	57 901	487	4 502	5 101	62	3 084
1977	923	5 139	59 657	492	4 657	5 232	63	3 142
1978	935	5 294	61 533	497	4 819	5 366	64	3 203
1979	955	5 459	63 548	502	4 991	5 501	65	3 267
1980	975	5 629	65 699	507	5 170	5 640	66	3 333
1981	988	5 806	67 905	512	5 362	5 783	68	3 403
1982	1 011	5 988	70 094	518	5 583	5 931	68	3 476
1983	1 045	6 189	71 202	523	5 802	6 083	69	3 553
1984	1 080	6 389	72 597	533	5 984	6 240	70	3 634
1985	1 116	6 589	74 697	542	6 157	6 402	71	3 719
1986	1 154	6 802	76 558	552	6 335	6 569	71	3 809
1987	1 196	7 016	78 892	563	6 539	6 742	72	3 904
1988	1 256	7 237	81 330	575	6 759	6 920	72	4 003
1989	1 339	7 436	83 874	588	6 968	7 159	73	4 109
1990	1 409	7 644	86 530	600	7 161	7 408	73	4 283
1991	1 438	7 863	89 263	613	7 359	7 667	74	4 407
1992	1 464	8 093	92 057	626	7 547	7 935	75	4 348
1993	1 491	8 333	94 934	640	7 721	8 211	76	4 318
1994	1 518	8 583	97 900	653	6 682	8 497	76	4 434
1995	1 544	8 844	100 959	666	5 980	8 790	77	4 589
1996	1 570	9 113	104 095	679	6 273	9 093	78	4 734
1997	1 596	9 389	107 286	692	7 718	9 404	78	4 892
1998	1 622	9 672	110 532	705	7 956	9 723	79	5 080

Table C4–a. **Population in 57 African Countries, Annual Estimates, 1950–98**
(000 at mid–year)

	Somalia	*South Africa*	*Sudan*	*Swaziland*	*Tanzania*	*Togo*	*Tunisia*	*Uganda*
1950	2 438	13 596	8 051	277	8 909	1 172	3 517	5 522
1951	2 482	13 926	8 275	284	9 061	1 195	3 583	5 671
1952	2 527	14 265	8 505	290	9 222	1 219	3 648	5 825
1953	2 574	14 624	8 741	297	9 392	1 244	3 713	5 983
1954	2 623	14 992	8 984	304	9 572	1 271	3 779	6 148
1955	2 673	15 369	9 233	311	9 762	1 298	3 846	6 317
1956	2 726	15 755	9 490	319	9 963	1 327	3 903	6 493
1957	2 780	16 152	9 753	327	10 175	1 357	3 951	6 676
1958	2 837	16 558	10 024	335	10 398	1 389	4 007	6 864
1959	2 895	16 975	10 303	343	10 632	1 422	4 075	7 059
1960	2 956	17 417	10 589	352	10 876	1 456	4 149	7 262
1961	3 017	17 870	10 882	361	11 135	1 491	4 216	7 472
1962	3 080	18 357	11 183	370	11 409	1 528	4 287	7 689
1963	3 145	18 857	11 493	380	11 693	1 566	4 374	7 914
1964	3 213	19 371	11 801	389	11 990	1 606	4 468	8 147
1965	3 283	19 898	12 086	399	12 301	1 648	4 566	8 389
1966	3 354	20 440	12 377	410	12 620	1 691	4 676	8 640
1967	3 429	20 997	12 716	421	12 952	1 736	4 787	8 900
1968	3 506	21 569	13 059	432	13 296	1 782	4 894	9 170
1969	3 585	22 157	13 403	443	13 657	1 830	4 996	9 450
1970	3 667	22 740	13 788	455	14 038	1 964	5 099	9 728
1971	3 752	23 338	14 182	467	14 430	2 019	5 198	9 984
1972	3 840	23 936	14 597	480	14 843	2 075	5 304	10 191
1973	3 932	24 549	15 113	493	15 321	2 133	5 426	10 386
1974	4 027	25 179	15 571	507	15 792	2 192	5 556	10 621
1975	4 128	25 815	16 056	521	16 250	2 254	5 704	10 891
1976	4 238	26 468	16 570	536	16 704	2 317	5 859	11 171
1977	4 354	27 130	17 105	551	17 195	2 382	6 005	11 459
1978	4 678	27 809	17 712	566	17 633	2 450	6 136	11 757
1979	5 309	28 506	18 387	585	18 155	2 521	6 280	12 034
1980	5 791	29 252	19 064	607	18 690	2 596	6 443	12 298
1981	5 825	30 018	19 702	625	19 240	2 686	6 606	12 597
1982	5 829	30 829	20 367	641	19 802	2 775	6 734	12 941
1983	6 003	31 664	21 751	661	20 385	2 870	6 860	13 323
1984	6 207	32 523	22 544	682	20 987	2 970	7 185	13 765
1985	6 446	33 406	23 459	705	21 603	3 075	7 362	14 232
1986	6 700	34 156	24 181	728	22 240	3 185	7 545	14 747
1987	6 922	34 894	24 738	762	22 913	3 301	7 725	15 350
1988	6 900	35 640	25 250	792	23 582	3 422	7 895	15 991
1989	6 748	36 406	25 844	813	24 227	3 548	8 053	16 627
1990	6 675	37 191	26 628	840	24 886	3 680	8 207	17 227
1991	6 427	37 962	27 441	867	25 567	3 818	8 364	17 833
1992	6 057	38 746	28 218	894	26 261	3 959	8 522	18 465
1993	6 044	39 481	28 946	916	27 093	4 105	8 680	19 150
1994	6 174	40 165	29 710	912	28 032	4 255	8 831	19 846
1995	6 256	40 864	30 556	909	28 825	4 410	8 972	20 401
1996	6 420	41 551	31 548	928	29 341	4 571	9 108	20 929
1997	6 590	42 209	32 594	947	29 899	4 736	9 245	21 544
1998	6 842	42 835	33 551	966	30 609	4 906	9 380	22 167

Table C4–a. **Population in 57 African Countries, Annual Estimates, 1950–98**
(000 at mid–year)

	Zambia	*Zimbabwe*	*Total 42 countries*	*Total other 15 countries*	*Total 57 countries*
1950	2 553	2 853	178 488	49 852	228 341
1951	2 611	2 951	182 351	50 688	233 039
1952	2 672	3 081	186 396	51 549	237 944
1953	2 734	3 191	190 552	52 435	242 986
1954	2 800	3 307	194 671	53 353	248 024
1955	2 869	3 409	199 069	54 305	253 374
1956	2 941	3 530	203 599	55 295	258 894
1957	3 016	3 646	208 253	56 324	264 577
1958	3 094	3 764	213 064	57 393	270 456
1959	3 173	3 887	218 047	58 500	276 547
1960	3 254	4 011	223 226	59 649	282 876
1961	3 337	4 140	228 354	60 847	289 201
1962	3 421	4 278	233 414	62 239	295 653
1963	3 508	4 412	239 124	63 658	302 782
1964	3 599	4 537	245 137	64 969	310 107
1965	3 694	4 685	251 355	66 351	317 706
1966	3 794	4 836	257 755	67 845	325 600
1967	3 900	4 995	264 369	69 474	333 843
1968	4 009	5 172	271 142	71 171	342 313
1969	4 123	5 353	278 105	72 886	350 991
1970	4 247	5 515	284 921	74 580	359 501
1971	4 368	5 684	292 306	76 320	368 625
1972	4 493	5 861	299 828	78 018	377 846
1973	4 625	6 041	307 751	79 900	387 651
1974	4 761	6 222	315 794	81 900	397 693
1975	4 895	6 403	323 884	84 066	407 950
1976	5 032	6 570	332 681	86 343	419 024
1977	5 176	6 728	342 148	88 376	430 525
1978	5 324	6 866	352 124	90 312	442 436
1979	5 478	6 999	362 794	92 466	455 260
1980	5 638	7 298	373 902	94 355	468 257
1981	5 832	7 574	385 008	96 373	481 381
1982	6 059	7 798	396 330	99 053	495 383
1983	6 311	8 053	408 360	101 796	510 156
1984	6 555	8 320	420 338	104 766	525 104
1985	6 793	8 597	433 006	107 334	540 340
1986	7 054	8 881	445 493	110 258	555 751
1987	7 314	9 189	457 793	113 875	571 668
1988	7 543	9 493	469 784	117 903	587 687
1989	7 754	9 745	482 024	122 038	604 062
1990	7 957	9 958	494 785	125 980	620 765
1991	8 158	10 157	507 781	129 957	637 738
1992	8 361	10 365	520 795	133 548	654 343
1993	8 561	10 556	534 482	137 169	671 651
1994	8 762	10 612	547 686	140 488	688 174
1995	8 915	10 646	560 972	144 585	705 557
1996	9 068	10 778	575 156	147 594	722 750
1997	9 265	10 915	590 817	150 790	741 607
1998	9 461	11 044	605 442	154 512	759 955

Table C4–b. **Levels of GDP in 57 African Countries, Annual Estimates, 1950–98**
(million 1990 international Geary–Khamis dollars)

	Algeria	Angola	Benin	Botswana	Cameroon	Cape Verde	Central African Republic	Chad
1950	12 136	4 331	1 813	150	3 279	66	972	1 240
1951	12 221	4 491	1 813	155	3 401	69	1 008	1 286
1952	12 767	4 660	1 813	159	3 525	71	1 045	1 333
1953	13 046	4 833	1 762	164	3 653	75	1 083	1 381
1954	13 811	4 703	1 813	169	3 788	76	1 123	1 432
1955	14 224	5 080	1 813	174	3 929	78	1 165	1 485
1956	15 619	4 985	1 813	179	4 073	82	1 207	1 540
1957	17 391	5 461	1 813	184	4 224	81	1 252	1 597
1958	18 022	5 751	1 880	189	4 381	83	1 299	1 657
1959	21 323	5 777	1 950	195	4 542	93	1 346	1 717
1960	22 780	6 011	2 010	200	4 666	100	1 358	1 730
1961	20 013	6 635	2 075	207	4 722	107	1 409	1 753
1962	15 765	6 444	2 005	213	4 867	113	1 373	1 846
1963	19 928	6 791	2 097	220	5 047	120	1 369	1 819
1964	20 971	7 587	2 240	228	5 227	127	1 391	1 773
1965	22 367	8 194	2 356	235	5 332	133	1 409	1 783
1966	21 287	8 635	2 443	258	5 581	140	1 420	1 752
1967	23 277	9 064	2 467	284	5 736	147	1 487	1 764
1968	25 996	8 947	2 561	313	6 109	153	1 494	1 756
1969	28 484	9 255	2 637	344	6 411	160	1 565	1 876
1970	31 336	9 909	2 692	378	6 605	166	1 638	1 912
1971	28 666	9 943	2 704	448	6 801	155	1 590	1 948
1972	34 685	10 091	2 942	592	7 096	148	1 557	1 815
1973	35 814	10 784	3 011	722	7 201	147	1 627	1 726
1974	37 999	10 242	2 784	873	7 523	143	1 580	1 963
1975	40 705	6 314	2 904	862	7 910	147	1 609	2 301
1976	43 387	5 669	3 029	1 024	8 061	147	1 679	2 267
1977	47 319	5 799	3 199	1 061	8 520	148	1 816	2 098
1978	53 387	6 037	3 301	1 264	8 985	164	1 848	2 088
1979	58 193	6 184	3 565	1 391	9 474	182	1 745	1 640
1980	59 273	6 483	3 901	1 589	10 441	249	1 730	1 541
1981	60 766	6 353	4 122	1 736	12 222	271	1 757	1 557
1982	64 662	6 050	4 566	1 865	13 147	279	1 790	1 640
1983	68 012	5 851	4 366	2 159	14 068	306	1 681	1 897
1984	71 774	5 881	4 713	2 400	15 170	317	1 803	1 937
1985	75 512	5 911	5 068	2 577	16 528	345	1 826	2 361
1986	74 747	5 379	5 182	2 773	17 722	355	1 859	2 264
1987	74 225	5 985	5 104	3 017	16 839	380	1 812	2 208
1988	72 672	6 843	5 258	3 492	16 072	392	1 845	2 551
1989	75 123	6 959	5 144	3 944	14 632	413	1 913	2 698
1990	73 934	7 202	5 347	4 178	14 393	430	1 982	2 537
1991	73 047	7 252	5 598	4 379	13 846	283	1 970	2 801
1992	74 216	7 180	5 822	4 510	13 417	231	1 844	2 868
1993	72 583	5 241	6 026	4 600	12 987	434	1 850	2 816
1994	71 784	5 315	6 291	4 757	12 663	490	1 940	2 977
1995	74 584	5 915	6 581	4 980	13 081	500	2 057	3 004
1996	77 418	6 607	6 942	5 324	13 735	513	1 989	3 115
1997	78 270	7 043	7 338	5 739	14 435	525	2 102	3 243
1998	81 948	7 029	7 668	6 083	15 157	544	2 203	3 463

Table C4–b. **Levels of GDP in 57 African Countries, Annual Estimates, 1950–98**
(million 1990 international Geary–Khamis dollars)

	Comoros	*Congo*	*Côte d'Ivoire*	*Djibouti*	*Egypt*	*Gabon*	*Gambia*	*Ghana*
1950	83	990	2 977	90	15 224	1 292	165	5 943
1951	88	1 027	3 087	95	15 498	1 340	174	6 163
1952	90	1 064	3 201	98	15 788	1 389	180	6 050
1953	94	1 103	3 317	102	16 062	1 440	187	6 888
1954	99	1 144	3 439	108	16 351	1 493	197	7 755
1955	102	1 186	3 567	111	16 655	1 548	203	7 256
1956	106	1 230	3 698	115	17 447	1 605	211	7 684
1957	110	1 275	3 835	120	18 269	1 665	219	7 933
1958	113	1 323	3 978	123	19 137	1 727	225	7 803
1959	120	1 372	4 123	130	20 050	1 791	238	8 932
1960	130	1 419	4 493	139	21 010	1 866	254	9 591
1961	132	1 465	4 912	150	22 395	2 090	296	9 930
1962	144	1 513	5 130	158	23 887	2 153	292	10 412
1963	174	1 563	5 972	171	25 485	2 229	294	10 774
1964	188	1 616	7 041	182	27 191	2 268	314	11 006
1965	188	1 670	6 886	194	28 987	2 306	348	11 154
1966	208	1 757	7 431	209	29 155	2 409	406	11 166
1967	217	1 850	7 538	224	28 789	2 508	421	11 368
1968	218	1 948	8 714	239	29 246	2 572	427	11 529
1969	221	2 050	9 098	256	31 255	2 780	473	11 939
1970	238	2 158	10 087	327	33 235	3 020	426	12 515
1971	280	2 333	10 593	361	34 620	3 330	475	13 514
1972	258	2 523	11 179	385	35 275	3 708	509	13 109
1973	229	2 727	12 064	412	36 249	4 086	533	13 484
1974	279	2 947	12 412	412	37 634	5 699	638	14 411
1975	219	3 185	12 400	430	41 441	6 090	598	12 616
1976	194	3 199	13 886	468	47 850	8 487	668	12 171
1977	190	2 934	14 541	410	54 092	6 732	701	12 450
1978	197	2 883	15 982	427	58 248	4 883	665	13 508
1979	202	3 323	16 282	444	62 846	4 814	773	13 163
1980	215	3 891	17 539	464	69 636	4 837	697	12 747
1981	226	4 697	18 152	491	72 407	4 780	691	12 765
1982	235	5 072	18 188	513	80 141	4 685	779	11 879
1983	244	5 327	17 479	519	86 307	4 756	685	11 339
1984	252	5 667	16 902	521	91 574	4 946	665	12 319
1985	259	5 412	17 732	521	97 618	4 846	609	12 943
1986	266	5 044	18 262	521	100 191	4 603	641	13 621
1987	277	5 079	17 970	521	102 718	4 005	676	14 274
1988	289	5 089	17 646	521	107 027	4 086	747	15 077
1989	290	5 277	17 542	526	110 239	4 261	799	15 843
1990	294	5 394	16 330	530	112 873	4 500	833	16 372
1991	278	5 523	16 330	533	109 261	4 775	851	17 240
1992	302	5 667	16 297	532	112 867	4 617	889	17 912
1993	311	5 610	16 265	511	114 673	4 728	943	18 808
1994	294	5 302	16 590	496	117 998	4 888	979	19 522
1995	283	5 514	17 768	478	120 948	5 231	942	20 401
1996	282	5 861	18 976	460	126 995	5 497	992	21 115
1997	282	5 750	20 115	464	133 345	5 789	999	22 002
1998	285	5 951	21 201	467	140 546	5 901	1 098	23 014

Table C4–b. **Levels of GDP in 57 African Countries, Annual Estimates, 1950–98**
(million 1990 international Geary–Khamis dollars)

	Kenya	*Liberia*	*Madagascar*	*Mali*	*Mauritania*	*Mauritius*	*Morocco*	*Mozambique*
1950	3 982	869	4 394	1 685	467	1 198	13 598	7 084
1951	4 851	919	4 557	1 747	484	1 267	14 046	7 332
1952	4 313	947	4 724	1 811	502	1 306	14 509	7 594
1953	4 205	984	4 895	1 879	520	1 356	14 987	7 857
1954	4 695	1 039	5 075	1 946	539	1 433	15 481	8 041
1955	5 050	1 073	5 264	2 018	559	1 479	15 991	8 537
1956	5 329	1 113	5 457	2 093	580	1 535	16 093	8 579
1957	5 504	1 155	5 660	2 170	601	1 594	16 195	8 770
1958	5 563	1 188	5 870	2 249	623	1 638	16 299	9 188
1959	5 699	1 257	6 086	2 333	647	1 733	16 402	9 684
1960	5 918	1 297	6 169	2 399	698	1 842	16 507	9 918
1961	5 775	1 328	6 297	2 414	817	2 261	17 085	10 202
1962	6 085	1 345	6 442	2 428	799	2 278	17 684	10 903
1963	6 392	1 377	6 380	2 591	750	2 595	18 303	10 513
1964	7 013	1 447	6 635	2 714	974	2 417	18 944	10 967
1965	7 093	1 472	6 604	2 753	1 109	2 495	19 608	11 215
1966	8 005	1 751	6 741	2 869	1 115	2 406	20 700	11 576
1967	8 419	1 740	7 114	2 964	1 154	2 510	21 853	12 369
1968	9 028	1 823	7 597	3 075	1 256	2 338	23 071	13 758
1969	9 590	1 955	7 883	3 060	1 237	2 453	24 356	15 394
1970	10 291	2 083	8 296	3 248	1 365	2 443	25 713	16 216
1971	10 944	2 186	8 621	3 361	1 378	2 563	27 154	17 321
1972	11 509	2 269	8 511	3 535	1 396	2 817	27 807	17 881
1973	12 107	2 212	8 292	3 449	1 309	3 169	28 800	18 894
1974	12 704	2 375	8 459	3 365	1 443	3 511	30 351	17 463
1975	12 652	2 017	8 564	3 831	1 351	3 514	32 385	14 643
1976	13 162	2 096	8 300	4 352	1 459	4 086	35 950	13 942
1977	14 369	2 079	8 498	4 648	1 440	4 353	37 711	14 055
1978	15 663	2 161	8 274	4 524	1 434	4 520	38 808	14 162
1979	16 252	2 257	9 087	5 612	1 500	4 679	40 584	14 367
1980	17 160	2 149	9 157	4 953	1 560	4 208	44 278	14 771
1981	17 555	2 197	8 366	4 787	1 619	4 455	43 054	15 040
1982	18 614	2 134	8 213	4 512	1 586	4 701	47 203	14 629
1983	18 729	2 119	8 278	4 711	1 663	4 719	46 930	13 581
1984	19 056	2 100	7 975	4 918	1 543	4 940	48 894	13 212
1985	19 876	2 071	8 155	5 029	1 587	5 285	51 955	12 022
1986	21 302	2 131	8 213	5 348	1 676	5 817	56 023	12 199
1987	22 569	2 189	8 393	5 449	1 727	6 408	54 762	12 639
1988	23 927	2 189	8 525	5 440	1 792	6 844	60 367	13 361
1989	25 018	2 216	8 867	5 995	1 852	7 145	61 748	13 900
1990	26 093	2 245	9 210	6 040	1 825	7 652	64 082	14 105
1991	26 458	2 281	8 630	5 986	1 872	8 142	68 504	14 796
1992	26 247	2 321	8 733	6 488	1 904	8 533	65 764	13 598
1993	26 352	2 374	8 917	6 333	2 009	9 104	65 106	14 781
1994	27 037	2 426	8 917	6 472	2 101	9 496	71 877	15 889
1995	28 226	2 492	9 068	6 886	2 196	9 828	67 133	16 572
1996	29 384	2 541	9 259	7 162	2 299	10 329	75 256	17 749
1997	30 001	2 555	9 601	7 642	2 410	10 897	73 751	19 755
1998	30 451	2 580	9 976	7 917	2 494	11 508	78 397	22 125

Table C4–b. **Levels of GDP in 57 African Countries, Annual Estimates, 1950–98**
(million 1990 international Geary–Khamis dollars)

	Namibia	Niger	Nigeria	Reunion	Rwanda	Senegal	Seychelles	Sierra Leone
1950	1 002	2 018	23 933	485	1 334	3 341	63	1 370
1951	1 033	2 093	25 728	512	1 410	3 464	67	1 448
1952	1 065	2 170	27 571	528	1 454	3 591	69	1 493
1953	1 106	2 248	28 217	549	1 510	3 721	71	1 550
1954	1 168	2 331	30 299	580	1 596	3 858	75	1 638
1955	1 206	2 418	31 089	598	1 646	4 002	78	1 696
1956	1 251	2 507	30 371	621	1 709	4 149	81	1 760
1957	1 299	2 600	31 615	645	1 773	4 303	84	1 826
1958	1 335	2 697	31 256	663	1 824	4 463	86	1 878
1959	1 412	2 797	32 621	701	1 929	4 627	91	1 986
1960	1 545	2 977	34 081	756	1 989	4 724	99	2 050
1961	1 562	3 100	35 229	796	1 904	4 937	94	2 087
1962	1 783	3 427	37 240	859	2 120	5 101	101	2 182
1963	1 961	3 766	40 734	925	1 912	5 298	111	2 219
1964	2 279	3 776	42 481	1 004	1 673	5 452	116	2 245
1965	2 433	4 061	45 353	1 101	1 790	5 656	116	2 405
1966	2 526	4 010	43 893	1 170	1 916	5 816	119	2 559
1967	2 424	4 029	37 072	1 256	2 051	5 746	119	2 542
1968	2 444	4 061	36 665	1 347	2 193	6 107	129	2 791
1969	2 529	3 940	46 502	1 477	2 435	5 709	129	3 045
1970	2 540	4 061	60 814	1 540	2 702	6 197	139	3 149
1971	2 627	4 291	67 970	1 575	2 734	6 187	162	3 120
1972	2 783	4 069	70 530	1 757	2 742	6 588	172	3 086
1973	2 895	3 377	76 585	1 771	2 826	6 217	187	3 180
1974	3 021	3 671	85 465	1 876	2 959	6 478	190	3 309
1975	3 052	3 570	82 904	1 838	3 510	6 965	197	3 408
1976	3 221	3 595	91 927	1 636	3 450	7 587	217	3 305
1977	3 424	3 873	95 277	1 603	3 629	7 383	234	3 353
1978	3 651	4 394	89 653	1 730	3 985	7 092	250	3 363
1979	3 806	4 709	95 852	1 815	4 360	7 590	292	3 554
1980	3 986	4 937	97 646	1 869	4 892	7 339	284	3 721
1981	4 110	4 995	89 820	1 913	5 210	7 283	265	3 951
1982	4 164	4 935	89 007	2 057	5 646	8 388	260	4 019
1983	4 057	4 844	83 000	2 157	5 984	8 602	255	3 961
1984	4 006	4 025	79 290	2 181	5 730	8 205	265	4 014
1985	4 023	4 095	86 302	2 205	5 982	8 515	290	3 904
1986	4 147	4 283	87 930	2 230	6 309	8 926	297	3 767
1987	4 268	4 130	87 284	2 248	6 261	9 290	311	3 965
1988	4 368	4 362	95 947	2 383	6 046	9 765	325	4 072
1989	4 738	4 368	102 146	2 454	6 168	9 598	343	4 164
1990	4 619	4 289	107 459	2 694	6 125	10 032	366	4 335
1991	4 882	4 396	113 907	2 863	5 862	9 992	376	3 988
1992	5 346	4 110	116 868	2 863	6 248	10 212	402	3 605
1993	5 239	4 168	119 439	2 863	5 730	9 987	428	3 609
1994	5 590	4 335	118 723	2 863	2 951	10 277	425	3 735
1995	5 780	4 447	121 809	2 863	3 919	10 842	422	3 362
1996	5 948	4 599	129 605	3 012	4 538	11 406	442	3 530
1997	6 055	4 750	133 623	3 136	5 119	11 976	461	2 817
1998	6 158	5 149	136 162	3 174	5 605	12 659	471	2 837

Table C4–b. **Levels of GDP in 57 African Countries, Annual Estimates, 1950–98**
(million 1990 international Geary–Khamis dollars)

	Somalia	South Africa	Sudan	Swaziland	Tanzania	Togo	Tunisia	Uganda
1950	2 576	34 465	6 609	200	3 362	673	3 920	3 793
1951	2 724	36 085	6 926	211	3 786	698	3 963	3 641
1952	2 810	37 360	7 270	218	3 863	723	4 450	3 868
1953	2 915	39 117	7 613	226	3 725	749	4 618	4 039
1954	3 083	41 427	7 983	239	4 028	777	4 720	3 982
1955	3 183	43 494	8 373	247	4 125	806	4 477	4 244
1956	3 301	45 907	9 259	256	4 176	836	4 775	4 479
1957	3 425	47 665	9 133	266	4 277	867	4 579	4 673
1958	3 520	48 664	9 510	273	4 314	899	5 175	4 703
1959	3 726	50 835	10 640	289	4 525	932	4 959	4 942
1960	3 775	52 972	10 838	329	4 710	1 016	5 571	5 177
1961	3 956	55 247	10 838	371	4 657	1 085	6 053	5 124
1962	4 130	58 349	11 592	449	5 080	1 125	5 912	5 332
1963	4 290	62 622	11 261	475	5 400	1 181	6 806	5 943
1964	3 826	66 827	11 142	545	5 695	1 351	7 100	6 394
1965	3 572	70 825	11 896	630	5 901	1 535	7 547	6 535
1966	4 079	73 892	11 717	657	6 657	1 676	7 735	6 941
1967	4 313	78 959	11 354	719	6 926	1 769	7 684	7 312
1968	4 388	82 371	12 048	686	7 282	1 859	8 491	7 498
1969	3 840	87 437	12 781	715	7 417	2 060	8 793	8 325
1970	4 174	91 986	12 246	926	7 847	2 112	9 315	8 450
1971	4 282	96 501	13 092	942	8 177	2 262	10 302	8 700
1972	4 717	98 362	12 814	1 057	8 725	2 340	12 129	8 757
1973	4 625	102 498	11 783	1 114	9 007	2 245	12 051	8 704
1974	3 682	108 254	12 966	1 238	9 216	2 340	13 019	8 719
1975	4 960	110 253	14 612	1 282	9 693	2 326	13 952	8 541
1976	4 944	112 941	17 302	1 324	10 386	2 315	15 054	8 606
1977	6 185	112 734	19 932	1 364	10 678	2 441	15 567	8 738
1978	6 500	116 077	19 621	1 399	10 987	2 689	16 571	8 260
1979	6 270	120 627	17 586	1 424	11 122	2 851	17 657	7 350
1980	6 005	128 416	17 758	1 466	11 216	2 721	18 966	7 100
1981	6 482	135 171	18 128	1 566	11 092	2 551	20 013	7 373
1982	6 716	134 619	20 421	1 656	11 236	2 453	19 915	7 980
1983	6 098	132 172	20 844	1 664	11 186	2 320	20 848	8 571
1984	6 306	138 893	19 800	1 698	11 465	2 389	22 040	7 843
1985	6 816	137 239	18 557	1 804	11 438	2 502	23 279	7 999
1986	7 056	137 307	19 291	1 872	11 811	2 580	22 918	8 025
1987	7 409	140 099	19 720	2 031	12 413	2 616	24 451	8 533
1988	7 359	145 855	19 952	1 984	12 937	2 733	24 478	9 148
1989	7 349	148 888	21 518	2 111	13 371	2 834	25 384	9 815
1990	7 231	147 509	19 793	2 154	13 852	2 805	27 387	10 206
1991	6 505	146 034	21 179	2 208	14 143	2 785	28 455	10 308
1992	5 536	142 967	22 280	2 237	14 228	2 674	30 675	10 628
1993	5 536	144 683	22 904	2 310	14 398	2 235	31 349	11 520
1994	5 701	149 313	24 118	2 391	14 629	2 611	32 384	12 131
1995	5 867	153 941	25 179	2 463	15 155	2 789	33 161	13 405
1996	6 048	160 407	26 362	2 552	15 837	3 059	35 482	14 490
1997	6 044	164 417	28 128	2 646	16 392	3 191	37 399	15 244
1998	6 044	165 239	29 535	2 699	16 933	3 159	39 306	16 082

Table C4–b. **Levels of GDP in 57 African countries, Annual Estimates, 1950–98**
(million 1990 international Geary–Khamis dollars)

	Zambia	Zimbabwe	Total 42 countries	Total other 15 countries	Total 57 countries
1950	1 687	2 000	176 858	17 709	194 568
1951	1 795	2 130	184 831	18 968	203 798
1952	1 910	2 232	191 583	20 059	211 642
1953	2 032	2 424	198 303	21 072	219 375
1954	2 161	2 554	208 248	21 873	230 121
1955	2 111	2 756	215 096	22 965	238 060
1956	2 362	3 148	223 320	24 392	247 712
1957	2 465	3 368	231 939	24 971	256 911
1958	2 401	3 412	237 382	25 267	262 649
1959	2 902	3 596	251 054	26 221	277 275
1960	3 123	3 762	261 999	27 609	289 608
1961	3 130	3 956	268 595	27 166	295 761
1962	3 096	4 016	276 171	30 854	307 024
1963	3 164	3 976	295 000	33 783	328 783
1964	3 586	4 326	310 279	36 203	346 482
1965	4 239	4 608	326 095	39 309	365 404
1966	4 007	4 678	333 469	42 439	375 908
1967	4 318	5 068	338 924	44 622	383 546
1968	4 379	5 168	354 074	49 389	403 463
1969	4 355	5 812	382 032	53 292	435 325
1970	4 562	7 072	416 129	55 239	471 369
1971	4 561	7 692	436 466	56 113	492 579
1972	4 979	8 342	455 548	55 180	510 728
1973	4 930	8 594	471 638	57 549	529 186
1974	5 332	8 810	497 754	56 400	554 154
1975	5 124	8 890	503 766	56 651	560 418
1976	5 426	8 816	537 581	59 988	597 569
1977	5 163	8 108	558 850	62 738	621 588
1978	5 195	8 338	573 167	63 348	636 515
1979	5 037	8 338	598 798	67 113	665 911
1980	5 190	9 288	626 270	68 617	694 886
1981	5 509	10 454	635 952	65 439	701 392
1982	5 354	10 726	656 633	65 340	721 973
1983	5 249	10 896	658 433	66 285	724 718
1984	5 231	10 688	673 549	65 872	739 421
1985	5 317	11 430	697 747	64 757	762 503
1986	5 354	11 732	711 972	66 283	778 255
1987	5 497	11 588	721 343	68 259	789 602
1988	5 841	12 672	752 279	69 913	822 192
1989	5 900	13 498	776 990	70 750	847 740
1990	6 432	13 766	789 435	70 352	859 787
1991	6 432	14 523	799 473	68 642	868 115
1992	6 323	13 216	803 175	66 447	869 622
1993	6 753	13 388	809 901	67 746	877 647
1994	6 172	14 298	829 146	68 002	897 149
1995	5 906	14 212	850 191	70 894	921 084
1996	6 284	15 250	898 652	75 305	973 958
1997	6 504	15 738	927 690	77 901	1 005 591
1998	6 374	15 990	961 581	77 825	1 039 407

Table C4–c. **Levels of Per Capita GDP in 57 African Countries, Annual Estimates, 1950–98**
(1990 international Geary–Khamis dollars)

	Algeria	Angola	Benin	Botswana	Cameroon	Cape Verde	Central African Republic	Chad
1950	1 365	1 052	1 084	349	671	450	772	476
1951	1 347	1 076	1 063	355	687	455	790	486
1952	1 376	1 101	1 043	359	704	461	809	497
1953	1 369	1 126	994	366	720	467	827	507
1954	1 437	1 079	1 002	372	737	460	845	518
1955	1 445	1 148	982	377	754	463	864	529
1956	1 553	1 110	962	383	771	469	881	540
1957	1 693	1 197	941	388	788	453	899	552
1958	1 719	1 241	956	392	805	449	917	563
1959	1 994	1 225	970	399	822	486	934	574
1960	2 088	1 253	978	403	832	508	925	569
1961	1 799	1 396	987	410	829	525	943	566
1962	1 433	1 335	932	415	840	539	901	586
1963	1 768	1 380	952	422	857	553	881	567
1964	1 806	1 510	993	430	872	564	878	542
1965	1 870	1 596	1 020	437	874	575	866	533
1966	1 725	1 660	1 032	473	898	585	844	513
1967	1 824	1 727	1 016	513	905	594	860	505
1968	1 977	1 672	1 029	557	946	602	851	492
1969	2 105	1 691	1 033	601	973	611	877	514
1970	2 249	1 768	1 027	647	982	619	896	512
1971	2 000	1 728	1 006	747	990	566	851	510
1972	2 350	1 712	1 065	956	1 011	536	815	465
1973	2 357	1 789	1 061	1 122	1 003	529	837	432
1974	2 428	1 710	955	1 299	1 024	512	797	480
1975	2 522	1 072	969	1 222	1 052	525	792	550
1976	2 608	952	983	1 380	1 044	520	811	530
1977	2 759	938	1 010	1 355	1 070	518	860	479
1978	3 016	957	1 013	1 534	1 094	567	858	466
1979	3 186	952	1 063	1 609	1 120	622	794	363
1980	3 143	954	1 132	1 760	1 192	841	771	342
1981	3 119	914	1 164	1 853	1 351	904	767	338
1982	3 212	850	1 254	1 919	1 417	916	765	340
1983	3 269	806	1 164	2 140	1 471	988	705	378
1984	3 340	795	1 220	2 291	1 537	1 009	736	383
1985	3 404	781	1 272	2 370	1 620	1 079	726	464
1986	3 272	694	1 261	2 457	1 681	1 091	727	433
1987	3 161	756	1 204	2 576	1 546	1 148	697	409
1988	3 015	846	1 201	2 875	1 430	1 163	695	459
1989	3 038	844	1 137	3 133	1 266	1 205	701	472
1990	2 916	854	1 144	3 204	1 210	1 231	708	431
1991	2 811	836	1 158	3 310	1 129	796	686	463
1992	2 788	801	1 165	3 362	1 062	638	626	461
1993	2 663	568	1 166	3 382	998	1 179	610	440
1994	2 573	560	1 178	3 450	945	1 305	622	452
1995	2 613	599	1 192	3 565	948	1 312	646	443
1996	2 653	645	1 216	3 763	967	1 324	613	446
1997	2 624	668	1 243	4 008	988	1 332	635	452
1998	2 689	647	1 257	4 200	1 008	1 360	653	471

Table C4–c. **Levels of Per Capita GDP in 57 African Countries, Annual Estimates, 1950–98**
(1990 international Geary–Khamis dollars)

	Comoros	Congo	Côte d'Ivoire	Djibouti	Egypt	Gabon	Gambia	Ghana
1950	560	1 289	1 041	1 500	718	3 108	540	1 122
1951	581	1 315	1 058	1 546	714	3 204	557	1 134
1952	587	1 340	1 075	1 554	710	3 302	560	1 084
1953	598	1 364	1 092	1 575	706	3 401	567	1 202
1954	619	1 388	1 110	1 622	702	3 504	584	1 317
1955	625	1 412	1 127	1 632	698	3 611	588	1 200
1956	635	1 436	1 144	1 651	714	3 718	596	1 236
1957	645	1 459	1 162	1 668	730	3 827	604	1 241
1958	649	1 482	1 179	1 665	747	3 939	606	1 187
1959	671	1 506	1 191	1 711	765	4 052	625	1 321
1960	712	1 523	1 256	1 771	783	4 184	650	1 378
1961	703	1 539	1 328	1 783	814	4 639	738	1 388
1962	749	1 553	1 339	1 759	848	4 725	711	1 416
1963	887	1 569	1 499	1 774	884	4 832	698	1 424
1964	932	1 584	1 697	1 758	921	4 851	727	1 414
1965	913	1 599	1 592	1 754	958	4 860	787	1 393
1966	984	1 642	1 642	1 761	941	5 003	896	1 354
1967	999	1 688	1 589	1 758	909	5 130	904	1 339
1968	973	1 732	1 749	1 746	904	5 176	894	1 318
1969	963	1 779	1 738	1 742	948	5 518	965	1 325
1970	1 009	1 825	1 833	2 069	990	5 874	848	1 424
1971	1 154	1 922	1 831	2 142	1 013	6 347	922	1 495
1972	1 032	2 025	1 841	2 150	1 013	6 922	963	1 409
1973	889	2 132	1 899	2 185	1 022	7 337	976	1 407
1974	1 055	2 243	1 874	2 080	1 039	9 635	1 133	1 467
1975	804	2 345	1 800	2 065	1 121	9 521	1 030	1 259
1976	692	2 275	1 942	2 154	1 268	12 549	1 114	1 190
1977	624	2 014	1 960	1 794	1 396	9 497	1 134	1 194
1978	627	1 911	2 078	1 724	1 458	6 426	1 044	1 274
1979	624	2 126	2 042	1 687	1 528	6 124	1 178	1 224
1980	643	2 402	2 123	1 661	1 641	5 990	1 030	1 172
1981	664	2 796	2 121	1 674	1 648	5 596	992	1 158
1982	675	2 912	2 052	1 676	1 767	5 185	1 086	1 057
1983	683	2 948	1 903	1 643	1 848	5 022	926	946
1984	688	3 009	1 776	1 802	1 904	5 025	867	974
1985	691	2 795	1 798	1 756	1 972	4 773	764	992
1986	691	2 535	1 787	1 712	1 966	4 438	775	1 002
1987	701	2 486	1 698	1 669	1 966	3 816	786	1 021
1988	712	2 427	1 611	1 587	2 001	3 860	837	1 048
1989	694	2 453	1 544	1 490	2 015	3 989	862	1 072
1990	685	2 445	1 372	1 432	2 012	4 176	864	1 078
1991	630	2 443	1 314	1 400	1 900	4 379	850	1 104
1992	664	2 448	1 274	1 360	1 922	4 173	855	1 117
1993	664	2 366	1 230	1 272	1 913	4 212	873	1 143
1994	610	2 184	1 208	1 202	1 930	4 292	873	1 157
1995	569	2 219	1 251	1 135	1 939	4 526	810	1 180
1996	549	2 306	1 295	1 077	1 997	4 687	823	1 193
1997	533	2 212	1 334	1 068	2 057	4 864	801	1 216
1998	522	2 239	1 373	1 061	2 128	4 886	850	1 244

Table C4–c. **Levels of Per Capita GDP in 57 African Countries, Annual Estimates, 1950–98**
(1990 international Geary–Khamis dollars)

	Kenya	*Liberia*	*Madagascar*	*Mali*	*Mauritania*	*Mauritius*	*Morocco*	*Mozambique*
1950	651	1 055	951	457	464	2 490	1 455	1 133
1951	771	1 090	972	465	477	2 540	1 458	1 155
1952	667	1 097	992	472	490	2 528	1 460	1 178
1953	633	1 113	1 012	480	504	2 530	1 468	1 199
1954	687	1 147	1 032	488	517	2 587	1 476	1 207
1955	718	1 156	1 052	496	531	2 587	1 483	1 259
1956	736	1 170	1 072	504	545	2 594	1 451	1 242
1957	738	1 183	1 092	513	558	2 613	1 420	1 246
1958	725	1 187	1 112	521	572	2 610	1 389	1 280
1959	720	1 223	1 132	530	586	2 685	1 358	1 323
1960	726	1 230	1 125	535	625	2 777	1 329	1 327
1961	686	1 226	1 126	528	722	3 319	1 341	1 337
1962	701	1 209	1 129	520	697	3 249	1 354	1 400
1963	714	1 204	1 096	544	645	3 629	1 367	1 321
1964	758	1 231	1 116	558	827	3 283	1 381	1 349
1965	743	1 218	1 088	555	928	3 302	1 394	1 351
1966	812	1 408	1 087	566	920	3 108	1 436	1 364
1967	826	1 360	1 123	572	938	3 180	1 480	1 425
1968	857	1 384	1 174	581	1 006	2 907	1 524	1 549
1969	881	1 442	1 192	566	975	3 006	1 570	1 693
1970	913	1 492	1 226	588	1 059	2 945	1 616	1 743
1971	937	1 519	1 246	595	1 051	3 047	1 665	1 816
1972	949	1 530	1 202	612	1 047	3 309	1 669	1 823
1973	961	1 447	1 144	584	966	3 680	1 694	1 873
1974	971	1 508	1 139	556	1 046	4 020	1 751	1 684
1975	929	1 242	1 126	619	962	3 969	1 831	1 404
1976	929	1 251	1 063	687	1 020	4 551	1 992	1 295
1977	973	1 203	1 061	724	988	4 768	2 050	1 263
1978	1 018	1 212	1 007	694	965	4 863	2 069	1 235
1979	1 013	1 226	1 076	848	989	4 943	2 122	1 215
1980	1 029	1 131	1 055	736	1 006	4 367	2 272	1 220
1981	1 012	1 120	938	699	1 021	4 550	2 169	1 208
1982	1 033	1 054	895	647	978	4 738	2 337	1 143
1983	1 001	1 013	877	663	1 001	4 708	2 263	1 034
1984	981	972	822	678	906	4 882	2 296	980
1985	986	927	817	679	909	5 173	2 377	869
1986	1 020	923	799	707	936	5 635	2 499	864
1987	1 044	917	793	704	940	6 146	2 382	899
1988	1 071	887	783	690	949	6 504	2 563	962
1989	1 087	869	792	745	958	6 725	2 560	1 000
1990	1 102	991	799	734	922	7 128	2 596	1 003
1991	1 080	1 137	728	711	920	7 505	2 714	1 035
1992	1 033	1 082	716	757	901	7 784	2 549	936
1993	1 011	1 046	710	725	914	8 221	2 471	982
1994	1 020	1 053	690	725	925	8 493	2 671	983
1995	1 051	1 092	682	750	941	8 711	2 445	966
1996	1 076	1 060	677	755	963	9 059	2 686	1 003
1997	1 078	982	683	781	984	9 441	2 582	1 087
1998	1 075	931	690	783	993	9 850	2 693	1 187

Table C4–c. **Levels of Per Capita GDP in 57 African Countries, Annual Estimates, 1950–98**
(1990 international Geary–Khamis dollars)

	Namibia	Niger	Nigeria	Reunion	Rwanda	Senegal	Seychelles	Sierra Leone
1950	2 160	813	753	1 989	547	1 259	1 912	656
1951	2 176	825	793	2 044	567	1 281	2 019	685
1952	2 191	835	832	2 051	574	1 303	2 050	697
1953	2 223	846	835	2 067	584	1 324	2 084	714
1954	2 292	856	878	2 113	604	1 346	2 174	744
1955	2 310	867	882	2 091	610	1 367	2 164	760
1956	2 339	877	844	2 098	620	1 388	2 143	777
1957	2 370	887	860	2 089	628	1 409	2 186	795
1958	2 376	897	832	2 085	631	1 429	2 200	807
1959	2 451	907	850	2 142	652	1 448	2 254	841
1960	2 616	940	869	2 239	656	1 445	2 367	856
1961	2 579	953	879	2 288	625	1 475	2 176	858
1962	2 869	1 025	909	2 394	695	1 487	2 306	884
1963	3 076	1 096	972	2 495	611	1 507	2 458	886
1964	3 486	1 069	991	2 617	525	1 499	2 488	883
1965	3 626	1 118	1 035	2 803	548	1 511	2 435	932
1966	3 668	1 074	979	2 901	570	1 508	2 434	976
1967	3 430	1 049	808	3 033	594	1 449	2 381	955
1968	3 369	1 028	780	3 169	618	1 499	2 522	1 032
1969	3 396	969	967	3 391	666	1 362	2 455	1 109
1970	3 321	971	1 233	3 463	717	1 435	2 570	1 129
1971	3 342	997	1 345	3 473	705	1 390	2 910	1 101
1972	3 443	919	1 362	3 807	687	1 436	3 013	1 072
1973	3 486	741	1 442	3 774	688	1 315	3 224	1 087
1974	3 539	782	1 565	3 946	700	1 329	3 203	1 113
1975	3 473	738	1 475	3 821	806	1 396	3 251	1 126
1976	3 559	721	1 588	3 361	766	1 487	3 507	1 072
1977	3 712	754	1 597	3 258	779	1 411	3 691	1 067
1978	3 906	830	1 457	3 480	827	1 322	3 885	1 050
1979	3 986	863	1 508	3 615	874	1 380	4 460	1 088
1980	4 089	877	1 486	3 686	946	1 301	4 274	1 117
1981	4 159	860	1 323	3 738	972	1 259	3 914	1 161
1982	4 120	824	1 270	3 972	1 011	1 414	3 794	1 156
1983	3 884	783	1 166	4 124	1 031	1 414	3 695	1 115
1984	3 710	630	1 092	4 094	957	1 315	3 799	1 105
1985	3 606	622	1 155	4 068	972	1 330	4 116	1 050
1986	3 593	630	1 149	4 039	996	1 359	4 163	989
1987	3 569	589	1 106	3 990	958	1 378	4 335	1 016
1988	3 478	603	1 180	4 141	894	1 411	4 483	1 017
1989	3 539	587	1 218	4 176	885	1 341	4 706	1 013
1990	3 278	561	1 242	4 488	855	1 354	4 984	1 012
1991	3 396	559	1 276	4 668	797	1 303	5 065	905
1992	3 651	508	1 270	4 570	828	1 287	5 360	829
1993	3 514	500	1 258	4 476	742	1 216	5 656	836
1994	3 684	505	1 213	4 385	442	1 210	5 562	842
1995	3 744	503	1 207	4 298	655	1 233	5 484	733
1996	3 788	505	1 245	4 435	723	1 254	5 697	746
1997	3 793	506	1 245	4 530	663	1 274	5 900	576
1998	3 796	532	1 232	4 502	704	1 302	5 994	558

Table C4–c. **Levels of Per Capita GDP in 57 African Countries, Annual Estimates, 1950–98**
(1990 international Geary–Khamis dollars)

	Somalia	South Africa	Sudan	Swaziland	Tanzania	Togo	Tunisia	Uganda
1950	1 057	2 535	821	721	377	574	1 115	687
1951	1 098	2 591	837	745	418	584	1 106	642
1952	1 112	2 619	855	751	419	593	1 220	664
1953	1 132	2 675	871	762	397	602	1 244	675
1954	1 175	2 763	889	787	421	611	1 249	648
1955	1 191	2 830	907	793	423	621	1 164	672
1956	1 211	2 914	976	803	419	630	1 223	690
1957	1 232	2 951	936	814	420	639	1 159	700
1958	1 241	2 939	949	817	415	647	1 291	685
1959	1 287	2 995	1 033	843	426	656	1 217	700
1960	1 277	3 041	1 024	935	433	698	1 343	713
1961	1 311	3 092	996	1 028	418	728	1 436	686
1962	1 341	3 179	1 037	1 214	445	736	1 379	694
1963	1 364	3 321	980	1 252	462	754	1 556	751
1964	1 191	3 450	944	1 399	475	841	1 589	785
1965	1 088	3 559	984	1 577	480	932	1 653	779
1966	1 216	3 615	947	1 602	527	991	1 654	803
1967	1 258	3 760	893	1 709	535	1 019	1 605	822
1968	1 252	3 819	923	1 588	548	1 043	1 735	818
1969	1 071	3 946	954	1 612	543	1 126	1 760	881
1970	1 138	4 045	888	2 036	559	1 075	1 827	869
1971	1 141	4 135	923	2 015	567	1 121	1 982	871
1972	1 228	4 109	878	2 201	588	1 128	2 287	859
1973	1 176	4 175	780	2 258	588	1 053	2 221	838
1974	914	4 299	833	2 443	584	1 067	2 343	821
1975	1 202	4 271	910	2 462	597	1 032	2 446	784
1976	1 167	4 267	1 044	2 472	622	999	2 569	770
1977	1 421	4 155	1 165	2 477	621	1 025	2 592	763
1978	1 390	4 174	1 108	2 470	623	1 098	2 700	703
1979	1 181	4 232	956	2 434	613	1 131	2 811	611
1980	1 037	4 390	931	2 416	600	1 048	2 944	577
1981	1 113	4 503	920	2 507	576	950	3 030	585
1982	1 152	4 367	1 003	2 581	567	884	2 957	617
1983	1 016	4 174	958	2 518	549	808	3 039	643
1984	1 016	4 271	878	2 491	546	805	3 068	570
1985	1 057	4 108	791	2 560	529	814	3 162	562
1986	1 053	4 020	798	2 572	531	810	3 038	544
1987	1 070	4 015	797	2 666	542	793	3 165	556
1988	1 067	4 092	790	2 506	549	799	3 101	572
1989	1 089	4 090	833	2 597	552	799	3 152	590
1990	1 083	3 966	743	2 565	557	762	3 337	592
1991	1 012	3 847	772	2 546	553	730	3 402	578
1992	914	3 690	790	2 501	542	675	3 599	576
1993	916	3 665	791	2 521	531	545	3 612	602
1994	923	3 717	812	2 621	522	614	3 667	611
1995	938	3 767	824	2 709	526	632	3 696	657
1996	942	3 860	836	2 749	540	669	3 896	692
1997	917	3 895	863	2 793	548	674	4 045	708
1998	883	3 858	880	2 793	553	644	4 190	726

Table C4–c. **Levels of Per Capita GDP in 57 African Countries, Annual Estimates, 1950–98**
(1990 international Geary–Khamis dollars)

	Zambia	Zimbabwe	Total 42 countries	Total other 15 countries	Total 57 countries
1950	661	701	991	355	852
1951	688	722	1 014	374	875
1952	715	724	1 028	389	889
1953	743	760	1 041	402	903
1954	772	772	1 070	410	928
1955	736	808	1 081	423	940
1956	803	892	1 097	441	957
1957	817	924	1 114	443	971
1958	776	906	1 114	440	971
1959	915	925	1 151	448	1 003
1960	960	938	1 174	463	1 024
1961	938	956	1 176	446	1 023
1962	905	939	1 183	496	1 038
1963	902	901	1 234	531	1 086
1964	996	953	1 266	557	1 117
1965	1 147	984	1 297	592	1 150
1966	1 056	967	1 294	626	1 155
1967	1 107	1 015	1 282	642	1 149
1968	1 092	999	1 306	694	1 179
1969	1 056	1 086	1 374	731	1 240
1970	1 074	1 282	1 461	741	1 311
1971	1 044	1 353	1 493	735	1 336
1972	1 108	1 423	1 519	707	1 352
1973	1 066	1 423	1 533	720	1 365
1974	1 120	1 416	1 576	689	1 393
1975	1 047	1 388	1 555	674	1 374
1976	1 078	1 342	1 616	695	1 426
1977	998	1 205	1 633	710	1 444
1978	976	1 214	1 628	701	1 439
1979	919	1 191	1 651	726	1 463
1980	920	1 273	1 675	727	1 484
1981	945	1 380	1 652	679	1 457
1982	884	1 375	1 657	660	1 457
1983	832	1 353	1 612	651	1 421
1984	798	1 285	1 602	629	1 408
1985	783	1 330	1 611	603	1 411
1986	759	1 321	1 598	601	1 400
1987	752	1 261	1 576	599	1 381
1988	774	1 335	1 601	593	1 399
1989	761	1 385	1 612	580	1 403
1990	808	1 382	1 596	558	1 385
1991	788	1 430	1 574	528	1 361
1992	756	1 275	1 542	498	1 329
1993	789	1 268	1 515	494	1 307
1994	704	1 347	1 514	484	1 304
1995	663	1 335	1 516	490	1 305
1996	693	1 415	1 562	510	1 348
1997	702	1 442	1 570	517	1 356
1998	674	1 448	1 588	504	1 368

Table C5–a. **World Population by Regions, Annual Estimates, 1950–98**
(000 at mid–year)

	Western Europe	*Western Offshoots*	*Eastern Europe*	*Former USSR*	*Latin America*	*Asia*	*Africa*	*World*
1950	305 060	176 094	87 288	180 050	165 837	1 381 877	228 341	2 524 547
1951	307 154	179 291	88 374	183 200	170 311	1 407 273	233 039	2 568 643
1952	308 930	182 674	89 487	186 400	174 875	1 435 051	237 944	2 615 361
1953	310 831	185 936	90 770	189 500	179 565	1 463 989	242 986	2 663 577
1954	312 709	189 438	92 045	192 700	184 466	1 495 286	248 024	2 714 668
1955	314 704	193 001	93 439	196 150	189 580	1 526 504	253 374	2 766 752
1956	316 866	196 630	94 721	199 650	194 851	1 558 521	258 894	2 820 132
1957	319 075	200 534	95 801	203 150	200 315	1 593 917	264 577	2 877 369
1958	321 368	204 130	96 919	206 700	205 990	1 630 911	270 456	2 936 474
1959	323 864	207 743	98 003	210 450	211 871	1 664 465	276 547	2 992 943
1960	326 354	211 193	99 056	214 350	217 946	1 686 557	282 876	3 038 332
1961	329 208	214 864	100 112	218 150	224 038	1 703 159	289 201	3 078 732
1962	332 429	218 306	101 010	221 750	230 359	1 732 466	295 653	3 131 974
1963	335 473	221 617	101 914	225 100	236 870	1 773 369	302 782	3 197 125
1964	338 094	224 890	102 783	228 150	243 570	1 813 771	310 107	3 261 365
1965	340 921	227 923	103 610	230 900	250 412	1 856 142	317 706	3 327 615
1966	343 368	230 857	104 412	233 500	257 334	1 901 077	325 600	3 396 148
1967	345 536	233 617	105 195	236 000	264 325	1 946 334	333 843	3 464 850
1968	347 492	236 170	106 264	238 350	271 436	1 993 712	342 313	3 535 737
1969	349 730	238 721	107 101	240 600	278 694	2 041 981	350 991	3 607 818
1970	351 931	241 676	107 927	242 757	286 046	2 092 669	359 501	3 682 507
1971	354 396	245 618	108 782	245 083	293 473	2 145 313	368 625	3 761 291
1972	356 490	248 398	109 628	247 459	300 949	2 196 790	377 846	3 837 560
1973	358 390	250 945	110 490	249 747	308 451	2 247 814	387 651	3 913 488
1974	359 954	253 474	111 461	252 131	316 009	2 297 965	397 693	3 988 687
1975	361 201	256 162	112 468	254 469	323 578	2 344 965	407 950	4 060 793
1976	362 292	258 702	113 457	256 760	331 230	2 391 244	419 024	4 132 709
1977	363 464	261 355	114 442	259 029	338 887	2 436 979	430 525	4 204 680
1978	364 667	264 109	115 300	261 253	346 560	2 483 071	442 436	4 277 395
1979	365 931	266 986	116 157	263 425	354 366	2 532 205	455 260	4 354 330
1980	367 487	270 158	116 921	265 542	362 041	2 580 039	468 257	4 430 445
1981	368 676	272 946	117 661	267 722	370 010	2 626 190	481 381	4 504 586
1982	369 472	275 757	118 323	270 042	378 155	2 669 253	495 383	4 576 385
1983	370 073	278 382	118 926	272 540	386 211	2 728 122	510 156	4 664 410
1984	370 613	280 887	119 503	275 066	394 093	2 777 658	525 104	4 742 924
1985	371 282	283 468	120 062	277 537	401 985	2 829 821	540 340	4 824 495
1986	372 073	286 150	120 574	280 236	410 109	2 882 336	555 751	4 907 229
1987	372 903	288 922	121 051	283 100	418 332	2 936 981	571 668	4 992 957
1988	374 053	291 675	121 253	285 463	426 621	2 992 382	587 687	5 079 134
1989	375 569	294 798	121 650	287 845	434 950	3 047 480	604 062	5 166 354
1990	377 324	298 150	121 866	289 350	443 049	3 102 758	620 765	5 253 262
1991	380 150	301 442	122 049	291 060	451 153	3 154 518	637 738	5 338 109
1992	381 043	304 764	122 070	292 422	459 285	3 206 375	654 343	5 420 302
1993	382 862	308 010	121 632	292 417	467 406	3 260 457	671 651	5 504 436
1994	384 221	311 090	121 323	292 407	475 526	3 312 538	688 174	5 585 279
1995	385 412	314 143	121 126	292 196	483 645	3 366 441	705 557	5 668 520
1996	386 514	317 175	120 980	291 660	491 723	3 416 609	722 750	5 747 411
1997	387 570	320 311	120 977	291 027	499 724	3 466 589	741 607	5 827 805
1998	388 399	323 420	121 006	290 866	507 623	3 516 411	759 955	5 907 680

Table C5–b. **World GDP by Regions, Annual Estimates, 1950–98**
(million 1990 International Geary–Khamis dollars)

	Western Europe	Western Offshoots	Eastern Europe	Former USSR	Latin America	Asia	Africa	World
1950	1 401 551	1 635 490	185 023	510 243	423 556	985 669	194 567	5 336 099
1951	1 484 940	1 753 540	195 667	512 566	445 119	1 054 754	203 798	5 650 385
1952	1 539 065	1 821 083	198 287	545 792	460 258	1 142 584	211 641	5 918 710
1953	1 619 122	1 903 763	209 197	569 260	477 777	1 221 578	219 375	6 220 072
1954	1 706 591	1 898 106	218 949	596 910	507 335	1 273 820	230 122	6 431 833
1955	1 813 957	2 032 869	233 875	648 027	538 673	1 333 611	238 060	6 839 072
1956	1 896 446	2 082 376	239 574	710 065	560 393	1 424 286	247 712	7 160 852
1957	1 980 883	2 123 207	257 645	724 470	600 946	1 489 000	256 911	7 433 062
1958	2 028 388	2 111 417	272 649	778 840	631 022	1 585 962	262 649	7 670 927
1959	2 124 669	2 261 993	286 878	770 244	648 142	1 662 352	277 275	8 031 553
1960	2 261 553	2 320 141	304 633	843 434	690 323	1 741 230	289 608	8 450 922
1961	2 381 945	2 374 411	322 781	891 763	722 982	1 749 488	295 761	8 739 132
1962	2 497 074	2 518 521	328 253	915 928	752 895	1 827 737	307 025	9 147 433
1963	2 613 049	2 630 968	344 112	895 016	775 494	1 956 643	328 783	9 544 065
1964	2 766 560	2 785 505	364 518	1 010 727	828 073	2 130 607	346 483	10 232 473
1965	2 886 298	2 962 352	380 016	1 068 117	869 320	2 239 319	365 404	10 770 826
1966	2 998 658	3 151 817	404 452	1 119 932	911 730	2 402 366	375 909	11 364 864
1967	3 104 789	3 234 760	420 645	1 169 422	951 067	2 520 293	383 547	11 784 523
1968	3 274 469	3 389 792	436 444	1 237 966	1 009 134	2 686 873	403 463	12 438 141
1969	3 467 301	3 507 231	449 862	1 255 392	1 074 640	2 945 818	435 325	13 135 568
1970	3 623 854	3 527 862	465 695	1 351 818	1 148 713	3 214 519	471 368	13 803 829
1971	3 745 279	3 647 077	499 790	1 387 832	1 214 030	3 393 670	492 579	14 380 257
1972	3 911 812	3 836 032	524 971	1 395 732	1 289 774	3 596 029	510 728	15 065 078
1973	4 133 780	4 058 289	550 756	1 513 070	1 397 698	3 876 398	529 186	16 059 177
1974	4 219 829	4 067 628	583 528	1 556 984	1 476 432	3 962 794	554 155	16 421 350
1975	4 193 760	4 069 398	604 251	1 561 399	1 518 608	4 149 379	560 418	16 657 212
1976	4 370 938	4 280 195	619 961	1 634 589	1 602 069	4 362 806	597 568	17 468 126
1977	4 492 840	4 459 671	641 681	1 673 159	1 677 493	4 605 841	621 588	18 172 272
1978	4 621 755	4 700 723	662 328	1 715 215	1 748 846	4 879 019	636 515	18 964 401
1979	4 785 340	4 866 597	672 299	1 707 083	1 858 391	5 080 598	665 912	19 636 220
1980	4 860 483	4 878 155	675 819	1 709 174	1 959 670	5 252 833	694 887	20 031 021
1981	4 869 363	5 006 126	667 932	1 724 741	1 970 328	5 470 912	701 392	20 410 793
1982	4 909 494	4 912 862	674 202	1 767 262	1 947 932	5 712 862	721 973	20 646 587
1983	4 996 928	5 103 869	684 326	1 823 723	1 899 843	6 007 357	724 718	21 240 764
1984	5 117 924	5 467 359	705 274	1 847 190	1 973 180	6 360 902	739 421	22 211 250
1985	5 244 501	5 687 354	706 201	1 863 687	2 033 805	6 680 912	762 503	22 978 964
1986	5 391 139	5 875 446	725 733	1 940 363	2 115 920	6 964 379	778 255	23 791 235
1987	5 545 984	6 086 756	721 188	1 965 457	2 181 077	7 367 697	789 602	24 657 761
1988	5 768 451	6 344 832	727 564	2 007 280	2 201 800	7 849 814	822 192	25 721 933
1989	5 964 036	6 560 368	718 039	2 037 253	2 229 366	8 186 193	847 741	26 542 996
1990	6 032 764	6 665 584	662 604	1 987 995	2 239 427	8 627 846	859 787	27 076 007
1991	6 132 835	6 639 812	590 231	1 863 524	2 321 984	8 990 515	868 115	27 407 016
1992	6 202 821	6 845 134	559 157	1 592 085	2 395 605	9 504 173	869 621	27 968 596
1993	6 182 869	7 012 226	550 466	1 435 008	2 478 695	10 018 478	877 647	28 555 388
1994	6 354 267	7 301 903	572 173	1 235 701	2 604 645	10 558 894	897 148	29 524 731
1995	6 506 423	7 506 406	605 352	1 169 446	2 642 585	11 175 854	921 085	30 527 151
1996	6 613 161	7 770 948	628 154	1 137 039	2 732 722	11 880 966	973 958	31 736 947
1997	6 780 168	8 114 193	646 234	1 156 028	2 876 155	12 408 761	1 005 591	32 987 130
1998	6 960 616	8 456 135	660 861	1 132 434	2 941 609	12 534 570	1 039 407	33 725 631

Table C5–c. World Per Capita GDP by Regions, Annual Estimates, 1950-98
(million 1990 international Geary–Khamis dollars)

	Western Europe	Western Offshoots	Eastern Europe	Former USSR	Latin America	Asia	Africa	World
1950	4 594	9 288	2 120	2 834	2 554	713	852	2 114
1951	4 835	9 780	2 214	2 798	2 614	750	875	2 200
1952	4 982	9 969	2 216	2 928	2 632	796	889	2 263
1953	5 209	10 239	2 305	3 004	2 661	834	903	2 335
1954	5 457	10 020	2 379	3 098	2 750	852	928	2 369
1955	5 764	10 533	2 503	3 304	2 841	874	940	2 472
1956	5 985	10 590	2 529	3 557	2 876	914	957	2 539
1957	6 208	10 588	2 689	3 566	3 000	934	971	2 583
1958	6 312	10 343	2 813	3 768	3 063	972	971	2 612
1959	6 560	10 888	2 927	3 660	3 059	999	1 003	2 683
1960	6 930	10 986	3 075	3 935	3 167	1 032	1 024	2 781
1961	7 235	11 051	3 224	4 088	3 227	1 027	1 023	2 839
1962	7 512	11 537	3 250	4 130	3 268	1 055	1 038	2 921
1963	7 789	11 872	3 376	3 976	3 274	1 103	1 086	2 985
1964	8 183	12 386	3 546	4 430	3 400	1 175	1 117	3 137
1965	8 466	12 997	3 668	4 626	3 472	1 206	1 150	3 237
1966	8 733	13 653	3 874	4 796	3 543	1 264	1 155	3 346
1967	8 985	13 846	3 999	4 955	3 598	1 295	1 149	3 401
1968	9 423	14 353	4 107	5 194	3 718	1 348	1 179	3 518
1969	9 914	14 692	4 200	5 218	3 856	1 443	1 240	3 641
1970	10 297	14 597	4 315	5 569	4 016	1 536	1 311	3 748
1971	10 568	14 849	4 594	5 663	4 137	1 582	1 336	3 823
1972	10 973	15 443	4 789	5 640	4 286	1 637	1 352	3 926
1973	11 534	16 172	4 985	6 058	4 531	1 725	1 365	4 104
1974	11 723	16 048	5 235	6 175	4 672	1 724	1 393	4 117
1975	11 611	15 886	5 373	6 136	4 693	1 769	1 374	4 102
1976	12 065	16 545	5 464	6 366	4 837	1 824	1 426	4 227
1977	12 361	17 064	5 607	6 459	4 950	1 890	1 444	4 322
1978	12 674	17 798	5 744	6 565	5 046	1 965	1 439	4 434
1979	13 077	18 228	5 788	6 480	5 244	2 006	1 463	4 510
1980	13 226	18 057	5 780	6 437	5 413	2 036	1 484	4 521
1981	13 208	18 341	5 677	6 442	5 325	2 083	1 457	4 531
1982	13 288	17 816	5 698	6 544	5 151	2 140	1 457	4 512
1983	13 503	18 334	5 754	6 692	4 919	2 202	1 421	4 554
1984	13 809	19 465	5 902	6 715	5 007	2 290	1 408	4 683
1985	14 125	20 063	5 882	6 715	5 059	2 361	1 411	4 763
1986	14 489	20 533	6 019	6 924	5 159	2 416	1 400	4 848
1987	14 872	21 067	5 958	6 943	5 214	2 509	1 381	4 939
1988	15 421	21 753	6 000	7 032	5 161	2 623	1 399	5 064
1989	15 880	22 254	5 902	7 078	5 126	2 686	1 403	5 138
1990	15 988	22 356	5 437	6 871	5 055	2 781	1 385	5 154
1991	16 133	22 027	4 836	6 403	5 147	2 850	1 361	5 134
1992	16 279	22 460	4 581	5 444	5 216	2 964	1 329	5 160
1993	16 149	22 766	4 526	4 907	5 303	3 073	1 307	5 188
1994	16 538	23 472	4 716	4 226	5 477	3 188	1 304	5 286
1995	16 882	23 895	4 998	4 002	5 464	3 320	1 305	5 385
1996	17 110	24 501	5 192	3 899	5 557	3 477	1 348	5 522
1997	17 494	25 332	5 342	3 972	5 755	3 580	1 356	5 660
1998	17 921	26 146	5 461	3 893	5 795	3 565	1 368	5 709

Table C–6a. **Year to Year Percentage Change in World Population, by Regions, 1950–98**

	Western Europe	Western Offshoots	Eastern Europe	Former USSR	Latin America	Asia	Africa	World
1950								
1951	0.7	1.8	1.2	1.7	2.7	1.8	2.1	1.7
1952	0.6	1.9	1.3	1.7	2.7	2.0	2.1	1.8
1953	0.6	1.8	1.4	1.7	2.7	2.0	2.1	1.8
1954	0.6	1.9	1.4	1.7	2.7	2.1	2.1	1.9
1955	0.6	1.9	1.5	1.8	2.8	2.1	2.2	1.9
1956	0.7	1.9	1.4	1.8	2.8	2.1	2.2	1.9
1957	0.7	2.0	1.1	1.8	2.8	2.3	2.2	2.0
1958	0.7	1.8	1.2	1.7	2.8	2.3	2.2	2.1
1959	0.8	1.8	1.1	1.8	2.9	2.1	2.3	1.9
1960	0.8	1.7	1.1	1.9	2.9	1.3	2.3	1.5
1961	0.9	1.7	1.1	1.8	2.8	1.0	2.2	1.3
1962	1.0	1.6	0.9	1.7	2.8	1.7	2.2	1.7
1963	0.9	1.5	0.9	1.5	2.8	2.4	2.4	2.1
1964	0.8	1.5	0.9	1.4	2.8	2.3	2.4	2.0
1965	0.8	1.3	0.8	1.2	2.8	2.3	2.5	2.0
1966	0.7	1.3	0.8	1.1	2.8	2.4	2.5	2.1
1967	0.6	1.2	0.7	1.1	2.7	2.4	2.5	2.0
1968	0.6	1.1	1.0	1.0	2.7	2.4	2.5	2.0
1969	0.6	1.1	0.8	0.9	2.7	2.4	2.5	2.0
1970	0.6	1.2	0.8	0.9	2.6	2.5	2.4	2.1
1971	0.7	1.6	0.8	1.0	2.6	2.5	2.5	2.1
1972	0.6	1.1	0.8	1.0	2.5	2.4	2.5	2.0
1973	0.5	1.0	0.8	0.9	2.5	2.3	2.6	2.0
1974	0.4	1.0	0.9	1.0	2.5	2.2	2.6	1.9
1975	0.3	1.1	0.9	0.9	2.4	2.0	2.6	1.8
1976	0.3	1.0	0.9	0.9	2.4	2.0	2.7	1.8
1977	0.3	1.0	0.9	0.9	2.3	1.9	2.7	1.7
1978	0.3	1.1	0.7	0.9	2.3	1.9	2.8	1.7
1979	0.3	1.1	0.7	0.8	2.3	2.0	2.9	1.8
1980	0.4	1.2	0.7	0.8	2.2	1.9	2.9	1.7
1981	0.3	1.0	0.6	0.8	2.2	1.8	2.8	1.7
1982	0.2	1.0	0.6	0.9	2.2	1.6	2.9	1.6
1983	0.2	1.0	0.5	0.9	2.1	2.2	3.0	1.9
1984	0.1	0.9	0.5	0.9	2.0	1.8	2.9	1.7
1985	0.2	0.9	0.5	0.9	2.0	1.9	2.9	1.7
1986	0.2	0.9	0.4	1.0	2.0	1.9	2.9	1.7
1987	0.2	1.0	0.4	1.0	2.0	1.9	2.9	1.7
1988	0.3	1.0	0.2	0.8	2.0	1.9	2.8	1.7
1989	0.4	1.1	0.3	0.8	2.0	1.8	2.8	1.7
1990	0.5	1.1	0.2	0.5	1.9	1.8	2.8	1.7
1991	0.7	1.1	0.2	0.6	1.8	1.7	2.7	1.6
1992	0.2	1.1	0.0	0.5	1.8	1.6	2.6	1.5
1993	0.5	1.1	−0.4	0.0	1.8	1.7	2.6	1.6
1994	0.4	1.0	−0.3	0.0	1.7	1.6	2.5	1.5
1995	0.3	1.0	−0.2	−0.1	1.7	1.6	2.5	1.5
1996	0.3	1.0	−0.1	−0.2	1.7	1.5	2.4	1.4
1997	0.3	1.0	0.0	−0.2	1.6	1.5	2.6	1.4
1998	0.2	1.0	0.0	−0.1	1.6	1.4	2.5	1.4

Table C6–b. **Year to Year Percentage Change in World GDP Volume, by Regions, 1950–98**

	Western Europe	Western Offshoots	Eastern Europe	Former USSR	Latin America	Asia	Africa	World
1950								
1951	5.9	7.2	5.8	0.5	5.1	7.0	4.7	5.9
1952	3.6	3.9	1.3	6.5	3.4	8.3	3.8	4.7
1953	5.2	4.5	5.5	4.3	3.8	6.9	3.7	5.1
1954	5.4	−0.3	4.7	4.9	6.2	4.3	4.9	3.4
1955	6.3	7.1	6.8	8.6	6.2	4.7	3.4	6.3
1956	4.5	2.4	2.4	9.6	4.0	6.8	4.1	4.7
1957	4.5	2.0	7.5	2.0	7.2	4.5	3.7	3.8
1958	2.4	−0.6	5.8	7.5	5.0	6.5	2.2	3.2
1959	4.7	7.1	5.2	−1.1	2.7	4.8	5.6	4.7
1960	6.4	2.6	6.2	9.5	6.5	4.7	4.4	5.2
1961	5.3	2.3	6.0	5.7	4.7	0.5	2.1	3.4
1962	4.8	6.1	1.7	2.7	4.1	4.5	3.8	4.7
1963	4.6	4.5	4.8	−2.3	3.0	7.1	7.1	4.3
1964	5.9	5.9	5.9	12.9	6.8	8.9	5.4	7.2
1965	4.1	6.3	4.3	5.7	5.0	5.1	5.5	5.2
1966	4.1	6.4	6.4	4.9	4.9	7.3	2.9	5.6
1967	3.5	2.6	4.0	4.4	4.3	4.9	2.0	3.7
1968	5.5	4.8	3.8	5.9	6.1	6.6	5.2	5.5
1969	5.9	3.5	3.1	1.4	6.5	9.6	7.9	5.6
1970	4.5	0.6	3.5	7.7	6.9	9.1	8.3	5.1
1971	3.4	3.4	7.3	2.7	5.7	5.6	4.5	4.2
1972	4.4	5.2	5.0	0.6	6.2	6.0	3.7	4.8
1973	5.7	5.8	4.9	8.4	8.4	7.8	3.6	6.6
1974	2.1	0.2	6.0	2.9	5.6	2.2	4.7	2.3
1975	−0.6	0.0	3.6	0.3	2.9	4.7	1.1	1.4
1976	4.2	5.2	2.6	4.7	5.5	5.1	6.6	4.9
1977	2.8	4.2	3.5	2.4	4.7	5.6	4.0	4.0
1978	2.9	5.4	3.2	2.5	4.3	5.9	2.4	4.4
1979	3.5	3.5	1.5	−0.5	6.3	4.1	4.6	3.5
1980	1.6	0.2	0.5	0.1	5.4	3.4	4.4	2.0
1981	0.2	2.6	−1.2	0.9	0.5	4.2	0.9	1.9
1982	0.8	−1.9	0.9	2.5	−1.1	4.4	2.9	1.2
1983	1.8	3.9	1.5	3.2	−2.5	5.2	0.4	2.9
1984	2.4	7.1	3.1	1.3	3.9	5.9	2.0	4.6
1985	2.5	4.0	0.1	0.9	3.1	5.0	3.1	3.5
1986	2.8	3.3	2.8	4.1	4.0	4.2	2.1	3.5
1987	2.9	3.6	−0.6	1.3	3.1	5.8	1.5	3.6
1988	4.0	4.2	0.9	2.1	1.0	6.5	4.1	4.3
1989	3.4	3.4	−1.3	1.5	1.3	4.3	3.1	3.2
1990	1.2	1.6	−7.7	−2.4	0.5	5.4	1.4	2.0
1991	1.7	−0.4	−10.9	−6.3	3.7	4.2	1.0	1.2
1992	1.1	3.1	−5.3	−14.6	3.2	5.7	0.2	2.0
1993	−0.3	2.4	−1.6	−9.9	3.5	5.4	0.9	2.1
1994	2.8	4.1	3.9	−13.9	5.1	5.4	2.2	3.4
1995	2.4	2.8	5.8	−5.4	1.5	5.8	2.7	3.4
1996	1.6	3.5	3.8	−2.8	3.4	6.3	5.7	4.0
1997	2.5	4.4	2.9	1.7	5.2	4.4	3.2	3.9
1998	2.7	4.2	2.3	−2.0	2.3	1.0	3.4	2.2

Table C6–c. **Year to Year Percentage Change in World Per Capita GDP, by Regions, 1950–98**

	Western Europe	Western Offshoots	Eastern Europe	Former USSR	Latin America	Asia	Africa	World
1950								
1951	5.2	5.3	4.5	−1.3	2.3	5.1	2.6	4.1
1952	3.0	1.9	0.1	4.7	0.7	6.2	1.7	2.9
1953	4.6	2.7	4.0	2.6	1.1	4.8	1.5	3.2
1954	4.8	−2.1	3.2	3.1	3.4	2.1	2.8	1.5
1955	5.6	5.1	5.2	6.7	3.3	2.6	1.3	4.3
1956	3.8	0.5	1.1	7.7	1.2	4.6	1.8	2.7
1957	3.7	0.0	6.3	0.3	4.3	2.2	1.5	1.7
1958	1.7	−2.3	4.6	5.7	2.1	4.1	0.0	1.1
1959	3.9	5.3	4.1	−2.9	−0.1	2.7	3.2	2.7
1960	5.6	0.9	5.1	7.5	3.5	3.4	2.1	3.6
1961	4.4	0.6	4.8	3.9	1.9	−0.5	−0.1	2.1
1962	3.8	4.4	0.8	1.0	1.3	2.7	1.5	2.9
1963	3.7	2.9	3.9	−3.7	0.2	4.6	4.6	2.2
1964	5.1	4.3	5.0	11.4	3.8	6.5	2.9	5.1
1965	3.3	4.9	3.4	4.4	2.1	2.7	2.9	3.1
1966	3.4	5.0	5.6	3.7	2.1	4.7	0.4	3.4
1967	2.9	1.4	3.2	3.3	1.6	2.5	−0.5	1.6
1968	4.9	3.7	2.7	4.8	3.3	4.1	2.6	3.4
1969	5.2	2.4	2.3	0.5	3.7	7.0	5.2	3.5
1970	3.9	−0.6	2.7	6.7	4.1	6.5	5.7	3.0
1971	2.6	1.7	6.5	1.7	3.0	3.0	1.9	2.0
1972	3.8	4.0	4.2	−0.4	3.6	3.5	1.2	2.7
1973	5.1	4.7	4.1	7.4	5.7	5.3	1.0	4.5
1974	1.6	−0.8	5.0	1.9	3.1	0.0	2.1	0.3
1975	−1.0	−1.0	2.6	−0.6	0.5	2.6	−1.4	−0.4
1976	3.9	4.1	1.7	3.8	3.1	3.1	3.8	3.0
1977	2.5	3.1	2.6	1.5	2.3	3.6	1.2	2.3
1978	2.5	4.3	2.4	1.6	1.9	4.0	−0.4	2.6
1979	3.2	2.4	0.8	−1.3	3.9	2.1	1.7	1.7
1980	1.1	−0.9	−0.1	−0.7	3.2	1.5	1.5	0.3
1981	−0.1	1.6	−1.8	0.1	−1.6	2.3	−1.8	0.2
1982	0.6	−2.9	0.4	1.6	−3.3	2.7	0.0	−0.4
1983	1.6	2.9	1.0	2.2	−4.5	2.9	−2.5	0.9
1984	2.3	6.2	2.6	0.4	1.8	4.0	−0.9	2.8
1985	2.3	3.1	−0.3	0.0	1.0	3.1	0.2	1.7
1986	2.6	2.3	2.3	3.1	2.0	2.3	−0.8	1.8
1987	2.6	2.6	−1.0	0.3	1.1	3.8	−1.4	1.9
1988	3.7	3.3	0.7	1.3	−1.0	4.6	1.3	2.5
1989	3.0	2.3	−1.6	0.7	−0.7	2.4	0.3	1.4
1990	0.7	0.5	−7.9	−2.9	−1.4	3.5	−1.3	0.3
1991	0.9	−1.5	−11.1	−6.8	1.8	2.5	−1.7	−0.4
1992	0.9	2.0	−5.3	−15.0	1.3	4.0	−2.4	0.5
1993	−0.8	1.4	−1.2	−9.9	1.7	3.7	−1.7	0.5
1994	2.4	3.1	4.2	−13.9	3.3	3.7	−0.2	1.9
1995	2.1	1.8	6.0	−5.3	−0.2	4.1	0.1	1.9
1996	1.4	2.5	3.9	−2.6	1.7	4.7	3.2	2.5
1997	2.2	3.4	2.9	1.9	3.6	2.9	0.6	2.5
1998	2.4	3.2	2.2	−2.0	0.7	−0.4	0.9	0.9

Appendix D

Growth and Levels of Performance in 27 Formerly Communist Countries

Table D–1a. GDP in East European Countries, 1990–99
(million 1990 international dollars)

	Albania	Bulgaria	Czech Republic	Slovakia	Hungary	Poland	Romania	Former Yugoslavia	Total
1990	8 125	49 779	91 706	40 854	66 990	194 920	80 277	129 953	662 604
1991	5 850	45 617	81 057	34 904	59 019	181 245	69 902	112 637	590 231
1992	5 426	42 277	80 640	32 641	57 212	185 958	63 779	91 224	559 157
1993	5 949	41 674	80 690	31 468	56 884	192 982	64 800	76 019	550 466
1994	6 446	42 441	82 481	32 977	58 561	202 934	67 351	78 982	572 173
1995	7 303	43 646	87 381	35 281	59 430	217 060	72 113	83 138	605 352
1996	7 963	39 210	90 725	37 586	60 227	230 188	75 005	87 250	628 154
1997	7 403	36 472	91 016	40 058	62 981	245 841	69 817	92 646	646 234
1998	7 999	37 786	88 897	41 818	66 089	258 220	64 715	95 337	660 861
1999	8 639	38 731	88 719	42 623	69 063	258 549	62 191		

Source: 1990–98 from OECD, *National Accounts of OECD Countries, 1988–1998,* Paris, 2000, and Statistics Division of Economic Commission for Europe, Geneva. 1999 Czech Republic, Hungary and Poland from OECD *Economic Outlook,* June 2000; 1999 Slovakia from OECD *Main Economic Indicators,* April 2000, p. 242; 1999 Bulgaria and Romania from IMF, *World Economic Outlook,* April 2000.

Table D–1b. Population in East European Countries,1990–99
(000)

	Albania	Bulgaria	Czech Republic	Slovakia	Hungary	Poland	Romania	Former Yugoslavia
1990	3 273	8 966	10 310	5 263	10 352	38 109	22 775	22 819
1991	3 259	8 914	10 309	5 283	10 352	38 242	22 728	22 961
1992	3 189	8 869	10 319	5 307	10 343	38 359	22 692	22 993
1993	3 154	8 495	10 329	5 329	10 326	38 456	22 660	22 883
1994	3 178	8 448	10 333	5 352	10 307	38 537	22 627	22 541
1995	3 219	8 399	10 327	5 368	10 285	38 590	66 582	22 357
1996	3 263	8 345	10 313	5 379	10 259	38 611	22 524	22 287
1997	3 300	8 291	10 298	5 388	10 232	38 615	22 463	22 390
1998	3 331	8 240	10 286	5 393	10 208	38 607	22 396	22 545
1999	3 365	8 195	10 281	5 396	10 186	38 609	22 234	22 679

Source: International Programs Center, US Bureau of the Census.

Table D–1c. GDP Per Capita in East European Countries, 1990–99
(1990 international $)

	Albania	Bulgaria	Czech Republic	Slovakia	Hungary	Poland	Romania	Former Yugoslavia
1990	2 482	5 552	8 895	7 762	6 471	5 115	3 525	5 695
1991	1 795	5 117	7 863	6 607	5 701	4 739	3 076	4 906
1992	1 701	4 767	7 815	6 151	5 531	4 848	2 811	3 967
1993	1 886	4 906	7 812	5 905	5 509	5 018	2 860	3 322
1994	2 028	5 024	7 982	6 162	5 682	5 266	2 977	3 504
1995	2 269	5 197	8 461	6 572	5 778	5 625	1 083	3 719
1996	2 440	4 699	8 797	6 988	5 871	5 962	3 330	3 915
1997	2 243	4 399	8 838	7 435	6 155	6 366	3 108	4 138
1998	2 401	4 586	8 643	7 754	6 474	6 688	2 890	4 229
1999	2 567	4 726	8 629	7 899	6 780	6 697	2 797	

Source: Derived from Tables D–1a and D–1b.

Table D–2a. **GDP in Successor Republics of Former Yugoslavia, 1990–98**
(million 1990 international dollars)

	Bosnia	*Croatia*	*Macedonia*	*Slovenia*	*Serbia–Montenegro*
1990	16 530	33 139	7 394	21 624	51 266
1991	14 610	26 147	6 875	19 695	45 310
1992	10 535	23 080	6 323	18 612	32 674
1993	7 287	21 225	5 755	19 153	22 599
1994	7 484	22 473	5 648	20 165	23 212
1995	7 933	24 007	5 583	21 012	24 603
1996	8 400	25 434	5 624	21 742	26 050
1997	9 028	27 182	5 706	22 730	28 000
1998	9 261	27 858	5 871	23 625	28 722

Source: Statistics Division of Economic Commission for Europe, Geneva, and national sources (see Table A–f in Appendix A).

Table D–2b. **Population in Successor Republics of Former Yugoslavia,1990–99**
(000)

	Bosnia	*Croatia*	*Macedonia*	*Slovenia*	*Serbia–Montenegro*
1990	4 360	4 754	2 031	1 969	9 705
1991	4 371	4 796	2 039	1 966	9 790
1992	4 327	4 714	2 056	1 959	9 937
1993	4 084	4 687	2 071	1 960	10 080
1994	3 686	4 723	1 946	1 965	10 220
1995	3 282	4 701	1 967	1 970	10 437
1996	3 111	4 661	1 982	1 974	10 558
1997	3 223	4 665	1 996	1 973	10 534
1998	3 366	4 672	2 009	1 972	10 526
1999	3 482	4 677	2 023	1 971	10 526

Source: International Programs Center, US Bureau of the Census.

Table D–2c. **GDP Per Capita in Successor Republics of Former Yugoslavia,1990–98**
(000)

	Bosnia	*Croatia*	*Macedonia*	*Slovenia*	*Serbia–Montenegro*
1990	3 791	6 971	3 641	10 982	5 282
1991	3 342	5 452	3 372	10 018	4 628
1992	2 435	4 896	3 075	9 501	3 288
1993	1 784	4 528	2 779	9 772	2 242
1994	2 030	4 758	2 902	10 262	2 271
1995	2 417	5 107	2 838	10 666	2 357
1996	2 700	5 457	2 838	11 014	2 467
1997	2 801	5 827	2 859	11 521	2 658
1998	2 751	5 963	2 922	11 980	2 729

Source: Derived from D–2a and D–2b.

Table D–3a. **GDP in Successor States of Former USSR, 1990–98**
(million 1990 international dollars)

	Europe							Europe/Asia
	Belarus	*Estonia*	*Latvia*	*Lithuania*	*Moldova*	*Ukraine*	*6 Country Total*	*Russian Federation*
1990	73 389	16 980	26 413	32 010	27 112	311 112	487 016	1 151 040
1991	72 491	15 280	23 666	30 189	22 362	284 003	447 991	1 094 081
1992	65 534	13 118	15 427	23 768	15 889	255 602	389 288	935 072
1993	60 596	12 010	13 117	19 928	15 695	219 457	340 803	853 194
1994	52 966	11 770	13 117	17 975	10 834	169 111	275 773	745 209
1995	47 430	12 268	13 091	18 570	10 639	148 456	250 454	714 357
1996	48 776	12 749	13 527	19 431	9 806	133 610	237 899	690 624
1997	54 315	14 098	14 709	20 855	9 972	129 423	243 372	696 609
1998	58 799	14 671	15 222	21 914	9 112	127 151	246 869	664 495

West Asia

	Armenia	*Azerbaijan*	*Georgia*	*3 Country Total*
1990	20 483	33 397	41 325	99 205
1991	18 077	33 159	32 612	83 848
1992	10 534	25 673	17 961	54 168
1993	9 602	19 736	12 704	42 042
1994	10 122	15 842	11 390	37 354
1995	10 816	13 989	11 682	36 487
1996	11 444	14 141	12 996	38 581
1997	11 835	14 979	14 455	41 269
1998	12 679	16 365	14 894	43 938

Central Asia

	Kazakhstan	*Kyrgyzstan*	*Tajikistan*	*Turkmenistan*	*Uzbekistan*	*5 Country Total*
1990	122 295	15 787	15 884	13 300	87 468	254 734
1991	108 830	14 537	14 537	12 673	87 027	237 604
1992	103 024	12 533	9 844	10 778	77 328	213 507
1993	93 636	10 590	8 243	10 935	75 565	198 969
1994	81 777	8 466	6 484	9 041	71 597	177 365
1995	75 106	7 999	5 675	8 388	70 980	168 148
1996	75 477	8 571	4 724	8 949	72 214	169 935
1997	76 716	9 415	4 803	7 931	75 913	174 778
1998	74 857	9 595	5 073	8 335	79 272	177 132

Source: Derived from indices in the statistical database of the Statistics Division, Economic Commission for Europe, Geneva.

Table D–3b. **Population in Successor States of Former USSR, 1990–98**

			Europe					Europe/Asia
	Belarus	*Estonia*	*Latvia*	*Lithuania*	*Moldova*	*Ukraine*	*6 Country Total*	*Russian Federation*
1990	10 260	1 582	2 684	3 726	4 365	51 891	74 508	148 290
1991	10 271	1 566	2 662	3 742	4 363	52 001	74 605	148 624
1992	10 313	1 544	2 632	3 742	4 334	52 150	74 715	148 689
1993	10 357	1 517	2 586	3 730	3 618	52 179	73 987	148 520
1994	10 356	1 449	2 548	3 721	3 618	51 921	73 613	148 336
1995	10 329	1 484	2 516	3 715	3 611	51 531	73 186	148 141
1996	10 298	1 469	2 491	3 710	3 599	51 114	72 681	147 739
1997	10 268	1 458	2 469	3 706	3 587	50 697	72 185	147 304
1998	10 239	1 450	2 449	3 703	3 649	50 295	71 785	146 909

West Asia

	Armenia	*Azerbaijan*	*Georgia*	*3 Country Total*
1990	3 335	7 134	5 460	15 929
1991	3 612	7 242	5 464	16 318
1992	3 686	7 332	5 455	16 473
1993	3 732	7 399	5 440	16 571
1994	3 748	7 459	5 425	16 632
1995	3 760	7 511	5 417	16 688
1996	3 774	7 555	5 419	16 748
1997	3 786	7 603	5 431	16 820
1998	3 795	7 666	5 442	16 903

Central Asia

	Kazakhstan	*Kyrgyzstan*	*Tajikistan*	*Turkmenistan*	*Uzbekistan*	*5 Country Total*
1990	16 742	4 395	5 303	3 668	20 515	50 623
1991	16 878	4 453	5 465	3 762	20 958	51 516
1992	16 975	4 493	5 571	4 032	21 445	52 516
1993	16 964	4 482	5 638	4 308	21 948	53 340
1994	16 775	4 473	5 745	4 406	22 378	53 777
1995	16 540	4 514	5 835	4 508	22 784	54 181
1996	16 166	4 576	5 927	4 597	23 225	54 491
1997	15 751	4 367	6 018	4 657	23 656	54 449
1998	15 567	4 699	6 115	4 838	24 050	55 269

Source: As for Table D–3a.

Table D–3c. **GDP Per Capita in Successor States of Former USSR, 1990–98**
(1990 international dollars)

	Europe							Europe/Asia
	Belarus	**Estonia**	**Latvia**	**Lithuania**	**Moldova**	**Ukraine**	**6 Country Total**	**Russian Federation**
1990	7 153	10 733	9 841	8 591	6 211	5 995	6 536	7 762
1991	7 058	9 757	8 890	8 068	5 125	5 461	6 005	7 361
1992	6 355	8 496	5 861	6 352	3 666	4 901	5 210	6 289
1993	5 851	7 917	5 072	5 343	4 338	4 206	4 606	5 745
1994	5 115	8 123	5 148	4 831	2 994	3 257	3 746	5 024
1995	4 592	8 267	5 203	4 999	2 946	2 881	3 422	4 822
1996	4 736	8 679	5 430	5 237	2 725	2 614	3 273	4 675
1997	5 290	9 669	5 957	5 627	2 780	2 553	3 372	4 729
1998	5 743	10 118	6 216	5 918	2 497	2 528	3 439	4 523

West Asia

	Armenia	**Azerbaijan**	**Georgia**	**3 Country Total**
1990	6 142	4 681	7 569	6 228
1991	5 005	4 579	5 969	5 138
1992	2 858	3 502	3 293	3 288
1993	2 573	2 667	2 335	2 537
1994	2 701	2 124	2 100	2 246
1995	2 877	1 862	2 157	2 186
1996	3 032	1 872	2 398	2 304
1997	3 126	1 970	2 662	2 454
1998	3 341	2 135	2 737	2 599

Central Asia

	Kazakhstan	**Kyrgyzstan**	**Tajikistan**	**Turkmenistan**	**Uzbekistan**	**5 Country Total**
1990	7 305	3 592	2 995	3 626	4 264	5 032
1991	6 448	3 265	2 660	3 369	4 152	4 612
1992	6 069	2 789	1 767	2 673	3 606	4 066
1993	5 520	2 363	1 462	2 538	3 443	3 730
1994	4 875	1 893	1 129	2 052	3 199	3 298
1995	4 541	1 772	973	1 861	3 115	3 103
1996	4 669	1 873	797	1 947	3 109	3 119
1997	4 871	2 156	798	1 703	3 209	3 210
1998	4 809	2 042	830	1 723	3 296	3 205

Source: Derived from Tables D–3a and D–3b.

Table D–4. **Confrontation of OECD and Maddison Estimates of 1990 Real GDP Levels in 15 Successor States of the Former Soviet Union**

	1996 GDP in million 1996 EKS dollars	*GDP Volume Ratio 1990–96*	*1990 GDP Level in 1996 EKS dollars*	*1990 GDP Level in 1990 EKS dollars*	*Maddison Estimates of 1990 GDP Level in 1990 Geary–Khamis dollars*
Armenia	7 423	1.7898	13 286	11 467	20 483
Azerbaijan	14 501	2.31265	33 536	28 944	33 397
Belarus	53 198	1.5046	80 042	69 083	73 389
Estonia	9 761	1.33187	13 000	11 220	16 980
Georgia	15 844	3.1798	50 381	43 483	41 325
Kazakhstan	71 548	1.620295	115 929	100 056	122 295
Kyrgyzstan	9 547	1.8419	17 585	15 177	15 787
Latvia	12 584	1.9526	24 572	21 208	26 413
Lithuania	21 320	1.647368	35 122	30 313	32 010
Moldova	7 558	2.764838	20 897	18 036	27 112
Russian Federation	996 051	1.66667	1 660 085	1 432 790	1 151 040
Tajikistan	5 455	3.362405	18 342	15 831	15 884
Turkmenistan	13 510	1.4862	20 079	17 330	13 300
Ukraine	169 933	2.3285	395 690	341 513	311 112
Uzbekistan	46 350	1.211234	56 141	48 454	87 468
Total	1 454 583		2 554 687	2 204 905	1 987 995

Source: First column from *A PPP Comparison for the NIS, 1994, 1995 and 1996,* OECD, Paris, February 2000, Annex B, Table B–1. Column 2 is the ratio of 1990 GDP to that of 1996 (derived from Table D–3 above). Third column is column 1 multiplied by column 2. Fourth column is column 3 multiplied by US GDP deflator 1990–96 (0.863082). Last column shows my estimates (from Table A1–b of Appendix A). My figures are based on the ECE estimates for the former USSR (as shown in Table A1–h of Appendix A). The breakdown by republic for 1990 is from Bolotin (1992). Bolotin also used the ICP approach. I prefer my estimates because they are consistent with those I used for East European countries, because the Geary–Khamis approach is distinctly superior to the EKS approach, and because the quality of the data was probably better in the 1990 comparison than in 1996.

Appendix E

Employment, Working Hours and Labour Productivity

Table E–1. **Total Employment in Europe, Japan, and Western Offshoots, 1870–1998**
(000 at mid–year)

	1870	*1913*	*1950*	*1973*	*1990*	*1998*
Austria	2 077	3 122	3 215	3 160	3 412	3 723
Belgium	2 141	3 376	3 341	3 748	3 815	3 766
Denmark	820	1 277	1 978	2 426	2 672	2 693
Finland	785	1 323	1 959	2 194	2 487	2 245
France	17 800	19 373	19 663	21 434	22 632	22 693
Germany	16 184	30 333	28 745	35 487	36 808	36 094
Italy	13 770	17 644	18 875	22 708	25 624	24 343
Netherlands	1 382	2 330	4 120	5 150	6 356	7 465
Norway	706	984	1 428	1 676	2 030	2 241
Sweden	1 923	2 602	3 422	3 879	4 465	3 979
Switzerland	1 285	1 904	2 237	3 277	3 563	3 850
United Kingdom	13 157	19 884	22 400	25 076	26 942	27 121
Total 12 West Europe	**72 030**	**104 152**	**111 383**	**130 215**	**140 806**	**140 213**
Ireland			1 220	1 067	1 126	1 503
Spain		7 613	11 662	13 031	12 890	13 378
Australia	630	1 943	3 459	5 838	7 938	8 652
Canada	1 266	3 014	5 030	8 843	13 244	14 386
United States	14 720	38 821	61 651	86 838	120 960	132 953
Czechoslovakia		5 854	5 972	7 092	7 679	7 374
a) Czech Republic					5 201	5 207
b) Slovakia					2 478	2 167
Hungary		3 285	4 379	5 008	4 808	3 698
Poland			12 718	17 319	16 840	15 477
Romania		6 877	9 710	10 015	10 865	10 845
USSR		64 664	85 246	128 278	132 546	
Russian Federation					75 325	64 500
East Germany			7 581	8 327	8 820	6 055
Japan	18 684	25 751	35 683	52 590	62 490	65 141

Source: 1870–1973 from Maddison (1995a), updated from OECD, *Labour Force Statistics 1978–1998,* Paris 1999 for West European countries, Japan and Western Offshoots. In the case of Germany, the 1870–1913 figures refer to the 1913 boundaries (excluding Alsace–Lorraine) and for 1950–98 to 1991 boundaries; for 1950–98, the figures for East Germany (given in the table) were added to those for the Federal Republic. For 1870, and 1913 employment in the territory of the Federal Republic, as given in Maddison (1995a) was adjusted upwards by the ratio of population within the 1913 frontiers including Alsace–Lorraine to population in the territory of the Federal Republic (see Table A–d in Appendix A). For the United Kingdom, the 1870 and 1913 figures include Southern Ireland; the employment estimates in Maddison (1995a) for 1870 and 1913 were adjusted upwards by the population ratio. For the other countries in this group the figures refer throughout to employment within present frontiers.
For Eastern Europe; 1870–1973 from Maddison (1995a). East Germany 1950 and 1973 derived from Merkel and Wahl (1991) p. 73; 1990 and 1998 from Van Ark (1999). The latter source was also used for Hungary, Poland, Romania, Russian Federation and Slovakia for 1990. Czech Republic 1990 and 1998; Hungary and Poland 1998 from OECD, *Labour Force Statistics 1978–1998,* OECD, Paris; Romania, Russian Federation and Slovakia 1998 from OECD, *Main Economic Indicators,* April 2000. USSR 1990 from Maddison (1995b).

Table E–2. **Total Employment in Latin America and Asia, 1950–98**
(000 at mid–year)

	1950	*1973*	*1990*	*1998*
Argentina	6 821	9 402	11 932	13 060
Brazil	17 657	33 164	56 108	63 966
Chile	2 256	2 894	4 429	5 541
Colombia	3 844	6 616	10 747	12 673
Mexico	8 766	15 180	24 905	31 519
Peru	2 799	4 471	7 446	9 444
Venezuela	1 571	3 338	5 859	7 716
China	184 984	362 530	567 400	626 630
Hong Kong			2 710	3 140
India	161 386	239 645	324 885	377 548
Indonesia	30 863	46 655	75 851	87 672
Malaysia			6 686	8 563
Pakistan	14 009	50 144	31 290	35 430
Philippines	8 525	14 195	22 532	28 262
Singapore			1 486	1 870
South Korea	6 377	11 140	18 085	19 926
Sri Lanka			4 951	6 085
Taiwan	2 872	5 327	8 283	9 289
Thailand	10 119	18 576	30 844	32 138

Source: Latin American estimates supplied by Andre Hofman. Asia 1950–73 from Maddison (1995a), p. 247, 1990 and 1998 generally from Asian Development Bank, *Key Indicators for Developing Asian and Pacific Countries,* China 1999 and 1998 from SSB, *China Statistical Yearbook 1999,* Beijing. Korea 1990 and 1998 from OECD, *Labour Force Statistics* 1978–1998, Paris, 1999.

Table E–3. **Annual Hours Worked Per Person Employed, 1870–1998**

	1870	*1913*	*1950*	*1973*	*1990*	*1998*
Austria	2 935	2 580	1 976	1 778	1 590	1 515
Belgium	2 964	2 605	2 283	1 872	1 638	1 568
Denmark	2 945	2 553	2 283	1 742	1 638	1 664
Finland	2 945	2 588	2 035	1 707	1 668	1 637
France	2 945	2 588	1 926	1 771	1 539	1 503
Germany	2 841	2 584	2 316	1 804	1 566	1 523
Italy	2 886	2 536	1 997	1 612	1 500	1 506
Netherlands	2 964	2 605	2 208	1 751	1 347	1 389
Norway	2 945	2 588	2 101	1 721	1 460	1 428
Sweden	2 945	2 588	1 951	1 571	1 508	1 582
Switzerland	2 984	2 624	2 144	1 930	1 644	1 595
United Kingdom	2 984	2 624	1 958	1 688	1 637	1 489
Ireland			2 250	2 010	1 700	1 657
Spain			2 200	2 150	1 941	1 908
Australia	2 945	2 588	1 838	1 708	1 645	1 641
Canada	2 964	2 605	1 967	1 788	1 683	1 663
United States	2 964	2 605	1 867	1 717	1 594	1 610
Argentina			2 034	1 996	1 850	1 903
Brazil			2 042	2 096	1 879	1 841
Chile			2 212	1 955	1 984	1 974
Colombia			2 323	2 141	1 969	1 956
Mexico			2 154	2 061	2 060	2 073
Peru			2 189	2 039	1 930	1 926
Venezuela			2 179	1 965	1 889	1 931
Japan	2 945	2 588	2 166	2 042	1 951	1 758

Source: 1870-1973 from Maddison (1995a), p. 248, 1990 for OECD countries from Maddison (1996), p. 41 and worksheets from Maddison (1991a). Movement in hours 1992-98 linked to 1992 level shown in Maddison (1995a) p. 248, except for the United States which is derived from estimates of the US Bureau of Labor Statistics of average weekly hours of production workers in the private sector, multiplied by average weeks worked per year. Latin American estimates supplied by Andre Hofman (updating those in Hofman, 2000).

Table E–4. **Total Hours Worked, 1870–1998**
(million hours)

	1870	1913	1950	1973	1990	1998
Austria	6 096	8 055	6 353	5 618	5 425	5 640
Belgium	6 346	8 794	7 628	7 016	6 249	5 905
Denmark	2 415	3 260	4 516	4 226	4 377	4 481
Finland	2 312	3 424	3 987	3 745	4 148	3 675
France	52 421	50 137	37 871	37 960	34 831	34 108
Germany	45 979	78 380	66 573	64 019	57 641	54 971
Italy	39 740	44 745	37 693	36 605	38 436	36 661
Netherlands	4 096	6 070	9 097	9 018	8 562	10 369
Norway	2 079	2 547	3 000	2 884	2 964	3 200
Sweden	5 663	6 734	6 676	6 094	6 733	6 295
Switzerland	3 834	4 996	4 796	6 325	5 858	6 141
United Kingdom	39 260	52 176	43 859	42 328	44 104	40 383
Total 12 West Europe	**210 242**	**269 318**	**232 049**	**225 838**	**219 327**	**211 829**
Ireland			2 745	2 145	1 914	2 490
Spain			25 656	28 017	25 019	25 525
Australia	1 855	5 028	6 358	9 971	13 058	14 198
Canada	3 752	7 851	9 894	15 811	22 290	23 924
United States	43 630	101 129	115 102	149 101	192 810	214 054
Argentina			13 874	18 766	22 074	24 853
Brazil			36 056	69 512	105 427	117 761
Chile			4 990	5 658	8 787	10 938
Colombia			8 930	14 165	21 161	24 788
Mexico			18 882	31 286	51 304	65 339
Peru			6 127	9 116	14 371	18 189
Venezuela			3 423	6 559	11 068	14 900
Japan	55 024	66 644	77 289	107 389	121 918	114 518

Table E–5. **GDP Per Person Employed in Europe, Japan and Western Offshoots, 1870–1998**
(1990 international $)

	1870	1913	1950	1973	1990	1998
Austria	4 053	7 512	7 994	26 971	38 240	41 019
Belgium	6 420	9 581	14 125	31 621	44 939	52 642
Denmark	4 612	9 139	14 992	28 867	35 503	43 564
Finland	2 546	4 829	8 704	23 575	33 817	42 058
France	4 051	7 458	11 214	31 910	45 356	50 680
Germany	4 414	7 824	9 231	26 623	34 352	40 452
Italy	3 037	5 412	8 739	25 661	36 124	42 015
Netherlands	7 201	10 710	14 719	34 134	40 606	42 534
Norway	3 520	6 218	12 492	26 578	38 588	46 792
Sweden	3 602	6 688	13 813	28 305	33 920	41 564
Switzerland	4 566	8 657	19 019	35 780	41 229	39 570
United Kingdom	7 614	11 296	15 529	26 956	35 061	40 875
Weighted Average						
12 West Europe	**4 702**	**8 072**	**11 551**	**28 109**	**37 476**	**43 108**
Ireland				19 778	36 820	44 822
Spain		6 001	5 727	23 346	36 801	41 870
Australia	10 241	14 180	17 714	29 516	36 682	44 190
Canada	5 061	11 585	20 311	35 302	39 601	43 298
United States	6 683	13 327	23 615	40 727	47 976	55 618
Czechoslovakia		4 741	7 262	14 445	17 263	17 726
a) Czech Republic					17 632	17 073
b) Slovakia					16 487	19 298
Hungary		5 007	5 288	11 649	13 933	17 872
Poland			4 776	10 276	11 575	16 684
Romania			1 985	7 230	7 389	5 967
USSR		3 593	5 986	11 795	14 999	
Russian Federation					15 281	10 302
East Germany			6 782	15 608	9 317	20 319
Japan	1 359	2 783	4 511	23 634	37 144	39 631

Table E–6. **GDP Per Person Employed in Latin America and Asia, 1950–98**
(1990 international $)

	1950	1973	1990	1998
Argentina	12 538	21 349	17 811	25 598
Brazil	5 060	12 111	13 256	14 491
Chile	10 316	17 416	18 974	26 038
Colombia	6 492	12 202	14 799	16 187
Mexico	7 685	18 399	20 747	20 810
Peru	6 170	12 685	8 727	10 135
Venezuela	23 792	37 856	27 419	26 495
China	1 297	2 041	3 718	6 181
Hong Kong			36 815	43 022
India	1 377	2 065	3 380	4 510
Indonesia			5 945	7 157
Malaysia			13 434	17 356
Pakistan			5 817	7 381
Philippines	2 653	5 809	6 348	6 236
Singapore			29 159	42 259
South Korea	2 516	8 689	20 633	28 315
Sri Lanka			8 501	10 420
Taiwan	2 569	11 924	24 203	35 198
Thailand	1 618	4 065	8 291	11 591

Table E–7. **Labour Productivity (GDP Per Hour Worked), 1870–1998**
(1990 international $ per hour)

	1870	1913	1950	1973	1990	1998
Austria	1.38	2.91	4.05	15.17	24.05	27.07
Belgium	2.17	3.68	6.19	16.89	27.44	33.57
Denmark	1.57	3.58	6.57	16.57	21.67	26.18
Finland	0.86	1.87	4.28	13.81	20.27	25.69
France	1.38	2.88	5.82	18.02	29.47	33.72
Germany	1.55	3.03	3.99	14.76	21.94	26.56
Italy	1.05	2.13	4.38	15.92	24.08	27.90
Netherlands	2.43	4.11	6.67	19.49	30.15	30.62
Norway	1.20	2.40	5.95	15.44	26.43	32.77
Sweden	1.22	2.58	7.08	18.02	22.49	26.27
Switzerland	1.53	3.30	8.87	18.54	25.08	24.81
United Kingdom	2.55	4.31	7.93	15.97	21.42	27.45
Weighted Average						
12 West Europe	**1.61**	**3.12**	**5.54**	**16.21**	**24.06**	**28.53**
Ireland			3.73	9.84	21.66	27.05
Spain			2.60	10.86	18.96	21.94
Australia	3.48	5.48	9.64	17.28	22.30	26.93
Canada	1.71	4.45	10.33	19.74	23.53	26.04
United States	2.25	5.12	12.65	23.72	30.10	34.55
Argentina			6.16	10.70	9.63	13.45
Brazil			2.48	5.78	7.05	7.87
Chile			4.66	8.91	9.56	13.19
Colombia			2.79	5.70	7.52	8.28
Mexico			3.57	8.93	10.07	10.04
Peru			2.82	6.22	4.52	5.26
Venezuela			10.92	19.27	14.52	13.72
Japan	0.46	1.08	2.08	11.57	19.04	22.54

Table E–8. **Rate of Growth of GDP Per Hour Worked, 1870–1998**
(annual average compound growth rates)

	1870–1913	1913–50	1950–73	1973–98	1973–90	1990–98
Austria	1.75	0.89	5.91	2.34	2.75	1.49
Belgium	1.24	1.42	4.46	2.79	2.89	2.56
Denmark	1.94	1.65	4.11	1.85	1.59	2.39
Finland	1.80	2.27	5.23	2.51	2.28	3.00
France	1.74	1.92	5.03	2.54	2.94	1.70
Germany	1.56	0.75	5.86	2.38	2.36	2.42
Italy	1.66	1.96	5.77	2.27	2.47	1.86
Netherlands	1.23	1.31	4.78	1.82	2.60	0.20
Norway	1.64	2.48	4.24	3.05	3.21	2.72
Sweden	1.75	2.76	4.14	1.52	1.31	1.96
Switzerland	1.80	2.71	3.26	1.17	1.79	−0.14
United Kingdom	1.22	1.67	3.09	2.19	1.74	3.15
Weighted Average						
12 West Europe	**1.55**	**1.56**	**4.77**	**2.29**	**2.35**	**2.16**
Ireland			4.31	4.13	4.75	2.82
Spain			6.41	2.85	3.33	1.84
Australia	1.06	1.54	2.57	1.79	1.51	2.39
Canada	2.25	2.30	2.86	1.11	1.04	1.27
United States	1.92	2.48	2.77	1.52	1.41	1.74
Argentina			2.42	0.92	−0.62	4.27
Brazil			3.75	1.24	1.18	1.38
Chile			2.85	1.58	0.42	4.10
Colombia			3.15	1.50	1.64	1.21
Mexico			4.07	0.47	0.71	−0.04
Peru			3.50	−0.67	−1.86	1.91
Venezuela			2.50	−1.35	−1.65	−0.70
Japan	1.99	1.80	7.74	2.70	2.97	2.13

Table E–9. **Levels of GDP Per Hour Worked, 1870–1998**
(United States = 100)

	1870	*1913*	*1950*	*1973*	*1990*	*1998*
Austria	61	57	32	64	80	78
Belgium	96	72	49	71	91	97
Denmark	69	70	52	70	72	76
Finland	38	36	34	58	67	74
France	61	56	46	76	98	98
Germany	69	59	32	62	73	77
Italy	47	42	35	67	80	81
Netherlands	108	80	53	82	100	89
Norway	53	47	47	65	88	95
Sweden	54	51	56	76	75	76
Switzerland	68	64	70	78	83	72
United Kingdom	113	84	63	67	71	79
Weighted Average						
12 West Europe	**71**	**61**	**44**	**68**	**80**	**83**
Ireland					72	78
Spain					63	64
Australia	154	107	76	73	74	78
Canada	76	87	82	83	78	75
Argentina			49	45	32	39
Brazil			20	24	23	23
Chile			37	38	32	38
Colombia			22	24	25	24
Mexico			28	38	33	29
Peru			22	26	15	15
Venezuela			86	81	48	40
Japan	20	21	16	49	63	65

Table E-10. **Annual Hours Worked Per Head of Population, 1870–1998**
(hours)

	1870	*1913*	*1950*	*1973*	*1990*	*1998*
Austria	1 349	1 190	916	741	702	698
Belgium	1 245	1 147	883	721	627	579
Denmark	1 279	1 093	1 058	842	852	845
Finland	1 318	1 131	994	803	832	713
France	1 364	1 209	905	728	614	580
Germany	1 172	1 205	974	811	726	670
Italy	1 425	1 201	800	669	678	637
Netherlands	1 133	985	899	671	573	660
Norway	1 198	1 041	919	728	699	722
Sweden	1 360	1 198	952	749	786	711
Switzerland	1 439	1 293	1 022	982	862	861
United Kingdom	1 251	1 143	871	753	766	682
Weighted Average						
12 West Europe	1 295	1 181	904	750	701	657
Ireland			925	698	546	672
Spain			921	805	644	648
Australia	1 048	1 043	778	738	764	757
Canada	992	1 000	720	701	805	790
United States	1 084	1 036	756	704	771	791
Argentina			809	745	676	685
Brazil			675	672	698	694
Chile			819	572	669	740
Colombia			770	614	642	643
Mexico			663	543	605	663
Peru			803	635	654	697
Venezuela			683	552	573	653
Japan	1 598	1 290	925	988	987	905

Table E–11. **Employment in Europe, Japan and Western Offshoots, as Per Cent of Population, 1870–1998**
(percentage)

	1870	1913	1950	1973	1990	1998
Austria	46.0	46.1	46.4	41.7	44.1	46.1
Belgium	42.0	44.0	38.7	38.5	38.3	36.9
Denmark	43.4	42.8	46.3	48.3	52.0	50.8
Finland	44.8	43.7	48.9	47.0	49.9	43.6
France	46.3	46.7	47.0	41.1	39.9	38.6
Germany	41.3	46.6	42.0	44.9	46.4	44.0
Italy	49.4	47.4	40.1	41.5	45.2	42.3
Netherlands	38.2	37.8	40.7	38.3	42.5	47.5
Norway	40.7	40.2	43.7	42.3	47.9	50.6
Sweden	46.2	46.3	48.8	47.7	52.1	45.0
Switzerland	48.2	49.3	47.7	50.9	52.4	54.0
United Kingdom	41.9	43.6	44.5	44.6	46.8	45.8
Weighted Average						
12 West Europe	**44.4**	**45.7**	**43.4**	**43.3**	**45.0**	**43.5**
Ireland			41.1	34.7	32.1	40.6
Spain		37.6	41.8	37.4	33.2	34.0
Australia	35.6	40.3	42.3	43.2	46.5	46.1
Canada	33.5	38.4	36.6	39.2	47.8	47.5
United States	36.6	39.8	40.5	41.0	48.4	49.1
Czechoslovakia		44.2	48.2	48.7	49.3	47.0
a) Czech Republic					50.4	50.6
b) Slovakia					47.1	40.2
Hungary		41.9	46.9	48.0	46.4	36.2
Poland		0.0	51.2	52.0	44.2	40.1
Romania		54.9	59.5	48.1	47.7	48.4
USSR		41.4	47.3	51.4	45.8	
Russian Federation					50.8	43.9
Japan	54.3	49.8	42.7	48.4	50.6	51.5

Table E-12. **Employment in Latin America and Asia, as Per Cent of Population, 1950–1998**

(percentage)

	1950	1973	1990	1998
Argentina	39.8	37.3	36.6	36.0
Brazil	33.0	32.1	37.1	37.7
Chile	37.0	29.2	33.7	37.5
Colombia	33.2	28.7	32.6	32.8
Mexico	30.8	26.3	29.4	32.0
Peru	36.7	31.2	33.9	36.2
Venezuela	31.4	28.1	30.3	33.8
China	33.8	41.1	50.0	50.4
Hong Kong			47.5	46.9
India	45.0	41.3	38.7	38.7
Indonesia	39.0	37.5	42.3	42.9
Malaysia			38.2	40.9
Pakistan	35.5	70.5	27.5	26.2
Philippines	40.3	33.7	34.6	36.4
Singapore			48.9	53.6
South Korea	30.6	32.7	42.2	42.9
Sri Lanka			28.8	32.1
Taiwan	36.4	34.5	40.9	42.6
Thailand	50.5	46.1	56.0	53.5

Appendix F

Value and Volume of Exports, 1870–1998

Table F–1. **Value of Merchandise Exports at Current Prices (56 Countries), 1870–1998**
(million dollars at current exchange rate)

	1870	*1913*	*1929*	*1950*	*1973*	*1990*	*1998*
Austria	160	561	308	326	5 283	41 138	62 746
Belgium	133	717	884	1 652	22 450	118 328	177 662
Denmark	42[a]	171	433	665	6 248	35 135	46 915
Finland	9	78	162	390	3 837	26 572	42 963
France	541	1 328	1 965	3 082	36 675	210 169	305 492
Germany	424	2 454	3 212	1 993	67 563	409 958	543 292
Italy	208	485	783	1 206	22 226	170 383	242 147
Netherlands	158[b]	413	800	1 413	27 348	131 787	182 753
Norway	22	105	199	390	4 726	34 045	39 649
Sweden	41	219	486	I 103	12 201	57 542	84 739
Switzerland	132[b]	226	404	894	9 538	63 793	75 439
United Kingdom	971	2 555	3 550	6 325	29 640	185 326	271 850
Total	2 841	9 352	13 186	19 439	247 735	1 484 176	2 075 627
Australia	98	382	592	1 668	9 559	39 760	55 896
Canada	58	421	1 141	3 020	26 437	127 634	214 335
New Zealand	12	112	259	514	2 596	9 394	12 071
United States	403	2 380	5 157	10 282	71404	393 592	682 497
Total	571	3 295	7 149	15 484	109 996	570 380	964 799
Greece	7	23	91	90	I 456	8 106	9 559
Ireland	–	–	225	203	2129	23 747	64 333
Portugal	22	38	48	186	1 842	16 419	24 218
Spain	76	183	407	389	5 200	55 528	109 231
Total	105	244	771	868	10 627	103 800	207 341
Bulgaria	5[b]	94	46	116	3 301	6 836	4292
Czechoslovakia	–	–	606	779	6 035	11 882	37 083
Hungary	–	–	182	329	3 354	9 597	22 955
Poland	–	–	316	634	6 374	13 627	27 191
Romania	32[b]	130	173	300	3 691	5 775	8 300
USSR	216	783	482	1 801	21458	104 177	119 798
Yugoslavia	6[b]	18	139	154	2 853	14 312	I7 324
Total	259	1 025	1 944	4 113	47 066	166 206	236 943

Table F–1. **Value of Merchandise Exports at Current Prices (56 Countries), 1870–1998**
(million dollars at current exchange rates)

	1870	1913	1929	1950	1973	1990	1998
Argentina	29	515	908	1 178	3 266	12 353	25 227
Brazil	76	317	462	1 359	6 199	31 414	51 120
Chile	27	149	283	281	1 231	8 373	14 895
Colombia	18	34	124	394	1 177	6 766	10 852
Mexico	28[a]	150	285	532	2 261	27 131	117 500
Peru	25[a]	43	117	193	1 112	3 231	5 736
Venezuela	15[a]	28	149	929	4 680	17 783	15 682
Total	218	1 236	2 328	4 866	19 926	107 051	241 012
Bangladesh	–	–	–	303	358	1 671	3 831
Burma	–	–	–	139	140	325	1 067
China	102	299	660	550	5 876	62 091	183 589
India	255	786	1 177	1 145	2 917	17 970	33 656
Indonesia	31	270	582	800	3 211	25 675	48 847
Japan	15	315	969	825	37 017	287 648	388 117
Pakistan	–	–	–	330	955	5 589	8 501
Philippines	29	48	163	331	1 885	8 068	27 783
South Korea	0	15	159	23	3 225	65 016	132 313
Taiwan	–	26	125	73	4 483	67 142	110 454
Thailand	7	43	94	304	1 564	23 071	54 455
Turkey	49[b]	94	139	159	1 317	12 959	25 938
Total	488	1 896	4 068	4 982	62 948	577 225	1 018 549
Côte d'Ivoire	–	–	–	79	857	3 072	4 504
Egypt	66[a]	156	253	504	1 121	4 957	3 130
Ethiopia	n.a.	n.a.	n.a.	37	239	298	560
Ghana	2	26	60	217	628	863	1 788
Kenya	n.a.	n.a.	34	57	516	1 031	2 007
Morocco	n.a.	n.a.	48	190	910	4 265	12 480
Nigeria	4	36	86	253	3 462	12 961	37 029
South Africa	14	342	454	1 158	6 114	22 834	25 396
Tanzania	n.a.	n.a.	18	68	61	331	675
Zaire	n.a.	n.a.	40	261	1 013	999	592
Total	n.a.	n.a.	n.a.	2 824	14 921	51 611	73 333

a) 1874; b) 1872; c) 1991.

Source: Maddison (1962 and 1989); League of Nations, *Review of World Trade 1938*, Geneva, 1939; UN. *Yearbook of International Trade Statistics*, New York, various issues; IMF, *International Financial Statistics*, Washington, D.C., various issues.

Table F–2. **Value of Merchandise Exports at Constant Prices (35 Countries), 1820–1998**
(million 1990 dollars)

	1820	1870	1913	1929	1950	1973	1998
Austria	47	467	2 024	1 746	1 348	13 899	69 519
Belgium	92	1 237	7 318	7 845	8 182	61 764	175 503
Denmark		314	1 494	2 705	3 579	16 568	49 121
Finland		310	1 597	2 578	3 186	15 641	48 697
France	487	3 512	11 292	16 600	16 848	104 161	329 597
Germany		6 761	38 200	35 068	13 179	194 171	567 372
Italy	339	1 788	4 621	5 670	5 846	72 749	267 378
Netherlands		1 727[a]	4 329	7 411	7 411	71 522	194 430
Norway		223	854	1 427	2 301	11 687	58 141
Sweden		713	2 670	4 167	7 366	34 431	103 341
Switzerland	147	1 107	5 735	5 776	6 493	38 972	78 863
United Kingdom	1 125	12 237	39 348	31 990	39 348	94 670	277 243
Total	n.a.	30 396	119 482	122 983	115 087	730 235	2 219 205
Australia		455	3 392	3 636	5 383	18 869	69 324
Canada		724	4 044	7 812	12 576	60 214	243 015
United States	251	2 495	19 196	30 368	43 114	174 548	745 330
Total	n.a.	3 674	26 632	41 816	61 073	253 631	1 057 669
Spain	137	850	3 697	3 394	2 018	15 295	131 621
USSR		n.a.	6 666	3 420	6 472	58 015	119 978
Argentina		222	1 963	3 096	2 079	4 181	23 439
Brazil		854	1 888	2 592	3 489	9 998	49 874
Chile		166	702	1 352	1 166	2 030	18 228
Colombia		114	267	811	1 112	2 629	11 117
Mexico		242	2 363	3 714	1 999	5 238	70 261
Peru		202	409	1 142	1 172	4 323	6 205
Venezuela		n.a.	1 374	2 593	9 722	23 779	29 411
Total		2 126	8 966	15 300	20 739	52 178	208 535
Bangladesh		-	-	-	284	445	4 146
Burma		-	-	-	269	235	1 075
China		1 398	4 197	6 262	6 339	11 679	190 177
India		3 466	9 480	8 209	5 489	9 679	40 972
Indonesia		172	989	2 609	2 254	9 605	56 232
Japan		51	1 684	4 343	3 538	95 105	346 007
Pakistan		-	-	-	720	1 626	9 868
Philippines		55	180	678	697	2 608	22 712
South Korea		0	171	1 292	112	7 894	204 542
Taiwan		-	70	261	180	5 761	100 639
Thailand		88	495	640	1 148	3 081	48 752
Total		5 230	17 266	24 294	21 030	147 733	1 025 122

a) 1872

Source: Volume movement in Western Europe, Western Offshoots and Japan from A. Maddison, *Dynamic Forces in Capitalist Development*, OUP, 1991, Appendix F, updated from OECD, *Economic Outlook*, December 1999. Spain 1826-1980 from A. Carreras, ed., *Estadisticas Historicas de España: Siglos XIX-XX*, Fundacion Banco Exterior, Madrid, 1989, pp. 346-7. USSR, Latin America and Asia from sources cited in A. Maddison, *The World Economy in the Twentieth Century*, OECD Development Centre, 1989, p. 140, updated with volume movements derivable from IMF, *International Financial Statistics*, various issues. Brazil 1870-1913 from R.W. Goldsmith, *Brasil 1850-1984: Desenvolvimento Financeiro Sob um Secolo de Inflacâo*, Harper and Row, Sao Paulo, 1986, pp. 54-5 and 110-111: Peru 1870-1950 from S.J. Hunt, "Price and Quantum Estimates of Peruvian Exports, 1830-1962", Discussion Paper 33, Research Program in Economic Development, Princeton University, January 1973, (1929 weights for 1900-50, 1900 weights for 1870-1900): Venezuela 1913-29 from A. Baptista, *Bases Cuantitativas de la Economia Venezolana 1830-1989*, C. Corporativas, Caracas, 1991, and 1929-92 from ECLAC sources. 1990-8 movements from ADB, OECD, ECLAC, IMF.

Table F–3. **Value of World Exports by Region at Constant Prices, 1870–1998**
(million 1990 dollars)

	1870	1913	1950	1973	1990	1998
Western Europe	32 428	127 839	121 535	773 726	1 597 933	2 490 596
Western Offshoots	3 783	27 425	62 892	254 128	570 380	1 071 432
Eastern Europe & former USSR	2 100	8 726	14 780	127 285	166 252	237 148
Latin America	2 709	10 910	25 235	66 155	139 611	286 043
Asia	7 000	22 900	41 800	372 170	883 309	1 577 571
Africa	2 325	14 625	29 379	97 184	99 277	154 290
World	50 345	212 425	295 621	1 690 648	3 456 762	5 817 080

Source: 1950–98 from IMF *International Financial Statistics,* various issues, supplemented by UN *Yearbook of International Trade Statistics,* various issues. 1870–1950 export volume movement for Western Europe as a whole assumed to move parallel to the 13 country total shown in Table F–2; for Western Offshoots parallel to the three country total in Table F–2; Latin America parallel to the seven country total in Table F–2 (adjusted to include Venezuela for 1870). Asian total assumed to move parallel to sum of the Asian countries shown in Table F–2, with adjustment to include West Asian oil exports. Eastern Europe and former USSR and Africa 1870–1913 are guesstimates based on partial value figures of Table F–1 and unit value estimates for areas with similar commodity structures.

Table F–4. **Rate of Growth in Volume of Merchandise Exports, 11 Countries and World, 1870–1998**
(annual average compound growth rates)

	1870–1913	1913–50	1950–73	1973–98
France	2.8	1.1	8.2	4.7
Germany	4.1	–2.8	12.4	4.4
Netherlands	2.3	1.5	10.4	4.1
United Kingdom	2.8	0.0	3.9	4.4
Spain	3.5	–1.6	9.2	9.0
United States	4.9	2.2	6.3	6.0
Mexico	5.4	–0.5	4.3	10.9
Brazil	1.9	1.7	4.7	6.6
China	2.6	1.1	2.7	11.8
India	2.4	–1.5	2.5	5.9
Japan	8.5	2.0	15.4	5.3
World	3.4	0.9	7.9	5.1

Source: Derived from Tables F–2 and F–3.

Table F–5. **Merchandise Exports as Per Cent of GDP in 1990 Prices, 11 Countries and World, 1870–1998**

	1870	*1913*	*1929*	*1950*	*1973*	*1998*
France	4.9	7.8	8.6	7.6	15.2	28.7
Germany	9.5	16.1	12.8	6.2	23.8	38.9
Netherlands	17.4	17.3	17.2	12.2	40.7	61.2
United Kingdom	12.2	17.5	13.3	11.3	14.0	25.0
Spain	3.8	8.1	5.0	3.0	5.0	23.5
United States	2.5	3.7	3.6	3.0	4.9	10.1
Mexico	3.9	9.1	12.5	3.0	1.9	10.7
Brazil	12.2	9.8	6.9	3.9	2.5	5.4
China	0.7	1.7	1.8	2.6	1.5	4.9
India	2.6	4.6	3.7	2.9	2.0	2.4
Japan	0.2	2.4	3.5	2.2	7.7	13.4
World	4.6	7.9	9.0	5.5	10.5	17.2

Source: Tables F–2, F–3, and B–18. See Maddison (1997), Table 13 for a comparison of ratios at current and constant prices. As export prices have risen less over the long run than GDP deflators, the ratios for earlier years are higher in current than in 1990 prices, e.g. the UK ratio in current prices for 1870 was 17.3; for 1913, 20.9; for 1950, 14.4 and for 1973, 16.3.

Bibliography

ABEL, W. (1978), *Agrarkrisen und Agrarkonjunktur*, Parey, Hamburg and Berlin.

ABRAMOVITZ, M. (1989), *Thinking About Growth*, Cambridge University Press, Cambridge.

ABULAFIA, D. (1987), "Asia, Africa and the Trade of Medieval Europe", in POSTAN *et al.*, (eds.), vol. II, pp. 402–73.

ABU–LUGHOD, J.L. (1989), *Before European Hegemony: The World System AD 1250–1350*, Oxford University Press, Oxford.

ABU–LUGHOD, J.L. (1971), *Cairo, 1001 Years of the City Victorious*, Princeton University Press, New Jersey.

ADB (Asian Development Bank) (1999), *Key Indicators of Developing Asian and Pacific Countries*, Oxford University Press, Oxford.

ALDEN, D. (1973), *The Colonial Roots of Modern Brazil,* University of California Press, Berkeley.

ALLEN, R.C. (1991), "The Two English Agricultural Revolutions, 1450–1850", in CAMPBELL AND OVERTON.

AMIN, S. (1966), *L'économie du Maghreb*, Editions de Minuit, Paris.

ARASARATNAM, S. (1990), "Recent Trends in the Historiography of the Indian Ocean, 1500 to 1800", *Journal of World History,* Fall, pp. 225–48.

ARK, B. VAN (1999), "Economic Growth and Labour Productivity in Europe: Half a Century of East–West Comparisons", Research Memorandum GD–41, Groningen Growth and Development Centre.

ARK, B. VAN (2000), "Measuring Productivity in the 'New Economy': Towards a European Perspective", *De Economist*, 148,1, pp. 87–105.

ARK, B. VAN AND N. CRAFTS (1996), *Quantitative Aspects of Post–War European Economic Growth,* Cambridge University Press, Cambridge.

ARK, B. VAN , S. KUIPERS AND G. KUPER (2000), *Productivity, Technology and Economic Growth*, Kluwer, Dordrecht.

ASHTOR, E. (1976), *A Social and Economic History of the Near East in the Middle Ages,* University of California Press, Berkeley.

ASHTOR, E. (1980), "The Volume of Medieval Spice Trade", *Journal of European Economic History,* vol. 9, No. 3, Winter, pp. 753–763.

AUBIN, F. (ed.) (1970), *Études Song in Memoriam Etienne Balazs,* Mouton, Paris.

BAGNALL, R.S. AND B.W. FRIER (1994), *The Demography of Roman Egypt*, Cambridge University Press, Cambridge.

BAIROCH, P. (1967), *Diagnostic de l'évolution économique du tiers–monde 1900–1966,* Gauthiers–Villars, Paris.

BAIROCH, P. AND ASSOCIATES (1968), *The Working Population and Its Structure*, Université Libre de Bruxelles, Brussels.

BAIROCH, P. AND M. LEVY–LEBOYER (1981), *Disparities in Economic Development since the Industrial Revolution,* Macmillan, London.

BALCEROWICZ, L. (1995), *Socialism, Capitalism, Transformation*, Central European University Press, Budapest, London and New York.

BANENS, M. (2000), "Vietnam: a Reconstitution of its 20th Century Population History", in BASSINO, GIACOMETTI AND ODAKA (2000).

BARAN, P.A. (1957), *The Political Economy of Growth*, Prometheus Paper Back, New York.

BARCLAY, G.W. *et al.* (1976), "A Reassessment of The Demography of Traditional Rural China", *Population Index*, Winter, pp. 606–35.

BARDET, J–P. AND J. DUPAQUIER (1997), *Histoire des populations de l'Europe*, Fayard, Paris, 2 vols.

BASSINO, J–P., J–D. GIACOMETTI AND K. ODAKA (2000), *Quantitative Economic History of Vietnam, 1900–1990*, Institute of Economic Research, Hitotsubashi University.

BATISTA, D, C. MARTINS, M. PINHEIRO AND J. REIS (1997), "New Estimates of Portugal's GDP, 1910–1958", Bank of Portugal, Lisbon.

BAUGH, A.C. AND T. CABLE (1993), *A History of the English Language*, Macmillan, London.

BAUMOL, W.J. (1986), "Productivity Growth, Convergence and Welfare: What the Long Run Data Show", *American Economic Review*, December.

BELOCH, J. (1886), *Die Bevölkerung der griechisch–römischen Welt*, Duncker and Humblot, Leipzig.

BELOCH, K.J. (1961), *Bevölkerungsgeschichte Italiens*, de Gruyter, Berlin.

BERGSON, A. (1953), *Soviet National Income and Product in 1937*, Columbia University Press, New York.

BERTOLA, L., L. CALICCHIO, M. CAMOU AND L. RIVERO (1998), *El PIB de Uruguay*, Universidad de la Republica, Montevideo.

BETHELL, L. (ed.) (1984–1991), *Cambridge History of Latin America*, 8 vols., Cambridge University Press, Cambridge.

BEVAN, D., P. COLLIER AND J. GUNNING (1999), *The Political Economy of Poverty, Equity and Growth: Indonesia and Nigeria*, Oxford University Press, Oxford.

BHANOJI RAO, V.V. (1976), *National Accounts of West Malaysia, 1947–1971*, Heinemann, Singapore.

BHATTACHARYA, D. (1987), "A Note on the Population of India, 1000–1800 AD" in *Le Peuplement du Monde avant 1800*, Société de Démographie Historique, Paris.

BIDEAU, A., B. DESJARDINS AND H. PEREZ–BRIGNOLI (1997), *Infant and Child Mortality in the Past*, Clarendon Press, Oxford.

BIELENSTEIN, H. (1987), "Chinese Historical Demography AD 2 – 1982", *Bulletin of the Museum of Far Eastern Antiquities*, Stockholm, No. 59.

BIRABEN, J.N. (1972), "Certain Demographic Characteristics of the Plague Epidemic in France, 1720–1722" in GLASS AND REVELLE.

BIRABEN, J.N. (1979), "Essai sur l'évolution du nombre des hommes", *Population*, Jan–Feb., pp. 13–25.

BLACKBURN, R. (1997), *The Making of New World Slavery*, Allen and Unwin, London.

BLAYO, Y. (1975), "La population de la France de 1740 à 1860" and "La mortalité en France de 1740 à 1829", *Population*, November, pp. 71–122 and 124–142, respectively.

BLOMME, J. AND H. VAN DER WEE (1994), "The Belgian Economy in a Long–Term Historical Perspective: Economic Development in Flanders and Brabant, 1500–1812", in MADDISON AND VAN DER WEE.

BLOOM, D.E. AND J.D. SACHS (1998), "Geography, Demography and Economic Growth in Africa", *Brookings Papers on Economic Activity*, 2, pp. 207–296.

BOLOTIN, B.M. (1992), "The Former Sovient Union as Reflected in National Accounts Statistics", in HIRSCH.

BOOMGAARD, P. (1993), "Economic Growth in Indonesia, 500–1990", in SZIRMAI, VAN ARK AND PILAT.

BOOTH, A. AND A. REID (1994), "Population, Trade and Economic Growth in South–East Asia in the Long Term: An Exploratory Analysis 1400–1990", in MADDISON AND VAN DER WEE.

BORAH, W.C. (1976), "The Historical Demography of Aboriginal and Colonial America: An Attempt at Perspective", in DENEVAN, pp. 13–34.

BORAH, W. AND S.F. COOK (1963), *The Aboriginal Population of Central Mexico on the Eve of the Spanish Conquest*, University of California, Berkeley.

BOSERUP, E. (1965), *The Conditions of Agricultural Growth*, Allen and Unwin, London.

BOSERUP, E. (1981), *Population and Technology*, Blackwell, Oxford.

BOWLEY, A.L. (1942), *Studies in the National Income*, Cambridge University Press, Cambridge.

BOWMAN, A.K. AND E. ROGAN (1999), *Agriculture in Egypt from Pharaonic to Modern Times*, Oxford University Press, Oxford.

BOXER, C.R. (1974), *Four Centuries of Portuguese Expansion, 1414–1825: A Succinct Survey*, Witwatersrand University Press, Johannesburg.

BRAUDEL, F. (1985), *Civilisation and Capitalism, 15th–18th Century*, 3 vols., Fontana, London.

BRAUDEL, F. AND F. SPOONER (1967), "Prices in Europe from 1450 to 1750", in RICH AND WILSON.

BRAUDEL, F. AND E. LAROUSSE (eds.) (1977), *Histoire économique et sociale de la France*, Vol. 2, P.U.F., Paris.

BRAY, F. (1984), *Agriculture*, Vol. VI:2 in NEEDHAM (1954–2000).

BRAY, F. (1986), *The Rice Economies: Technology and Development in Asian Societies*, Blackwell, Oxford.

BREWER, J. (1989), *The Sinews of Power: War, Money and the English State, 1688–1783*, Unwin Hyman, London.

BREWER, J. AND R. PORTER (eds.) (1993), *Consumption and the World of Goods*, Routledge, London.

BRUIJN, J.R. AND F.S. GAASTRA (eds.) (1993), *Ships, Sailors and Spices, East India Companies and their Shipping in the 16th, 17th and 18th Centuries*, NEHA, Amsterdam.

BULBECK, D., A. REID, L.C. TAN AND Y. WU (1998), *Southeast Asian Exports since the Fourteenth Century*, KITLV Press, Leiden.

BUTLIN, N.G. (1983), *Our Original Aggression*, Allen and Unwin, Sydney.

BUTLIN, N.G. (1993), *Economics and the Dreamtime*, Cambridge University Press, Melbourne.

CAMPBELL, B.M.S. AND M. OVERTON (eds.), (1991), *Land, Labour and Livestock: Historical Studies in European Agricultural Productivity*, Manchester University Press.

CARR–SAUNDERS, A.M. (1964), *World Population*, Cass, London.

CASELLI, G. (1991), "Health Transition and Cause Specific Mortality", in SCHOFIELD, REHER AND BIDEAU.

CHANDLER, A.D., JR. (1990), *Scale and Scope: The Dynamics of Industrial Capitalism*, Harvard.

CHANG, CHUNG–LI (1962), *The Income of the Chinese Gentry*, Greenwood, Westport.

CHAO, K. (1986), *Man and Land in Chinese History*, Stanford.

CHAUDHURI, K.N. (1978), *The Trading World of Asia and the English East India Company, 1660–1760*, Cambridge University Press, Cambridge.

CHAUDHURI, K.N. (1982), "Foreign Trade", in RAYCHAUDHURI AND HABIB.

CHAUDHURY, S. (1999), *From Prosperity to Decline: Eighteenth Centry Bengal*, Manohar, New Delhi.

CHAUDHURY, S. AND M. MORINEAU (1999), *Merchants, Companies and Trade: Europe and Asia in the Early Modern Era*, Cambridge University Press, Cambridge.

CHESNAIS, J.–C. (1987), *La revanche du tiers–monde*, Laffont, Paris.

CHOU, K.R. (1966), *The Hong Kong Economy*, Academic Publications, Hong Kong.

CIPOLLA, C.M. (1969), *Literacy and Development in the West*, Penguin Books, London.

CIPOLLA, C.M. (1970), *European Culture and Overseas Expansion*, Pelican, London.

CIPOLLA, C.M. (ed.) (1972–76), The Fontana Economic History of Europe, 6 vols., Collins/Fontana Books, London

CIPOLLA, C.M. (1976), *Before the Industrial Revolution: European Society and Economy, 1000–1700*, Norton, New York.

CLARK, C. (1940), *The Conditions of Economic Progress*, Macmillan, London.

CLARK, C. (1967), *Population Growth and Land Use,* Macmillan, London.

CLARK, G. (1991), "Yields per Acre in English Agriculture, 1250–1860: Evidence from Labour Inputs", *Economic History Review*, August, pp. 445–60.

CLARK, G.N. (1968), *Science and Social Welfare in the Age of Newton*, Clarendon Press, Oxford.

COALE, A.J. AND P. DEMENY (1983), *Regional Model Life Tables and Stable Populations*, Academic Press, New York.

COATSWORTH, J.H. (1978), "Obstacles to Economic Growth in Nineteenth Century Mexico", *American Historical Review*, February, pp. 80–100.

COATSWORTH, J.H. (1989), "The Decline of the Mexican Economy, 1800–1860" in LIEHR.

COLLIER, P. AND J.W. GUNNING (1999), "Explaining African Performance", *Journal of Economic Literature*, March, pp. 64–111.

COOK, D.N. (1981), *Demographic Collapse: Indian Peru, 1520–1620*, Cambridge University Press, Cambridge.

COOK, S.F. AND L.B. SIMPSON (1948), *The Population of Central Mexico in the Sixteenth Century*, University of California, Berkeley.

COOPER, J.P. (1967), "The Social Distribution of Land and Men in England, 1436–1700", *Economic History Review* 20, pp. 419–440.

CRAFTS, N.F.R. (1983), "British Economic Growth, 1700–1831: A Review of the Evidence", *Economic History Review*, May, pp. 177–199.

CRAFTS, N.F.R. AND C.K. HARLEY (1992), "Output Growth and the British Industrial Revolution: A Restatement of the Crafts–Harley View", *Economic History Review*, November, pp. 703–730.

CRAIG, A.M. (1961), *Choshu in the Meiji Restoration*, Harvard University Press, Cambridge, Ma.

CRAWCOUR, E.S. (1963), "Changes in Japanese Commerce in the Tokugawa Period", *Journal of Asian Studies*, pp. 387–400.

CROSBY, A.W. (1972), *The Columbian Exchange: Biological and Cultural Consequences of 1492*, Greenwood Press, Westport, Connecticut.

CROSBY, A.W. (1986), *Ecological Imperialism: The Biological Expansion of Europe, 900–1900*, Cambridge University Press, Cambridge.

CROUZET, F. (1964), "Wars, Blockade, and Economic Change in Europe, 1792–1815", *Journal of Economic History*, December, pp. 567–88.

CROUZET, F. (1985), *De la supériorité de l'Angleterre sur La France*, Perrin, Paris.

CURTIN, P.D. (1969), *The Atlantic Slave Trade: A Census,* University of Wisconsin Press, Madison.

CURTIN, P.D. (1984), *Cross–cultural Trade in World History,* Cambridge University Press, Cambridge.

DANIELS, J.D. (1992), "The Indian Population of North America in 1492", *William and Mary Quarterly*, pp. 298–320.

DAS GUPTA, A. AND M.N. PEARSON (1987), *India and the Indian Ocean, 1500–1800,* New Delhi.

DAVID, P.A. (1967), "The Growth of Real Product in the United States Before 1840: New Evidence, Controlled Conjectures", *Journal of Economic History*, June.

DAVID, P.A. (1991), "Computer and Dynamo: The Modern Productivity Paradox in a Not Distant Mirror", in *Technology and Productivity: The Challenge for Economic Policy*, OECD, Paris, pp. 315–48.

DAVIES, R.T. (1964), *The Golden Century of Spain,* Macmillan, London.

DAVIS, K. (1951), *The Population of India and Pakistan*, Princeton.

DAVIS, L. AND ASSOCIATES (eds.) (1972), *American Economic Growth: An Economist's History of the United States,* Harper and Row, New York.

DAVIS, R. (1962), *The Rise of the English Shipbuilding Industry*, Macmillan, London.

DAY, C. (1921), *A History of Commerce*, Longmans Green, New York.

DEANE, P. (1955), "The Implications of Early National Income Estimates for the Measurement of Long–Term Economic Growth in the United Kingdom", *Economic Development and Cultural Change*, pp. 3–38.

DEANE, P. (1995–6), "Contemporary Estimates of National Income in the First Half of the Nineteenth Century", *Economic History Review*, VIII, 3, pp. 339–354.

DEANE, P. (1956–7), "Contemporary Estimates of National Income in the Second Half of the Nineteenth Century", *Economic History Review*, IX, 3, pp. 451–61.

DEANE P. (1957), "The Industrial Revolution and Economic Growth: The Evidence of Early British National Income Estimates", *Economic Development and Cultural Change*, pp. 159–74.

DEANE, P. AND W.A. COLE (1964), *British Economic Growth 1688–1958*, Cambridge University Press, Cambridge.

DEANE, P. (1968), "New Estimates of Gross National Product for the United Kingdom, 1830–1914", *Review of Income and Wealth*, June, pp. 95–112.

DENEVAN, W.M. (ed.) (1976), *The Native Population of the Americas in 1492*, University of Wisconsin.

DENISON, E.F. AND W.C. HARALDSON (1945), "The Gross National Product of Germany 1936–1944", Special Paper 1, (mimeographed appendix to Galbraith, *et al.*

DICKSON, D., C. O'GRADA AND S. DAULTREY (1982), "Hearth Tax, Household Size and Irish Population Change 1672–1981", *Proceedings of the Royal Irish Academy*, Vol. 82 C, No. 6, Dublin.

DICKSON, P.M.G. (1967), *The Financial Revolution in England,* Macmillan, London.

DOMAR, E.D. (1989), *Capitalism, Socialism and Serfdom*, Cambridge University Press, Cambridge.

DORE, R.P. (1965), *Education in Tokugawa Japan*, University of California Press, Berkeley.

DUBLIN, L.I., A.J. LOTKA AND M. SPIEGELMAN (1963), *Length of Life,* Ronald Press, New York.

DUPAQUIER, J. (1997), "La connaissance démographique", in BARDET AND DUPAQUIER, Vol. 1, pp. 218–38.

DURAND, J.D. (1974), *Historical Estimates of World Population: An Evaluation*, University of Pennsylvania, Philadelphia.

DYSON, T. (ed.) (1989), *India's Historical Demography*, Curzon, Riverdale.

EBRD (European Bank for Reconstruction and Development), (1999), *Transition Report 1999*, London.

ECE (Economic Commission for Europe), (1994), *International Comparison of Gross Domestic Product in Europe 1990*, Geneva.

ECLAC, (Economic Commission for Latin America and the Caribbean) (1978), *Series Historicas del Crecimiento de America Latina.*

ECLAC (1996), *Preliminary Overview of the Economy of Latin America and the Caribbean*, Santiago, Chile.

EISNER, G. (1961), *Jamaica, 1830–1930: a Study in Economic Growth*, Manchester University Press.

ELTIS, D. (1995), "The Total Product of Barbados 1667–1701", *Journal of Economic History,* vol. 55:2, pp. 321–38

ENGERMAN, S.L. AND R.E. GALLMAN (1986), *Long Term Factors in American Economic Growth,* NBER, University of Chicago Pr'ess, Chicago.

ENGERMAN, S.L. AND R.E. GALLMAN (1996), *The Cambridge History of the United States,* Vol. 1, Cambridge University Press, Cambridge.

ESCAP (Economic and Social Commission for Asia and the Pacific), (1999), *Escap Comparisons of Real Gross Domestic Product and Purchasing Power Parities, 1993,* Bangkok.

EUROSTAT (Statistical Office of the European Communities), (1989), *Comparison of Price Levels and Economic Aggregates 1985: The Results for 22 African Countries,* Luxemburg.

FAGERBERG, J. (1994), "Technology and International Differences in Growth Rates", *Journal of Economic Literature,* September.

FAIRBANK, J.K. (ed.) (1968), *The Chinese World Order,* Harvard University Press, Cambridge, Ma.

FAIRBANK, J.K. (ed.) (1983), *The Cambridge History of China,* Vol. 12, Cambridge University Press, Cambridge.

FAROQHI, S., B. MCGOWAN, D. QUATAERT, AND S. PAMUK (1994), *An Economic and Social History of the Ottoman Empire, 1600–1914,* Vol. 2, Cambridge University Press, Cambridge.

FARRIS, W.W. (1985), *Population, Disease and Land in Early Japan, 645–900,* Harvard.

FEINSTEIN, C.H. (1998), "Pessimism Perpetuated: Real Wages and the Standard of Living in Britain during and after the Industrial Revolution", *Journal of Economic History,* September, pp. 625–58.

FERNANDES, F. (1969), *The Negro in Brazilian Society,* Columbia University Press, New York.

FEUERWERKER, A. (1983), "The Foreign Presence in China", IN FAIRBANK.

FIRESTONE, O.J. (1958) *Canada's Economic Development, 1867–1953,* Bowes and Bowes, London

FOGEL, R.W. (1964), *Railroads and American Economic Growth,* Johns Hopkins, Baltimore.

FOGEL, R.W. (1986), "Nutrition and the Decline in Mortality since 1700: Some Preliminary Findings", in ENGERMAN AND GALLMAN.

FOGEL, R.W. AND S.L. ENGERMAN (1974), *Time on the Cross: The Economics of American Negro Slavery,* Little Brown, London.

FOY, C., Y.–H. KIM AND H. REISEN (2000), *Sustainable Recovery in Asia: Mobilising Resources for Development,* OECD Development Centre, Paris (Preface by Braga de Macedo and Chino).

FRANK, A.G. (1998), *Reorient: Global Economy in the Asian Age,* University of California Press, Berkeley.

FREYRE, G. (1959), *New World in the Tropics,* Knopf, New York.

GALBRAITH, J.K., et al. (1945), *The Effects of Strategic Bombing on the German War Economy,* US Strategic Bombing Survey, Washington, D.C.

GALENSON, D.W. (1996), "The Settlement and Growth of the Colonies, Population, Labour and Economic Development", in ENGERMAN AND GALLMAN.

GALLOWAY, P.R. (1994), "A Reconstitution of the Population of North Italy from 1650 to 1881 using Annual Inverse Projection with Comparisons to England, France and Sweden", *Journal of Population,* 10, pp. 222–74.

GALLMAN, R.E. (1972), "The Pace and Pattern of American Economic Growth", in DAVIS AND ASSOCIATES.

GERSCHENKRON, A. (1965), *Economic Backwardness in Historical Perspective,* Praeger, New York.

GILBERT, M. AND I.B. KRAVIS (1954), *An International Comparison of National Products and Purchasing Power of Currencies,* OEEC, Paris.

GILLE, H. (1949), "The Demographic History of the Northern European Countries in the Eighteenth Century", *Population Studies,* III:1, June, pp. 3–65.

GLAMANN, K. (1981), *Dutch Asiatic Trade, 1620–1740,* Nijhoff, the Hague.

GLASS, D.V. (1965), "Two Papers on Gregory King", in GLASS AND EVERSLEY (1965), pp. 159–221.

GLASS, D.V. (1966), *London Inhabitants Within the Walls 1695*, London Record Society, London.

GLASS, D.V. AND D.E.C. EVERSLEY (eds.) (1965), *Population in History: Essays in Historical Demography*, Arnold, London.

GLASS, D.V. AND E. GREBENIK (1966), "World Population, 1800–1950", in H.J. HABAKKUK AND M. POSTAN, *Cambridge Economic History of Europe*, Vol. VI:1, Cambridge University Press, Cambridge.

GLASS, D.V. AND R. REVELLE (1972), *Population and Social Change*, Arnold, London.

GOITEIN, S.D. (1967), *A Mediterranean Society,* vol. 1, *Economic Foundations,* University of California Press, Berkeley.

GOLDSMITH, R.W. (1984), "An Estimate of the Size and Structure of the National Product of the Roman Empire", *Review of Income and Wealth*, September.

GOODMAN, D. AND C.A. RUSSELL (1991), *The Rise of Scientific Europe, 1500–1800*, Hodder and Stoughton, London.

GORDON, R.J. (2000), "Interpreting the 'One Big Wave in US Long–Term Productivity Growth", in VAN ARK, KUIPERS AND KUPER.

GOUBERT, P. (1965), "Recent Theories and Research in French Population Between 1500 and 1700", in GLASS AND EVERSLEY.

GRAUNT, J. (1676), *Natural and Political Observations upon the Bills of Mortality,* fifth edition, reprinted in Hull (1899).

HABAKKUK, H.J. AND M. POSTAN (eds.) (1966), *The Cambridge Economic History of Europe,* vol. VI, Cambridge University Press, Cambridge.

HABIB, I. (1982), "Technology and Economy of Moghul India", *Indian Economic and Social History Review,* XVII(1), pp. 1–34.

HABIB, I. (1995), *Essays in Indian History,* Tulika, New Delhi.

HALL, J.W. (ed.) (1991), *Early Modern Japan*, Vol. 4 of *The Cambridge History of Japan*, Cambridge University Press, Cambridge.

HALL, J.W., N. NAGAHARA, AND K. YAMAMURA (1981), *Japan Before Tokugawa*, Princeton.

HALLEY, E. (1693), "An Estimate of the Degrees of Mortality of Mankind, drawn from curious tables of the births and funerals at the city of Breslaw; with an attempt to ascertain the price of annuities upon lives", *Philosophical Transactions of the Royal Society,* Vol. XVII, No. 198, pp. 596–610.

HANLEY, S.B. AND K. YAMAMURA (1977), *Economic and Demographic Change in Preindustrial Japan*, Princeton.

HANLEY, S.B. (1997), *Everyday Things in Premodern Japan*, University of California Press, Berkeley.

HANSEN, B. AND G.A. MARZOUK (1965), *Development and Economic Policy in the UAR (Egypt)*, North Holland, Amsterdam.

HARLEY, C.K. (1988), "Ocean Freight Rates and Productivity, 1740–1913: The Primacy of Mechanical Invention Reaffirmed", *Journal of Economic History,* December, pp. 851–76.

HAWKE, G.R. (1985), *The Making of New Zealand,* Cambridge Univerity Press, Melbourne.

HAYAMI, A. (1973), *Kinsei Noson no Rekishi Jinkogakuteki Kenkyu* (A Study of Historical Demography of Pre–Modern Rural Japan), Toyo Keizai Shimposha, Tokyo.

HAYAMI, A. (1986a), "Population Trends in Tokugawa Japan, 1600–1868", paper presented at the 46th session of the International Statistical Institute Congress.

HAYAMI, A. (ed.) (1986b), *Preconditions to Industrialization in Japan*, International Economic History Conference, Berne.

HAYAMI, A. AND M. MIYAMOTO (eds.) (1988), *Keizai Shakai no seritsu: 17–18 seiki, Nihon keizai-shi*, Vol. 1, Iwanami Shoten, Tokyo.

HAYAMI, Y., V.W. RUTTAN AND H.M. SOUTHWORTH (eds.) (1979), *Agricultural Growth in Japan, Taiwan, Korea and the Philippines*, Asian Productivity Center, Honolulu.

HAYAMI, Y. AND V.W. RUTTAN (1985), *Agricultural Development*, second edition, Johns Hopkins, Baltimore.

HEMMING, J. (1978), *Red Gold: The Conquest of the Brazilian Indians*, Macmillan.

HENRY L. AND D. BLANCHET (1983), "La population de l'Angleterre de 1514 à 1871", *Population*, 4–5, pp. 781–826.

HENRY L. AND Y. BLAYO (1975), "La population de la France de 1740 à 1860", *Population*, November.

HIGMAN, B.W. (1996), "Economic and Social Development in the British West Indies", in ENGERMAN AND GALLMAN.

HIRSCH, S. (ed.) (1992), *Memo 3: In Search of Answers in the Post–Soviet Era*, Bureau of National Affairs, Washington, D.C.

HLAING, A. (1964), "Trends of Economic Growth and Income Distribution in Burma 1870–1940", *Journal of the Burma Research Society*.

HO, P.T. (1959), *Studies on the Population of China, 1368–1953*, Harvard University Press, Cambridge, Ma.

HO, P.T. (1970), "An Estimate of the Total Population of Sung–Chin China", in AUBIN

HOFFMANN, W.G. (1965), *Das Wachstum der deutschen Wirtschaft seit der Mitte des 19. Jahrhunderts*, Springer, Berlin.

HOFMAN, A.A. (2000), *The Economic Development of Latin America in the Twentieth Century*, Elgar, Cheltenham.

HODGES, R. AND D. WHITEHOUSE (1998), *Mohammed, Charlemagne and the Origins of Europe*, Duckworth, London.

HOLMES, G.S. (1977), "Gregory King and the Social Structure of Pre–Industrial England", *Transactions of the Royal Historical Society*, 5th series, Vol. 27, pp. 41–68.

HOOLEY, R.W. (1968), "Long Term Growth of the Philippine Economy, 1902–1961", *Philippine Economic Journal*.

HONDA, G. (1997), "Differential Structure, Differential Health: Industrialisation in Japan, 1868–1940", in STECKEL AND FLOUD.

HONJO, E. (1935), *The Social and Economic History of Japan*, Kyoto.

HOPKINS, K. (1980), "Taxes and Trade in the Roman Empire (200 B.C.–400 A.D.)", *Journal of Roman Studies*, Vol. LXX, pp. 101–25.

HORIOKA, C.Y. (1990), "Why is Japan's Household Saving Rate So High? A Literature Survey", *Journal of Japanese and International Economies*, 4.

HOURANI, G.F. (1951), *Arab Seafaring in the Indian Ocean in Ancient and Early Medieval Times*, Princeton.

HSUEH, TIEN–TUNG AND LI, QIANG (1999), *China's National Income, 1952–1995*, Westview Press, Boulder, Colorado.

HULL, C.H. (ed.) (1899), *The Economic Writings of Sir William Petty*, 2 vols, Cambridge University Press, Cambridge.

IBGE (1960), *O Brasil em Numeros*, Rio de Janeiro.

IKRAM, K. (1980), *Egypt: Economic Management in a Period of Transition*, Johns Hopkins, Baltimore.

IMF (International Monetary Fund) (1999), *World Economic Outlook*, Washington, D.C.

INALCIK, H. (1994), *An Economic and Social History of the Ottoman Empire, 1300–1600*, Vol. 1, Cambridge University Press, Cambridge.

ISHII, R. (1937), *Population Pressure and Economic Life in Japan*, King, London.

ISRAEL, J.I. (1989), *Dutch Primacy in World Trade, 1585–1740*, Clarendon Press, Oxford.

ISRAEL, J. (1995), *The Dutch Republic*, Clarendon Press, Oxford.

JANNETTA, A.B. (1986), *Epidemics and Mortality in Early Modern Japan*, Princeton.

JANNETTA, A.B. AND S.H. PRESTON (1991), "Two Centuries of Mortality Change in Central Japan: The Evidence from a Temple Death Register", *Population Studies*, 45, pp. 417–36.

JARRETT, H.S. AND S–N. SARKAR (1949), *Ain–I–Akbari of Abul Fazl–I–Allami*, Royal Asiatic Society of Bengal, Calcutta.

JONES, E.L. (1981), *The European Miracle*, Cambridge University Press, Cambridge.

JONES, V. (1978), *Sail the Indian Sea*, Gordon and Cremonesi, London.

JORGENSON, D.W. AND K.J. STIROH (2000), "Raising the Speed Limit: US Economic Growth in the Information Age", *Brookings Papers on Economic Activity I*, pp. 125–236

KALLAND, A. AND J. PEDERSON (1984), "Famine and Population in Fukuoka Domain during the Tokugawa Period", *Journal of Japanese Studies*, 10, pp. 31–72.

KEENE, D. (1969), *The Japanese Discovery of Europe, 1720–1820*, Stanford.

KENDRICK, J.W. (1961), *Productivity Trends in the United States*, Princeton.

KENNEDY, P. (1987), *The Rise and Fall of the Great Powers*, Random House, New York.

KEYNES, J.M. (1919), *The Economic Consequences of the Peace*, Macmillan, LONDON.

KIM, K.S. AND M. ROEMER (1979), *Growth and Structural Transformation: The Republic of Korea*, Harvard University Press, Cambridge, Mass.

KING, G. (1696), *Natural and Political Observations and Conclusions upon the State and Condition of England*, in BARNETT (ed.) Johns Hopkins (1936).

KIRSTEN, E., E.W. BUCHHOLZ AND W. KÖLLMANN (1956), *Raum und Bevölkerung in der Weltgeschichte*, Ploetz–Verlag, Würzburg.

KLEIN, H.S. (1999), *The Atlantic Slave Trade*, Cambridge University Press, Cambridge.

KNODEL, J.E. (1988), *Demographic Behavior in the Past*, Cambridge University Press, Cambridge.

KORNAI, J. (1992), *The Socialist System: The Politicial Economy of Communism*, Clarendon Press, Oxford.

KRAVIS, I.B., A. HESTON AND R. SUMMERS (1982), *World Product and Income, International Comparisons of Real Gross Product*, Johns Hopkins, Baltimore.

KROEBER, A.L. (1939), *Cultural and National Areas of Native North America*, Berkeley.

KUHN, D. (1988), *Textile Technology: Spinning and Reeling*, Vol. 5, Part IX of Needham, Cambridge University Press, Cambridge.

KUMAR, D. AND M. DESAI (1983), *Cambridge Economic History of India*, Vol. 2, Cambridge.

KUZNETS, S. (1966), *Modern Economic Growth*, Yale.

KUZNETS, S. (1971), *Economic Growth of Nations*, Harvard.

KUZNETS, S. (1973), *Population, Capital and Growth: Selected Essays*, Norton, New York.

KUZNETS, S. (1979), *Growth, Population and Income Distribution*, Norton, New York.

KWON, T.H. (1993) "Reconstructing Population Phenomena in Chosun Korea",International Workshop on Historical Demography, Reitaku University, Chiba, Japan.

KWON, T.H. AND Y–H. SHIN (1977), "On Population Estimates of the Yi Dynasty, 1392–1910", *Tong–A Munhwa*, 14 (in Korean).

LAL, D. (1988), *The Hindu Equilibrium: Cultural Stability and Economic Stagnation*, Oxford University Press, Oxford.

LANDERS, J. (1993), *Death and the Metropolis: Studies in the Demographic History of London, 1670–1830*, Cambridge Universtiy Press, Cambridge.

LANDES, D.S. (1966), "Technological Change and Development in Western Europe, 1750–1914", IN HABAKKUK AND POSTAN.

LANDES, D.S. (1969), *The Unbound Prometheus,* Cambridge University Press, Cambridge.

LANDES, D.S. (1998), *The Wealth and Poverty of Nations,* Little Brown, London.

LANE, F.C. (1966), *Venice and History: Collected Papers,* Johns Hopkins Press, Baltimore.

LANE, F.C. (1973), *Venice: A Maritime Republic,* Johns Hopkins Press, Baltimore.

LANE, F.C. AND R.C. MUELLER (1985) *Money and Banking in Medieval and Renaissance Venice,* vol. 1, Johns Hopkins Press, Baltimore.

LASLETT, P. (1969), "John Locke, the Great Recoinage, and the Origins of the Board of Trade" in YOLTON.

LASLETT, P. (ed.) (1973), *The Earliest Classics: John Graunt and Gregory King,* Gregg International, London.

LEBERGOTT, S. (1984), *The Americans: An Economic Record,* Norton, New York.

LEBOUTTE, R. (ed.) (1996), *Proto–industralization,* Droz, Geneva.

LEE, H.K. (1936), *Land Utilization and Rural Economy in Korea,* Oxford University Press.

LEE, J.Z AND C. CAMPBELL (1997), *Fate and Fortune in Rural China,* Cambridge University Press, Cambridge.

LEE, J.Z. AND F. WANG (forthcoming*), Malthusian Mythology and Chinese Reality: The Population History of One Quarter of Humanity: 1700–2000.*

LEFF, N.H. (1982), *Underdevelopment and Development in Brazil,* 2 vols., Allen and Unwin, London.

LENIHAN, P. (1997), "War and Population, 1649–52", *Irish Economic and Social History, XXIV,* pp. 1–21.

LE ROY LADURIE, E. (1966), *Les paysans de Languedoc,* Mouton, Paris.

LE ROY LADURIE, E. (1977), "Les masses profondes: la paysannenerie", in BRAUDEL AND LAROUSSE.

LE ROY LADURIE, E. (1978), *Le territoire de l'historien,* 2 vols., Gallimard, Paris.

LEVATHES, L. (1994), *When China Ruled the Seas,* Simon and Schuster, New York.

LIEHR, R. (1989), *La formacion de las economias latinoamericanos en la epoca de Simon Bolivar,* Colloquium Verlag, Berlin.

LIM, C.H. (1967), *Economic Development of Modern Malaya,* Oxford University Press, Kuala Lumpur.

LINDERT, P.H. (1980), "English Occupations, 1670–1811", *Journal of Economic History, XL,* 4, pp. 685–713.

LINDERT, P.H. AND J.G. WILLIAMSON (1982), "Revising England's Social Tables, 1688–1812", *Explorations in Economic History,* 19, 1982, pp. 385–408.

LIVI BACCI, M. AND D.S. REHER (1993), "Other Paths to the Past: from Vital Series to Population Patterns", in REHER AND SCHOFIELD.

LORIMER, F. (1946), *The Population of the Soviet Union: History and Prospects,* League of Nations, Geneva.

LOVEJOY, P.E. (1982), "The Volume of the African Slave Trade: A Synthesis", *Journal of African History,* pp. 473–75.

LUNDBERG, E. (1968), *Instability and Economic Growth,* Yale University Press, New Haven.

MACEDO, J. BRAGA DE (1995), "Convertibility and Stability 1834–1994: Portuguese Currency Experience Revisited", in *Ensaios de Homenagem a Francisco Pereira de Moura,* UTL, Lisbon.

MACFARLANE, A. (1997), *The Savage Wars of Peace,* Blackwell, Oxford.

MADDISON, A. (1962), "Growth and Fluctuation in the World Economy, 1870–1960", *Banca Nazionale del Lavoro Quarterly Review,* June.

MADDISON, A. (1969), *Economic Growth in Japan and the USSR,* Allen and Unwin, London.

MADDISON, A. (1970), *Economic Progress and Policy in Developing Countries,* Allen and Unwin, London.

MADDISON, A. (1971), *Class Structure and Economic Growth: India and Pakistan Since the Moghuls*, Allen and Unwin, London.

MADDISON, A. (1972), "Explaining Economic Growth", *Banca Nazionale del Lavoro Quarterly Review*, 102, September.

MADDISON, A. (1976), "Economic Policy and Performance in Europe, 1913–70", in CIPOLLA.

MADDISON, A. (1980), "Monitoring the Labour Market", *Review of Income and Wealth*, June.

MADDISON, A. (1982), *Phases of Capitalist Development*, Oxford University Press, Oxford.

MADDISON, A. (1983), "A Comparison of Levels of GDP Per Capita in Developed and Developing Countries, 1700–1980", *Journal of Economic History*, March, pp. 27–41.

MADDISON, A. (1985), *Two Crises: Latin America and Asia, 1929–38 and 1973–83*, OECD Development Centre, Paris.

MADDISON, A. (1987a), "Growth and Slowdown in Advanced Capitalist Economies: Techniques of Quantitative Assessment", *Journal of Economic Literature*, June.

MADDISON, A. (1987b), "Recent Revisions to British and Dutch Growth, 1700–1870 and their Implications for Comparative Levels of Performance", in MADDISON AND VAN DER MEULEN (1987).

MADDISON, A. (1989a), *The World Economy in the Twentieth Century*, OECD Development Centre, Paris.

MADDISON, A. (1989b), "Dutch Income in and from Indonesia 1700–1938", *Modern Asian Studies*, pp. 645–70.

MADDISON, A. (1990a), "The Colonial Burden: A Comparative Perspective", in SCOTT AND LAL.

MADDISON, A. (1990b), "Measuring European Growth: the Core and the Periphery", in E. AERTS AND N. VALERIO, *Growth and Stagnation in the Mediterranean World*, Tenth International Economic History Conference, Leuven.

MADDISON, A. (1991a), *Dynamic Forces in Capitalist Development*, Oxford University Press, Oxford.

MADDISON, A. (1991b), *A Long Run Perspective on Saving*, Research Memorandum 443, Institute of Economic Research, University of Groningen (a shorter version appeared in the *Scandinavian Journal of Economics*, June 1992, pp. 181–96).

MADDISON, A. (1995a), *Monitoring the World Economy 1820–1992*, OECD Development Centre, Paris.

MADDISON, A. (1995b) *Explaining the Economic Performance of Nations: Essays in Time and Space*, Elgar, Aldershot.

MADDISON, A. (1995c), "The Historical Roots of Modern Mexico: 1500–1940", in MADDISON (1995b).

MADDISON, A. (1996), "Macroeconomic Accounts for European Countries", in VAN ARK AND CRAFTS.

MADDISON, A. (1997), "The Nature and Functioning of European Capitalism: A Historical and Comparative Perspective", *Banca Nazionale del Lavoro Quarterly Review*, December.

MADDISON, A. (1998a), *Chinese Economic Performance in the Long Run*, OECD Development Centre, Paris.

MADDISON, A. (1998b), "Measuring the Performance of A Communist Command Economy: An Assessment of the CIA Estimates for the USSR", *Review of Income and Wealth*, September.

MADDISON, A. (1999a), "Poor until 1820", *Wall Street Journal*, January 11th, p.8.

MADDISON, A. (1999b), "Book Review", of Hanley (1997), *Journal of Japanese and International Economies*, 13, pp. 150–151.

MADDISON, A. AND B. VAN ARK (1994), "The International Comparison of Real Product and Productivity", paper presented at IARIW meetings, St. Andrews, New Brunswick, Canada.

MADDISON, A. AND ASSOCIATES (1992), *The Political Economy of Economic Growth: Brazil and Mexico*, Oxford University Press, New York.

MADDISON, A. AND G. PRINCE (eds.) (1989), *Economic Growth in Indonesia, 1820–1940*, Foris, Dordrecht.

MADDISON, A. AND H. VAN DER MEULEN (eds.) (1987), *Economic Growth in Northwestern Europe: The Last 400 Years*, Research Memorandum 214, Institute of Economic Research, University of Groningen.

MADDISON, A. AND H. VAN DER WEE (eds.) (1994), *Economic Growth and Structural Change: Comparative Approaches over the Long Run*, Proceedings of the Eleventh International Economic History Congress, Milan, September.

MADDISON, A., D.S. PRASADA RAO AND W. SHEPHERD (eds.) (2001) *The Asian Economies in the Twentieth Century*, Elgar, Aldershot.

MALANIMA, P. (1995), *Economia Preindustriale*, Mondadori, Milan.

MALANIMA, P. (1998a), *La Fina del Primato*, Mondadori, Milan.

MALANIMA, P. (1998b), "Italian Cities 1300–1800: A Quantitative Approach", *Revista de Storia Economica*, August, pp. 91–126.

MANCALL, P.C. AND T. WEISS (1999), "Was Economic Growth Likely in British North America?", *Journal of Economic History*, March, pp. 17–40.

MARCILIO, M.L. (1984), "The Population of Colonial Brazil", in BETHELL (1984), Vol. 2.

MARCZEWSKI, J. (1961), "Some Aspects of the Economic Growth of France, 1660–1958", *Economic Development and Cultural Change*, April.

MARI BHAT, P.N. (1989), "Mortality and Fertility in India, 1881–1961: A Reassessment", in DYSON.

MATHIAS, P. (1957), "The Social Structure in the Eighteenth Century: A Calculation by Joseph Massie", *Economic History Review*, pp. 30–45.

McEVEDY, C. (1967), *The Penguin Atlas of Ancient History*, Penguin Books, London.

McEVEDY, C. (1997), *The New Penguin Atlas of Medieval History*, Penguin Books, London.

McEVEDY, C. AND R. JONES (1978), *Atlas of World Population History*, Penguin, Middlesex.

McNEILL, W.H. (1964), *Europe's Steppe Frontier*, University of Chicago Press, Chicago.

McNEILL, W.H. (1974), *Venice: The Fringe of Europe, University of Chicago Press*, Chicago.

McNEILL, W.H. (1977), *Plagues and Peoples*, Anchor Books, Doubleday, New York.

MEIER, G.M. AND D. SEERS (eds.) (1984), *Pioneers in Development*, Oxford University Press, Oxford.

MERKEL, W. AND S. WAHL (1991), *Das geplünderte Deutschland*, IWG, Bonn.

MERRICK, T.W. AND D.H. GRAHAM (1979), *Population and Development in Brazil 1800 to the Present*, Johns Hopkins University Press, Baltimore and London.

METZER, J. (1998), *The Divided Economy of Mandatory Palestine*, Cambridge University Press, Cambridge.

MITCHELL, B.R. (1975), *European Historical Statistics, 1750–1970*, Macmillan, London.

MITCHELL, B.R. AND P. DEANE (1962), *Abstract of British Historical Statistics*, Cambridge University Press, Cambridge.

MITCHELL, B.R. AND H.G. JONES (1971), *Second Abstract of British Historical Statistics*, Cambridge University Press, Cambridge.

MIZOGUCHI, T. (1999), *Long Term Economic Statistics of Taiwan: 1905–1990*, Institute of Economic Research, Hitotsubashi University, Tokyo.

MIZOGUCHI, T. AND M. UMEMURA (1988), *Basic Economic Statistics of Japanese Colonies, 1895–1938*, Toyo Keizai Shinposha, Tokyo.

MOOSVI, S. (1987), *The Economy of the Moghul Empire c.1595: A Statistical Study*, Oxford University Press, Delhi.

MORELAND, W.H. (1920), *India at the Death of Akbar: An Economic Study*, Atmar Ram, Delhi (1962 reprint).

MORINEAU, M. (1985), *Incroyable gazettes et fabuleux métaux*, Cambridge University Press, Cambridge.

MORISON, S.E. (1971), *The European Discovery of America: The Northern Voyages, A.D. 500–1600,* Oxford Univeristy Press, Oxford.

MORISON, S.E. (1974), *The European Discovery of America: The Southern Voyages, A.D. 1492–1616,* Oxford University Press, Oxford.

MOTE, F.W. AND D. TWITCHETT (eds.) (1988), *The Cambridge History of China, The Ming Dynasty, 1368–1644,* Part 1, Cambridge University Press, Cambridge.

MOWERY, D.C. AND N. ROSENBERG (1989), *Technology and the Pursuit of Economic Growth,* Cambridge University Press, Cambridge.

MULHALL, M.G. (1896), *Industries and Wealth of Nations,* Longmans, London.

MULHALL, M.G. (1899), *The Dictionary of Statistics,* Routledge, London, 4th edition.

MYERS, R.H. (ed.) (1996), *The Wealth of Nations in the Twentieth Century,* Hoover Institution, Stanford.

NAKAMURA, J.I. (1966), *Agricultural Production and the Economic Development of Japan, 1873–1922,* Princeton.

NAKAMURA, S. (1968), *Meiji Ishin no Kiso Kozo.*

NAOROJI, D. (1901), *Poverty and Un–British Rule in India,* London, Government of India Reprint, Delhi, 1962.

NDULU, B. AND S.A. O'CONNELL (1999), "Governance and Growth in Sub–Saharan Africa", *Journal of Economic Perspectives,* Summer, pp. 41–66.

NEEDHAM, J. AND ASSOCIATES (1954–2000), *Science and Civilisation in China,* 50 major sections, many co–authors, many volumes, Cambridge University Press, Cambridge.

NEF, J.U. (1987), "Mining and Metallurgy in Medieval Civilisation", in POSTAN *et al.* (eds.), vol. II, pp. 693–762.

NISHIKAWA, S. (1987), "The Economy of Choshu on the Eve of Industrialisation", *Economic Studies Quarterly,* December.

NORTH, D.C. (1966), *Growth and Welfare in the American Past,* Prentice Hall, New Jersey.

NORTH D.C. (1968), "Sources of Productivity Change in Ocean Shipping, 1600–1850", *Journal of Political Economy,* September–October, pp. 953–70.

NORTH D.C. (1990), *Institutions, Institutional Change and Economic Performance,* Cambridge University Press, Cambridge.

Ó GRÁDA, C. (1988), *Ireland Before and After the Famine,* Manchester University Press, Manchester.

OECD (1979), *Demographic Trends 1950–1990,* Paris.

OHKAWA, K. (1957), *The Growth Rate of the Japanese Economy since 1878,* Kinokuniya, Tokyo.

OHKAWA, K., M. SHINOHARA, AND M. UMEMURA (eds.) (1966–1988), *Estimates of Long–Term Economic Statistics of Japan since 1868,* 14 volumes, Toyo Keizai Shinposha, Tokyo.

OHKAWA, K. AND M. SHINOHARA (eds.) (1979), *Patterns of Japanese Economic Development: A Quantitative Appraisal,* Yale.

OHLIN, G. (1955), *The Positive and Preventive Check: A Study of the Rate of Growth of Pre–Industrial Populations,* Harvard Ph.D thesis, reprinted by Arno Press, New York, 1981.

OKAMOTO, Y. (1972), *The Namban Art of Japan,* Heibonsha, Tokyo.

OLINER. S.D. AND D.E. SICHEL (2000), "The Resurgence of Growth in the Late 1990s: Is Information Technology the Story?", Federal Reserve Board, Washington, D.C., February.

OLIVER, R. AND J.D. FAGE (1995), *A Short History of Africa,* Penguin Books, London.

O'ROURKE, K.H. AND J.G. WILLIAMSON (1999), *Globalization and History,* MIT Press, Cambridge, Ma.

OVERTON, M. (1996), *Agricultural Revolution in England: The Transformation of the Agrarian Economy, 1500–1850,* Cambridge University Press, Cambridge.

PAIGE, D. AND G. BOMBACH (1959), *A Comparison of National Output and Productivity of the UK and the United States*, OECD, Paris.

PANNIKAR, K.M. (1953), *Asian and Western Dominance*, Allen and Unwin, London.

PARKER, G. (1979), *Spain and the Netherlands, 1599–1659*, Fontana/Collins, London.

PARRY, J.H. (1967), "Transport and Trade Routes", in RICH AND WILSON.

PARRY, J.H. (1974), *The Discovery of the Sea*, Weidenfeld and Nicolson, London.

PATINKIN, D. (1960), *The Israeli Economy: The First Decade*, Falk Project, Jerusalem.

PEBRER, P. (1833), *Taxation, Revenue, Expenditure, Power, Statistics of the Whole British Empire*, Baldwin and Cradock, London.

PERKINS, D.W. (1969), *Agricultural Development in China, 1368–1968*, Aldine, Chicago.

PERRIN, N. (1979), *Giving up the Gun: Japan's Reversion to the Sword, 1543–1879*, Godine, Boston.

PETTY, W. (1690), *Political Arithmetick*, in Hull (1899), Vol. 1.

PETTY, W. (1997), *The Collected Works of Sir William Petty*, 8 volumes, Routledge/Thoemes Press, London (includes Hull's (1899) collection of Petty's economic writings; E.G. Fitzmaurice's (1895) biography of Petty; Lansdowne's (1927 and 1928) collection of Petty papers and the Southwell–Petty correspondence; Larcom's (1851) edition of Petty's Irish Land Survey, and critical appraisals by T.W. Hutchinson and others).

PHELPS BROWN, H. AND S.V. HOPKINS (1981), *A Perspective on Wages and Prices*, Methuen, London.

PIRENNE, H. (1939), *Mohammed and Charlemagne*, Allen and Unwin, London.

POLAK, J.J. (1943), *The National Income of the Netherlands Indies, 1921–1939*, New York.

POMERANZ, K. (2000), *The Great Divergence*, Princeton University Press, Princeton.

POSTAN, M.M., et al. (eds.) (1963–87), *The Cambridge Economic History of Europe*, vol. I (1966), vol. II (1987) and vol. III (1963), Cambridge University Press, Cambridge.

POTTER, J. (1965), "The Growth of Population in America, 1700–1860", in GLASS AND EVERSELEY.

PRAKASH, O. (1998), *European Commercial Enterprise in Pre–colonial India*, Cambridge University Press, Cambridge.

PRESTON, S.H AND E. VAN DER WALLE (1978), "Urban French Mortality in the Nineteenth Century", *Population Studies*, 32, 2, pp. 275–297.

PROCACCI, G. (1978), *History of the Italian People*, Penguin Books, London.

PURCELL, V. (1965), *The Chinese in Southeast Asia*, Oxford University Press, Kuala Lumpur.

QAISAR, A.J. (1982), *The Indian Response to European Techgnology and Culture, A.D. 1498–1707*, Oxford University Press, Bombay.

RANIS, G. AND T.P. SCHULTZ (eds.) (1988), *The State of Development Economics*, Blackwell, Oxford.

RAPP, R.T. (1976), *Industry and Economic Decline in Seventeenth Century Venice*, Harvard University Press, Cambridge, Ma.

RAYCHAUDHURI, T. AND I. HABIB (1982) (eds.) *The Cambridge Economic History of India*, Cambridge University Press, Cambridge.

REHER, D.S. AND R. SCHOFIELD (eds.) (1993), *Old and New Methods in Historical Demography*, Clarendon Press, Oxford.

REID, A. (1988), *Southeast Asia in the Age of Commerce, 1450–1680, Vol. 1, The Lands Below the Winds*, Yale, New Haven,

REID, A. (1993), *Southeast Asia in the Age of Commerce, 1450–1680, Vol. 2, Expansion and Crisis*, Yale, New Haven.

REISEN, H. AND M. SOTO (2000), "The Need for Foreign Savings in Post–Crisis Asia" (see FOY, KIM AND REISEN) in BRAGA DE MACEDO AND CHINO (Preface by).

REN, R. (1997), *China's Economic Performance in An International Perspective*, OECD Development Centre, Paris.

RICCIOLI, G.B. (1672), *Geographiae et Hydrographiae Reformatae, Libri Duodecim*, Venice.

RICH, E.E. AND C.H. WILSON (1967), *The Cambridge History of Europe*, Vol. IV, Cambridge University Press, Cambridge.

RICHARDS, E.G. (1998), *Mapping Time*, Oxford University Press, Oxford.

RICHARDS, J.F. (1983), *Precious Metals in the Later Medieval and Early Modern Worlds,* Carolina Academic Press, Durham, North Carolina.

ROBERTSON, J. (1984), "Japanese Farm Manuals: A Literature of Discovery", *Peasant Studies*, 11, Spring, pp. 169–194.

ROMANELLI, G. (ed.) (1997), *Venice: Art and Architecture,* Könemann, Cologne.

ROMER, P.M. (1986), "Increasing Returns and Long Run Growth", *Journal of Political Economy*, 94, No. 5.

ROSENBLAT, A. (1945), *La Poblacion Indigena de America Desde 1492 Hasta la Actualidad*, ICE, Buenos Aires.

ROSENBLAT, A. (1967), *La Poblacion de America en 1492*, Colegio de Mexico, Mexico D.F.

ROSTOW, W.W. (1960), *The Stages of Economic Growth*, Cambridge University Press, Cambridge.

ROSTOW, W.W. (ed.) (1963), *The Economics of Take–Off into Sustained Growth*, Macmillan, London.

ROSTOW, W.W. (1990), *Theorists of Economic Growth from David Hume to the Present*, Oxford University Press, Oxford.

ROTHERMUND, D. (1999), "The Changing Pattern of British Trade in Indian Textiles, 1701–57", in CHAUDHURY AND MORINEAU.

ROSENZWEIG, F. (1963), "La economia Novo–Hispaña al comenzar del siglo XIX", *Revista de Sciencias Politicas y Sociales,* UNAM, July–September.

ROZMAN, G. (1973), *Urban Networks in Ch'ing China and Tokugawa Japan*, Princeton University Press, Princeton.

RUSSELL, J.C. (1948), *British Medieval Population,* University of New Mexico, Albuquerque.

RUSSELL, J.C. (1958), *Late Ancient and Medieval Population*, American Philosophical Society, Philadelphia.

RUSSELL, P. (2000), *Prince Henry "The Navigator": A Life,* Yale University Press, New Haven.

SAITO, O. (1979), "Who Worked When: Life Time Profiles of Labour Force Participation in Cardington and Corfe Castle in the Late Eighteenth and Mid–Nineteenth Centuries", *Local Population Studies*, pp. 14–29.

SAITO, O. (1996), "Gender, Workload and Agricultural Progress: Japan's Historical Experience in Perspective", in LEBOUTTE.

SAITO, O. (1997), "Infant Mortality in Pre–Transition Japan: Levels and Trends", in BIDEAU, DESJARDINS AND PEREZ BRIGNOLI.

SALTER, W.E.G. (1960), *Productivity and Technical Change*, Cambridge University Press, Cambridge.

SANCHEZ–ALBORNOZ, N. (1984), "The Population of Colonial Spanish America", in BETHELL, vol. 2.

SANCHEZ–ALBORNOZ, N. (1986), "The Population of Latin America, 1850–1930", in BETHELL, vol. 4.

SARKAR, N.K. (1957), *The Demography of Ceylon*, Ceylon Government Press, Colombo.

SCHMOOKLER, J. (1966), *Invention and Economic Growth*, Harvard University Press, Cambridge, Ma.

SCHOFIELD, R., D. REHER AND A. BIDEAU (1991), *The Decline of Mortality in Europe*, Clarendon Press, Oxford.

SCHULTZ, T.W. (1961), "Investment in Human Capital", *American Economic Review*, March.

SCHUMPETER, J.A. (1939), *Business Cycles*, McGraw Hill, New York.

SCHWARTZ, S.B., (1985), *Sugar Plantations in the Formation of Brazilian Society*: Bahià, 1550–1835, Cambridge University Press, Cambridge.

SCOTT, M. AND D. LAL (eds.) (1990), *Public Policy and Economic Development: Essays in Honour of Ian Little*, Clarendon Press, Oxford.

SELLA, D. (1979), *Crisis and Continuity: The Economy of Spanish Lombardy in the Seventeenth Century*, Harvard University Press, Cambridge, Ma.

SHAMMAS, C. (1993), "Changes in English and Anglo–American Consumption from 1550 to 1800", in BREWER AND PORTER.

SHEA, D.E. (1976), "A Defence of Small Population Estimates for the Central Andes in 1520", in DENEVAN (1976), pp. 157–80.

SIMONSEN, R.C. (1962), *Historia Economica do Brasil (1500–1820)*, Editora Nacional, Sao Paulo.

SIVASUBRAMONIAN, S. (2000), *The National Income of India in the Twentieth Century*, Oxford University Press, New Delhi.

SIVASUBRAMONIAN, S. (2001), "Twentieth Century Economic Performance of India", in MADDISON, PRASADA RAO AND SHEPHERD.

SLICHER VAN BATH, B.H. (1963), *The Agrarian History of Western Europe, AD 500–1850*, Arnold, London.

SMITH, A. (1776), *An Inquiry into the Nature and Causes of the Wealth of Nations*, University of Chicago Reprint, 1976.

SMITH, T.C. (1959), *The Agrarian Origins of Modern Japan*, Stanford.

SMITH, T.C. (1969), "Farm Family By-Employments in Preindustrial Japan", *Journal of Economic History*, December.

SMITH, T.C. (1977), *Nakahara: Family Farming and Population in a Japanese Village, 1717–1830*, Stanford University Press, Stanford, California.

SMITH, T.C. (1988), *Native Sources of Japanese Industrialization, 1750–1920*, University of Claifornia, Berkeley.

SMITS, J.P., E. HORLINGS AND J.L. VAN ZANDEN (2000), *The Measurement of Gross National Product and Its Components, 1800–1913*, Groningen Growth and Development Centre Monograph Series, No. 5.

SNODGRASS, D.R. (1966), *Ceylon: An Export Economy in Transition*, Irwin, Illinois.

SNOOKS, G.D. (1993), *Economics Without Time*, Macmillan, London.

SNOOKS, G.D. (1996), *The Dynamic Society: Exploring the Sources of Global Change*, Routledge, London.

SNOOKS, G.D. (1997), *The Ephemeral Civilisation*, Routledge, London.

SOLOW, R.M. (1956), "A Contribution to the Theory of Economic Growth", *Quarterly Journal of Economics*, February.

SOLOW, R.M. (1960), "Investment and Technical Progress", in ARROW, KARLIN AND SUPPES (eds.) *Mathematical Methods in the Social Sciences*, Stanford University Press.

SOLOW, R.M. (1962), "Technical Progress, Capital Formation and Eonomic Growth", *American Economic Review*, May.

SPOONER, F.C. (1972), *The International Economy and Monetary Movements in France, 1493–1725*, Harvard University Press, Cambridge, Ma.

SPULBER, N. (1966), *The State and Economic Development in Eastern Europe*, Random House, New York.

STECKEL, R.H. AND R. FLOUD (1997), *Health and Welfare during Industrialisation*, University of Chicago Press, Chicago.

STEENSGAARD, N. (1972), *Carracks, Caravans and Companies*, Copenhagen.

STONE, R. (1997), *Some British Empiricists in the Social Sciences 1650–1900*, Cambridge University Press, Cambridge.

STUDENSKI, P. (1958), *The Income of Nations: Theory, Measurement and Analysis: Past and Present*, New York University Press, Washington Square.

SUBRAHMANYAM, S. (1997), *The Career and Legend of Vasco de Gama*, Cambridge University Press, Cambridge.

SUH, S.C. (1978), *Growth and Structural Changes in the Korean Economy, 1910–40*, Harvard University Press, Cambridge, Ma.

SUMMERS, R. AND A. HESTON (1991), "The Penn World Table (Mark 5): An Expanded Set of International Comparisons 1950–1988", *Quarterly Journal of Economics*, May, supplemented by January 1995 diskette of P.W.T. Mark 5.6.

SZERESZEWSKI, R. (1965), *Structural Changes in the Economy of Ghana*, Weidenfeld and Nicolson, London.

SZERESZEWSKI, R. (1968), *Essays on the Structure of the Jewish Economy in Palestine and Israel*, Falk project, Jerusalem.

SZIRMAI, A., B. VAN ARK AND D. PILAT (eds.) (1993), *Explaining Economic Growth: Essays in Honour of Angus Maddison*, North Holland, Amsterdam.

TAEUBER, I.B. (1958), *The Population of Japan*, Princeton University Press, New Jersey.

TAWNEY, A.J. AND R.H. (1934), "An Occupational Census of the Seventeenth Century", *Economic History Review*, October.

TAYLOR, G.R. (1964), "American Economic Growth Before 1840: An Exploratory Essay", *Journal of Economic History*, December, pp. 427–444.

TEMPLE, W. (1693), *Observations upon the United Provinces of the Netherlands*, Tonson, London.

TERRISE, M. (1975), "Aux origines de la méthode de reconstitution des familles: les Suédois d'Estonie", *Population*, numéro spécial.

THIRSK, J. (1978), *Economic Policies and Projects: The Development of a Consumer Society in Early Modern England*, Oxford University Press, Oxford.

THOMAS, R.P. (1965), "A Quantitative Approach to the Study of the Effects of British Imperial Policy upon Colonial Welfare: Some Preliminary Findings", *Journal of Economic History*, December.

THOMAS, R.P. (1968), "The Sugar Colonies of the Old Empire: Profit and Loss to Great Britain", *Economic History Review*.

THORNTON, R. (1987), *American Indian Holocaust and Survival: A Population History since 1492*, University of Oklahoma, Norman.

TIBBETTS, G.R. (1981), *Arab Navigation in the Indian Ocean before the Coming of the Portuguese*, Royal Asiatic Society of Great Britain and Ireland

TRACY, J.D. (ed.) (1990), *The Rise of Merchant Empires: Long Distance Trade in the Early Modern Period, 1350–1750*, Cambridge University Press.

TWITCHETT, D. AND F.W. MOTE (eds.) (1998), *The Cambridge History of China*, Vol. 8, *The Ming Dynasty*, Part 2, *1368–1644*, Cambridge University Press, Cambridge.

UBELAKER, D.H. (1976), "Prehistoric New World Population Size: Historical Review and Current Appraisal of North American Estimates", *American Journal of Physical Anthropology*, pp. 661–6.

UNGER, R.W. (1980), *The Ship in the Medieval Economy, 600–1600*, Croom Helm, London.

UNGER, R.W. (1992), "The Tonnage of Europe's Merchant Fleets, 1300–1800", *The American Neptune (52)*, pp. 247–61.

UN POPULATION DIVISON (1973), *The Determinants and Consequences of Population Trends*, New York.

UN POPULATION DIVISON (1999), *World Population Prospects: The 1998 Revision*, New York.

URLANIS, B.TS. (1941), *Rost Naselennie v Evrope*, Ogiz, Moscow.

VALLIN, J. (1991), "Mortality in Europe from 1720 to 1914", in SCHOFIELD, REHER AND BIDEAU.

VAMPLEW, W. (ed.) (1987), *Australians: Historical Statistics,* Cambridge University Press, Cambridge.

VAN DER ENG, P. (1998), "Exploring Exploitation: The Netherlands and Colonial Indonesia, 1870–1940", *Revista de Historia Economica* XVI, 1, pp. 291–320.

VAUBAN, S. (1707), *La dixme royale* (1992 edition, with introduction by E. Le Roy Ladurie, Imprimerie nationale, Paris).

VERLINDEN, C. (1963), "Markets and Fairs", in POSTAN *et al.* (eds.) Vol. III, pp. 126–136.

VERLINDEN, C. (1972), "From the Mediterranean to the Atlantic", *Journal of European Economic History,* pp. 625-46.

VISARIA, L. AND P. VISARIA (1983), "Population: 1757–1947", IN KUMAR AND DESAI.

VOGEL, W. (1915), "Zur Grösse der europaischen Handelsflotten im 15., 16. und 17. Jahrhundert", in D. Schäfer (ed.) *Forschungen und Versuche zur Geschichte des Mitelalters und der Neuzeit,* Fischer, Jena.

VON GLAHN, R. (1996), *Fountain of Fortune: Money and Monetary Policy in China, 1000–1700,* University of California Press, California.

VRIES, J. DE (1974), *The Dutch Rural Economy in the Golden Age, 1500–1700,* Yale.

VRIES, J. DE (1976), *Economy of Europe in an Age of Crisis, 1600–1750,* Cambridge University Press, Cambridge.

VRIES, J. DE (1984), *European Urbanization 1500–1800,* Methuen, London.

VRIES, J. DE (1985), "The Population and Economy of the Preindustrial Netherlands", *Journal of Interdisciplinary History,* XV:4, pp. 661–82.

VRIES, J. DE (1993), "Between Purchasing Power and the World of Goods: Understanding the Household Economy in Early Modern Europe" in BREWER AND PORTER.

VRIES, J. DE AND A. VAN DER WOUDE (1997), *The First Modern Economy: Success, Failure and Perseverance of the Dutch Economy, 1500–1815,* Cambridge University Press, Cambridge.

WAKE, C.H.H. (1979), "The Changing Pattern of Europe's Pepper and Spice Imports, ca 1400–1700", *Journal of European Economic History,* vol. 8(2), pp. 361–403.

WAKE, C.H.H. (1986), "The Volume of European Spice Imports at the Beginning and End of the Fifteenth Century", *Journal of European Economic History,* vol 15(3), pp. 621–35.

WALL, R. (1983), "The Household: Demographic and Economic Change in England, 1650–1970" in WALL *et al.*

WALL, R., J. ROBIN AND P. LASLETT (1983), *Family Forms in Historic Europe,* Cambridge University Press, Cambridge.

WALTER, J. AND R. SCHOFIELD (1989), *Famine, Disease and the Social Order in Early Modern Society,* Cambridge University Press, Cambridge.

WARMINGTON, E.H. (1928), *The Commerce Between the Roman Empire and India,* Cambridge University Press, Cambridge.

WESTERGAARD, H. (1932), *Contributions to the History of Statistics,* King, London (Kelley reprint, 1969).

WHITE, L. (1962), *Medieval Tehnology and Social Change, Clarendon Press,* Oxford.

WHITWORTH, C. (ed.) (1771), *The Political and Commercial Works of Charles Davenant,* 5 vols., Horsefield, London.

WILLCOX, W.F. (1931), "Increase in the Population of the Earth and of the Continents since 1650", in W.F. WILLCOX (ed.) *International Migrations,* Vol. II, National Bureau of Economic Research, New York, pp. 33–82.

WILLIAMS, E. (1970), *From Columbus to Castro: The History of the Caribbean 1492–1969,* Deutsch, London.

WILLIAMSON, J.G. (1995), "The Evolution of Global Markets Since 1830: Background Evidence and Hypotheses", *Explorations in Economic History,* 32, pp. 141–196.

WILSON, C. AND G. PARKER (eds.) (1977), *An Introduction to the Sources of European Economic History, 1500–1800,* Weidenfeld and Nicolson, London.

WOLF, J. (1912), *Die Volkswirtschaft der Gegenwart und Zukunft,* Deichert, Leipzig, 1912.

WORLD BANK (2000), *Global Development Finance,* Washington, D.C.

WRIGLEY, E.A. (1967), "A Simple Model of London's Importance in Changing English Society and Economy 1650–1750", *Past and Present,* July, pp. 44–70.

WRIGLEY, E.A. (1988), *Continuity, Chance and Change,* Cambridge.

WRIGLEY, E.A. AND R.S. SCHOFIELD (1981), *The Population History of England 1541–1871,* Arnold, London.

WRIGLEY, E.A., R.S. DAVIES, J.E. OEPPEN AND R.S. SCHOFIELD (1997), *English Population History from Family Reconstitution 1580–1837,* Cambridge University Press, Cambridge.

WYCKOFF, A.W. (1995), "The Impact of Computer Prices on International Comparisons of Labour Productivity", *Economies of Innovation and New Technology,* vol. 3, pp. 277–93.

XU, XIANCHUN (1999), "Evaluation and Adjustments of China's Official GDP by the World Bank and Prof. Maddison", *Journal of Econometric Study of Northeast Asia,* Vol. 1, No. 2.

YAMADA, S. AND Y. HAYAMI (1979), "Agricultural Growth in Japan, 1880–1970", in HAYAMI, RUTTAN AND SOUTHWORTH, pp. 33–48 and 230–64.

YAMAMURA, K. (1974), *A Study of Samurai Income and Entrepreneurship,* Harvard.

YAMAMURA, K. (1981), "Returns on Unification Economic Growth in Japan, 1550–1650", in HALL *et al.*

YAMAMURA, K. AND T. KAMIRI (1983), "Silver Mines and Sung Coins — A Monetary History of Medieval and Modern Japan in International Perspective", IN RICHARDS.

YASUBA, Y. (1987), "The Tokugawa Legacy: A Survey", *Economic Studies Quarterly,* December, pp. 290–308.

YOLTON, J.W. (ed.) (1969), *John Locke: Problems and Perspectives.*

YOSHIDA, T. (1911), *Ishinshi Hachi Ko,* Fuzanbo, Tokyo.

YUN, B. (1994), "Proposals to Quantify Long–Run Performance in the Kingdom of Castile, 1550–1800", in MADDISON AND VAN DER WEE.

ZAMBARDINO, R.A. (1980), "Mexico's Population in the Sixteenth Century: Demographic Anomaly or Mathematical Illusion?", *Journal of Interdisciplinary History,* pp. 1–27.

ZANDEN, J.L. VAN (1987), "De economie van Holland in de periode 1650–1805: groei of achteruitgang? Een overzicht van bronnen, problemen en resultaten", *Bijdrage en Mededelingen Geschiedenis der Nederlanden.*

OECD PUBLICATIONS, 2, rue André-Pascal, 75775 PARIS CEDEX 16
PRINTED IN FRANCE
(41 2001 01 1 P) ISBN 92-64-18608-5 – No. 51519 2001